D0166203

CE4V-CG8J-YMDR-MWGM-7YRA

IMPORTANT

HERE IS YOUR REGISTRATION CODE TO ACCESS MCGRAW-HILL PREMIUM CONTENT AND MCGRAW-HILL ONLINE RESOURCES

For key premium online resources you need THIS CODE to gain access. Once the code is entered, you will be able to use the web resources for the length of your course.

Access is provided only if you have purchased a new book.

If the registration code is missing from this book, the registration screen on our website, and within your WebCT or Blackboard course will tell you how to obtain your new code. Your registration code can be used only once to establish access. It is not transferable.

To gain access to these online resources

1. USE your web browser to go to: **www.mhhe.com/chambers9**

2. CLICK on "First Time User"

3. ENTER the Registration Code printed on the tear-off bookmark on the right

4. After you have entered your registration code, click on "Register"

5. FOLLOW the instructions to setup your personal UserID and Password

6. WRITE your UserID and Password down for future reference. Keep it in a safe place.

If your course is using WebCT or Blackboard, you'll be able to use this code to access the McGraw-Hill content within your instructor's online course.

To gain access to the McGraw-Hill content in your instructor's WebCT or Blackboard course simply log into the course with the user ID and Password provided by your instructor. Enter the registration code exactly as it appears to the right when prompted by the system. You will only need to use this code the first time you click on McGraw-Hill content.

These instructions are specifically for student access. Instructors are not required to register via the above instructions.

REGISTRATION CODE
REGISTRATION CODE

The McGraw-Hill Companies

Mc Graw Hill **Higher Education**
ISBN 13: 978-0-07-325089-2
ISBN 10: 0-07-325089-9

Thank you, and welcome to your McGraw-Hill Online Resources.

The McGraw-Hill Companies **Higher Education**

THE WESTERN EXPERIENCE

VOLUME C:
THE MODERN ERA

THE WESTERN EXPERIENCE

Ninth Edition

MORTIMER CHAMBERS
University of California, Los Angeles

BARBARA HANAWALT
The Ohio State University

THEODORE K. RABB
Princeton University

ISSER WOLOCH
Columbia University

RAYMOND GREW
University of Michigan

LISA TIERSTEN
Barnard College

Boston   Burr Ridge, IL   Dubuque, IA   Madison, WI   New York   San Francisco   St. Louis
Bangkok   Bogotá   Caracas   Kuala Lumpur   Lisbon   London   Madrid   Mexico City
Milan   Montreal   New Delhi   Santiago   Seoul   Singapore   Sydney   Taipei   Toronto

Higher Education

THE WESTERN EXPERIENCE, VOLUME C: THE MODERN ERA
Published by McGraw-Hill, a business unit of The McGraw-Hill Companies, Inc., 1221 Avenue of the Americas, New York, NY, 10020.
Copyright © 2007, 2003, 1999, 1995, 1991, 1987, 1983, 1979, 1974 by The McGraw-Hill Companies, Inc. All rights reserved. No part of this publication may be reproduced or distributed in any form or by any means, or stored in a database or retrieval system, without the prior written consent of The McGraw-Hill Companies, Inc., including, but not limited to, in any network or other electronic storage or transmission, or broadcast for distance learning.

Some ancillaries, including electronic and print components, may not be available to customers outside the United States.

This book is printed on acid-free paper.

1 2 3 4 5 6 7 8 9 0 DOW/DOW 0 9 8 7 6

ISBN-13: 978-0-07-325085-4
ISBN: 0-07-325085-6

Vice President and Editor-in-Chief: *Emily Barrosse*
Publisher: *Lyn Uhl*
Senior Sponsoring Editor: *Monica Eckman*
Director of Development: *Lisa Pinto*
Developmental Editor: *Angela W. Kao*
Permissions Coordinator: *The Permissions Group*
Marketing Manager: *Katherine Bates*
Managing Editor: *Jean Dal Porto*
Project Manager: *Emily Hatteberg*
Art Director: *Jeanne Schreiber*
Art Editor: *Ayelet Arbel*
Lead Designer: *Gino Cieslik*
Cover and Interior Designer: *Ellen Pettengell*
Cover credit: *Andre Lhote,* Entree du bassin à flot à Bordeaux (Entrance to the wet dock of Bordeaux), *1912; Musée des Beaux-Arts, Bordeaux, France. Erich Lessing/Art Resource, NY/© 2005 Artists Rights Society (ARS), New York/ADAGP, Paris*
Senior Photo Research Coordinator: *Alexandra Ambrose*
Photo Research: *Photosearch, Inc., New York*
Senior Production Supervisor: *Carol A. Bielski*
Lead Media Producer: *Sean Crowley*
Media Project Manager: *Kate Boylan*
Composition: *9.5/12 Trump, by Carlisle Publishing Services*
Printing: *45 # Pub Matte Plus, R.R. Donnelley & Sons*

Credits: The credits section for this book begins on page C-1 and is considered an extension of the copyright page.

Library of Congress Cataloging-in-Publication Data

The Western experience / Mortimer Chambers ... [et al,].—9th ed. [main text]
    6 v. cm.
  Includes bibliographical references and index.
  ISBN-13: 978-0-07-288369-5 (alk. paper)
  ISBN-10: 0-07-288369-3 (alk. paper)
  1. Civilization—History. 2. Civilization, Western—History. I. Chambers, Mortimer.
CB59.W38 2007
909'.09821—dc22

                      2006041940

The Internet addresses listed in the text were accurate at the time of publication. The inclusion of a Web site does not indicate an endorsement by the authors or McGraw-Hill, and McGraw-Hill does not guarantee the accuracy of the information presented at these sites.

www.mhhe.com

About the Authors

Mortimer Chambers is Professor of History at the University of California at Los Angeles. He was a Rhodes Scholar from 1949 to 1952 and received an M.A. from Wadham College, Oxford, in 1955 after obtaining his doctorate from Harvard University in 1954. He has taught at Harvard University (1954–1955) and the University of Chicago (1955–1958). He was Visiting Professor at the University of British Columbia in 1958, the State University of New York at Buffalo in 1971, the University of Freiburg (Germany) in 1974, and Vassar College in 1988. A specialist in Greek and Roman history, he is coauthor of *Aristotle's History of Athenian Democracy* (1962), editor of a series of essays entitled *The Fall of Rome* (1963), and author of *Georg Busolt: His Career in His Letters* (1990) and of *Staat der Athener*, a German translation and commentary to Aristotle's *Constitution of the Athenians* (1990). He has edited Greek texts of the latter work (1986) and of the *Hellenica Oxyrhynchia* (1993). He has contributed articles to the *American Historical Review* and *Classical Philology* as well as to other journals, both in America and in Europe. He is also an editor of *Historia*, the international journal of ancient history.

Barbara Hanawalt holds the King George III Chair of British History at The Ohio State University and is the author of numerous books and articles on the social and cultural history of the Middle Ages. Her publications include *The Middle Ages: An Illustrated History* (1999), *'Of Good and Ill Repute': Gender and Social Control in Medieval England* (1998), *Growing Up in Medieval London: The Experience of Childhood in History* (1993), *The Ties That Bound: Peasant Life in Medieval England* (1986), and *Crime and Conflict in English Communities, 1300–1348* (1979). She received her M.A. in 1964 and her Ph.D. in 1970, both from the University of Michigan. She has served as president of the Social Science History Association and the Medieval Academy of America and has been on the Council of the American Historical Association and the Medieval Academy of America. She was a fellow of the Netherlands Institute for Advanced Study (2005–2006), a fellow of the Guggenheim Foundation (1998–1999), an ACLS Fellow in 1975–1976, a fellow at the National Humanities Center (1997–1998), a fellow at the Wissenschaftskolleg in Berlin (1990–1991), a member of the School of Historical Research at the Institute for Advanced Study, and a senior research fellow at the Newberry Library in 1979–1980.

Theodore K. Rabb is Professor of History at Princeton University. He received his Ph.D. from Princeton in 1961 and subsequently taught at Stanford, Northwestern, Harvard, and Johns Hopkins universities. He is the author of numerous articles and reviews in journals such as *The New York Times* and the *Times Literary Supplement*, and he has been editor of *The Journal of Interdisciplinary History* since its foundation. Among his books are *The Struggle for Stability in Early Modern Europe* (1975), *Renaissance Lives* (1993), and *Jacobean Gentleman* (1999). He has won awards from the Guggenheim Foundation, the National Endowment for the Humanities, the American Historical Association, and the National Council for History Education. He was the principal historian for the PBS series *Renaissance*, which was nominated for an Emmy.

Isser Woloch is Moore Collegiate Professor of History at Columbia University. He received his Ph.D. (1965) from Princeton University in the field of eighteenth- and nineteenth-century European history. He has taught at Indiana University and at the University of California at Los Angeles, where, in 1967, he received a Distinguished Teaching Citation. He has been a fellow of the ACLS, the National Endowment for the Humanities, the Guggenheim Foundation, and the Institute for Advanced Study at Princeton. His publications include *Jacobin Legacy: The Democratic Movement under the Directory* (1970), *The Peasantry in the Old Regime: Conditions and Protests* (1970), *The French Veteran from the Revolution to the Restoration* (1979), *Eighteenth-Century Europe: Tradition and Progress, 1715–1789* (1982), *The New Regime: Transformations of the French Civic Order, 1789–1820s* (1994), *Revolution and the Meanings of Freedom in the Nineteenth Century* (1996), and *Napoleon and His Collaborators: The Making of a Dictatorship* (2001).

Raymond Grew is Professor of History Emeritus at the University of Michigan. He has also taught at Brandeis University, Princeton University, and at the Écoles des Hautes Études en Sciences Sociales in Paris. He earned both his M.A. and Ph.D. from Harvard University in the field of modern European history. He has been a Fulbright Fellow to Italy and a Fulbright Travelling Fellow to Italy and to France, a Guggenheim Fellow, and a Fellow of the National Endowment for the Humanities. In 1962 he received the Chester Higby Prize from the American Historical Association, and in 1963 the Italian government awarded him the Unità d'Italia Prize; in 1992 he received the David Pinkney Prize of the Society for French Historical Studies and in 2000 a citation for career achievement from the Society for Italian Historical Studies. He has twice served as national chair of the Council for European Studies, was for many years the editor of the international quarterly *Comparative Studies in Society and History*, and is one of the directors of the Global History Group. His recent publications include essays on historical comparison, global history, Catholicism in the nineteenth century, fundamentalism, and Italian culture and politics. His books include *A Sterner Plan for Italian Unity* (1963),

Crises of Development in Europe and the United States (1978), *School, State, and Society: The Growth of Elementary Schooling in Nineteenth-Century France* (1991), with Patrick J. Harrigan, and two edited volumes: *Food in Global History* (1999) and *The Construction of Minorities* (2001).

Lisa Tiersten is Associate Professor of History at Barnard College, Columbia University. She received her Ph.D. (1991) at Yale University and has taught at Wellesley College and Barnard College. She has been the recipient of a Chateaubriand Fellowship, a French Historical Studies Society Fellowship, and a Getty Fellowship. She also received the Emily Gregory Teaching Award at Barnard College in 1996. Her publications include *Marianne in the Market: Envisioning Consumer Society in Fin-de-Siècle France* (2001). She is currently at work on a history of bankruptcy and the culture of credit in modern France, entitled *Terms of Trade: The Capitalist Imagination in Modern France*, and on an edited volume on the comparative history of children's rights in twentieth-century Europe. Her research interests include modern France, gender, consumer culture, empire, and the comparative culture of capitalism.

This book is dedicated to the memory of David Herlihy, whose erudition and judgment were central to its creation and whose friendship and example continue to inspire his coauthors.

Brief Contents

Contents

Maps

Boxes

Chronological Boxes

Global Moment Boxes

Preface

When *The Western Experience* was originally conceived, we sought to write a textbook that would introduce students to the growing field of social history and exciting new ways of thinking about history. We wanted the textbook not merely to set forth information but to serve as an example of historical writing. That means we cared a lot about the quality of the writing itself and also that we wanted the chapters to be examples of a historical essay that set up a historical problem and developed arguments about that problem using historical evidence. We also recognized that for American students the Western Civilization textbook needed to provide an overview of that civilization, giving students an introduction to the major achievements in Western thought, art, and science as well as the social, political, and economic context for understanding them. And lastly, we were determined that our book would treat all these various aspects of history in an integrated way. Too many books, we felt, dealt with cultural or social change entirely separately, even in separate chapters, and we sought to demonstrate and exemplify the connections. To that end, *The Western Experience* is designed to provide an analytical and reasonably comprehensive account of the contexts within which, and the processes by which, European society and civilization evolved.

Now in the ninth edition, this book has evolved with the strength of prior revisions, including Barbara Hanawalt's impressive rewriting and reordering of the six chapters that cover the Middle Ages for the seventh edition. To continue that evolution, we are proud to welcome another distinguished scholar, Lisa Tiersten of Barnard College, to our author team. She has written a new chapter on nineteenth-century empires (chapter 26), one of the first among western civilization textbooks, and she has undertaken the substantial revision and reorganization of chapters 25 and 27. With a fresh voice and lucid approach, Dr. Tiersten has greatly enriched the coverage in these chapters by incorporating recent research on gender, bourgeois and consumer culture, imperialism, technology, and globalization.

EXPERIENCING HISTORY

Everyone uses history. We use it to define who we are and to connect our personal experience to the collective memory of the groups to which we belong, including a particular region, nation, and culture. We invoke the past to explain our hopes and ambitions and to justify our fears and conflicts. The Charter of the United Nations, like the American Declaration of Independence, is based on a view of history. When workers strike or armies march, they cite the lessons of their history. Because history is so important to us psychologically and intellectually, historical understanding is always shifting and often controversial.

Historical knowledge is cumulative. Historians may ask many of the same questions about different periods of history or raise new questions or issues; they integrate the answers, and historical knowledge grows. The study of history cannot be a subjective exercise in which all opinions are equally valid. Regardless of the impetus for a particular historical question, the answer to it stands until overturned by better evidence. We now know more about the past than ever before, and we understand it as the people we study could not. Unlike them, we know the outcome of their history; we can apply methods they did not have, and often we have evidence they never saw.

Humans have always found pleasure in the reciting and reading of history. The poems about the fall of Troy or the histories of Herodotus and Thucydides entertained the ancient Greeks. The biographies of great men and women, dramatic accounts of important events, colorful tales of earlier times can be fascinating in themselves. Through these encounters with history we experience the common concerns of all people; and through the study of European history, we come to appreciate the ideals and conflicts, the failures and accidents, the social needs and human choices that formed the Western world in which we live. Knowing the historical context also enriches our appreciation for the achievements of European culture, enabling us to see its art, science, ideas, and politics in relationship to real people, specific interests, and burning issues.

We think of Europe's history as the history of Western civilization because the Greeks gave the names east and west to the points on the horizon at which the sun rises and sets. Because the Persian Empire and India lay to their east, the Greeks labeled their own continent, which they called Europe, the west. However, we need to be cautious about the view that Western civilization is a united whole, entirely distinct from other civilizations, except perhaps in its cultural development. We will see many occasions when a larger context is appropriate.

The Western Experience thus gives primary attention to a small part of the world and honors a particular cultural tradition. Yet the concentration on Europe does allow us to explore contrasts of worldwide significance; between city and rural life; among empires and monarchies and republics; in life before and after industrialization; among societies that organized labor through markets, serfdom, and slavery; between cultures little concerned with science and those that used changing scientific knowledge; among different ways of creating and experiencing forms of literature and the arts; and among Christian and non-Christian religions and all the major forms of Christianity.

A college course alone cannot create an educated citizen. Moreover, Western history is not the only history a person should know, and an introductory survey is not necessarily the best way to learn it. Yet, as readers consider and then challenge interpretations offered in this text, they will exercise critical and analytical skills. They can begin to overcome the parochialism that attributes importance only to the present. To learn to think critically about historical evidence and know how to formulate an argument on the bases of this evidence is to experience the study of history as one of the vital intellectual activities by which we come to know who and where we are.

A BALANCED, INTERPRETIVE, AND FLEXIBLE APPROACH

At the same time, we recognize that the professional scholar's preference for new perspectives over familiar ones makes a distinction that students may not share. For them, the latest interpretations need to be integrated with established understandings and controversies, with the history of people and events that are part of our cultural lore. We recognize that a textbook

should provide a coherent presentation of the basic information from which students can begin to form their historical understanding. We believe this information must be part of an interpretive history but also that its readers—teachers, students, and general readers—should be free to use it in many different ways and in conjunction with their own areas of special knowledge and their own interests and curiosity.

USE OF THEMES

Throughout this book, from the treatment of the earliest civilizations to the discussion of the present, we pursue certain key themes. These seven themes constitute a set of categories by which societies and historical change can be analyzed.

Social Structure   In early chapters, social structure involves how the land was settled, divided among its inhabitants, and put to use. Later discussions of how property is held must include corporate, communal, and individual ownership, then investment banking and companies that sell shares. Similarly, in each era we treat the division of labor, noting whether workers are slave or free, male or female, and when there are recognized specialists in fighting or crafts or trade. The chapters covering the ancient world, the Middle Ages, and the early modern period explore social hierarchies that include nobles, clergy, commoners, and slaves or serfs; the treatments of the French Revolution, the Industrial Revolution, and twentieth-century societies analyze modern social classes.

The Body Politic   Another theme we analyze throughout this book is what used to be called the body politic. Each era contains discussions of how political power is acquired and used and of the political structures that result. Students learn about the role of law from ancient codes to the present, as well as problems of order, and the formation of governments, including why government functions have increased and political participation of the population has changed.

Technology   From cultivation in the plains of the Tigris and Euphrates to the global economy, we follow changes in the organization of production and in the impact of technology. We note how goods are distributed, and we observe patterns of trade as avenues of cultural exchange in addition to wealth. We look at the changing economic role of governments and the impact of economic theories.

Gender Roles and Family   The evolution of the family and changing gender roles are topics fundamental to every historical period. Families give form to daily life and kinship structures. The history of demography, migration, and work is also a history of the family. The family has always been a central focus of social organization and religion, as well as the principal instrument by which societies assign specific practices, roles, and values to women and men. Gender roles have changed from era to era, differing according to social class and between rural and urban societies. Observing gender roles across time, the student discovers that social, political, economic, and cultural history are always interrelated; that the present is related to the past; and that social change brings gains and losses rather than evolution in a straight line—three lessons all history courses teach.

War   No history of Europe could fail to pay attention to war, which, for most polities, has been their most demanding activity. Warfare has strained whatever resources were available from ancient times to the present, leading governments to invent new ways to extract wealth and mobilize support. War has built and undermined states, stimulated science and consumed technology, made heroes, and restructured nobility, schooling, and social services. Glorified in European culture and often condemned, war in every era has affected the lives of all its peoples. This historical significance, more than specific battles, is one of the themes of *The Western Experience.*

Religion   Religion has been basic to the human experience, and our textbook explores the different religious institutions and experiences that societies developed. Religion affects and is affected by all the themes we address, creating community and causing conflict, shaping intellectual and daily life, providing the experiences that bind individual lives and society within a common system of meaning.

Cultural Expression   For authors of a general history, no decision is more difficult than the space devoted to cultural expression. In this respect, as elsewhere, we have striven for a balance between high and popular culture. We present as clearly and concisely as possible the most important formal ideas, philosophies, and ideologies of each era. We emphasize concepts of recognized importance in the general history of ideas and those concepts that illuminate behavior and discourse in a given period. We pay particular attention to developments in science that we believe are related to important intellectual, economic, and social trends. Popular culture appears both in specific sections and throughout the book. We want to place popular culture within its social and historical con-text but not make the gulf too wide between popular and high or formal culture. Finally, we write about many of the great works of literature, art, architecture, and music. Because of the difficulties of selection, we have tried to emphasize works that are cultural expressions of their time but that also have been influential over the ages and around the globe.

Attention to these seven themes occasions problems of organization and selection. We could have structured this book around a series of topical essays, perhaps repeating the series of themes for each of the standard chronological divisions of European history. Instead, we chose to preserve a narrative flow that emphasizes interrelationships and historical context. We wanted each chapter to stand as an interpretive historical essay, with a beginning and conclusion. As a result, the themes emerge repeatedly within discussions of a significant event, an influential institution, an individual life, or a whole period of time. Or they may intersect in a single institution or historical trend. Nevertheless, readers can follow any one of these themes across time and use that theme as a measure of change and a way to assess the differences and similarities between societies.

CHANGES TO THE NINTH EDITION

For us the greatest pleasure in a revision lies in the challenge of absorbing and then incorporating the latest developments in historical understanding. From its first edition, this book included more of the results of quantitative and social history than most general textbooks of European history, an obvious reflection of our own research. Each subsequent edition provided an occasion to incorporate current methods and new knowledge, such as the rise of gender studies: a challenge that required reconsidering paragraphs, sections, and whole chapters in the light of new theories and new research, sometimes literally reconceptualizing part of the past.

Newly Revised Chapter 25: "Progress and Its Discontents"

From the last edition, chapters 25 and 26, "European Power: Wealth, Knowledge, and Imperialism" and "The Age of Progress," have been combined into a new chapter 25, "Progress and Its Discontents." Relevant material on imperial Europe has been moved to chapter 26. This new chapter 25 treats late-nineteenth-century economic transformations that brought the bourgeoisie to power along with the intellectual developments that both reinforced that power and raised doubts about its bases and its legitimacy. It also explores the class identity of the new ruling elite and examines both the pleasures and anxieties evoked by the mass commercial culture it created.

New Chapter 26: "Nineteenth-Century Empires"

In the past fifteen years, European historians increasingly have acknowledged the centrality of imperial experience to European history. Spanning a long nineteenth century from 1780 to 1914, this chapter not only explores the impact of major European economic, cultural, and political developments on imperial practice and attitudes, but also explores the profound impact of imperialism on Europe itself (making use of new scholarship on gender and popular culture, for example, to show how empire increasingly touched upon the lives of everyday Europeans). The chapter thus argues that empire did not happen "out there," but at the center of nineteenth-century European society and culture. This chapter includes fresh new illustrations and photographs, primary source boxes, and a Global Moment box on the Indian Rebellion of 1857.

Newly Revised Chapter 27: "World War I and the World It Created"

The revised chapter 27 brings to bear new scholarship on the war, including research on gender relations and the home front and on the imperial dimension of war. It emphasizes in particular how the military mobilization of the colonies—combined with the postwar rhetoric of national self-determination—raised expectations of colonial reform and gradual self-government. When these hopes were disappointed in the postwar period, the chapter shows, colonial reform movements were transformed into militant movements for colonial independence.

Streamlined Narrative throughout the Book

All of the chapters in the ninth edition have been substantially shortened and streamlined. We have worked to make difficult concepts more understandable and to remove material that interfered with the general flow of the text.

New Global Moment Features

The process whereby worldwide connections have intensified in the past two centuries, usually referred to as globalization, has caused a revision in the way we think about the histories of individual states and regions. Although revolutions in communications and transport have made the interconnections inescapable since the 1800s, it is important to see them in perspective and to pay attention to early signs of cross-cultural activity. Five Global Moment boxed essays highlight significant occasions when Europeans had to come to terms with neighbors in other continents. And we have tried, throughout, to keep students aware of the larger context within which European history has developed.

PEDAGOGICAL FEATURES

Each generation of students brings different experiences, interests, and training into the classroom—changes that are important to the teaching-learning process. The students we teach have taught us what engages or confuses them, what impression of European history they bring to college, and what they can be expected to take from a survey course. Current political, social, and cultural events also shape what we teach and how we teach. Our experience as teachers and the helpful comments of scores of other teachers have led to revisions and new additions throughout the book as we have sought to make it clearer and more accessible without sacrificing our initial goal of writing a reasonably sophisticated, interpretive, and analytic history.

Primary Source Boxes

These excerpts from primary sources are designed to illustrate or supplement points made in the text, to provide some flavor of the issues under discussion, and to allow beginning students some of that independence of judgment that comes from a careful reading of historical sources.

"THEY HAVE A MASTER CALLED LAW"

As King Xerxes leads his army into Greece in 480 B.C., he asks a former king of Sparta, who is accompanying him, whether the Greeks will really fight against the Persians.

"Now, Demaratus, I will ask you what I want to know. You are a Greek and one from no minor or weak city. So now tell me, will the Greeks stand and fight me?" Demaratus replied, "Your Majesty, shall I tell you the truth, or say what you want to hear?" The king ordered him to tell the truth, saying that he would respect him no less for doing so.

"Your Majesty," he said, "I am not speaking about all of them, only about the Spartans. First, I say they will never accept conditions from you that would enslave Greece; second, that they will fight you in battle even if all the other Greeks join your side."

Xerxes said, "Demaratus, let's look at it in all logic: why should a thousand, or ten thousand, or fifty thousand men, if they are all free and not ruled by a single master, stand up against such an army as mine? If they were ruled by one man, like my subjects, I suppose they might, out of fear, show more bravery than usual and, driven into battle by the lash, go up against a bigger force; but if allowed their freedom, they wouldn't do either one."

Demaratus said, "Your Majesty, I knew from the beginning that if I spoke the truth you wouldn't like my message, but, since you ordered me to do so, I told you about the Spartans. They are free men, but not wholly free: They have a master called Law, whom they fear far more than your soldiers fear you. And his orders are always the same—they must not run away from any army no matter how big, but must stand in their formation and either conquer or die. But, your Majesty, may your wishes be fulfilled."

From *Herodotus*, book VII, M. H. Chambers (tr.).

Historical Issues Boxes

These boxes explain major controversies over historical interpretations so that students can see how historical understanding is constructed. They encourage students to participate in these debates and formulate their own positions.

New *Global Moment Boxes*

These boxes focus on particularly vivid occasions when Europeans encountered other world civilizations, in order to suggest the broader context within which Western history unfolded.

HISTORICAL ISSUES: TWO VIEWS OF LOUIS XIV

Implicit in any assessment of the reign of Louis XIV in France is a judgment about the nature of absolutism and the kind of government the continental European monarchies created in the late seventeenth and eighteenth centuries. From the perspective of Frenchman Albert Sorel, a historian of the French Revolution writing at the end of the nineteenth century, the Revolution had been necessary to save France from Louis' heritage. For the American John Rule, a historian who concerned himself primarily with the development of political institutions during the seventeenth century, the marks of Louis XIV's rule were caution, bureaucracy, and order.

Sorel: "The edifice of the state enjoyed incomparable brilliance and splendor, but it resembled a Gothic cathedral in which the height of the nave and the arches had been pushed beyond all reason, weakening the walls as they were raised ever higher. Louis XIV carried the principle of monarchy to its utmost limit, and abused it in all respects to the point of excess. He left the nation crushed by war, mutilated by banishments, and impatient of the yoke which it felt to be ruinous. Men were worn-out, the treasury empty, all relationships strained by the violence of tension, and in the immense framework of the state there remained no institution except the accidental appearance of genius. Things had reached a point where, if a great king did not appear, there would be a great revolution."

From Albert Sorel, *L'Europe et la révolution française*, 3rd ed., Vol. 1, Paris, 1893, p. 199, as translated in William F. Church (ed.), *The Greatness of Louis XIV: Myth or Reality?*, Boston: D. C. Heath, 1959, p. 63.

Rule: "As Louis XIV himself said of the tasks of kingship, they were at once great, noble, and delightful. Yet Louis' enjoyment of his craft was tempered by political prudence. At an early age he learned to listen attentively to his advisers, to speak when spoken to, to ponder evidence, to avoid confrontations, to dissemble, to wait. He believed that time and tact would conquer. Despite all the evidence provided him by his ministers and his servants, Louis often hesitated before making a decision; he brooded, and in some instances put off decisions altogether. As he grew older, the king tended to hide his person and his office. Even his officials seldom saw the king for more than a brief interview. And as decision-making became centralized in the hands of the ministers, [so] the municipalities, the judges, the local estates, the guilds and at times the peasantry contested royal encroachments on their rights. Yet to many in the kingdom, Louis represented a modern king, an agent of stability whose struggle was their struggle and whose goal was to contain the crises of the age."

From John C. Rule, "Louis XIV, *Roi-Bureaucrate*," in Rule (ed.), *Louis XIV and the Craft of Kingship*, Columbus: Ohio State University Press, 1969, pp. 91–92.

Global Moment

THREE EMPIRES AND AN ELEPHANT

Although trade and diplomatic ties between the West and the East diminished in the period of the seventh through the tenth centuries, merchants, pilgrims, envoys, and religious officials still traveled extensively and spread news. If we look at events surrounding the year 800, we find that diplomatic missions among the Franks (a Germanic kingdom), the Byzantines (the Eastern Roman Empire), and the Abbasid caliphate (an Arabic-speaking Muslim empire) continued. The main actors in these negotiations and contacts were Charles the Great or Charlemagne (r. 768–814), king of the Franks and, as of Christmas Day 800, Roman emperor in the West; Irene (r. 796–802), who became empress of Roman Empire in the East after she blinded her son, who subsequently died; and the Caliph Harun al-Rashid (786–809), heir to the Abbasid Dynasty, centered in Baghdad in Persia.

These three rulers dominated the area around the Mediterranean, but their empires were vastly different in terms of economic sophistication, religion, and in

the scholars were the world's leaders in medicine and science. A great hospital flourished in this period. Harun al-Rashid was said to have sponsored the "golden age" for the Arabic world. It took centuries for Arab learning in geography, astronomy, and medicine to reach the West. Charlemagne's court in Aachen was a long way from this intellectual achievement and cultural splendor.

The three empires had a history of clashes. The Arabic expansions had left the Eastern Roman Empire with far less territory. The Franks and other Germanic tribes had taken over the Western Empire and established independent kingdoms, with the Franks conquering most of them. Charlemagne, as King of the Franks, wanted the title of emperor. But before 800, no other Germanic ruler had had the audacity to take the title of emperor of the Romans, and he had some trepidation over assuming the title without permission or blessings of the real successor to the title in Constantinople. The Franks and the Arabs also had considerable conflicts. After all, Charlemagne's grandfather, Charles Martel, had defeated the Arabs 70 years before (732) and he,

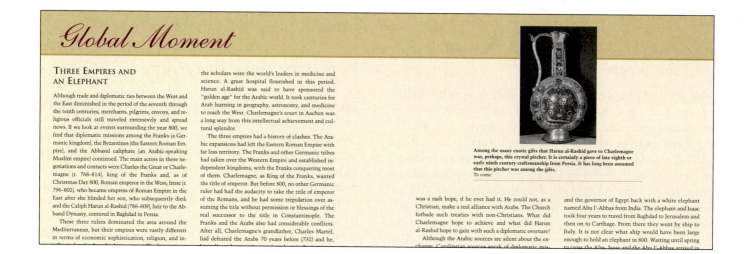

Among the many exotic gifts that Harun al-Rashid gave to Charlemagne was, perhaps, this crystal pitcher. It is certainly a piece of late eighth or early ninth century craftsmanship from Persia. It has long been assumed that this pitcher was among the gifts.
To come

was a rash hope, if he ever had it. He could not, as a Christian, make a real alliance with Arabs. The Church forbade such treaties with non-Christians. What did Charlemagne hope to achieve and what did Harun al-Rashid hope to gain with such a diplomatic overture?

Although the Arabic sources are silent about the exchange, Carolingian sources speak of diplomatic mis...

and the governor of Egypt back with a white elephant named Abu l'-Abbas from India. The elephant and Isaac took four years to travel from Baghdad to Jerusalem and then on to Carthage. From there they went by ship to Italy. It is not clear what ship would have been large enough to hold an elephant in 800. Waiting until spring to cross the Alps, Isaac and the Abu l'-Abbas arrived in

New *Chapter-Opening Timelines*

Each chapter now opens with a new timeline. These timelines are meant to offer students a visual aid with which to track simultaneous developments and important dates to remember. Ultimately, we hope that they will help give readers a grounded sense of chronology.

1800	1820	1840	1860	1880	1900

Indian Rebellion 1857

Taiping Rebellion in China 1850–1864

The Great Trek of the Afrikaners in southern Africa 1835–1845

Britain abolishes slavery 1834

1807 Britain abolishes the slave trade

1804–1825 Latin American liberation from colonial rule

1791 Haitian Revolution

1859 Darwin, *On the Origin of Species*

1869 Opening of the Suez Canal

1884–1885 Berlin Conference

1885 Indian National Congress established

1894–1895 zz War

1896 Ethiopian defeat of the Italians at Adowa

1898 Fashoda Crisis

1900 Boxer Rebellion in China

1899–1902 Boer War in southern Africa

1904–1905 Russo-Japanese War

New *Chapter-Opening Outlines*

Each chapter now opens with a short outline to give students a sense of what's to come in each chapter.

Chapter Twenty

THE FRENCH REVOLUTION

REFORM AND POLITICAL CRISIS • 1789: THE FRENCH REVOLUTION •
THE RECONSTRUCTION OF FRANCE • THE SECOND REVOLUTION

Well into the eighteenth century, the long-standing social structures and political institutions of Europe were securely entrenched. Most monarchs still claimed to hold their authority directly from God. In cooperation with their aristocracies, they presided over realms composed of distinct orders of citizens, or *estates* as they were sometimes known. Each order had its particular rights, privileges, and obligations. But pressures for change were building during the century. In France, the force of public opinion grew increasingly potent by the 1780s. A financial or political crisis that could normally be managed by the monarchy threatened to snowball in this new environment. Such vulnerability was less evident in Austria, Prussia, and Russia, however, where strong monarchs instituted reforms to streamline their governments. Similarly, in Britain the political system proved resilient despite explosions of discontent at home and across the Atlantic.

Unquestionably, then, the French Revolution constituted the pivotal event of European history in the late eighteenth century. From its outbreak in 1789, the Revolution transformed the nature of sovereignty and law in France. Under its impetus, civic and social institutions were renewed, from local government and schooling to family relations and assistance for the poor. Soon its ideals of liberty, equality, and fraternity resonated across the borders of other European states, especially after war broke out in 1792 and French armies took the offensive.

The French Revolution's innovations defined the foundations of a liberal society and polity. Both at home and abroad, however, the new regime faced formidable opposition, and its struggle for survival propelled it in unanticipated directions. Some unforeseen turns, such as democracy and republicanism, became precedents for the future even if they soon aborted. Other developments, such as the Reign of Terror, seemed to nullify the original liberal values of 1789. The bloody struggles of the Revolution thus cast a shadow over this transformative event as they dramatized the brutal dilemma of means versus ends.

New *Glossary and Key Terms*

Reviewers of the last edition requested this new feature. Glossary words are bolded in each chapter and compiled in the end-of-book glossary.

Cahiers and Elections   For the moment, however, patriot spokesmen stood far in advance of their grass roots. The king had invited all citizens in their local parishes to elect delegates to electoral assemblies and to draft grievances (*cahiers*) setting forth their views. The great majority of rural cahiers were highly traditional in tone and complained only of particular local ills or hardships, expressing confidence that the king would

Anabaptists Individuals who, citing that the Bible nowhere mentions infant baptism, argued that the sacrament was effective only if the believer understood what was happening and that therefore adults ought to be rebaptized. Opponents argued that infant baptism was necessary so that a baby would not be denied salvation if it died young.

anarchists Radical activists who called for the abolition of the state, sometimes by violent means.

The Art

The ninth edition of *The Western Experience* continues the precedent of earlier editions, with more than four hundred full-color reproductions of paintings and photographs and over one hundred clearly focused maps.

The Maps

The maps in *The Western Experience* are already much admired by instructors. Each carries an explanatory caption that enhances the text coverage to help students tackle the content without sacrificing subtlety of interpretation or trying to escape the fact that history is complex. In the ninth edition, each caption has been further improved with a thought question.

MAP 3.2 THE EMPIRE OF ALEXANDER THE GREAT AND THE ROUTE OF HIS CONQUESTS
Alexander formed the largest empire known down to his own time. He even conquered some territory across the Indus River in India. What were the two major Persian cities near the Persian Gulf?
◆ For an online version, go to www.mhhe.com/chambers9 > chapter 3 > book maps

---

QUESTIONS FOR FURTHER THOUGHT

1. The Greeks invented historical writing. In looking at the past, what are the most important questions a historian should ask?

2. The Greek city-states and their system of alliances gave way to the rising power of Macedonia. How might the Greek states have preserved their strength and political power?

Questions for Further Thought

To encourage students to move beyond rote learning of historical "facts" and to think broadly about history, the authors have added "Questions for Further Thought" at the end of each chapter. These are too broad to be exam questions; instead, they are meant to be questions that stimulate the students to think about history and social, political, and economic forces. Some are comparative, some require students to draw on knowledge of a previous chapter, some ask about the role of great leaders in politics, and some ask about how the less famous people living at the time perceived the events surrounding them.

More Heading Levels

We have given particular attention to adding more descriptive content guides, such as the consistent use of three levels of headings. We believe these will help students identify specific topics for purposes of study and review as well as give a clear outline of a chapter's argument.

Chronological Charts

Nearly every chapter employs charts and chronological tables that outline the unfolding of major events and social processes and serve as a convenient reference for students.

CHRONOLOGY
The Persian Wars
(All dates B.C.)

499, autumn	Greek cities of Ionia in Asia Minor revolt from Persian Empire.
498	Athens and Eretria (on island of Euboea) take part in burning Sardis in Persian Empire.
496	Persians besiege Miletus, the leading city in the revolt.
494	Fall of Miletus.
493	End of Ionian revolt.
492, spring	Persian expedition to northern Greece suffers heavy losses in storms.
490, mid-August	Battle of Marathon near Athens; Persians defeated.
486, November	Death of King Darius of Persia; accession of Xerxes.
484, spring–480, spring	Xerxes prepares for new invasion of Greece.
480, spring	Persian army sets out from Sardis.
480, late August	Battles of Thermopylae and Artemisium.
480, late September	Battle of Salamis.
479, early August	Battle of Plataea.

AVAILABLE FORMATS

To provide an alternative to the full-length hardcover edition, *The Western Experience* Ninth Edition, is available in two-volume and three-volume paperbound editions.

- Volume I includes chapters 1–17 and covers material through the eighteenth century.
- Volume II includes chapters 15–30 and covers material since the sixteenth century.
- Volume A includes chapters 1–12, Antiquity and the Middle Ages.
- Volume B includes chapters 11–21, The Early Modern Era.
- Volume C includes chapters 19–30, The Modern Era.

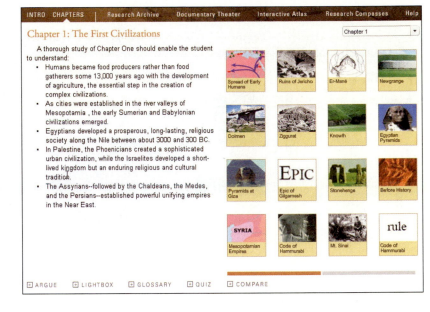

SUPPLEMENTARY INSTRUCTIONAL MATERIALS

McGraw-Hill offers instructors and students a wide variety of ancillary materials to accompany *The Western Experience*. Please contact your local McGraw-Hill representative for details concerning policies, prices, and availability.

For the Instructor

Instructor's Resource CD-ROM   The Instructor's Resource CD-ROM (IRCD) contains several instructor tools on one easy CD-ROM. For lecture preparation, teachers will find an Instructor's Manual with PowerPoint samples by chapter. For quizzes and tests, the IRCD contains a test bank and *EZ Test*, McGraw-Hill's flexible and easy-to-use electronic testing program. Extras on the IRCD also include map images from the book as well as extra photographs and art images.

Online Learning Center for Instructors   At www.mhhe.com/chambers9. At this home page for the text-specific website, instructors will find a series of online tools to meet a wide range of classroom needs. The Instructor's Manual, PowerPoint presentations, and blank maps can be downloaded by instructors, but are password protected to prevent tampering. Instructors can also create an interactive course syllabus using McGraw-Hill's *PageOut* (www.mhhe.com/pageout).

Overhead Transparency Acetates   This expanded full-color transparency package includes all the maps and chronological charts in the text.

For the Student

McGraw-Hill's *Primary Source Investigator* (PSI) CD-ROM   This CD-ROM, bound into each copy of *The Western Experience*, provides students with instant access to hundreds of world history documents, images, artifacts, audio recordings, and videos. PSI helps students practice the art of "doing history" on a real archive of historical sources. Students follow the three basic steps of *Ask, Research,* and *Present* to examine sources, take notes on them, and then save or print copies of the sources as evidence for their papers or presentations. After researching a particular theme, individual, or time period, students can use PSI's writing guide to walk them through the steps of developing a thesis, organizing their evidence, and supporting their conclusion.

More than just a history or writing tool, the PSI is also a student study tool that contains interactive maps, quiz questions, and an interactive glossary with audio pronunciation guide.

Student Study Guide/Workbook with Map Exercises, Volumes I and II   Includes the following features for each chapter: chapter outlines, chronological diagrams, four kinds of exercises—map exercises, exercises in document analysis, exercises that reinforce the book's important overarching themes, exercises in matching important terms with significant individuals—and essay topics requiring analysis and speculation.

The Online Learning Center   At www.mhhe.com/chambers9. The Online Learning Center is a fully interactive, book-specific website featuring numerous student study tools such as multiple-choice and true-false practice quizzes; interactive, drag-and-drop games about significant individuals and chronologies; key terms with correct identifications; an audio function to help students pronounce difficult terms; and drag-and-drop map exercises. Animated maps from the book are also available through the site. These maps carry a specific URL in their caption.

ACKNOWLEDGMENTS

Manuscript Reviewers, Ninth Edition

Robert Bast, University of Tennessee; Stephen Blumm, Montgomery County Community College; Nathan Brooks, New Mexico State University; Susan Carrafiello, Wright State University; Steven Fanning, University of Illinois at Chicago; Betsy Hertzler, Mesa Community College; Paul Hughes, Sussex County Community College; Mary Kelly, Franklin Pierce College; Paul Lockhart, Wright State University; Eileen Moore, University of Alabama at Birmingham; Penne Prigge, Rockingham Community College; William Roberts, Fairleigh Dickinson University; Steven Ross, Louisiana State University; Charles Sullivan, University of Dallas; Robert Thurston, Miami University.

Manuscript Reviewers, Eighth Edition

Tyler Blethen, West Carolina University; Owen Bradley, University of Tennessee; Dan Brown, Moorpark College; Richard Cole, Luther College; Vickie Cook, Pima Community College; Mary DeCredico, U.S. Naval Academy; Gunar Freibergs, Los Angeles Valley College; Ron Goldberg, Thomas Nelson Community College; Neil Heyman, San Diego State University; Elizabeth McCrank, Boston University; Edrene Stephens McKay, Northwest Arkansas Community College; George Monahan, Suf-folk Community College; Fred Murphy, Western Kentucky University; Laura Pintar, Loyola University; Anne Quartararo, U.S. Naval Academy; Thomas Rowland, University of Wisconsin–Oshkosh; Charles Steen, University of New Mexico; Sig Sutterlin, Indian Hills Community College; John Tanner, Palomar College; Valentina Tikoff, DePaul University; Guangquin Xu, Northwest Arkansas Community College.

Manuscript Reviewers, Seventh Edition

Frank Baglione, Tallahassee Community College; Paul Goodwin, University of Connecticut; Robert Herzstein, University of South Carolina; Carla M. Joy, Red Rocks Community College; Kathleen Kamerick, University of Iowa; Carol Bresnahan Menning, University of Toledo; Eileen Moore, University of Alabama at Birmingham; Frederick Murphy, Western Kentucky University; Michael Myers, University of Notre Dame; Robert B. Patterson, University of South Carolina at Columbia; Peter Pierson, Santa Clara University; Alan Schaffer, Clemson University; Marc Schwarz, University of New Hampshire; Charles R. Sullivan, University of Dallas; Jack Thacker, Western Kentucky University; Bruce L. Venarde, University of Pittsburgh.

Manuscript Reviewers, Sixth Edition

S. Scott Bartchy, University of California, Los Angeles; Thomas Blomquist, Northern Illinois University; Nancy Ellenberger, U.S. Naval Academy; Steven Epstein, University of Colorado at Boulder; Laura Gellott, University of Wisconsin at Parkside; Drew Harrington, Western Kentucky University; Lisa Lane, Mira Costa College; William Matthews, S.U.N.Y. at Potsdam; Carol Bresnahan Menning, University of Toledo; Sandra Norman, Florida Atlantic University; Peter Pierson, Santa Clara University; Linda Piper, University of Georgia; Philip Racine, Wofford College; Eileen Soldwedel, Edmonds Community College; John Sweets, University of Kansas; Richard Wagner, Des Moines Area Community College.

Focus Group Reviewers from Spring 1992

Michael DeMichele, University of Scranton; Nancy Ellenberger, U.S. Naval Academy; Drew Harrington, Western Kentucky University; William Matthews, S.U.N.Y. at Potsdam.

We would like to thank Lyn Uhl, Monica Eckman, Angela Kao, and Emily Hatteberg of McGraw-Hill for their considerable efforts in bringing this edition to fruition.

THE WESTERN EXPERIENCE

Pietro Longhi
THE GEOGRAPHY LESSON
This painting of *The Geography Lesson* **evokes the interest in exotic places among Europe's educated elites, male and female, during the eighteenth centruy.**
Cameraphoto/Art Resource, NY

Chapter Nineteen

THE AGE OF ENLIGHTENMENT

THE ENLIGHTENMENT • EIGHTEENTH-CENTURY ELITE CULTURE • POPULAR CULTURE

Sharp breaks have been rare in Europe's intellectual and religious life—two of the defining themes in the Western experience—but we are about to witness one. During the eighteenth century, the great scientific and philosophical innovations of the previous century evolved into a naturalistic worldview divorced from religion. Scientific knowledge and religious skepticism, previously the concerns of an extremely narrow group of learned people, entered the consciousness of Europe's elites in a way that would have startled Descartes or Newton. Displacing the authority of religion with that of reason, the new outlook offered an optimistic vision of future progress in human affairs. Known as the Enlightenment, this movement formed the intellectual foundation for a new sense of modernity.

Never since pagan times, certainly not during the Renaissance, was religious belief so directly challenged. Many important eighteenth-century intellectuals no longer believed in Christianity and wished to reduce its influence in society. They argued that there was no divine standard of morality, no afterlife to divert humanity from worldly concerns. These writers developed a strong, sometimes arrogant, sense of their own capacity to ignore traditional authority and guide society toward change.

The evolution of cultural institutions and the media of the day gave these writers an increasingly wide forum. While aristocratic patronage and classical culture remained influential, a new kind of middle-class culture was developing alongside a much wider reading public and an expanding sphere of public discussion.

Yet, as we turn to consider the Enlightenment within the varied cultural environments of the eighteenth century, we should not exaggerate. Although they were critics of their society, most eighteenth-century intellectuals lived comfortably amid Europe's high culture. They had scant interest in or understanding of the vibrant popular culture around them. On the contrary, their growing belief in "public opinion" referred solely to the educated elites of the aristocracy and the middle classes.

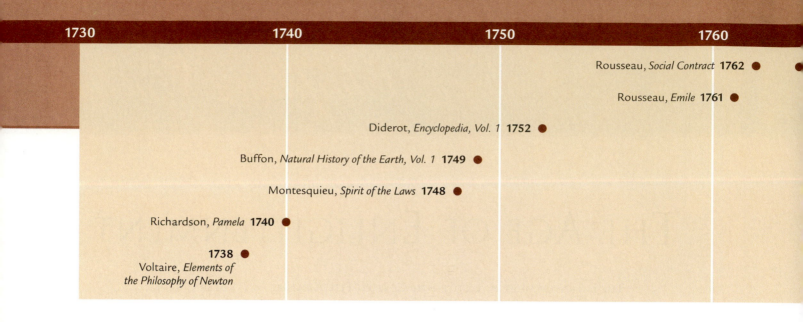

Rousseau, *Social Contract* **1762**

Rousseau, *Emile* **1761**

Diderot, *Encyclopedia, Vol. 1* **1752**

Buffon, *Natural History of the Earth, Vol. 1* **1749**

Montesquieu, *Spirit of the Laws* **1748**

Richardson, *Pamela* **1740**

1738
Voltaire, *Elements of
the Philosophy of Newton*

THE ENLIGHTENMENT

Building on seventeenth-century science, skepticism in matters of religion, and a heightened appreciation for the culture of classical antiquity, eighteenth-century intellectuals approached their calling in a new spirit. They believed that human behavior and institutions could be studied rationally, like Newton's universe, and that their faults could be corrected. They saw themselves as participants in a movement—which they called the Enlightenment—that could make educated men and women more rational, tolerant, and virtuous. While the Enlightenment had creative adherents across the Western world, its capital was undoubtedly in Paris, where an ideology of progress and freedom gradually took shape. Renowned writers such as Voltaire, Diderot, and Rousseau produced a steady flow of remarkable works across a wide range of subjects, which governmental censorship could not suppress, try as it might.

The Broadening Reverberations of Science

It is hard to think of two men less revolutionary in temperament than the seventeenth century's René Descartes and Isaac Newton. Both were conservative on matters outside the confines of science, had relatively little concern for social institutions, remained practicing Christians, and wrote only for small learned audiences. Yet their legacy of insight into the world of nature produced in succeeding generations what has been described as "a permanent intellectual insurrection," which unfolded in a spirit undreamed of by either man.

The Popularization of Science While eighteenth-century scientists pondered the cosmologies of Descartes and Newton, nonscientists in England and on the Continent applied the methodologies of Descartes, Newton, and the philosopher John Locke to other realms of human thought. They fused the notion of methodical doubt and naturalistic explanations of phenomena into a scientific or mathematical spirit, which at bottom simply meant confidence in reason and a skeptical attitude toward accepted dogmas. They attempted to popularize scientific method, with the aim of transforming the values of Western civilization. Writers translated the discoveries of scientists into clear and even amusing general reading. The literary talents of these enthusiasts helped make household words of Newton and Descartes among educated Europeans.

A more calculating and ambitious propagandist of the scientific spirit was the Frenchman François-Marie Arouet, who wrote under the pen name of Voltaire and is virtually synonymous with the Enlightenment. While his chief talents lay in literature and criticism, Voltaire also spent some time studying Newton's work. In 1738, in collaboration with his friend Madame du Châtelet, he published a widely read popularization called *Elements of the Philosophy of Newton.* However dry the study of physics, Voltaire argued, it frees the mind from dogma, and its experimental methods provide a model for the liberation of human thought. Moreover, Voltaire related Newton's achievement to the environment of a liberal England that also produced Francis Bacon and John Locke, the three of whom Voltaire adopted as his personal Trinity. In his *Philosophical Letters on the English* (1734)—a celebration of English toleration and an indirect attack on religious bigotry, censorship, and social snobbery in France—Voltaire had already noted the respect enjoyed in England by its writers and scientists.

Popularizations of scientific method stimulated public interest in science, as mathematicians, cartogra-

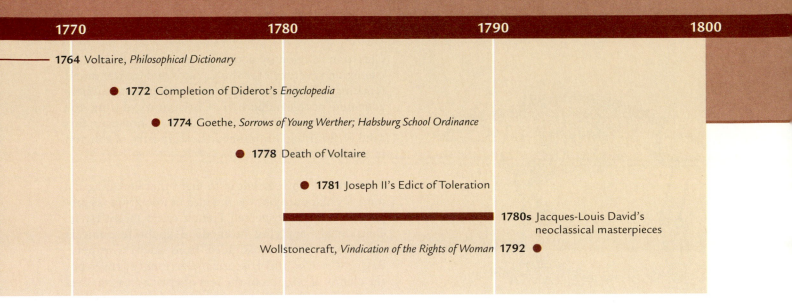

1770   **1780**   **1790**   **1800**

1764 Voltaire, *Philosophical Dictionary*

1772 Completion of Diderot's *Encyclopedia*

1774 Goethe, *Sorrows of Young Werther; Habsburg School Ordinance*

1778 Death of Voltaire

1781 Joseph II's Edict of Toleration

1780s Jacques-Louis David's neoclassical masterpieces

Wollstonecraft, *Vindication of the Rights of Woman* **1792**

French chemist Lavoisier conducts an experiment in his laboratory to study the composition of air during the process of respiration. Bettmann/Corbis

phers, and astronomers made notable advances in their fields. But further scientific progress was far from automatic. In chemistry, for example, the traditions of alchemy persisted, and phenomena such as fire long escaped objective analysis. At the end of the century, however, a major breakthrough occurred when the Englishman Joseph Priestley isolated oxygen and the Frenchman Antoine Lavoisier analyzed the components of air and water and came close to explaining the process of combustion.

The vogue for science also had a dubious side, apparent, for example, in the great popularity of mesmerism. This pseudoscience of magnetic fields purported to offer its wealthy devotees relief from a variety of ailments by the use of special "electrical" baths and treatments. Although repeatedly condemned by the Academy of Sciences in Paris, mesmerism continued to attract educated followers.

Natural History   The most widely followed scientific enterprise in the eighteenth century was **natural history,** the science of the earth's development—a combination of geology, zoology, and botany. This field of study was easy for the nonscientist to appreciate. Its foremost practitioner was G. L. Buffon, keeper of the French Botanical Gardens—a patronage position that allowed him to produce a multivolume *Natural History of the Earth* between 1749 and 1778. Drawing on a vast knowledge of phenomena such as fossils, Buffon went beyond previous attempts to classify the data of nature and provided both a description and a theory of the earth's development.

An image of a mastadon from the section on fossil remains in Buffon's *Natural History*.
Courtesy Brooklyn Public Library

Although he was a nonbeliever, Buffon did not explicitly attack religious versions of such events as the Creation; he simply ignored them, an omission of obvious significance to his readers. Similarly, while he did not specifically contend that human beings have evolved from beasts, he implied it. "It is possible," he wrote, "to descend by almost insensible degrees from the most perfect creature to the most formless matter." Buffon's earth did not derive from a singular act of divine creation that would explain the origins of human beings. The readers of his *Natural History* or its numerous popularizations in several languages thus encountered a universe that had developed through evolution.

Beyond Christianity

The erosion of biblical revelation as a source of authority is one hallmark of the Enlightenment. This shift derived some of its impetus from seventeenth-century scientists and liberal theologians who were themselves believing Christians but who opposed religious superstition or "enthusiasm," as they called it. They had hoped to accommodate religion to new philosophical standards and scientific formulations by eliminating the superstitious imagery that could make religion seem ridiculous and by treating the world of nature as a form of revelation in which God's majesty could be seen. The devil, for example, could be considered as a category of moral evil rather than as a specific horned creature with a pitchfork. They hoped to bolster the

Christian religion by deemphasizing miracles and focusing on reverence for the Creator and on the moral teachings of the Bible. Their approach did indeed help educated people adhere to Christianity during the eighteenth century. In the final analysis, however, this kind of thinking diminished the authority of religion in society.

Toleration   One current of thought that encouraged a more secular outlook was the idea of toleration, as propounded by the respected French critic Pierre Bayle. Consciously applying methodical doubt to subjects that Descartes had excluded from such treatment, Bayle's *Critical and Historical Dictionary* (1697) put the claims of religion to the test of critical reason. Certain Christian traditions emerged from this scrutiny as the equivalent of myth and fairy tale, and the history of Christianity appeared as a record of fanaticism and persecution. Bayle's chief target was Christianity's attempts to impose orthodoxy at any cost (for example, the Spanish Inquisition and Louis XIV's revocation of the Edict of Nantes and persecution of French Protestants). Though a devout Calvinist himself, Bayle advocated complete toleration, which would allow any person to practice any religion or none at all. An individual's moral behavior rather than his or her creed is what mattered, according to Bayle.

The most striking success of the eighteenth-century campaign for toleration came with the Edict of Toleration issued by the Habsburg emperor Joseph II on his ascendancy to the throne in 1781. For the first time, a Catholic Habsburg ruler recognized the right of Protestants and Jews in his realm to worship freely and to hold property and public office (see "Joseph II on Religious Toleration," p. 559). Joseph also tried to reduce the influence of the Catholic Church by ordering the dissolution of numerous monasteries on the grounds that they were useless and corrupt. Part of their confiscated wealth was used to support the medical school at the University of Vienna.

Deism   Voltaire became the Enlightenment's most vigorous antireligious polemicist. This prolific writer was one of the century's most brilliant literary stylists, historians, and poets. Those talents alone would have ensured his fame. But Voltaire was also a dedicated antagonist of Christianity. For tactical reasons, much of his attack against *l'infame* ("the infamous thing"), as he called Christianity, targeted such practices as monasticism or the behavior of priests. His ultimate target, though, was Christianity itself, which, he declared, "every sensible man, every honorable man must hold in horror."

Voltaire's masterpiece, a best seller called *The Philosophical Dictionary* (1764), had to be published

JOSEPH II ON RELIGIOUS TOLERATION

Between 1765 and 1781 Joseph II was joint ruler of the Habsburg Empire with his pious mother, Empress Maria Theresa. Joseph advocated a utilitarian approach to religious toleration (Document 1) but made little headway against Maria Theresa's traditional insistence that the state must actively combat religious dissent. Soon after Maria Theresa's death, Joseph promulgated a series of decrees on religion, including a landmark Toleration Edict for Protestants (Document 2) and even a special, if somewhat less sweeping, edict of toleration for the Jews of his domains.

1. LETTER TO MARIA THERESA, JULY 1777

"The word toleration has caused misunderstanding. . . . God preserve me from thinking it a matter of indifference whether the citizens turn Protestant or remain Catholics. . . . I would give all I possess if all the Protestants of your States would go over to Catholicism. The word *toleration* as I understand it, means only that I would employ any persons, without distinction of religion, in purely temporal matters, allow them to own property, practice trades, be citizens if they were qualified and if this would be of advantage to the State and its industry. . . . The undisturbed practice of their religion makes them far better subjects and causes them to avoid irreligion, which is a far greater danger to our Catholics."

2. TOLERATION EDICT OF OCTOBER 1781

"We have found Ourselves moved to grant to the adherents of the Lutheran and Calvinist religions, and also to the non Uniat Greek religion, everywhere, the appropriate private practice of their faith. . . . The Catholic religion alone shall continue to enjoy the prerogative of the public practice of its faith. . . . Non-Catholics are in future admitted under dispensation to buy houses and real property, to acquire municipal domicile and practice as master craftsmen, to take up academic appointments and posts in the public service, and are not to be required to take the oath in any form contrary to their religious tenets. . . . In all choices or appointments to official posts . . . difference of religion is to be disregarded."

From C. A. Macartney (ed.), *The Habsburg and Hohenzollern Dynasties in the 17th and 18th Centuries*, HarperCollins, 1970, pp. 151, 155–157.

anonymously and was burned by the authorities in Switzerland, France, and the Netherlands. Modeled after Bayle's dictionary, it was far more blunt. Of theology, he wrote, "We find man's insanity in all its plenitude." Organized religion is not simply false but pernicious, he argued. Voltaire believed that religious superstition inevitably bred fanaticism and predictably resulted in bloody episodes like the Saint Bartholomew's Day Massacre.

Voltaire hoped that educated Europeans would abandon Christianity in favor of **deism,** a belief that recognized God as the Creator but held that the world, once created, functions according to natural laws without interference by God. Humanity thus lives essentially on its own in an ordered universe, without hope or fear of divine intervention and without the threat of damnation or the hope of eternal salvation. For deists, religion should be a matter of private contemplation rather than public worship and mythic creeds. Although certain figures in the Enlightenment went beyond deism to a philosophical atheism, which rejected any concept of God as unprovable, Voltaire's mild deism remained a characteristic view of eighteenth-century writers. At bottom, however, this form of spirituality was essentially secular. Broad-minded clergy could accept many of the arguments of eighteenth-century science and philosophy, but they could not accept deism.

The Philosophes

Science and secularism became the rallying points of a group of French intellectuals known as the **philosophes.** Their traditionalist opponents employed this term to mock the group's pretensions, but the philosophes themselves used that label with pride. They saw themselves as a vanguard, the men who raised the Enlightenment to the status of a self-conscious movement. The leaders of this influential coterie of writers were Voltaire and Denis Diderot. Its ranks included mathematicians Jean d'Alembert and the Marquis de Condorcet, the magistrate Baron de Montesquieu, the government official Jacques Turgot, and the atheist philosopher Baron d'Holbach. Thus, the French philosophes came from both the aristocracy and the middle class. Outside of France their kinship extended to a group of brilliant Scottish philosophers, including David Hume and Adam Smith; to the German

In 1745 the Habsburg monarchy expelled an estimated seventy thousand Jews from Prague to appease anti-Semitic sentiment.

playwright Gotthold Lessing and the philosopher Immanuel Kant; to the Italian economist and penal reformer the Marquis of Beccaria; and to such founders of the American Philosophical Society as Benjamin Franklin and Thomas Jefferson.

Intellectual Freedom   The philosophes shared above all else a critical spirit, the desire to reexamine the assumptions and institutions of their societies and expose them to the tests of reason, experience, and utility. Today this might sound banal, but it was not so at a time when almost everywhere religion permeated society. Asserting the primacy of reason meant turning away from faith, the essence of religion. It meant a decisive break with the Christian worldview, which placed religious doctrine at the center of society's values. The philosophes invoked the paganism of ancient Greece and Rome, where the spirit of rational inquiry prevailed among educated people. They ridiculed the Middle Ages as the "Dark Ages" and contrasted the religious spirit of that era to their own sense of liberation and modernity. In *The Decline and Fall of the Roman Empire* (1776–1788), the historian Edward Gibbon declared that Christianity had eclipsed a Roman civilization that had sought to live according to reason rather than myths.

The inspiration of antiquity was matched by the stimulus of modern science and philosophy. The philosophes laid claim to Newton, who made the universe intelligible without the aid of revelation, and Locke, who uncovered the workings of the human mind. From Locke they went on to argue that human

personality is malleable: Its nature is not fixed, let alone corrupted by original sin. People are, therefore, ultimately responsible to themselves for what they do with their lives. Existing arrangements are no more nor less sacred than experience has proved them to be. As the humanists had several centuries before, the philosophes placed human beings at the center of thought. Unlike most humanists, however, philosophes placed thought in the service of change and launched a noisy public movement.

Persecution and Triumph   Philosophes appeared clamorous to their contemporaries because they had to battle entrenched authority. Religious traditionalists and the apparatus of censorship in almost all countries threatened the intellectual freedom demanded by the philosophes. They often had to publish their works clandestinely and anonymously. Sometimes they were pressured into withholding manuscripts from publication altogether or into making humiliating public apologies for controversial books. Even with such caution, almost all philosophes saw some of their publications confiscated and burned. A few were forced into exile or sent to jail: Voltaire spent several decades across the French border in Switzerland, and Voltaire and Diderot both spent time in prison. Although the notoriety produced by these persecutions stimulated the sale of their works, the anxiety took its toll.

By the 1770s, however, the philosophes had survived their running war with the authorities. Some of them lived to see their ideas widely accepted and their works acclaimed. In 1778, the last year of his life, Voltaire

WHAT IS ENLIGHTENMENT?

The most concise formulation of the Enlightenment's spirit is conveyed in an essay of the 1780s by the German philosopher Immanuel Kant. As Kant makes clear, intellectual freedom and the role of public opinion refer not so much to the average person in the street as to the educated classes—serious writers (whom he calls "scholars") and their public. Note that in drawing the distinction between the public realm (where freedom is vital) and the private realm (where obedience is rightly expected), Kant reverses the labels that we would likely assign to the two realms today.

"Enlightenment is man's emergence from his self-imposed nonage. Nonage is the inability to use one's own understanding without another's guidance. This nonage is self-imposed if its cause lies not in lack of understanding but in indecision and lack of courage to use one's own mind without another's guidance. Dare to know. (*Sapere aude*). 'Have the courage to use your own understanding,' is therefore the motto of the Enlightenment.

"Laziness and cowardice are the reasons why such a large part of mankind gladly remain minors all their lives, long after nature has freed them from external guidance. They are the reasons why it is so easy for others to set themselves up as guardians. It is so comfortable to be a minor. If I have a book that thinks for me, a pastor who acts as my conscience, then I have no need to exert myself. . . .

"This enlightenment requires nothing but freedom: freedom to make public use of one's reason in all matters. . . . On the other hand, the private use of reason may frequently be narrowly restricted without especially hindering the progress of enlightenment. By 'public use of reason' I mean that use which man, as a scholar, makes of it before the reading public. I call 'private use' that use which a man makes of his reason in a civic post that has been entrusted to him . . . and where arguing is not permitted: one must obey. . . . Thus it would be very unfortunate if an officer on duty and under orders from his superiors should want to criticize the appropriateness or utility of his orders. He must obey. But as a scholar he could not rightfully be prevented from taking notice of the mistakes in the military service and from submitting his views to his public for its judgement."

returned triumphantly to Paris. When he attended a performance of one of his plays at the national theater, the audience greeted him with tumultuous enthusiasm. Even if the philosophes had contributed little else to the Western experience, their struggle for freedom of expression would merit them a significant place in its history.

Pioneering in the Social Sciences But the philosophes achieved far more. In their scholarly and polemical writings, they investigated a wide range of subjects and pioneered in several new disciplines. Some philosophes—Voltaire, for example—were pathbreaking historians. Moving beyond traditional chronicles of battles and rulers' biographies, they studied culture, social institutions, and government structures in an effort to understand past societies as well as describe major events. Practically inventing the notion of social science, they investigated the theoretical foundations of social organization (sociology) and the workings of the human mind (psychology). On a more practical level, they proposed fundamental reforms in such areas as the penal system and education.

The philosophes embedded their study of social science in questions of morality and the study of ethics. Enlightenment ethics were generally utilitarian. Such philosophers as David Hume tried to define good and evil in pragmatic terms; they argued that social utility should become the standard for public morality. This approach to moral philosophy in turn raised the question of whether any human values were absolute and eternal. Among the philosophers who grappled with this challenge, Kant tried to harmonize the notion of absolute moral values with practical reason.

Political Liberty The most influential work of social science produced by the Enlightenment was probably *The Spirit of the Laws* (1748) by the French magistrate Montesquieu. The book offered a comparative study of governments and societies. On the one hand, Montesquieu introduced the perspective of relativism: He tried to analyze the institutions of government in relation to the special customs, climate, religion, and commerce of various countries. He thus argued that no single, ideal model of government existed. On the other hand, he deeply admired his own idealized version of the British system of government; he thereby implied that all societies could learn from the British about liberty.

Montesquieu's sections on liberty won a wide readership in Europe and in America, where the book was influential among the drafters of the U.S. Constitution.

An English engraving entitled "Voltaire's Staircase" suggests how the great writer stood at the center of Europe's literary and intellectual life. The fifth figure from the right at the top, Voltaire is bidding good-bye to d'Alembert, coeditor of the *Encyclopedia*.
Bettmann/Corbis

Political liberty, said Montesquieu, requires checks on those who hold power in a state, whether that power is exercised by a king, an aristocracy, or the people. Liberty can thrive only with a balance of powers, preferably by the separation of the executive, the legislative, and the judicial branches of government. Montesquieu ascribed a central role to aristocracies as checks on royal despotism. Indeed, many eighteenth-century writers on politics considered strong privileged groups, independent from both the crown and the people, as the only effective bulwarks against tyranny. To put it another way, Montesquieu's followers thought that the price for a society free from despotism was privilege for some of its members.

Liberal Economics   French and British thinkers of the Enlightenment transformed economic theory with attacks against mercantilism and government regulation. We noted in chapter 18 Adam Smith's critique of artificial restraints on individual economic initiative. In France, the Physiocrats similarly argued that economic progress depended on freeing agriculture and trade from restrictions. Since in their view (unlike Adam Smith's) land was the only real source of wealth, they also called for reforms in the tax structure, with a uniform and equitable land tax. In opposition to a traditional popular insistence on government intervention to maintain supplies of grain and flour at fair prices, the Physiocrats advocated freedom for the grain trade to operate according to the dictates of supply and demand. The incentive of higher prices would encourage growers to expand productivity, they believed, and in this way the grain shortages that plagued Europe could eventually be eliminated, although at the cost of temporary hardship for most consumers.

Diderot and the Encyclopedia

The Enlightenment thus produced not only a new intellectual spirit but also a wide range of critical writings on various subjects. In addition, the French philosophes collectively generated a single work that exemplified their notion of how knowledge could be useful: Diderot's *Encyclopédie* (*Encyclopedia*).

Within a few years of arriving in Paris as a young man, Denis Diderot had published novels, plays, treatises on mathematics and moral philosophy, and critical essays on religion. His most original writings examined the role of passion in human personality and in any system of values derived from an understanding of human nature. Specifically, Diderot affirmed the role of sexuality, arguing against artificial taboos and repression. As an advocate of what was sometimes called "the natural man," Diderot belies the charge leveled against the philosophes that they overemphasized reason to the neglect of feeling.

Diderot's unusual boldness in getting his works published brought him a considerable reputation but also some real trouble. Two of his books were condemned by the authorities as contrary to religion, the state, and morals. In 1749 he spent one hundred days in prison and was released only after making a humiliating apology. At about that time, Diderot was approached by a publisher to translate a British encyclopedic reference work into French. After a number of false starts, he persuaded the publisher to sponsor instead an entirely new and more comprehensive work that would reflect the interests of the philosophes.

The Encyclopedia   The *Encyclopedia, or Classified Dictionary of the Sciences, Arts, and Occupations*, an inventory of all fields of knowledge from the most theoretical to the most mundane, constituted an arsenal of critical concepts. As the preface stated: "Our Encyclopedia is a work that could only be carried out in a

Diderot's *Encyclopedia* focused much of its attention on technology. Illustrations of mechanical processes, such as the one shown here for making plate glass, filled eleven folio volumes.

philosophic century. . . . All things must be examined without sparing anyone's sensibilities. . . . The arts and sciences must regain their freedom." The ultimate purpose of the *Encyclopedia*, wrote its editors, was "to change the general way of thinking." Written in this spirit by an array of talented collaborators, the expensive twenty-eight-volume *Encyclopedia* (1752–1772) fulfilled the fondest hopes of its editors and four thousand initial subscribers.

In such a work, religion could scarcely be ignored, but neither could it be openly attacked. Instead, the editors treated religion with artful satire or else relegated it to a philosophical or historical plane. Demystified and subordinated, religion was probed and questioned like any other subject, much to the discomfort of learned but orthodox critics.

Science stood at the core of the *Encyclopedia*, but the editors emphasized the technological or practical side of science with numerous articles and plates illustrating machines, tools, and manufacturing processes. They praised the roles of mechanics, engineers, and artisans in society and stressed the benefits of efficient production in the advance of civilization. Such emphasis implied that technology and artisanal skills constituted valuable realms of knowledge comparable to theoretical sciences such as physics and mathematics.

On economic topics the encyclopedists tended to echo the Physiocratic crusade against restrictions on trade and agriculture. On questions of government, the authors generally endorsed absolute monarchy, provided it was reasonably efficient and just. The major political concerns of the editors were civil rights, freedom of expression, and the rule of law.

The Encyclopedia's Impact   In retrospect, after the French Revolution, the *Encyclopedia* does not seem very revolutionary. Yet in the context of the times, it assuredly was. The revolution that Diderot sought was intellectual. As he wrote in a letter to a friend, the encyclopedists were promoting "a revolution in the minds of men to free them from prejudice." Judging by the reaction of religious and government authorities, they were eminently successful. "Up till now," commented one French bishop, "hell has vomited its venom drop by drop." Now, he concluded, it could be found assembled between the *Encyclopedia's* covers.

After allowing the first three volumes to appear, the French government banned the *Encyclopedia* in 1759 and revoked the bookseller's license to issue the remaining volumes. As the attorney general of France put it: "There is a project formed, a society organized to propagate materialism, to destroy religion, to inspire a spirit of independence, and to nourish the corruption of morals." Most of the *Encyclopedia's* contributors prudently withdrew from the project, but Diderot went underground and continued the herculean task until the subscribers received every promised volume, including eleven magnificent folios of illustrations. By the time these appeared, the persecutions had receded. Indeed, the *Encyclopedia* was reprinted in cheaper editions (both legal and pirated) that sold out rapidly, earning fortunes for their publishers. This turn of events ensured the status of Diderot's project as the landmark of its age.

Jean-Jacques Rousseau

Arguably the most original and influential eighteenth-century thinker, Jean-Jacques Rousseau stood close to but self-consciously outside the coterie of the philosophes, for Rousseau provided in his life and writing a critique not only of the status quo but of the

Enlightenment itself. Obsessed with the issue of moral freedom, Rousseau found society far more oppressive than most philosophes would admit, and he considered the philosophes themselves to be part of the problem.

Young Rousseau won instant fame when he submitted a prize-winning essay in a contest sponsored by a provincial academy on the topic, "Has the restoration of the arts and sciences had a purifying effect upon morals?" Unlike most respondents, Rousseau answered that it had not. He argued that the lustrous cultural and scientific achievements of recent decades were producing pretension, conformity, and useless luxury. Most scientific pursuits, he wrote, "are the effect of idleness which generate idleness in their turn." The system of rewards in the arts produces "a servile and deceptive conformity . . . the dissolution of morals . . . and the corruption of taste." Against the decadence of high culture, he advocated a return "to the simplicity which prevailed in earliest times"—manly physical pastimes, self-reliance, independent citizens instead of fawning courtiers.

Rousseau's Moral Vision

Rousseau had no wish to return to a state of nature, a condition of anarchy in which force ruled and people were slaves of appetite. But the basis of morality, he argued, was conscience, not reason. "Virtue, sublime science of simple minds: are not your principles graven on every heart?" This became one of his basic themes in two popular works of fiction, *Julie, or the New Héloise* (1761), and *Emile, or Treatise on Education* (1762).

In the first novel, Julie is educated in virtue by her tutor St. Preux but allows herself to fall in love with and be seduced by him. In the second half of the novel, Julie breaks away from St. Preux and marries Monsieur de Wolmar, her father's wealthy friend. She maintains a distant friendship with her old lover and rears her children in exemplary fashion, overseeing their education. In the end she overcomes her past moral lapse and sacrifices her own life to save one of her children. Wolmar then brings in the chastened St. Preux to continue the children's education. This tale of love, virtue, and motherhood won an adoring audience of male and female readers who identified with the characters, shed tears over their moral dilemmas, and applauded Rousseau for this superb lesson in the new sensibility.

Emile recounts the story of a young boy raised to be a moral adult by a tutor who emphasized experience over book learning and who considered education a matter of individual self-development. This new kind of man of course required a comparably sensitive wife, attuned to practical matters and without vain aristocratic pretenses. Sophie, the girl in question, received a very different type of education, however, one concerned with virtue but far more limited in its scope. Rousseau depicted men and women liberating themselves from stultifying traditional values, yet in the new relation-

Nicolas Henri Jeaurat de Bertry
ALLEGORY OF THE REVOLUTION WITH A PORTRAIT MEDALLION OF J. J. ROUSSEAU
The French revolutionaries acclaimed both Voltaire and Rousseau and transferred their remains to a new Pantheon. But Rousseau was the man considered by many French people to be the Revolution's spiritual father, as suggested by his position in this allegorical painting of 1793, filled with the new symbolism of liberty and equality.
Musée de la Ville de Paris, Musée Carnavalet, Paris, France. Giraudon/Art Resource, NY

ships he portrayed in these novels, women held a decidedly subordinate position. Their virtues were to be exclusively domestic in character, while the men would be prepared for public roles—a distinction that deeply troubled feminist thinkers in the future (see "Mary Wollstonecraft on the Education of Women," p. 565).

The Rebel as Cultural Hero

Rousseau himself was by no means a saint. His personal weaknesses—including the illegitimate child that he fathered and abandoned—doubtless contributed to his preoccupation with morality and conscience. Nonetheless, his rebellious life as well as his writings greatly impressed the generation of readers and writers coming of age in the 1770s and 1780s. Not only did he quarrel with the repressive authorities of Church and state—who repeatedly

MARY WOLLSTONECRAFT ON THE EDUCATION OF WOMEN

The sharpest challenge to Rousseau's widely shared attitude toward women came only in 1792, with the publication of Mary Wollstonecraft's A Vindication of the Rights of Woman. *Inspired by the French Revolution's doctrine of natural rights, this spirited writer deplored the fact that society kept women (in her words) frivolous, artificial, weak, and in a perpetual state of childhood. While men praised women for their beauty and grace, they hypocritically condemned them for a concern with vanity, fashion, and trivial matters, yet refused to treat them as rational human beings who could contribute to society as much as men. Her book emphasized the need for educational reform that would allow women to develop agile bodies and strong minds. Along the way Wollstonecraft took particular aim at Rousseau's* Emile.

"The conduct and manners of women, in fact, evidently prove that their minds are not in a healthy state; for, like the flowers which are planted in too rich a soil, strength and usefulness are sacrificed to beauty. . . . One cause of this barren blooming I attribute to a false system of education, gathered from the books written on this subject by men who, considering females rather as women than human creatures, have been more anxious to make them alluring mistresses than affectionate wives and rational mothers. The understanding of the sex has been so bubbled by this specious homage, that the civilized women of the present century, with a few exceptions, are only anxious to inspire love, when they ought to cherish a nobler ambition, and by their abilities and virtues exact respect.

"[T]he most perfect education, in my opinion, is such an exercise of the understanding as is best calculated to strengthen the body and form the heart. Or, in other words, to enable the individual to attain such habits of virtue as will render it independent. In fact, it is a farce to call any being virtuous whose virtues do not result from the exercise of its own reason. This was Rousseau's opinion respecting men: I extend it to women, and confidently assert that they have been drawn out of their sphere by false refinement, and not by an endeavor to acquire masculine qualities. Still the regal homage which they receive is so intoxicating, that till the manners of the times are changed, and formed on more reasonable principles, it may be impossible to convince them that the illegitimate power, which they obtain by degrading themselves, is a curse, and that they must return to nature and equality."

From Sandra M. Gilbert and Susan Gubar (eds.), *The Norton Anthology of Literature by Women: The Tradition in English*, W. W. Norton Co, 1985.

banned his books—but he also attacked the pretensions of his fellow philosophes, whom he considered arrogant, cynical, and lacking in spirituality.

By the 1770s the commanding figures of the Enlightenment, such as Voltaire and Diderot, had won their battles and had become masters of the most prestigious academies and channels of patronage. In a sense, they had themselves become the establishment. For younger writers frustrated by the existing distribution of influence and patronage, Rousseau became the inspiration.

Rousseau's Concept of Freedom What proved to be Rousseau's most enduring work, *The Social Contract*, published in 1762, became famous only after the French Revolution dramatized the issues that the book had raised. (The Revolution, it could be said, did more for the book than Rousseau did for the Revolution, which he neither prophesied nor advocated.) *The Social Contract* was not meant as a blueprint for revolution but rather as an ideal standard against which readers might measure their own society. Rousseau did not expect that this standard could be achieved in practice, since existing states were too large and complex to allow the kind of participation that he considered essential.

For Rousseau, a government distinct from the individuals over whom it claims to exercise authority has no validity. Rousseau denied the almost universal idea that some people are meant to govern and others to obey. In the ideal polity, Rousseau said, individuals have a role in making the law to which they submit. By obeying it, they are thus obeying themselves as well as their fellow citizens. For this reason, they are free from arbitrary power. To found such an ideal society, each citizen would have to take part in creating a social contract laying out the society's ground rules. By doing so, these citizens would establish themselves as "the sovereign." This sovereign—the people—then creates a government that will carry on the day-to-day business of applying the laws.

Rousseau was not advocating simple majority rule but rather a quest for consensus as to the best interests of all citizens. Even if it *appears* contrary to the welfare of some or even many citizens, Rousseau believed, the best interest of the community must be every individual's best interest as well, since that individual is a member of the community. Rousseau called this difficult concept the **"general will."** Deferring to the general will means that an individual ultimately must do what

ROUSSEAU'S CONCEPT OF THE GENERAL WILL

"The essence of the social compact reduces itself to the following terms: Each of us puts his person and all his power in common under the supreme direction of the general will, and, in our collective capacity, we receive each member as an indivisible part of the whole. . . .

"In fact, each individual, as a man, may have a particular will contrary or dissimilar to the general will which he has as a citizen. His particular interest may speak to him quite differently from the common interest: his absolute and naturally independent existence may make him look upon what he owes to the common cause as a gratuitous contribution, the loss of which will do less harm to others than the payment of it is burdensome to himself. . . . He may wish to enjoy the rights of citizenship without being ready to fulfill the duties of a subject. The continuance of such an injustice could not but prove the undoing of the body politic.

"In order then that the social compact may not be an empty formula, it tacitly includes the undertaking, which alone can give force to the rest, that whoever refuses to obey the general will shall be compelled to do so by the whole body. This means nothing less than that he will be forced to be free; for this is the condition which, by giving each citizen to his country, secures him against all personal dependence. In this lies the key to the working of the political machine."

From Jean-Jacques Rousseau, *The Social Contract*, Book 1, David Campbell Publishers.

---

one *ought*, not simply what one *wants*. This commitment derives from conscience, which must do battle within the individual against passion, appetite, and mere self-interest. Under the social contract, to use Rousseau's most striking phrase, the individual "will be forced to be free" (see "Rousseau's Concept of the General Will," above). Thus, for Rousseau, individual freedom depends on a political framework involving consent and participation as well as subordination of individual self-interest to the commonweal. More than any of the philosophes, Rousseau argued that individual freedom depends on the arrangements governing the collectivity.

EIGHTEENTH-CENTURY ELITE CULTURE

The Enlightenment was merely one dimension of Europe's vibrant cultural life in the eighteenth century. An explosive increase in publishing activity, legal and underground, served diverse audiences. New cultural forums and institutions, such as salons and freemasons lodges, combined with new media to create a **"public sphere"** for the uninhibited exchange of ideas. Meanwhile, the realm of literature saw remarkable innovation, including the rise of the novel. Royal courts and aristocracies still dominated most activity in music and the fine arts through their patronage, but here too the presence of a growing middle-class audience made itself felt and offered new opportunities of recognition for composers and artists.

Cosmopolitan High Culture

As the expansive, cosmopolitan aspects of European high culture are described here, it must be remembered that the mass of Europe's peasants and workers remained virtually untouched by these developments, insulated within their local environments and traditions. But the educated and wealthy, the numerically small and influential elites, enjoyed a sense of belonging to a common European civilization. French was the international language of this culture; even King Frederick II of Prussia favored French over German. Whatever the effects of Frederick's attitude might have been—the German dramatist Lessing, for one, considered it a deplorable cultural prejudice—the widespread knowledge of French meant that ideas and literature could circulate easily past language barriers.

The Appeal of Travel Europeans sharpened their sense of common identity through travel literature and by their appetite for visiting foreign places. Although transportation was slow and uncomfortable, many embarked on a "grand tour," whose highlights included visits to Europe's large cities (such as London, Paris, Rome, and Vienna) and to the ruins of antiquity—to the glories of the modern and the ancient worlds.

Kings, princes, and municipal authorities were embellishing their towns with plazas, public gardens, theaters, and opera houses. Toward the end of the century, amenities such as street lighting and public transportation began to appear in a few cities, with London leading the way. From the private sector came two notable additions to the urban scene: the coffeehouse and the storefront window display. Coffeehouses, where customers

Anicet Charles G. Lemonnier
READING OF VOLTAIRE'S TRAGEDY "L'ORPHELIN DE LA CHINE" AT THE SALON OF MADAME GEOFFRIN, 1755
This 1814 painting of Mme. Geoffrin's Salon in 1755 reflects the artist Lemonnier's imagination rather than historical reality. His canvas depicts an assemblage of all the major philosophes and their patrons that never actually took place. Yet it does accurately convey the social atmosphere and serious purpose of the Parisian salons. At the center is a bust of Voltaire, who lived in exile at the time.
Giraudon/Art Resource, NY

could chat or read, and enticing shop windows, which added to the pleasures of city walking (and stimulated consumer demand), enhanced the rhythms of urban life for tourists and residents alike. When a man is tired of London, Samuel Johnson remarked, he is tired of life.

Travelers on tour invariably passed from the attractions of bustling city life to the silent monuments of antiquity. As the philosophes recalled the virtues of pagan philosophers like Cicero, interest grew in surviving examples of Greek and Roman architecture and sculpture. Many would have agreed with the German art historian Johann Winckelmann that Greek sculpture was the most worthy standard of aesthetic beauty in all the world.

The Republic of Letters   Among writers, intellectuals, and scientists, the sense of a cosmopolitan European culture devolved into the concept of a "republic of letters." The phrase, introduced by sixteenth-century French humanists, was popularized by Pierre Bayle (noted earlier as a proponent of religious toleration), who published a critical journal that he called *News of the Republic of Letters*. The title implied that the realm of culture and

ideas stretched across Europe's political borders. In one sense, it was an exclusive republic, limited to the educated; but it was also an open society to which people of talent could belong regardless of their social origins.

Aside from the medium of the printed word, the republic of letters was organized around the salons and the academies. Both institutions encouraged social interchange by bringing together socially prominent men and women with talented writers. The philosophes themselves exemplified this social mixture, for their "family" was composed in almost equal measures of nobles (Montesquieu, Holbach, Condorcet) and commoners (Voltaire, Diderot, d'Alembert). Voltaire, while insisting that he was as good as any aristocrat, had no desire to topple the aristocracy from its position; rather, he sought amalgamation. As d'Alembert put it, talent on the one hand and birth and eminence on the other both deserve recognition.

The Salons and Masonic Lodges   Usually organized and led by women of wealthy bourgeois or noble families, the **salons** sought to bring together important writers with the influential persons they needed for favors and patronage. The salon of Madame Tencin, for example, helped launch Montesquieu's *Spirit of the Laws* in the 1740s, while the salon of Madame du Deffand in the 1760s became a forum in which the philosophes could test their ideas (see figure, p. 567). The salons also helped to enlarge the audience and contacts of the philosophes by introducing them to a flow of foreign visitors, ranging from German princes to Benjamin Franklin. Private newsletters kept interested foreigners and provincials abreast of activities in the Parisian salons when they could not attend personally, but salons also operated in Vienna, London, and Berlin.

The salons placed a premium on elegant conversation and wit. The women who ran them insisted that intellectuals make their ideas lucid and comprehensible, which increased the likelihood that their thought and writings would have some impact. The salons were also a forum in which men learned to take women seriously, and they constituted a unique cultural space for women between the domestic and public spheres. But the salons' emphasis on style over substance led Rousseau to denounce them as artificial rituals that prevented the display of genuine feeling and sincerity.

Throughout Europe, freemasonry was another important form of cultural sociability that often crossed the lines of class and (less commonly) of gender. Operating in an aura of secretiveness and symbolism, the masonic lodges fostered a curious mixture of spirituality and rationalism. Originating as clubs or fraternities dedicated to humane values, they attracted a wide range of educated nobles, commoners, and liberal clergy, while some lodges accepted women as well. But toward the end of the century, freemasonry was torn by sectarian controversies, and its influence seemed to be diminishing.

The Learned Academies As important for the dissemination of ideas in the eighteenth century as the salons were the learned academies. These ranged from the Lunar Society in Birmingham, a forum for innovative British industrialists and engineers, to state-sponsored academies in almost every capital of Southern and Central Europe, which served as conduits for advanced scientific and philosophical ideas coming from Western Europe. In France, moreover, academies were established in more than thirty provincial cities, most of which became strongholds of advanced thinking outside the capital.

These provincial academies were founded after the death of Louis XIV in 1715, as if in testimony to the liberating effect of his demise. Most began as literary institutes, concerned with upholding the purity of literary style. A few academies adhered to such goals well into midcentury, but most gradually shifted their interests from literary matters to scientific and practical questions in such areas as commerce, agriculture, and local administration. They became offshoots, so to speak, of the *Encyclopedia's* spirit. Indeed, when a Jesuit launched an attack against the *Encyclopedia* in the Lyons Academy, many members threatened to resign unless he retracted his remarks.

By the 1770s the essay contests sponsored by the provincial academies and the papers published by their members had turned to such topics as population growth, capital punishment and penology, education, poverty and welfare, the grain trade, the guilds, and the origins of sovereignty. A parallel shift in membership occurred. The local academies began as privileged corporations, dominated by the nobility of the region. Associate membership was extended to commoners from the ranks of civil servants, doctors, and professionals. Gradually, the distinction between regular and associate participants crumbled. The academies admitted more commoners to full membership, and a fragile social fusion took place.

Publishing and Reading

The eighteenth century saw a notable rise in publishing geared to several kinds of readers. Traveling circulating libraries originated in England around 1740 and opened untapped markets for reading material; by the end of the century almost one thousand traveling libraries had been established. "Booksellers," or publishers—the intermediary between author and reader—combined the functions of a modern editor, printer, salesperson, and (if need be) smuggler. Their judgment and marketing techniques helped create as well as fill the demand for books, since they conceived and financed a variety of works. The *Encyclopedia* originated as a bookseller's project; so, too, did such enduring masterpieces as Samuel Johnson's *Dictionary*, a monumental lexicon that helped purify and standardize the English language. Booksellers commissioned talented stylists to write popular versions of serious scientific, historical, and philosophical works. Recognizing a specialized demand among women readers, they increased the output of fictional romances and fashion magazines and also began to publish more fiction and poetry by women.

Journals and Newspapers The eighteenth century saw a proliferation of periodicals. In England, which pioneered in this domain, the number of periodicals increased from 25 to 158 between 1700 and 1780. In one successful model, Addison and Steele's *Spectator* (1711), each issue consisted of a single essay that sought in elegant but clear prose to raise the reader's standards of morality and taste. Their goal was "to enliven Morality with Wit, and to temper Wit with Morality. . . . To bring Philosophy . . . to dwell in clubs and assemblies, at tea-tables and coffeehouses." Eliza

A

DICTIONARY

OF THE

ENGLISH LANGUAGE:

IN WHICH

The WORDS are deduced from their ORIGINALS,

AND

ILLUSTRATED in their DIFFERENT SIGNIFICATIONS

BY

EXAMPLES from the beſt WRITERS.

TO WHICH ARE PREFIXED,

A HISTORY of the LANGUAGE,

AND

AN ENGLISH GRAMMAR.

BY SAMUEL JOHNSON, A. M.

IN TWO VOLUMES.

VOL. I.

Cum tabulis animum cenſoris ſumet honeſti :
Audebit quæcumque parum ſplendoris habebunt,
Et ſine pondere erunt, et honore indigna ferentur,
Verba movere loco ; quamvis invita recedant,
Et verſentur adhuc intra penetralia Veſtæ ;
Obſcurata diu populo bonus eruet, atque
Proferet in lucem ſpecioſa vocabula rerum,
Quæ priſcis memorata Catonibus atque Cethegis,
Nunc ſitus informis premit et deſerta vetuſtas.   Hor.

LONDON

Printed by W. STRAHAN,

For J. and P. KNAPTON ; T. and T. LONGMAN ; C. HITCH and L. HAWES ;
A. MILLAR· and R. and J. DODSLEY.

MDCCLV.

The title page of Samuel Johnson's pioneering *Dictionary of the English Language* (1755 edition), one of the masterpieces of eighteenth-century literature.
The Mary Evans Picture Library

Haywood adapted this format in her journal, *The Female Spectator* (1744–1756), in which she advocated improvement in the treatment of women and greater "opportunities of enlarging our minds." Another type of journal published extracts and summaries of books and covered current events and entertainment; one such journal, the *Gentleman's Magazine,* reached the impressive circulation of fifteen thousand in 1740. More learned periodicals specialized in book reviews and serious articles on science and philosophy.

Most important for the future of reading habits in Europe was the daily newspaper, which originated in England. Papers like the *London Chronicle* at first provided family entertainment and then took on classified advertisements (thereby spurring consumerism and the notion of fashion). English newspapers of course published news of current events, but only after strenuous battles for permission from a reluctant government did they win the right to report directly on parliamentary debates. In France, a handful of major Parisian newspapers enjoyed privileged monopolies in exchange for full compliance with government censorship. This arrangement severely restricted their ability to discuss government and politics, although other periodicals published outside France's borders helped satisfy the demand for such coverage in France.

"Bad Books" The demand for books and the dynamism of the publishing industry created new employment opportunities for men and women. Although the number of would-be writers swelled, relatively few could achieve financial independence without patronage. Many remained poverty-stricken and frustrated.

Publishers thus could hire legions of otherwise unemployed writers to turn out the kinds of books for which they sensed a great demand: potboilers, romances, salacious pamphlets, and gossip sheets, which pandered to low tastes. Paid for quantity and speed rather than quality, these hack writers led a precarious, humiliating existence. Booksellers and desperate writers saw money to be made in sensational pamphlets assailing the character of notorious aristocrats; in partisan pamphlets attacking a particular faction in court politics; and in pornography. Sometimes they combined character assassination and pornography in pamphlets dwelling on the alleged perversions of rulers or courtiers. For all its wild exaggeration, such material helped "desacralize" monarchy and created a vivid image of a decadent aristocracy.

To satisfy the public's demand for gossip, character assassination, and pornography in violation of laws regulating the book trade in France, publishers located just across the French border marketed such books and pamphlets clandestinely. They smuggled this material into France, along with banned books by writers like Voltaire and Rousseau, using networks of couriers and distributors. In their sales lists of what they called Philosophic Books, the clandestine publishers lumped together banned books by serious writers along with such illicit publications as *The Scandalous Chronicles, The Private Life of Louis XV,* and *Venus in the Cloister* (a pornographic account of the alleged perversions of the clergy). The police made the same judgment. In attempting to stop the flow of "bad books," they scarcely distinguished between a banned work by Voltaire assaulting religious bigotry and a libelous pamphlet depicting the queen as a corrupt pervert.

Literature, Music, and Art

Unlike the artistic style of the seventeenth century, generally classified as baroque, the artistic style of the eighteenth century cannot be given a single stylistic label. The nature of the audience and the sources of support for writers and composers also varied considerably. But several trends proved to be of lasting importance: the rise of the novel in England, the birth of Romantic poetry, the development of the symphony in Austria, and the changing social context of French painting late in the century.

The Rise of the Novel The modern novel had its strongest development in England, where writers and booksellers cultivated a growing middle-class reading public. The acknowledged pioneer of this new genre was Samuel Richardson. With a series of letters telling the story, Richardson's *Pamela, or Virtue Rewarded* (1740) recounted the trials and tribulations of an honest if somewhat hypocritical servant girl. Pamela's sexual virtue is repeatedly challenged but never conquered by her wealthy employer, Mr. B., who finally agrees to marry her. An instant success, this melodrama broke from the standard forms and heroic subjects of most narrative fiction. Richardson dealt with recognizable types of people.

Pamela's apparent hypocrisy, however, prompted a playwright and lawyer named Henry Fielding to pen a short satire called *Shamela*, which he followed with his own novel *Joseph Andrews*. Here comedy and adventure replaced melodrama; Fielding prefaced *Joseph Andrews* with a manifesto claiming that the novel was to be "a comic epic in prose." Fielding realized the full potential of his bold experimentation with literary forms in *Tom Jones* (1749), a colorful, robust, comic panorama of English society featuring a gallery of brilliantly developed characters and vivid depictions of varied social environments.

The novel was thus emerging as a form of fiction that told its story and treated the development of personality in a realistic social context. It seemed to mirror its times better than other forms of fiction. Like the dramas that filled the stage in the second half of the century, most novels focused on family life and everyday problems of love, marriage, and social relations. Novelists could use broad comedy, or they could be totally serious; they could experiment endlessly with forms and techniques and could deal with a wide range of social settings.

In *Evelina, or A Young Lady's Entrance into the World* (1778), the writer Fanny Burney used the flexibility of the novel to give a woman's perspective on eighteenth-century English social life. In the form of letters, like *Pamela* and Rousseau's *Julie, Evelina* traces a provincial girl's adventures in London as she discovers her true father and finds a suitable husband. While falling back on conventional melodrama, in which marriage is the only happy ending for a young woman, Burney also uses social satire to suggest how society restricts, and even endangers, an independent woman's life. If Burney was ambivalent about the possibilities for female independence in the social world, her own writing, together with that of other women writers of the period, demonstrated the opportunities for female artistic achievement.

The Birth of Romantic Poetry During most of this century of innovation in prose fiction, poetry retained its traditional qualities. Still the most prized form of literary expression, poetry followed unchanging rules on what made good literature. Each poetic form had its particular essence and rules, but in all types of poems diction was supposed to be elegant and the sentiments refined. Poets were expected to transform the raw materials of emotion into delicate language and references that only the highly educated could appreciate. In this neoclassical tradition, art was meant to echo eternal standards of truth and beauty. Poets were not permitted to unburden their souls or hold forth on their own experiences. The audience for poetry was the narrowest segment of the reading public—"the wealthy few," in the phrase of William Wordsworth, who criticized eighteenth-century poets for pandering exclusively to that group.

By the end of the century, however, the restraints of **Neoclassicism** finally provoked rebellion in the ranks of English and German poets. Men like Friedrich von Schiller and Wordsworth defiantly raised the celebration of individual feeling and inner passion to the level of a creed, which came to be known as **Romanticism.** These young poets generally prized Rousseau's writings, seeing the Genevan rebel as someone who had forged a personal idiom of expression and who valued inner feeling, moral passion, and the wonders of nature. Hoping to appeal to a much broader audience, these poets decisively changed the nature of poetic composition and made this literary form, like the novel, a flexible vehicle of artistic expression.

Goethe   The writer who came to embody the new ambitions of poets, novelists, and dramatists was Johann von Goethe, whose long life (1749–1832) spanned the beginnings and the high point of the Romantic movement. A friend of Schiller and many of the German writers and philosophers of the day, he soon came to tower over all of them. Goethe first inspired a literary movement known as ***Sturm und Drang*** (Storm and Stress), which emphasized strong artistic emotions and gave early intimations of the Romantic temperament. The best-known work of Sturm und Drang was Goethe's *The Sorrows of Young Werther* (1774), a novel about a young man driven to despair and suicide by an impossible love.

Courted by many of the princes and monarchs of Germany, Goethe soon joined the circle of the duke who ruled the small city-state of Weimar, where he remained for the rest of his life. There flowed from his pen an astonishing stream of works—lyrical love poetry, powerful dramas, art and literary criticism, translations, philosophic reflections, an account of his travels in Italy, and studies of optics, botany, anatomy, and mathematics. Even though he held official posts in the duke's court, Goethe's literary output never flagged. His masterpiece, *Faust,* occupied him for nearly fifty years and revealed the progress of his art. The first part (published in 1808) imbued with romantic longing the story of a man who yearns to master all of knowledge and who makes a pact with the devil to achieve his goal. But the second part (1831) emphasized the determination that came to be Goethe's credo. The final lines are:

> He only earns his freedom and existence
> Who daily conquers them anew.

What had begun in the youthful exuberance and energy of Romanticism ended in an almost classical mood of discipline. No wonder that Goethe seemed to his contemporaries to be the last "universal man," the embodiment of conflicting cultural values and Western civilization's struggle to resolve them.

The Symphony   For Europe's elites, music offered the supreme form of entertainment, and the development of the symphony in music paralleled the rise of the novel in literature. For much of the century, composers still served under royal, ecclesiastical, or aristocratic patronage. They were bound by rigid formulas of composition and by prevailing tastes tyrannically insistent on conventions. Most listeners wanted little more than pleasant melodies in familiar forms; instrumental music was often commissioned as background fare for balls or other social occasions.

The heartland of Europe's music tradition shifted during the eighteenth century from Italy and France to Austria. Here a trio of geniuses transformed the routines of eighteenth-century composition into original and enduring masterpieces. True, the early symphonies of Franz Joseph Haydn and young Wolfgang Amadeus Mozart were conventional exercises. As light and tuneful as its audience could wish, their early music had little emotional impact. By the end of their careers, however, these two composers had altered the symphonic form from three to four movements, had achieved extraordinary harmonic virtuosity, and had brought a deep if restrained emotionalism to their music. Haydn and Mozart had changed the symphony radically from the elegant trifles of earlier years.

Beethoven   Ludwig van Beethoven consummated this development and ensured that the symphony, like the novel and Romantic poetry, would be an adaptable vehicle for the expression of creative genius. In each of his nine symphonies, as well as in his five piano concertos, Beethoven progressively modified the standard formulas, enlarged the orchestra, and wrote movements of increasing intricacy. His last symphony burst the bonds of the form altogether. Beethoven introduced a large chorus singing one of Schiller's odes to conclude his *Ninth Symphony* (1824), making it a celebration in music of freedom and human kinship. Laden with passion, the music is nevertheless recognizable as an advanced form of the classical symphony. Thus, it provides a bridge between the music of two periods:

Jean-Baptiste Greuze
THE FATHER'S CURSE, 1777
Instead of the aristocrats or
classical figures that most artists
chose for their subjects, Jean-
Baptiste Greuze painted ordinary
French people. His portraits and
dramatic scenes (such as *The
Father's Curse*) seemed to echo
Rousseau's call for honest,
"natural" feeling.
Louvre, Paris, France. Giraudon/
Arts Resource, NY

Élisabeth Vigée-Le Brun
MARIE ANTOINETTE WITH A ROSE
One of the leading French portrait painters, and the most
successful female artist of the era anywhere, was Élisabeth
Vigée-Le Brun, who enjoyed the patronage of Queen Marie
Antoinette. Shown here is one of several portraits that she
painted of the French queen.
Giraudon/Art Resource, NY

eighteenth-century classicism and nineteenth-century
Romanticism.

Aristocratic and court patronage remained the surest
foundation for a career in music during the eighteenth
century. Haydn, for example, worked with mutual
satisfaction as the court composer for one prince from
1761 to 1790. At the end of his long life, however,
Haydn moved out on his own, having won enough international recognition to sign a lucrative contract
with a London music publisher who underwrote performances of his last twelve symphonies. In contrast,
Mozart had an unhappy experience trying to earn his
living by composing. After a few miserable years as
court composer for the Archbishop of Salzburg, Mozart
escaped to Vienna but could not find a permanent employer. He was obliged to eke out an inadequate living
by teaching, filling private commissions, and giving
public concerts. Beethoven did much better at freeing
himself from dependence on a single patron through individual commissions and public concerts.

The Social Context of Art   Unlike the situation in literature and music, there were no notable innovations
in the field of painting during most of the eighteenth
century. With the exception of the Frenchman Jacques-

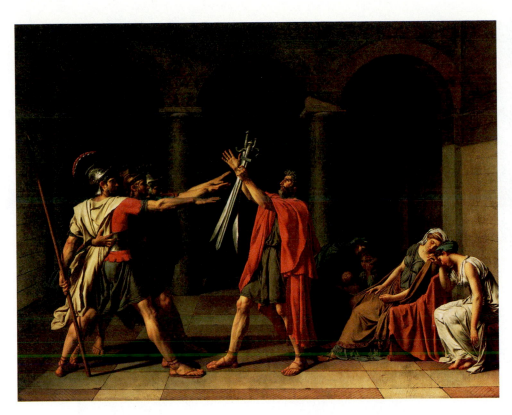

Jacques-Louis David
THE OATH OF THE HORATII
The greatest innovation in French painting came in reaction to the artificiality of the rococo style and subject matter, with a return to favor of "noble simplicity and calm grandeur." This Neoclassical style found its supreme expression in the work of Jacques-Louis David. Such history paintings as *The Oath of the Horatii* evoked the ideal of civic virtue in ancient Greek and Roman civilization.
Louvre, Paris, France. Erich Lessing/ Art Resource, NY

Louis David, eighteenth-century painters were overshadowed by their predecessors. Neoclassicism remained a popular style in the late eighteenth century, with its themes inspired by antiquity and its timeless conceptions of form and beauty, comparable to the rules of Neoclassical poetry.

The social context of painting, however, was changing. Most commissions and patronage still depended on aristocrats and princes, but the public was beginning to claim a role as the judge of talent in the visual arts. Public opinion found its voice in a new breed of art critics, unaffiliated with official sources of patronage, who reached their new audience through the press in the second half of the century. The Royal Academy of Art in France created the opening for this new voice by sponsoring an annual public exhibition, or "salon," starting in 1737. People could view the canvases chosen by the Academy for these exhibitions and could reach their own judgments about the painters.

David and Greuze   David, a brilliant painter in the Neoclassical style, won the greatest renown in this arena of public opinion during the 1780s. He skillfully celebrated the values of the ancient world in such historical paintings as *The Oath of the Horatii* (see figure, above), *The Death of Socrates*, and *Brutus*. Discarding many of the standard conventions for history painting (and thereby drawing criticism from the Academy), David overwhelmed the public with his vivid imagery and the emotional force of his compositions. His paint-

ings of the 1780s unmistakably conveyed a yearning for civic virtue and patriotism that had yet to find its political outlet in France. Not surprisingly, David became the most engaged and triumphant painter of the French Revolution.

In an entirely different vein, a few eighteenth-century artists chose more mundane and "realistic" subjects or themes for their canvases, parallel in some respects to what novelists and playwrights were doing. Jean-Baptiste Greuze, for example, made a hit in the Parisian exhibitions of the 1770s with his sentimentalized paintings of ordinary people in family settings caught in a dramatic situation, such as the death of a father or the banishment of a disobedient son. William Hogarth, a superb London engraver who worked through the medium of prints and book illustrations, went further down the social pyramid with his remarkable scenes of life among the working classes and the poor.

POPULAR CULTURE

While the cultural world of aristocratic and middle-class elites has been extensively studied, the culture of artisans, peasants, and the urban poor remains more dimly known. In those sectors of society, culture primarily meant recreation, and it was essentially public and collective. Despite traditions of elementary schooling in certain regions and the spread of literacy among some groups, literacy rates remained generally low. Popular

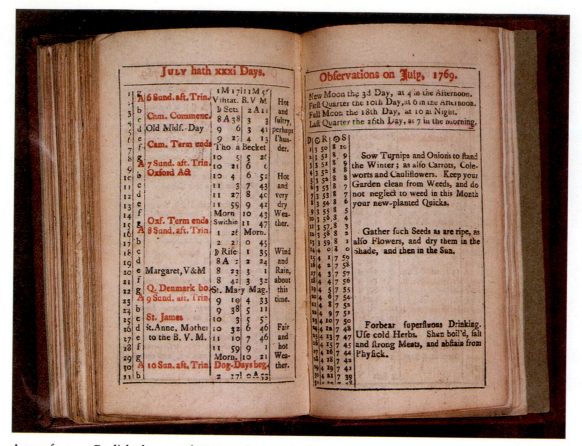

A page from an English almanac of 1769 on the month of July includes saints' days, information about likely weather patterns, and advice about agricultural matters and health care.
New York Public Library, Astor, Lenox, and Tilden Foundations

culture did have its written forms, but these were less prevalent than the oral traditions embodied in songs, folktales, and proverbs. Despite the rare firsthand traces of popular culture in the historical record, it is possible to suggest the rich variety of sociability and recreational practice among working people in traditional society.

Popular Literature

Far removed from the markets for Voltaire and the *Gentleman's Magazine* existed a distinct world of popular literature—the reading matter consumed by journeymen and peasants, the poor and the almost poor, those who could barely read and those who could not read at all. From the seventeenth through the early nineteenth century, publishers produced for this audience small booklets written anonymously, printed on cheap paper, costing only a few pennies, and sold by itinerant peddlers who knew the tastes of their customers. Presumably the booklets were often read aloud by those who could read to those who could not.

This popular literature took three major forms. Religious material included devotional tracts, saints' lives, catechisms, manuals of penitence, and Bible stories, all written simply and generously laced with miracles. Readers who were preoccupied with fears of death and damnation sought reassurance in these works that a virtuous life would end in salvation. Almanacs constituted a second type of popular literature, which appealed to the readers' concern for getting along in this life. Almanacs discussed things like the kinds of potions to take for illnesses, and featured astrology—how to read the stars and other signs for clues about the future. The third type of popular literature provided entertainment: tales and fables, burlesques and crude satires, mixtures of fiction and history in which miraculous events frequently helped bring the story to a satisfactory conclusion.

Although useful information may have trickled down through these booklets, most of them were escapist. The religiosity and supernatural events of popular literature separate it from the growing rationalism and secularism of elite culture. Moreover, it could be argued that by ignoring such problems as food shortages, high taxes, and material insecurity, popular writings fostered submissiveness, a fatalistic acceptance of

Most eighteenth-century elementary school teachers used the extremely inefficient individual method of instruction, in which pupils read to the teacher from whatever book they happened to bring from home, while the other pupils occupied themselves as best they could. Tallandier, Bibliothèque des Arts Décoratifs, Paris. Editions

a dismal status quo. Glimpsing the content of this popular literature helps us understand why Voltaire had no hope of extending his ideas on religion to the masses.

Oral Tradition   **Oral tradition** encompassed folktales told at the fireside on long winter nights, songs passed on from generation to generation, and sayings that embodied the conventional wisdom of the people.

Themes touching on hunger, sex, or oppression were more likely to turn up in songs or oral tales than in booklets. Songs and tales expressed the joyful bawdiness of ordinary men and women but also the ever-present hardships and dangers of daily life: the endless drudgery of work in the fields, the gnawing ache of an empty stomach, the cruelty of parental neglect or mean stepparents, the desperation of beggars on the road. The most fantastic tales evoked a threatening world in which strangers might turn out to be princes or good fairies but might just as well turn into wolves or witches. Oral tradition also celebrated the shrewdness and cunning of ordinary people struggling for survival, in the spirit of the saying: "Better a knave than a fool."

Literacy and Primary Schooling

The wars of religion had spurred the spread of literacy and elementary schooling in Europe. Protestantism explicitly promoted literacy so that Christians could read their Bibles directly; strongly Protestant societies such as Scotland, Switzerland, and Sweden had unusually high rates of literacy by the eighteenth century. The Catholic Church, as well, believed that the spread of lit-

eracy would serve its cause in the battle against heresy. While teaching reading, Catholic schoolmasters could provide religious instruction and could socialize children into the beliefs and behavior of a Catholic way of life.

A unique study of literacy in France carried out in the late nineteenth century, based on signatures versus *X*s on parish marriage registers all across the country, indicates a national literacy rate (meaning the ability to read) in 1686 of about 21 percent, which reached 37 percent a century later. These national averages, however, conceal striking regional and social disparities. The south of France had much lower rates than the north/northeast, and rural literacy rates lagged significantly behind those of the towns. While agricultural laborers rarely could read, urban artisans were generally literate. The widest gap of all separated men from women, the rates in 1786 being 47 and 27 percent, respectively. Similarly, estimates for England suggest a male literacy rate of slightly under 60 percent and a female rate of about 40 percent.

Primary Education   Schooling was not intended to transform society or lift the mass of people out of the situations into which they were born. On the contrary, it was supposed to maintain the social order and reinforce the family in promoting piety and decent behavior among the young. Many among the elites (including Voltaire) were skeptical about the value of education for peasants and laborers. Might it not confuse them, or make it more difficult for them to accept the drudgery to which they seemed destined? Peasant or laboring parents might well have shared such skepticism about educating their young. Education could seem a waste of time when their children could be contributing to the family's livelihood; they might especially begrudge spending the money on tuition that most elementary schooling required.

A village usually hired a schoolmaster in consultation with the pastor or priest; schools usually straddled community and church, since the schoolmaster often served as the pastor's aide. Except in towns that had charitable endowments to support schooling, the parents, the village, or some combination of the two paid the schoolmaster, and for that reason numerous villages did without any schooling. Even a modest tuition could deter impoverished parents from hiring a master, enrolling their children, or keeping them in school for a sufficient time. Since schoolmasters taught reading first and writing separately and later, many pupils, especially girls, were not kept in school long enough to learn how to write anything but their names. Schooling, in other words, was largely demand-driven, the product of a community's level of wealth and interest.

Schooling in Central Europe

While England and France left primary schooling entirely to the chance of local initiative, the Habsburg monarchy seriously promoted primary education and thereby became the first Catholic realm to do so. The Habsburg General School Ordinance of 1774 authorized state subsidies, in combination with local funds, for the support of a school in almost every parish. Attendance was supposed to be compulsory, though the state had no way to enforce it. The state also intended to train future teachers at institutions called normal schools. A similar two-pronged strategy was adopted in Prussia under Frederick II at about the same time, although little was done to implement it.

In Prussia, as in most of Europe, schoolmasters remained barely competent and poorly paid. Frederick II indeed had a limiting vision of popular education: "It is enough for the country people to learn only a little reading and writing. . . . Instruction must be planned so that they receive only what is most essential for them but which is designed to keep them in the villages and not influence them to leave." As elsewhere in Europe, the goals of elementary schooling were to inculcate religion and morality, propagate the virtues of hard work, and promote deference to one's superiors.

Sociability and Recreation

If the educated elites had their salons, masonic lodges, and learned academies, the common people also formed organized cultural groups. Many artisans, for example, belonged to secret societies that combined fraternal and trade-union functions. Young unmarried artisans frequently traveled the country, stopping periodically to work with comrades in other towns in order to hone their skills. Artisans also relied on their associations for camaraderie and ritual celebrations. Married artisans often joined religious confraternities, which honored a patron saint and ensured a dignified funeral when they died, or mutual aid societies to which they contributed small monthly dues to pay for assistance if illness or accident should strike.

Taverns and Festivals

Corresponding to the coffeehouses of the urban middle classes were the taverns in working-class neighborhoods. These noisy, crowded places catered to a poor clientele, especially on Sunday and on Monday, which workingmen often took as a day off, honoring (as they put it) "Saint Monday." The urban common people were first beginning to consume wine in the eighteenth century, still something of a luxury except in its cheapest watered form. In England gin was the poor person's drink, cheap and plentiful until the government levied a hefty excise tax after realizing that too many people were drinking themselves into disability and death—a concern depicted in Hogarth's etchings, p. 577.

More commonly, drinking was not done in morbid fashion but as part of a healthy and vibrant outdoor life. Popular pastimes followed a calendar of holidays that provided occasions for group merrymaking, eating, drinking, dressing-up, contests, and games. Local festivals were particularly comfortable settings for single young men and women to meet each other. The highlight of a country year usually came in early autumn after the summer harvest was in, when most villages held a public feast that lasted several days. In Catholic countries similar festivities were often linked with church rituals. Popular observances included the commemoration of local patron saints, pilgrimages to holy places, and the period of Carnival before Lent. More generally, a growing "commercialization of leisure" in the eighteenth century supported new spectator sports, such as horse racing and boxing matches.

In early modern Europe, gentlefolk and commoners had been accustomed to mixing in recreational and religious settings: fairs and markets, sporting events, village or town festivals, Carnival in Catholic countries. But in the eighteenth century, as aristocrats and bourgeois alike became more concerned with good manners and refinement, these elite groups began to distance themselves from the bawdy and vulgar behavior of ordinary people. With growing intolerance, they censured popular recreational culture in the hope of "reforming" the people into a more sober and orderly lifestyle. Social status was based on birth or wealth, but cultural taste was becoming its behavioral marker.

William Hogarth
GIN LANE AND *BEER STREET*
In his *Gin Lane* etching of 1750, Hogarth depicted the results of excessive gin drinking by the English common people as death, apathy, and moral decay. A cheerful companion piece called *Beer Street*, however, suggested that drinking in moderation was an acceptable practice.

Hogarth, *Gin Lane.* The Metropolitan Museum of Art, Harris Brisbane Dick Fund, 1932. Photography © 2002 The Metropolitan Museum of Art, New York.

Hogarth, *Beer Street.* The Metropolitan Museum of Art, Harris Brisbane Dick Fund, 1932. [32.35 (123)]. Photograph © 2002 The Metropolitan Museum of Art, New York.

Summary

The philosophes, celebrated members of Europe's cultural establishment by the 1770s, hoped that their society would gradually reform itself under their inspiration. Although these writers criticized their society, they were not its subverters. Distrustful of the uneducated masses and afraid of popular emotion, superstition, and disorder, the philosophes were anything but democrats. Nonetheless, the Enlightenment challenged basic traditional values of European society: from Voltaire's polemics against Christianity through the sober social science of Diderot's *Encyclopedia* to the impassioned writings of Rousseau. Along with a flood of "bad books"—the pornography and scandal sheets of the clandestine publishers—booksellers, writers, and journalists disseminated critical ideas among Europe's educated men and women. The philosophes challenged the automatic respect for convention and authority, promoted the habit of independent reflection, and implanted the conviction that the reform of institutions was both necessary and possible. They promoted a climate that put the status quo on the defensive and in which revolution—when provoked under particular circumstances—would not be unthinkable.

QUESTIONS FOR FURTHER THOUGHT

1. What were the core values of the Enlightenment and how would you assess their strengths and weaknesses? What might have produced a backlash against Enlightenment values in subsequent periods? How might one defend them today?
2. How does the music, painting, and literature of the eighteenth century compare to the high culture of earlier periods you have studied, such as the Renaissance or the seventeenth century? Has the social or political context of cultural life changed? Were there comparable changes in the realm of popular culture?
3. What do you make of Jean-Jacques Rousseau?

RECOMMENDED READING

Sources

Gay, Peter (ed.). *The Enlightenment: A Comprehensive Anthology.* 1973.

Gendzier, Stephen (ed.). *Denis Diderot: The Encyclopedia: Selections.* 1967.

*Jacob, Margaret C. *The Enlightenment: A Brief History with Documents.* 2001.

Mohl, Mary R., and Helene Koon (eds.). *The Female Spectator: English Women Writers Before 1800.* 1977.

Vigée-Le Brun, Marie-Louise . . . Élisabeth. *Memoirs.* S. Evans (ed.). 1989. Memoirs of the most notable female painter in eighteenth-century France.

Studies

*Brewer, John. *The Pleasures of the Imagination: English Culture in the Eighteenth Century.* 1997. A lively, panoramic survey of the production and consumption of high culture in all its forms.

Bruford, W. H. *Germany in the Eighteenth Century: The Social Background of the Literary Revival.* 1952. A useful survey.

Buchan, James. *Crowded with Genius: The Scottish Enlightenment: Edinburgh's Moment of the Mind.* 2003. A popular history of the remarkable circle of Scottish philosophes, including Adam Smith and David Hume.

Capp, Bernard. *English Almanacs, 1500–1800: Astrology and the Popular Press.* 1979. A probing study of the most important genre of popular literature.

*Chartier, Roger. *The Cultural Origins of the French Revolution.* 1991. A synthesis of recent research on publishing, the public sphere, and the emergence of new political attitudes.

Cranston, Maurice. *Jean-Jacques, The Noble Savage,* and *The Solitary Self.* 1982, 1991, and 1995. A three-volume study of the life and work of Rousseau, critical but sympathetic.

*Crow, Thomas. *Painters and Public Life in Eighteenth-Century Paris.* 1985. A pioneering work on the development of a public sphere of critical discourse about art.

*Darnton, Robert. *The Forbidden Best Sellers of Pre-Revolutionary France.* 1995. A pathbreaking work on the circulation, content, and impact of banned books.

*Gay, Peter. *The Enlightenment: An Interpretation.* 2 vols. 1966 and 1969. A masterly, full-bodied exposition of Enlightenment thought.

*Goodman, Dena. *The Republic of Letters: A Cultural History of the French Enlightenment.* 1994. Focuses on the salons and the roles of women in cultural and intellectual life.

*Isherwood, Robert. *Farce and Fantasy: Popular Entertainment in Eighteenth-Century Paris.* 1986. A cultural and institutional history of fairs and popular theater.

Malcolmson, R. W. *Popular Recreations in English Society, 1700–1850.* 1973. A good survey of a neglected subject.

May, Gita. *Elisabeth Vigée-Le Brun: The Odyssey of an Artist in an Age of Revolution.* 2005. The public and private life of the period's most prominent female painter.

*Maza, Sarah. *Private Lives and Public Affairs: The Causes Célèbres of Pre-Revolutionary France.* 1993. An original analysis of scandals and lawsuits that raised social consciousness in the later eighteenth century.

McClellan, James. *Science Reorganized: Scientific Societies in the Eighteenth Century.* 1985.

Melton, James Van Horn. *Absolutism and the Eighteenth-Century Origins of Compulsory Schooling in Prussia and Austria.* 1988.

———. *The Rise of the Public in Enlightenment Europe.* 2001. An excellent comparative survey of the developing "public sphere" in Europe.

Palmer, Robert R. *Catholics and Unbelievers in Eighteenth-Century France.* 1939. The response of Catholic intellectuals to the century's philosophic thought.

Porter, Roy, and Mikulas Teich (eds.). *The Enlightenment in National Context.* 1981. A comprehensive geographic overview.

*Roche, Daniel. *France in the Enlightenment*. 1998. A masterly synthesis, especially on the Enlightenment and French society.

*Spencer, Samia (ed.). *French Women and the Age of Enlightenment*. 1984. A pioneering collection of essays on a variety of literary and historical themes.

Venturi, Franco. *Italy and the Enlightenment*. 1972. Essays on important Italian philosophes by a leading historian.

*Watt, Ian. *The Rise of the Novel: Studies of Defoe, Richardson, and Fielding*. 1957. The view from England.

Wilson, Arthur. *Diderot*. 1972. An exhaustive, reliable biography of the consummate French philosophe.

*Available in paperback.

Jean Duplessis-Bertaux
STORMING OF THE TUILERIES, COURS DU CAROUSSEL, AUGUST 10, 1792
The armed assault on the Tuileries Palace of August 10, 1792, brought an end to the monarchy and led directly to the founding of the first French Republic.
Giraudon/Art Resource, NY

Chapter Twenty

THE FRENCH REVOLUTION

REFORM AND POLITICAL CRISIS • 1789: THE FRENCH REVOLUTION •
THE RECONSTRUCTION OF FRANCE • THE SECOND REVOLUTION

Well into the eighteenth century, the long-standing social structures and political institutions of Europe were securely entrenched. Most monarchs still claimed to hold their authority directly from God. In cooperation with their aristocracies, they presided over realms composed of distinct orders of citizens, or *estates* as they were sometimes known. Each order had its particular rights, privileges, and obligations. But pressures for change were building during the century. In France, the force of public opinion grew increasingly potent by the 1780s. A financial or political crisis that could normally be managed by the monarchy threatened to snowball in this new environment. Such vulnerability was less evident in Austria, Prussia, and Russia, however, where strong monarchs instituted reforms to streamline their governments. Similarly, in Britain the political system proved resilient despite explosions of discontent at home and across the Atlantic.

Unquestionably, then, the French Revolution constituted the pivotal event of European history in the late eighteenth century. From its outbreak in 1789, the Revolution transformed the nature of sovereignty and law in France. Under its impetus, civic and social institutions were renewed, from local government and schooling to family relations and assistance for the poor. Soon its ideals of liberty, equality, and fraternity resonated across the borders of other European states, especially after war broke out in 1792 and French armies took the offensive.

The French Revolution's innovations defined the foundations of a liberal society and polity. Both at home and abroad, however, the new regime faced formidable opposition, and its struggle for survival propelled it in unanticipated directions. Some unforeseen turns, such as democracy and republicanism, became precedents for the future even if they soon aborted. Other developments, such as the Reign of Terror, seemed to nullify the original liberal values of 1789. The bloody struggles of the Revolution thus cast a shadow over this transformative event as they dramatized the brutal dilemma of means versus ends.

Civil Constitution of the Clergy **1790** ●

Peasant revolts and August 4 decree **July–August 1789** ●

Storming of the Bastille **July 1789** ●

Estates General become National Assembly **June 1789** ●

Failed Assembly of Notables in France **1787** ●

1780s
Joseph II's authoritarian reforms in Habsburg Empire

● **1776** American Declaration of Independence

REFORM AND POLITICAL CRISIS

To put the French Revolution into perspective, it helps to compare political tensions and conflicts elsewhere in Europe. Strong monarchs with reputations for being "enlightened" reigned in Prussia, Austria, Spain, and even Russia. Their stature seemingly contrasts with the mediocrity of Louis XV and Louis XVI, who ruled in France. Yet the former did not get far in reforming their realms or granting rights and freedom to their subjects. The limits of "enlightened absolutism," therefore, should be kept in mind when considering the crisis that confronted France. Meanwhile, in Britain energetic movements for political reform ran into determined opposition. This rigidity had a particular impact across the Atlantic, where Britain's thirteen colonies in North America were driven to rebellion and a revolutionary war for independence.

Enlightened Absolutism in Central and Eastern Europe

During the late nineteenth century, German historians invented the concept of enlightened absolutism to describe the Prussian and Habsburg monarchies of the eighteenth century. Critical of the ineptitude and weakness of French monarchs in that period, these historians argued that the strength of an enlightened ruler had been the surest basis for progress in early modern Europe. A king who ruled in his subjects' interest, they implied, avoided violent conflicts like those of the French Revolution. Earlier strong monarchs, such as Philip II of Spain and France's Louis XIV (who had once declared: "I am the state"), had been irresponsible; in contrast, these German historians argued, Frederick II of Prussia symbolized the enlightened phase of abso-

lutism with his comment that the ruler is the "first servant of the state."

Previous chapters, however, have demonstrated that monarchs dealt with the same fundamental issues during all stages of absolutism. They always strove to assert their authority over their subjects and to maximize the power of their state in relation to other realms, principally by means of territorial expansion. Any notion that Enlightenment thinking caused monarchs to abandon these efforts is misleading. Still, several eighteenth-century monarchs did initiate reforms and did modify their styles of ruling in order to appear more modern or enlightened. Frederick II of Prussia and Catherine II of Russia, for example, lavished praise on Voltaire and Diderot, and those philosophes returned the compliment. These rulers may simply have been engaging in public relations. Yet the fact that they seemed supportive of such writers suggests that absolutism had indeed adopted a new image.

Catherine the Great (r. 1762–1796) played this game to its limit. In 1767 she announced a new experiment in the direction of representative government—a policy hailed as a landmark by her philosophe admirers, who were too remote from St. Petersburg to see its insincerity. Catherine convened a Legislative Commission, a body of delegates from various strata of Russian society who were invited to present grievances, propose reforms, and then debate the proposals. In the end, however, she sent the delegates home under the pretext of having to turn her attention to a war with Turkey. Little came of the Legislative Commission except some good publicity for Catherine. In fact, she later promulgated a Charter of the Nobility, which, instead of limiting the nobility's privileges, strengthened their corporate status and increased their control over their serfs in exchange for their loyalty to the throne.

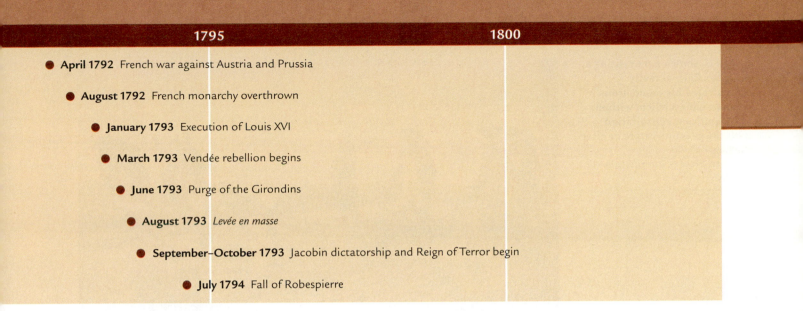

1795

1800

- **April 1792** French war against Austria and Prussia
- **August 1792** French monarchy overthrown
- **January 1793** Execution of Louis XVI
- **March 1793** Vendée rebellion begins
- **June 1793** Purge of the Girondins
- **August 1793** *Levée en masse*
- **September–October 1793** Jacobin dictatorship and Reign of Terror begin
- **July 1794** Fall of Robespierre

Conceptions of Enlightened Rule in Germany In justification of absolute monarchy, eighteenth-century German writers depicted the state as a machine and the ruler as its mainspring. Progress came from sound administration, through an enlightened monarch and well-trained officials. In keeping with this notion, German universities began to train government bureaucrats, and professors offered courses in the science of public finance and administration called *cameralism*.

The orders for the bureaucracy came from the monarchs, who were expected to dedicate themselves to the welfare of their subjects in return for their subjects' obedience. The framework for this command-obedience chain was to be a coherent body of public law, fairly administered by state officials. According to its advocates, this system would produce the rule of law, without the need for a written constitution or a representative parliament. The ruler and his or her officials, following their sense of public responsibility and rational analysis, would ensure the citizens' rights and well-being.

Joseph II and the Limits of Absolutism

Joseph II, coruler of the Habsburg Empire with his mother, Maria Theresa, from 1765 and sole ruler in the 1780s, vigorously promoted reform from above. Unlike Frederick or Catherine, he did not openly identify with the philosophes, and he maintained his own Catholic faith. But Joseph proved to be the most innovative of the century's major rulers as well as one of its most autocratic personalities. It was a problematic combination.

Sound rule for Emperor Joseph involved far more than the customary administrative and financial reform necessary for survival in the competitive state system. With startling boldness he implemented several reforms long advocated by Enlightenment thinkers: freedom of expression, religious toleration, greater state control over the Catholic Church, and legal reform. A new criminal code, for example, reduced the use of the death penalty, ended judicial torture, and allowed for no class differences in the application of the laws. By greatly reducing royal censorship, Joseph made it possible for Vienna to become a major center of literary activity. And we have already noted Joseph's remarkable Edicts of Religious Toleration for Protestants and for Jews. But Joseph's religious policies did not stop there. To make the Catholic Church serve its parishioners better, Joseph forced the clergy to modernize its rituals and services. Most of his Catholic subjects, however, preferred their traditional ways to Joseph's streamlined brand of Catholicism. These "reforms" proved extremely unpopular.

Agrarian Reform Joseph's most ambitious policies aimed to transform the economic and social position of the peasants. Elsewhere, agrarian reform was generally the weak side of enlightened absolutism, since Frederick II and Catherine II did little to improve the lot of the peasants or serfs in their realms. Joseph, however, set out to eradicate serfdom and to convert Habsburg peasants into free individuals in command of their persons and of the land they cultivated.

By royal decree, Joseph abolished personal servitude and gave peasants the right to move, marry, and enter any trade they wished. He then promulgated laws to secure peasants' control over the land they worked. Finally and most remarkably, he sought to limit the financial obligations of peasant tenants to their lords and to the state. All land was to be surveyed and subject to a uniform tax. Twelve percent of the land's annual yield would go to the state and a maximum of 18 percent would go to the lord. This tax replaced

Joseph II, shown here visiting a peasant's field, actually promulgated his momentous agrarian reform edicts without any significant consultation with the peasants before or after the fact.
Austrian Press & Information Service

previous seigneurial obligations in which peasants owed service to their lord that could consume more than one hundred days of labor a year.

Joseph ordered these reforms in an authoritarian fashion, with little consultation and no consent from any quarter. Predictably, these reforms provoked fierce opposition among the landowning nobles. But they also perplexed most peasants, who already distrusted the government because of its arbitrary religious policies. Joseph made no effort to build support among the peasants by carefully explaining the reforms, let alone by modifying their details after getting feedback from the grass roots.

His arbitrary manner, however, was not incidental. Joseph acknowledged no other way of doing things, no limitation on his own sovereignty. In reaction to the opposition that his reforms aroused, he moved to suppress dissent in the firmest possible way. Not only did he restore censorship in his last years, but he elevated the police department to the status of an imperial ministry and gave it unprecedented powers. By the time he died, in 1790, Joseph was a disillusioned man. His realm resembled a police state, and his successors quickly restored serfdom.

Upheavals in the British Empire

An aggressive monarch, George III, helped ignite political unrest in Great Britain. He was intent on advancing royal authority, but rather than bypass Parliament altogether, he simply tried, as Whig ministers had before him, to control its members through patronage and influence. The Whig aristocrats saw this operation as a threat to their own traditional power. Not only did they oppose the king and his ministers in Parlia-

ment, but they enlisted the support of citizens' groups outside of Parliament as well. These organizations were calling for political reform, including representation in Parliament proportionate to population, stricter laws against political corruption, and greater freedom of the press.

"Wilkes and Liberty"   John Wilkes, a member of Parliament and a journalist, became the center of this rising storm. Wilkes viciously attacked the king's prime minister, and by implication the king himself, over the terms of the Treaty of Paris, which ended the Seven Years' War in 1763. The government arrested him for seditious libel on a general warrant. When the courts quashed the indictment, the government then accused Wilkes of having authored a libelous pornographic poem, and this time he fled to France to avoid prison. He stayed in France for four years; but in 1768, still under indictment, he returned to stand once more for Parliament. Three times he was reelected, and three times the House of Commons refused to seat him. With the ardent support of radicals and to the acclaim of crowds in London, who marched to the chant of "Wilkes and Liberty," Wilkes finally took his seat in 1774.

Agitation for parliamentary reform drew support primarily from shopkeepers, artisans, and property owners, who had the franchise in a few districts but were denied it in most others. Thus, even without a right to vote, English citizens could engage in politics and mobilize the power of public opinion, in this case by rallying to Wilkes. Most radicals called only for political reform, not for the overthrow of the British political system. They retained a measure of respect for the nation's political traditions, which ideally guaranteed the rights of "freeborn Englishmen."

The committee that drafted the American Declaration of Independence included John Adams, Thomas Jefferson, and Benjamin Franklin, all shown here standing at the desk.
The Library of Congress

Rebellion in America   Great Britain did face revolutionary action in the thirteen North American colonies. George III and his prime minister, Lord North, attempted to force the colonies to pay the costs, past and present, of their own defense. The policy would have meant an increase in taxes and a centralization of authority in the governance of the British Empire. Colonial landowners, merchants, and artisans of the eastern seaboard organized petitions and boycotts in opposition to the proposed fiscal and constitutional changes.

The resistance in North America differed fundamentally from comparable movements in Europe. American political leaders did not appeal to a body of privileges that the actions of the monarchy were allegedly violating. Instead, they appealed to traditional rights supposedly enjoyed by all British subjects, regardless of status, and to theories of popular sovereignty and natural rights advanced by John Locke and other English libertarian writers. When conciliation and compromise with the British government failed,

the American Declaration of Independence in 1776 gave eloquent expression to those concepts. The lack of a rigid system of estates and hereditary privileges in American society, the fluid boundaries that separated the social strata, and the traditions of local government in the colonies—from town meetings in New England to the elected legislatures that had advised colonial governors—blunted the kinds of conflicts between aristocrats and commoners that derailed incipient revolutionary movements in Ireland, Belgium, and the Dutch Netherlands.

These differences help to explain the unique character of the American rebellion, which was simultaneously a war for independence and a political revolution. The theories that supported the rebellion, and the continuing alliance between social strata, made it the most democratic revolution of the eighteenth century before 1789. The American Revolution created the first state governments, and ultimately a national government, in which the exercise of power was grounded not on royal sovereignty or traditional privilege but on the participation and consent of male citizens (apart from the numerous black slaves, whose status did not change). Even more important as a historical precedent, perhaps, it was the first successful rebellion by overseas colonies against their European masters.

1789: THE FRENCH REVOLUTION

Although the rebellion in America stirred sympathy and interest across the Atlantic, it seemed remote from the realities of Europe. The French Revolution of 1789 proved to be the turning point in European history. Its sheer radicalism, creativity, and claims of universalism made it unique. Its ultimate slogan—"Liberty, Equality, Fraternity"—expressed social and civic ideals that became the foundations of modern Western civilization. In the name of individual liberty, French revolutionaries swept away the institutionalized constraints of the old regime: seigneurial charges upon the land, tax privileges, guild monopolies on commerce, and even (in 1794) black slavery overseas. The revolutionaries held that legitimate governments required written constitutions, elections, and powerful legislatures. They demanded equality before the law for all persons and uniformity of institutions for all regions of the country, denying the claims to special treatment of privileged groups, provinces, towns, or religions. The term *fraternity* expressed a different kind of revolutionary goal. Rousseauist in inspiration, it meant that all citizens, regardless of social class, or region, shared a common fate in society and that the nation's well-being could override the interests of individual citizens.

Origins of the Revolution

Those who made the Revolution believed they were rising against despotic government, in which citizens had no voice, and against inequality and privilege. Yet the government of France at that time was no more tyrannical or unjust than it had been in the past. On the contrary, a process of modest reform had been under way for several decades. What, then, set off the revolutionary upheaval? What had failed in France's long-standing political system?

An easy answer would be to point to the incompetence of King Louis XVI (r. 1774–1792) and his queen, Marie Antoinette. Louis was good-natured but weak and indecisive, a man of limited intelligence who lacked self-confidence and who preferred hunting deer to supervising the business of government. By no stretch of the imagination was he an enlightened absolutist. Worse yet, his young queen, a Habsburg

princess, was frivolous, meddlesome, and tactless. But even the most capable French ruler could not have escaped challenge and unrest in the 1780s.

The Cultural Climate   In eighteenth-century France, as we have seen, intellectual ferment preceded political revolt. For decades the philosophes had questioned accepted political and religious beliefs. They undermined confidence that traditional ways were the best ways. But the philosophes harbored deep-seated fears of the uneducated masses and did not question the notion that educated and propertied elites should rule society; they wished only that the elites should be more enlightened and more open to new ideas. Indeed, the Enlightenment had become respectable by the 1770s, a kind of intellectual establishment. Rousseau damned that establishment and wrote of the need for simplicity, sincerity, and virtue, but the word *revolution* never flowed from his pen either.

More subversive perhaps than the writings of Enlightenment intellectuals were several sensational lawsuits centered on the scandalous doings of high aristocrats. The melodramatic legal briefs published by the lawyers in such cases were eagerly snatched up by the reading public along with prohibited "bad books"—the clandestine gossip sheets, libels, exposés, and pornography—discussed earlier. All this material—indirectly, at least—portrayed the French aristocracy as decadent and the monarchy as a ridiculous despotism. Royal officials and philosophes alike regarded the authors of this material as "the excrement of literature," as Voltaire put it. And writers forced to earn their living by turning out such stuff were no doubt embittered at being stuck on the bottom rung in the world of letters. Their resentment would explode once the Revolution began in 1789, and many became radical journalists either for or against the new regime. In itself, however, the "literary underground" of the old regime did not advocate, foresee, or directly cause the Revolution.

Class Conflict?   Did the structure of French society, then, provoke the Revolution? Karl Marx, and the many historians inspired by him, certainly believed so. Marx saw the French Revolution as the necessary break marking the transition from the aristocratic feudalism of the Middle Ages to the era of middle-class capitalism. In this view, the French bourgeoisie, or middle classes, had been gaining in wealth during the eighteenth century and resented the privileges of the nobility, which created obstacles to their ambition. Though they framed their ideology in universal terms in 1789, the middle classes led the Revolution in order to change the political and social systems in their own interests.

Three decades of research have rendered this theory of the Revolution's origins untenable. Whether a sizable and coherent capitalist middle class actually existed in eighteenth-century France is questionable. In any case, the leaders of the Revolution in 1789 were lawyers, administrators, and liberal nobles, and rarely merchants or industrialists. Moreover, the barrier between the nobility of the Second Estate and the wealthy and educated members of the Third Estate was porous, the lines of social division frequently (though not always) blurred. Many members of the middle class identified themselves on official documents as "living nobly," as substantial property owners who did not work for a living. Conversely, wealthy nobles often invested in mining, overseas trade, and finance—activities usually associated with the middle classes. Even more important, the gap between the nobility and the middle classes was nothing compared with the gulf that separated both from the working people of town and country. In this revisionist historiography, the bourgeoisie did not make the Revolution so much as the Revolution made the bourgeoisie (see "On the Origins of the French Revolution," p. 588).

Yet numerous disruptive pressures were at work in French society. A growing population left large numbers of young people in town and country struggling to attain a stable place in society. New images and attitudes rippled through the media of the day, despite the state's efforts to censor material it deemed subversive. The nobility, long since banished by Louis XIV from an independent role in government, chafed at its exclusion, although it continued to enjoy a near monopoly on positions in the officer corps. The prosperous middle classes too aspired to a more active role in government. The monarchy struggled to contain these forces within the established social and political systems. Until the 1780s it succeeded, but then its troubles began in earnest.

Fiscal Crisis and Political Deadlock

When he took the throne in 1774, Louis XVI tried to conciliate elite opinion by recalling the parlements, or sovereign law courts, that his grandfather had banished in 1770 for opposing his policies. This concession to France's traditional "unwritten constitution" did not suffice to smooth the new sovereign's road. Louis' new controller-general of finances, Jacques Turgot, encountered a storm of opposition from privileged groups to the reforms he proposed.

The Failure of Reform   Turgot, an ally of the philosophes and an experienced administrator, hoped to encourage economic growth by a policy of nonintervention, or *laissez-faire*, that would give free play to economic markets and allow individuals maximum freedom to pursue their own economic interests. He proposed to remove all restrictions on commerce in grain and to abolish the guilds. In addition, he tried to cut down on expenses at court and to replace the obligation of peasants to work on the royal roads (the *corvée*) with a small new tax on all landholders. Privately, he also considered establishing elected advisory assemblies of landowners to assist in local administration. Vested interests, however, viewed Turgot as a dangerous innovator. When agitation against him mounted in the king's court at Versailles and in the Paris parlement, Louis took the easy way out and dismissed his contentious minister. With Turgot went perhaps the last hope for significant reform in France under royal leadership.

Deficit Financing   The king then turned to Jacques Necker, a banker from Geneva who had a reputation for financial wizardry. Necker had a shrewd sense of public relations. To finance the heavy costs of France's aid to the rebellious British colonies in North America, Necker avoided new taxes and instead floated a series of large loans at exorbitant interest rates as high as 10 percent.

By the 1780s royal finances hovered in a state of permanent crisis. Direct taxes on land, borne mainly by the peasants, were extremely high but were levied inequitably. The great variations in taxation from province to province and the numerous exemptions for privileged groups were regarded by those who benefited from them as traditional liberties. Any attempt to revoke these privileges therefore appeared to be tyrannical. Meanwhile, indirect taxes on commercial activity (customs duties, excise or sales taxes, and royal monopolies on salt and tobacco) hit regressively at consumers, especially in the towns. At the same time, the cycle of borrowing—the alternative to increased taxes—had reached its limits. New loans would only raise the huge interest payments already being paid out. By the 1780s those payments accounted for about half the royal budget and created additional budget deficits each year.

Calonne and the Assembly of Notables   When the king's new controller-general, Charles Calonne, pieced all this information together in 1787, he warned that, contrary to Necker's rosy projections, the monarchy was facing outright bankruptcy. Though no way had yet been found to win public confidence and forge a consensus for fiscal reform, the monarchy could no longer rely on old expedients. Calonne accordingly proposed to establish a new tax, called the *territorial subvention*, to be levied on the yield of all landed property without exemptions. At the same time, he proposed

HISTORICAL ISSUES: ON THE ORIGINS OF THE FRENCH REVOLUTION

A long-held view of the French Revolution's origins attributed the starring role to the middle class, "the rising bourgeoisie." Liberal historians of the nineteenth century regarded the middle class as the carrier of liberal ideals—individual freedom, civil equality, representative government—that finally came to fruition in the French Revolution. Marxists considered the triumph of capitalism to be the pivotal issue in modern history and linked it to the political ascendancy of the middle class in the French Revolution. In a sense, both versions of this "social interpretation" of the French Revolution read its causes back from its results. In his classic synthesis of 1939 embodying the social interpretation, for example, Georges Lefebvre begins with these observations:

"The ultimate cause of the French Revolution of 1789 goes deep into the history of France and of the western world. At the end of the eighteenth century the social structure of France was aristocratic. It showed the traces of having originated at a time when land was almost the only form of wealth, and when the possessors of land were the masters of those who needed it to work and to live. It is true that in the course of age-old struggles the king had been able gradually to deprive the lords of their political powers and subject nobles and clergy to his authority. But he had left them the first place in the social hierarchy.

"Meanwhile the growth of commerce and industry had created, step by step, a new form of wealth, mobile or commercial wealth, and a new class, called in France the bourgeoisie. . . . In the eighteenth century commerce, in-

dustry and finance occupied an increasingly important place in the national economy. It was the bourgeoisie that rescued the royal treasury in moments of crisis. . . . The role of the nobility had correspondingly declined; and the clergy, as the ideal which it proclaimed lost prestige, found its authority growing weaker. These groups preserved the highest rank in the legal structure of the country, but in reality economic power, personal abilities and confidence in the future had passed largely to the bourgeoisie. Such a discrepancy never lasts forever. The Revolution of 1789 restored the harmony between fact and law."

From Georges Lefebvre, *The Coming of the French Revolution*, R. R. Palmer (trans.), Princeton University Press, 1989.

Since the 1950s, revisionist historians have challenged this "social interpretation" of the French Revolution. In his synthesis, William Doyle summarizes some of their research and arguments.

"Money, not privilege, was the key to pre-revolutionary society in France. Wealth transcended all social barriers and bound great nobles and upper bourgeois together into an upper class unified by money. . . . Eighteenth-century capitalism was far from a bourgeois monopoly. One of its basic features was the heavy involvement of nobles. . . . [On the other hand,] the wealth of all social groups in pre-revolutionary France was overwhelmingly non-capitalist in nature. Capitalism had not become the dominant mode of production in the French economy before 1789. . . . there was between most of the nobility and the proprietary sectors of the middle class, a continuity of investment forms and socioeconomic values that made them, economically, a single group.

"If the nobility and the bourgeoisie had so much in common, why did they become such implacable enemies in 1789? [Since] the Revolution could not be explained in economic terms as a clash of opposed interests. . . . it was time to revert to a political explanation of the Revolution's outbreak. The radical reforms of 1789 were products of a political crisis, and not the outcome of long-maturing social and economic trends. [As historian George Taylor concluded:] 'It was essentially a political revolution with social consequences and not a social revolution with political consequences.' "

From William Doyle, *Origins of the French Revolution*, Oxford University Press, 1988.

to convene *provincial assemblies* elected by large landowners to advise royal officials on the collection and allocation of revenues.

Certain that the parlements would reject this scheme, Calonne convinced the king to convene an Assembly of Notables, comprising about 150 influential men, mainly but not exclusively from the aristocracy, who might more easily be persuaded to support the re-

forms. To Calonne's shock, the Assembly of Notables refused to endorse the proposed decrees. Instead, they denounced the lavish spending of the court and insisted on auditing the monarchy's financial accounts. Moreover, when the government now submitted Calonne's proposals to the parlement, it not only rejected them but demanded that Louis convene the **Estates General,** a body representing the clergy, nobility, and Third

Estate, which had not met since 1614. Louis responded by sending the members of the parlements into exile. But a huge outcry in Paris and in the provinces against this arbitrary act forced the king to back down: After all, the whole purpose of Calonne's proposals had been to build public confidence in the government.

Facing bankruptcy and unable to float new loans in this atmosphere, the king recalled the parlements, reappointed Necker, and agreed to convene the Estates General in May 1789. In the opinion of the English writer Arthur Young, who was visiting France, the kingdom was "on the verge of a revolution, but one likely to add to the scale of the nobility and clergy." The aristocracy's determined opposition was putting an end to absolutism in France. But it was not clear what would take its place.

From the Estates General to the National Assembly

The calling of the Estates General in 1789 created extraordinary excitement across the land. The king invited his subjects to express their opinions about this great event, and thousands did so in pamphlet form. Here the "patriot," or liberal, ideology first took shape. Self-styled patriots came from the ranks of the nobility and clergy as well as from the middle classes; they opposed traditionalists, whom they labeled as "aristocrats." Their top priority was the method of voting to be used in the Estates General. While the king accorded the Third Estate twice as many delegates as the two higher orders, he refused to promise that the deputies would all vote together (by head) rather than separately in three chambers (by order). Voting by order would mean that the two upper chambers would outweigh the Third Estate no matter how many deputies it had. Patriots had hoped that the lines dividing the nobility from the middle class would crumble in a common effort by France's elites at reform. Instead, it appeared as if the Estates General might sharpen the lines of separation between the orders.

The Critique of Privilege   It did not matter that the nobility had led the fight against absolutism. Even if they endorsed new constitutional checks on absolutism and accepted equality in the allocation of taxes, nobles would still hold vastly disproportionate powers if the Estates General voted by order. In the most influential pamphlet about the Estates General, Emmanuel Sieyès posed the question, "What is the Third Estate?" and answered flatly, "Everything." "And what has it been until now in the political order?" he asked. Answer: "Nothing." The nobility, he claimed, monopolized all the lucrative positions in society while doing little of its productive work. In the manifestos of Sieyès

THE AWAKENING OF THE THIRD ESTATE
Thousands of pamphlets discussed the calling of the Estates General in 1789, but the grievances of the Third Estate translated most readily into vivid imagery and caricature.
Roger-Viollet/Bibliothèque Nationale de France, Paris

and other patriots, the enemy was no longer simply absolutism but privilege as well.

Unlike reformers in England or the American revolutionaries of 1776, the French patriots did not simply claim that the king had violated historic traditions of liberty. Rather, they contemplated a complete break with a discredited past. As a basis for reform, they would substitute reason for tradition. It is this frame of mind that made the French Revolution so radical.

Cahiers and Elections   For the moment, however, patriot spokesmen stood far in advance of opinion at the grass roots. The king had invited all citizens to meet in their local parishes to elect delegates to district electoral assemblies and to draft grievance petitions (**cahiers**) setting forth their views. The great majority of rural cahiers were highly traditional in tone and complained only of particular local ills or high taxes, expressing confidence that the king would redress them. Only a few cahiers from cities like Paris invoked concepts of natural rights and popular sovereignty or demanded that France must have a written constitution, that sovereignty belonged to the nation, or that feudalism and regional privileges should be abolished. It is impossible, in other words, to read in the cahiers the future course of the Revolution. Still, these gatherings of citizens promoted reflection on France's problems and encouraged expectations for change. They thereby raised the nation's political consciousness.

So too did the local elections, whose royal ground rules were remarkably democratic. Virtually every

When the king opened the meeting of the Estates General, the deputies for each estate were directed to sit in three separate sections of the hall.
Bulloz/© Photo RMN/Art Resource, NY

adult male taxpayer was eligible to vote for electors, who, in turn, met in district assemblies to choose representatives of the Third Estate to the Estates General. The electoral assemblies were a kind of political seminar, where articulate local leaders emerged to be sent by their fellow citizens as deputies to Versailles. Most of these deputies were lawyers or officials, without a single peasant or artisan among them. In the elections for the First Estate, meanwhile, parish priests rather than Church notables formed a majority of the deputies. And in the elections for the Second Estate, about one-third of the deputies could be described as liberal nobles or patriots, the rest traditionalists.

Deadlock and Revolution Popular expectation that the monarchy would provide leadership in reform proved to be ill-founded. When the deputies to the Estates General met on May 5, Necker and Louis XVI spoke to them only in generalities and left unsettled whether the estates would vote by order or by head. The upper two estates proceeded to organize their own chambers, but the deputies of the Third Estate balked. Vainly inviting the others to join them, the Third Estate took a decisive revolutionary step on June 17 by proclaiming that it formed a "National Assembly." A few days later more than a third of the deputies from

the clergy joined them. The king, on the other hand, decided to cast his lot with the nobility and locked the Third Estate out of its meeting hall until he could present his own program. But the deputies moved to an indoor tennis court and swore that they would not separate until they had given France a constitution.

The king ignored this act of defiance and addressed the delegates of all three orders on June 23. He promised equality in taxation, civil liberties, and regular meetings of the Estates General at which, however, voting would be by order. France would be provided with a constitution, he pledged, "but the ancient distinction of the three orders will be conserved in its entirety." He then ordered the three estates to retire to their individual meeting halls, but the Third Estate refused to move. "The assembled nation cannot receive orders," declared its spokesman. Startled by the determination of the patriots, the king backed down. For the time being, he recognized the National Assembly and ordered deputies from all three estates to join it.

Thus, the French Revolution began as a nonviolent, "legal" revolution. By their own will, delegates elected by France's three estates to represent their own districts to the king became instead the representatives of the entire nation. As such, they claimed to be the sovereign power in France—a claim that the king now

Jacques-Louis David
OATH OF THE TENNIS COURT, THE 20TH OF JUNE, 1789
Jacques-Louis David's depiction of the Tennis Court Oath, one of the great historical paintings, captures the deputies' sense of idealism and purpose.
Giraudon/Art Resource, NY

seemed powerless to contest. In fact, however, he was merely biding his time until he could deploy his army to subdue the capital and overwhelm the deputies at Versailles. The king ordered twenty thousand royal troops into the Paris region, due to arrive sometime in July.

The Convergence of Revolutions

The political struggle at Versailles was not occurring in isolation. The mass of French citizens, politically aroused by elections to the Estates General, was also mobilizing over subsistence issues. The winter and spring of 1788–1789 had brought severe economic difficulties, as crop failures and grain shortages almost doubled the price of flour and bread on which the population depended for subsistence. Unemployed vagrants filled the roads, angry consumers stormed grain convoys and marketplaces, and relations between town and country grew tense. Economic anxieties merged with rage over the obstructive behavior of aristocrats in Versailles. Parisians believed that food shortages and royal troops would be used to intimidate the people into submission. They feared an "aristocratic plot" against the National Assembly and the patriot cause.

The Fall of the Bastille   When the king dismissed Necker on July 11, Parisians correctly assumed that a counterrevolution was about to begin. They prepared to resist, and most of the king's military units pulled back in the face of determined crowds. On July 14 Parisian crowds searching for weapons and ammunition laid siege to the **Bastille,** an old fortress that had once served as a royal prison and in which gunpowder was stored. The small garrison resisted, and a fierce firefight erupted. Although the troops soon capitulated, dozens of citizens were hit, providing the first martyrs of the Revolution, and the infuriated crowd massacred several soldiers as they left the fortress. Meanwhile, patriot electors ousted royal officials of the Paris city government, replaced them with a revolutionary municipality, and organized a citizens' militia to patrol the city. Similar municipal revolutions occurred in twenty-six of the thirty largest French cities, thus ensuring that the defiance in the capital would not be an isolated act.

The Storming of the Bastille
The fall of the Bastille was understood at the time to be a great turning point in history, and July 14 eventually became the French national holiday. Numerous prints and paintings evoke the daunting qualities of the fortress, the determination of the besieging crowd, and the valor of individuals in that crowd.
Bulloz/© Photo RMN/Art Resource, NY

The Parisian insurrection of July 14 not only saved the National Assembly but altered the Revolution's course by giving it a far more popular dimension. Again the king capitulated. He traveled to Paris on July 17 and, to please the people, donned a ribbon bearing three colors: white for the monarchy and blue and red for the capital. This *tricolor* would become the emblem of the new regime.

Peasant Revolts and the August 4 Decree   These events did not pacify the anxious and hungry people of the countryside. Peasants had numerous and long-standing grievances. Population growth and the parceling of holdings reduced the margin of subsistence for many families, while the purchase of land by rich townspeople further shrank their opportunities for economic advancement. Seigneurial dues and church tithes weighed heavily on many peasants. Now, in addition, suspicions were rampant that nobles were hoarding grain in order to stymie the patriotic cause. In July peasants in several regions sacked the houses of the nobles and burned the documents that recorded their seigneurial obligations.

This peasant insurgency blended into a vast movement known to historians as "the Great Fear." Rumors abounded that the vagrants who swarmed through the countryside were actually "brigands" in the pay of nobles, who were marching on villages to destroy the new harvest and cow the peasants into submission. The fear was baseless, but it stirred up the peasants' hatred and suspicion of the nobles, prompted armed mobilizations in hundreds of villages, and set off new attacks on manor houses.

Peasant revolts worried the deputies of the National Assembly, but they decided to appease the peasants rather than simply denounce their violence. On the night of August 4, therefore, certain deputies of the nobility and clergy dramatically renounced their ancient privileges. This action set the stage for the Assembly to decree "the abolition of feudalism" as well as the end of the church tithe, the sale of royal offices, regional tax privileges, and social privilege of all kinds. Later, it is true, the Assembly clarified the August 4 decree to ensure that property rights were maintained. While personal servitudes such as hunting rights, manorial justice, and labor services were suppressed outright, the Assembly decreed that most seigneurial dues would end only after the peasants had paid compensation to their lords. Peasants resented this onerous requirement, and most simply refused to pay the dues; pressure built until all seigneurial dues were finally abolished without compensation by a more radical government in 1793.

THE RECONSTRUCTION OF FRANCE

The summer of 1789 had seen a remarkable sequence of unprecedented events. A bloodless, juridical revolution from above (engineered by the patriot deputies to the Estates General) combined with popular mobilization from below in town and country made the French Revolution seem irresistible. After the clearing operations of August 4, the National Assembly set out not simply to enact reforms but to reconstruct French institutions on entirely new principles. With sovereignty wrested from the king and vested in the people's deputies, no aspect of France's social or political system was immune to scrutiny, not even slavery in the colonies. First, the Assembly adopted a set of general principles known as the Declaration of the Rights of Man and Citizen. Then it proceeded to draft a constitution, settle the question of voting rights (where the issue of women's citizenship first came up), reorganize the structures of public life, and determine the future of the Catholic clergy. None of this occurred without intense disagreement, especially over the religious issue and the role of the king. Moreover, Austria and Prussia eventually decided on armed intervention against revolutionary France. In 1792 war broke out, which led directly to the fall of the monarchy and to a new, violent turn in the Revolution.

The Declaration of the Rights of Man and Citizen

By sweeping away the old web of privileges, the August 4 decree permitted the Assembly to construct a new regime. Since it would take months to draft a constitution, the Assembly drew up a Declaration of the Rights of Man and Citizen to indicate its intentions (see "Two Views of the Rights of Man," p. 594). The Declaration was the death certificate of the old regime and a rallying point for the future. It affirmed individual liberties but also set forth the basic obligation of citizenship: obedience to legitimate law. The Declaration enumerated **natural rights,** such as freedom of expression and freedom of religious conscience, but (unlike the America Bill of Rights) stipulated that even these rights could be circumscribed by law. It proclaimed the sovereignty of the nation and sketched the basic criteria for a legitimate government, such as representation and the separation of powers. The Declaration's concept of natural rights meant that the new regime would be based on the principles of reason rather than history or tradition.

In his *Reflections on the Revolution in France,* published in 1790, the Anglo-Irish statesman Edmund Burke condemned this attitude, as well as the violence of 1789. In this influential counterrevolutionary tract, Burke argued that France had passed from despotism to anarchy in the name of misguided, abstract principles. Burke distrusted the simplicity of reason that the Assembly celebrated. In his view, the complexity of traditional institutions served the public interest. Burke attacked the belief in natural rights that guided the revolutionaries; something was natural, he believed, only if it resulted from long historical development and habit. Trying to wipe the slate of history clean was a grievous error, he wrote, since society "is a contract between the dead, the living, and the unborn." Society's main right, in Burke's view, was the right to be well-governed by its rulers. Naturally this argument did not go unchallenged, even in England. Mary Wollstonecraft countered with *A Vindication of the Rights of Man,* followed shortly by her seminal *Vindication of the Rights of Woman,* while Thomas Paine published *The Rights of Man* in 1792 to refute Burke.

The New Constitution

Representative Government   From 1789 to 1791, the National Assembly acted as a Constituent Assembly to produce a constitution for France. While proclaiming equal civil rights for all French citizens, it effectively transferred political power from the monarchy and the privileged estates to the body of propertied citizens; in 1790 nobles lost their titles and became indistinguishable from other citizens. The new constitution created a limited monarchy with a clear separation of powers. Sovereignty effectively resided in the representatives of the people, a single-house legislature to be elected by a system of indirect voting. The king was to name and dismiss his ministers, but he was given only a suspensive or delaying veto over legislation; if a bill passed the Assembly in three successive years, it would become law even without royal approval.

TWO VIEWS OF THE RIGHTS OF MAN

The radical theoretical and practical implications of French revolutionary ideology are suggested in a comparison of two essentially contemporaneous documents. The Prussian General Code, a codification initiated by Frederick the Great and issued in its final form in 1791 after his death, reinforced the traditional prerogatives of the nobility under an umbrella of public law. The French National Assembly's Declaration of the Rights of Man and Citizen (1789) established the principle of civil equality alongside the doctrines of national sovereignty, representation, and the rule of law. While the Prussian General Code exemplifies the old order against which French revolutionary ideology took aim, the Declaration became a foundational document of the liberal tradition.

EXCERPTS FROM THE PRUSSIAN GENERAL CODE, 1791

- This general code contains the provisions by which the rights and obligations of inhabitants of the state, so far as they are not determined by particular laws, are to be judged.
- The rights of a man arise from his birth, from his estate, and from actions and arrangements with which the laws have associated a certain determinate effect.
- The general rights of man are grounded on the natural liberty to seek and further his own welfare, without injury to the rights of another.
- Persons to whom, by their birth, destination or principal occupation, equal rights are ascribed in civil society, make up together an *estate* of the state.
- The nobility, as the first estate in the state, most especially bears the obligation, by its distinctive destination, to maintain the defense of the state. . . .
- The nobleman has an especial right to places of honor in the state for which he has made himself fit.
- Only the nobleman has the right to possess noble property.
- Persons of the burgher [middle-class] estate cannot own noble property except by permission of the sovereign.
- Noblemen shall normally engage in no burgher livelihood or occupation.

From R. R. Palmer (trans.), *The Age of Democratic Revolution*, Princeton University Press, 1959, pp. 510–511.

EXCERPTS FROM THE FRENCH DECLARATION OF THE RIGHTS OF MAN AND CITIZEN, 1789

1. Men are born and remain free and equal in rights. Social distinctions may be based only on common utility.
3. The principle of all sovereignty rests essentially in the nation. No body and no individual may exercise authority which does not emanate expressly from the nation.
4. Liberty consists in the ability to do whatever does not harm another; hence the exercise of the natural rights of each man has no limits except those which assure to other members of society the enjoyment of the same rights. These limits can only be determined by law.
6. Law is the expression of the general will. All citizens have the right to take part, in person or by their representatives, in its formation. It must be the same for all whether it protects or penalizes. All citizens being equal in its eyes are equally admissible to all public dignities, offices and employments, according to their capacity, and with no other distinction than that of their virtues and talents.
13. For maintenance of public forces and for expenses of administration common taxation is necessary. It should be apportioned equally among all citizens according to their capacity to pay.
14. All citizens have the right, by themselves or through their representatives, to have demonstrated to them the necessity of public taxes, to consent to them freely, to follow the use made of the proceeds, and to determine the shares to be paid, the means of assessment and collection and the duration.

Under the French Constitution of 1791, every adult male of settled domicile who satisfied minimal tax-paying requirements (roughly two-thirds of all adult males) gained the right to vote, with a higher qualification needed to serve as an elector. Although it favored the propertied, France's new political system was vastly more democratic than Britain's. Still, the National Assembly considered the vote to be a civic function rather than a natural right. "Those who contribute nothing to the public establishment should have no direct influence on government," declared Sieyès. In the same frame of mind the Assembly excluded all women from voting.

Women in the Revolution   That the Assembly even debated political rights for women testifies to the potential universalism of the Revolution's principles. A brief but spirited drive for women's suffrage advanced through pamphlets, petitions, and deputations to the Assembly—most notably the "Declaration of the Rights of Women" (1791) drafted by the playwright Olympe de Gouges. But the notion of gender difference

In October 1789 Parisian women were furious over the high cost of bread and suspicious of the king and queen. In concert with the National Guard, they set out on an armed march to confront the royal couple in Versailles. To appease the menacing crowd, Louis XVI agreed to return to Paris and to cooperate with revolutionary authorities.
Giraudon/Art Resource, NY

and separate spheres, popularized by Rousseau, easily prevailed. The great majority of deputies believed women to be too emotional. Too easily influenced to be independent, they must be excluded from the new public sphere—the more so because of the deputies' belief that elite women had used their sexual powers nefariously behind the scenes during the old regime to influence public policy. Now public life would be virtuous and transparent, uninfluenced by feminine wiles. Instead, women would devote themselves to their crucial nurturing and maternal roles in the domestic sphere.

This type of discourse has prompted some feminist scholars to claim that the revolutionary public sphere "was constructed not merely without women but against them." Balanced against this argument, however, is an offsetting consideration. Male revolutionaries may have distrusted women, and some were overt misogynists, yet their own ideology and political culture created unprecedented public space for women. True, women could not vote or hold office, but otherwise *citoyennes* had extensive opportunity for political participation. Women actively engaged in local conflicts over the Assembly's religious policy (discussed later in this chapter). In the towns they agitated over

food prices, and in October 1789 Parisian women led a mass demonstration to Versailles that forcibly returned the king and queen to Paris. Combining traditional concerns over food scarcities with antiaristocratic revolutionary ideology, women frequently goaded authorities like the national guard into action.

In unprecedented numbers women also took up the pen to publish pamphlets and journals. Their physical presence in public spaces was even more important. Women helped fill the galleries of the Assembly, of the Paris Jacobin Club, and later of the Revolutionary Tribunal—shouting approval or disapproval and in general monitoring their officials. In at least sixty towns women formed auxiliaries to the local Jacobin club, where they read newspapers, debated political issues, and participated in revolutionary festivals.

Nor did Rousseauian antifeminism prevent the revolutionaries from enacting dramatic advances in the civil status of women. Legislation between 1789 and 1794 created a more equitable family life by curbing paternal powers over children, lowering the age of majority, and equalizing the status of husbands and wives in regard to property. Viewing marriage as a contract between a free man and a free woman, the revolutionaries

MAP 20.1 REDIVIDING THE NATION'S TERRITORY IN 1789
The old regime provinces (left) were replaced by revolutionary departments (right). What advantages did this change bring for the French state?

◆ For an online version, go to www.mhhe.com/chambers9 > chapter 20 > book maps

provided the right of divorce to either spouse should the marriage go sour. A remarkably egalitarian inheritance law stipulated that daughters as well as sons were entitled to an equal share of a family's estate. Finally, in the domain of education—central to the feminist vision of Mary Wollstonecraft that the French Revolution had crystalized—an unprecedented system of universal and free primary schooling in 1794 extended to girls as well as boys and provided for state-salaried teachers of both sexes.

Race and Slavery   As the Assembly excluded women from voting citizenship without much debate, other groups posed challenges on how to apply "the rights of man" to French society. In eastern France, where most of France's forty thousand Jews resided amid discrimination, public opinion scorned them as an alien race not entitled to citizenship. Eventually, however, the Assembly rejected that argument and extended civil and political equality to Jews. A similar debate raged over the status of the free Negroes and mulattoes in France's Caribbean colonies. White planters, in alliance with the merchants who traded with the islands, were intent on preserving slavery and demanded local control over the islands' racial policy as their best defense. The planters argued that they could not maintain slavery, which was manifestly based on race, unless free people of color were disenfranchised.

When the Assembly accepted this view, the mulattoes rebelled. But their abortive uprising had the unintended consequence of helping ignite a slave rebellion. Led by Toussaint-L'Ouverture, the blacks turned violently on their white masters and proclaimed the independence of the colony, which became known as Haiti. In 1794 the French revolutionary government abolished slavery in all French colonies. (For further discussion see "The Fight for Liberty and Equality in Saint-Domingue," p. 598.)

Unifying the Nation   Within France the Assembly obliterated the political identities of the country's historic provinces and instead divided the nation's territory into eighty-three departments of roughly equal size (see map 20.1). Unlike the old provinces, each new department was to have exactly the same institutions. The departments were, in turn, subdivided into districts, cantons, and communes (the common designation for a village or town). On the one hand, this administrative transformation promoted local autonomy: The citizens of each department, district, and commune elected their own local officials, and in that sense political power was decentralized. On the other hand, these local governments were subordinated to the national legislature in Paris and became instruments for promoting national integration and uniformity.

The new administrative map also created the boundaries for a new judicial system. Sweeping away the parlements and law courts of the old regime, the revolutionaries established a justice of the peace in each canton, a civil court in each district, and a criminal court in each department. The judges on all tribunals were to be elected. The Assembly rejected the use of juries in civil cases but decreed that felonies would be tried by juries; also, criminal defendants for the first time gained the right to counsel. In civil law, the Assembly encouraged arbitration and mediation to avoid the time-consuming and expensive processes of formal litigation. In general, the revolutionaries hoped to make the administration of justice faster and more accessible.

Economic Individualism   The Assembly's clearing operations extended to economic institutions as well. Guided by the dogmas of laissez-faire theory and by its uncompromising hostility to privileged corporations, the Assembly sought to open up economic life to individual initiative, much as Turgot had attempted in the 1770s. Besides dismantling internal tariffs and chartered trading monopolies, it abolished merchants' and artisans' guilds and proclaimed the right of every citizen to enter any trade and conduct it freely. The government would no longer concern itself with regulating wages or the quality of goods. The Assembly also insisted that workers bargain in the economic marketplace as individuals, and it therefore banned workers' associations and strikes. The precepts of economic individualism extended to the countryside as well. At least in theory, peasants and landlords were free to cultivate their fields as they saw fit, regardless of traditional collective practices. In fact, those deep-rooted communal restraints proved to be extremely resistant to change.

The Revolution and the Church

To address the state's financial problems, the National Assembly acted in a way that the monarchy had never dared contemplate. Under revolutionary ideology, the French Catholic Church could no longer exist as an independent corporation—as a separate estate within the state. The Assembly, therefore, nationalized Church property (about 10 percent of the land in France), placing it "at the disposition of the nation," and made the state responsible for the upkeep of the Church. It then issued paper notes called *assignats,* which were backed by the value of these "national lands." The property was to be sold by auction at the district capitals to the highest bidders. This plan favored the bourgeois and rich peasants with ready capital and made it difficult for needy peasants to acquire the land, though some pooled their resources to do so.

The sale of Church lands and the issuance of assignats had several consequences. In the short run, they eliminated the need for new borrowing. Second, the hundreds of thousands of purchasers gained a strong vested interest in the Revolution, since a successful counterrevolution was likely to reclaim their properties for the Church. Finally, after war broke out with an Austrian-Prussian coalition in 1792, the government made the assignats a national currency and printed a volume of assignats way beyond their underlying value in land, thereby touching off severe inflation and new political turmoil.

Religious Schism   The issue of Church reform produced the Revolution's first and most fateful crisis. The Assembly intended to rid the Church of inequities that enriched the aristocratic prelates of the old regime. Many Catholics looked forward to such healthy changes that might bring the clergy closer to the people. In the **Civil Constitution of the Clergy** (1790), the Assembly reduced the number of bishops from 130 to 83 and reshaped diocesan boundaries to conform exactly with those of the new departments. Bishops and parish priests were to be chosen by the electoral assemblies in the departments and districts and were to be paid according to a uniform salary scale that favored those currently at the lower end. Like all other public officials, the clergy was to take an oath of loyalty to the constitution.

The clergy generally opposed the Civil Constitution because it had been dictated to them by the National Assembly; they argued that such questions as the selection of bishops and priests should be negotiated either with the Pope or with a National Church Council. But the Assembly asserted that it had the sovereign power to order such reforms, since they affected temporal rather than spiritual matters. In November 1790 the Assembly demanded that all clergy take the loyalty oath forthwith; those who refused would lose their positions and be pensioned off. In all of France only seven bishops and about 54 percent of the parish clergy swore the oath; but in the west of France only 15 percent of the priests complied. A schism tore through French Catholicism, since the laity had to take a position as well: Should parishioners remain loyal to their priests who had refused to take the oath (the nonjuring, or refractory, clergy) and thus be at odds with the state? Or should they accept the unfamiliar "constitutional clergy" designated by the districts to replace their own priests?

The Assembly's effort to impose reform in defiance of religious sensibilities and Church autonomy was a grave tactical error. The oath crisis polarized the nation. It seemed to link the Revolution with impiety and the Church with counterrevolution. In local

Global Moment

THE FIGHT FOR LIBERTY AND EQUALITY IN SAINT-DOMINGUE

The French colony Saint-Domingue shared the Caribbean island of Hispaniola with Spain's colony, Santo Domingo (today's Dominican Republic). The crown jewel of France's colonial empire, Saint-Domingue was responsible for about two-fifths of its overseas trade. Worked by about 500,000 slaves from Africa, its 8,000 plantations produced half of all the sugar consumed in continental Europe and the Americas. In the decade before the French Revolution, 30,000 to 40,000 new slaves had to be imported from Africa annually, to compensate for the loss of life from the brutal regimen of slavery on the plantations.

Forty thousand white people (including planters, tradesmen, and soldiers) inhabited this colony alongside the 500,000 black slaves and 30,000 free people of color—freed slaves and their descendants, who often intermarried with whites. Many of these free coloreds managed or possessed estates and slaves of their own. By the 1789s, however, the colony's white authorities were subjecting free people of color to stringent racial laws barring them from the professions and positions in the armed forces, and restricting them to wearing certain types of dress.

The outbreak of the French Revolution in 1789 had a profoundly unsettling effect on the island. While the revolutionaries fought for the principles of liberty, equality, and fraternity in Europe, the members of the National Assembly rebuffed similar demands from delegates of Saint-Domingue's people of color. Racial laws, the Assembly insisted, were a local matter for white planters and merchants, and revolutionary principles did not apply across the color line. In their view, plantation slavery contributed to French economic prosperity, and the maintenance of slavery depended on white supremacy. The Assembly gave in to pressure from the white colonial lobby in the belief that this alone would keep Saint-Domingue under French control.

Thwarted in Paris, the free colored people attempted to achieved liberation by force of arms, which the colony's whites, rich and poor alike, repelled. Neither side realized that a restive slave population was about to seize the initiative itself. In November 1791 thousands of slaves in the north of the colony rose up, setting fire to over a thousand plantations and massacring hundreds of whites. Still, as the free people of color and whites continued their own battle, each side began to recruit slaves as their foot soldiers. Finally, in April 1792 a more liberal Legislature in Paris granted members of the free colored community full French citizenship. Furious at this decision, royalist planters (who soon heard that the king himself had been overthrown) were ready to break free of France, its new Republic, and its new emissary to Saint-Domingue, a man named L.-F. Sonthonax. The son of a French planter, Sonthonax had risen through the ranks of the French Revolution. His main supporters on the island were the free people of color.

To complicate matters, in 1793 Britain and Spain declared war on France, and each sent military forces to wrest Saint-Domingue from the French. Sonthonax now had another fight on his hands. In return for their service as French soldiers, he freed many slaves, and in August 1793 he proclaimed the abolition of slavery in Saint-Domingue. This move then spurred abolitionist sentiment in the National Convention. In an historic decree of February 1794 it abolished slavery in all French colonies—a radical expansion of democratic ideals with enormous implications for the rest of the Atlantic world.

But the story does not end there. If the decrees of the Convention and its commissioner abolished slavery in Saint-Domingue, only the rebellion of the island's slaves and their continued fight for freedom under a forceful leader made emancipation permanent. That leader, Toussaint (1743–1803), was born on the island into slavery and served as a coachman on the Bréda sugar plantation until he was freed sometime in the 1770s. A man with great military aptitude, in 1793 he

Rebellious slaves in pitched battle with French soldiers on Saint-Domingue.
Bettmann/Corbis

joined the Spanish forces and earned the nickname *L'Ouverture* ("the opening") because "he could make an opening anywhere" in the French defenses. But in 1794 he changed sides, organized a new army for the French out of freed slaves, and led his troops into battles that eventually pushed out the Spanish and the British forces. By the time the British left in 1798, Toussaint had eliminated other political rivals to emerge as the supreme authority in the colony. Supporting emancipation, Toussaint proclaimed: "I want liberty and equality to reign in Saint-Domingue." To keep the economy and his army afloat, however, Toussaint reinstated the plantation system of cultivation, and used his army to impose forced labor and corporal punishment. In the constitution he promulgated in 1801, he made himself governor for life with the right to choose his successor.

By that time things had changed dramatically in France as well. Napoleon Bonaparte sought to regain full control of the colony. Toussaint L'Ouverture led the fight against the invading French army, but one of his own generals, J.-J. Dessalines, betrayed him. In June 1802 the first black leader in the Western world was handed over to French troops and sent to France, where he soon died in prison. Around that time news arrived that Bonaparte intended to restore slavery. Large numbers of former slaves and free coloreds joined the remnants of Toussaint's army, now led by Dessalines, who exhorted his troops to "burn houses, cut off heads"— brutality that the French returned in kind. Decimated by fever, however, and unable to receive reinforcements or supplies because of an English naval blockade, the remaining French force withdrew in 1804, and Dessalines declared full independence from France. To symbolize this dramatic break, he renamed his country Haiti, a term used on the island before the French had arrived.

continued

"I have given the French cannibals blood for blood," Dessalines declared; "I have avenged America."

The repercussions of the Haitian revolution spread throughout the Americas. The loss of life and property in the Haitian upheaval encouraged plantation societies elsewhere to reinforce their grip on slave labor. Cuba, Brazil, and the Southern United States tightened their slave and race codes, making it more difficult to free slaves and restricting free people of color. Napoleonic France restored slavery in Guadeloupe, another French colony in the Caribbean. Scorned or ignored by other governments and commercial interests, Haiti became an isolated backwater until the twentieth century.

But the Haitian slave rebellion also stimulated antislavery movements. Abolitionists in Britain and the United States argued that unless their governments moved toward gradual emancipation, similar violence would occur in British colonies and the American South. A reenergized British antislavery movement finally convinced Parliament to abolish the African slave trade in 1807. In the United States, New York and New Jersey passed emancipation laws, although similar legislation had failed in those states in the 1780s.

Despite the bitterness and bloodshed, the events in Haiti shook the rationale for slavery in the Atlantic world. The National Convention's pioneering decree of 1794 established emancipation as a legitimate goal of any democratic society. (It was France's democratic Second Republic of 1848 that definitively abolished slavery in all French colonies.) More fundamentally the Haitian revolution demonstrated the fervent desire of black slaves for freedom. Haiti's independence became irrefutable proof that slavery was not a natural condition for blacks; already in 1791, news of the uprising inspired Jamaican slave songs, and whites throughout the West Indies and North America noticed a growing insolence among the black population. In subsequent insurrections in Havana and Charleston, black militants tried to imitate the actions of Toussaint L'Ouverture and other leaders of the revolt. Haiti provided millions of blacks with a sense of identity apart from that of slave, and a ray of inspiration for their own liberation.

communities, refractory clergy began to preach against the entire Revolution. Local officials fought back by arresting them and demanding repressive laws. Civil strife rocked hundreds of communities.

Counterrevolution, Radicalism, and War

The King's Flight Opposition to the Revolution had actually begun much earlier. After July 14 some of the king's relatives had left the country in disgust, thus becoming the first émigrés, or political exiles, of the Revolution. During the next three years, thousands of nobles, including two-thirds of the royal army's officer corps, joined the emigration. Across the Rhine River in Coblenz, émigrés formed an army that threatened to overthrow the new regime at the first opportunity. The king himself publicly submitted to the Revolution, but privately he smoldered in resentment. Finally, in June 1791, Louis and his family fled in secret from Paris, hoping to cross the Belgian frontier and enlist the aid of Austria. But Louis was stopped at the French village of Varennes and was forcibly returned to Paris.

Moderates hoped that this aborted escape would finally end the king's opposition to the Revolution. The Assembly, after all, needed his cooperation to make its constitutional monarchy viable. It did not wish to open the door to a republic or to further unrest. Radicals such as the journalist Jean-Paul Marat, on the other hand, had long thundered against the treachery of the king and the émigrés and against the Assembly itself for not acting vigorously against aristocrats and counterrevolutionaries. But the Assembly was determined to maintain the status quo and adopted the fiction that the king had been kidnapped. The Assembly reaffirmed the king's place in the new regime, but Louis' treasonous flight to Varennes ensured that radical agitation would continue.

The Outbreak of War When the newly elected Legislative Assembly convened on October 1, 1791, the questions of counterrevolution at home and the prospect of war abroad dominated its stormy sessions. Both the right and the left saw advantages to be gained in a war between France and Austria. The king and his court hoped that a military defeat would discredit the new regime and restore full power to the monarchy. Most members of the **Jacobin Club**—the leading radical political club in Paris—wanted war to strike down the foreign supporters of the émigrés along with domestic counterrevolutionaries.

When Francis II ascended the throne of the Habsburg monarchy in March 1792, the stage was set for war. Unlike his father, Leopold, who had rejected intervention in France's affairs, Francis fell under the influence of émigrés and bellicose advisers. He was determined to assist the French queen, his aunt, and he also expected to make territorial gains. With both sides thus eager for battle, France went to war in April 1792 against a coalition of Austria, Prussia, and the émigrés.

Each camp expected rapid victory, but both were deceived. The French offensive quickly faltered, and invading armies soon crossed France's borders. The Legislative Assembly ordered the arrest of refractory clergy and called for a special corps of twenty thousand national guardsmen to protect Paris. Louis vetoed both measures and held to his decisions in spite of demonstrations against them in the capital. For all practical purposes, these vetoes were his last acts as king. The legislature also called for one hundred thousand volunteers to bolster the French army and defend the homeland.

The Fall of the Monarchy   As Prussian forces began a drive toward Paris, their commander, the Duke of Brunswick, rashly threatened to level the city if it resisted or if it harmed the royal family. When Louis XVI published this Brunswick Manifesto, it seemed proof that he was in league with the enemy. Far from intimidating the revolutionaries, the threat drove them forward. Since a divided Legislative Assembly refused to act decisively in the face of royal obstructionism, Parisian militants, spurred on by the Jacobin Club, organized an insurrection.

On August 10, 1792, a crowd of armed Parisians stormed the royal palace at the Tuileries, literally driving the king from the throne. The Assembly then had no choice but to declare Louis XVI suspended. That night more than half the Assembly's members themselves fled Paris, making it clear that the Assembly too had lost its legitimacy. The deputies who remained ordered elections for a National Convention to decide the king's fate, to draft a republican constitution, and to govern France during the current emergency. What the events of 1789 in Versailles and Paris had begun, the insurrection of August 10, 1792,

completed. The old regime in France had truly been destroyed.

THE SECOND REVOLUTION

By 1792—just three years after the fall of the Bastille—the Revolution had profoundly altered the foundations of government and society in France. The National Assembly introduced constitutional government, legislative representation, and a degree of local self-government. It repudiated absolutism, as well as aristocratic and group privilege; established civil equality and uniform institutions across the country; freed peasants from much of the seigneurial system and religious minorities from persecution. Yet the Revolution was far from over, for these changes had been won only against intense opposition, and the old order was far from vanquished. European monarchs and aristocrats encouraged refractory priests, émigrés, and royalists in France to resist.

The patriots, threatened in 1792 by military defeat and counterrevolution, were themselves divided. Some became radicalized, while others grew alienated from the Revolution's increasingly radical course. But each increment of opposition stiffened the resolve of the Revolution's strongest partisans. The dominant Jacobins forged an alliance with Parisian militants known as the **sans-culottes** (literally, men who wore trousers rather than fashionable knee breeches). Together they propelled France into a second revolution: a democratic republic that espoused a broadening notion of equality. At the same time, however, the Jacobin government instituted an improvised revolutionary dictatorship and a reign of terror against "the enemies of the people." Thus, the second revolution was distorted, as the ideals of equality became confused with the impulse to repress any opposition by the most drastic means.

The National Convention

The insurrection of August 10, 1792, created a vacuum of authority until the election of a National Convention was completed. A revolutionary Paris Commune, or city government, became one power center, but that bastion of radicalism could not control events even within its own domain. As thousands of volunteers left for the battlefront, Parisians nervously eyed the capital's jails, which overflowed with political prisoners and common criminals. Radical journalists like Marat saw these prisoners as a counterrevolutionary striking force and feared a plot to open the prisons. A growing sense of alarm finally exploded early in September. For three days groups of Parisians invaded the

Beset by invasion jitters and fearing a plot to force open the capital's overcrowded jails, mobs of Parisians invaded the prisons and over the course of three days in September 1792 slaughtered more than two thousand prisoners.
Bulloz/© Photo RMN/Art Resource, NY

prisons, set up "popular tribunals," and slaughtered more than two thousand prisoners. No official dared intervene to stop the carnage, known since as the September massacres.

The sense of panic eased, however, with the success of the French armies. Bolstered by units of volunteers, the army finally halted the invaders at the Battle of Valmy on September 20. Two months later it defeated the allies at Jemappes in the Austrian Netherlands, which the French now occupied. Meanwhile, the Convention convened and promptly declared France a republic.

Settling Louis XVI's fate proved to be extremely contentious. While the deputies unanimously found the former king guilty of treason, they divided sharply over the question of his punishment. Some argued for clemency, while others insisted that his execution was a necessary symbolic gesture as well as a fitting punishment for his betrayal. Finally, by a vote of 387 to 334, the Convention sentenced Louis to death and voted down efforts to reprieve this sentence or delay it for a popular referendum. On January 21, 1793, Louis was guillotined, put to death like an ordinary citizen. The deputies to the Convention had become regicides

(king killers) and would make no compromise with counterrevolution.

Factional Conflict From the Convention's opening day, two bitterly hostile groups of deputies vied for leadership and almost immobilized it with their rancorous conflict. One group became known as the *Girondins,* since several of its spokesmen were elected as deputies from the Gironde department. The Girondins were fiery orators and ambitious politicians who advocated provincial liberty and laissez-faire economics. They reacted hostilely to the growing radicalism of Paris and broke with or were expelled by the Jacobin Club, to which some had originally belonged. Meanwhile Parisian electors chose as their deputies leading members of the Jacobin Club, such as Danton, Robespierre, and Marat. The Parisian deputation to the Convention became the nucleus of a group known as the *Mountain,* so-called because it occupied the upper benches of the Convention's hall. The Mountain attracted the more militant provincial deputies and attacked the Girondins as treacherous compromisers unwilling to adopt bold measures in the face of crisis. The Girondins, in turn, denounced the Mountain as

After the National Convention concluded its trial of former King Louis XVI and voted to impose the death penalty without reprieve, "Louis Capet" was guillotined and the leaders of the Republic became regicides, king killers.
Bulloz/© Photo RMN/Art Resource, NY

would-be tyrants and captives of Parisian radicalism and held them responsible for the September prison massacres.

Several hundred deputies stood between these two factions. These centrists (known as the *Plain*) were committed to the Revolution but were uncertain which path to follow. The Plain detested popular agitation, but they were reluctant to turn against the sans-culottes.

The Revolutionary Crisis

By the spring of 1793 the National Convention faced a perilous convergence of invasion, civil war, and economic crises that demanded imaginative responses. Austria and Prussia had mounted a new offensive in 1793, their alliance strengthened by the addition of Spain, Piedmont, and Britain. Between March and September, military reversals occurred on every front. The Convention reacted by introducing a military draft, which in turn touched off a rebellion in western France by peasants and rural weavers, who had long resented the patriot middle class in the towns for monopolizing local political power and for persecuting their priests. In the isolated towns of the Vendée re-

gion, south of the Loire River, the rebels attacked the Republic's supporters. Priests and nobles offered leadership to the insurgents, who first organized into guerrilla bands and finally into a "Catholic and Royalist Army." The Vendée rebels briefly occupied several towns, massacred local patriots, and even threatened the port of Nantes, where British troops could have landed.

Meanwhile, economic troubles were provoking the Parisian sans-culottes. By early 1793 the Revolution's paper money, the assignat, had declined to 50 percent of its face value. Inflation was compounded by a poor harvest, food shortages, hoarding, and profiteering. Municipal authorities fixed the price of bread but could not always secure adequate supplies. Under these conditions the government could not even supply its armies.

The Purge of the Girondins   Spokesmen for the sans-culottes demanded that the Convention purge the Girondins and adopt a program of "public safety," including price controls for basic commodities, execution of hoarders and speculators, and forced requisitions of grain. Behind these demands lay the threat of armed

MAP 20.2 CONFLICTS IN REVOLUTIONARY FRANCE
According to this map, what were three types of conflicts challenging revolutionary France?
◆ For an online version, go to www.mhhe.com/chambers9 > chapter 20 > book maps

insurrection. This pressure from the sans-culottes aided the Mountain in their struggle against the Girondins, but it could easily have degenerated into anarchy. In a sense, all elements of the revolutionary crisis hinged on one problem: the lack of an effective government that would not simply respond to popular pressures but would organize and master them. When the sans-culottes mounted a massive armed demonstration for a purge of the Girondins on June 2, centrist deputies reluctantly agreed to go along. The Convention expelled twenty-three Girondin deputies, who were subsequently tried and executed for treason.

Factionalism in the Convention reflected conflict in the provinces. Moderate republicans in several cities struggled with local Jacobin radicals and sympathized with the Girondin deputies in their campaign against the Parisian sans-culottes. In the south, local Jacobins lost control of Marseilles, Bordeaux, and Lyons to their rivals, who then repudiated the Convention. As in the Vendée revolt, royalists soon took over the resistance in Lyons, France's second largest city. This act was an intolerable challenge to the Convention. Labeling the anti-Jacobin rebels in Lyons and elsewhere as "federal-

ists," the Convention dispatched armed forces to suppress them (see map 20.2). In the eyes of the Jacobins, to defy the Convention's authority was to betray France itself.

The Jacobin Dictatorship

Popular radicalism in Paris had helped bring the Mountain to power in the Convention. The question now was: Which side of this coalition between the Mountain and the sans-culottes would dominate the other? The sans-culottes seemed to believe that the sovereign people could dictate their will to the Convention. Popular agitation peaked on September 5, when a mass demonstration in Paris demanded new policies to ensure food supplies. To give force to the law, urged the sans-culottes, "Let terror be placed on the order of the day." The Convention responded with the Law of the Maximum, which imposed general price controls, and with the Law of Suspects, which empowered local revolutionary committees to imprison citizens whose loyalty they suspected.

Revolutionary Government   In June the triumphant Mountain had drafted a new democratic constitution for the French Republic and had submitted it to an unprecedented referendum, in which almost 2 million citizens had overwhelmingly voted yes. But the Convention formally laid the constitution aside and proclaimed the government "revolutionary until the peace." Elections, local self-government, and guarantees of individual liberty were to be suspended until the Republic had defeated its enemies within and without. The Convention placed responsibility for military, economic, and political policy, as well as control over local officials, in the hands of a twelve-man **Committee of Public Safety.** Spontaneous popular action was about to give way to revolutionary centralization.

Maximilien Robespierre emerged as the Committee's leading personality and tactician. An austere bachelor in his mid-thirties, Robespierre had been a provincial lawyer before the Revolution. As a deputy to the National Assembly he had ardently advocated greater democracy. His main political forum was the Paris Jacobin Club, which by 1793 he more or less dominated. In the Convention, Robespierre was inflexible and self-righteous in his dedication to the Revolution. He sought to appease the sans-culottes but also to control them, for he placed the Revolution's survival above any one viewpoint (see "Robespierre's Justification of the Terror," p. 606).

Local political clubs (numbering more than five thousand by 1794) formed crucial links in the chain of

Jules Benoit-Levy
BATTLE OF CHOLET OR THE SUICIDE OF GENERAL MOULININ, **1794**
Bitter fighting in the Vendée between counterrevolutionaries and republicans caused a profound split in the loyalties of western France, which endured for at least the next hundred years. Each side cultivated its own memories of the event and honored its own martyrs.
Musée d'Art et d'Histoire, Cholet, France. Giraudon/Art Resource, NY

The Paris Jacobin Club began as a caucus for a group of liberal deputies to the National Assembly. During the Convention it became a bastion of democratic deputies and middle-class Parisian radicals while continuing to serve as a "mother club" for affiliated clubs in the provinces.
Bibliothèque Nationale, Paris, France. Giraudon/Art Resource, NY

ROBESPIERRE'S JUSTIFICATION OF THE TERROR

"If the spring of popular government in time of peace is virtue, the springs of popular government in revolution are at once *virtue and terror:* virtue, without which terror is fatal; terror, without which virtue is powerless. Terror is nothing other than justice, prompt, severe, inflexible; it is therefore an emanation of virtue. . . . It is a consequence of the general principle of democracy applied to our country's most urgent needs.

"It has been said that terror is the principle of despotic government. Does your government therefore resemble despotism? Yes, as the sword that gleams in the hands of the heroes of liberty resembles that with which the henchmen of tyranny are armed. Let the despot govern his brutalized subjects by terror; he is right, as a despot. Subdue by terror the enemies of liberty, and you will be right, as founders of the Republic. The government of the revolution is liberty's despotism against tyranny. Is force made only to protect crime?

"Society owes protection only to peaceable citizens; the only citizens in the Republic are the republicans. For it, the royalists, the conspirators are only strangers or, rather, enemies. This terrible war waged by liberty against tyranny—is it not indivisible? Are the enemies within not the allies of the enemies without? The assassins who tear our country apart, the intriguers who buy the consciences that hold the people's mandate; the traitors who sell them; the mercenary pamphleteers hired to dishonor the people's cause, to kill public virtue, to stir up the fire of civil discord, and to prepare political counterrevolution—are all those men less guilty or less dangerous than the tyrants [abroad] whom they serve?

"We try to control revolutions with the quibbles of the courtroom; we treat conspiracies against the Republic like lawsuits between individuals. Tyranny kills, and liberty argues."

From Robespierre's speech to the Convention on "The Moral and Political Principles of Domestic Policy," February 1794.

revolutionary government. The clubs nominated citizens for posts on local revolutionary institutions, exercised surveillance over those officials, and served as "arsenals of public opinion." The clubs fostered the egalitarian ideals of the second revolution and supported the war effort. They also saw it as their civic duty to denounce fellow citizens for unpatriotic behavior and thereby sowed fear and recrimination across the land.

The Jacobins tolerated no serious dissent. The government's demand for unity during the emergency nullified the right to freedom of expression. Among those to fall were a group of ultrarevolutionaries led by Jacques-René Hébert, a leading radical journalist and Paris official. The extremists were accused of a plot against the Republic and were guillotined. In reality, Hébert had questioned what he deemed the Convention's leniency toward "enemies of the people." Next came the so-called indulgents. Headed by Georges-Jacques Danton, a leading member of the Jacobin Club, they publicly argued for a relaxation of rigorous measures. For this dissent they were indicted on trumped-up charges of treason and were sentenced to death by the revolutionary tribunal. This succession of purges, which started with the Girondins and later ended with Robespierre himself, suggested, as one victim put it, that "revolutions devour their own children."

The Reign of Terror   Most of those devoured by the French Revolution, however, were not its own children but a variety of armed rebels, counterrevolutionaries, and unfortunate citizens swept into the vortex of war and internal strife. As an official policy, the Reign of Terror sought to organize repression so as to avoid anarchic violence like the September massacres. It reflected a state of mind that saw threats and plots everywhere (some real, most imagined). The laws of the Terror struck most directly at the people perceived to be enemies of the Revolution: Refractory priests and émigrés, for instance, were banned from the Republic upon pain of death. But the Law of Suspects also led to the incarceration of as many as 300,000 ordinary citizens for their opinions, past behavior, or social status.

The Terror produced its own atrocities: the brutal drowning of imprisoned priests at Nantes; the execution of thousands of noncombatants during the military campaigns of the Vendée; and the summary executions of about two thousand citizens of Lyons, more than two-thirds of them from the wealthy classes. ("Lyons has made war against liberty," declared the Convention, "thus Lyons no longer exists.") But except in the two zones of intense civil war—western France and the area of "federalist" rebellion in the south (see map 20.2)—the Terror struck by examples, not by mass executions.

CHRONOLOGY

Turning Points in the French Revolution

June 17, 1789	Third Estate declares itself a National Assembly.
July 14, 1789	Storming of the Bastille and triumph of the patriots.
August 10, 1792	Storming of the Tuileries and the end of the monarchy (followed by the September prison massacres).
January 21, 1793	Execution of Louis XVI.
March 1793	Vendée rebellion begins.
June 2, 1793	Sans-culottes intimidate the Convention into purging the Girondin deputies. "Federalist" rebellion begins in Lyons.
September 5, 1793	Sans-culottes demonstrate for the enactment of economic controls and Terror.
October 1793	The Jacobin dictatorship and the Terror begin: The Convention declares that "the government is revolutionary until the peace."
9 Thermidor year II (July 27, 1794)	Fall of Robespierre.
1–2 Prairial year III (May 20–21, 1795)	Failed insurrection by Parisian sans-culottes for "Bread and the Constitution of 1793."
18 Brumaire year VIII (November 9, 1799)	Coup d'état by General Bonaparte and the "revisionists."

The Sans-Culottes: Revolution from Below

The Parisian sans-culottes formed the crowds and demonstrations that produced the Revolution's dramatic turning points, but they also threw themselves into a daily routine of political activism during the second revolution of 1792–1794. The sans-culottes were mainly artisans, shopkeepers, and workers—building contractors, carpenters, shoemakers, wine sellers, clerks, tailors, cafe keepers. Many owned their own businesses; others were wage earners. But they shared a strong sense of local community in the capital's varied neighborhoods.

Popular Attitudes   The supply and price of bread obsessed the sans-culottes. As consumers, they faced inflation and scarcities with fear and rage and demanded forceful government intervention to ensure the basic necessities of life. Sans-culotte militants believed in property rights, but they insisted that people did not have the right to misuse property by hoarding food or speculating. As one petition put it, "What is the meaning of freedom, when one class of men can starve another? What is the meaning of equality, when the rich, by their monopolies, can exercise the right of life and death over their equals?" The sans-culotte call for price controls clashed dramatically with the dogma of laissez-faire. By 1793, however, the Jacobins had acknowledged "the right to subsistence" in their new constitution and had instituted price controls under the Law of the Maximum to regulate the economy during the emergency.

Bitterly antiaristocratic, the sans-culottes displayed their social attitudes in everyday behavior. They advocated simplicity in dress and manners and attacked opulence and pretension wherever they found or imagined them to be. Under the sans-culottes' disapproving eye, high society and fancy dress generally disappeared from view. Vices like prostitution and gambling were attributed to aristocrats and were denounced in the virtuous society of the Revolution; drinking, the common people's vice, was tolerated.

The revolutionaries symbolized their break with the past by changing the names of streets and public places to eliminate signs of royalism, religion, or aristocracy. The Palais Royal thus became the Palais d'Egalité (Equality Palace). Some citizens exchanged their Christian names for the names of secular heroes from antiquity, like Brutus. And all citizens were expected to drop honorifics like *monsieur* and *madame* in favor of the simple, uniform designation of citizen. Even the measurement of time changed when the Convention decreed a new republican calendar that renamed the months and replaced the seven-day week with a symmetrical ten-day *décadi*. The year I dated from the establishment of the Republic in 1792.

Popular Politics   The Convention believed in representative democracy with an active political life at the grass roots, but during the emergency it decreed a centralized revolutionary dictatorship. The sans-culottes preferred a more decentralized style of participatory democracy. They believed that the local assembly of citizens was the ultimate sovereign body. At the beginning of the year II (1793–1794), the forty-eight sections of Paris functioned almost as autonomous republics in which local activists ran their own affairs. Political life in Paris and elsewhere had a naive, breathless quality and made thousands of ordinary citizens feel that they held real political power (see "A Portrait of the Parisian Sans-Culotte," p. 608).

A PORTRAIT OF THE PARISIAN SANS-CULOTTE

"A Sans-Culotte is a man who goes everywhere on his own two feet, who has none of the millions you're all after, no mansions, no lackeys to wait on him, and who lives quite simply with his wife and children, if he has any, on the fourth or fifth floor. He is useful, because he knows how to plough a field, handle a forge, a saw, or a file, how to cover a roof or how to make shoes and to shed his blood to the last drop to save the Republic. And since he is a working man, you will never find him in the Cafe de Chartres where they plot and gamble. . . . In the evening, he is at his Section, not powdered and perfumed and all dolled up to catch the eyes of the *citoyennes* in the galleries, but to support sound resolutions with all his power and to pulverize the vile faction [of moderates]. For the rest, a Sans-Culotte always keeps his sword with a sharp edge, to clip the ears of the malevolent. Sometimes he carries his pike and at the first roll of the drum, off he goes to the Vendée, to the Army of the Alps or the Army of the North."

From a pamphlet attributed to the Parisian militant Vingternier: "A Reply to the Impertinent Question: But What Is a Sans-Culotte?" 1794.

At the height of a radical "dechristianization" movement (which lasted for about eight months in 1793–1794), more than eighteen thousand priests renounced their vocations under pressure from militant revolutionaries. About a third also agreed to marry as a way of proving the sincerity of their resignations. (The print's caption states: "They shave me in the morning and have me married by evening.")
Bibliothèque Nationale de France, Paris

Within this upsurge of activism, the Society of Revolutionary-Republican Women, founded in Paris in the spring of 1793, constituted a vanguard of female radicals. The members of this club were undeterred by their exclusion from the vote, which did not much concern them at this point. Even without voting rights, women considered themselves citizens in revolutionary France.

In agitating for severe enforcement of price controls and the compulsory use of republican symbols, however, these women irritated the revolutionary government. Before long the ruling Jacobins perceived them as part of an irresponsible ultra-left opposition, whom they denounced as *enragés*, rabid ones. In October the government arrested the most prominent *enragés*, male and female, closed down the Society of Revolutionary-Republican Women, and forbade the formation of female political clubs in the future. The government's spokesman derided these activists as "denatured women," viragos who neglected their maternal duties. Behind this bitter antifeminist rhetoric lay a

The Revolutionary Wars

Ultimately, the Revolution's fate rested in the hands of its armies, although no one had thought in such terms in 1789. France's revolutionary ideology had initially posed no direct threat to the European state system. Indeed, the orators of the National Assembly had argued that the best foreign policy for a free society was peace, neutrality, and isolation from the diplomatic intrigues of monarchs. But peaceful intentions did not imply pacifism. When counterrevolution at home coalesced with threats from abroad, the revolutionaries vigorously confronted both. As in most major wars, however, the initial objectives were soon forgotten. As the war expanded, it brought revolution to other states.

The revolutionary wars involved standard considerations of international relations as well as new and explosive purposes. On the one hand, France pursued the traditional aim of extending and rounding off its frontiers. On the other hand, France now espoused revolutionary principles such as the right of a people to self-determination. As early as September 1791, the National Assembly had declared that "the rights of peoples are not determined by the treaties of princes."

Foreign Revolutionaries and French Armies   Even before 1789 "patriots" in Geneva, the Dutch Netherlands, and the Austrian Netherlands (Belgium) had unsuccessfully challenged the traditional arrangements that governed their societies, and the French Revolution rekindled those rebellious sentiments. Foreign revolutionaries were eager to challenge their governments again, and they looked to revolutionary France for assistance. Refugees from these struggles had fled to France and now formed pressure groups to lobby French leaders for help in liberating their own countries during France's war against Austria and Prussia. Some revolutionaries from areas contiguous to France (Belgium, Savoy, and the Rhineland) hoped that the French Republic might simply annex those territories. Elsewhere—in the Dutch Netherlands, Lombardy, Ireland, and the Swiss Confederation—insurgents hoped that France would help establish independent republics by overthrowing the ruling princes or oligarchies.

Few French leaders were interested in leading a European crusade for liberty, but practical considerations led them to intervene. As the war spilled over into Belgium and the Rhineland, the French sought to establish support abroad by incorporating the principles of the Revolution into their foreign policy. Thus, in December 1792 the Convention decided that feudal practices and hereditary privileges would be abolished wherever French armies prevailed. The people thus liberated, however, would have to pay for their liberation with special taxes

The radical activists of the *aris* sections—the sans-culottes and their female counterparts—made a point of their plebeian forms of dress, their freedom to bear arms, and their egalitarian insignias, such as the red liberty cap.
Bulloz/© Photo RMN/Art Resource, NY

sense of anxiety. In the virile and punitive world of radical republicanism (see the illustration of Hercules on p. 610), the Jacobins yearned for an offsetting feminine virtue to soften the severity required in the public sphere.

To Robespierre, in any case, the notion of direct democracy appeared unworkable and akin to anarchy. The Convention watched the sans-culottes with concern, supportive of their democratic egalitarianism but fearful of the unpredictability, disorder, and inefficiency of this popular movement. The Mountain attempted to encourage civic participation yet control it. From the forty-eight sections of Paris, however, came an endless stream of petitions, denunciations, and veiled threats to the government. In the spring of 1794 the Convention finally curbed the power of the sections by drastically restricting their rights and activities. But in forcibly cooling down the ardor of the sans-culottes, the revolutionary government necessarily weakened its own base of support.

Amidst elaborate arrays of symbolism, revolutionary iconography generally used the figure of a woman to represent its ideals. Briefly in the period 1793–1794, however, the Jacobins introduced the more aggressive masculine figure of Hercules to represent the Republic.
Bulloz/© Photo RMN/Art Resource, NY   Roger-Viollet/Getty Images

and requisitions of supplies for French troops. By 1794 France had a permanent foothold in Belgium and soon annexed that territory to the Republic. Yet Robespierre was dubious about foreign entanglements; he believed that liberty had to be secured in France before it could be exported abroad. The Committee of Public Safety thus declined to support a distant Polish revolutionary movement, refused to invade Holland, and attempted to avoid any involvements in Italy.

Citizen-Soldiers The fighting men who defended France and carried its revolution abroad were a far different body from the old royal army. The National Assembly of 1789 retained the notion of a professional army but opened officers' careers to ordinary soldiers, especially after most of the royal officer corps emigrated or resigned. At the same time, the concept of the citizen-soldier was introduced in the newly organized national guard, which had elected officers. When the

war against the coalition began in 1792, the government enrolled more than 100,000 volunteers for short-term service at the front. But when the coalition launched its second offensive in 1793, the inadequacy of the French army demanded drastic innovations.

The Convention responded with the mass levy of August 1793 (***levée en masse***). All able-bodied unmarried men between the ages of eighteen and twenty-five were drafted for military service, without the option of buying themselves a replacement. About 300,000 new recruits poured into the armies, while perhaps 200,000 draftees fled to avoid service. By the end of 1794 the French had almost 750,000 men under arms. With elected officers at their head, the citizen-soldiers marched off to the front under banners that read "The French people risen against the tyrants." The Convention merged these recruits with the regulars of the line army, so that the professionals could impart their military skills to the new troops.

Attributed to Louis Joseph Watteau
THE DEPARTURE OF THE VOLUNTEERS
To bolster the professional troops of the line army in 1791 and again in 1792 after the war began, the government called for volunteers, one of whom is shown in this sentimental and patriotic portrait bidding farewell to his family. By 1793, the National Convention had to go further and draft all able-bodied young, single men.
Musée Carnavalet, Paris, France/Giraudon/Bridgeman Art Library

Revolutionary Warfare   Military tactics in the field reflected a combination of revolutionary spirit and pragmatism. The new units did not have the training to be deployed in the well-drilled line formations of old-regime armies. Commanders instead favored mass columns that could move quickly without much drilling. Mass and mobility characterized the armies of the French Revolution. The Committee of Public Safety advised its commanders, "Act offensively and in masses. Use the bayonet at every opportunity. Fight great battles and pursue the enemy until he is destroyed."

The revolutionary government fostered new attitudes toward military life. The military was under civilian control. Discipline applied equally to officers and men, and wounded soldiers received generous veterans benefits. The Convention insisted that generals show not only military talent but the will to win. Many young officers rose quickly to command positions, but some generals fared badly. The commander of the defeated Rhine army in early 1793, for example, was branded a traitor, tried, and guillotined. Meanwhile, economic mobilization at home produced the weapons, ammunition, clothing, and food necessary to support this mass army.

In late 1793 and early 1794 the armies of the Republic won a string of victories, culminating in the Battle of Fleurus in June 1794, which liberated Belgium for the second time. French armies also triumphed at the Péyérnes and the Rhine and forced their enemies one by one to the peace table—first Spain and Prussia, then Piedmont. An army crippled at the outset by treason and desertion, defeat, lack of training and discipline, and collapsing morale had been forged into a potent force in less than two years. Militarily, at least, the revolutionary government had succeeded brilliantly.

Summary

To its most dedicated supporters, the revolutionary government had two major purposes: first, to surmount a crisis and steer the Republic to victory; and second, to democratize France's political and social fabric. Only the first objective, however, won widespread adherence. The National Convention held a polarized nation together, consolidated the Republic, and defeated its foreign enemies, but only at enormous and questionable costs. Moderates and ultrarevolutionaries alike resented the stifling political conformity imposed by the revolutionary government. Wealthy peasants and businesspeople chafed under the economic regimentation, and Catholics bitterly resented local "dechristianization" campaigns. The Jacobins increasingly isolated themselves, making enemies on every side. It is not surprising, then, that the security provided by the military victories of 1793–1794 would permit the Convention to end the Jacobin dictatorship and abandon its rhetoric of radical egalitarianism. But the question remained: What would take its place?

QUESTIONS FOR FURTHER THOUGHT

1. How do you explain the onset of the French Revolution? Was it an accident, so to speak, or did it have long-term causes that made it in some sense inevitable?
2. How do you see the relationship between the liberal phase of the French Revolution (1789–1792) and its radical phase (1792–1794)? Why do revolutions often "devour their own children"?
3. The slogan of the French Revolution eventually became "Liberty, Equality, Fraternity." What was meant by fraternity? Are liberty and equality inherently in tension or are they complementary and mutually reinforcing?

RECOMMENDED READING

Sources

Beik, Paul H. (ed.). *The French Revolution.* 1971. A comprehensive anthology.

*Hunt, Lynn (ed.). *The French Revolution and Human Rights: A Brief Documentary History.* 1996. Excerpts from revolutionary debates on the rights of the poor, free blacks and slaves, Jews, and women.

*Levy, Darlene, H. Applewhite, and M. Johnson (eds.). *Women in Revolutionary Paris, 1789–1795.* 1979. A documentary history of women activists.

Stewart, J. H. *A Documentary Survey of the French Revolution.* 1951. A compendium of important official documents.

*Walzer, Michael (ed.). *Regicide and Revolution: Speeches at the Trial of Louis XVI.* 1992. Documents and penetrating analysis.

Studies

*Blanning, T. C. W. *The French Revolutionary Wars, 1787–1802.* 1996. A brief but comprehensive synthesis.

———. *Joseph II and Enlightened Despotism.* 1970. A convenient synthesis on a fundamental subject.

*Christie, Ian. *Wars and Revolutions: Britain, 1760–1815.* 1982. Focuses on British government policy in the age of revolutions.

*Cobb, Richard. *The French and Their Revolution: Selected Writings.* D. Gilmour (ed.). 1998. An anthology of writings by a great historian of ordinary people caught up in the French Revolution. Should be compared to Soboul's account of the popular movement.

Desan, Suzanne. *The Family on Trial in Revolutionary France.* 2004. Changing law, institutions, and social practice on a variety of gender and family issues.

*De Tocqueville, Alexis. *The Old Regime and the French Revolution.* Stuart Gilbert (tr.). 1955. A classic interpretation of the Revolution's genesis, first published in the 1850s.

*Doyle, William. *Origins of the French Revolution.* 1999. A reliable synthesis of revisionist historiography.

*———. *The Oxford History of the French Revolution.* 1989. A readable, detailed narrative.

Dubois, Laurent. *Avengers of the New World: The Story of the Haitian Revolution.* 2004. The most recent study of Toussaint L'Ouverture and the Saint-Domingue slave revolt during the French Revolution.

Fitzsimmons, Michael. *The Night the Old Regime Ended: August 4, 1789, and the French Revolution.* 2003. Illuminates a major and dramatic leap forward in the Revolution.

*Forrest, Alan. *Soldiers of the French Revolution.* 1990. A deft synthesis of recent research.

Furet, Francois, and Mona Ozouf (eds.). *A Critical Dictionary of the French Revolution.* 1989. A collection of essays, some brilliant and some idiosyncratic, on selected events, actors, institutions, ideas, and historians of the French Revolution.

*Godineau, Dominique. *The Women of Paris and Their French Revolution.* 1998. The best account of ordinary Parisian women's participation in the French Revolution—a story of citizenship without voting rights.

*Hunt, Lynn. *Politics, Culture, and Class in the French Revolution.* 1984. A pioneering analysis of the imagery and sociology of revolutionary politics.

*Jones, Peter. *The Peasantry in the French Revolution.* 1988. A comprehensive study of the impact of the Revolution on rural society.

*Kennedy, Emmet. *A Cultural History of the French Revolution.* 1989. The Revolution's impact on cultural institutions and artistic activity.

McManners, John. *The French Revolution and the Church.* 1970. A superb synthesis on a major issue.

*Middlekauff, Robert. *The Glorious Cause: The American Revolution 1763–1789.* 1982. A comprehensive and balanced synthesis.

*Palmer, Robert R. *The Age of the Democratic Revolution: A Political History of Europe and*

America, 1760–1800. 2 vols. 1959 and 1962. A magisterial comparative survey of the origins and course of revolutionary movements in the eighteenth century, from America to Poland.

*———. *Twelve Who Ruled: The Year of the Terror in the French Revolution.* 1941. A modern classic, by far the best book on the subject.

*Popkin, Jeremy. *Revolutionary News: The Press in France 1789–1799.* 1990. An excellent analysis of journalism and the impact of journalists in the revolutionary decade.

Scott, H. M. (ed.). *Enlightened Absolutism: Reforms and Reformers in Later Eighteenth-Century Europe.* 1990. A comprehensive assessment.

*Soboul, Albert. *The Parisian Sans-Culottes and the French Revolution.* 1964. An abridgement of a landmark French thesis; should be compared to Cobb's study.

*Sutherland, Donald. *France 1789–1815: Revolution and Counter-revolution.* 1985. A fine general history of the period.

Tackett, Timothy. *When the King Took Flight.* 2003. A lively account of the flight to Varennes in 1791 and its explosive aftermath.

*Woloch, Isser. *The New Regime: Transformations of the French Civic Order, 1789–1820s.* 1994. A thematic study of new civic institutions and how they fared, from the beginning of the Revolution to the Restoration of the Bourbons.

*Available in paperback.

Jacques-Louis David
NAPOLEON BONAPARTE, SKETCH
General Bonaparte, in an uncompleted portrait by Jacques-Louis David.
Giraudon/Art Resource, NY

Chapter Twenty-One

THE AGE OF NAPOLEON

FROM ROBESPIERRE TO BONAPARTE • THE NAPOLEONIC SETTLEMENT IN FRANCE •
NAPOLEONIC HEGEMONY IN EUROPE • RESISTANCE TO NAPOLEON

The second phase of the French Revolution (1792–1794) left a stark legacy of contradictions. On the one hand, the National Convention moved for the first time since ancient Athens to institute a democratic republic: a government without kings, based on universal male suffrage and affirming such popular rights as the right to subsistence and to education for all. On the other hand, the Convention responded to foreign military threats, internal rebellion, and intense factionalism by establishing a revolutionary dictatorship. Individual liberties disappeared, and terror against "enemies of the people" became the order of the day. With the crisis finally surmounted by repression and military victories in 1794, most members of the Convention wearied of those repressive policies and wished to terminate the Revolution as quickly as possible.

Ending the Terror while preserving the Revolution's positive gains, however, proved extremely difficult. By 1794 too much blood had been spilled, too much social hatred and recrimination had accumulated. The new regime could not easily be steered toward the safe har-

bor of republican liberty in such a polarized atmosphere. In the end General Napoleon Bonaparte replaced the Republic with a personal dictatorship—an outcome that the men of 1789 (schooled in the history of the Roman Republic) had feared from the start.

Would Bonaparte betray the Revolution or consolidate it, as he transformed the Republic's political institutions and social policies? And, since the struggle for and against revolution had long since spilled across France's borders, what would be the consequences for Europe of Napoleon's ascendancy? After 1800 the public life of both France and Europe hinged to an unparalleled degree on the will of a single man. Gradually his designs became clear: a strong centralized state ruled from the top down in France and an imperial reorganization of Europe totally dominated by France. Undergirding both developments was arguably the most significant priority of Napoleon: the implementation of mass conscription and the consequent militarization of European society. On a vast new scale, war once again became the central motif of the Western experience.

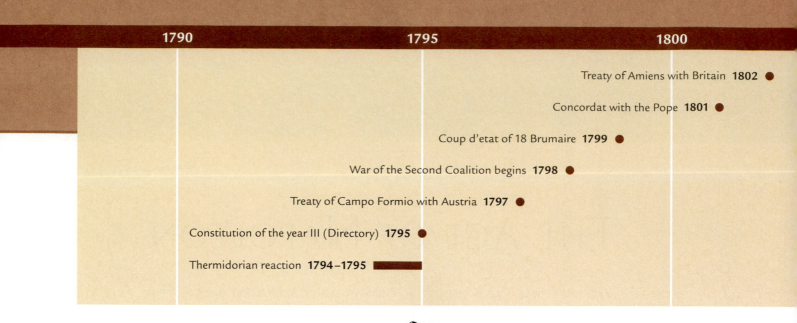

1790	1795	1800

Treaty of Amiens with Britain **1802** ●

Concordat with the Pope **1801** ●

Coup d'etat of 18 Brumaire **1799** ●

War of the Second Coalition begins **1798** ●

Treaty of Campo Formio with Austria **1797** ●

Constitution of the year III (Directory) **1795** ●

Thermidorian reaction **1794–1795** ▬

FROM ROBESPIERRE TO BONAPARTE

Relatively secure after the military victories of 1793–1794, the National Convention repudiated the Terror and struck at the leading terrorists in a turnabout known as the Thermidorian reaction. Jacobinism, however, was now a permanent part of French political experience, along with antirevolutionary royalism. The political spectrum of modern European history was beginning to emerge. Most revolutionaries now attempted to establish a moderate or centrist position, but they proved unequal to the task. During the four unsteady years of the Directory regime (1795–1799), meanwhile, French armies helped bring revolution to other parts of Western Europe, only to provoke a second anti-French coalition. This new challenge brought the weaknesses of the Republic to a head and allowed an ambitious general and hero of the Republic to seize power. With the backing of disillusioned civilian politicians, Napoleon Bonaparte emerged as the head of the French state.

The Thermidorian Reaction (1794–1795)

When the military victories over the coalition and the Vendée rebels in the year II (1793–1794) eased the need for patriotic unity, long-standing clashes over personalities and policies exploded in the Convention. Robespierre prepared to denounce yet another group of unspecified intriguers, presumably to send them to the guillotine as he had Hébert and Danton. But his enemies made a preemptive strike and denounced Robespierre to the Convention as a tyrant. The Convention no longer needed Robespierre's uncompromising style of leadership. Moderate deputies now repudiated him along with his policies of terror. The Parisian sansculottes might have intervened to keep Robespierre in power, but the Jacobins had alienated their one-time

ROBESPIERRE GUILLOTINING THE EXECUTIONER
With its field of guillotines, this Thermidorian caricature portrays Robespierre as a murderous tyrant who had depopulated France.
Giraudon/Art Resource, NY

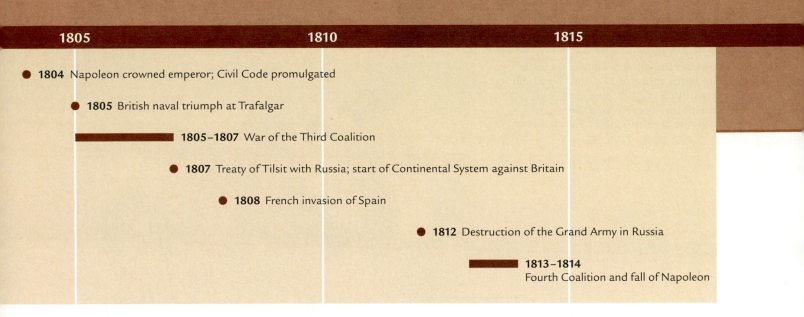

1804 Napoleon crowned emperor; Civil Code promulgated

1805 British naval triumph at Trafalgar

1805–1807 War of the Third Coalition

1807 Treaty of Tilsit with Russia; start of Continental System against Britain

1808 French invasion of Spain

1812 Destruction of the Grand Army in Russia

1813–1814
Fourth Coalition and fall of Napoleon

allies when they curbed the sans-culottes' political activities several months earlier. On July 27, 1794 (9 Thermidor year II in the revolutionary calendar), the Convention declared Robespierre an outlaw; he was guillotined the following day, along with several loyal associates.

Anti-Jacobinism   As the Convention dismantled the apparatus of the Terror, suspects were released from jail, the revolutionary committees were abolished, and some of their members were arrested in turn. The Convention closed the Paris Jacobin Club, once the main forum for Robespierre's influence, while the political clubs in the provinces gradually withered away. The Convention also extended an amnesty to the surviving Girondins and arrested a few leading deputies of the Mountain. Those who had established the Terror in the year II now found themselves under attack. The anti-Jacobin thirst for retribution eventually produced a "white terror" against the Jacobins and the sans-culottes that resulted in arrests, assassinations, and, in the south of France, wholesale massacres.

The **Thermidorian reaction** also released France from the social austerity of the year II. The Jacobins' insistence on public virtue gave way to the toleration of luxury and self-indulgence among the wealthy. The titles *monsieur* and *madame* reappeared, replacing the republican designation of *citizen*. In keeping with laissez-faire ideology, the Thermidorians rescinded economic controls. With the marketplace again ruled by supply and demand, skyrocketing inflation reignited. Worse yet, the harvest of 1795 proved mediocre, and many consumers suffered worse privations than those during the shortages of 1793. In near-famine conditions, mortality rates rose markedly; police reports spoke of little but popular misery.

The Last Revolutionary Uprising   Former militants attempted to spark a political reversal and halt the Thermidorian reaction. In the spring of 1795 sans-culottes began to demonstrate in Paris with the slogan "Bread and the Constitution of 1793." The Thermidorians, however, were moving in the opposite direction. They viewed the Jacobin Constitution of 1793 as far too democratic and looked for an excuse to scrap it altogether. In May sans-culottes launched a poorly organized insurrection (the revolt of Prairial year III). In a grim and desperate gamble, they invaded the Convention's hall, where they won the sympathy of only a handful of deputies. Their hours were numbered. In two days of street fighting, government forces overwhelmed the insurgents. Afterward, thirty-six sans-culottes were executed, and twelve hundred more were imprisoned for their activism during the Terror. This event proved to be the last mobilization of the Parisian revolutionary crowd and the final eclipse of the egalitarian movement.

The Directory (1795–1799)

By the end of 1795, the remaining members of the Convention considered the Revolution over. The extremes had been vanquished, and the time for the "peaceable enjoyment of liberty" seemed at hand. The Thermidorians drafted a new constitution—the constitution of the year III (1795)—proclaimed a general amnesty, and hoped to turn a new page. The revolutionary government, which had replaced the fallen constitutional monarchy in 1793, gave way to a constitutional republic, known as the **Directory** after its five-man executive.

The Directory's proponents declared that the Republic should "be governed by the best citizens, who are found among the property-owning class." The new constitution

The Parisian sans-culottes launched a futile rebellion in the spring of 1795 for "Bread and the Constitution of 1793" in response to hyperinflation and severe food shortages.
© Photothèque des Musées de la Ville de Paris

said little about the popular rights proclaimed by the Constitution of 1793, like the right to subsistence, public assistance, or free education. The constitution also abandoned the universal male suffrage promised in 1793 and restored the propertied franchise of 1791 and the system of indirect elections. The regime's two-house legislature was designed to moderate the political process, while its five-man executive was meant to prevent the rise of a dictator. The Directory also feared a royalist resurgence. Since genuinely free elections at this point might be carried by the antirepublicans of the right, the outgoing Convention decided to coopt two-thirds of its members into the new legislature, thereby ensuring a substantial degree of political continuity. Government troops led by an officer named Napoleon Bonaparte easily crushed a royalist revolt against this power grab.

The Political Spectrum   The Directory wished to command the center of the political spectrum, which one historian has aptly called "the mirage of the moderates." To maintain themselves in power, however, the directorials violated the liberties pledged in their own constitution. They repeatedly purged elected officials and periodically suppressed political clubs and newspapers on the left and right. In general they refused to acknowledge the legitimacy of organized opposition of any kind. This attitude explains the succession of coups and purges that marked the Directory's four years. Although the repressive measures were mild compared with those of the Terror, they ultimately undermined the regime's viability. In the end many moderate republicans would walk away from their own creation.

For all its repressive qualities, however, the Directory regime was democratic enough to allow most shades of the political spectrum some visibility. The full range of opinions in France, obscured previously by the Terror, was evident during the years of the Directory and would persist with some modifications into the twentieth century. The most important legacy of all, no doubt, was the apathy born of exhaustion or cynicism. Most citizens, especially peasants, had wearied of politics and distrusted all officials, whatever government they served. Participation in the Directory regime's annual elections was extremely low.

Within this context of massive apathy, politically conscious minorities showed fierce partisanship. On the right, ultraroyalists (including émigrés, refractory priests, and armed rebels in western France) hoped to overthrow the Republic altogether. Some worked with the exiled Bourbon princes and with British secret agents. More moderate royalists hoped to win control of the Republic's political institutions lawfully and then bring back the émigrés and refractory priests while stamping out the last vestiges of Jacobinism.

On the left of the spectrum stood the Neo-Jacobins—democrats in their own eyes, anarchists to their opponents. The Neo-Jacobins adhered to the moderate Republic of 1795 but identified positively with the experience of 1793. They did not advocate a return to the Terror or the use of force to regain power. Instead, the Neo-Jacobins promoted grassroots activism through local political clubs, petition drives, newspapers, and electoral campaigns to keep alive the egalitarian ideals of the year II, such as free public education and progressive taxation.

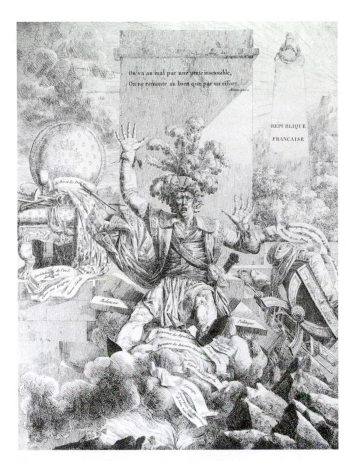

THE DIRECTORY FALLS BETWEEN TWO STOOLS
This caricature depicts the political dilemma of the Directory, which vainly sought a centrist position between the left and right.
Bulloz/© Photo RMN/Art Resource, NY

At the far end of the spectrum stood a tiny group of radicals whose significance would loom larger in the next century than it did in 1796. Their leader was François-Noël Babeuf, who had changed his name to Gracchus Babeuf in 1793. The Babeuvists viewed the revolutionary government of the year II as a promising stage that had to be followed by a final revolution in the name of the masses. The Babeuvists advocated a vaguely defined material equality, or communism, for all citizens—a "community of goods," as they called it. They also assigned a key role to a small revolutionary vanguard in carrying out this final revolution. Regarding the present Republic as simply a new form of oppression by the elites, they conspired to overthrow it.

The Elusive Center The Directory's adherents stood somewhere in the center of this broad spectrum, hostile to royalists and Neo-Jacobins alike and ready to shift their ground with any change in the political balance. Thus, although the Neo-Jacobins had spurned Babeuf's calls for insurrection, after Babeuf's plot was

exposed the Directory joined forces with the right. But when the first regular elections in the year V (1797) produced a royalist victory, the Directory reversed field. Backed by influential generals, the government purged newly elected royalist deputies, suppressed royalist newspapers, and allowed the Neo-Jacobins to open new clubs.

After a few months, however, the Directory grew fearful of the revived left. During the elections of the year VI (1798), Neo-Jacobins and Directorial moderates vied for influence in what almost amounted to party rivalry. But in the end the Directory would not risk the results of free elections. Again it intervened: It closed down clubs and newspapers, manipulated electoral assemblies, and purged those Neo-Jacobins who were elected anyway. Interestingly, at almost the same moment that France's government was quashing its political rivals, leaders of the American republic were reluctantly coming to accept opposition parties as legitimate. In France, however, the Directory would not tolerate organized opposition, and that rigidity contributed to the Republic's demise.

The Rise of Bonaparte

Meanwhile, the Directory years provided unexpected impetus for revolutionary expansion in Europe, which brought into being a half-dozen **sister republics** (see map 21.1), including the Batavian Republic in the Netherlands and the Helvetic Republic in the Swiss Confederation. Revolutionary change also spread through the entire Italian peninsula, as French commanders in the field began to make their own diplomacy. Among them was a young brigadier general, Napoleon Bonaparte.

Bonaparte personifies the world-historic individual—the rare person whose life decisively dominates the course of historical events. Born in 1769 of an impoverished but noble family on the French-controlled island of Corsica, Napoleon scarcely seemed destined to play such a historic role. His youthful ambitions and fantasies involved little more than leading Corsica to independence from France. Sent to French military academies, he proved a diligent student, adept at mathematics. Aloof from his aristocratic classmates, whose pretensions he resented, self-reliant and energetic, Bonaparte became an expert on artillery.

After 1789 the young officer returned to Corsica, but his ambitions ran up against more conservative forces on the island. Eventually, local factional conflict drove him and his family off Corsica altogether. Bonaparte then moved onto a much larger stage. He rose steadily and rapidly through the military ranks, based in part on the luck of opportunities but equally on his ability to act decisively. While on leave in Paris in 1795, Bonaparte was assigned to the planning bureau of the war

MAP 21.1 FRANCE AND ITS SISTER REPUBLICS, 1798
Notice the locations of France's sister republics. Which republics were likely to be the most viable?
◆ For an online version, go to www.mhhe.com/chambers9 > chapter 21 > book maps

ministry. There he advocated a new strategy: opening a front in Italy to strike at Austrian forces from the south, while French armies on the Rhine pushed as usual from the west. The strategy was approved, and Bonaparte gained command of the Army of Italy in 1796.

The Making of a Hero Austria's forces outnumbered the French in Italy, but Bonaparte moved his troops rapidly to achieve surprise and numerical superiority in specific encounters. The end result was a major victory that brought the French into the Habsburg domain of Lombardy and its capital, Milan. Bonaparte's overall plan almost miscarried, since the Army of the Rhine did not advance as planned. But this mishap made his own triumphs all the more important to the Directory. And Bonaparte ensured his popularity with the government by making his campaign self-supporting through organized levies on the Italians.

Bonaparte brought a great sense of excitement and drama to the French occupation of Lombardy. His personal magnetism and his talent in manipulating people attracted many Italians. The general encouraged the Italians to organize their own revolutionary movement; the liberation of northern Italy, he believed, would solidify support for his army and enhance his own reputation. This policy distressed the Directory, since it had intended to trade back conquests in Italy in exchange for security on the Rhine frontier. But in the end the Directory endorsed the Treaty of Campo Formio, in which Bonaparte personally negotiated a peace settlement with Austria in October 1797. Austria recognized a new, independent state in northern Italy, the Cisalpine Republic, and left the Rhine question to future negotiations. The Directory regime had found the hero it desperately needed.

The French now focused their patriotic aspirations on defeating the last member of the coalition: the hated British enemy. Bonaparte naturally yearned for the glory of accomplishing this feat, and he was authorized to prepare an invasion force. Previous seaborne landings directed at Ireland had failed, however, and Bonaparte too finally had to abandon the scheme because of France's insufficient naval force.

Instead, in the spring of 1798 Bonaparte launched an expedition to Egypt intended to strike at Britain's approaches to India. But British naval superiority, in the form of Admiral Horatio Nelson's fleet, turned the expedition into a debacle. The British destroyed the French fleet at the Battle of the Nile, thereby marooning a French army in North Africa. Worse yet, the French were beaten back in several engagements with Turkish forces. Only cynical news management prevented the full story of this defeat from reaching France. Instead, the expedition's exotic details and scientific explorations held the attention of the French public. Bonaparte extricated himself from this mess by slipping off through the British blockade, in effect abandoning his army as he returned to France.

The Brumaire Coup

While Bonaparte floundered in Egypt, the Directory was faltering under political pressures at home. Charges of tyranny and ineptitude accumulated against the directors. Further French expansion into Italy, which produced new sister republics centered in Rome and Naples, precipitated a new coalition against France, consisting of Britain, Russia, and Austria. In June 1799 ill-supplied French forces were driven out of most of Italy and Switzerland.

The legislature ousted four of the five directors and named Sieyès, a respected leader of the patriots in 1789, among the replacements. Sieyès and his supporters secretly wished to alter the constitution itself, for they had lost confidence in the regime's institutions, especially its annual elections. These "revisionists" wanted to redesign the Republic along more oligarchic lines, as opposed to the Neo-Jacobins, who wished to democratize the Republic. The centrist position had virtually disappeared. The revisionists blocked emergency measures proposed by the Neo-Jacobins in reaction to the new war crisis and breathed a sigh of relief as French armies rallied and repulsed Anglo-Russian forces in the Batavian Republic and Switzerland. Most of Italy was lost for the time being, but the threat to France itself had passed. Sieyès and the revisionists moved against the Neo-Jacobins by closing their clubs and newspapers and prepared for a coup.

A General Comes to Power   Although no dire military threat remained to propel the country into the arms of a general, the revisionists wished to establish a more centralized, oligarchic republic, and they needed a general's support. Generals were the only national heroes in France, and only a general could organize the force necessary to ensure the coup's success. Bonaparte's return to France from Egypt thus seemed most timely. Bonaparte was not the revisionists' first choice, but he proved to be the best available one.

Contrary to the intentions of Sieyès and his fellow conspirators, Bonaparte became the tail that wagged the dog. Once the coup began, he proved to be far more ambitious and energetic than the other conspirators and thrust himself into the most prominent position. Bonaparte addressed the legislature to denounce a mythical Jacobin plot and to demand emergency powers for a new provisional government. Intimidated into submission, a cooperative rump of the legislature approved the new arrangements. Along with Sieyès, Bonaparte was empowered to draft a new constitution. Thus unfolded the coup of 18 Brumaire (November 9, 1799).

The **Brumaire** coup had not been intended to install a dictatorship, but that was its eventual result. In the maneuvering among the revisionists, Bonaparte's ideas and personality prevailed. The plotters agreed to eliminate meaningful elections, which they saw as promoting political instability. They agreed also to enshrine the social ideals of 1789, such as civil equality, and to bury those of the year II, such as popular democracy. The vague notion of popular sovereignty gave way to concentrated authority. The general came out of the coup as the regime's strongman, and Sieyès' elaborate plans for a republican oligarchy ended up in the wastebasket. On one other point, the plotters were particularly deceived. With General Bonaparte's leadership they hoped to achieve durable peace through military victory. Instead, the Napoleonic regime promoted unbounded expansion and endless warfare.

THE NAPOLEONIC SETTLEMENT IN FRANCE

Bonaparte's prime asset in his rapid takeover of France was the apathy of its citizens. Most French people were so weary politically that they saw in Bonaparte what they wished to see.[1] The Committee of Public Safety had won grudging submission through its terroristic policies; Bonaparte achieved the same result almost by default. As a brilliant propagandist for himself and a man of great personal appeal, he soothed a divided France. Ultraroyalists and dedicated Jacobins never warmed to his regime, but most citizens fell between those positions. They relished the prospect of a strong, reliable government, a return to order and stability, a codification of basic revolutionary gains, and settlement of the religious conflict.

The Napoleonic Style

Napoleon Bonaparte was not a royalist or a Jacobin, not a conservative or a liberal, though his attitudes were flavored by a touch of each viewpoint. Authority, not ideology, was his great concern, and he justified his actions by their results. The revolutionaries of 1789 could consider Napoleon one of theirs because of his hostility toward the unjust and ineffective institutions of the old regime. He had little use for seigneurialism, the cumbersome institutions of Bourbon absolutism, or the congealed structures of aristocratic privilege, which the Revolution had destroyed. Napoleon valued the Revolution's commitment to equality of opportunity and continued to espouse that liberal premise. Other rights and liberties of 1789 he curtailed or disdained.

Ten years of upheaval had produced a grim paradox: The French Revolution had proceeded in the name of liberty, yet successive forms of repression had been mounted to defend it. Napoleon fit comfortably into this history; unlike the Directory, he made no pretense about it. The social gains of the Revolution would be preserved through political centralization and authoritarian control. Napoleon's field of action was in fact far greater than that of the most powerful eighteenth-century monarch, for no entrenched aristocracy existed to resist him. Thanks to the clearing operations of the Revolution, he could reconstruct at will.

Tragically, however, Napoleon drifted away from his own rational ideals. Increasingly absorbed in his personal power, he began to force domestic and foreign policies on France that were geared to his imperial ambitions. Increasingly he concentrated his government on raising men and money for his armies and turned his back on revolutionary liberties.

Political and Religious Settlements

Centralization Bonaparte gave France a constitution, approved in a plebiscite, that placed almost unchecked authority in the hands of a First Consul (himself) for ten years. Two later constitutional revisions, also approved overwhelmingly in plebiscites, increased executive power and diminished the legislative branch until it became simply a rubber stamp. The first revision, in 1802, converted the consulship into a lifetime post; the second, in 1804, proclaimed Napoleon hereditary emperor. The task of proposing new laws passed from elected representatives to appointed experts in the Council of State. This new body advised the ruler, drafted legislation under his direction, and monitored public officials. Such government by experts stood as an alternative to meaningful parliamentary democracy for the next century.

The system of local government established by Bonaparte in 1800 came ironically close to the kind of royal centralization that public opinion had roundly condemned in 1789. Bonaparte eliminated the local elections that the Revolution had emphasized. Instead, each department was now administered by a **prefect** appointed by the ruler. The four-hundred-odd subprefects on the district level as well as the forty thousand mayors of France's communes were likewise appointed. With minor changes, the unquestionably efficient prefectorial system survived in France for 150 years, severely limiting local autonomy and self-government.

Police-state methods finished what constitutional change began: the suppression of independent political activity. From the legislature to the grass roots, France was depoliticized. The government permitted no organized opposition, reduced the number of newspapers drastically, and censored the remaining ones. The free journalism born in 1789 gave way to government press releases and news management. In 1811 only four newspapers remained in Paris, all hewing to the official line. Political clubs were prohibited, outspoken dissidents deported, and others placed under police surveillance. All these restrictions silenced liberal intellectuals as well as former political activists.

The Concordat Napoleon's religious policies promoted tranquillity at home and a good image abroad. Before Brumaire the Republic tolerated Catholic worship in theory but severely restricted it in practice. Continued proscription of the refractory clergy; insistence on the republican calendar, with its ten-day weeks that made Sunday a workday; and a drive to keep religious instruction out of elementary schools

---

[1] It is customary to refer to him as Bonaparte until 1804, when the general crowned himself Emperor Napoleon I.

Antoine Jean Gros
PORTRAIT OF BONAPARTE AS FIRST CONSUL
Napoleon Bonaparte as First Consul, at the height of his popularity, painted by his admirer J.-B. Gros.
Bulloz/© Photo RMN/Art Resource, NY

the state. Though nominated by the ruler, bishops would again be consecrated by the pope. But as a major concession to the Revolution, the Concordat stipulated that land confiscated from the Church and sold during the Revolution would be retained by its purchasers. On the other hand, the government dropped the ten-day week and restored the Gregorian calendar.

The balance of church-state relations tilted firmly in the state's favor, for Napoleon intended to use the clergy as a major prop of his regime. The pulpit and the primary school became instruments of social control, to be used, as a new catechism stated, "to bind the religious conscience of the people to the august person of the Emperor." As Napoleon put it, the clergy would be his "moral prefects." Devout Catholics came to resent this subordination of the Church. Eventually Pope Pius renounced the Concordat, to which Napoleon responded by removing the pontiff to France and placing him under house arrest.

The Era of the Notables

With civil equality established and feudalism abolished, Napoleon believed that the Revolution was complete. It remained to encourage an orderly hierarchical society to counteract what he regarded as the excessive individualism of revolutionary social policy. Napoleon intended to reassert the authority of the state, the elites, and, in family life, the father.

In the absence of electoral politics, Napoleon used the state's appointive powers to confer status on prominent local individuals, or **notables,** thus associating

curtailed the free and familiar exercise of Catholicism. These policies provoked wide resentment among the mass of citizens whose commitment to Catholicism remained intact throughout the Revolution.

Though not a believer himself, Napoleon judged that major concessions to Catholic sentiment were in order, provided that the Church remained under the control of the state. In 1801 he negotiated a **Concordat,** or agreement, with Pope Pius VII. It stipulated that Catholicism was the "preferred" religion of France but protected religious freedom for non-Catholics. The Church was again free to operate in full public view and to restore the refractory priests. Primary education would espouse Catholic values and use Catholic texts, as it had before the Revolution, and clerical salaries would be paid by

FAMILY AND GENDER ROLES UNDER THE NAPOLEONIC CIVIL CODE

"Art. 148. The son who has not attained the full age of 25 years, the daughter who has not attained the full age of 21 years, cannot contract marriage without the consent of their father and mother; in case of disagreement, the consent of the father is sufficient.

"Art. 212. Married persons owe to each other fidelity, succor, assistance.

"Art. 213. The husband owes protection to his wife, the wife obedience to her husband.

"Art. 214. The wife is obliged to live with her husband, and to follow him to every place where he may judge it convenient to reside: the husband is obliged to receive her, and to furnish her with everything necessary for the wants of life, according to his means and station.

"Art. 215. The wife cannot plead [in court] in her own name, without the authority of her husband, even though she should be a public trader . . . or separate in property.

"Art. 217. A wife . . . cannot give, alienate, pledge, or acquire by free or chargeable title, without the concurrence of her husband in the act, or his consent in writing.

"Art. 219. If the husband refuses to authorize his wife to pass an act, the wife may cause her husband to be cited directly before the court of first instance . . . which may give or refuse its authority, after the husband shall have been heard, or duly summoned.

"Art. 229. The husband may demand a divorce on the ground of his wife's adultery.

"Art. 230. The wife may demand divorce on the ground of adultery in her husband, when he shall have brought his concubine into their common residence.

"Art. 231. The married parties may reciprocally demand divorce for outrageous conduct, ill-usage, or grievous injuries, exercised by one of them towards the other."

---

them with his regime. These local dignitaries were usually chosen from among the largest taxpayers: prosperous landowners, former nobles, businessmen, and professionals. Those who served the regime with distinction were honored by induction into the Legion of Honor, nine-tenths of whose members were military men. "It is with trinkets that mankind is governed," Napoleon once said. Legion of Honor awards and appointments to prestigious but powerless local bodies were precisely such trinkets.

Napoleon offered more tangible rewards to the country's leading bankers when he chartered a national bank that enjoyed the credit power derived from official ties to the state. In education, Napoleon created elite secondary schools, or *lycées*, to train future government officials, engineers, and officers. The *lycées* embodied the concept of careers open to talent and became part of a highly centralized French academic system called the *University*, which survived into the twentieth century.

The Civil Code Napoleon's most important legacy was a civil code regulating social relations and property rights. Baptized the Napoleonic Code, it was in some measure a revolutionary law code that progressives throughout Europe embraced. Wherever it was implemented, the **Civil Code** swept away feudal property relations and gave legal sanction to modern contractual notions of property. The code established the right to choose one's occupation, to receive equal treatment under the law, and to enjoy religious freedom. At the same time, it allowed employers to dominate their

workers by prohibiting strikes and trade unions. Nor did the code match property rights with popular rights like the right to subsistence.

Revolutionary legislation had emancipated women and children by establishing their civil rights. Napoleon undid most of this by restoring the father's absolute authority in the family. "A wife owes obedience to her husband," said the code, which proceeded to deprive wives of property and juridical rights established during the 1790s. The code curtailed the right to divorce, while establishing a kind of double standard in the dissolution of a marriage (see "Family and Gender Roles under the Napoleonic Civil Code," above). The code also expanded the husband's options in disposing of his estate, although each child was still guaranteed a portion.

The prefectorial system of local government, the Civil Code, the Concordat, the University, the Legion of Honor, and the local bodies of notables all proved to be durable institutions. They fulfilled Napoleon's desire to create a series of "granite masses" on which to reconstruct French society. His admirers emphasized that these institutions contributed to social stability as skillful compromises between revolutionary liberalism and an older belief in hierarchy and central authority. Detractors point out that these institutions were class oriented and excessively patriarchal. Moreover, they fostered overcentralized, rigid structures that might have sapped the vitality of French institutions in succeeding generations. Whatever their merits or defects, these institutions took root, unlike Napoleon's attempt to dominate all of Europe.

Nicolas Andre Monsiau
Deputies from the Cisalpine Republic of Italy proclaim Napoleon Bonaparte their president in 1802.
Chateaux de Versailles et de Trianon, Versailles, France. Erich Lessing/Art Resource, NY

NAPOLEONIC HEGEMONY IN EUROPE

After helping to give France a new government, Bonaparte turned to do battle against the second anti-French coalition in northern Italy. The outcome of his campaign against Austria would either solidify or destroy his regime. Within a few years, in the arena of international relations his ambitions lost all semblance of restraint. Bonaparte evolved from a winning general of the Republic to an imperial conqueror. After defeating his continental opponents on the battlefield in a series of ever more murderous campaigns, he still faced an implacable enemy in Britain. Unable to invade Britain, he resorted to economic warfare and blockade, but Britain withstood that assault as well. Meanwhile, the raw militarism of Napoleon's rule became evident in the relentless expansion of military conscription within the empire.

Military Supremacy and the Reorganization of Europe

Bonaparte's strategy in 1800 called for a repeat of the 1797 campaign: He would strike through Italy while the Army of the Rhine pushed eastward against Vienna. Following French victories at Marengo in Lombardy and in Germany, Austria sued for peace. The Treaty of Lunéville (February 1801) essentially restored France to the position it had held after Bonaparte's triumphs in Italy in 1797.

In Britain a war-weary government now stood alone against France and decided to negotiate. The Treaty of Amiens (March 1802) ended hostilities and reshuffled territorial holdings outside Europe, such as the Cape Colony in South Africa, which passed from the Dutch to the British. But this truce proved precarious since it did not settle the future of French influence in Europe or of commercial relations between the two great powers. Napoleon abided by the letter of the treaty but soon violated its spirit. Britain and Austria alike were dismayed by further expansion of French influence in Italy and Switzerland. Most important, perhaps, France seemed determined to exclude British trade rather than restore normal commercial relations. Historians agree that the Treaty of Amiens failed to keep the peace because neither side was ready to abandon its century-long struggle for predominance.

The Third Coalition   A third anti-French coalition soon took shape, a replay of its predecessors. France ostensibly fought to preserve the new regime at home and

Nicholas Pocock
NELSON'S FLAGSHIPS AT ANCHOR,
1807
**Admiral Nelson's heavily armed
three-decker ship of the line,
which inflicted devastation on
the French fleet at Trafalgar.**
National Maritime Museum,
Greenwich, London

its sister republics abroad. The coalition's objectives included the restoration of the Netherlands and Italy to
"independence," the limitation of French influence
elsewhere, and, if possible, a reduction of France to its
prerevolutionary borders. Like most such alliances, the
coalition would be dismembered piecemeal.

French hopes of settling the issue directly by invading Britain proved impossible once again. At the Battle
of Trafalgar (October 1805), Admiral Nelson's fleet
crushed the combined naval forces of France and its
ally Spain. Nelson, an innovative tactician who broke
rule-book procedures on the high seas just as French
generals did on land, died of his wounds in the battle
but ensured the security of the British Isles for the remainder of the Napoleonic era.

Napoleon, meanwhile, had turned against the Austro-
Russian forces. Moving 200,000 French soldiers with unprecedented speed across the Continent, he took his
enemies by surprise and won a dazzling succession of
victories. After occupying Vienna he proceeded against
the coalition's main army in December. Feigning weakness and retreat at the moment of battle, he drew his numerically superior opponents into an exposed position,
crushed the center of their lines, and inflicted a decisive
defeat. This Battle of Austerlitz was Napoleon's most
brilliant tactical achievement, and it forced the Habsburgs to the peace table. The resulting Treaty of Press-
burg (December 1805), extremely harsh and humiliating
for Austria, imposed a large indemnity and required the
Habsburgs to cede their Venetian provinces.

France and Germany   By now the French sphere of
influence had increased dramatically to include most
of southern Germany, which Napoleon reorganized
into the Confederation of the Rhine, a client realm of

France (see map 21.2). France had kept Prussia neutral
during the war with Austria by skillful diplomacy.
Only after Austria made peace did Prussia recognize its
error in failing to join with Austria to halt Napoleon.
Belatedly, Prussia mobilized its famous but antiquated
army; it was rewarded with stinging defeats by France
in a number of encounters culminating in the Battle of
Jena (October 1806). With the collapse of Prussian military power, the conquerors settled in Berlin and
watched the prestige of the Prussian ruling class crumble. Napoleon was now master of northern Germany
as well as the south. For a while it appeared that he
might obliterate Prussia entirely, but he restored its
sovereignty—after amputating part of its territory and
imposing a crushing indemnity.

Napoleon was free to reorganize central Europe as he
pleased. After formally proclaiming the end of the Holy
Roman Empire in 1806, he liquidated numerous small
German states and merged them into two new ones: the
Kingdom of Westphalia, with his brother Jérôme on the
throne, and the Grand Duchy of Berg, to be ruled by his
brother-in-law Joachim Murat. His ally Saxony became
a full-scale kingdom, while a new duchy of Warsaw was
carved out of Prussian Poland. This "restoration" of
Poland had propaganda value; it made the emperor appear as a champion of Polish aspirations, compared to
the rulers of Prussia, Russia, and Austria, who had dismembered Poland in a series of partitions between 1772
and 1795. Moreover, Napoleon could now enlist a Polish army and use Polish territory as a base of operations
against his remaining continental foe, Russia.

France and Russia   In February 1807 Napoleon confronted the colossus of the east in the Battle of Eylau;
the resulting carnage was horrifying but inconclusive.

Charles Meynier
THE DAY AFTER THE BATTLE OF EYLAU, 9 FEBRUARY 1807
Napoleon amidst the carnage on the battlefield of Eylau, the bloodiest engagement to date of the revolutionary-Napoleonic era, where the French and Russians fought each other to a stalemate in 1807.
Versailles, France. Giraudon/Art Resource, NY

When spring came, only a dramatic victory could preserve his conquests in central Europe and vindicate the extraordinary commitments of the past two years. The Battle of Friedland in June was a French victory that demoralized Russia's Tsar Alexander I and persuaded him to negotiate.

Meeting at Tilsit, the two rulers buried their differences and agreed, in effect, to partition Europe into eastern and western spheres of influence. Each would support the other's conquests and mediate in behalf of the other's interests. The Treaty of Tilsit (July 1807) sanctioned new annexations of territory directly into France and the reorganization of other conquered countries. The creation of new satellite kingdoms became the vehicle for Napoleon's domination of Europe. Like the French Republic, the sister republics became kingdoms between 1805 and 1807. And it happened that Napoleon had a large family of brothers ready to wear those new royal crowns.

The distorted shape of Napoleonic Europe is apparent on maps dating from 1808 to 1810 (see map 21.2). His chief satellites included the Kingdom of Holland, with brother Louis on the throne; the Kingdom of Italy, with Napoleon himself as king and his stepson Eugène de Beauharnais as viceroy; the Confederation of the Rhine, including brother Jérôme's Kingdom of Westphalia; the Kingdom of Naples, covering southern Italy, with

brother Joseph the ruler until Napoleon transferred him to Spain and installed his brother-in-law Murat; and the Duchy of Warsaw. Belgium, the Rhineland, Tuscany, Piedmont, Genoa, and the Illyrian provinces had been annexed to France. Switzerland did not become a kingdom, but the Helvetic Republic (as it was now called) received a new constitution dictated by France. In 1810, after yet another war with Austria, a marriage was arranged between the house of Bonaparte and the house of Habsburg. Having divorced Joséphine de Beauharnais, Napoleon married princess Marie Louise, daughter of Francis II, who bore him a male heir the following year.

Naval War with Britain

For a time it seemed that Britain alone stood between Napoleon and his dream of hegemony over Europe. Since Britain was invulnerable to invasion, Napoleon hoped to destroy its influence by means of economic warfare. Unable to blockade British ports directly, he could try to close off the Continent: keep Britain from its markets, stop its exports, and thus ruin its trade and credit. Napoleon reasoned that if Britain had nowhere to sell its manufactured goods, no gold would come into the country and bankruptcy would eventually ensue. Meanwhile, overproduction would cause unemployment and labor unrest, which would turn the

MAP 21.2 EUROPE AROUND 1810
Note the extent of the French Empire as well as its satellite territories and allies. Was it plausible that the Napoleonic Empire could sustain its military power from Madrid to Warsaw?
◆ For an online version, go to www.mhhe.com/chambers9 > chapter 21 > book maps

British people against their government and force the latter to make peace with France. At the same time, French advantages in continental markets would increase with the elimination of British competition.

The Continental System Napoleon therefore launched his **Continental System** to prohibit British trade with all French allies. Even neutral ships were banned from European ports if they carried goods coming from the British Isles. Britain responded in 1807 with the Orders in Council, which in effect reversed the blockade: It *required* all neutral ships to stop at British ports to procure trading licenses and pay tariffs. In other words, the British insisted on regulating all

trade between neutral states and European ports. Ships that failed to obey would be stopped on the high seas and captured. In an angry response, Napoleon, in turn, threatened to seize any neutral ship that obeyed the Orders in Council by stopping at British ports.

Thus, a total naval war between France and Britain enveloped all neutral nations. Indeed, neutral immunity virtually disappeared, since every ship was obliged to violate one system or the other and thus run afoul of naval patrols or privateers. While the British captured only about forty French ships a year after 1807 (for few were left afloat), they seized almost three thousand neutral vessels a year, including many from the United States.

Jean-Auguste-Dominique Ingres
NAPOLEON ON HIS IMPERIAL THRONE, 1806
Emperor Napoleon I on his imperial throne in 1806, by the great portrait painter Ingres. Note the dramatic contrast in appearance with the young, intense military hero of the Republic in David's portrait at the beginning of this chapter.
Musée des Beaux-Arts, Rennes, France. Erich Lessing/Art Resource, NY

CHRONOLOGY
Napoleon and Europe

June 1800	Battle of Marengo and defeat of the Second Coalition.
Feb. 1801	Treaty of Lunéville with Austria.
March 1802	Treaty of Amiens with Britain.
Sept. 1802	Annexation of Piedmont.
1805–1806	Third Coalition forms.
Oct. 1805	Battle of Trafalgar and defeat of French fleet.
Dec. 1805	Battle of Austerlitz; defeat of Austria.
1806	Battle of Jena and humiliation of Prussia.
1807	Battles of Eylau and Friedland; stalemate with Russia.
July 1807	Treaty of Tilsit with Russia. Consolidation of satellite kingdoms.
1807	Launching of Continental System against British trade.
Feb. 1808	Invasion of Spain.
July 1809	Battle of Wagram; Austria defeated again.
April 1810	Napoleon weds princess Marie Louise of Austria.
Dec. 1810	Annexation of Holland.
July 1812	Invasion of Russia.
Oct. 1812	Retreat and destruction of Grand Army.
Oct. 1813	Battle of Leipzig and formation of Fourth Coalition.
March 1814	Battle of France and Napoleon's abdication.

The Continental System did hurt British trade. British gold reserves dwindled, and 1811 saw widespread unemployment and rioting. France was affected, in turn, by Britain's counterblockade, which cut it off from certain raw materials necessary for industrial production. But the satellite states, as economic vassals of France, suffered the most. In Amsterdam, for example, shipping volume declined from 1,350 ships entering the port in 1806 to 310 in 1809, and commercial revenues dropped calamitously. Out of loyalty to the people whom he ruled, Holland's King Louis Bonaparte tolerated smuggling. But this action so infuriated Napoleon that he ousted his brother from the throne and annexed the Kingdom of Holland directly to France. Smuggling

was, in fact, the weak link in the system, for it created holes in Napoleon's wall of economic sanctions that constantly needed plugging. This problem drove the emperor to ever more drastic actions.

The Napoleonic Conscription Machine

One key to Napoleon's unrestrained ambitions in Europe was the creation of an efficient administrative state in France and its annexed territories with the ability to continuously replenish the ranks of the imperial army.

The National Convention's mass levy of August 1793 had drafted all able-bodied unmarried men between the ages of eighteen and twenty-five. But this unprecedented mobilization had been meant as a one-time-only emergency measure, a temporary "requisition." There was no implication that subsequent cohorts of young men would face conscription into the army as part of their civic obligations. When the war resumed in 1798, however, the Directory passed a conscription law that made successive "classes" of young men (that is, those born in a particular year) subject to a military draft should the need arise. The Directory immediately implemented this law and called up three classes, but local officials reported massive draft evasion in most of the departments. Many French youths found the prospect of military service repugnant. From this shaky foundation, however, the Napoleonic regime developed a remarkably successful conscription system.

The Rules of the Game   After much trial and error with the details, timetables, and mechanisms, the system began to operate efficiently within a few years. The government assigned an annual quota of conscripts for each department. Using parish birth registers, the mayor of every community compiled a list of men reaching the age of nineteen that year. These youths were then led by their mayor to the cantonal seat on a specified day for a draft lottery. Panels of doctors at the departmental capitals later verified or rejected claims for medical exemptions. In all, about a third of French youths legally avoided military service because they were physically unfit—too short, lame, or suffering from poor eyesight, chronic diseases, or other infirmities.

In the draft lottery, youths picked numbers out of a box; marriage could no longer be used as an exemption, for obvious reasons. Those with high numbers were spared (for the time being), while those who drew low numbers filled the local induction quota. Two means of avoiding service remained: The wealthy could purchase a replacement, and the poor could flee. True, the regime had a bad conscience about allowing draftees to hire replacements, because the practice made its rhetoric about the duties of citizenship sound hollow. But to placate wealthy notables and peasants with large holdings (who were sometimes desperate to keep their sons on the farm), the government permitted the hiring of a replacement under strict guidelines that made it difficult and expensive but not impossible. The proportion of replacements was somewhere between 5 and 10 percent of all draftees.

Draft Evasion   For Napoleon's prefects, conscription levies were always the top priority among their duties, and draft evasion was the number one problem. Dogged persistence, bureaucratic routine, and various forms of coercion gradually overcame this chronic resistance. From time to time, columns of troops swept through areas in which evasion and desertion were most common and arrested culprits by the hundreds. But draft evaders

Royalist caricatures often depicted Napoleon as an ogre whose conscription machine devoured the nation's young men.
Bibliothèque Nationale de France, Paris

usually hid out in remote places—mountains, forests, marshes—so coercion had to be directed against their families as well. Heavy fines assessed against the parents did little good, since most were too poor to pay anything. A better tactic was to billet troops in the draft evaders' homes; if their families could not afford to feed the troops, then the community's wealthy taxpayers were required to do so. All these actions created pressure on the youths to turn themselves in. By 1811 the regime had broken the habit of draft evasion, and conscription was grudgingly becoming accepted as a disagreeable civic obligation, much like taxes. Just as draft calls began to rise sharply, draft evasion fell dramatically.

Napoleon had begun by drafting 60,000 Frenchmen annually, but by 1810 the annual quotas had risen steadily to 120,000, and they continued to climb. Moreover, in 1810 the emperor ordered the first of many "supplementary levies," calling up men from earlier classes who had drawn high lottery numbers. In January 1813, to look ahead, Napoleon replenished his armies by calling up the class of 1814 a year early and by making repeated supplementary calls on earlier classes.

RESISTANCE TO NAPOLEON

By 1808, with every major European power except Britain vanquished on the battlefield, Napoleon felt that nothing stood in his way. Since Spain and, later, Russia seemed unable or unwilling to stop smuggling from Britain, thus thwarting his strategy of economic warfare, the emperor decided to deal with each by force of arms. His calculations proved utterly mistaken, and in both places he ultimately suffered disastrous defeats. More generally, Napoleon's intrusion into Italy, Germany, Spain, and Russia set in motion various responses and movements of resistance. French expansion sparked new forms of nationalism in some quarters, but also liberalism and reaction. Finally, all his opponents coalesced, defeated Napoleon on the battlefield, and drove him from his throne.

The "Spanish Ulcer"

Spain and France shared a common interest in weakening British power in Europe and the colonial world. But the alliance they formed after making peace with each other in 1795 brought only troubles for Spain, including the loss of its Louisiana Territory in America and (at the Battle of Trafalgar) most of its naval fleet. The Spanish royal household, meanwhile, was mired in scandal. Prime Minister Manuel de Godoy, once a lover of the queen, was a corrupt opportunist and extremely unpopular with the people. Crown Prince Ferdinand despised Godoy and

Godoy's protectors, the king and queen, while Ferdinand's parents actively returned their son's hostility.

Napoleon looked on at this farce with irritation. At the zenith of his power, he concluded that he must reorganize Spain himself to bring it solidly into the Continental System. As a pretext for military intervention, he set in motion a plan to invade Portugal, supposedly to partition it with Spain. Once the French army was well inside Spain, however, Napoleon intended to impose his own political solution to Spain's instability.

Napoleon brought the squabbling king and prince to France, where he threatened and bribed one and then the other into abdicating. The emperor then gathered a group of handpicked Spanish notables who followed Napoleon's scenario by petitioning him to provide a new sovereign, preferably his brother Joseph. Joseph was duly proclaimed king of Spain. With 100,000 French troops already positioned around Madrid, Joseph prepared to assume his new throne, eager to rule under a liberal constitution and to believe his brother's statement that "all the better Spanish people are on your side." As he took up the crown, however, an unanticipated drama erupted.

Popular Resistance   Faced with military occupation, the disappearance of their royal family, and the crowning of a Frenchman, the Spanish people rose in rebellion. It began on May 2, 1808, when an angry crowd in Madrid rioted against French troops, who responded with firing squads and brutal reprisals. This bloody incident, known as the Dos de Mayo and captured in

Francisco Goya
THE THIRD OF MAY, **1808**
The great Spanish artist Francisco Goya memorably captured the brutality of French reprisals against the citizens of Madrid who dared to rebel against the Napoleonic occupation on May 2, 1808.
Painted in 1814. Museo del Prado, Madrid, Spain. Erich Lessing/Art Resource, NY

Francisco de Goya
THE DISASTERS OF WAR: POPULACHO
In a relentlessly bleak series of drawings collectively entitled *The Horrors of War,* Goya went on to record the savagery and atrocities committed by both sides of the struggle in Spain.
The Norton Simon Art Foundation, Pasadena, CA

SPANISH LIBERALS DRAFT A CONSTITUTION, 1812

"The general and extraordinary Cortes of the Spanish nation, duly organized . . . in order duly to discharge the lofty objective of furthering the glory, prosperity and welfare of the Nation as a whole, decrees the following political Constitution to assure the well-being and upright administration of the State.

"Art. 1: The Spanish Nation is the union of all Spaniards from both hemispheres.

"Art. 3: Sovereignty resides primarily in the Nation and because of this the right to establish the fundamental laws belongs to it exclusively.

"Art. 4: The Nation is obligated to preserve and protect with wise and just laws civil liberty, property and the other legitimate rights of all the individuals belonging to it.

"Art. 12: The religion of the Spanish Nation is and always will be the Catholic, Apostolic, Roman and only true faith. The Nation protects it with wise and just laws and prohibits the exercise of any other.

"Art. 14: The Government of the Spanish Nation is an hereditary limited Monarchy.

"Art. 15: The power to make laws resides in the Cortes with the King.

"Art. 16: The power to enforce laws resides in the King.

"Art. 27: The Cortes is the union of all the deputies that represent the Nation, named by the citizens.

"Art. 34: To elect deputies to the Cortes, electoral meetings will be held in the parish, the district, and the province.

"Art. 59: The electoral meetings on the district level will be made up of the electors chosen at the parish level who will convene at the seat of every district in order to name the electors who will then converge on the provincial capital to elect the deputies to the Cortes.

"Art. 338: The Cortes will annually establish or confirm all taxes, be they direct or indirect, general, provincial or municipal. . . .

"Art. 339: Taxes will be apportioned among all Spaniards in proportion to their abilities [to pay], without exception to any privilege."

From *Political Constitution of the Spanish Monarchy*, proclaimed in Cádiz, March 19, 1812, James B. Tueller (tr.).

Goya's famous paintings, has remained a source of Spanish national pride, for it touched off a sustained uprising against the French. Local notables created committees, or *juntas*, to organize resistance and to coordinate campaigns by regular Spanish troops. These troops were generally ineffective against the French, but they did produce one early victory: A half-starved French army was cut off and forced to surrender at Bailén in July 1808. This defeat broke the aura of Napoleonic invincibility.

The British saw a great opportunity to attack Napoleon in concert with the rebellious Spanish people. Landing an army in Portugal, the British bore the brunt of anti-French military operations in Spain. In what they called the Peninsular War, a grueling war of attrition, their forces drove the French out of Portugal. After five years of fighting and many reversals, they pushed the French back across the Pyrénées in November 1813. The British commander, the Duke of Wellington, grasped the French predicament when he said: "The more ground the French hold down in Spain, the weaker they will be at any given point."

About 30,000 Spanish **guerilla** fighters helped wear down the French and forced the occupiers to struggle for survival in hostile country. The guerillas drew French forces from the main battlefields, inflicted casualties, impeded the French access to food, and punished Spanish collaborators. Their harassment kept the invaders in a constant state of anxiety, which led the French to adopt harsh measures in reprisal. But these "pacification" tactics only escalated the war's brutality and further enraged the Spanish people.

Together, the Spanish regulars, the guerillas, and the British expeditionary force kept a massive French army of up to 300,000 men pinned down in Spain. Napoleon referred to the war as his "Spanish ulcer," an open sore that would not heal. Though he held the rebel fighters in contempt, other Europeans were inspired by their example of armed resistance to France.

The Spanish Liberals The war, however, proved a disaster for Spanish liberals. Torn between loyalty to Joseph, who would have liked to be a liberal ruler, and nationalist rebels, liberals faced a difficult dilemma. Those who collaborated with Joseph hoped to spare the people from a brutal war and to institute reform from above in the tradition of Spanish enlightened absolutism. But they found that Joseph could not rule independently; Napoleon gave the orders in Spain and relied on his generals to implement them. The liberals who joined the rebellion organized a provisional government by reviving the ancient Spanish parliament, or Cortes, in the southern town of Cádiz. Like the French National Assembly of 1789, the Cortes of Cádiz drafted a liberal constitution in 1812 (see "Spanish Liberals Draft a Constitution, 1812," above), which pleased the

British and was therefore tolerated for the time being by the juntas.

In reality, most nationalist rebels despised the liberals. They were fighting for the Catholic Church, the Spanish monarchy, and the old way of life. When in 1814 Wellington finally drove the French out of Spain and former crown prince Ferdinand VII took the throne, the joy of the Cádiz liberals quickly evaporated. As a royalist mob sacked the Cortes building, Ferdinand tore up the constitution of 1812, reinstated absolutism, restored the monasteries and the Inquisition, revived censorship, and arrested the leading liberals. Nationalist reactionaries emerged as the victors of the Spanish rebellion.

Independence in Spanish America   The Creoles, descendants of Spanish settlers who were born in the New World, also profited from the upheaval in Spain. Spain had been cut off from its vast empire of American colonies in 1805, when the British navy won control of the Atlantic after the Battle of Trafalgar. In 1807 a British force attacked Buenos Aires in Spain's viceroyalty of the Río de la Plata (now Argentina). The Argentines—who raised excellent cattle on the *pampas*, or grassy plains—were eager to trade their beef and hides for British goods, but Spain's rigid mercantilism had always prevented such beneficial commerce. The Argentines welcomed the prospect of free trade, but not the prospect of British conquest. With Spain unable to defend them, the Creoles organized their own militia and drove off the British, pushed aside the Spanish viceroy, and took power into their own hands. The subsequent upheaval in Spain led the Argentines to declare their independence. After Ferdinand regained the Spanish throne in 1814, he sent an army to reclaim the colony, but the Argentines, under General José de San Martín, drove it off, and Argentina made good on its claim to full independence.

Rebellion spread throughout Spanish America, led above all by Simón Bolívar, revered in the hemisphere as "The Liberator." After Napoleon removed the king of Spain in 1808, the Creoles in Spain's viceroyalty of New Granada (encompassing modern-day Venezuela, Colombia, and Ecuador) elected a congress, which declared independence from Spain. An arduous, protracted war with the Spanish garrisons followed, and by 1816 Spain had regained control of the region.

Bolívar resumed the struggle and gradually wore down the Spanish forces; in one campaign his army marched six hundred miles from the torrid Venezuelan lowlands over the snow-capped Andes Mountains to Colombia. Finally in 1819 the Spanish conceded defeat. Bolívar's dream of one unified, conservative republic of Gran Colombia soon disintegrated under regional pres-

MAP 21.3 SOUTH AMERICA AFTER INDEPENDENCE
◆ For an online version, go to www.mhhe.com/chambers9 > chapter 21 > book maps

sures into several independent states, but not before Bolívar launched one final military campaign and liberated Peru, Spain's remaining colony in South America (see map 21.3).

MAP 21.4 THE RUSSIAN CAMPAIGN OF 1812
◆ For an online version, go to www.mhhe.com/chambers9 > chapter 21 > book maps

The Russian Debacle

Napoleon did not yet realize in 1811 that his entanglement in Spain would drain French military power and encourage resistance in Central Europe. On the contrary, never were the emperor's schemes more grandiose. Surveying the crumbling state system of Europe, he imagined that it could be replaced with a vast empire, ruled from Paris and based on the Napoleonic Code. He mistakenly believed that the era of the balance of power among Europe's states was over and that nationalist sentiments need not constrain his actions.

Russia now loomed as the main obstacle to Napoleon's imperial reorganization and domination of Europe. Russia, a restive ally with ambitions of its own in Eastern Europe, resented the restrictions on its trade under the Continental System. British diplomats, anti-Napoleonic exiles such as Baron Stein of Prussia, and nationalist reactionaries at court all pressured the tsar to resist Napoleon. Russian court liberals, more concerned with domestic reforms, hoped on the contrary that Alexander would maintain peace with France, but by 1812 their influence on the tsar had waned. For his part, Napoleon wanted to enforce the Continental System and humble Russia. As he bluntly put it: "Let Alexander defeat the Persians, but don't let him meddle in the affairs of Europe."

Napoleon prepared for his most momentous military campaign. His objective was to annihilate Russia's army or, at the least, to conquer Moscow and chase the army to the point of disarray. To this end he marshaled a "Grand Army" of almost 600,000 men (half of them French, the remainder from his satellite states and allies) and moved them steadily by forced marches across Central Europe into Russia. The Russians responded by retreating in orderly fashion and avoiding a fight. Many Russian nobles abandoned their estates and burned their crops to the ground, leaving the Grand Army to operate far from its supply bases in territory stripped of food. At Borodino the Russians finally made a stand and sustained a frightful 45,000 casualties, but the remaining Russian troops managed to withdraw in order. Napoleon lost 35,000 men in that battle, but far more men and horses were dying from hunger, thirst, fatigue, and disease in the march across Russia's unending, barren territory. The greatly depleted ranks of the Grand Army staggered into Moscow on September 14, 1812, but the Russian army was still intact and far from demoralized.

The Destruction of the Grand Army In fact, the condition of Moscow demoralized the French. They found the city deserted and bereft of badly needed supplies. The next night Moscow was mysteriously set ablaze, causing such extensive damage as to make it unfit to be the Grand Army's winter quarters. Realistic advisers warned the emperor that his situation was dangerous, while others told him what he wished to hear—that

Just as Goya's drawings captured the unique ferocity of the Spanish campaign, this illustration evokes the particular agonies of climate and logistics in the Russian debacle.
Photo Archive, Nationalbibliothek Austria

Russian resistance was crumbling. For weeks Napoleon hesitated. Logistically it was imperative that the French begin to retreat immediately, but that would constitute a political defeat. Only on October 19 did Napoleon finally order a retreat, but the order came too late.

The delay forced an utterly unrealistic pace on the bedraggled army as it headed west. Supplies were gone, medical care for the thousands of wounded nonexistent, horses lacking. Food shortages compelled foraging parties to sweep far from the main body of troops, where these men often fell prey to Russian guerillas. And there was the weather—Russia's bitter cold and deep snow, in which no commander would wish to find himself leading a retreat of several hundred miles, laden with wounded and loot but without food, fuel, horses, or proper clothing. Napoleon's poor planning, the harsh weather, and the operation of Russian guerilla bands made the long retreat a nightmare of suffering for the Grand Army. No more than 100,000 troops survived the ordeal. Worse yet, the Prussian contingent took the occasion to desert Napoleon, opening the possibility of mass defections and the formation of a new anti-Napoleonic coalition.

German Resistance and the Last Coalition

Napoleon was evidently impervious to the horror around him. On the sleigh ride out of Russia, he was al-ready planning how to raise new armies and set things aright. Other European statesmen, however, were ready to capitalize on Napoleon's defeat in Russia and demolish his empire once and for all. Provocative calls for a national uprising in various German states to throw off the tyrant's yoke reinforced the efforts of diplomats like Prussia's Baron Stein and Austria's Klemens von Metternich to revive the anti-Napoleonic coalition.

Reform from Above in Prussia In Prussia after the defeat of 1806, the government had introduced reforms intended to improve the quality of the bureaucracy by offering nonnobles more access to high positions and by reducing some of the nobility's privileges. The monarchy hoped thereby to salvage the position of the nobility and the authority of the state. Prussian military reformers adopted new methods of recruitment to build up a trained reserve force that could be rapidly mobilized, along with a corps of reserve officers to take command of these units. Prussia, in other words, hoped to achieve French-style efficiency and military mobilization without resorting to new concepts of citizenship, constitutions, legislatures, or the abolition of seigneurialism. On the level of propaganda and the symbolic gesture, writers in Prussia and other German states called for a popular war of liberation under the slogan "With God for King and Fatherland."

Against this background of Prussian military preparation and growing nationalist sentiment, the diplomats maneuvered and waited. Finally, in March 1813, King Frederick William III of Prussia signed a treaty with Russia to form an offensive coalition against Napoleon. A great struggle for Germany ensued between the Russo-Prussian forces and Napoleon and his allies. Austria continued to claim neutrality and offered to mediate the dispute, but at a meeting in Prague, Napoleon rejected an offer of peace in exchange for restoring all French conquests since 1802.

In August, as Napoleon learned of new defeats in Spain, Habsburg Emperor Francis finally declared war on his son-in-law. Napoleon called up underage and overage conscripts and was able to field one last army, but his major southern German ally, Bavaria, finally changed sides. A great battle raged around Leipzig for three days in October, and when the smoke cleared, Napoleon was in full retreat. German states were free from Napoleon's domination, but Prussia's rulers were also free from the need to concede further reforms in the political and social order.

The Fall of Napoleon   In the belief that he could rely on his conscription machine, Napoleon had rebuffed offers by the allies to negotiate peace in 1813. In fact, however, he reached the end of the line in November 1813 with a desperate call for 300,000 more men to defend France against the allies. Difficulties were inevitable, wrote one prefect, "when the number of men required exceeds the number available." Another reported: "There is scarcely a family that is not oppressed by conscription." Alongside sizable contingents of Italians, Germans, and other foreigners from the annexed territories and satellite states, nearly 2.5 million Frenchmen had been drafted by Napoleon. At least 1 million of those conscripts never returned.

With Napoleon driven back into France, British troops reinforced the coalition to ensure that it would not disintegrate once Central Europe had been liberated. The coalition offered final terms to the emperor: He could retain his throne, but France would be reduced to her "normal frontiers." (The precise meaning of this term was left purposely vague.) Napoleon, still hoping for a dramatic reversal, chose to fight, and with some reluctance the allies invaded France. Napoleon led the remnants of his army skillfully but to no avail. The French had lost confidence in him, conscription had reached its limits, and no popular spirit of resistance to invasion developed as it had in 1792. Paris fell in March 1814. The price of this defeat was unconditional surrender and the emperor's abdication. Napoleon was transported to the island of Elba, between Corsica and Italy, over which he was granted sovereignty. After twenty-two years of exile, the Bourbon Dynasty returned to France.

The Napoleonic Legend

For Napoleon, imperial authority—originating with him in France and radiating throughout Europe—represented the principle of rational progress. In his view, the old notion of balance of power among European states merely served as an excuse for the British to pursue their selfish interests. While paying lip service to the notion of Italian, Spanish, and Polish nationhood, Napoleon generally scorned patriotic opposition to his domination as an outmoded, reactionary sentiment—exemplified by the "barbaric" guerillas in Spain fighting for king and religion. Modern-minded Europeans, he believed, would see beyond historic, parochial traditions to the prospect of a new European order. Indeed, Napoleon's credibility with some reformers in Europe was considerable. The Bavarian prime minister, for instance, justified his collaboration with France in 1810 in these words: "The spirit of the new age is one of mobility, destruction, creativity. . . . The wars against France offer the [unfortunate] possibility of bringing back old constitutions, privileges, and property relations."

During his final exile, however, Napoleon came to recognize that nationalism was not necessarily reactionary—as one could plainly see in the nationalistic but liberal Cortes of Cádiz of 1812. Progressive thinking and nationalist aspirations could coexist. From exile Napoleon rewrote his life story to portray his career as a series of defensive wars against selfish adversaries (especially Britain) and as a battle in behalf of the nations of Europe against reactionary dynasties. In this way, Napoleon brilliantly (if falsely) put himself on the side of the future.

These memoirs and recollections from exile formed the basis of the Napoleonic legend, as potent a force historically, perhaps, as the reality of the Napoleonic experience. The image they projected emphasized how General Bonaparte had consolidated what was best about the French Revolution while pacifying a bitterly divided nation and saving it from chaos. They cast the imperial experience in a deceptively positive light, glossed over the tyranny and unending military slaughter, and aligned Napoleon with reason, efficiency, and modernity (see "Napoleon Justifies Himself in 1815," p. 638).

The Napoleonic legend also evoked a sense of grandeur and glory that moved ordinary people in years to come. Napoleon's dynamism and energy became his ultimate inspirational legacy to succeeding generations. In this way, the Napoleonic legend fed on the Romantic movement in literature and the arts. Many young romantics (including the poet William Wordsworth and

NAPOLEON JUSTIFIES HIMSELF IN 1815

"I have cleansed the Revolution, ennobled the common people, and restored the authority of kings. I have stirred all men to competition, I have rewarded merit wherever I found it, I have pushed back the boundaries of greatness. Is there any point on which I could be attacked and on which a historian could not take up my defense? My despotism? He can prove that dictatorship was absolutely necessary. Will it be said that I restricted freedom? He will be able to prove that license, anarchy, and general disorder were still on our doorstep. Shall I be accused of having loved war too much? He will show that I was always on the defensive. That I wanted to set up a universal monarchy? He will explain that it was merely the fortuitous result of circumstances and that I was led to it step by step by our very enemies. My ambition? Ah, no doubt he will find that I had ambition, a great deal of it—but the grandest and noblest perhaps, that ever was: the ambition of establishing and consecrating at last the kingdom of reason and the full exercise, the complete enjoyment, of all human capabilities!"

From B. Las Cases (ed.), *Mémorial de Sainte-Hélène.*

the composer Ludwig van Beethoven) saw in the French Revolution a release of creativity and a liberation of the individual spirit. Napoleon's tyranny eventually alienated most such creative people. But the Napoleonic legend, by emphasizing the bold creativity of his career, meshed nicely with the sense of individual possibility that the romantics cultivated. Napoleon's retrospective justifications of his reign may not be convincing, but one can only marvel at the irrepressible audacity of the man.

Summary

In the confrontations between Napoleon and his European adversaries, France still embodied the specter of revolution. Even if the revolutionary legacy in France amounted by that time to little more than Napoleon's contempt for the inefficiency and outmoded institutions of the old regime, France after Brumaire remained a powerful challenge to the status quo. Napoleon intended to abolish feudalism, institute centralized administrations, and implant the French Civil Code in all of France's satellite states. But by 1808 his extravagant international ambitions relied on increasingly tyrannical and militaristic measures. These in turn provoked a range of responses, including nationalist rebellions. Britain and Russia, then Prussia and Austria, joined forces once more to bring the Napoleonic Empire down, to restore the balance of power in Europe, and to reinstall the Bourbons in France. But the clock could not really be set back from Europe's experience of revolution and Napoleonic transformation. The era of modern political and social conflicts had begun.

QUESTIONS FOR FURTHER THOUGHT

1. Apart from Jesus, more books have probably been written about Napoleon than any other historical figure. What accounts for this enduring fascination? Compare Napoleon to dominant leaders of the past whom you have studied (e.g., Alexander the Great, Caesar, Philip II, and Louis XIV).

2. Was Napoleon a revolutionary? Did he consolidate or betray the French Revolution?
3. Using the boxed excerpt in which Napoleon justifies his conduct as a starting point, what is *your* assessment of his reign?

Recommended Reading
(See also chapter 20)

Sources

De Caulaincourt, Armand. *With Napoleon in Russia.* 1935. A remarkable account of the diplomacy and warfare of the 1812 debacle by a man at Napoleon's side.

Herold, J. C. (ed.). *The Mind of Napoleon.* 1961.

Thompson, J. M. (ed.). *Napoleon Self-Revealed.* 1934.

*Walter, Jakob. *The Diary of a Napoleonic Foot Soldier.* M. Raeff (ed.). 1991. A vivid and appalling account of the Russian campaign.

Studies

*Bergeron, Louis. *France under Napoleon.* 1981. A fresh and insightful evaluation of the Napoleonic settlement in France.

*Broers, Michael. *Europe under Napoleon, 1799–1815.* 1996. An incisive and up-to-date synthesis on French expansion in Europe.

Chandler, David. *Napoleon's Marshals.* 1986. By a leading expert on Napoleonic military history.

*Connelley, Owen. *Blundering to Glory: Napoleon's Military Campaigns.* 1988. An irreverent but incisive account of Napoleon's military leadership.

———. *Napoleon's Satellite Kingdoms.* 1965. A study of the states conquered by France and ruled by the Bonaparte family.

*Dwyer, Philip (ed.). *Napoleon and Europe.* 2001. A well-focused yet wide-ranging collection of essays with a comprehensive bibliography.

*Ellis, Geoffrey. *Napoleon.* 1997. A concise profile of the era.

Elting, John. *Swords around a Throne: Napoleon's Grande Armée.* 1988. An eminently readable military history.

*Englund, Steven. *Napoleon: A Political Life.* 2004. The most recent, and perhaps the best, one-volume biography in English.

Esdaile, Charles. *Fighting Napoleon: Guerrillas, Bandits, and Adventurers in Spain, 1808–1814.* 2004.

Forrest, Alan. *Conscripts and Deserters: The Army and French Society during the Revolution and Empire.* 1988. A study of popular resistance to revolutionary and Napoleonic conscription.

Gates, David. *The Spanish Ulcer: A History of the Peninsular War.* 1986. On the Spanish rebellion, the French response, and Wellington's expeditionary force.

*Geyl, Pieter. *Napoleon, For and Against.* 1949. Napoleon and the historians, as reviewed by a Dutch scholar with no illusions.

Hazareesingh, Sudhir. *The Legend of Napoleon.* 2004. A lively and suggestive study of an elusive subject.

*Lynch, John. *The Spanish American Revolutions, 1808–1826.* 1986. A comprehensive account of the independence movements in Spanish America and their aftermath.

Lyons, Martyn. *France under the Directory.* 1975. A brief topical survey of the Revolution's later, unheroic phase.

*———. *Napoleon Bonaparte and the Legacy of the French Revolution.* 1994. A good recent textbook.

Marcus, G. J. *A Naval History of England, II: The Age of Nelson.* 1971. The standard history of British naval supremacy.

Palmer, Robert R. *The World of the French Revolution.* 1971. Emphasizes the interplay of French power and revolutionary movements outside of France.

Rothenberg, Gunther. *The Art of Warfare in the Age of Napoleon.* 1978. A good analysis of strategy and tactics.

*Sheehan, James. *German History, 1770–1866.* 1989. An outstanding overview of this and other periods in German history.

*Sutherland, D. M. G. *France, 1789–1815: Revolution and Counter-revolution.* 1985. A fine general history of France in this period.

Tulard, Jean. *Napoleon: The Myth of the Savior.* 1984. A synthesis by the leading French expert on Napoleon.

*Woloch, Isser. *Napoleon and His Collaborators: The Making of a Dictatorship.* 2001.

Woolf, Stuart. *A History of Italy, 1700–1860.* 1979. An authoritative general history, with fine chapters on this period.

*Available in paperback.

Leander Russ
THE AUSTRIAN SOUTHERN RAILWAY FROM VIENNA TO BADEN, **1847**
The contrast of new and old: The train from Vienna to Baden frightened the horses in this
watercolor done in 1847.
AKG London

Chapter Twenty–Two

FOUNDATIONS OF THE NINETEENTH CENTURY: POLITICS AND SOCIAL CHANGE

THE POLITICS OF ORDER • THE PROGRESS OF INDUSTRIALIZATION •
THE SOCIAL EFFECTS

After twenty-five years of war, peace was a dramatic change. The first concern of the powers that had opposed Napoleon was to guarantee that no one state would be able to dominate the Continent again.

The wars against France had been about more, however, than territory or the balance of power. The allies had fought to preserve monarchy and social hierarchy, and they sought a peace that would prevent events like the French Revolution in the future. The first step was to impose regimes that would be safely conservative. For the most part, they restored the dynasties that had been overturned. These restored regimes were nonetheless new, and establishing them raised classical questions about the body politic—how power should be organized, what institutions should direct society, and who should participate in deciding policy. The possibility of revolution thus remained a fact of life, dreaded by some and hoped for by others, reinvoked in each country by the risings, acts of repression, and major reforms of the next thirty years.

The challenge to the restoration experiment was not just political. Enforced stability was expected to bring social peace and economic benefits. In some parts of Europe, however, industrialization was under way and beginning to transform society. The technologies that stimulated economic development and the changing economy's impact on social structure and family were also part of the political and social system of the restoration and are treated in this chapter. Coming after the French Revolution and Napoleon, these changes opened the way to a new era of passionate politics and pervasive social change. How Europeans dealt with the resulting tensions is the subject of chapter 23.

1815	1820	1825	1830

Charles X crowned King of France **1824** ●

Greek Revolution begins **1821** ●

Uprisings in Italy and Spain **1820–1821** ▬

Carlsbad Decrees **1819** ●

● **1815** Napoleon's "Hundred Days"

▬ **1814–1815** Congress of Vienna

THE POLITICS OF ORDER

Allied leaders wanted to design a peace that would impose order across the continent. Once they settled the boundaries between states, they placed crowned heads on hereditary thrones and pressed these conservative monarchs to prevent disorder in their own lands. Internationally, they sought to establish an intricate balance of power that would make war unlikely and ensure that the major powers would join in stamping out any future threat of revolution. But revolutions broke out in 1820–1821 and 1830, an early measure of the limited effectiveness of the experiment in international conservatism.

The Congress of Vienna

To forge these arrangements, the great international conference known as the **Congress of Vienna** met in September 1814, an occasion for serious deliberations and elaborate pomp centered on the crowned heads of Austria, Prussia, Russia, and dozens of lesser states. Officials, expert advisers, princesses and countesses, dancers and artists, and the ambitious of every rank flocked to the Austrian capital. Their contrived gaiety and bewigged elegance made the Congress a symbol of aristocratic restoration.

The business of the Congress remained the responsibility of the four great powers—Austria, Great Britain, Russia, and Prussia—an inner circle to which France was soon admitted. Prince Klemens von Metternich, who had led the Austrian Empire to this triumph, conducted the affairs of the Congress with such skill that its provisions can be seen as largely his work. Handsome, elegant, and arrogant, Metternich was the epitome of an aristocrat, fluent in all the ma-

In the tradition of aristocratic portraits, Prince Metternich is conveyed as a polished courtier; the medals, symbolic of his position and power, are also a reminder of the purpose of his policies.
Mansell/TimePix/Getty Images

jor European languages, a dandy who dabbled in science and shone in the ballroom. More consistently than any other single figure, he had understood the extent of Napoleon's ambitions and had welded the international alliance that defeated the French emperor.

642

1833 *Zollverein* in Germany

Abolition of Corn Laws in Britain; economic depression sweeps Europe **1846** ●

Crystal Palace Exhibition **1851** ●

The Congress of Vienna is portrayed here as a kind of elegant salon in which the very clothes these statesmen wore mix the styles of the old regime and the new century.
AKG London

Metternich was named foreign minister of Austria in 1809 and would hold that position for nearly forty years, tying his vision of European order to Austria's interests. Metternich was generally supported by Lord Castlereagh, England's able foreign minister. Russia's Tsar Alexander I, who acted as his own chief diplomat, was more unpredictable. Educated in the ideas of enlightened absolutism, Alexander was now more given to mysticism and conservative fear and was attracted to grandiose programs upsetting to the careful calculations of self-interest by which the Congress reached agreement.

The Peace Terms The most pressing issue these statesmen faced was the future of France. Most of the allies favored restoring some sort of monarchy, and the Treaty of Paris, signed in May 1814, had recognized as king Louis XVIII, a brother of the executed Bourbon, Louis XVI. The treaty also restored France to its slightly expanded frontiers of 1792. A settlement covering all the territory affected by the Napoleonic wars would take longer. Warily watching one another, the allies soon included Prince Talleyrand, the French representative, in their deliberations. A former bishop who had served the Directory, he had helped Napoleon to power and been his foreign minister for eight years. Talleyrand was now the indispensable servant of Louis XVIII, using all his famous shrewdness to regain for France its former influence.

The concerns of these men focused on continental Europe, for only Great Britain among the victors had extensive interests overseas, and British designs on South Africa, Ceylon, and Malta were modest enough to be accepted by the other European states. Europe was considered the sphere of the great powers; each closely weighed the claims of the others, and all especially watched Russia, with its mammoth armies, undefined ambitions, and quixotic tsar.

Conflicting interests kept Austria, Prussia, and Russia from dividing up Poland as they had in the eighteenth century, but neither did they want to risk creating an independent Poland. So Russia received most of Poland to be ruled as a separate kingdom, and Prussia took about half of Saxony—a triumph of old regime diplomacy in which each of the powers got something (see map 22.1). Prussia was also given greatly enlarged territories in the Rhineland, ensuring that formidable Prussian armies would stand along the French border. The former Austrian Netherlands were absorbed into a new, independent Kingdom of the Netherlands, which created another strong buffer against France. It also met the British desire that no major power control the Low Countries' important river ports across the channel from England. Austria, in return for ceding the southern Netherlands, acquired Venetia and recovered Lombardy, which greatly strengthened Austrian dominance of northern Italy. The other duchies of northern Italy went to dukes with close Austrian ties.[1]

The terms agreed on at Vienna constituted the most extensive European peace settlement since the treaty of Westphalia in 1648. Each of the victors had gained territory, and France was surrounded by states capable of resisting any future French aggression. The final act was signed in June 1815 by the five great powers and by Sweden, Spain, and Portugal, a gracious recognition of their past importance.

Napoleon's Hundred Days The deliberations of the Congress were interrupted in March 1815 by the terrifying news of Napoleon's escape from exile. He had tried to make the best of ruling the island of Elba and had even showed something of his old flair as he designed uniforms, held receptions, and inquired into the local economy. But the island principality was far too small to contain an emperor's ambition. Landing in the south of France, he was joined by units of the French army as he moved toward Paris. Louis XVIII waited for signs of resistance that did not develop, then climbed into his carriage and once again headed for the eastern border. Napoleon became the ruler of France without firing a shot. He then tried to negotiate with the powers allied against him, but they declared him an outlaw and quickly assembled their troops. After several minor battles, allied armies led by Wellington defeated Napoleon for the last time at Waterloo on June 18. They dispatched him to the more distant island of St. Helena, in the South Atlantic.

Napoleon's dashing venture lasted only a hundred days, but its effects were felt far longer. The terms of peace were altered: France was required to pay an indemnity, and its boundaries were reduced to those of 1789. The Bourbons again returned to the French throne, haunted by the specter of renewed revolution and permanently embarrassed by the ease with which Napoleon had retaken power. Napoleon had used his Hundred Days to soften the memory of his despotism with the promise of a more liberal constitution. Even from St. Helena, he continued to propagandize for Bonapartism, redefining it as a system for achieving both national strength and social change. Allied statesmen, with power on their side, did not pay so much attention to popular opinion.

Principles of International Order The **restorations** of 1815 acknowledged many of the changes of the past twenty-five years. The Bourbons were restored in France but now governed with a constitution. In Germany, the Holy Roman Empire and hundreds of minor German principalities, all abolished by Napoleon, were not restored but were consolidated into thirty-nine states, including Prussia and Austria, and joined in a loose confederation. The Congress established the principle that navigation on international riverways should be open to all and set down rules of diplomatic conduct useful to this day. For the next hundred years the Continent would be free of a general European war, due in part to the complicated arrangements negotiated at Vienna.

[1] The Kingdom of Sardinia would have liked Lombardy but got Genoa, the ancient Italian maritime republic. Russia took Finland from Sweden, which in turn got Norway from Denmark.

MAP 22.1 EUROPE, 1815
Examine the territorial boundaries of Europe after the Congress of Vienna. What do you notice about the extent of the French and Austrian empires in 1815 compared to 1810 (see map 21.1)? Compare the compact nation-states of Western Europe to the geographically fragmented areas of Italy and Germany, and to the multinational Habsburg, Ottoman, and Russian empires.
◆ For an online version, go to www.mhhe.com/chambers9 > chapter 22 > book maps

The Congress was less impressive in the realm of ideas. Recognizing the need to invoke some general principle to justify such far-reaching arrangements, Talleyrand suggested they were only restoring governments made legitimate by tradition and public support; but that justification gave more weight to public opinion than his colleagues could accept. Aiming for something more stirring, Tsar Alexander proposed a Holy Alliance, an agreement that all states would conduct their affairs according to Christian teachings. The prin-

ciple seemed vague enough; and though some were publicly skeptical, nearly all European governments agreed. Three refused: The Ottoman sultan cared too little for Christian teachings, the pope cared too much, and Britain rejected any permanent commitments on the Continent. Historians, too, have tended to dismiss the Holy Alliance as a meaningless expression of Alexander's mysticism. Yet there was something modern in the tsar's recognition that the international order should make some moral appeal to public opinion.

METTERNICH ANALYZES THE THREAT TO STABILITY

On December 15, 1820, Metternich wrote the Habsburg emperor from the international conference he had called to deal with the threat of revolution. Metternich argued that all monarchs must act together against the common threat, which he blamed on the middle class.

"Europe presents itself to the impartial observer under an aspect at the same time deplorable and peculiar. We find everywhere the people praying for the maintenance of peace and tranquillity, faithful to God and their Princes. . . . The governments, having lost their balance, are frightened, intimidated, and thrown into confusion by the cries of the intermediary class of society, which, placed between the Kings and their subjects, breaks the scepter of the monarch, and usurps the cry of the people—that class so often disowned by the people, and nevertheless too much listened to. . . .

"We see this intermediary class abandon itself with a blind fury and animosity. . . . to all the means which seem proper to assuage its thirst for power, applying itself to the task of persuading Kings that their rights are confined to sitting upon a throne, while those of the people are to govern, and to attack all that centuries have bequeathed as holy and worthy of man's respect—denying, in fact, the value of the past, and declaring themselves the masters of the future.

". . . The evil is plain; the means used by the faction which causes these disorders are so blamable in principle, so criminal in their application, and expose the faction itself to so many dangers, that . . . we are convinced that society can no longer be saved without strong and vigorous resolutions on the part of the Governments. . . .

"By this course the monarchs will fulfill the duties imposed upon them by Him who, by entrusting them with power, has charged them to watch the maintenance of justice, and the rights of all, to avoid the paths of error. . . . and to show themselves as they are, fathers invested with the authority belonging by right to the heads of families, to prove that, in days of mourning, they know how to be just, wise, and therefore strong. . . .

"The Governments, in establishing the principle of stability, will in no wise exclude the development of what is good, for stability is not immobility. But it is for those who are burdened with the heavy task of government to augment the well-being of their people! It is for Governments to regulate it according to necessity and to suit the times. It is not by concessions, which the factious strive to force from legitimate power, . . . that wise reforms can be carried out. That all the good possible should be done is our most ardent wish; but . . . even real good should be done only by those who unite to the right of authority the means of enforcing it."

From Prince Richard Metternich (ed.), *Memoirs of Prince Metternich, 1815–1829*, Mrs. Alexander Napier (tr.), Scribner's Sons Publishers, 1970.

Opposition to the Settlement   Proponents of change—Europe's liberals, reformers, and nationalists—would later recall the Congress of Vienna as the occasion during which aristocrats danced while foisting reactionary regimes on the people of Europe. Such critics cited the brutal shuffling of territory without regard to the claims of nationality or constitutions.

In fact, the new order was not so solid as it seemed. In 1820 and 1821 uprisings occurred in both Italy and Spain, led by young army officers who were influenced by memories of Napoleonic reforms and convinced that individual advancement and efficient government required a constitution. Metternich quickly called for a **"Concert of Europe"** to snuff the flames of revolution by force, but unanimity among the former allies was breaking down. Great Britain disapproved sending foreign troops to put down a constitutional government in Naples and did not attend the conference, which approved Austrian intervention in Naples and called on France to send troops against an uprising in Spain. French forces met little resistance in Spain, and their royal parade was welcomed by conservatives throughout Europe as evidence of the French monarchy's revived prestige.

The next step, some suggested, was to put down the revolts in Latin America, where leaders cited principles associated with the French and American revolutions. Movements for independence from Spain and Portugal, which had steadily gained ground from the time of Napoleon, burst forth anew with the 1820 revolution in Spain. But talk of intervention brought stern warnings from Britain and the proud announcement of the Monroe Doctrine from the United States, declaring the Americas outside the sphere of European power politics.

The Concert of Europe was hardly invoked at all when Greeks revolted against Ottoman Turk rule in 1821. Cries for freedom from that home of ancient democracy excited liberals throughout Europe, an early

Eugène Delacroix
GREECE EXPIRING ON THE RUINS OF MISSOLONGHI, **1826**
The Greek revolution captured the imagination of many Europeans, and Delacroix's *Greece Expiring* has all the elements of that fascination. Greece is symbolized by an ordinary peasant girl who is also a classical figure of liberty, come alive. The Turk in the background, a colorful and exotic figure of oppression, evokes centuries of conflict. Romanticism, nationalism, and political liberty come together on the stones of Greek culture and the arm of a martyred freedom fighter.
Musée des Beaux-Arts, Bordeaux, France. Erich Lessing/Art Resource, NY

demonstration of the power of nationalist movements that would be repeated throughout the century. Metternich restrained Russia from rushing to war against the Ottomans as it often had in the past, but he could not keep the British and French fleets from intervening in 1827, when the sultan seemed about to subdue the Greeks. Russia declared war a few months later. Greece was granted independence in 1829 on terms arranged by the European powers, stipulating that it must have a king but one who was not a member of the ruling fam-

CHRONOLOGY
Challenges to the Vienna Settlement

May 1814	Treaty of Paris.
September 1814– June 1815	Congress of Vienna.
March 1815–June 1815	Napoleon's 100 days.
1817	German students at Wartburg.
1820–1821	Revolts in Spain and Italy.
1821–1829	Greek war of independence.
1825	Decembrist rising in Russia.
1830	Revolution in France, Belgium.

ily of a major power. With that policy, the leading European states altered the status quo after all. They did so partly in response to public opinion, but they also made sure that the Greek rising would go no further. In the name of Greek freedom, Britain, France, and Russia displayed a willingness to use force and an eagerness to carve up the Ottoman Empire that foreshadowed the practice of imperialism later in the century.

The Pillars of the Restoration: Russia, Austria, Prussia

Even the most reactionary rulers accepted some of the changes (and the potential for increased power) brought by revolution, war, and Napoleonic occupation. To maintain social order in the nineteenth century, the state would need to be more effective than before in order to sustain large armies and collect more taxes, support a better-trained bureaucracy, dispense justice more evenly, and provide more services. Because they would thus affect the lives of their subjects more directly, governments would have to be more concerned with popular sentiment. For these reasons, the organization of the state became an issue even in conservative Russia, Austria, and Prussia, the guardians of the European restoration.

The Russian Empire   By 1820 Tsar Alexander had abandoned his earlier enthusiasm for new ideas. As Metternich's staunchest ally, Alexander imposed harsh censorship, increased restrictions on universities, and made sure that the constitution granted to the newly organized Kingdom of Poland was largely ignored. On Alexander's death in 1825, a group of young army officers, the Decembrists, attempted a coup and called for a constitution in Russia. Like the leaders of the revolts in Naples and Spain a few years earlier, the Decembrists saw a constitution as an essential step toward a more efficient and progressive administration. Their poorly planned and isolated conspiracy was easily defeated, but it would be remembered by conservatives as an ever-present danger and by revolutionaries as part of Russia's radical tradition.

Alexander's younger brother, Nicholas I, succeeded him, convinced that only a loyal army and his own decisiveness had prevented revolution. He turned Russia into Europe's strongest pillar of reaction by his example at home and his willingness to use force abroad. He was a diligent administrator who gave his closest attention to the army and the police and who established a more effective bureaucracy by making it less attached to the nobility.

Nevertheless, petty corruption, the arrogance of local officials, and fear of change continued to undermine the government's capacity to manage a vast land of varied peoples in which communication was poor and few had the means or the will to effect reform. Most thoughtful people, including the state's highest officials, agreed that serfdom had become a hindrance to Russia's development, but they proposed no solution. Despite fears that education bred discontent, the government built schools.

Intellectuals who expected Russia to develop along familiar European lines were known as Westernizers. Those who stressed the uniqueness of Russia were called **Slavophiles,** and they argued that Russia's Orthodox Christian religion, peasant communes, and traditional culture gave Russia a unique destiny. Despite this urgent questioning about Russia's place in a changing world and despite bitter Poles, angry peasants, and its own immobility, the authority of the Russian state remained. Nicholas would watch with pride in 1848 as his empire escaped the revolutions that swept over most thrones of Europe.

The Habsburg Empire   Habsburg rule over German, Italian, and Eastern European lands relied on a well-organized bureaucracy. Forged by Maria Theresa and Joseph II, that system of government had enabled Austria to survive the Napoleonic wars without dramatic transformation despite repeated defeat. Metternich and others recognized the need for domestic reform, but their projects for better fiscal planning, stronger local government, and recognition of the empire's diverse nationalities came to nothing. Habsburg rule remained locked in stalemate between an increasingly cautious central bureaucracy and selfish local aristocracies.

Hungary proved particularly troublesome for the Habsburg Empire, for the dominant **Magyar** aristocracy had a strong sense of their historical identity and a good deal of power, although they remained an ethnic minority in their own country. Emperor Francis I grudgingly acknowledged many of their claims, and by the 1840s Magyar had replaced German as the official language of administration and schooling in Hungary. More demands followed. The campaign for a more representative parliament and related reforms was led by Lajos Kossuth, who became Hungary's leading statesman, able through newspapers and public meetings to reach much of the nation.

This widespread agitation, encouraged other groups subject to Habsburg rule to claim national rights of their own (see map 22.1). Much of Polish Galicia rose in revolt in 1846; but weakened by the bitter antagonism between Polish peasants and their masters, the uprising was soon suppressed. In Croatia and Bohemia, too, angry peasants and nationalists often had different aims. The various national groups opposed to Habsburg rule, often hostile to each other, were also internally divided by class, religion, and language. Their divisions helped sustain Habsburg rule. Throughout the empire, however, growing nationalist movements sought to overcome these social divisions, giving broader appeal to criticisms of Habsburg rule that came mainly from merchants and lawyers. At the center, in Vienna, despite much good advice and many promising plans, inaction remained the safest course.

Prussia and the German Confederation   Germans called the later battles against Napoleon (1813–1814) the Wars of Liberation; and after that common national experience, talk of "Germany" meant more than it had before. The Congress of Vienna acknowledged this awareness with the creation of the German Confederation. A cautious gesture toward national sentiment that preserved the position of the strongest local rulers, a confederation required some coordination among Germany's many states. Any stronger union was prevented by the rivalry of Austria and Prussia, distaste for reform among restoration regimes, and the conflicting ambitions of German princes. The Confederation's diet, a council of ambassadors from member states rather than a representative assembly, was permitted to legislate only on certain matters—characteristically, restriction of the press was one of them.

In practice, the German Confederation was important in German politics largely when Metternich wished it to be. He used it, for example, to suppress agitation led by nationalist and reformist student groups in the universities. In 1817 some of these groups organized a celebration of the three hundredth anniversary of Luther's theses with a rally, the Wartburg Festival. Several hundred young people gathered to drink, listen to speeches full of mystical nationalist rhetoric,

German authorities worried greatly that university students would be a center of political agitation, and this print from a series on student life in the 1820s suggests why. Privileged, educated, and idle young men meeting to drink and smoke were all too likely to talk about politics, spread radical ideas, and maybe even hatch plots.
AKG London

sing songs, and cheer as a Prussian military manual was tossed into a bonfire. Even such symbolic challenges to military authority alarmed governments in Berlin and Vienna. When a well-known reactionary writer was assassinated, the Confederation was pressed into issuing the Carlsbad Decrees of 1819, which intensified censorship, proscribed dangerous professors and students, outlawed fraternities and political clubs, and required each state to guarantee that its universities would be kept safely conservative (see "Policing Universities . . . ," p. 650).

Despite these fears, there was less agitation within the German Confederation than in most of the rest of Europe. Meanwhile, Prussian influence increased. Its national educational system was capped by the new but prestigious University of Berlin, its administration and its army seemed models of modern efficiency, and its policies included measures that stimulated economic growth. In 1818 Prussia lowered tariffs, allowing raw materials free entry into both its eastern and western Prussian territories. The results were so impressive

that within a decade the Prussian tariff was adopted by many of the smaller states that were nearly surrounded by Prussian territory. By 1833 most German governments except Austria had joined Prussia's customs union, the **Zollverein,** which proved a further spur to commerce. One of the most important steps toward German unification under Prussia had been taken without clear nationalist intent.

The Test of Restoration: Spain, Italy, and France

The durability of the conservative order that the Congress of Vienna sought to impose would depend less on the autocracies in Russia, Austria, and Prussia than on the new regimes imposed in Spain, Italy, and France. There, the effects of revolution and Bonapartism had been woven into the fabric of public life. Intensely divided over questions of government—its form, powers, and policies—conservatives and liberals alike considered politics central to everything else.

POLICING UNIVERSITIES—THE CARLSBAD DECREES

The Carlsbad Decrees, drafted by Metternich, were adopted by the Diet of the German Confederation in 1819 to be applied in all its member states. Their spirit is in complete opposition to the ideal of academic freedom.

"1. There shall be appointed for each university a special representative of the ruler of each state, the said representatives to have appropriate instructions and extended powers, and they shall have their place of residence where the university is located. . . .

"This representative shall enforce strictly the existing laws and disciplinary regulations, he shall observe with care the attitude shown by the university instructors in their public lectures and registered courses; and he shall, without directly interfering in scientific matters or in teaching methods, give a beneficial direction to the teaching, keeping in view the future attitude of the students. Finally, he shall give unceasing attention to everything that may promote morality . . . among the students. . . .

"2. The confederated governments mutually pledge themselves to eliminate from the universities or any other public educational institutions all instructors who shall have obviously proved their unfitness for the important work entrusted to them by openly deviating from their duties, or by going beyond the boundaries of their functions, or by abusing their legitimate influence over young minds, or by presenting harmful ideas hostile to public order or subverting existing governmental instructions. . . .

"Any instructor who has been removed in this manner becomes ineligible for a position in any other public institution of learning in another state of the Confederation.

"3. The laws that for some time have been directed against secret and unauthorized societies in the universities shall be strictly enforced. . . . The special representatives of the government are enjoined to exert great care in watching these organizations.

"The governments mutually agree that all individuals who shall be shown to have maintained their membership in secret or unauthorized associations, or shall have taken membership in such associations, shall not be eligible for any public office.

"4. No student who shall have been expelled from any university by virtue of a decision of the university senate ratified or initiated by the special representative of the government, shall be admitted by any other university. . . .

"As long as this edict remains in force, no publication which appears daily, or as a serial not exceeding twenty sheets of printed matter, shall be printed in any state of the Confederation without the prior knowledge and approval of the state officials. . . ."

Excerpt from Louis L. Snyder (ed.), *Documents of German History*, Rutgers University Press, 1958, pp. 158–159.

Spain and Italy In Spain the Bourbon king Ferdinand VII regained his throne in 1814 when Napoleon's army was expelled. Strong enough to denounce the constitution he had promised, Ferdinand was too weak to do much more. He benefited from patriotic resentment against French rule, but his government found no solution for its own inefficiency or the nation's poverty. In Spain's American colonies, the revolts led by José de San Martín and Simón Bolívar gained strength, and in 1820 the army that was assembled in Spain to reconquer the colonies mutinied instead and marched on Madrid. The king was then forced to grant a constitution after all, and for three years the constitutional regime struggled to cope with Spain's enormous problems, weakened by its own dissension and its uncooperative monarch. The regime's restrictions on religious orders raised powerful opposition from the Church, freedom of the press produced more devastating criticism, and a constitution in Spain was no help in reconquering the rebellious colonies.

When a French army once again crossed into Spain in 1823, this time with the blessing of the Concert of Europe and in the name of order, the Spaniards who had fought French invasion so heroically just ten years earlier were strangely acquiescent. The constitution disappeared again, but the threat of revolution did not.

In Italy restoration meant the return to power of the aristocracies the French had ousted and reestablishment of the separate Italian states.[2] Yet the years of Napoleonic rule had established institutions (and hopes) that the new regimes could not ignore, and they promised constitutions, enlightened administration,

---

[2]Italy was divided into three monarchies, four duchies, and a republic. The Kingdom of Sardinia (Sardinia and Piedmont), the Papal States, and the Kingdom of the Two Sicilies were monarchies. The Grand Duchy of Tuscany and the duchies of Lucca, Modena, and Parma were all tied to the Habsburgs, who annexed Lombardy and Venetia. The disappearance of the republics of Genoa (part of Piedmont) and Venice left tiny San Marino, safe on its mountaintop, the oldest republic in the world.

peace, and lower taxes—even though their insecure rulers were hardly prepared to take such initiatives. Cautious, moderately repressive, and conveniently corrupt, these regimes provided the sleepy stability Metternich thought appropriate for Italians. Such an atmosphere bred some conspiracy and rumors of far more. Secret groups began to meet across Italy. Known collectively as the *Carbonari* (charcoal burners), they varied in membership and program. Most were middle class, although their name suggested a life of rural simplicity. Some talked of tyrannicide, some promised equality and justice, and some sought mild reform; they had in common the excitement of secret meetings, terrifying oaths, and ornate rituals.

By 1820 news of revolution in Spain was enough to prompt revolts in Italy. Young army officers led the demand for a constitution in Naples; but as the Neapolitan army turned to put down a rising in Sicily, an Austrian army was dispatched to Naples to remove the new constitutional regime. A similar revolt erupted in Piedmont, causing the king to abdicate in favor of his son, and Charles Albert, the prince regent, hastily granted a constitution. But when the new monarch arrived, the Austrian army was with him. Piedmont's constitution lasted two weeks. These revolutions, which left Italy's reactionary governments more rigid and Austrian influence more naked, demonstrated the inadequacy of romantic conspiracies but affirmed an Italian radical and patriotic tradition that would continue to grow.

The Bourbons Restored in France

More than anything else, Europe's conservative order was meant to prevent France from again becoming the center of military aggression or revolutionary ideas, and the restoration there was an especially complex compromise. France was permitted a constitution called the Charter, presented as a gift from Louis XVIII and not as a right. It granted the legislature more authority than Napoleon had allowed but left the government largely in the hands of the king. The old estates were wisely forgotten, replaced by a Chamber of Peers with hereditary members and a Chamber of Deputies chosen by an electorate limited to prosperous landowners. Napoleon's centralized administration and effective system of taxation were willingly kept intact.

The regime's supporters, shaken by Napoleon's easy return during the Hundred Days, were determined to crush their enemies. A violent "white terror" broke out in parts of the countryside as those tainted with a revolutionary past were ousted from local office or even killed. Yet Louis XVIII resisted as best he could the more extreme demands of the reactionary ultraroyalists; land confiscated from the Church and from the émigré aristocracy during the Revolution was not re-turned to them, and most of those who had gained office or wealth since 1789 were allowed quietly to live out their lives. From 1816 to 1820 the Bourbons governed well in a relatively peaceful and prosperous country, and Paris became again Europe's most brilliant center of science and the arts.

The Catholic Church, weakened in the intervening years by the loss of property and a decline in the number of new priests, revived remarkably. Missions of preachers toured the countryside calling for a return to the faith, praising the monarchy, and ceremonially planting crosses of repentance for the sins of revolution. The nobles, traditionally rather skeptical in matters of religion, were now more pious; and so, too, for the first time in more than a century, were France's leading writers. To the surprise of many Catholics, however, Napoleon's 1801 Concordat with the Church remained in effect.

From Opposition to Revolution in France

Despite its achievements, the regime remained insecure and uncertain, satisfying neither Catholics nor anticlericals, neither **ultraroyalists** nor liberals. The assassination of the duke of Berry, the son of Louis' younger brother, in 1820 reminded everyone how fragile the monarchy was. Louis XVIII reacted to the assassination by naming more conservative ministers, increasing restrictions on the press, and dismissing some leading professors. The air of reaction grew heavier in 1824 when his brother succeeded to the throne as Charles X. A leader of the ultraroyalists, Charles had himself crowned at Reims in medieval splendor, in a ceremony redolent with symbols of the divine right of kings and the alliance of throne and altar.

The new government gave the Church fuller control of education, declared sacrilege a capital crime, and granted a cash indemnity to those who had lost land in the Revolution. In reality, the law against sacrilege was never enforced, and the indemnity, which helped end one of the most dangerous issues left from the Revolution, was a limited one. France still remained freer than most European countries, but Charles's subjects worried about the intentions of an ultraroyalist regime that disliked the compromises on which it rested. Public criticism increased, radical secret societies blossomed, and liberals made gains in the elections of 1827.

By 1829 the king could stand no more. While political disputes grew more inflamed, he appointed a cabinet of ultraroyalists only to have the Chamber of Deputies reject them. He called new elections, but instead of regaining seats the ultraroyalists lost still more. Determined not to show the hesitancy of Louis XVI, Charles X reacted with firmness. In 1830 he and his ministers suddenly issued a set of secretly drafted

François Pascal Simon Gerard
***CHARLES X*, 1825**
This official portrait of Charles X, in the up-to-date Romantic style, echoes the portraits of Louis XIV and suggests the way a regime that looked to the past wanted to be seen.
Château de Versailles, France/Giraudon/Bridgeman Art Library

decrees, the July Ordinances, which dissolved the new Chamber of Deputies even before it met, further restricted suffrage, and muzzled the press. Having shown his fiber, the king went hunting.

A shocked Paris slowly responded. Crowds began to mill about, some barricades went up, and stones were thrown at the house of the prime minister. Newspapers disregarded the ordinances and denounced the violation of the constitution, and the government responded with enough troops to raise tempers but too few to enforce order. Charles began to back down, but people were being killed (nearly seven hundred died in the three days of Paris fighting), some of the soldiers were mingling with the crowds, and liberal leaders were planning for a new regime. Once again, Paris was the scene of a popular uprising, and Charles X, victim of what he most detested, abdicated

on August 2. For fifteen years, and for the only time in its history, France had been administered by its aristocracy, but the monarchy had been meant above all to provide political stability. This the Bourbon regime, the restoration's most important experiment, had failed to do.

THE PROGRESS OF INDUSTRIALIZATION

Political instability was one aspect of the larger process of change. In parts of Europe economic growth of a distinctive kind was creating a dynamic of continuing expansion in which the elements of growth—new inventions, demand for more capital, factory organization, more efficient transportation, and increased consumption—stimulated each other and thus led to further growth. Particular historical conditions had begun in the previous century to bring these factors together (see chapter 18), but once the pattern of industrial development was clearly established in the nineteenth century, it began to spread, creating new challenges for governments.

The Technology to Support Machines

Industrialization required the efficient use of raw materials, beginning with cheap metals, such as iron, which could be formed into machines, and cheap fuel, such as coal. The increased importance of iron and coal gave England an important advantage, for it was well supplied with deposits of coal that lay conveniently close to its iron ore.

Coal and Iron The English had increasingly turned to the use of coal as the once-great forests were cut down, and miners had begun taking coal from deeper veins, often beneath the water table. The need for powerful pumps to remove the water stimulated experiments to harness steam. Coal was not useful in smelting iron, however, because its impurities combined with the iron, resulting in an inferior product. For high-quality wrought iron, ironmasters therefore traditionally used charcoal, which was expensive. This problem stimulated experiments by eighteenth-century engineers in smelting with coke (a purified form of coal) to produce pig iron, which could be cast but not worked or machined. As demand for iron and steel increased, the search for new techniques continued, resulting in the 1780s in the puddling process, the first commercially feasible effort to purify iron using coke alone.

It was a breakthrough that convinced ironmasters like John Wilkinson that iron would be the building material of a new age. His improved techniques for bor-

The crucial resource of industrialization was coal, and coal mining was one of the earliest industrial activities, employing steam engines to pump water and creating large, polluting enterprises in which hundreds of workers labored painfully, as at this English mine in Northumberland.
The Mary Evans Picture Library

ing cylinders made it possible to make better cannons and steam engines, and he built the world's first iron bridge over the Severn River in 1779, experimented with iron rails, launched an iron boat, and at his death was buried in an iron coffin.

The Steam Engine   The development of steam power also had a long history. In the seventeenth century several scientists proved that the atmosphere has weight; one used atmospheric pressure to push a piston through a cylinder, overcoming the efforts of twenty men to restrain it. Such sensational experiments encouraged construction of an "atmospheric engine," which required creating a partial vacuum, and before the end of the seventeenth century, atmospheric machines using the condensation of steam to create the needed vacuum were being designed both in England and on the Continent.

The first commercially successful atmospheric engine was invented in England by Thomas Savery, who described it in a book published in 1702 and significantly entitled *The Miner's Friend.* Used as a pump, Savery's engine was woefully inefficient; but a decade later another Englishman, Thomas Newcomen, returned to the piston and cylinder design, which completely separated engine and pump and proved a third more efficient. Newcomen engines were soon being used to remove water from mines not only in Great Britain but in France, Denmark, Austria, and Hungary.

The most fundamental step in the development of steam was the work of James Watt, a young mechanic and instrument maker working at the University of Glasgow. In the 1760s he made important improvements on the Newcomen engine, while still relying on atmospheric pressure pushing against a vacuum. But he also recognized the enormous potential in the direct pressure created when expanding steam pushed against a piston. His work took years, for it required new levels of precision in machining cylinders and pistons, new designs for valves, and new knowledge of lubricants and the properties of steam itself. Finally patented in 1782, Watt's first practical model was nearly three times more efficient than the Newcomen engine. Once he added a system of gears for converting the piston's reciprocating motion to the rotary motion needed to drive most machines, the **steam engine** had become much more than a pump.

Getting these inventions into use required the business talents of Watt's partner, the Birmingham industrialist Matthew Boulton. He recognized that the demand for cheap power had become more critical with the new inventions in the textile industry (including Arkwright's water frame, Crompton's spinning mule, and Cartwright's power loom, discussed in chapter 18). From the 1780s on, the steam engine was being used in factories, and some five hundred were built before 1800. Even these early machines represented a remarkable improvement over traditional sources of power. They produced between six and twenty horsepower, comparable to the largest windmills and water mills, and did so more reliably and wherever they were needed. An economy traditionally starved for sources of power had overcome that obstacle.

The Economic Effects of Revolution and War

Great Britain's lead over continental countries in goods produced, capital invested, and machinery employed had widened steadily from 1789 to 1815. Nonetheless, there had been economic growth on the Continent, too, where the exploitation of resources became more systematic, population increased, transportation generally improved, the means of mobilizing capital for investment expanded, and more and more political and business leaders were concerned with speeding industrial growth. In important respects the French Revolution and the Napoleonic era had cleared the way for future industrialization. In France, western Germany, northern Italy, and the Low Countries, land tenure was no longer the most pressing economic and social issue. Less constrained by custom and legal restrictions, landowners, including peasant proprietors, could more easily shift their production to meet the demands of a national market. The abolition of guilds and old commercial restrictions had eliminated some obstacles to the free movement of workers and the establishment of new enterprises.

The Napoleonic Code and French commercial law not only favored free contracts and an open marketplace but also introduced the advantages of uniform and clear commercial regulations. The French government had exported a common and sensible standard of weights and measures, encouraged the establishment of technical schools (the Polytechnic School in Paris long remained the world's best), and honored inventors and inventions of every sort, from improved gunpowder to new techniques for raising sugar beets. Under Napoleon, Europe had benefited from improved highways and bridges and a large zone of free trade; and the Bank of France, as restructured in 1800, had become the European model of a bank of issue providing a reliable currency.

In the short run, however, the years of war had slowed and disrupted Europe's economic growth. Vast resources in material and men were destroyed or wastefully used up. When peace came, governments were burdened with heavy debts, and returning soldiers had to find ways to support themselves in a changed economy. The Continental System, which had initially swung production and trade in France's favor, had collapsed with Napoleon's fall, bringing down many of the enterprises that it had artificially sustained. Both political change and renewed British competition discouraged daring capital investment. During the war, Great Britain had found compensation in American markets for its exclusion from continental ones and had avoided the shock of military invasion; but it, too, suffered a severe slump in the postwar years when the anticipated continental demand for British goods failed to materialize and the transition to a peacetime economy proved difficult to achieve.

Patterns of Industrialization

By the mid-1820s, however, British trade was reviving, and by 1830 its economy was being transformed. Growth in one economic sector stimulated growth in others. Increased textile production, for example, accel-

erated the use of chemical dyes; greater iron production required more coal. A few factories in one place encouraged the growth of others in the same region, where they could take advantage of the available workforce and capital; this concentration of production in turn increased the demand for roads, canals, and, later, railways. All this growth required more capital, and on the cycle went. In continuity, range of industries affected, national scope, and rate of increase, Great Britain's industrial growth in the first half of the nineteenth century was the greatest humankind had ever experienced.

Cotton: The Leading Sector In 1760 Britain imported only 2.5 million pounds of raw cotton; by 1830 it was importing 366 million pounds. Spurred by consumer demand, cotton textiles had become the single most important industrial product in terms of output, capital investment, and number of workers. Its production was almost exclusively organized in factories using power-driven machinery for spinning yarn and weaving cloth. In the process, the price of cotton yarn fell to about one-twentieth of what it had been in the 1760s. Lancashire, with its abundant waterways and coal deposits to fuel steam engines, became the center of a booming cotton cloth industry, and Manchester, its leading city, became the cotton capital of the world.

Railroads New inventions became whole industries and were integrated into the economy with dazzling speed. The steam engine's application to rail travel is a classic case. The first successful steam railway line was

Stephenson's North Star engine of 1837 was meant to be an object of beauty, combining technology and craftsmanship.
Science Museum, London, UK/Bridgeman Art Library

built in England in 1825; a few years later an improved engine impressed spectators by outracing a horse, and in 1830 the first passenger line took its riders the thirty-two miles from Liverpool to Manchester in an hour and a quarter. Just more than a decade later, there were 2,000 miles of such rail lines in Great Britain; by 1851 there were 7,000.

Railroads constituted a new industry that stimulated further industrialization. They bought huge quantities of coal and of iron for rails. They carried food and raw materials to cities, manufactured products to consumers, and building materials and fertilizers to the countryside. And they made it easier for the men and women who crowded into dirt-stained railway cars to travel in search of work. Similarly, the telegraph, developed by a generation of scientists working in many countries and quickly adopted as an adjunct of railroading, expanded to other uses, becoming a military necessity and a conveyor of news to the general public.

Yet the leap from new invention to industrialization was not necessarily direct or predictable. Often dozens of subsidiary inventions or improvements were necessary to make a new machine competitive. Everywhere, but more often on the Continent than in Britain, small-scale manufacturing and crafts persisted alongside the new. But the water-driven mills, charcoal-fired smelters, and hand-powered looms that dotted the countryside were gradually but relentlessly displaced, as were hundreds of thousands of skilled artisans and rural families working in their homes to make products in the old ways—a transformation that accounted for much of the human suffering occasioned by industrialization.

National Differences In 1815 many regions of the Continent, including such traditional commercial centers as Barcelona and Naples, had seemed ready to follow the British example of industrial growth, but by the 1850s the zone of industrialization had narrowed to include only northeastern France, Belgium and the Netherlands, western Germany, and northern Italy. Industrial change in this zone was uneven but more extensive than outside it. Countries poorly endowed in coal and iron, such as Italy, faced formidable obstacles. Although Saxony in eastern Germany was an early industrial center, most of Germany remained an area of quiet villages in which commerce relied on peddlers and trade fairs, even though by midcentury the German states were crisscrossed by the Continent's largest railway network. Except for pockets of industrial development, Eastern Europe remained a world of agricultural estates.

Belgium, which had prospered from its former connections with Holland, built on its tradition of technological skill, its geographical advantages as a trade center accessible by water, and its excellent supplies of

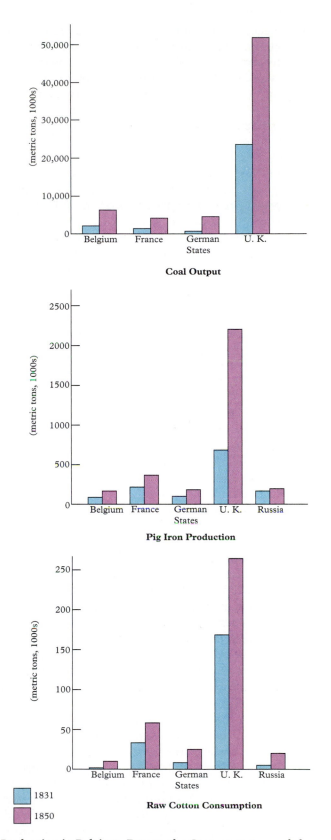

Production in Belgium, France, the German states, and the United Kingdom
From B. R. Mitchel, *European Historical Statistics, 1750–1970,* Columbia University Press, 1975, pp. 360–361, 428–429.

coal to become the Continent's first industrialized nation. Belgium extracted more coal than did France or Germany and was the first country to complete a railway network. The French railway system, on the other hand, was not finished until after Germany's, for it was slowed by political conflict despite early and ambitious plans. France's production of iron, coal, and textiles increased severalfold between 1815 and 1848. This growth would have been impressive a generation earlier, but Britain's expansion in each of these sectors was several times greater. In iron production, for example, the two countries were about equal in 1800, but by 1850 Britain's output was six or seven times greater. Britain outstripped France still more in textiles and coal, producing by midcentury half the world total of these items.

Everywhere, increased production led to more commerce and closer international ties as capital, techniques, workers, and managers moved from Britain across the channel and spread from Belgium and France into the rest of Europe. Finance became so internationally linked that the Bank of France granted an emergency loan to the Bank of England in 1825, only a decade after Waterloo. The domestic banking policies of the United States, in response to a financial panic in 1837, led to a wave of crises in the financial centers of Europe.

State Politics Although many writers argued that the new prosperity followed from natural economic laws that worked best unimpeded by government, by midcentury the state was centrally involved in the process of economic growth even in Britain. Railroads required franchises and the power of eminent domain before a spike was pounded. Inevitably, routes, rates, and even the gauge of the track became political matters to be settled by parliaments or special commissions. In Belgium and in most of Germany, railroads were owned as well as planned by the state.

Tariffs, the dominant issue in British politics in the 1840s, became a critical question in every country. In 1846, after a wrenching public campaign, Britain abolished the tariff on imported grain, known as the Corn Laws. In doing so, the nation expressed confidence in its position as the world's greatest center of manufacture and sided with those who favored trade and a lower price for bread rather than with the landowners who benefited from higher, protected grain prices. Equally important to economic development was the role of government in banking and currency. Just before the middle of the century, Parliament granted the Bank of England a monopoly on issuing money and required companies to register with the government and publish their annual budget as a guide to investors. Similar steps were taken across Europe. Before industries could effectively tap private wealth, investors needed assurance that they risked only the money they invested, without being liable (as in a partnership) for all a firm's debts. That assurance required new legislation establishing limited liability and encouraging the formation of corporations, and every major country passed such measures.

The Role of Government The growth of cities and the benefits of new technology created additional social demands on government. By the 1840s most cities had a public omnibus, some sidewalks, and gas lighting in certain areas. Such services, usually provided by private companies, had to be subsidized, regulated, and given legal protection by the government. As the cost and importance of these services increased, so did the state's participation in them, often extending to full ownership.

The growing role of government was exemplified by the postal service, which most states had provided since the seventeenth and eighteenth centuries. These postal systems proved inadequate for an industrial era. In Britain demands for improvement led a little-known inventor to propose a solution that captured the thinking of the new age. He called for standard envelopes and payment in advance by means of an adhesive stamp. These innovations would not only eliminate graft and reduce costs, he argued, but the service would pay for itself because lower rates would increase volume. His reforms, denounced as dangerous and impractical, passed nevertheless in 1840; and within twenty years the volume of mail in Britain increased sixfold. By then, money orders, savings accounts, and the telegraph had been added to postal services. In France mail delivery was extended to rural areas, and by the 1850s every major government was adopting the new system, including the postage stamp.

Effective government, in short, was now expected to further economic development—by subsidizing ports, transportation, and new inventions; by registering patents and sponsoring education; by encouraging investment and enforcing contracts; and by maintaining order and preventing strikes. In the 1840s the leaders of Britain, France, and Belgium busily did these things—in Great Britain the number of government employees increased about fourfold in the first half of the century—and the desire in other countries to have governments similarly foster economic development was an important element in the revolutions of 1848 and the nationalist movements of the period that followed.

The Crystal Palace The British celebrated their position as the masters of industrialization in 1851 with the first international industrial exhibition. Prominent people from the aristocracy, business, and gov-

Henry Thomas Alken
A VIEW OF THE WHITECHAPEL ROAD, **1828**
By 1830 it was possible to conceive of life transformed by technology, as in this imagined view of what London's important White Chapel road might soon become, with traffic jams and smog but on an unpaved road with room for dogs.
National Railway Museum, York, UK/Bridgeman Art Library

ernment joined in the planning, and a specially designed pavilion was built in London, a sort of giant greenhouse called the Crystal Palace, which proved to be an architectural milestone. Many governments feared that Britain risked revolution by attracting huge throngs to London, but the admiring crowds proved well behaved.

The exhibition provided a significant comparison of the relative economic development of the participating countries. Russia displayed primarily raw materials; Austria showed mainly luxury handicrafts. So did the German *Zollverein* and the Italian states, whose appearance as single economic units foretold the advantages of national unification. Although unable to fill all the space it had demanded, the United States impressed viewers with collections of fossils, cheap manufactured products for use in the home, mountains of dentifrice and soap, and a series of new

inventions, including Colt revolvers, a sewing machine, and McCormick's reaper. French machines, which ranged from a much-admired device for folding envelopes to a submarine, were generally considered the most elegant. But British machines surpassed everyone's in quantity, size, and variety. It is, explained London's *Morning Chronicle*, "to our wonderful industrial discipline—our consummately arranged organization of toil, and our habit of division of labour—that we owe all the triumph." By 1850 Great Britain was the wealthiest nation in history,[3] and over the next twenty years, it would continue to increase its lead in goods produced.

[3]Although all estimates for this period are uncertain, it seems likely that by 1860 the per capita wealth of the French was about two-thirds and of the Germans about two-fifths that of the British.

EXTERIOR OF THE CRYSTAL PALACE,

London's imposing Crystal Palace was designed to house the first international industrial exhibition, held there in 1851. The building was constructed of cast iron and glass, a significant innovation in architecture. The exhibits held here were organized as a kind of encyclopedia of world industry, with subcategories for different products.
Hulton Archive/Getty Images

British products dominated the machinery section of the Crystal Palace Exhibition. Here men and women marveled at Joseph Whitworth's lathe for forming railway wheels, a machine for making machines.
Guildhall Library, Corporation of London, UK/Bridgeman Art Library

THE SOCIAL EFFECTS

Economic growth on such a scale was accompanied by far-reaching social change. Even in its early stages, industrialization impinged on all of society, from the state to the family, affecting governmental functions, the nature of work, women's roles, and childhood. Child labor, tyrannical foremen, teeming slums, and unemployment brought new social problems and required new social policies as the growing prosperity and security of the middle class contrasted all the more sharply with the destitution of the urban poor.

The Division of Labor

The Factory   The factory quickly became the symbol of the age. Well before industrialization, there had been workplaces in which hundreds of people labored under one roof; conversely, even in industrialized societies, most wage earners did not work in factories. But the factory symbolized a different kind of power—the power of steam and of technology, the power of capital to assemble machinery and laborers, the power of competition to drive down prices and wages, the power of markets to absorb ever more production and determine what would be produced. Above all, the factory symbolized the capacity of this whole system to change the landscape, to erect or transform cities, and to reshape the lives of masses of men, women, and children.

The factory model was most clearly triumphant in the production of textiles. Spinning and weaving had always been domestic tasks; even in Europe's most important textile centers, where merchants collected the output from hundreds of looms, the actual work had been done primarily in the home, where it might involve all the family. The most successful weavers often employed other workers, so that the average domestic establishment contained about a half-dozen weavers. Pay and working conditions varied with the region, the season, and the ability of middlemen to control the prices of the yarn they supplied and the cloth they purchased and resold. Textile factories, on the other hand, required an investment in buildings, machinery, and raw materials far beyond the reach of most weavers; and production per worker increased more than a thousandfold with the factory's efficient organization and power-driven machinery. By the 1830s cotton factories in Manchester, larger than most, averaged nearly three hundred employees.

This Nasmyth steam hammer looms above the men who endured heat and noise to feed it—in every way the symbol of a new era.
The Science Museum, London

These factories would slowly drive the older forms of textile production out of business, although the flexibility of domestic production (and the weavers' hatred of factories) long kept the older ways alive in some regions and for special products. Those who came to work in a factory might be former weavers, but they were likely to be less skilled laborers (often migrants) driven by poverty. Most were women and children, hired to tend power looms, splice thread, or sweep the floor. Children were paid less than women and women less than men, who did the heaviest work and served as carpenters and mechanics. At first, children usually worked with their parents, even in the factories; but increased specialization meant that, like their mothers and fathers, children came to be employed and supervised without regard to family ties.

Factory Life   The workday usually began at 5:30 or 6:00 in the morning and lasted for twelve hours of work plus whatever time was allotted for meals and for recesses (when belts were replaced and machinery fixed). The workroom, hot in summer and cold in winter, was usually kept moist so the taut thread would break less readily. Employers, concerned about keeping the expensive machinery running, found their workers too often lethargic and sullen, prone to drunkenness and indifference. To maintain the discipline that efficient production demanded, foremen used whips, curses, and most of all, fines (fines for lateness, for slacking off, for flawed work, for talking, and sometimes even for singing or whistling).

The best employers and the inspectors subsequently appointed as the result of factory legislation were shocked by these conditions and by the workers themselves, in whom they discovered foul language, filthiness, poor health, ignorance, and promiscuity. Factory owners could see no solution beyond more discipline, and nearly all employers opposed such measures as the law finally passed in England in 1847 that limited the workday to ten hours. Even that legislation was primarily an embarrassed response to the evils of child labor, which had been bitterly criticized by reformers and intellectuals.

Many workers, especially those with established skills—hatters, masons, tanners, typesetters, bakers, and eventually, steam-engine makers—took the lead in forming labor organizations and agitating for political redress. Although skilled laborers tended to look down on factory workers, the latter were, in income at least, better off than about half of all laborers; and their lot improved a bit as legislation hesitantly restricted hours and set some standards of hygiene and safety.

Differentiation   The increased division of labor was not limited to the allocation of work within factories,

Under the foreman's close supervision, women kept the textile looms running.

and sociologists use the term *differentiation* to describe the spread of specialization among groups and institutions that was a characteristic of the nineteenth century. Just as factories separated work from family life, so money exchange and legal contracts differentiated economic from personal or social relationships. Business affairs and governmental functions became more specialized, matters determined by calculation or regulation rather than status or social connection. Maintaining the peace, collecting taxes, inspecting factories and schools, and administering welfare measures fell to separate agencies.

Just as each trade and each locality followed its own course of social change, so each nation differed in the pace and manner of institutional differentiation. Britain, more than continental states, left many public matters to local government and private groups; in France the role of the national government increased; and the German states tended to combine centralizing bureaucracies with considerable local autonomy. Whatever the pattern, the growth of differentiation brought increased professionalization and exposed tensions between government and established interests, between national policy and local custom.

The Family

To a great many nineteenth-century observers, social change threatened to undermine the family, and moralists of every sort warned that the very institution most central to civilization was in danger. Recent research

has suggested a different view. The heightened concern for the family was a response to real stress, but it was also an expression of a growing belief in the importance of the family, which would prove to be an extraordinarily adaptable institution.

Traditional Roles   Family life in Europe had always been related to social status. For the aristocracy, family encompassed a wide network of relatives, privilege, and power. Women played a critical but subordinate role as carriers of the dowries that joined estates, as managers of large domestic staffs, and as centers of the social circles in which aristocrats met. Among peasants, the family unit might include grandparents or, where plots were large enough, even in-laws, cousins, and nephews. Particularly in the Mediterranean regions, such extended families often shared housing in the village but worked in different nearby fields. When they could, however, a young couple generally set up a household of their own. In regions where peasants owned land, they had difficulty keeping it intact while giving something to all their children. Law and custom might require equal division of inheritance (as in France), primogeniture (inheritance by the eldest son, as in England), or other more complicated arrangements. But everywhere bitter disputes were frequent, for the elderly feared dispossession and the children feared that they would not get their share in time.

The family was the basic economic unit, pooling income from various sources and dividing labor in customary ways. Women usually handled household chores and the smaller animals, the men were responsible for the heavier work, and everyone worked together in critical periods of planting and harvest. Often the women had more access than the men to additional sources of income—piecework from a nearby mill or domestic service for the well-to-do—and they played a central role in marketing. Men, on the other hand, were more likely to travel considerable distances, especially in difficult times, in order to pick up a bit of work on roads or docks or at some great landlord's harvest. As population increased, the children were more often pushed out to seek employment in the nearest mills and towns.

The Impact of Industrialization   For artisans as well as peasants, the family was often the unit of production, although the division of tasks by sex was usually more explicit, and even small workshops had long tended to exclude women, at least from the better-paid tasks. Working-class women and children were accustomed to long hours of labor. The strain on the family in the industrial age came rather from the lack of housing, the conditions of work, and the need for cash, which was compounded by the risk of unemployment. Not only did women and children have to supplement the father's income, but they were less and less likely to work side by side; if taught a trade, children were less likely to learn it from their parents. Sometimes the father, with his preindustrial skills, remained unemployed and did housework while his wife and children earned wages, which the socialist Friedrich Engels believed was another source of "the righteous indignation of the workers at being virtually turned into eunuchs."

Adolescents in factory towns, hardened at an early age, were probably more likely to leave home when their pay allowed, and urban conditions made it more difficult for the family to support the aged and the sick. Such factors did weaken family ties, as did—at least in the eyes of the upper classes—the common practice for working men and women to live together without the trouble or expense of formal marriage rites. Yet among workers, too, the family survived, and the home remained a special place expected to provide protection for small children, a haven for wage earners, and temporary shelter for relatives come to seek a job.

Middle-Class Women   The fact that women worked for pay may also have slowly lessened their domestic subordination. In the lower-middle class, especially in France, women were as important as and frequently more visible than men in operating small shops. The life of the middle-class woman, however, contrasted greatly with that of her poorer sisters, and the role allotted to wife and mother became one of the most apparent and important indicators of social status. Women continued to be the organizers, patrons, critics, and ornaments of

Francois Bonvin
THE IRONSMITHS, 1857
Ironsmiths at work in France in a characteristically small workshop: A master, young helper, and boy already learning the trade. Living quarters were probably overhead.
Musée des Augustins, Toulouse. Giraudon/Art Resource, NY

many of Europe's most cultivated circles; but the middle class isolated women from the harsh competition of business and politics. As the contemporary French historian Jules Michelet complained, "By a singular set of circumstances—social, economic, religious—man lives separated from woman." In Victorian England gentlemen met in their clubs or withdrew from the ladies after dinner for their cigars and weighty talk.

Except for the well-to-do who had domestic (female) servants, wives of every class—no matter what their other burdens—were expected to prepare and serve the food, wash and mend clothes, and clean the home. Victorian discourse often made the ideal of femininity appear to be an idle and pallid creature, encased in corset or bustle, whose tendency to faint was a sign of delicacy. In reality women's roles were far more significant and varied, but the image may well have reflected values widely shared.

Allowing a wife to be idle even if her husband worked hard was a kind of conspicuous consumption, a partial imitation of aristocratic elegance. There were signs, too, of an unconscious effort to sustain a sort of

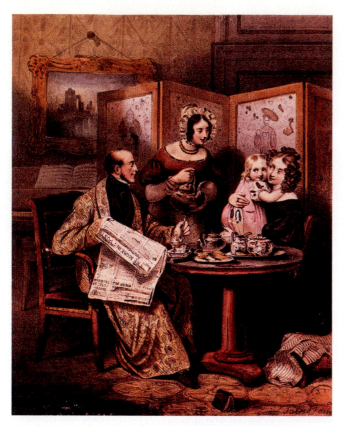

The bourgeois family at breakfast: perfect domestic harmony, father looks up from the morning newspaper to enjoy the scene of an angelic child and adoring wife, while a servant tends to them in front of the Chinese screen that sets off the eating space.
Editions Tallandier

counterculture. If men must be competitive, hard, and practical, women should be tender, innocent, and gracious—the weak but pure upholders of morality and taste. The middle-class woman with no estate to manage and few servants to direct was almost literally placed on a pedestal. Neither her needlework nor her piano playing was viewed as serious, but her role in maintaining the protective calm of the home and as exemplar of the moral virtues was.

Moral Seriousness Middle-class concern with the family also emphasized the special moral role of women within the home, conceived as a private citadel largely closed to the outside world. The liberal dream of combining individualism and social order found its model in the family, where the patriarchal father, devoted mother, and carefully trained children were meant to live in disciplined harmony. Childhood itself lasted longer in the middle class, for manners, education, and character required elaborate preparation. The mother was the core of this home; and books, newspapers, magazines, and sermons enthusiastically de-

scribed the talents her role required. Motherhood was treated as an honored occupation, fondly depicted in novels and in the new women's magazines founded, like the Parisian *Journal des Femmes* of 1832, to make women "skilled in their duties as companions and mothers."

Clearly, these attitudes were related to the famous prudery of the age and the distrust of sexual passion. In 1818 Thomas Bowdler produced his *Family Shakespeare*, a "bowdlerized" version "in which . . . those words and phrases are omitted which cannot with propriety be read in a family," a strange sensitivity after two hundred years of admiration for Shakespeare's dramas. And "the anti-English pollution of the waltz . . . the most degenerating that the last or present century can see" was denounced in *The Ladies' Pocket Book of Etiquette* of 1840. The middle classes sought to maintain an orderly world through convention. At a time when prostitution and drunkenness were believed to have reached new heights, prudery was more than repression; it was an effort to bend society to the self-discipline on which morality, a thriving commerce, the advancement of knowledge, and personal fulfillment were thought to rest.

The Standard of Living

Historians agree more about the general pattern of social change in the first half of the nineteenth century than about its effects on the standard of living, particularly of the working class. For this period, England is the critical case; scholars agree that between 1790 and 1840 national wealth about doubled but that the upper classes were the principal beneficiaries. Did workers gain, too? Certainly they were poor, but poverty, even of the bleakest sort, was not new (and the growing protest against such destitution was in itself one of the important changes of the period). The poorest peasants of Sicily who lived in caves were hardly victims of industrialization.

Living Conditions What *was* new was the terrible crowding in industrial areas and the workers' helpless dependence on their employers. The conditions in which workers lived made poverty more miserable, more obvious to all, and more threatening to the general welfare. The crowding was partly the result of increased population, but it followed directly from the rapid growth of factory towns. There, hastily built housing may often have been drier and cleaner than peasant hovels that had served for centuries, but squeezing whole families into a single room and cramming hundreds and thousands of people into slums with little light, with a single source of insalubrious water, and with no means for disposing of sewage created problems so different in scale as to be different in kind (see "The Housing Crisis

THE HOUSING CRISIS IN FRANCE AND GERMANY

The housing crisis was not limited to cities with a lot of new industry, as these two descriptions, expressing the shock of middle-class reformers, show. The first is from André Guépin, Nantes au XIXe siècle (Nantes, 1835); the second, giving Dr. Bluemner's impression of Breslau, is from Alexander Schneer, Über die Zuständer der arbeitenden Klassen in Breslau (Berlin, 1845).

"If you want to know how he [the poorer worker] lives, go—for example—to the Rue des Fumiers which is almost entirely inhabited by this class of worker. Pass through one of the drain-like openings, below street-level, that lead to these filthy dwellings, but remember to stoop as you enter. One must have gone down into these alleys where the atmosphere is as damp and cold as a cellar; one must have known what it is like to feel one's foot slip on the polluted ground and to fear a stumble into the filth: to realise the painful impression that one receives on entering the homes of these unfortunate workers. Below street-level on each side of the passage there is a large gloomy cold room. Foul water oozes out of the walls. Air reaches the room through a sort of semi-circular window which is two feet high at its greatest elevation. Go in—if the fetid smell that assails you does not make you recoil. Take care, for the floor is uneven, unpaved and untiled—or if there are tiles, they are covered with so much dirt that they cannot be seen. And then you will see two or three rickety beds fitted to one side because the cords that bind them to the worm-eaten legs have themselves decayed. Look at the contents of the bed—a mattress; a tattered blanket of rags (seldom washed since there is only one); sheets sometimes; and a pillow sometimes. No wardrobes are needed in these homes. Often a weaver's loom and a spinning wheel complete the furniture. There is no fire in the winter. No sunlight penetrates [by day], while at night a tallow candle is lit. Here men work for fourteen hours [a day]."

"*Question:* What is the condition of the living quarters of the class of factory workers, day labourers and journeymen?

"*Reply of the City Poor Doctor, Dr. Bluemner:* It is in the highest degree miserable. Many rooms are more like pigsties than quarters for human beings. The apartments in the city are, if possible, even worse than those in the suburbs. The former are, of course, always in the yard, if places in which you can hardly turn round can be called apartments. The so-called staircase is generally completely in the dark. It is also so decrepit that the whole building shakes with every firm footstep; the rooms themselves are small and so low that it is hardly possible to stand upright, the floor is on a slope, since usually part of the house has to be supported by struts. The windows close badly, the stoves are so bad that they hardly give any heat but plenty of smoke in the room. Water runs down the doors and walls. The ground-floor dwellings are usually half underground."

From Sidney Pollard and Colin Holmes (eds.), *Documents of European Economic History*, Vol. 1, St. Martin's Press, 1968, pp. 494–495, 497–498.

in France and Germany," above). The assault on the lungs of coal mining, cotton spinning, and machine grinding combined with poor nutrition to make tuberculosis widespread. Everywhere in Europe members of the working class were recognizably thinner, shorter, and paler than other people.

The work available had always changed with the seasons, and laborers in many regions and trades were accustomed to migrating to follow harvests and other temporary opportunities for work. Industrialization, however, often brought a demoralizing dependence. Most new factories employed between 150 and 300 men, women, and children whose well-being was largely tied to a single employer. A high proportion of these people were new to the area in which they lived, starkly dependent on cash to pay their rent, to purchase rough cotton for clothes, to provide the bread that was the staple of their diet, and to buy some candles and coal. For millions, employment was never steady; for millions of others, unemployment was the norm. It was common for a third of the adult males of a town to be without work, especially in the winter, and pauperism was acknowledged to be the social disease of the century, a condition that included some 10 percent of the population in Britain and only slightly less in France.

Workers, of course, suffered most in the periodic economic depressions that baffled even the most optimistic observers. The depression of 1846 was nearly universal, and that of 1857 extended from North America to Eastern Europe. Layoffs in the Lancashire cotton industry ran so high in the 1860s as a result of the American Civil War that at one time more than 250,000 workers, better than half the total, lived by what they could get on relief. The recipes for watery soup handed out by the charitable agencies of every city define the thinness of survival.

J. Leonard
THE DOCTOR FOR THE POOR
Hopelessness dominates J. Leonard's painting of the poor coming to the charitable doctor in an endless stream.
Musée des Beaux-Arts, Valenciennes/Giraudon/Bridgeman Art Library

Purchasing Power Although most workers everywhere suffered from the changing conditions of employment, workers in some trades and places were distinctly better off. Overall, real wages—measured, that is, in terms of what they could buy—may have begun to increase somewhat even before the general rise in wages in the mid-1840s and notably again in the 1850s, though these gains meant less in new factory towns, where workers could be forced to buy shoddy goods at high prices in company stores. Alcoholism was so extensive that in many a factory town paydays were staggered in order to reduce the dangerous number of drunks, a sign of alienation that may also have reflected an increase in available money. Technology brought benefits as well. The spread of the use of soap and cotton underwear was a boon to health, and by midcentury brick construction and iron pipes had improved housing even for many of the relatively poor. Luxuries such as sugar, tea, and meat were becoming available to the lower-middle class and to the more prosperous artisans.

The vigorous debate among historians over whether industrialization raised or lowered workers' standard of living in the first half of the century has become in large measure a judgment about the effects of capitalism (see "Industrialization and the Standard of Living," p. 665). But historians generally agree that whatever improvements occurred reached the masses slowly and often could not compensate for the added burdens of industrial employment or the growing chasm between the destitute and the regularly employed. In industrial Europe the urban poor remained a subject of baffled concern. The more fortunate workers and the middle classes were unquestionably more prosperous than they had been in the recent past, which made the contrast with the poverty of those beneath them even more striking. A luxury restaurant in Paris (by 1830 Paris had more than three thousand restaurants of every type, in contrast to only fifty or so before the Revolution) might charge twenty-five or thirty times an average worker's daily wage for a single meal; even modest restaurants charged twice a worker's daily wage—to a clientele that ate three or four times a day, in contrast to the two meals of many workers. From the top to the bottom of society, the gradations in status and wealth were subtle, but the differences between the comfortable minority and the poor majority were palpable in every aspect of daily life.

HISTORICAL ISSUES: INDUSTRIALIZATION AND THE STANDARD OF LIVING

These excerpts show the diverse emphases and shifting conclusions in this debate but not the careful reasoning and the extraordinary range of the research that makes this literature still worth reading. The first four excerpts are anthologized in Philip A. M. Taylor (ed.), The Industrial Revolution in Britain: Triumph or Disaster?, *D. C. Heath, 1970.*

JOHN L. AND BARBARA HAMMOND

"The apologies for child labour were precisely the same as the apologies for the slave trade. This was no travesty of their argument. The champions of the slave trade pointed to the £70,000,000 invested in the sugar plantations, to the dependence of our commerce on the slave trade. . . . The argument for child labour followed the same line. . . . Sir James Graham thought that the Ten Hours Bill would ruin the cotton industry and with it the trade of the country. . . . Our population, which had grown rapidly in the Industrial Revolution was no longer able to feed itself; the food it bought was paid for by its manufactures: those manufactures depended on capital: capital depended on profits: profits depended on the labour of the boys and girls who enabled the manufacturer to work his mills long enough at a time to repay the cost of the plant and to compete with foreign rivals. This was the circle in which the nation found its conscience mangled.

". . . Thus England asked for profits and received profits. Everything turned to profit. The towns had their profitable dirt, their profitable smoke, their profitable slums, their profitable disorder, their profitable ignorance, their profitable despair. The curse of Midas was on this society. . . . For the new town was not a home where man could find beauty, happiness, leisure, learning, religion, the influences that civilize outlook and habit, but a bare and desolate place. . . . The new factories and the new furnaces were like the Pyramids, telling of man's enslavement, rather than of his power, casting their long shadow over the society that took such pride in them."

From John L. and Barbara Hammond, *The Rise of Modern Industry*, M. S. G. Haskell House, 1925.*

THOMAS S. ASHTON

"Let me confess at the start that I am of those who believe that, all in all, conditions of labour were becoming better, at least after 1820, and that the spread of the factory played a not inconsiderable part in the improvement. . . . One of the merits of the factory system was that it offered, and required, regularity of employment and hence stability of consumption. During the period 1790–1830 factory production increased rapidly. A greater proportion of the people came to benefit both as producers and as consumers. The fall in the price of textiles reduced the price of clothing. Government contracts for uniforms and army boots called into being new industries, and after the war the products of these found a market among the better-paid artisans. Boots began to take the place of clogs and hats replaced shawls, at least for wear on Sundays. Miscellaneous commodities, ranging from clocks to pocket handkerchiefs, began to enter into the scheme of expenditure, and after 1820 such things as tea and coffee and sugar fell in price substantially. The growth of trade-unions, friendly societies, savings banks, popular newspapers and pamphlets, schools, and nonconformist chapels—all give evidence of the existence of a large class raised well above the level of mere subsistence."

From Thomas S. Ashton, "The Standard of Life of the Workers in England, 1790–1830," *Journal of Economic History*, Vol. 9, 1949.*

ERIC J. HOBSBAWM

"We may consider three types of evidence in favour of the pessimistic view: those bearing on (a) mortality and health, (b) unemployment and (c) consumption. . . . The rise in mortality rates in the period 1811–41 is clearly of *some* weight for the pessimistic case, all the more as modern work . . . tend[s] to link such rates much more directly to the amount of income and food consumption than to other social conditions.

". . . It is too often forgotten that something like 'technological' unemployment was not confined to those workers who were actually replaced by new machines. It could affect almost all pre-industrial industries and trades. . . . Doubtless the general expansion of the early industrial period (say 1780–1811) tended to diminish unemployment except during crises: doubtless the decades of difficulty and adjustment after the wars tended to make the problem more acute. From the later 1840s, the working classes began to adjust themselves to life under a new set of economic rules . . . but it is highly probable that the period 1811–42 saw abnormal problems and abnormal unemployment. . . . These notes on unemployment are sufficient to throw doubt upon the less critical statements of the optimistic view, but not to establish any alternative view. . . . Per capita consumption can hardly have risen. The discussion of food consumption thus throws considerable doubt on the optimistic view."

From Eric J. Hobsbawm, "The British Standard of Living, 1790–1850," *Economic History Review*, 1957.*

continued

RONALD M. HARTWELL

[I]ncreasing life expectation and increasing consumption are no measures of ultimate well-being, and to say that the standard of living for most workers was rising, is *not* to say that it was high, *nor* that there was no dire poverty, and cyclical fluctuations and technological unemployment of a most distressing character.

"... Thus much misunderstanding has arisen because of assumptions—mainly misconceptions—about England before the Industrial Revolution; assumptions, for example, that rural life was naturally better than town life, that working for oneself was better and more secure than working for an employer, that child and female labour was something new, that the domestic system . . . was preferable to the factory system, that slums and food adulteration were peculiar products of industrialization, and so on. . . . The new attitude to social problems that emerged with the industrial revolution was that ills should be identified, examined, analysed, publicised and remedied, either by voluntary or legislative action. Thus evils that had long existed—child labour, for example—and had long been accepted as inevitable, were regarded as new ills to be remedied rather than as old ills to be endured. It was during the industrial revolution, moreover, and largely because of the economic opportunities it afforded to the working class women, that there was the beginning of the most important and most beneficial of all the social revolutions of the last two centuries, the emancipation of women."

From Ronald M. Hartwell, "The Rising Standard of Living in England, 1800–1850," *Economic History Review*, 1961.*

THEODORE S. HAMMEROW

"For most [workers] the coming of the industrial revolution made little difference with regard to income, workday, diet, or housing. This was especially true of those employed in agriculture, who still made up the great bulk of the labor force. Yet even those engaged in manufacture experienced only minor changes in their accustomed level of subsistence. The goods and services generated by early industrialization remained largely inaccessible to them. But the new hardships imposed on the working population by the rationalization of production were less the result of a long-term decline in income than of psychological disorientation. Millions of people who had grown up amid the certainties and traditions of the village or small town were suddenly thrown into an alien environment of factories, shops, tenements, and slums, where the values of rural society soon disintegrated before the hard realities of the urban experience. The outcome was a profound demoralization, which primarily reflected not a change in the standard of living but a change in the way of life.

"Such generalizations about the initial effect of the industrial revolution may be open to challenge, but there can be little doubt about what happened subsequently. Within fifty years the standard of living of the lower classes began to rise. The evidence on this point is incontrovertible."

From Theodore S. Hamerow, *The Birth of a New Europe: State and Society in the Nineteenth Century*, University of North Carolina Press, 1983, pp. 140–141.

Summary

The reorganization of Europe in 1815 had focused on politics as the key to social order. The system of international relations that the victors established proved reasonably effective, but the conservative domestic arrangements they favored were challenged from the start. In trying various combinations of repression and compromise, the restoration regimes acknowledged that they had not achieved the stability hoped for. At the same time, accelerating industrial growth made new demands of government and placed new strains on society. Not stability but change would be the central reality of the new century. While Europe's leaders chose different means for containing change, millions dealt with it in daily struggles over wages and housing, food and family.

QUESTIONS FOR FURTHER THOUGHT

1. Following the French Revolution and Napoleon, Europe's leaders sought to create peace and lasting stability through international agreements and political firmness at home. Was that possible? Is it ever?
2. Do historical explanations as to why industrialization began when it did, spread from country to country, and became a self-perpetuating process of change indicate that economic growth can spread almost anywhere?
3. Moralists then, like moralists now, worried that industrialization might undermine the family. Were their fears misplaced?

RECOMMENDED READING

Sources

The published memoirs and correspondence of diplomats are a wonderful source. *The Memoirs of Prince Metternich* (5 vols., published in the United States in the 1890s), and *The Memoirs and Correspondence of Viscount Castlereagh* (12 vols.), and the *Memoirs of the Prince of Talleyrand* (5 vols.) give a lively picture of the Congress of Vienna.

Ure, Andrew. *The Philosophy of Manufactures.* 1835. A classic justification of liberal economics, emphasizing its promised benefits for all.

Studies

Carr, Raymond. *Spain, 1808–1975.* 1982. The most balanced and comprehensive account in any language.

Davies, Norman. *God's Playground: A History of Poland.* Vol. 2: *From 1789 to the Present.* 1981. Effectively studies the development of a nation without a national government.

*Frader, Laura L., and Sonya O. Rose. *Gender and Class in Modern Europe.* 1996. Essays exploring the relationship between social change and conceptions of gender and class.

*Gash, Norman. *Aristocracy and People: Britain, 1815–1865.* 1979. An incisive and balanced account of how British politics adapted to social and economic change.

*Gideon, Sigfried. *Mechanization Takes Command.* 1948. This provocative analysis of the social and aesthetic implications of the machine age has become a classic.

Goodman, J., and K. Honeyman. *Gainful Pursuits: The Making of Industrial Europe, 1600–1914.* 1988. Attentive to the variety of interests that made industrialization a continuing process.

Hamerow, Theodore S. *The Birth of a New Europe: State and Society in the Nineteenth Century.* 1983. On the major social changes of the nineteenth century, noting their connection to industrialization and the role of the state.

*Hobsbawm, E. J. *Industry and Empire.* 1969. A lively account of British economic transformation by an influential Marxist historian.

*Kemp, Tom. *Industrialization in Nineteenth-Century Europe.* 2nd ed. 1985. Comparative analysis of differences and similarities in the process of industrialization as it spread across Europe.

Kissinger, Henry A. *A World Restored: Metternich, Castlereagh, and the Problems of Peace, 1812–22.* 1957. The author's subsequent fame adds to the interest of this account, which is very sympathetic to Metternich.

Kossman, Ernst H. *The Low Countries, 1780–1940.* 1978. Balanced treatment of a region that was an important participant in all the trends of modern European history.

*Landes, David S. *The Unbound Prometheus: Technological Change and Development in Western Europe from 1750 to the Present Day.* 1969. Emphasizes the role of technology.

*Macartney, C. A. *The Habsburg Empire, 1790–1918.* 1968. Detailed and authoritative.

Magraw, Roger. *France, 1815–1914: The Bourgeois Century.* 1986. A clear general account attentive to social change.

*More, Charles. *Understanding the Industrial Revolution.* 2000. Applies modern theory to rethinking the origins, nature, and development of the industrial revolution in Britain.

*Nicolson, Harold. *The Congress of Vienna: A Study in Allied Unity, 1812–1822.* 1970. A classic account of the process of peacemaking by a British diplomat.

Nipperdey, Thomas. *Germany from Napoleon to Bismarck, 1800–1866.* 1996. An invaluable modern synthesis.

O'Brien, Patrick, and Caglar Keyder. *Economic Growth in Britain and France, 1780–1914.* 1978. A thorough examination of statistical methods and data for the period, focusing in particular on wages and productivity.

668 Chapter Twenty-Two Foundations of the Nineteenth Century: Politics and Social Change

*Pollard, Sidney. *Peaceful Conquest: The Industrialization of Europe 1760–1970.* 1981. A provocative study that focuses on the importance of geographical regions and not political units.

Price, Roger. *An Economic History of Modern France, 1730–1914.* 1981. Underlines the importance of modes of communication and transportation in the development of the marketplace.

*Rémond, René. *Religion and Society in Modern Europe.* 1999. An impressive overview of a topic too often neglected.

*Schroeder, Paul. *The Transformation of European Politics, 1763–1848.* 1994. An authoritative synthesis on Europe's state system.

Seton-Watson, Hugh. *The Russian Empire, 1801–1917.* 1967. A solid, largely political survey.

*Smith, Bonnie G. *Changing Lives: Women in European History Since 1700.* 1989. Discussion of the major trends affecting all classes; excellent bibliographies.

*Tilly, Louise, and Joan Scott. *Women, Work, and Family.* 1978. Discusses the impact of industrialization on women and on the family economy.

*Trebilcock, Clive. *The Industrialization of the Continental Powers, 1780–1914.* 1981. A synthesis that uses modern research to emphasize the political implications of industrialization.

*Woloch, Isser (ed.). *Revolution and the Meanings of Freedom in the Nineteenth Century.* 1996. Ten specialists assess the political culture of different European countries (and Latin America) in an era obsessed with the promise and dangers that revolution might bring.

*Available in paperback.

This painting of a copper foundry in the 1830s evokes the grandeur and ugliness of early industrialization.
The Art Archive/Bibliothéque des Arts Decoratifs. Paris/Dagli Orti

Chapter Twenty-Three

LEARNING TO LIVE WITH CHANGE

IDEAS OF CHANGE • THE STRUCTURE OF SOCIETY •
THE SPREAD OF LIBERAL GOVERNMENT

Everyone knew that after twenty-five years of revolution and war Europe was not the same as before, and even in 1814 it was clear to many that economic developments were bringing further change. Thus, change itself became the central preoccupation of philosophy and the arts as well as politics. And that was as true of those who decried what was lost from the past as of those who welcomed the prospects of a new kind of society. While intellectuals wrestled with these issues, the very structure of society (and the ways of describing it) continued to be transformed. Social relations based on custom were giving way to ones seemingly controlled by the impersonal rules of law and economics. Populations were growing larger, and more people lived in cities, where lifestyles and social problems were different. Industrialization subjected millions to hardships for which neither individual charity nor government had adequate answers. These changes, experienced more intensely in cities than in the countryside and more in Western than in Southern or Eastern Europe, raised explosive questions and in Western Europe led to new liberal regimes.

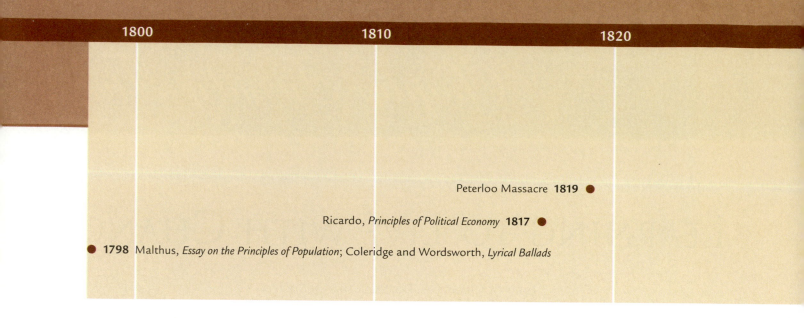

Peterloo Massacre **1819** ●

Ricardo, *Principles of Political Economy* **1817** ●

● **1798** Malthus, *Essay on the Principles of Population*; Coleridge and Wordsworth, *Lyrical Ballads*

IDEAS OF CHANGE

Political ideas, social theories, and new movements in the arts were all closely interconnected in the early nineteenth century. They altered the way people painted pictures, wrote poetry, collected statistics, analyzed society, studied biology, and understood history. Several elements served to connect all this creative diversity and increase its impact. The writers, scientists, artists, and professors whose works were most influential increasingly saw themselves as having a special place in society because of their talents and knowledge. Primarily male and largely from the middle class, they depended less on patronage than on their connections to established institutions such as academies, universities, publishing houses, magazines, and newspapers. Through exhibitions, public lectures, and publications, they sought to reach others like themselves and then a broader audience. Their need to explain modern society, like their effort to comprehend the French Revolution, produced competing interpretations that were, in fact, debates about the nature of society and the sources of historical change.

Romanticism

Romanticism, a movement in philosophy and the arts, cannot be captured in any simple definition. Associated with the great burst of creativity in Germany in the latter part of the eighteenth century and with the ideas of Jean-Jacques Rousseau (see chapter 19), the Romantic movement, initially strongest in Germany and England, rapidly spread across the Continent and to North America. Romanticism affected every aspect of culture and in such a variety of ways that it is best understood as a set of attitudes and aesthetic preferences rather than as a defined doctrine. Although by midcentury

other styles and concerns challenged Romanticism, its influence continued into the twentieth century.

Certain themes were characteristic: an emphasis on feeling, emotion, and direct experience more than on universal principles and abstract logic; a preoccupation with erotic love, often unrequited, and mortality; fascination with nature understood as an unconquerable power, raw and unpredictable; a search for the organic relatedness of all life that went beyond the cold analysis of cause and effect; a concern for spirituality, deep and mysterious, that tended to dismiss thinkers of the Enlightenment as shallow; interest in the momentary, the accidental, and the uniquely colorful in human affairs; and an admiration for imagination and originality that hailed the individual genius who was capable of experiences and feelings more profound than those of ordinary mortals.

These preferences were revealed in matters of fashion as well as content. English gardens became the vogue. Carefully arranged to look natural, with great trees and hidden copses along a rolling terrain dappled with flowers of varied colors and heights, gardens in the English style replaced, or were added to, the geometrical plots and cropped hedges of the classical garden. Romantic artists and writers favored flamboyant dress that distinguished them from aristocrats or bourgeois and presented themselves as pensive and passionate.

Romantic Philosophy and Literature Romantic modes of thought flourished in conjunction with the revival of religion, the increased interest in history, and rising nationalism, all of which are discussed in the next chapter; but their core was philosophical. Romantic thinkers wrote about metaphysics, aesthetics, and the philosophy of nature. While envisioned in terms of grand systems, Romantic philosophies were often expressed piecemeal in poetry, aphorisms, meditations on death, and autobiographical accounts of youthful

1830 Revolutions in France and Belgium

1832 Reform Act for British Parliament

1830s Cholera epidemics

1834 Spanish constitution; new Poor Law in Britain; silk workers uprising in Lyon

1842 Parliament rejects the Great Charter

1846–1847 Potato famine in Ireland

1848 Abolition of serfdom in Prussia and Austria

Mill, *On Liberty* **1859**

Joseph Severn
SHELLY AT THE BATHS OF CARACALLA
Notebook at the ready, the English romantic poet Shelley seeks inspiration in contemplating the ancient ruins at Caracalla.
Keats-Shelley Memorial House, Rome.
Scala/Art Resource, NY

yearning for truth. In Germany August Wilhelm Schlegel and in England Samuel Taylor Coleridge (heavily influenced by German philosophy) were among the most influential Romantic thinkers, through intense personal friendships with other intellectuals as well as their published work. Both wrote poetry, drama, and essays on philosophy and theology.

Coleridge's *Rime of the Ancient Mariner*, one of the great long poems in English, is a tale of guilt, redemption, and the supernatural. Full of evocative nautical lore, the poem tells of a seaman cursed to wear a dead albatross around his neck, a result of his violence against nature. He is released from that weight only in the end, as he comes to feel God's love. With William Wordsworth, his closest friend, Coleridge campaigned for a new kind of poetry, direct and emotive. Wordsworth's poems contrasted the beauty of nature with urban corruption, the clear-eyed and innocent responsiveness of youth with the jaded sadness of age. Like William Blake before him, he denounced the materialism of his age. Blake, whose drawings and poems were filled with religious mystery, also believed that poets had a special wisdom that society should heed. Many other Romantics could have joined in Blake's cry:

673

Augustus Pugin
A convert to Catholicism and a leading student of Gothic architecture, Augustus Pugin was one of the architects of the Houses of Parliament. These illustrations, part of a book on *Contrasts* comparing Catholic and Protestant society, sum up the romantic and conservative critique of modern society for replacing church spires with smokestacks, cottages and artisanship with massive tenements and factories, and charities with prisons. (The new prison in the foreground is Jeremy Bentham's Panopticon, designed so that a single guard can see down all the cellblocks.)
New York Public Library

Hear the voice of the Bard,
Who present, past, and future, sees
The Holy Word
That walk'd among the ancient trees.

The anguish, depression, and despair experienced in their personal lives became for Romantic poets a sign of their own sensitivity and a summons to a higher vision of the meaning of life.

In France, where Romanticism developed somewhat later, Madame Anne-Louise de Staël's essays on the German thinkers stimulated a whole generation of philosophers, historians, and novelists. These ranged from the young Victor Hugo, whose plays and novels (*The Hunchback of Notre Dame* and *Les Misérables* are the best known) made him the towering figure of French letters through most of the century, to the swashbuckling stories of Alexander Dumas' *Three Musketeers.* Novelists and dramatists in Italy and Russia, as well as in England, France, and Germany, often set their tales in the distant past and tended to favor vivid description and singular settings appropriate to occurrences beyond rational understanding. Turning from the Enlightenment and its veneration for the Renaissance, they preferred the rougher, sprawling picture of human experience in seventeenth-century writers like Shakespeare and Cervantes (stimulating an important revival of interest in their work). They felt a kinship with the Middle Ages as an age of faith and spontaneity that produced such achievements as Dante's poetry and Gothic architecture.

Joseph Mallord William Turner
INTERIOR OF TINTURN ABBEY, EXHIBITED 1794
The evocation of nature and time, favorite Romantic themes, made the ruins of Tintern Abbey the subject of a poem by Wordsworth and of this watercolor by Turner.
Watercolor. Victoria and Albert Museum, London/Art Resource, NY

WORDSWORTH ON THE ROLE OF THE POET

Wordsworth was one of England's most popular poets, and the success of his Lyrical Ballads *may have encouraged him to write a preface to the second edition, explaining what he was up to. He points out that his poems differ from classical poetry with its greater formality and lofty themes, and he justifies his use of ordinary speech. In making his case, he touches on many of the themes characteristic of the Romantic movement.*

"The principle object of these Poems was to choose incidents and situations from common life, and to relate or describe them, throughout, as far as was possible in a selection of language really used by men, and, at the same time, to throw over them a certain colouring of imagination, whereby ordinary things could be presented to the mind in an unusual aspect. . . . Humble and rustic life was generally chosen because, in that condition, the essential passions of the heart find a better soil in which they can attain their maturity, are less under restraint, and speak a plainer and more emphatic language; because in that condition of life our elementary feelings co-exist in a state of greater simplicity, and, consequently, may be more accurately contemplated and more forcibly communicated; because the manners of rural life germinate from those elementary feelings . . . ; and, lastly, because in that condition the passions of men are incorporated with the beautiful and permanent forms of nature. . . .

" . . . For all good poetry is the spontaneous overflow of powerful feelings: and though this be true, Poems to which any value can be attached were never produced on any variety of subjects but by a man who, being possessed of more than usual organic sensibility, had also thought long and deeply. . . .

"The Man of science seeks truth as a remote and unknown benefactor; he cherishes and loves it in his solitude; the Poet, singing a song in which all human beings join with him, rejoices in the presence of truth as our visible friend and hourly companion. Poetry is the breath and finer spirit of all knowledge; it is the impassioned expression which is the countenance of all Science. Emphatically may it be said of the Poet, as Shakespeare hath said of man, 'that he looks before and after.' He is the rock of defence for human nature; an upholder and preserver, carrying everywhere with him relationship and love . . . ; the Poet binds together by passion and knowledge the vast empire of human society, as it is spread over the whole earth, and over all time."

From William Wordsworth, "Preface to the Second Edition of *Lyrical Ballads*," in *William Wordsworth: Selected Poems and Prefaces*, Jack Stillinger (ed.), Houghton-Mifflin, 1965.

The Wider Influence of Romanticism   The fairy tales of Hans Christian Andersen combined the Romantic delight in folk culture and affection for childhood. Throughout the Western world there was a new taste for tales of ghostly spirits (Edgar Allen Poe was one of the first American writers to achieve international recognition) and paintings of storms and ruins that evoked unseen powers, as in the landscapes of William Constable and J. M. W. Turner in England and Caspar David Friedrich in Germany.

Literary and artistic works thus burst beyond classical forms. Romantic painters like Théodore Géricault in France emphasized vibrant color and swirling lines without the sharp outlines and balanced composition so important to their predecessors. Like Eugène Delacroix (see his paintings on p. 699), they were drawn to exotic scenes from the past and from North Africa and the Middle East.

Romantic values came together with particular power in music, admired for its ability to communicate an ineffable understanding deeper than words. The response to the works of Beethoven had brought a self-conscious seriousness to music. Critics wrote of his symphonies and string quartets in terms of their philosophic profundity, and audiences listened in reverent silence, finding in that shared experience something akin to religion. Subsequent Romantic composers appealed even more directly to the heart, emphasizing melody and using freer harmonies. When words and music were combined, as in the song cycles of Franz Schubert and Robert Schumann, or in grand opera (often hailed as the highest of the arts), it was the music that mattered most.

Both conservatives and radicals drew upon the Romantic movement, for it was both a call for change and a response to it, attentive to politics as well as to philosophy and the arts. Conservatives found in Romantic values powerful arguments for rejecting the French Revolution and considered it the lamentable result of Enlightenment rationalism and of the universalism that ignored local variety and tradition. Stability, they argued, was possible only in a society organically connected, held together as it had been in the Middle Ages by respect for custom and religion. They contrasted their vision of an organic society with the competition and selfish individualism of modern capitalism.

Radicals, however, used Romantic themes to argue that a new era required shattering old institutional constraints, much as creativity in the arts fostered the breaking of established art forms. Romantic thinkers tended to see folk culture and language as natural expressions of the nation. For conservatives these values validated rural life and custom; for radicals the promise of this culture would be realized when the people spontaneously arose to achieve new freedoms. In Germany and England many Romantics had, like Wordsworth, initially welcomed the French Revolution only to turn away from it in disgust. Victor Hugo, on the other hand, turned from conservatism to become a lifelong advocate of radical change. A younger generation of English poets, led by Lord Byron, Percy Bysshe Shelley, and John Keats, were persistent critics of church and state drawn to the promise of revolution. In its aspirations and its tumultuousness Romanticism expressed the preoccupation with change that marked the age.

Social Thought

Conservatism   Conservatism grew from opposition to the French Revolution to become what today would be called an ideology—a coherent view of human nature, social organization, and political power that generally justified the status quo. This conservatism was not mere nostalgia for the past. Rather, like the restoration regimes established in 1815, conservatives advocated changes when designed to strengthen the kind of society they favored.

Not that conservatives always agreed. But in arguing for social order, they tended to emphasize the limitations of human understanding, the wisdom of established customs, the value of hierarchy, and the social importance of religion. From those concerns, conservatives mounted a powerful critique not just of radical programs but of modern society itself as perilously inclined toward antisocial individualism, materialism, and immorality. More than a matter of temperament or interest, conservatism would remain a vigorous part of European intellectual life and political discourse throughout the nineteenth century.

From the late eighteenth century on, the powerful English prose of Edmund Burke (see discussion on p. 593) provided what was perhaps the most influential formulation of the conservative position. Society, he argued, exists through continuity. By granting special privileges to certain groups, it fulfills social needs in a way that sustains order, achieving a delicate arrangement in which rank is related to social function and in which differences of status, having evolved through time, are acceptable to all. This "natural" historical order, Burke argued, was far wiser than the "artificial" plans of radicals, no matter how well intentioned. The Burkean view thus allowed for gradual change, at least in theory; in practice, such arguments could be used against any plan for general reform. This tendency was

George Cruikshank
DEATH OR LIBERTY, **1819**
This cartoon by George Cruikshank, the most famous cartoonist of the day, reflects the vitriolic quality of political debate in the early nineteenth century. A satanic figure of Reform (the Phrygian cap on a pike behind him was a symbol of the French Revolution) assaults Britannia, who relies on religion to save her. The cartoon is sarcastically entitled "Death or Liberty," but the subtitle is more straightforward: "or Britannia and the Virtues of the Constitution in Danger of Violation from the Great Political Libertine, Radical Reform."
Private Collection/Bridgeman Art Library

strengthened by a distrust of reason that rejected the ideas of the Enlightenment as dangerously abstract. No social schemes or written constitutions could reconstitute society, because it was a great interconnecting web, and slogans about rights or equality merely concealed selfish interests and encouraged false hopes.

Conservatives found in history the record of how painfully civilization had developed and how fragile it remained, and many saw evidence not only of human error but of divine will in events since the French Revolution. Christianity was the source of Europe's strength, and Christian fear a necessary restraint on humanity's selfish and prideful nature. Without it, society dissolved into revolution and anarchy. Political battles were part of a far larger millennial conflict.

Such views gave conservative thought both militancy and depth. Europeans were used to receiving radical ideas from France, and two of the most pungent exponents of conservatism were men who wrote in French, Joseph de Maistre and Louis de Bonald. Society's first task, they argued, is self-preservation. Only authority can check the selfish wills of individuals, and authority requires undivided sovereignty, social hierarchy, close links between church and state, and the vigilant suppression of dangerous ideas. These writers thus connected religion to politics and tied the Church to aristocracy and monarchy. Revolution, Maistre explained, is divine retribution for

MAISTRE'S OPPOSITION TO REFORM

Over the course of the past twenty years, most European governments had adopted constitutions when Joseph de Maistre, writing from exile in Russia, set forth his objections to them in his Essay on the Generative Principle of Political Constitutions. *First published in Russia in 1810 and in Paris in 1814, the essay was reprinted many times.*

"Every thing brings us back to the general rule—*man cannot create a constitution; and no legitimate constitution can be written.* The collection of fundamental laws, which must essentially constitute a civil or religious society, never has been written, and never will be, *a priori*. It is only when society finds itself already constituted, without being able to say how, that it is possible to make known, or explain, in writing, certain special articles; but in almost every case these declarations or explanations are the effect of very great evils, and always cost the people more than they are worth.

" . . . Not only does it not belong to man to create institutions, but it does not appear that his power, *unassisted*, extends even to change for the better institutions already established. . . . *Nothing* [says the philosopher, Origen] . . . *can be changed for the better among men, without God.* All men have a consciousness of this truth, without being in a state to explain it to themselves. Hence that instinctive aversion, in every good mind, to innovations. The word *reform*, in itself, and previous to all examinations, will be always suspected by wisdom, and the experience of every age justifies this sort of instinct.

" . . . To apply these maxims to a particular case . . . the great question of parliamentary reform, which has agitated minds in England so powerfully, and for so long a time, I still find myself constrained to believe, that this idea is pernicious, and that if the English yield themselves too readily to it, they will have occasion to repent."

From Joseph de Maistre, *Essay on the Generative Principle of Political Constitutions*, Boston: Little and Brown, 1847; reprint: Scholars' Facsimiles & Reprints, New York: Delmar, 1977.

false ideas (see "Maistre's Opposition to Reform," above). This hard-line conservatism, very different from Burke's, contained little that was humane or tolerant. With its praise of hangmen and censors, it spoke only to those who already shared its fears. Terrified of weakening the dikes that held back revolution, it left little room for compromise, divided while calling for unity, and relied on power while speaking of the social good. Nevertheless, as a way of understanding change, mobilizing opposition to liberal demands, and criticizing modern life, conservatism would be a profoundly influential element in modern thought.

Liberalism   Liberalism, like conservatism, was not so much a compact doctrine as a set of attitudes. Whereas conservatism emphasized tradition and hierarchy, liberalism was associated with ideas of social progress, belief in economic development, and values associated with the middle class. Confident that their ideas would triumph, liberals generally welcomed change.

They appraised society primarily in terms of freedom for individual choice and opportunities for individual growth, an emphasis that gave some ethical dignity to the pain of industrialization and lent promise to the process of social change. They believed their principles were universally valid; yet, to the perpetual surprise of its adherents, liberalism proved a creed of limited appeal, forever subject to attack and internal division. Enthusiasm for limited constitutional reform produced disagreements over how limited it should be. In practice, reconciling liberty with order or equal rights with private property proved contentious and led to attacks on liberalism and divisions among liberals themselves. Some theorists reduced liberalism to little more than the narrow justification of individual success. Others expanded it until the demand for social justice overshadowed its founding principles of competition and individualism. In each country the temper of liberalism was different, shaped by a national history liberals never wholly dominated.

Political Liberalism   Liberal political thought was rooted in the writings of John Locke and of the philosophes. Liberals in the nineteenth century believed that their programs would benefit individuals and society as a whole. A leading French liberal, Benjamin Constant, put the case succinctly: "The liberty of the individual is the object of all human association; on it rest public and private morality; on it are based the calculations of industry and commerce, and without it there is neither peace, dignity, nor happiness for men." By this creed, freedom would lead to morality, prosperity, and progress. The freedom that liberals sought was primarily political and legal, and they generally favored a constitution and representative institutions, freedom of the press and of assembly, an extension of the jury system, separation of church and state, public education, and administrative reform. Most liberals did not favor democracy—political wisdom, they thought, required the advantages of education and leisure and the restraint that came with owning property—but nearly all believed that giving ideas a free hearing and propertied voters a free voice would result in policies beneficial to all.

Economic Liberalism   Although liberal politics and liberal economic theory were closely related, they were nevertheless separable. The advocates of one were not always committed to the other. Still, England's example of economic growth as well as political liberty made it the model of nineteenth-century liberalism. Adam Smith's argument that government intervention in the free play of the market restricted economic forces, which if left to themselves would increase productivity and prosperity, became a dogma of liberalism. As systematically expounded by Englishman David Ricardo in his *Principles of Political Economy and Taxation* (1817), liberal theory became the keystone of modern economics. Ricardo, a financier who became wealthy during the Napoleonic wars and then retired from business, became an important public figure; but his great influence lay in his precise, flat prose that presented economics as a science.

The wealth of the community, Ricardo declared, comes from land, capital, and labor; and these three "classes" are compensated by rent, profit, and wages. A product's value results from the labor required to make it: This was the labor theory of value, which socialists would later use for very different purposes. For Ricardo, this theory led to principles of property similar to those of Locke and to an emphasis on labor saving as the source of profit, a view foreshadowed by Adam Smith. The value of land or of work was determined not by individual decisions but by economic laws. The poorest land in cultivation simply sustains those who work it; but the most fertile land produces more for the same labor, and that increment constitutes profit, paid to the landlord as rent. As population pressures bring more (and poorer) land into cultivation, rents rise because the difference between the best and worst land increases. Similarly, wages subtract from profit, but the rate of pay is set by an "iron law of wages." It decrees that when labor is plentiful, the workers tend to be paid at the subsistence level. Short-term fluctuations in prices are the natural regulator within this system, pushing people to activities for which demand is high.

For Ricardo, both land and labor are commodities, their value quite unaffected by any sentimental talk about the virtues of rural life or artisanship, and society is a collection of competing interests. Legislation cannot raise wages or prevent the marketplace from working in its natural way; but if people acknowledge economic laws and act in their own best interest, a natural harmony and progress follow.

While his opponents referred to it as "the dismal science," Ricardo called his subject *political economy*, and a powerful reform movement developed from it. Landed interests, liberals argued, had misused political power for their own benefit while harming the rest of society. Throughout Europe liberal economic theory thus added important weight to demands that special privilege be eliminated (as the French Revolution had done), that governments be responsive to their citizens (who best know their own interests), and above all that the state not try to regulate production and trade. As economic growth became more impressive, it was natural for liberals to add that politicians should adopt some of the efficiency and energy of the men of action who were transforming the economy.

Utilitarianism   The call for political and social reform could also lead to renewed emphasis on the role of the state, as it did in the **utilitarianism** of another Englishman, Jeremy Bentham. Like the philosophes, Bentham believed he could rationally deduce practical programs from universal principles, and he was ready to write a constitution for Russia or codify the laws of Latin American republics. Bentham began his reform campaign by criticizing the legal system, and he remained all his life an opponent of the precedent-bound courts of England. Some of his most important writings before 1789 appeared first in French (the revolutionaries gave him French citizenship).

But in contrast to most philosophes, he rejected the doctrine of natural rights as a meaningless abstraction. In his system utility replaced natural rights as the basis of public policy, and utility was measured by determining the greatest good for the greatest number. In the Enlightenment tradition, he combined plans of detailed reform with a theory of psychology. The good is that which avoids pain and gives pleasure—a calculation all people make for themselves anyway and that better education would enable them to make more wisely. In contrast to Burke's emphasis on tradition and many liberals' preference for limited government, Bentham gave the state a central role. It should assign penalties for undesirable actions and rewards for desirable ones, distributing them to induce socially beneficial behavior.

Bentham's followers, sober intellectuals who called themselves *philosophic radicals*, did not necessarily adopt all his doctrines, but they applied his principles in every sphere. By his death in 1832, they were among the most important reformers of Parliament, law, prisons, education, and welfare. A special group within a larger liberal movement, they shared and contributed to the tendency of liberals everywhere to press for hu-

MILL OPPOSES THE SUBJECTION OF WOMEN

John Stuart Mill published his essay The Subjection of Women *in 1869. His arguments were based on familiar ideas about individualism and modern progress, but their extension to women's rights and in such absolute terms went much further than most contemporary discussion.*

"The object of this Essay is to explain, as clearly as I am able, the grounds of an opinion which . . . has been constantly growing stronger by the progress of reflection and the experience of life: That the principle which regulates the existing social relations between the two sexes—the legal subordination of one sex to the other—is wrong in itself, and now one of the chief hindrances to human improvement; and that it ought to be replaced by a principle of perfect equality, admitting no power or privilege on the one side, nor disability on the other.

" . . . The masters of all other slaves rely, for maintaining obedience, on fear; either fear of themselves, or religious fears. The masters of women wanted more than simple obedience, and they turned the whole force of education to effect their purpose. All women are brought up from the very earliest years in the belief that their ideal of character is the very opposite to that of men; not self-will, and government by self-control, but submission, and yielding to the control of others. All the moralities tell them that it is the duty of women, and all the current sentimentalities that it is their nature, to live for others; to make complete abnegation of themselves, and to have no life but in their affections.

" . . . So far as the whole course of human improvement up to this time, the whole stream of modern tendencies, warrants any inference on the subject, it is, that this relic of the past is discordant with the future, and must necessarily disappear.

"For what is the peculiar character of the modern world—the difference which chiefly distinguishes modern institutions, modern social ideas, modern life itself, from those of times long past? It is, that human beings are no longer born to their place in life, and chained down by an inexorable bond to the place they are born to, but are free to employ their faculties, and such favourable chances as offer, to achieve the lot which may appear to them most desirable.

"If this general principle of social and economical sciences is . . . true, we ought to act as if we believed it, and not to ordain that to be born a girl instead of a boy, any more than to be born black instead of white, or a commoner instead of a nobleman, shall decide the person's position through all life. . . .

"At present, in the more improved countries, the disabilities of women are the only case, save one, in which laws and institutions take persons at their birth, and ordain that they shall never in all their lives be allowed to compete for certain things. The one exception is that of royalty.

" . . . The social subordination of women thus stands out an isolated fact in modern social institutions; a solitary breach of what has become their fundamental law; a single relic of an old world of thought and practice exploded in everything else, but retained in the one thing of most universal interest."

From John Stuart Mill, "The Subjection of Women," *Three Essays,* Oxford: Oxford University Press, 1975.

mane reforms on grounds of common sense and natural harmony.

John Stuart Mill   Liberalism's broader meaning is best exemplified in John Stuart Mill, the most important liberal thinker of the nineteenth century. Mill's father was a leading Benthamite, and he raised his son in the strictest utilitarianism, but the younger Mill gradually came to modify received doctrine. Mill was extraordinarily learned—a philosopher, economist, and publicist—and he wrote some of the most influential classics of modern thought. Fearful of the intolerance and oppression of which any social class or political majority was capable, he made freedom of thought a first principle. He advocated universal suffrage as a necessary check on the elite and proportional representation as a means of protecting minorities. Mill acknowledged that institutions,

even liberal ones, suited to one stage of historical development might not be appropriate for another.

To counterbalance the influence of the established elites, Mill favored a more open administration, organized interest groups, and workers' cooperatives. Moved by the problems of the industrial poor, he tried to distinguish between production (to which liberal economics could still apply) and distribution (in which the state might intervene in behalf of justice), and he came to see that collective action by the workers could enhance freedom rather than restrict it. In later years, under the influence of his companion, Harriet Taylor, Mill courageously advocated causes, such as the emancipation of women and the confiscation of excess profit, that seemed fearfully radical to most contemporaries (see "Mill Opposes the Subjection of Women," above). His liberalism, thus modified and extended,

A saintly father figure, Fourier instructs his disciples from a hill overlooking an idyllic setting and an imagined phalanstery, Fourier's orderly community for four hundred families.
AKG London

remained firm. His essay, *On Liberty*, published in 1859, stands as one of the important works of European political theory, a balanced but unyielding declaration that society can have no higher interest than the freedom of each of its members.

The Early Socialists

Socialist thought offered a radical alternative to conservative and liberal ideologies, varied as each of those were. Among scores of socialist schemes, those of Saint-Simon, Fourier, and Owen were notable for the attention they won among intellectuals and political leaders. All three men had lived through the French Revolution and had personal experience of burgeoning capitalism in the early stages of industrialization, and each of them founded a movement critical of capitalism. Competition, they argued, is wasteful and cruel, induces hard-hearted indifference to suffering, misuses wealth, and leads to frequent economic crises. They offered instead scores of suggestions for organizing production differently and creating a harmonious, orderly, and truly free society.

Saint-Simon As a young French officer, Comte Claude de Saint-Simon fought alongside George Washington at Yorktown. During the French Revolution, he abandoned his title, made and lost a fortune speculat-

ing in land, and then devoted himself to the difficult career of a seer. Injustice, social divisions, and inefficiency could be overcome, he believed, in a society directed by experts standing above the conflict: scientists, men of affairs (*industriels*), and artists. These specialists, chosen for their ability, would design plans to increase productivity and prosperity for the benefit of all. The integrated, organic quality of Greek city-states and of the Middle Ages could be recaptured in the industrial age with scientists and managers (who would have the authority once granted priests and soldiers) leading humanity to self-fulfillment.

Saint-Simon's theories won a significant following, especially among the bright engineers at France's Ecole Polytechnique, and an extraordinary number of France's leading engineers and entrepreneurs in the next generation fondly recalled the **Saint-Simonian** enthusiasms of their youth. In their penchant for planning, in their grand economic projects, and in their schemes for social reform, they carried elements of his teaching into the world of affairs and respectable politics. There were important Saint-Simonian movements in every country, and later socialists would long sustain his respect for industrialization and the power of planning.

Fourier Charles Fourier had been a traveling salesman before dedicating himself, at the same time as

Saint-Simon, to a theory that he firmly believed would rank among the greatest discoveries ever made. His cantankerous yet shrewd writings on contemporary society were so copious that his manuscripts have still not all been printed, despite the devotion of generations of admirers. His central concept, however, was an ideal community, the *phalanstery* (from *phalanx*). Once even one was created, the happiness and well-being of its members would inspire the establishment of others until all of society was converted.

A phalanstery should contain some sixteen hundred men, women, and children, representatives of all the types of personality identified in Fourier's elaborate psychology. He listed a dozen passions that move human beings and proposed to organize the phalanstery in such a way that individuals would accomplish the tasks society required simply by doing what they wanted. Each member would perform a variety of tasks, engaging in no one task for too long; pleasure and work would flow together. Largely self-sufficient, a phalanstery would produce some goods for export and pay its members according to the capital, labor, and talent that each contributed. Although no phalanstery was ever established exactly as Fourier planned (he even offered designs for the architecture), communities were founded on Fourierist principles from the United States to Romania; and if few of them survived for long, the vision endured of a society in which cooperation replaced compulsion and joy transformed drudgery.

Robert Owen

Robert Owen was one of the success stories of industrial capitalism: A self-made man, he rose from selling cloth to be the manager and part owner of a large textile mill in New Lanark, Scotland. Owen ran the mill in a way that transformed the whole town, and by the end of the Napoleonic wars, distinguished visitors were traveling from all over Europe to see the miracle he had wrought in New Lanark. The workday was shortened from fifteen to ten hours. New housing eventually allowed an employee's family several rooms; inspection committees maintained cleanliness; gardens were planted and sewers installed. In nursery schools with airy, pleasant rooms, children were given exercise, encouraged to sing and dance, taught without corporal punishment, and trained in the useful arts. Most promising of all, the subjects of this paternalistic kingdom developed a pride in their community, productivity rose, and profits increased.

Owen had, he felt, disproved Ricardo's dismal economic laws, and he set about establishing ideal communities elsewhere. Like Fourier's, they would be placed in a rural setting and would supply most of their own needs. Members would take meals and enjoy entertainment in common, and children would be raised communally. After five years in distributive or managerial jobs, adults would assume the tasks of government, cultivating the sciences and the arts in their increasing leisure time. The controlled environment would ensure good character among community members, and the division of tasks would provide them with varied and interesting lives. Standardized production would offer more goods at lower cost (the snobbery that made luxuries attractive would disappear), and higher wages would increase sales (see "Owen Tells Congress about the Science of Socialism," p. 682).

Even after losing most of his wealth when the community of New Harmony, which he founded in Indiana, failed, Owen remained the single most important figure in the labor movement and in the workers' cooperatives that he helped spread across England in the 1830s and 1840s.

The Socialist Critique

Although much in these socialist movements was easily ridiculed, the values they stressed echoed those of growing workers' movements everywhere. These early socialists sought to combine an older sense of community with the possibilities of a new era. They imagined a society enriched by new inventions and new means of production, in which new forms of social organization would foster cooperation and love. Their indictment of capitalism, their insights into the nature of productivity and exchange, and their attention to social planning and education had an impact far beyond their relatively small circles of believers. The dream of fraternity and of work that was fulfilling echoed through later socialist and anarchist movements; yet nearly everyone ultimately rejected their ideas as impractical and too radical. Bucolic isolation and artisanal production became increasingly unrealistic in the face of industrialization, and these theories were incredibly vague about problems of politics and power.

The nature of their radicalism, however, deserves a closer look. The criticisms of liberal society mounted by Saint-Simon, Fourier, and Owen were not so different overall from the conservative attack. With some restrictions (Saint-Simon, for example, insisted on the abolition of inheritance), they allowed private property, and none of them was thoroughly democratic. What most shocked contemporaries were their views on the status of women, sexual mores, and Christianity. All rejected the place allotted women in bourgeois society, and Owen not only specified that women should share in governing but believed that their emancipation required lessening their family responsibilities. All wrote of sensual

OWEN TELLS CONGRESS ABOUT THE SCIENCE OF SOCIALISM

Robert Owen made a number of trips to the United States in connection with the Owenite community on the Wabash River at New Harmony, Indiana. His international fame was such that on one of these trips he was invited to give two addresses to the U.S. Congress. In the first he called on Congress to adopt his principles; and in the second—delivered on March 7, 1825—he set out in some detail his plan for a community of up to five thousand people on one or two thousand acres, with a square of large buildings at the center. These buildings would house the "school, academy, and university" as well as washrooms, kitchens, dining halls, dormitories for children over the age of two, and apartments. Owen described the arrangements for central heating and cooling, gardens, manufacturing, and farms and discussed how the community would be governed by an elected committee. But before entering into such specific matters, he presented the general principles of his program:

"Then it should be ever remembered, that the first principle of the science is derived from the knowledge of the facts, *that external circumstances may be so formed as to have an overwhelming and irresistible influence over every infant that comes into existence, either for good or evil . . . and thus, at pleasure, make any portion, or the whole, of the human race, poor, ignorant, vicious, and wretched; or affluent, intelligent, virtuous, and happy.*

"And thus, also, form man to understand and to practice pure and genuine religion, which never did nor ever will consist in unmeaning phrases, forms, and ceremonies; but in the daily, undeviating practice . . . of charity, benevolence, and kindness . . . [this] is the *universal religion of human nature.*

" . . . Having then discovered, as I believe I have, the science of the influence of circumstances, and a rational, and therefore, a pure and genuine religion, the next important consideration is, to ascertain in what manner the new science and the new religion can be applied to produce the promised practical results. I have been frequently urged to apply these principles to the present state of society, and not attempt to disturb it, but endeavor to make them unite

harmoniously together. . . . The inventor of the Steam Engine might as well have been required to unite his new machinery with the inefficient and clumsy horse engine. . . . The fact is . . . the system which I propose now for the formation and government of society, is founded on principles, not only altogether different, but directly opposed to the system of society which has hitherto been taught and practised at all times, in all nations.

" . . . My conviction is, that, from necessity and inclination, the individual or old system of society would break up, and soon terminate; from necessity, because the new societies would undersell all individual producers, both of agricultural productions, and manufactured commodities. And from inclination, because it is scarcely to be supposed that anyone would continue to live under the miserable, anxious, individual system of opposition and counteraction, when they could with ease form themselves into, or become members of, one of these associations of union, intelligence, and kind feeling."

From Oakley C. Johnson (ed.), *Robert Owen in the United States*, Humanities Press, 1970.

---

pleasure as good and of its repression as a characteristic European error. The Saint-Simonians publicly advocated free love, and Fourier carefully provided that neither young nor old should be deprived of the pleasures of the flesh. Owen was only slightly less outspoken in his contempt for Christian marriage. At the same time, all three stressed religion as the source of community feeling, brotherhood, and ethics. Their efforts to replace what they had eliminated therefore led to imitations of Christian ritual and foggy mysticism that provided an easy target for their opponents. By the end of the nineteenth century, these thinkers would be remembered as "utopian socialists." For by then, socialist thought would center on the more hard-headed and systematic theories of Karl Marx.

THE STRUCTURE OF SOCIETY

Nineteenth-century politics, economies, and ideological conflict had to deal with fundamental changes in social organization. The idea that society consists of distinct social classes flourished because it took into account the spreading effects of industrialization. Population growth and urbanization altered the way people lived and raised new challenges to which individuals, families, groups, and governments had to respond.

Social Classes

Theories of change combined with everyday experience to alter the way nineteenth-century society was perceived. In the old regime, discussion of the "orders" or "ranks" in society had referred to an imaginary social pyramid rising from the lowliest peasant through all the ranks to the monarch. In this idealized picture, each person had an assigned place in that pyramid and social relations were governed by elaborate networks of reciprocal responsibilities. In the nineteenth century, society was most often described in terms of a few broad strata, called classes. A person was said to belong to a given social class less on the basis of connection to others than as an attribute of his, or her husband's, occupation. The source of income was assumed to imply something of the values held, the style of life led, and later, the political and social interests likely to be favored. Social relations were represented as matters of free contract between individuals, with middle-class mobility the model. Descriptive of an expanding, fluid, unequal, national society, the concept of class gained urgency with the sharpening contrast between the middle class and the urban poor.

The Aristocracy   The class most easily identified was the aristocracy. Recognized since the Middle Ages as a special group, it included all nobles (whose rank gave them a number of formal privileges) and their immediate relatives, whether they held noble titles or not; members of the upper gentry, who were large landholders and lived like nobles; and (in the ancient commercial cities of the Netherlands, northern Germany, and northern Italy) the established and wealthy patrician families, who dominated the cities though they might not bear titles.

In the nineteenth century, however, the aristocracy was on the defensive. It had been a principal target of the French Revolution, and its privileges and influence were subsequently challenged by new industrial wealth (which overshadowed the fortunes of large landholders), wider participation in politics, the growth of the state, and cultural change. The aristocracy's relative decline was so clear, in fact, that its continued importance is easily overlooked.

A member of France's parliament could rise in 1821 to ask, "What is the aristocracy?" and answer: "I am going to tell you: . . . it is the coalition of those who want to consume without producing, to live without working, to know everything without learning anything, to capture all the honors without having earned them, to occupy all the jobs without being able to fulfill them; that is the aristocracy."[1]

In most countries aristocrats continued to control most of the wealth, were closely allied to an established church, and dominated the upper levels of administration and the military. By training and tone the most international of social classes, aristocrats would remain the preeminent diplomats even in governments dominated by the middle class. Aristocrats also stimulated some of the most influential critiques of nineteenth-century society, denouncing the middle class for selfishness and materialism, proclaiming urban life morally inferior to rural, and lamenting the loss of gentlemanly honor.

National Differences in Aristocracies   In much of Europe, especially the south and east, the aristocracy held on to local power and tremendous wealth, a social pattern exemplified by the Kingdom of Naples and by Russia. In both states the nobility, constituting only about 1 percent of the population, in effect ruled over most of the peasant masses. Three-fifths of the people in southern Italy lived on baronial estates, and after the defeat of Napoleon the aristocracy there worked with king and church to reestablish its authority. In Russia a fraction of the nobility held one-third of the land, and most of the rest of the land, although owned by the state, was administered by nobles. Tyrants on their estates and dominant over local administration, Russia's aristocracy was a pillar of tsarist rule.

In countries in which the nobles made up a higher proportion of the population, the pattern was somewhat different. In Poland, Hungary, and Spain, many of the nobility were extremely poor, and they tended to alternate between desperate allegiance to an empty title and sympathy for radical change. In some countries, however, aristocrats sought to strengthen their influence through representative government and decentralization, thereby cooperating with political and economic reformers. The confident Magyars took this position in Hungary, and so, even more open-mindedly, did the aristocrats of northern Italy, Belgium, and Great Britain. They were thus prominent during the revolutions of 1848 in Hungary and northern Italy and in the subsequent nationalist movements in those countries.

In England, above all, the aristocracy proved willing to accept liberal programs in exchange for keeping their political prominence. Of the one hundred men who served as cabinet ministers in Britain between the electoral reforms of 1832 and 1867, sixty-four were sons of nobles; and perhaps four-fifths of the members of Parliament were landholders or their representatives, closely tied to the aristocracy. On the other hand, younger sons and lesser aristocrats in England were more closely associated with the upper-middle class, which lessened the sharpness of social division.

---

[1] Cited in Nicholas J. Richardson, *The French Prefectural Corps, 1814–1830*, Cambridge, 1966, p. 4.

In Prussia, the most influential aristocrats were the **Junkers** of east Prussia, owners of large estates, some of which included sizable villages. The Junkers maintained their traditional position even when the state became the instrument of dramatic and rapid change. Considered crude and ignorant by most of the aristocracies of Europe—which set great store by polished manners, elegant taste, and excellent French—the Junkers had a proud tradition of service to the state and loyalty to their king. In local government, in the bureaucracy, in the army, and at the court, their manners and their values—from rectitude to fondness for dueling, from arrogance to loyalty—set the tone of Prussian public life.

France is thus the European exception, for there the old aristocracy was reduced to a minor role in national politics after the revolution of 1830. Its members retained major influence in the Church, army, and foreign service, but those institutions were also on the defensive. Yet even in France, aristocrats maintained a strong voice in local affairs and were a major influence on manners and the arts. Everywhere, however, aristocrats were in danger of being isolated from important sources of political and economic power. Lineage was once of such importance that tracing family lines had been a matter of state; now, pride of family was becoming a private matter.

Peasants   The overwhelming majority of all Europeans were peasants, a social class as firmly tied to the land and to tradition as the aristocracy. Praised by conservatives for simple virtues and solid values, disparaged by progressives for their ignorance, peasants struggled to make ends meet in a changing world.

An important change occurred with the emancipation of peasants from traditional obligations to the lord whose land they worked. These "feudal" obligations typically might have required the peasant to give the lord a number of days of labor or to use the lord's grain mill at rates the lord set. The French Revolution abolished such requirements, a policy carried to much of Western Europe by Napoleon and spread to most of Eastern Europe with the revolutions of 1848. These changes encouraged peasant producers to enter the commercial market; but they also deprived peasants of such traditional protections against hard times as the use of a common pasture, the right to glean what was left after the first harvest, and the practice of foraging for firewood in forests owned by others.

Similarly, the decline of the putting-out system in textiles and of local industries took away critical income, especially during the winter months. Agriculture became more commercial, its production increasingly intended for market rather than for mere subsistence or local consumption. Profits increased with the cultivation of one or two cash crops and with the use of improved fertilizers and machinery, but these changes were easier for those farmers with more capital and bigger holdings than most peasants enjoyed. Because larger farms were more likely to be profitable, landed nobles, bourgeois investors, and richer peasants sought to expand and consolidate their holdings.

Peasant Activism   Peasants, however, were not just passive victims of outside forces. They tenaciously maintained old loyalties to their region, their priests, and their habitual ways; and they were the despair of reformers, who were often defeated by peasant suspicion of outsiders and opposition to change. But peasants also used elaborate ties of family and patronage to build effective social networks, and they were frequently shrewd judges of their interests, cooperating with measures that promised immediate benefits while resisting all others with the skepticism of experience.

Their hunger for land, resentment of taxes and military service, and sense of grievance against those above them could also become a major political force. Peasant involvement made a crucial difference in the early days of the French Revolution, in the Spanish resistance to Napoleon, in the wars of German liberation, and in the strength of nationalism in Germany and Italy. Rulers were kept on edge by eruptions of peasant violence in southern England in the 1820s; Ireland in the 1830s and 1840s; Wales, Silesia, and Galicia in the 1840s; and on a smaller scale in most other countries. The outbreaks of 1848 would topple the system of feudal service in the Austrian Empire and eastern Prussia, though rural indifference to constitutional claims and to workers' demands undermined the urban revolutions there.

The peasantry was deeply divided between those who owned land and those who were forced to sell their labor. Some of the former, especially in the West, grew relatively prosperous and joined the influential notables of their region. In most of Europe peasants were tenants who received only a part of the crops they raised, with the rest going to their landlords. Such arrangements could provide security, but they also tended to be inflexible, discouraging adaptation to changes in prices, markets, and technology. Rural laborers were the poorest and most insecure of all, the tinder of violence and the recruits for factory work.

Peasants and Social Change   A central problem for nineteenth-century European society was how to integrate the agricultural economy and the masses dependent on it into the developing commercial and

This idealized picture of prosperous peasants and bustling farmyard is a German lithograph of 1850.
AKG London

industrial economy. By the 1850s the process had gone farthest in France and Great Britain but by opposite means. In Britain the peasantry was largely eliminated as the continuing enclosures of great estates reduced the rural poor to laborers, shifting from place to place and hiring out for the season or by the day (see chapter 18). The concentration of landholding in Great Britain was one of the highest in Europe: Some 500 aristocratic families controlled half the land; and some 1,300 others, most of the rest. In France, on the other hand, peasants owned approximately one-third of the arable land and were gradually gaining more. They made the most of their situation by favoring crops that required intense cultivation, such as grapes and sugar beets, and by maintaining small-scale craft industries.

Patterns elsewhere lay between these two extremes. Small landholding persisted in western Germany, northern Italy, Switzerland, the Netherlands, Belgium, and Scandinavia alongside a trend toward the consolidation of larger farms that reduced millions to becoming day laborers. In Germany emancipation from personal obligations to the lord usually required peasants to pay for their freedom with part (often the best part) of the land they had previously cultivated.

The clear distinction remained, however, between these western and central regions and Eastern Europe, where peasants were more directly subject to the power of the lord, most of all under Russian serfdom. In the West, developments that increased agricultural productivity often made the life of peasants more precarious. In the East, the landowners' authority over their peasants included claims to their unpaid labor, which in

Russia ranged from a month or so of work each year to several days a week. The disadvantages of such a system were many, and the eventual emancipation of Russian serfs in the 1860s proved necessary for economic growth and minimal military and administrative efficiency. As urbanization and industrialization advanced, many writers waxed nostalgic for the bucolic purity and sturdy independence of peasant life, but the social and economic problems of the peasantry were, in fact, some of the gravest and most intractable of European society.

Workers and Artisans   Industrial workers attracted far more attention than did the peasantry; yet even in Britain industrial workers were a minority among paid laborers (there were more domestic servants than factory hands). Industrial workers, however, were taken to be indicative of the new age because of the environment in which they lived and worked and because of their absolute dependence on wages set by employers, who could fire them at will and who determined the tasks performed as well as the conditions of work and the length of the workday.

Most factory workers earned too little to sustain a family even when work was steady, and the employment of women and children became as necessary to the family's survival as it was advantageous to employers, who appreciated their greater dexterity and the lower wages they would accept. Awakened before dawn by the factory bell, they tramped to work, where the pace of production was relentless and the dangers from machinery and irate foremen were great. Any lapse of attention during a workday of fourteen hours or more,

An etching of Dean Mills in 1851 shows cotton spinning as contemporaries liked to think of it: women working together with nimble industriousness under the watchful but gentle eye of a sturdy foreman, all in the iron grandeur of an immaculate, orderly, huge new factory.
Mansell/TimePix/Getty Images

even stopping to help a neighbor, brought a fine and a harsh reprimand.

Industrial workers were set apart by the conditions of their labor, the slums in which they lived, and special restrictions such as the *livret*, or passport, that all French workers were required to present when applying for a job and on which previous employers recorded comments on the worker's conduct and performance. Life was still more precarious for the millions without regular employment, who simply did such tasks as they could find, hauling or digging for a few pence. Understandably, the powerful worried about the social volcano on which they lived.

The most independent workers were the artisans, who had been stripped of their tight guilds and formal apprenticeships by the French Revolution, by a series of laws passed in Britain in the years before the 1830s, and by a similar process in Germany that was completed by the revolutions of 1848. Nevertheless, artisans continued to ply their crafts in a hierarchy of masters, journeymen, and apprentices, working in small shops in which conditions varied as much ac-

cording to the temper of the master as to the pressures of the market. Skilled or semiskilled workers, from carpenters and shoemakers to mechanics, were distinctly better paid than the masses of the unskilled. Although they were vulnerable to unemployment during the frequent economic slumps, in general their real wages tended slowly to increase, and they could expect to earn enough to support their families in one or two bare rooms on a simple diet.

Uneducated and exhausted industrial workers, often strangers to one another, for the most part lacked the means necessary for effective concerted action to improve their lot. Their frequent outbursts of resentment and intermittent strikes usually ended in some bloodshed and sullen defeat. Most worker protests were led by artisans, who felt most keenly the threat of economic change and held clearer visions of their rights and dignity.

Early Labor Movements   Trade unions were banned everywhere except in England after 1824, and even there the laws against conspiracy restricted their activity. But various local organizations had developed in the eighteenth century for mutual aid. By 1850 more than 1.5 million British workers may have belonged to such groups, called friendly societies in England and confraternities in France, which tended to form around skilled workers and to meet in secret, often of necessity but also as a sign of brotherhood and trust. Although their members were fond of elaborate rituals, these societies served specific purposes, such as providing burial costs for members or assistance in times of illness. There were also movements that aimed to increase the workers' control over their lives, such as consumers' cooperatives and artisans' production cooperatives. Such programs sometimes became associated with radical politics, a specter likely to rouse crushing opposition even from liberal governments. For the most part, however, these expressions of workers' insistence on their rights and dignity remained small in scale and local in influence.

The hundreds of strikes that occurred throughout Western Europe in the first half of the century suggested what unions might accomplish, but without funds, organizational experience, or effective means of communication, these labor movements usually petered out after a few years or sometimes a few months. Not even the Workingman's Association for Benefiting Politically, Socially, and Morally the Useful Classes, launched with some fanfare in England in 1836, managed to survive for long or bring off the general strike its more radical members dreamed of. Yet these organizations did influence Parliament to favor factory legislation.

The meetings, torchlight parades, and special workers' tracts all contributed to the growing sense of belonging to a distinctive class. So, above all, did the repression by police and courts that usually followed. By midcentury millions of workers in Britain, somewhat fewer perhaps in France, and smaller numbers elsewhere shared heroes and rituals, believed they faced a common enemy, and adopted organization as the prime means of defending themselves in a hostile world. In Britain the national trade unions of skilled workers formed in the 1830s and 1840s (with only some 100,000 members then) steadily increased their size and influence, reaching more than a million members a generation later.

The vast majority of the working class, however, remained essentially defenseless, possessing meager skills, dependent on unstable employment, and living in the isolation of poverty. Ideas of *fraternité* and *égalité*, of the rights of freeborn English people, and of simple patriotism, often expressed in Biblical prose, communicated a common sense of hope and outrage to the millions of men and women who attended rallies, met in dingy cafés, and read the working-class press (or listened as it was read to them). Newspapers and pamphlets intended for workers were numerous in England after 1815, less widespread in France in the 1830s and 1840s, and present everywhere in 1848. The common themes were people's natural rights, pride of work, and the claims of social justice.

The Middle Classes   Of all the social classes, the most confident and assertive was the middle class. At the top stood the great bankers, who in London and Paris were often closely connected to the liberal aristocracy and whose political influence after 1830 was considerable. Just below them in status, the great industrialists and the wealthiest merchants were more separate from and a little contemptuous of the traditional elites. The bottom of the middle class consisted of office clerks, schoolteachers, and small shopkeepers, often distinguishable from artisans only by their pretensions. This petite bourgeoisie constituted most of the middle class numerically, but the class was epitomized by those neither at the top nor bottom but in between: most merchants, managers, and upper bureaucrats and nearly all lawyers, doctors, engineers, and professors. The view that such disparate groups made up a social class resulted as much from ideas shared as from common interests. Opposed to aristocratic privilege, they saw themselves as the beneficiaries of social changes that allowed talented people to gain security and influence.

They were primarily an urban class and intimately connected with the commerce and politics of city life. In Paris they constituted nearly all of that part of the population (between one-fourth and one-fifth) that was prosperous enough to pay some taxes, have at least one maid, and leave an estate sufficient to cover the costs of private burial. In other cities their proportion was probably somewhat smaller. Among nations, they were most numerous in Great Britain, a sizable fraction in France and Belgium, and a smaller minority elsewhere. The middle class was the only social class that it was possible to fall out of, and people established their membership in it by economic self-sufficiency, literacy, and respectability. Their manner, their dress, and their homes were thus symbols of their status and were meant to express values of probity, hard work, fortitude, prudence, and self-reliance. No matter how favored by birth or fortune, they tended to think of themselves as self-made.

Middle-Class Values   While industrial centers were notoriously drab, the middle-class home became more ornate, packed with furnishings that boasted of elaborate craftsmanship. Women's fashions similarly

Fashion magazines like *La Mode Illustré* kept middle-class women informed of the latest styles and elegant touches to which they might aspire.
Bulloz/© RMN/Art Resource, NY

featured ornamental frills, and shops translated Parisian elegance into forms available to more modest purses. Masculine garb, by contrast, grew plainer, a point of some pride in a practical age; and clerk and banker tended to dress alike. Those who forged great industries out of daring, foresight, and luck; those who invented or built; and those who taught or tended shop or wrote for newspapers came to share a certain pride in one another's achievements as proof that personal drive and social benefit were in harmony and as a harbinger of progress yet to come.

More than any other, the middle class was associated with an ideology; and the triumph of the middle class in this period—so heralded then and by historians since—related as much to constitutionalism and legal equality, individual rights, and economic opportunity as it did to any explicit transfer of power. The conquests of the middle class were measured not just by its rise in importance but also by a more general adoption of values associated with it. Even being in the middle, between the extremes of luxury and power and of poverty and ignorance, was seen as an advantage, a kind of inherent moderation. Most of Europe's writers, scientists, doctors, lawyers, and businesspeople would have felt no

need to blush on finding themselves called by a London paper in 1807 "those persons . . . always counted the most valuable, because the least corrupted, members of society," or on hearing John Stuart Mill speak a generation later of "the class which is universally described as the most wise and the most virtuous part of the community, the middle rank." Society was understood in terms of social class at a time when the hallmarks of the era—flourishing commerce, science, and technology; great works of art and institutions of culture; triumphant movements of liberalism and nationalism—were seen as achievements of the middle class.

The Changing Population

While Europeans grappled with political, economic, and social changes, they also faced the fact that there were more and more people—more people to feed, more seeking work, and more living in cities.

Demographic Growth   The effects of population growth were particularly visible in areas in which industrialization was under way, and historians used to think that industrialization had stimulated a rising birthrate with new opportunities for employment, particularly of children. But demographic research has challenged that view, and current explanations emphasize a decline in disease-carrying germs, an increase in the food supply, a lowering of the age at which people married, and, after 1870, some improvement in public sanitation.

Admittedly spotty data suggest that the world experienced a decline in some common diseases beginning in the eighteenth century. Microbes have cycles (like those of locusts but less regular), and remissions had undoubtedly occurred many times before. Now, however, better supplies of food allowed the larger number of babies surviving the perilous years of infancy to reach adulthood and form families of their own.

The food supply rose because of better transportation, more effective agricultural techniques, and the potato. Agricultural associations, usually led by enlightened aristocrats, campaigned for more scientific farming; and the humble potato, not common on the Continent before 1750, was a staple of the peasant's diet in most of Europe by 1830. Potatoes are easy to cultivate in a small space and can yield more calories per acre than any other crop. While infant mortality remained enormously high by modern standards, even a slight decline in death rates could make a great difference in the total number of people, so close to subsistence did most Europeans live.

Population and Society   The reasons for the trend toward earlier marriage are less clear, but peasants freed

Jean-Auguste-Dominique Ingres
Louis François Bertin, 1832
This painting portrays the entrepreneur Louis François Bertin as the very epitome of the self-reliant, aggressive man of the industrial middle class.
Giraudon/Art Resource, NY

from servile obligations apparently tended to marry and form new households at a younger age. Early marriage was facilitated by the spread of cottage industry, which preceded the new factories and enabled families to add to their income by spinning or weaving at home.

The increased number of people in a single generation multiplied in the next generation and led to an enormous increase in the aggregate. As population grew, the proportion who were in the childbearing years grew still faster, which increased the ratio of births to the total population. The net result was that the 180 to 190 million Europeans of 1800 had become 266 million by 1850 and 295 million by 1870.

The effects of a larger population were far-reaching. More people consumed more food, which necessitated more intensive cultivation and the use of land previously left fallow. An increasing population also meant an expanding market for goods other than food, an element of growth that would have stronger impact later in the century. More people meant a larger potential workforce readier to leave the countryside for industrial jobs; and this mobility became a social change of

immeasurable importance, for it reduced the isolation of country folk and stimulated a pattern of migration to the Americas that would become a flood. Young people constituted a greater proportion of the population, which may have made for increased restiveness and a larger pool of potential radical leaders.[2] There was also a distinction in birthrates by social class, which demographers call *differential fertility*. On the whole, the higher a man stood on the social scale, the fewer the children in his family, which led some to interpret the lower classes' fertility as a lack of foresight and moral restraint and to worry that they would eventually overwhelm society.

The most influential analysis of population was Thomas R. Malthus' *An Essay on the Principle of Population as It Affects the Future Improvement of Society*, first published in 1798 and reissued in many revisions. Observing the Britain of his time, Malthus argued that human population, unless checked by death (through war, famine, or pestilence) or deliberate sexual continence, increases faster than the supply of food. A clergyman, he advocated continence, but he remained pessimistic that human beings were capable of such restraint. An economist as well, Malthus presented demography as a science closely attached to liberal economic theory, with the convenient corollary that the misery of the poor resulted from their own improvidence.

Urbanization   At the turn of the century, greater London reached 1 million in population. No European city since imperial Rome had ever approached this size. Paris, with about half that number, would reach 1 million a generation later. The third largest European city in 1800, Naples, had some 350,000 inhabitants; and in all Europe there were then only twenty-two cities with populations of more than 100,000. By midcentury there were forty-seven. Great Britain was the leader, with six cities over the 100,000 mark; London's population had surpassed 2.5 million by 1856, Liverpool had grown from 80,000 to almost 400,000, and Manchester and Glasgow each had more than 300,000 people. By the 1850s, half of Britain's population lived in towns or cities, making it the most urbanized society since the Classical era.

On the Continent most old cities increased by at least 50 percent in the first half of the century, and many a town became a city. The major capitals burgeoned. Paris reached a population of nearly 1.5 million

[2] The nationalist organization Young Italy limited membership to those under forty, and probably most of the leaders of the revolutions of 1848 would have met that standard. The relation of youth to revolution is interestingly discussed in Herbert Moller, "Youth as a Force in the Modern World," *Comparative Studies in Society and History*, April 1968.

Gustave Doré
In this famous engraving of London, the rhythmic sameness and cramped efficiency of new housing suggest a machine for living appropriate to the age of the railroad.
New York Public Library

by 1850; Berlin almost trebled, to 500,000; and a similar growth rate pushed Brussels to 250,000. St. Petersburg, Vienna, and Budapest all had populations between 400,000 and 500,000.

By the 1860s the English countryside was actually losing people, as were some sections of France. The tide of urbanization was overwhelming, and nearly all the subsequent increase in European population would end up in cities swelling with immigrants, as rural folk moved to nearby villages, villagers to towns, and town dwellers to cities. Clearly, the tide of urbanization was strongest where industry was great, but the growth of ports and national capitals demonstrated the importance of great commercial, financial, and political centers as well.

Urban Problems   Society had neither the experience nor the means to cope very well with such an expansion. Urban conditions for all but the reasonably pros-

perous were unspeakable. Narrow alleys were littered with garbage and ordure that gave off an overpowering stench. The water supply in Paris, better than in most large cities, offered access to safe water only at fountains that dotted the city (the affluent paid carriers by the bucket), and in London the private companies that provided water allowed it to flow only a few hours a day. In most cities the water supply came from dangerously polluted rivers. Sewage was an even more serious problem. A third of Manchester's houses used privies in the 1830s, and a decade later the ratio of inside toilets to population was 1 to 212. In London cesspools menaced health only slightly less than still more public means of disposal.

The most dramatic inadequacy, however, was in housing. A third of Liverpool's citizens lived crowded into dark, cold cellars, and conditions in Lille were similar. In every city the poor of both sexes crowded into filthy, stuffy, unheated rooms; and over the cities,

Le Creusot was a carefully planned and controlled company town that provided housing for the workers in its foundries.
Roger-Viollet/Getty Images

especially manufacturing and mining towns, chemical smog and coal smoke darkened the sky. It is hardly surprising that crime was rampant, that often more than a third of the births were illegitimate, and that the number of prostitutes soared (reaching perhaps 80,000 in London, where 9,000 were officially registered; 3,600 were registered in Paris).

Maintaining public order became a new kind of problem. The protection of lives and property in great cities, the effective handling of crowds, and the enforcement of local ordinances required new police forces. London's force was established by Sir Robert Peel in 1829, and the Paris Municipal Guard was created under Guizot a few years later. The role played by Sir Robert Peel led to the nickname "Bobbies," by which the police are still called in London.

For all their misery, cities continued to grow; and through the century the worst conditions were slowly alleviated by housing codes, public sewers, and reliable water supplies. These improvements were made possible in part by industrialization, which gradually provided iron pipes, water closets, gas lighting, better heating, and sounder buildings. Urban life developed a style of its own, increasingly distinct from life in the countryside. Towns clustered around factories and railway stations, but cities teeming with the poor and indigent were also the thriving centers of communication, commerce, politics, and culture.

Social Welfare

Social questions were debated in hundreds of speeches and pamphlets and in newspaper articles that worried about public health and morals, class division, and pauperism. These discussions were filled with the appalling facts uncovered through parliamentary and private inquiries in Britain and scholarly investigations in France. These humanitarian attempts to improve the lot of the lower class had discouragingly modest results, although individual employers, especially in Britain and Alsace, improved conditions somewhat by building special housing for their workers, drab barracks that nonetheless seemed marvels of cleanliness and decency.

Charity Middle-class radicals supported efforts like those of England's Society for the Diffusion of Useful Knowledge, founded in 1826 to carry enlightenment to the lower classes. They contributed to and gave lectures for workers at night schools, many of which were run by the Mechanics' Institutes (of which there were more than 700 in Great Britain by 1850) and by the Polytechnic Association of France (which had more than 100,000 participants by 1848). Thousands of middle-class people personally carried the lamp of truth to the poor in the form of Bibles, pious essays, moral stories, and informative descriptions of how machines worked. Ambitious members of the lower-middle class were, however, more likely than workers to take advantage of these opportunities.

For the truly poverty-stricken, charities were established at an astounding rate; more than 450 relief organizations were listed in London alone in 1853, and whole encyclopedias cataloging these undertakings were published in France. A revival of Christian zeal provided powerful impetus to such groups in Britain, and on the Continent new Catholic religious orders, most with specific social missions, were founded by the hundreds. They sponsored lectures, organized wholesome recreation to compete with the temptations of the tavern, set up trade apprenticeships, provided expectant

The visitation of the poor by charitable members of the middle class was expected to bring a good example as well as food and clothes.
Jean-Loup Charmet/Bridgeman Art Library

mothers with a clean sheet and a pamphlet on child care, opened savings banks that accepted even the tiniest deposit, campaigned for hygiene and temperance, gave away soup and bread, supported homes for abandoned children and fallen women, and ran nurseries, schools, and hostels. These good works were preeminently the province of women. Catholic nuns and Protestant matrons in the middle class were expected to uplift the poor by example as well as charity. The Society of St. Vincent de Paul believed that pious men could have a similar effect. Organized in Paris in 1835, it soon spread to all of Catholic Europe, requiring thousands of educated and well-to-do men to visit the poor regularly so that they might teach thrift and give hope by their very presence. Although these efforts were important for some lucky individuals and were a significant means of informing the comfortable about the plight of the poor, they were never adequate to the social challenge. Most of Europe's urban masses remained largely untouched by charity or religion.

Public Health   In matters of public health, standards of housing, working conditions, and education, governments were forced to take a more active role. By modern standards the official measures were timid and hesitant. Vaccination, enforced by progressive governments, made smallpox less threatening. Beyond that, advances in medicine contributed little to public health. The great work of immunization would come later in the century. The most important medical gain of the 1840s was probably the use of anesthesia in surgery, dentistry, and childbirth.

Serious epidemics broke out in every decade. Typhus, carried by lice, was a constant threat, accounting

for one death in nine in Ireland between 1816 and 1819, and infected water spread typhoid fever in city after city. A cholera epidemic, which apparently began along India's Ganges River in 1826, spread through East Asia, reaching Moscow and St. Petersburg by 1830; 100,000 people died of cholera in Russia in two years. From Russia it spread south and west, to Egypt and North Africa, to Poland, Austria, and into Germany, where it was reported in Hamburg in 1831. Despite efforts to put ports in quarantine (a move opposed by shipping interests), the disease reached northern England and then France in that same year and continued slowly to the south, taking a ninth of Palermo's population in the period from 1836 to 1837.

Reaction to the cholera epidemic in Britain, France, and Germany revealed much about social change. An official day of fasting, prayer, and humiliation in England and warnings of the archbishop of Paris that the cholera was divine retribution expressed the strength of traditional faith and revealed widespread distrust of an era of materialism and its claims to progress.

But governments were expected to act. Torn between two inaccurate theories of how the disease spread, governments mobilized inspectors to enforce such sanitary regulations as existed. (Not infrequently the inspectors faced riots by a populace fearful of medical body snatchers eager to dissect corpses.) In Paris and Lille, tenements were whitewashed by the tens of thousands, foods inspected, and streets and sewers cleaned by official order; similar steps were taken in the German states and in Britain, where the demonstrated inadequacy of local government prompted establishment of a national Public Health Commission with extraordinary powers over towns and individuals.

Carefully collected statistics led to a new understanding of how disease spread and of the importance of social factors for public health. Over the years, doctors and inspectors reported with troubled consciences on the terrible conditions they had found among lower-class neighbors whose quarters they had never visited before. Another cholera epidemic followed in the 1840s and lesser ones thereafter, but the shock and uncertainty of what to do was never again so great. Gradually, hospitals, too, came under more direct state supervision as the cost and complexity of medical treatment increased. By midcentury housing and sanitary codes regulated most of urban construction throughout the West, and inspectors were empowered to enforce these rules.

The Irish Famine   Liberalism showed its other face in England's handling of the terrible potato famine in Ireland. As the potato blight struck late in 1845, disaster for a population so dependent on a single crop was not hard to predict. By winter hundreds of thousands of families sold what little they had to survive, were forced off the land, and began to suffer the diseases that accompany famine. Hope rested on a good harvest the following year. In spring and summer the potato plants emerged promisingly; but when desperate peasants dug them up, there was only stinking rot. In 1846 the blight was nearly total. In that year and the next, millions died, about a quarter of the population—the exact number will never be known. Roads were lined with bodies, huts abandoned. For several years some of England's ablest officials struggled with bureaucratic earnestness to collect information, organize relief, and maintain order in a corpse-strewn land; yet they were so inhibited by respect for the rules of liberal economics and the rights of property that their efforts had limited effect. In England, even those public figures most concerned to provide help to the Irish tended to view the famine as a natural disaster rather than a failure of policy; and many blamed Irish laziness for the country's dependence on potatoes, an easy crop to grow.

Ireland did produce grain, but that brought a better price in Britain. The landowners, mainly English and absentee, followed market principles and continued to export most of their wheat to England even as famine spread. Most Irish farmers rented the tiny plots they worked and paid for them principally by selling the pig or two they could raise on the same potatoes that provided their subsistence. When that crop failed and they had no money for rent, landlords usually forced them off the land. The relief law that denied aid to anyone who farmed more than a quarter acre of land had a similar effect, forcing tenants to abandon farming so their families might have food. The Irish famine, which made migration to the United States a part of Irish life and stimulated increased hatred of English rule, also fostered debate about what the responsibilities of a liberal government should be.

Government Regulation   In the 1830s and 1840s governments began reluctantly to regulate child labor, banning employment of those under nine years old in textile mills in Britain and factories in Prussia, under eight in factories in France, and under ten in mines in Britain. By the end of the 1840s, similar measures had been adopted in Bavaria, Baden, Piedmont, and Russia. Generally, the laws variously held the workday to eight or nine hours for children under twelve or thirteen years old and to twelve hours for those under sixteen or eighteen. Britain and France included additional requirements that the very young be provided with a couple of hours of schooling each day. To be effective, such regulations required teams of inspectors, provided for only in Britain, where earnest disciples of Jeremy Bentham applied the laws diligently. This expansion of government authority had been vigorously opposed by industrialists and many liberals; but mounting evidence of the harmful effects of industrial work made the need apparent, and the ability to gather such evidence became one of government's most important functions.

The most bitterly controversial welfare measure of the period was Britain's Poor Law of 1834. The old parish system of relief permitted each county to supplement local wages up to a level of subsistence determined by the price of bread. The system, expensive and inadequate to changing needs, was attacked by liberal economists, who charged that it cost too much and discouraged workers from migrating to new jobs. An extensive campaign for reform led to the Poor Law of 1834, based on the Benthamite notion that unemployment had to be made as unattractive as possible. Those receiving relief were required to live in workhouses, where discipline was harsh, conditions were kept suitably mean, and the sexes were separated. Workers bitterly resented the new law, and referred to the new institutions as Bastilles. On the Continent welfare measures kept more traditional forms while gradually shifting the responsibility for directing them from local and religious auspices to the state.

Education   Public education also became a matter of national policy. Prussia had declared local schooling compulsory in 1716, and efforts to enforce and regulate that requirement culminated in 1807 with the creation of a bureau of education. In the following decades the government, with the cooperation of the Lutheran clergy, established an efficient system of universal primary instruction with facilities now needed to train the teachers and to guarantee that the subject matter taught would remain rudimentary and politically safe. The network of secondary schools was also enlarged but kept quite separate, generally not admitting graduates of the ordinary primary schools. Most of the German states had similar arrangements, establishing nearly universal elementary education.

In France the French Revolution had provided the framework for a national system of free public schools meant as a substitute for the extensive but more informal and largely religious schools of the old regime. Slowly that vision of a national system of public schools took effect. By 1833 every commune was required to support a public school, and schooling steadily expanded while the quality of teachers improved and the power of inspectors over tightfisted local authorities increased. By the revolution of 1848, three-fourths of France's school-age children were receiving some formal instruction.

In Britain conflict between the Church of England and other Protestant churches prevented creation of a state-controlled system of elementary schools, a lack welcomed by those conservatives who opposed educating the masses. Nevertheless, Parliament voted in 1833 to underwrite the construction of private schools, and subsidies for education gradually increased in amount and scope each year thereafter. From Spain to Russia, elementary schools were favored by every government and passionately demanded by liberals. The public schools of Europe, inadequate and impoverished, offered little chance of social advancement to those forced to attend them, but few doubted that they could be a major instrument for improving society as well as a force for social peace.

THE SPREAD OF LIBERAL GOVERNMENT

These limited social programs were part of the great age of liberalism that began in 1830, made England its model, and spread to the Continent with revolution in France and the revolt that created Belgium. With the establishment of liberal governments, these representative monarchies of the West stood in sharp contrast to the autocratic governments of Central and Eastern Europe.

Great Britain

Britain's withdrawal in the 1820s from Metternich's Concert of Europe represented more than insular habit. The world's leading example of liberalism, Britain was coming to favor liberal programs in other countries, too. But the triumph of liberalism at home had not come without serious conflict.

Pressure for Change   The turmoil of the postwar years was heightened by the economic crisis that resulted from demobilization and the collapse of wartime markets, and popular meetings echoed with cries of class resentment. The government's economic policies—removal of the wartime income tax and a higher tariff on grains, which made bread more expensive—favored the rich. To change policies required reform of the political system; heated agitation for that reform swept the country.

The government at first responded with repression. Habeas corpus was suspended for the first time in English history in 1817. A mass meeting for reform at St. Peter's Field, Manchester, in 1819 so terrified the local magistrates that they called out troops. In the ensuing charge, hundreds of demonstrators, including women and children, were wounded, and several were killed. With bitter mockery people called it the Peter-

loo Massacre (see the illustration on p. 695). Parliament responded by passing the Six Acts of 1819, which restricted public meetings, facilitated the prosecution of radicals, and imposed a stamp tax intended to cripple the radical press. Support for the established order continued to ebb, and the scandal of George IV's personal life earned public contempt. Old restrictions on Protestant dissenters and Roman Catholics (they could not hold public office, for example) now brought rising criticism of the special privileges accorded the Church of England.

Even an unreformed Parliament could be sensitive to public opinion, however, and it began to support compromises on some critical issues. The government reduced some tariffs and repealed the Combination Acts that had banned unions, although an amendment effectively outlawing strikes was soon added. As the minister in charge of the Home Office, Sir Robert Peel ceased the prosecution of newspapers and the use of political spies, halved the list of capital crimes, and put domestic order in the hands of civil authority by creating a police force. The Tories, who opposed such measures, looked to the conservative Duke of Wellington, the prestigious victor over Napoleon at Waterloo, to resist further change. Yet as prime minister even he saw the need to push through Parliament a measure he himself disliked, allowing Catholics and religious dissenters to vote and to hold public office.

All of these issues—religious freedom, the legitimacy of labor unions, tariffs, restrictions on the press—led to agitation that from London to Ireland increasingly focused on the need to reform Parliament itself. Elections in 1830, required by the death of King George IV and the accession of William IV, raised the political temperature. In the countryside, disenfranchised laborers set haystacks afire by night; by day, stern magistrates ordered laborers accused of seditious activity transported to Australia.

The Reform Bill of 1832   As public turmoil rose (and British leaders watched with concern the revolution of 1830 in France), a new cabinet presented a bill to reform the electoral system. The measure was approved in the House of Commons only after a new election and was then rejected in the Lords until the king reluctantly threatened to create enough new peers to get it through. Each defeat made the public mood uglier, and the king's intervention came amid demonstrations, the burning of the town hall and the bishop's palace in Bristol, and much dark talk about the French example.

The bill itself offered a good deal less than the more outspoken radicals had wanted, but it marked a fundamental change in Britain's electoral system. Suffrage was increased, allowing some 800,000 well-to-do men to vote, based on the property they owned or the rents

This cartoon of the 1819 Peterloo Massacre captures the sense of class hatred it evoked. Citizens, peaceably seeking reform, are wantonly trampled by His Majesty's overfed officials.
The Granger Collection, New York

they paid.[3] More important was the elimination of local variation in favor of a uniform national standard which, as many Tories warned, could easily be broadened in the future. Before the Reform Bill was passed, many boroughs that sent representatives to Parliament were barely villages (the most notorious, Old Sarum, was uninhabited), and the bustling cities of Birmingham and Manchester had had no representatives at all. Perhaps a third of the members of Parliament owed their seats to the influence of some lord. Now representation was at least crudely related to population, and the voices of commerce and manufacturing would be more numerous.

Although restricted suffrage and social tradition (and open voting) guaranteed the continued dominance of the upper classes, Parliament was ready after 1832 to turn to other reforms. Slavery was abolished in Britain's colonies in 1833, a victory for Protestant reformers and humanitarian radicals. The Factory Act, limiting the hours children worked,[4] soon followed, as did the much-despised Poor Law of 1834. A law granting all resident taxpayers the right to vote in municipal elections challenged aristocratic influence even more directly than the Reform Bill of 1832. When young Victoria ascended the throne in 1837, representative government was stronger than ever. Her reign of more than six decades would rival that of Queen Elizabeth I as a period of British glory and power, but she would remain subordinate (often against her wishes) to an increasingly flexible political system.

[3] This electorate was considerably broader than that established in either France or Belgium in 1830, though Belgium, the only country to give elected representatives a salary, had in many respects Europe's most liberal constitution. About 1 Frenchman in 160 could vote in 1830; 1 Briton in 32, after the Reform Bill of 1832. About 1 Belgian in 95 could vote by 1840; and 1 in 20 by 1848. Universal male suffrage permits approximately one-fifth of the total population to go to the polls.

[4] The work week was limited to 48 hours for children between the ages of six and thirteen, and to 69 hours for those between ages fourteen and eighteen.

CHRONOLOGY
Major Reform Legislation in Britain

1828 Restrictions on non-Anglican Protestants lifted; London police force created.

1829 Catholic emancipation, Catholics allowed in Parliament.

1832 Parliament reformed.

1833 Slavery abolished in British Empire; child labor in factories restricted to nine hours for those more than nine years old.

1834 Poor Law.

1846 Corn Laws repealed.

1847 Ten-hour workday.

Joseph Nash
INTERIOR OF THE HOUSE OF COMMONS
The British House of Commons sat in a new building of Gothic splendor that made parliamentary liberty seem ancient and the two-party system inevitable.
Houses of Parliament, Westminster, London, UK/Bridgeman Art Library

Chartism and the Corn Laws   Two great popular movements helped define the limits of that political system. **Chartism** was a huge, amorphous workers' movement, the central aim of which was political democracy, spelled out in what was called the People's Charter.[5] With articulate leaders and a working-class base, Chartists propagandized widely; held huge demonstrations in 1839, 1840, and 1848; and were accused of causing riots that ended with scores of deaths. Although treated by the state as dangerous revolutionaries, their principal tactic was to present Parliament with petitions containing tens of thousands of signatures (see "The Great Charter," p. 697). These petitions were summarily rejected, however, and by 1842 the movement was weakening. It failed, despite its size, to find a program that could for long mobilize the masses struggling for survival. And it failed, despite its emphasis on political rather than more threatening economic goals, to stir the consciences of those in power. Angry or desperate workers could riot here or there, but in England they were too isolated from one another and from other classes to gain their political, let alone their social, goals.

The other great popular movement, against the grain tariff, was victorious. The Anti-Corn Law League grew out of urban resentment over the high cost of bread resulting from grain tariffs—the **Corn Laws**—that bene-

---

[5] The six points of the People's Charter were universal male suffrage, a written ballot, abolition of property qualifications for members of Parliament, payment of the members, constituencies of equal population, and annual elections. All but the last of these points had been adopted by 1918.

fited the landowning classes. From Manchester the movement spread throughout the country, becoming a kind of crusade, an attack on the privileges of aristocracy in the name of the "productive orders" of society, the middle and working classes. The league's propaganda used the new techniques of popular politics: parades and rallies, songs and speeches, pamphlets and cartoons. Its slogans were printed on trinkets for children, ribbons for women, drinking cups for men. Two manufacturers, Richard Cobden and John Bright, proved effective spokesmen who became influential figures in public life, spreading the gospel of free trade across the land. To the upper classes, such activity seemed in terrible taste; and conservatives argued that the nation's greatness was rooted in its landed estates.

In the face of this sort of coalition of the middle and working classes, however, British politics proved responsive. Twice Sir Robert Peel's government lowered duties on a wide range of items, including grain, but the league demanded more. Finally, in 1845, Peel an-

THE GREAT CHARTER

The Chartist movement reached its peak in 1842 with the presentation to the House of Commons of the Great Charter. There were more than 3 million signatures on this petition calling for universal male suffrage, annual parliaments, lower taxes, and greater attention to the needs of the poor.

TO THE HONOURABLE THE COMMONS OF GREAT BRITAIN AND IRELAND, IN PARLIAMENT ASSEMBLED.

"The petition of the undersigned people of the United Kingdom. . . .

"That as Government was designed for the benefit and protection of, and must be obeyed and supported by all, therefore all should be equally represented.

"That any form of Government which fails to effect the purposes for which it was designed, and does not fully and completely represent the whole people, who are compelled to pay taxes to its support, and obey the laws resolved upon by it, is unconstitutional, tyrannical, and ought to be amended or resisted.

"That your honourable House, as at present constituted, has not been elected by, and acts irresponsibly of, the people; and hitherto has only represented parties, and benefited the few, regardless of the miseries, grievances, and petitions of the many. Your honourable House has enacted laws contrary to the expressed wishes of the people, and by unconstitutional means enforced obedience to them, thereby creating an unbearable despotism on the one hand, and degrading slavery on the other. . . .

"That the existing state of representation is not only extremely limited and unjust, but unequally divided, and gives preponderating influence to the landed, and monied interests, to the utter ruin of the small-trading and labouring classes.

"That bribery, intimidation, corruption, perjury, and riot, prevail at all parliamentary elections, to an extent best understood by the Members of your honourable House. . . .

"That your petitioners would direct the attention of your honourable House to the great disparity existing between the wages of the producing millions, and the salaries of those whose comparative usefulness ought to be questioned, where riches and luxury prevail amongst the rulers, and poverty and starvation amongst the ruled. . . .

"That your petitioners believe all men have a right to worship God as may appear best to their consciences, and that no legislative enactments should interfere between man and his Creator.

"That your petitioners maintain that it is the inherent, indubitable, and constitutional right, founded upon the ancient practice of the realm of England, and supported by well approved statutes, of every male inhabitant of the United Kingdom, he being of age and of sound mind, non-convict of crime, and not confined under any judicial process, to exercise the elective franchise in the choice of Members to serve in the Commons House of Parliament."

---

nounced his support for outright repeal of the Corn Laws. In 1846 he shepherded the measure through both the Commons and the Lords. The grain tariff was reduced to almost nothing, and nearly all duties were abolished or greatly lowered. As in 1832, the political system had bent when demands for reform gained widespread support among the middle class, but Peel's courage split his party and ended his ministry. He was jeered by angry Tories as a young newcomer, Benjamin Disraeli, rose to decry Peel's treachery to the great landlords. Yet the growing weight of public opinion and the liberal creed had triumphed; the sphere of political debate had expanded to include vexing social issues.

The Revolutions of 1830

Uprisings across Europe   The cause of reform in Britain had benefited from fear of revolution, following a wave of revolutions on the Continent in 1830. The first of these occurred in France. Brief and largely limited to Paris, it was a revolution nevertheless, and any uprising in France was a European event. Minor revolts stimulated by the French example occurred in central Italy, Spain, Portugal, some of the German principalities, and Poland. Austria once again extinguished revolt in Italy, and the Russian army crushed Poland's rebels; elsewhere, the results were more lasting.

Belgium   In the southern Netherlands, Catholics and liberals took the occasion to rise against Dutch rule. This revolt was a direct challenge to the provisions of the Congress of Vienna. Britain opposed any intervention by the great powers, however, once convinced that France had no territorial designs on the Netherlands; and Britain led in arranging international guarantees for the independence of the southern Netherlands, which became Belgium. The British and French then pressured the Dutch to acquiesce.

The Belgian monarchy established in 1830 was one of the triumphs of liberal constitutionalism. The new

Mass meetings had been one of the Chartists' most effective devices, and this one held on Kensington Common in London, April 10, 1848, was one of the most publicized. With revolution on the Continent and famine in Ireland, radical hopes were as high as conservative fears. The twenty thousand who attended this meeting had passed armed soldiers, policemen, and special constables. The expectation of violence explains the small number of women and children in this photograph. What might have been the beginning of a revolution in England was instead the Chartists' last national demonstration.
The Royal Archives © 2002 Her Majesty Queen Elizabeth II

state, which owed its existence both to French restraint and British protection, took as its king Leopold I, who had lived long in England (he was an uncle of Queen Victoria) and who soon married the daughter of Louis Philippe. The constitution went further than France's in guaranteeing civil rights and the primacy of the Chamber of Deputies. Politics revolved around a coalition—rare in Europe—of Catholics and liberals, aristocrats and members of the upper-middle class.

Rapidly becoming the most industrialized nation on the Continent, Belgium was prosperous. Self-confident and satisfied with the new order of things, the Belgians built on the administrative traditions left from earlier Austrian and French rule as well as that of the Dutch and proved themselves remarkably adept at planning railroads, reforming taxes and schools, and making timely political concessions.

France's July Monarchy   In France, Charles X's abdication led not to the succession of his son, as the king had hoped, but to a provisional government. Organized largely in newspaper offices, it soon settled for a liberal monarchy. Most of France was ready to accept that compromise when the Marquis de Lafayette, still a republican and a popular hero, stepped out on the balcony of the town hall to present the candidate for the throne. Louis Philippe, head of the House of Orléans, the liberal branch of the royal line, whose father had voted with the Jacobins for the death of his cousin, Louis XVI. The symbols of revolution and moderation were neatly combined in France's new monarchy.

Louis Philippe's posters proclaimed him citizen-king, and the Revolution's tricolor replaced the Bourbon flag. Known as the **July Monarchy,** the new regime began with a constitution presented as a contract the king swore to keep, not as a gift he granted. Similar to the one it replaced, the contract offered stronger guarantees of political freedom, lowered property requirements for voters (nearly doubling their number to some 170,000, safely restricted to men of means), and replaced the hereditary upper house with lifetime peers. Because most of the old aristocracy resigned their offices, never to return to public life, there was an important change in government personnel. Those who replaced the aristocracy were professional people and bearers of newer (often Napoleonic) titles. In his appeal to the people of Paris, Louis Philippe sounded more radical than he was, and the new government hastened to assure Europe's other monarchs that this French revolution would send no militants to sponsor or support revolution elsewhere.

The overriding political question of the 1830s in France was the July Monarchy itself, which was attacked from left and right. Louis Philippe presented himself as a good bourgeois, while the regime's opponents on both sides sought broader support. With strong Catholic support, legitimists (those in favor of the Bourbons) campaigned in the countryside and the newspapers. In 1832 the duchess of Berry, whose infant son was now the legitimist claimant to the throne, tried to stage an uprising. Republicans were active, too, often in secret groups that had provocative names like

Eugène Delacroix
LIBERTY LEADING THE PEOPLE,
28 JULY 1830
Delacroix's painting presents the revolution of 1830 in France as the heroic rising of the people, poor and middle class together, being led by Liberty into a new era.
Louvre, Paris, France/Peter Willi/
Bridgeman Art Library

Jeanron's depiction of a Parisian barricade in 1830 (later used to illustrate Louis Blanc's socialist history of the period) presents a more realistic scene of the fighting than Delacroix's more famous version, but a similar heroic vision of workers and middle class together.
Roger-Viollet/Getty Images

the Society of the Rights of Man. When the silk workers of Lyons went on strike in 1834, it was viewed as a republican revolt and was suppressed with the bitterness of class hatred by the bourgeois National Guard.

Limited Liberalism in France   Despite such turbulence, the July Monarchy presented itself as a center of stability and patriotism, even laying claim to the cult

of Napoleon I by bringing the emperor's body back from St. Helena and placing it with nationalist pomp in the marble crypt of the Invalides. The government built on the administrative system that had developed under the Revolution and Napoleon to promote public education, new if limited social services, and industrialization. With time (and restrictions on the press) opposition quieted, and many of the

Carefully staged ceremonies marked the return of Napoleon's ashes from St. Helena for internment in Paris on December 15, 1840, as a national, patriotic event.
AKG London

middle-class notables of France rallied to a government of cautious moderation that talked of progress.

A regime largely isolated from workers, peasants, and the old aristocracy had found in nationalism its most effective means of propaganda. Yet it remained divided between those who wanted further reform and wider suffrage and those, like the king himself, who believed the proper balance between liberty and order had been achieved. The former were led by Adolphe Thiers; the latter, by François Guizot. Both were journalists and historians of great talent; but their skillful verbal duels in parliament failed to mobilize opinion in France as agitation over the Corn Laws had done in England. From 1840 to 1848 the government was dominated by Guizot. A Protestant in a Catholic country, an intellectual in politics, a man who held broad principles rigidly, Guizot had in excess failings common to many liberals of the nineteenth century. He spoke of liberty, progress, and law in eloquent terms that made his cautious practices seem hypocritical. In 1848 the whole regime fell as easily as incumbents losing an election.

The two freest and most prosperous of Europe's great nations had developed similarly since 1830. In both, liberal governments led by able men sought through reasonable compromise, the rule of law, and parliamentary politics to unify their nations and to make "progress" compatible with stability. Discontent and workers' misery, though frightening, were understood in the councils of government primarily as a threat to order. In England reform had to be wrung from a powerful aristocracy that was, in the end, secure enough to cede under pressure. In France the aristocracy counted for little after 1830; but the government, fearful of the more radical hopes for democracy and social justice that it excluded, remained uncertain of its popular support.

Spain   The victories of French and British liberalism seemed part of a general trend. In Spain the monarchy itself wooed liberals. When King Ferdinand VII died in 1833, he had carefully arranged for his three-year-old daughter, Isabella, to succeed him. But the king's brother, Don Carlos, denounced the arrangement as illegal and began an uprising that lasted until 1839. The Carlists, who favored autocracy and the traditional claims of Spanish Catholicism, found their greatest support in rural areas and regions of the north that were resentful of rule from Madrid. Despite eventual defeat, Don Carlos won a place in Spanish legend as a dashing and chivalric hero, protector of old Spanish virtues. Carlism would remain a conservative rallying cry in every subsequent Spanish revolution.

To win liberal support, the regency ruling in Isabella's name granted a constitution in 1834. Cautiously modeled on the French constitution of 1814, with narrow suffrage and protection of royal power, it established representative institutions as a lasting feature of Spanish politics. Even so modest a step placed Spain in the liberal camp, and Isabella's government relied on extensive support from Britain and France against threats from abroad. Internal war brought generals into politics and conflict between two camps: the moderates (who supported the constitution of 1834 and admired Guizot's France) and the anticlerical progressives (who demanded a democratic constitution and the election of local officials). Only after a couple of military coups did moderates establish a regime in the 1840s strong enough to hold power for a decade. Everywhere, the changes that brought constitutions, limited suffrage, and circumscribed freedoms were based on a delicate balance that proved difficult to maintain.

Summary

Clusters of ideas about the nature of historical change, about how to prevent revolutions or achieve them, and about the kind of future that industrialization might bring had grown into the ideologies that have divided Western social thought ever since. In the arts and philosophy, Romanticism pointed nostalgically to the past but also toward the new, hailing individual genius yet yearning for community. Conservatives sustained standards critical of the new age; liberals gained strength from their confidence in the future; and socialists envisioned an alternative to capitalist industrialization. From 1815 on, a variety of political experiments, each claiming to be permanent, had been tried in Europe. The problem for conservative regimes was to increase their political effectiveness while preserving as much of the old social order as possible. Although liberal regimes fostered the benefits of uniform justice, legal equality, individual rights, and broader political participation, they faced the question of how far such principles could be taken without creating instability. They, like the conservative regimes they replaced, were a compromise. In fact, all available ideas, institutions, and policies were challenged by the social changes that accompanied industrialization, factory labor, demographic growth, and urbanization. Living with change had become a definition of modernity. There was an explosive mixture in these intellectual, social, and political trends; and they came together in the revolutions that swept across Europe in 1848 and in the increased emphasis on the importance of the state, especially a national state that could demand the loyalty of its citizens.

QUESTIONS FOR FURTHER THOUGHT

1. What explains the relevance, two centuries later, of political and cultural ideologies that took shape during the French Revolution and early years of industrialization?

2. How is it that society can still be described in terms of social classes despite all the social and political changes that have occurred?

3. What kinds of people are most likely to be drawn to liberalism or to reject its appeal? Does that change over time?

RECOMMENDED READING

Sources

Engels, Friedrich. *The Condition of the Working Class in England.* Written in 1844 and available in many modern editions, this influential work by Karl Marx's friend and coauthor paints a dark picture of the working-class slum and conveys the moral outrage radicals felt.

Novels are important sources for understanding nineteenth-century society. Elizabeth Gaskell (*Mary Barton* and *North and South*) and Charles Dickens (*Hard Times* and *Oliver Twist*) provided contemporaries with an influential picture of social conditions in England; Honoré de Balzac's *Père Goriot* set the tone for criticisms of the selfishness of the middle class.

Studies

*Bellamy, Richard. *Liberalism and Modern Society: A Historical Argument.* 1992. Treats the changes over time and the national differences in the meanings of liberalism.

Berdahl, Robert M. *The Politics of the Prussian Nobility: The Development of a Conservative Ideology.* 1988. Shows how political interests and social structure led to the formation of a conservatism that dominated much of German history.

*Briggs, Asa. *Victorian Cities.* 1970. Colorful studies of the urban politics and social life of individual cities.

Brock, Michael. *The Great Reform Act.* 1974. Analyzes the significance of the Reform Bill of 1832 through a close examination of the political and social forces that brought it about.

Church, Clive H. *Europe in 1830: Revolution and Political Change.* 1983. A study that emphasizes the significance of the revolutions of 1830 by noting their transnational connections and impact.

Coffin, Judith G. *The Politics of Women's Work: The Paris Garment Trades, 1750–1915.* 1996. The quintessential women's work was in the garment industry, and this study reveals the long evolution of women in the labor movement and of ideas about gender.

*Davidoff, Leonore, and Catherine Hall. *Family Fortunes: Men and Women of the English Middle Class, 1780–1850.* 1985. A rich and concrete picture of the aspirations and concerns of middle-class life.

Dennis, Richard. *English Industrial Cities of the Nineteenth Century.* 1984. A comprehensive study of the special problems of this new kind of city.

Foster, R. F. *Modern Ireland 1600–1972.* 1988. A magisterial, well-written synthesis.

Franklin, S. H. *The European Peasantry: The Final Phase.* 1969. These essays on different countries reveal not only the striking differences in peasants' lives but the importance of the peasantry for understanding the general history of European nations.

*Hamerow, Theodore S. *Restoration, Revolution, and Reaction: Economics and Politics in Germany, 1815–1871.* 1958. A complex analysis of the relationship of social classes and the state to economic change in this revolutionary period.

Harrison, J. F. C. *The Early Victorians, 1832–1851.* 1971. A lively account of the personalities and issues that marked the beginning of a new era.

*Heilbroner, Robert L. *The Worldly Philosophers.* 1972. A good introduction to the ideas of the economic liberals.

Holmes, Stephen. *Benjamin Constant and the Making of Modern Liberalism.* 1984. The biographical focus offers a valuable insight into the evolution of liberalism on the Continent.

*Hopkins, Eric. *Industrialisation and Society: A Social History, 1830–1951.* 2000. A wide-ranging discussion of the impact of industrialization on British society through the nineteenth century and on to the welfare state.

Johnson, Douglas. *Guizot: Aspects of French History.* 1963. Essays on the dominant figure of the July Monarchy reveal the tensions between aspirations for a liberal society and conservative fear for order.

Katznelson, Ira, and Artistide R. Zolberg (eds.). *Working-Class Formation: Nineteenth-Century Patterns in Western Europe and the United States.* 1986. Interpretative essays by some leading scholars take a fresh look at how working-class awareness was formed.

*Lichtheim, George. *A Short History of Socialism.* 1975. Well-constructed treatment of the evolution of socialist ideas in their historical context.

*Lindemann, Albert S. *A History of European Socialism.* 1984. Establishes the line of continuity from the early socialists through labor movements and the eventual dominance of Marxism.

*Lukács, Georg. *The Historical Novel.* Hannah and Stanley Mitchell (trs.). 1962. Insightful study of the social significance of the nineteenth-century novel by one of Europe's leading Marxist scholars.

Perkin, Harold. *The Origins of Modern English Society, 1780–1860.* 1969. Provides a clear picture of the diverse sectors of English society and how they adapted to the changes of the period.

Porter, Roy, and Mikul Teich (eds.). *Romanticism in National Context.* 1988. Particularly useful for the student because this volume of interpretive essays includes many on smaller European nations.

Price, Roger. *A Social History of Nineteenth-Century France.* 1987. A clear synthesis of recent research that provides an excellent introduction.

*Riasanovsky, Nicholas V. *The Emergence of Romanticism.* 1992. An introduction to the origins of European Romanticism that emphasizes its importance for rising nationalism.

Saville, John. *1848: The British State and the Chartist Movement.* 1987. Why Chartism failed to win its aims.

Segalen, Martine. *Love and Power in the Peasant Family: Rural France in the Nineteenth Century.* J. C. Whitehouse and Sarah Mathews (trs.). 1983.

*Sewell, William H., Jr. *Work and Revolution in France: The Language of Labor from the Old Regime to 1848.* 1980. An important study that shows the radical potential and continuing strength of a preindustrial working-class culture.

*Thompson, Dorothy. *The Chartists: Popular Politics in the Industrial Revolution.* 1984. A lively and sympathetic account that relates working-class action to the larger social context.

*Thompson, Edward P. *The Making of the English Working Class.* 1964. A remarkable work of sympathetic insight and exhaustive research that continues to influence studies of the working class in all societies.

Walker, Mack. *German Home Towns: Community, State, and General Estate, 1648–1871.* 1971. Sensitive treatment of the response of small-town life to political and social change.

*Weiss, John. *Conservatism in Europe, 1770–1945: Traditionalism, Reaction, and Counter-Revolution.* 1977. A valuable survey of the rich variety and social insight in conservative thought and of its political importance.

*Available in paperback.

Anton von Werner
PROCLAMATION OF THE GERMAN EMPIRE ON JANUARY 18, 1871 AT THE HALL OF MIRRORS IN VERSAILLES, 1885
Victory and the birth of a new Germany: The halls of Versailles ring as Prussian officers hail the proclamation of Prussia's King Wilhelm as German Kaiser.
Bildarchiv Preussischer Kulturbesitz/Art Resource, NY

Chapter Twenty-Four

NATIONAL STATES AND NATIONAL CULTURES

THE REVOLUTIONS OF 1848 • THE POLITICS OF NATIONALISM •
NINETEENTH-CENTURY CULTURE

In the spring of 1848, revolution swept across Europe from France to Hungary. Popular uprisings seemed to transform Europe in a few dramatic months; yet the revolutionary regimes were soon suppressed. They nevertheless demonstrated that revolution could erupt at any time, that demands for political freedom could win passionate support, that class conflict could be explosive, that military power could be decisive, and that nationalism could make the broadest appeal of all. In the next thirty years, two new national states, Italy and Germany, came into being and governments everywhere took increased responsibility for shaping public life. That included supporting a formal culture that was both an expression of national identity and a means of defining and propagating it.

Cavour prime minister of Piedmont **1852** ●   ● **1854** Crimean War

Louis Napoleon's coup d'etat **1851** ●   Piedmont's war on Austria **1859** ●

● **1849** Hungary declares independence from Austria;
  Frederick William rejects crown of a unified Germany

● **December 1848** Louis Napoleon elected president of French Republic

● **June 1848** "June Days" uprisings in Paris

● **May 1848** Frankfurt Parliament opens

● **February–March 1848** Revolutions in Paris, Vienna, Berlin

THE REVOLUTIONS OF 1848

The revolutions of 1848 spread by a kind of spontaneous imitation from city to city, their causes, early successes, and ultimate defeat somewhat different in each case. Yet all of them went through comparable phases in which easy victory and initial euphoria was followed by rising social conflict and, ultimately, by the triumph of the forces of order.

Two years of poor harvests and industrial recession in most of Europe preceded these outbreaks, but economic crisis alone does not make a revolution. In Ireland more than a million people died from starvation during the famine years from 1846 to 1849, yet that tragedy did little more to shake British rule than the Chartist movement. In Switzerland, Belgium, and the Netherlands, major liberalization occurred without a serious revolt. Revolutions occurred where governments were distrusted and where the fear and resentment fed by rising food prices and unemployment found focus in specific political demands.

The Opening Phase

France   In France Guizot's government refused to widen the suffrage, and that led to the fall of the July Monarchy. The parliamentary opposition launched a protest movement that staged large banquets across the country. When a nervous government, aware of its unpopularity, banned the banquet scheduled for Paris in late February 1848, some members of the Chamber of Deputies announced they would attend anyway. Crowds gathered in the streets, and workers who could never have afforded banquet tickets started to build barricades. The rituals of revolution had begun. Louis Philippe, ever sensitive to middle-class opinion, held a review of his citizen militia, the National Guard. When

they sullenly refused to cheer him, Louis Philippe knew his days were numbered. He abdicated in favor of his grandson and left for England, much as Charles X had done just eighteen years before.

A provisional government of men chosen by two rival newspapers appeared at the Hôtel de Ville and declared France a republic. The Paris crowds cheered, and political clubs organized. The new cabinet—led by Alphonse de Lamartine, a handsome and much-admired Romantic poet—was dominated by moderates who at first cooperated with more radical members, including a socialist, Louis Blanc. They agreed that the republic should adopt universal male suffrage, a degree of democracy allowed in no other large nation. They proclaimed the citizens' right to work as a principle of government and established a commission to hold public hearings on problems of labor.

At the same time, the new regime was careful to demonstrate its restraint. It refused to intervene on behalf of revolutions in other countries, rejected proposals for adopting a red flag as the symbol of socialism and kept the familiar tricolor, and levied new taxes to balance the budget. Relations with the Catholic Church were the best in a generation, and April elections for a constituent assembly took place in good order. Nearly 85 percent of the eligible electorate voted, giving moderate republicans an overwhelming majority. The Second Republic seemed solidly established.

Revolution Spreads   As news of the events in France sped across Europe, a conservative nightmare became a reality. Nearly every capital had citizens who found exciting promise in words like *constitution*, *rights*, *liberty*, and *free press*. In Hungary the Diet cheered Lajos Kossuth, the Magyar leader, as he called on March 3 for representative government. In the same week, demon-

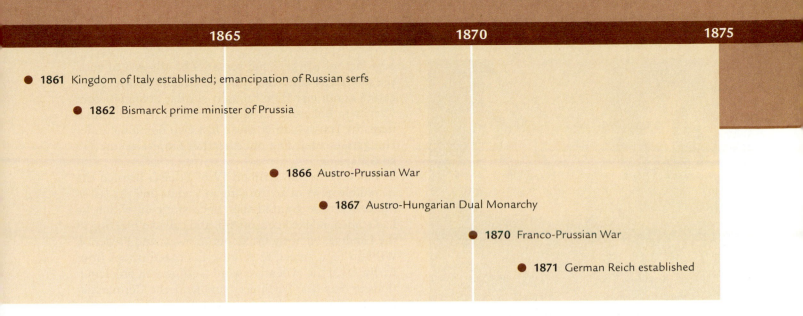

● **1861** Kingdom of Italy established; emancipation of Russian serfs

● **1862** Bismarck prime minister of Prussia

● **1866** Austro-Prussian War

● **1867** Austro-Hungarian Dual Monarchy

● **1870** Franco-Prussian War

● **1871** German Reich established

Felix Philippoteaux
LAMARTINE REJECTS THE RED FLAG, **1848**
Lamartine persuades the crowd to reject the red flag and let the new French republic keep the tricolor.
Musée du Petit Palais, Paris. Giraudon/Bridgeman Art Library

strations with similar demands erupted in the cities of the Rhineland, soon giving way to revolution there and then in Vienna (March 12), Berlin (March 15), Milan (March 18), and Venice (March 22). Each of these revolutions followed a similar pattern. The news from France would attract excited crowds; groups of men—especially journalists, lawyers, and students—would meet in cafés to discuss rumors and newspaper reports. Governments that did not quickly grant constitutions (as they had tended to do in Italy) would call out troops to maintain order; and with a kind of inevitability,

some incident would occur—a shot fired by a soldier insulted once too often or by someone in the crowd with an unfamiliar gun.

Then barricades would rise in the style that came from Paris, constructed of paving stones, a passing coach ceremoniously overturned, nearby trees, and furniture. Barricades became the people's voice, threatening but vague, as workers and professional people, men, women, and children labored together. When blood was shed, the crowd had its martyrs. In Paris corpses were carried around on a cart as a spur to revolutionary

In one of the early triumphs of the 1848 revolutions, the citizens of Milan forced the Austrian Army to leave the city. Everyone now knew how to build barricades, and the whole family helped, using whatever was available.
Museo del Risorgimento, Milan. © G. Costa/Index

determination; in Berlin the king, supporting his fainting queen, acceded to the crowd's demands and paid his respects, bareheaded, to the subjects his own troops had killed. When new concessions were won, the atmosphere would grow festive. New flags would fly, often a tricolor, an echo of the French Revolution but with colors symbolizing some other nation. In the almost universal dedication to politics, newspapers and pamphlets appeared in floods (one hundred new newspapers in Vienna, nearly five hundred in Paris). Radicals would seek ever after to recapture the unanimity and joy of those early days of revolution. Others, and not just conservatives, would never forget fearsome crowds, fanatical faces, and ugly threats.

Central Europe   In the Austrian Empire, the Hungarian Diet had by mid-March established a free press and a national guard, abolished feudal obligations (with compensation to the lords), and required nobles to pay taxes. Everyone noticed the parallel to 1789. Reluctantly Vienna agreed that Hungary could levy its own taxes and direct its own army. The Hungarian example encouraged students in Vienna to demand representative government for Austria as well, and crowds soon clashed with the troops and formed specific demands. In rapid order Metternich resigned, censorship was abolished, a constitution was promised, and firearms were passed out to the students. When students rejected the proposal that all men ex-

cept factory workers and servants be allowed to vote, the monarchy conceded universal male suffrage. Hungarian autonomy then brought similar demands from Czechs in Bohemia, Croatians in Croatia, and Romanians in Transylvania (these last two domains under Hungarian rule). The old Austrian Empire seemed to be collapsing.

When Frederick William IV of Prussia learned the incredible news of an uprising in Vienna and the fall of Metternich, he granted the concessions on which he had stalled, relaxed censorship, and called a meeting of the Landtag. Fighting broke out anyway, and Frederick William then agreed to remove his hated troops from Berlin, used the evocative word *Germany* in proclamations to "my dear Berliners," and wore the German national colors: black, gold, and red. A constituent assembly was elected in May by universal but indirect male suffrage, and when it met in Berlin, where a civic guard now kept order, revolution seemed to have triumphed in Prussia, too.

Events in the rest of Germany confirmed that victory. In May, 830 delegates elected in the various German states convened the **Frankfurt Parliament** to write a constitution for all of Germany. Mostly liberals, more than half of them were lawyers and professors, but there were also businessmen, members of the liberal gentry, and even nobles. The great majority favored a monarchical German state under a liberal constitution as the brilliant, difficult, and noisy assembly set about to write a constitution for a united Germany.

The arrangements contrived in 1815 at the Congress of Vienna were under siege in Italy as well, where in the 1820s and 1830s the kingdoms of Piedmont in the north and Naples (including Sicily) in the south had barely weathered earlier revolts, which had also threatened the smaller duchies in between. A well-organized rising in Palermo against rule from Naples was actually the first of the revolutions in 1848; but it was news of the revolution in Paris that made it possible to demand constitutions in Naples, Tuscany, and Piedmont. Even the Papal States got a constitution, though it awkwardly preserved a veto for the pope and the College of Cardinals. Lombardy and Venetia had been ruled as part of the Habsburg Empire since 1815, but shortly after the revolution in Vienna, a revolt broke out in Milan against the Austrian forces there. The Austrians were forced to retreat, and the "Five Glorious Days of Milan" were added to the heroic legends of March. Then Venice rose up to reestablish the Venetian republic of old, and the possibility that the Italian peninsula might be freed from foreign rule stimulated a nationalist fervor that forced Piedmont to join the war against Austria.

CHRONOLOGY
The Opening Phase
1848

France	Habsburg Empire	German States / Prussia	Italian States
Feb. 22 Barricades in Paris.	**Mar. 3** Hungarian demands.	**Mar. 15** Berlin rising.	**Jan. 12** Palermo revolt.
Feb. 23 Louis Philippe abdicates; Republic proclaimed.	**Mar. 12** Student risings in Vienna.	**Mar. 18–21** Prussian king calls Landtag.	**Feb. 10** King in Naples grants constitution.
Apr. 23 French elections.	**Mar. 13** Metternich resigns.	**May 18** Frankfurt national assembly meets.	**Mar. 4** Constitution granted in Piedmont.
	Mar. 15–31 Liberal legislation; Hungarian autonomy.	**May 22** Prussian constituent assembly meets.	**Mar. 14** Pope grants constitution.
	Apr. 25 Emperor proclaims constitution for Austria.		**Mar. 18–22** Milan revolt: Five Glorious Days.
	May 15 Demonstrators in Vienna demand democracy.		**Mar. 22** Venice declares republic.
			May 30 Italian troops defeat Austrians.

The Fatal Dissensions

Social Class   Everywhere, however, the new freedom exposed divisions among those who had fought for it. In France these divisions were primarily social— between Paris and the countryside, between the middle class and the workers. Workers agitated for a social program and pinned their hopes on the national workshops that had been established as an echo of ideas popularized by the socialist Louis Blanc. Imagined as cooperatives in which workers would work for themselves and share the profits, the workshops that the Republic established were in practice little more than a program of temporary public relief. Unemployed men from Paris and the countryside nevertheless enrolled by the tens of thousands. To moderate republicans the workshops represented a dangerous principle and outrageous waste. The government ordered them disbanded in June. To workers the workshops represented a symbolic promise and the beginning of a new era. They responded by building barricades in the working-class sections of Paris. For three days workers fought with the ferocity of hopelessness before the Republic's troops under General Cavaignac systematically crushed the threat to order.

More than a thousand people died; thousands more would be sent to prison or into exile. The **June Days** remained the very symbol of class conflict for socialists, and radicals never quite recaptured their faith that democracy alone would lead to social justice. Given almost dictatorial powers, Cavaignac took steps to restrict the press, suppress radical societies, and discipline workers. Yet Cavaignac remained a convinced republican, and the assembly continued to write a constitution that maintained universal suffrage and provided for a president directly elected by popular vote. But after June there was something a little hollow about the Second Republic.

National Ambitions   In Germany and Austria, also, revolution uncovered latent conflicts between workers and the middle class and among artisans, peasants, and nobles. But the outcome was determined more by competing nationalisms and the fact that kings still had their armies. The Frankfurt parliament felt little sympathy for uprisings by other nationalities against German rule. Instead of protesting the repression of revolution, it congratulated the Austrian field marshal who bombarded Prague (where Czechs had staged a Pan-Slav conference) on his German victory; and it applauded the Austrian forces that regrouped in northern Italy and fought their way back into Milan. It called on the Prussian army to put down a Polish uprising in Posen and to fight against Danes in

Ernest Meissonier
THE BARRICADE IN RUE MORTELLERIE, PARIS, JUNE 1848
A silent street in Paris after the June Days, its rubble, bodies, and blood—the emblems of revolution defeated.
Louvre, Paris, France. Erich Lessing/Art Resource, NY

Schleswig. In September, when riots broke out in Frankfurt itself, the assembly invited Prussian troops to restore order. Conflicts among multiple nationalities were also strengthening the Habsburgs at home, as the emperor mobilized Croatians demanding autonomy from Hungary much as Hungary had from Austria. In parts of the empire, Austrian officials were also able to win peasant support by abolishing serfdom and by playing on their distrust of local revolutionaries.

The armies that soon moved on Frankfurt and Vienna confronted resistance that, like the June Days in Paris, revealed popular fury and more radical demands than the risings of February and March. Politics turned more radical in Rome, too, where the pope had proved not to be an Italian nationalist; economic conditions worsened, and a government that had promised much accomplished little. When his prime minister was assassinated, Pius IX slipped across the border into the Kingdom of Naples, and a representative assembly gave the eternal city its ancient title of Roman Republic.

Venice and France were also republics, and assemblies were still busy drafting constitutions in Vienna, Berlin, and Frankfurt, but there could be no doubt that conservative forces were gaining ground.

The Final Phase

New Leaders In December, France elected a president, and the candidates who had been prominent in the new republic finished far behind Louis Napoleon Bonaparte, who won 70 percent of the votes. The ambitious nephew of Emperor Napoleon, he had campaigned as a republican. He had written more about social questions and workers' needs than any other candidate, and he was supported by the Catholic Church and the monarchists, for want of anyone else, as a man of order. Above all, he had his name.[1]

Austria, too, found a strong new leader in Prince Felix von Schwarzenberg, who filled the place Metternich left vacant. In December he persuaded the emperor to abdicate in favor of his eighteen-year-old nephew, Franz Joseph I, who could promise a fresh start. In Prussia the king felt confident enough to dissolve the Landtag and promulgate a constitution of his own. Ten months of turmoil had led back to the arrangements of February.

Military Force One by one, the remaining revolutionary regimes were subdued. The Frankfurt Assembly, having completed its constitution for a unified Germany, in March 1849 elected the Prussian king as German emperor, only to have him reject this "crown from the gutter," declaring that the ones he recognized came by grace of God. The Frankfurt constitution—with its list of old abuses to be abolished, its universal male suffrage and promises of civil rights and education—would never be tested (see "The Frankfurt Constitution," p. 713). New revolutions broke out in the Rhineland, Saxony, and Baden, but all were quashed in June and July with the aid of Prussian troops. The Habsburgs' multinational armies bombarded the revolutionaries of Vienna into submission and soon turned on Hungary, where a republic had been declared because Schwarzenberg refused to permit Hungary to have a constitution. The Hungarians battled for months against the armies of Austria and against Croatians and Romanians until Russia

---

[1] On trial for his attempted coup in 1840, Louis Napoleon had concluded his defense with these words: "I represent before you a principle, a cause, and a defeat: the principle is sovereignty of the people; the cause, that of the Empire; the defeat, Waterloo. The principle you have recognized; the cause you have served; the defeat you want to avenge."

CHRONOLOGY
Fatal Dissensions
1848

France	German States		Italy
	Habsburg Empire	*Prussia*	
June 23–26 June Days insurrection.	**June 12** Prague bombarded; Pan-Slav congress dissolved.	**June–Sept.** Frankfurt assembly supports Prussia against Danes in Schleswig.	**July 24** Austrians defeat Italian army.
Nov. 4 Constitution.	**June 22** Assembly in Vienna adopts constitution, peasants emancipated.		**Nov. 25** Pope flees Rome.
	Sept. 17 Habsburg army from Croatia invades Hungary.		
	Oct. 31 Vienna bombarded, occupied.		

An engraving of the violence in Frankfurt in September 1848 contrasts the fighting styles of troops and the defenders of revolution.
The Granger Collection, New York

intervened in June to seal the fate of the Hungarian republic.

In Italy, too, military force was decisive. Austria defeated Piedmont one more time, leaving it nothing to show for its support of Italian independence except an enormous debt, an unpopular government, a new ruler, a cautious constitution, and the red, white, and green flag of Italian nationalism. Ten years later the constitution and the flag would seem quite a lot; for the time being, Austrian power once again dominated

CHRONOLOGY
The Final Phase
1848–1849

France	German States		Italy
	Habsburg Empire	*Prussia*	
Dec. 20 Louis Napoleon elected president.	**Dec. 2.** Francis Joseph, emperor.	**Dec. 5** Prussian assembly dissolved.	**Feb. 9** Roman Republic established.
	Jan. 5 Budapest occupied.	**Mar. 27** Frankfurt constitution completed; rejected by Prussia on Apr. 21.	**Mar. 23** Decisive defeat of Piedmont by Austria.
	Mar. 4 Austrian Assembly dissolved.	**July** Last insurgents crushed in Baden.	**Apr. 24** French army lands in Papal States.
	Apr. 13 Hungary declares a republic.		**June 30** Rome falls to French.
	June 17 Russia invades Hungary.		**Aug. 28** Venice surrenders.
	Aug. 13 Hungary capitulates.		

the Italian peninsula. There was soon a further foreign presence in the center of Italy, for Louis Napoleon sent French armies to restore the pope and defeat the Roman Republic, which fought with heroic tenacity for three months before being overrun. The Kingdom of Naples did not reconquer Sicily until May 1849 and only after a bombardment of the city of Messina that gave Ferdinand II the nickname King Bomba. The last of the revolutionary regimes to fall was the Venetian republic, defeated in August 1849 more by starvation and cholera than by the Austrian artillery that accomplished the unprecedented feat of lobbing shells three miles from the mainland into the island city.

The Results A famous liberal historian, G. M. Trevelyan, called 1848 "the turning-point at which modern history failed to turn," and his epigram captures the sense of destiny thwarted that still colors the liberal view of 1848. Current historical analysis of the failures of 1848 generally makes five broad points. First, liberal constitutions and increased civil rights failed to pull strong and lasting support from artisans, peasants, and workers, whose more immediate needs were neither met nor understood. Second, the revolutions of February and March were made primarily by the middle classes, strengthened by popular discontent; but when radicals sought more than representative government and legal equality, the middle classes worried about order and private property. Isolated from the

masses, they were too weak to retain power except in France; and there order came only after repression of the urban poor and erosion of constitutional liberties. Third, the leaders of the revolutions, inexperienced in practical politics, often mistook parliaments for power and left intact the established authorities that would soon turn on them. Fourth, nationalism divided revolutionaries and prevented the cooperation that was essential for durable success. Fifth, no major nation was ready to intervene in behalf of change. Britain was sympathetic, France encouraging, and the United States (its consulates centers of republicanism) enthusiastic; but none of that sympathy matched the military assistance Russia gave the Austrian emperor or the formidable armies of Austria and Prussia.

The events of 1848 had significant effects nonetheless. Revolution so widespread reflected the failures of restoration, displayed again the power of political ideas, and uncovered the effects of a generation of social change. Many of the gains won in that year endured: The peasants of eastern Prussia and the Austrian Empire were emancipated from serfdom in 1848 and remained free of servile obligations; Piedmont and Prussia kept their new, limited constitutions. The monarchs triumphant in 1849 punished revolutionaries with execution, prison, and exile, but they also learned that they must pay more attention to winning some popular support. Liberals would never again depend so optimistically on the spontaneous power of the

THE FRANKFURT CONSTITUTION

The Frankfurt Parliament completed its work on a constitution for Germany in 1849. It was a long and detailed document, carefully proscribing the repressive acts that had been most common in the preceding years. Its proud assertions of German freedom remain significantly vague, however, about the enforcement of its provisions and what the boundaries of the German nation will be.

THE FUNDAMENTAL RIGHTS OF THE GERMAN PEOPLE

Article 1

¶ 131. The German people consists of the citizens of the states, which make up the Reich.

¶ 132. Every German has the right of German Reich's citizenship. He can exercise this right in every German land. Reich's franchise legislation shall provide for the right of the individual to vote for members of the national assembly.

¶ 133. Every German has the right to live or reside in any part of the Reich's territory, to acquire and dispose of property of all kinds, to pursue his livelihood, and to win the right of communal citizenship. . . .

¶ 134. No German state is permitted to make a distinction between its citizens and other Germans in civil, criminal, and litigation rights which relegates the latter to the position of foreigners.

¶ 135. Capital punishment for civil offenses shall not take place, and, in those cases where condemnation has already been made, shall not be carried out, in order not to infringe upon the hereby acquired civil law.

¶ 136. Freedom of emigration shall not be limited by any state; emigration levies shall not be established.

All matters of emigration remain under the protection and care of the Reich.

Article 2

¶ 137. There are no class differences before the law. The rank of nobility is abolished.

All special class privileges are abolished.

All Germans are equal before the law.

All titles, insofar as they are not bound with an office, are abolished and never again shall be introduced.

No citizen shall accept a decoration from a foreign state.

Public office shall be open to all men on the basis of ability.

All citizens are subject equally to military service; there shall be no draft substitutions.

Article 3

¶ 141. The confiscation of letters and papers, except at an arrest or house search, can take place with a legally executed warrant, which must be served on the arrested person at once or within the next twenty-four hours.

¶ 142. The secrecy of letters is inviolable.

Necessary exceptions in cases of criminal investigation and in the event of war shall be established by legislation.

Article 4

¶ 143. Every German shall have the right freely to express his opinion through speech, writing, publication, and illustration.

The freedom of the press shall be suspended under no circumstances through preventive measures, namely, censorship, concessions, security orders, imposts, limitation of publication or bookselling, postal bans, or other restraints.

From Louis L. Snyder (ed.), *The Documents of German History,* Rutgers University Press, 1958.

---

people, and advocates of social reform would be more skeptical of political liberalism. International power clearly constrained domestic policy, but political leaders of every hue now also recognized the potential force of nationalism.

THE POLITICS OF NATIONALISM

Why **nationalism** assumed such importance in the nineteenth century and has retained it to the present day remains one of the important questions of modern history. As an ideology, it represents itself as a natural, age-old sentiment arising spontaneously; yet national-

ism is essentially a modern phenomenon and often seems to require persistent propaganda. Associated with liberalism in the first part of the nineteenth century, nationalism came to be embraced and used by both the left and the right. And it affected politics on every level: international relations; the unification of Italy and Germany, which changed the map of Europe; and domestic policies in every sort of government.

The Elements of Nationalism

Nationalism's deepest roots lie in a shared sense of regional and cultural identity, especially as those roots are expressed in custom, language, and religion. This shared culture had been greatly affected, even shaped, by the development of the state, whose power and importance had increased since the state building of the seventeenth century. But it was the experience of the French Revolution that established nationalism as a political force capable of mobilizing popular enthusiasm, of reforming society, of creating seemingly irresistible political movements, and ultimately of greatly adding to the power of the state.

Liberation and Modernization   Napoleon I had appealed to national feeling in much of Europe, most notably Poland and Italy. In Germany the fight against Napoleon was called a national war of liberation, and the Allies had somewhat more timidly evoked national feeling to recruit opposition to the French in Spain and (less successfully) Italy. The association of liberation and nationalism had been particularly marked in the New World, where the American Revolution had fostered a fervent nationalism and where, as a result of their revolt against Spanish rule, elite groups had carved Central and South America into new states and claimed a national identity for each of them.

Nationalism was also a movement for self-conscious modernization, embraced by people who believed that their societies might equal the industrial wealth of England and acquire political systems as responsive and efficient as those of Britain and France. In the course of the nineteenth century, increased communication, literacy, and mobility further stimulated the sense of belonging to a larger but definable community. Nationalism was thus a response to social and economic change, one that promised to bring middle classes and masses together in support of common goals. Nationalists, like conservatives and socialists, stressed the values of community; like liberals, they tended to believe that change could bring progress.

National Identity   As an intellectual movement, nationalism was an international phenomenon, everywhere emphasizing the importance of culture. But it was also informed by cultural Romanticism, with its rejection of the universalism of the Enlightenment. Thus, German intellectuals such as Johann Gottlieb Fichte urged their countrymen to put aside values imported from France in favor of a uniquely German culture.

The exploration of ethnic origins took many forms. A group of German scholars made philology (the study of language) a science, and by the 1830s and 1840s an extraordinary revival of national languages had occurred across Europe. Gaelic was hailed as the national tongue of Ireland; in Finland the first public lecture in Finnish marked a break from the dominant Swedish culture; intellectuals in Bohemia began abandoning their customary German to write in Czech. More re-

markable still was the number of languages consciously contrived out of local dialects and invented vocabularies. Norwegian became distinct from Danish, Serbian from other Slavic languages, and Slovak from Czech—all literary languages by the 1840s, each the work of a handful of scholars whose task of establishing a national language was made easier by widespread illiteracy.

This fascination with folk culture and language was reinforced by an emphasis on history as a popular but scholarly form of knowledge that revealed each nation's historic character. Germans wrote of a special sense of freedom embodied in Germanic tribes, expanded in the Reformation, and now extended to the state. French historians wrote eloquently of France's call to carry reason and liberty across Europe, and Italian writers proclaimed that Italy was destined to lead Europe once again as it had as the home of Roman civilization and the center of Christianity. The poet Adam Mickiewicz, lecturing in Paris, inspired Polish nationalists with his descriptions of how Poland's history paralleled the life of Christ and had yet to achieve Resurrection. Francis Palacky pioneered in stressing the role of the Czechs as leaders of the Slavs. Such visions were repeated in poetry and drama, which now blossomed in the native tongue and justified resistance to alien rule. This cultural nationalism, which circulated among intellectuals, students, professional people, and journalists, served as a weapon of middle-class self-assertion, whereby people who felt cramped by their society's social hierarchy, unsympathetic bureaucracy, or stagnant economy could win broader support for their own dreams of progress.

Political Goals   In places subject to foreign rule, the political goal of nationalist movements was independence. Everywhere, economic issues were central. Campaigns for agricultural improvement, promoted by the liberal aristocracy, became nationalist programs in Hungary and Italy. In Germany Friedrich List, a leading liberal economist, argued that the American example proved the need for tariffs to protect fledgling industries and made his analysis into a nationalist battle cry. Only a united Germany with a national tariff, he insisted, could create an internal area of free trade sufficient to develop the industry and vigorous middle class necessary for competitive strength and independence. Everywhere nationalist groups demanded public education, more political freedom, and efficient government. Strengthened by its promises of economic growth and its respect for native traditions, nationalism generated political movements of broad appeal, capable of mobilizing popular enthusiasm. Daniel O'Connell's inflammatory speeches won thousands to his Young Ireland organization and its demands for the end of union with

In 1844 Daniel O'Connell was released from prison after having served three months on the charge of attempting to repeal the Act of Union that subordinated Ireland to England. His release was the occasion of a great parade in Dublin. Ordinary people celebrated, too, as shown here in an illustration from *The Illustrated London News*, a picture that must have frightened many English readers.
The Mary Evans Picture Library

Great Britain. In the 1830s and 1840s, he led the largest such protest movement Europe had yet seen.

A New Regime: The Second Empire in France

Elections in France had left the Second Republic ruled by a president, Louis Napoleon, who would eventually subvert it, and a Chamber of Deputies in which a majority were monarchists, who did not want a republic at all.

From Republic to Empire   Often at odds with the deputies, Napoleon continued to play to public opinion; and when, in the third year of his four-year term, the Chamber rejected a constitutional amendment that would have allowed him a second term, he struck. His coup d'état came on the eve of December 2, 1851—the anniversary of the first Napoleon's coronation as emperor in 1804 and of his victory at Austerlitz in 1805. Potential opponents, including two hundred deputies, were quickly taken into custody; troops occupied the streets and overran hastily built barricades. At the same time, Napoleon restored universal male suffrage, which the conservative Chamber had restricted. Resistance was serious in many parts of France—hundreds were killed and more than 20,000 people arrested—but brief. Three weeks later Napoleon's actions were ratified by more than 90 percent of the voters in a national

plebiscite. Exactly one year after this first coup, Napoleon had the Second Republic transformed into the **Second Empire** and became Emperor Napoleon III, a change even more overwhelmingly supported in another plebiscite. Citizens could do no more than vote yes or no, to accept changes already effected or risk whatever might follow from a negative vote.

The Second Empire claimed a democratic mandate but held authoritarian power. It was supported by most businessmen and the Catholic Church, accepted by most monarchists, local notables, and peasants. It sponsored programs for social welfare as well as economic growth and promised both peace and national glory. Napoleon III was influenced by Saint-Simonian socialism, attracted by liberal nationalism, and obsessed by belief in his own destiny—Napoleon the Little to his opponents, the Emperor to most of the French.

The economy boomed in the 1850s; and the French government fostered economic growth more systematically than any other government in Europe, using tax incentives to stimulate investment, making it easier to form companies with limited liability, and adding its own special investment funds. Among its many programs of public works, the rebuilding of Paris was one of the most elaborate.

A pioneering venture in city planning, the project typified the imperial style. Plans were reviewed by Napoleon III himself, who favored ostentatious structures of equal height, and directed by his extraordinarily able prefect Georges Haussmann. New parks were created and slums cleared, often with painful dislocation for their residents; wide boulevards, planned for their striking vistas and as an aid to traffic, incidentally made it hard to build barricades. Facades often received more attention than the buildings behind them, but the buildings were now served by a vast new sewer and water system. Such massive projects stimulated land speculation and profiteering; yet the result was a city healthier and more convenient, envied and imitated throughout the world. The court of Napoleon and Empress Eugnie was brilliant, and French prestige in the arts and sciences (enhanced by the fame of Louis Pasteur's discoveries in biology) was never higher. The emperor presented himself as the patron of educational and social reform and, in the Napoleonic tradition, rewarded talent with honors and promotions, taking credit for France's prestige.

The Liberal Empire   By the 1860s, however, the empire's fortunes were changing, its policies at home and abroad subject to rising criticism. The coalition of interests that had supported Napoleon was breaking up. Foreign ventures intended to extend French influence and satisfy national pride had their political costs. Support of Italian unification antagonized

Haussmann's rebuilding of Paris began with the demolition of buildings that had stood for centuries and included a ring of spacious boulevards around the city.
Giraudon/Art Resource, NY

French Catholics, and an attempt to gain imperial glory by intervention in Mexico ended in disaster. Steps toward free trade, including a major tariff agreement with Great Britain in 1860, appealed to liberal economists but upset many producers. At the same time, workers wanted more from the government than public works projects and support for mutual-aid societies. Restrictions of political freedom were increasingly resented, and opponents' criticisms became more intense.

Napoleon's response was a gradual liberalization that in 1860 enlarged the role of the legislature and by 1868 included freedom of the press and of assembly; a full-fledged parliamentary system was in place two years later. The government also encouraged workers' organizations and acknowledged the right to strike. Like the establishment of public secondary schools, which the Church opposed, these new measures alienated some old supporters without, however, mollifying an opposition that gained in each election. Republicans held nearly half the lower house in 1869, and a republican was prime minister the following year, which turned out to be the Second Empire's last.

The Second Empire had pioneered a new kind of regime, one that was authoritarian but played to public opinion, that imposed order but fostered social programs and economic growth, and that used national prestige to counter domestic division. Balancing those tensions became increasingly difficult.

Nationalism and International Relations

The Politics of Patriotism   The conflicts of 1848 and 1849 had suggested the political potential of nationalism, a lesson that Prussia, Austria, Britain, Piedmont, and France would all seek to apply. In 1849 Prussia still hoped to lead a confederation of North German states, finding the nationalist dreams of the Frankfurt Parliament more attractive once the assembly itself had no voice. Austria, eager to reassert Habsburg influence in Germany after revolution in Hungary had been quelled, promoted a competing solution. For the next decade the Prussian and Austrian monarchies vied for primacy among the other German states.

The British foreign secretary also exploited the nationalist appeal of an assertive policy. Viscount Palmer-

MAP 24.1 THE DECLINE OF THE OTTOMAN EMPIRE, 1683–1914
In the nineteenth century the Russian and Habsburg empires kept up the pressure against a weakening
Ottoman Empire in the Caucusus and the Balkans. But it remained a formidable presence in the Arab world
and in the Mediterranean region and was thus of great interest to Britain and France. How did the Ottoman
Empire's existence affect the balance of power in Europe?
◆ For an online version, go to www.mhhe.com/chambers9 > chapter 24 > book maps.

ston was a flamboyant aristocrat, frequently at odds
with his cabinet colleagues, but shrewdly alert to public opinion. Thus, he made an issue of national honor
out of one British citizen's claims against the Greek
government. An Athenian mob had burned the house
of one Don Pacifico, who had been born in Gibraltar
and held British citizenship. Palmerston vigorously
supported Pacifico's demands for compensation from

the Greek government, sending notes, threats, and finally a British fleet to Greece until an indemnity was
paid. Palmerston defended his stand in the House of
Commons. Dramatically, he recalled the pride of ancient Romans, who could say *"Civis Romanus sum"*
("I am a Roman citizen") and know themselves secure
throughout their empire. A British subject, Palmerston
declared, "in whatever land he may be, shall feel

The Crimean War generated considerable enthusiasm in Britain and France, with the help of colorful accounts from the front. This dramatic illustration from a British paper shows Florence Nightingale rushing to aid wounded soldiers, a service that made her and professional nurses famous.
The Granger Collection, New York

confident that the watchful eye and strong arm of England will protect him against injustice and wrong." To the public at least, Palmerston was vindicated.

The Crimean War The restless search for international prestige led France and Great Britain to war against Russia in 1854 over competing claims by Roman Catholic and Greek Orthodox monks to be the guardians of Jerusalem's holy places. France pressed the Ottoman sultan, whose empire included Jerusalem, to grant them specific privileges. Russia, as defender of the Orthodox faith, demanded a protectorate over Orthodox churches within the Ottoman Empire and showed its determination by occupying Wallachia and Moldavia, Danubian lands under Ottoman suzerainty. This Russian expansion, part of a long-term pattern, worried the English, who saw a threat to their own empire in any extension of Russian influence in the direction of Persia or Afghanistan. Britain encouraged the sultan to resist Russia's demands.

Negotiations repeatedly broke down; Britain and France sent their fleets into the Aegean Sea, and in October 1853 the sultan exuberantly declared war on Russia. Russian forces destroyed an Ottoman fleet, however, and Britain and France decided to fight Russia to preserve the balance of power in the Middle East. That announcement in March 1854 was greeted with patriotic enthusiasm in London and Paris. Six months after war was declared, not having found a more convenient battlefield, British and French forces landed in the Crimea, which juts into the Black Sea. The war was conducted with remarkable incompetence on both sides. Russia was unable to mobilize or effectively de-

ploy the large armies that made it so feared, and Britain's supply system proved inadequate for hostilities at such a distance. In 1855 the allies welcomed the aid of little Piedmont and, a full year after invading the Crimea, finally took Sevastopol. Russia sued for peace and agreed to accept terms to be defined at a European congress in Paris.

Congress of Paris The Congress signified an important shift in the European balance. It met in Paris rather than Vienna and was preoccupied with issues of nationalism. In 1856 Russia counted for less than it had in 1815, and the conservative alliance of Austria, Prussia, and Russia that had dominated the Continent for a generation had broken up over competing ambitions in the Balkans and Germany. The Congress required Russia to surrender its claims to any protectorate over Christians in the Ottoman Empire, and to accept a ban on warships in the Black Sea. Only this last point really rankled. The more troublesome issues all had to do with national claims. Britain and France did not want to give the Danubian principalities to either Russia or Austria. The issue was postponed because the obvious resolution—uniting the two territories and allowing them autonomy, a procedure that began a few years later—would create the basis for a Romanian national state, and Austria was learning to fear nationalism as a threat to the Habsburg Empire. Such fears prevented Napoleon III from putting the question of Polish independence on the agenda as he wanted to.

Almost 500,000 soldiers died in the Crimean War, the highest toll of any European conflict from the Napoleonic wars to World War I. Two-thirds of the casualties were Russian, and two-thirds of all losses resulted from sickness and bad care. Yet the outbreak of war produced a surge of enthusiasm no government could ignore. The public diplomacy that led to the war, the parades of magnificently uniformed soldiers, and the heroic stories reported by an aggressive journalism underscored its political importance. Under Western pressure, the Ottoman Empire began to adopt the modernizing institutions of the West; and Russia, sobered by defeat, launched an era of fundamental reform unequaled since the days of Peter the Great. In Italy and Germany the way was opening for still more drastic changes.

A New Nation: The Unification of Italy

Giuseppe Mazzini   Across the Italian peninsula, all the revolutions of 1848 had declared an independent nation to be a primary goal. In doing so, they employed the ideas of Giuseppe Mazzini, one of Europe's most important revolutionaries (see "Mazzini's Nationalism," p. 720). For fifteen years, Mazzini had lived in exile, mainly in London, organizing conspiracies and writing passionate propaganda in pamphlets and thousands of letters. His nationalist movement, Young Italy, had stimulated similar efforts in Ireland, Switzerland, and Hungary. Until 1848, the conspiracies he fostered had resulted in tragic failures; yet like the clandestine committees, secret meetings, and smuggled newspapers that surrounded them, these unsuccessful plots disseminated the belief that once corrupt regimes were toppled, the people would rise in common cause. Revolutionary and democratic, Mazzini was also a moralist who criticized the French Revolution for stressing rights over moral duty and who rejected socialism as materialistic. In nationalism he saw the expression of natural communities, the basis for popular democracy and international brotherhood.

Italy renewed would lead the way. A man of letters steeped in Romanticism, Mazzini nonetheless wrote tellingly about the specific grievances of peasants, artists, professionals, and intellectuals. His influence was especially strong in northern Italy, where in the 1830s and 1840s young lawyers and liberal landowners began to find national implications in nearly everything they did. Annual congresses of Italian scientists became quiet demonstrations of patriotic aspirations; disputes over where railroad lines should be built became means of expressing discontent with Austrian influence. Literary journals and societies for agricultural improvement took up the nationalist theme.

For Mazzinians, 1848 was the great chance (Mazzini himself was one of the leaders of the Roman Republic), and the defeats that followed were an even greater blow to Mazzinianism than to Italian nationalism. As Aus-

In his portraits and in his personal life, Mazzini seemed as much a romantic poet as a revolutionary agitator.
The Granger Collection, New York

tria regained dominance of the peninsula, Mazzini returned to exile and Italian nationalists began to look elsewhere for leadership. The papacy, restored by French arms, was no longer sympathetic to Italian unity; Austria ruled Lombardy and Venetia repressively, and all the other Italian regimes except Piedmont were Austrian dependencies.

The Role of Piedmont   Although a small state, Piedmont held some promise for patriots. It had fought Austria, and its young king, Victor Emmanuel II, though no liberal, ruled with a parliament. The kingdom had a tradition of military strength and bureaucratic rectitude. More recently, its government had encouraged commerce and industry, and its efforts to win trade away from Austria through commercial treaties excited Italians elsewhere. These policies acquired firmer purpose in 1852, when Count Camillo Cavour became prime minister. Cavour was a gentleman-farmer who had traveled in France and England. He believed in economic and scientific progress, representative government with limited suffrage, the rule of law, and religious tolerance. Nationalism he understood primarily as an avenue to modernization, and he

MAZZINI'S NATIONALISM

"On the Duties of Man" is one of Giuseppe Mazzini's most famous essays. It was first written in 1844 for Italian workers living in England; the excerpts here are from the fifth chapter, which was added for a new edition in 1858. Despite the events of the intervening years, Mazzini's romantic faith had changed little. The essay's title was meant to contrast with the French Revolution's "Declaration of the Rights of Man," which Mazzini criticized for encouraging selfishness and materialism.

"Your first duties—first as regards importance—are, as I have already told you, towards Humanity. . . . If you do not embrace the whole human family in your affection, . . . if, wheresoever a fellow-creature suffers, or the dignity of human nature is violated by falsehood or tyranny—you are not ready, if able, to aid the unhappy, and do not feel called upon to combat, if able, for the redemption of the betrayed or oppressed—you violate your law of life, you comprehend not that Religion which will be the guide and blessing of the future.

"But what can each of you, singly, *do* for the moral improvement and progress of Humanity? . . . The watchword of the faith of the future is *Association*, and . . . [the] means was provided for you by God when he gave you a country; when, even as a wise overseer of labour distributes the various branches of employment according to the different capacities of the workmen, he divided Humanity into distinct groups or nuclei upon the face of the earth, thus creating the germ of Nationalities. Evil governments have disfigured the divine design. Nevertheless you may still trace it, distinctly marked out—at least as far as Europe is concerned—by the course of the great rivers, the direction of the higher mountains, and other geographical conditions. They have disfigured it by their conquests, their greed, and their jealousy even of the righteous power of others. . . .

"These governments did not, and do not, recognize any country save their own families or dynasty, the egotism of caste. But the Divine design will infallibly be realized. Natural divisions, and the spontaneous, innate tendencies of the peoples, will take the place of the arbitrary divisions sanctioned by evil governments. The map of Europe will be redrawn. The countries of the Peoples, defined by the vote of free men, will arise upon the ruins of the countries of kings and privileged castes. . . .

"O my brothers, love your Country! Our country is our Home, the house that God has given us, placing therein a numerous family that loves us, and whom we love. . . . Our country is our common workshop, whence the products of our activity are sent forth for the benefit of the whole world. . . . In labouring for our own country on the right principle, we labour for Humanity."

From Giuseppe Mazzini, *On the Duties of Man*, Greenwood Publishing Group.

---

found in free trade, sound finances, and railroads a power that could remake Piedmont.

Cavour pursued his liberal goals with tactical brilliance, skillfully using newspapers and parliamentary debate to mold public opinion. He created a centrist parliamentary coalition with which he dominated both king and parliament from 1852 until his death in 1861. In that brief time he established himself as one of the outstanding statesmen of the century. Piedmont's internal strength was Cavour's first concern, but he also sought to make his state the center of Italy's resurgence, the **risorgimento**.[2] He welcomed exiles from other parts of the peninsula, encouraged the nationalist press, and sought every opportunity for symbolic gestures of patriotism. He was aided in this goal by the Italian National Society, one of whose founders was the president of the Venetian republic in 1848. The National Society propagandized for Italian unity under Piedmont's king and established secret committees in most of the cities of Italy. Its members were predominantly liberal aristocrats, local lawyers, and professors; and in calling for Italian unity, the society combined Mazzinian rhetoric with hardheaded insistence on the need for international alliances and military force. Economic liberalism largely replaced more generous and vaguer social theories.

War against Austria   Most of all, Cavour depended on astute foreign policy. He had pushed for Piedmont's participation in the Crimean War and was rewarded with the discussion of the Italian question at the Congress of Paris. Using his state's enhanced international position, he argued that Italy repressed would remain a danger to European order. He appealed for liberal sympathy throughout Western Europe, and he courted Napoleon III. At last, in July 1858, Cavour and Napoleon III met

[2] *Risorgimento*, now the historian's label for the whole period of Italian unification, was a term meaning "resurgence," often used by nationalists and made the title of a liberal newspaper that Cavour helped to found and edit.

secretly. It was easy to argue that war was inevitable, given Austria's resentment of Piedmont's growing prominence. If France would support Piedmont against Austria, Cavour promised to accept a complicated set of arrangements designed to benefit France and limit Piedmont's expansion.

Austria, watching young Lombards and Venetians escape conscription by streaming to Piedmont as volunteers, determined to end the nationalist threat once and for all. It sent Piedmont an ultimatum so strong that Cavour needed only to reply with cautious dignity in order to have his war. On April 29, 1859, Austria invaded Piedmont, and France went to the rescue of a small state attacked by her giant neighbor. The rapid movement of large French armies was impressive, but thereafter the war was fought with little tactical brilliance on either side. As the Austrians retreated to the fortresses controlling the Lombard plain, Napoleon suddenly lost his taste for war and unilaterally assented to a truce. The emperors of France and Austria agreed that Piedmont should have Lombardy but not Venetia and that the other Italian states should remain as before.

Formation of the Italian Kingdom

Those other Italian states, however, were not immune to the excitement of a national war. Gentle revolutions accompanied the march of Piedmontese troops throughout northern Italy. When local patriots gathered in the streets, the dukes of Modena, Parma, and Tuscany simply fled, to be replaced by provisional governments led by members of the National Society. These governments quickly adopted Piedmontese laws and held elections to representative assemblies. The terms of the truce arranged by France and Austria could not be carried out; and after a few months, the provisional governments held plebiscites—a device Napoleon could hardly reject—on the question of annexation to Piedmont. Italians trooped to the polls with bands playing and flags waving, peasants behind their lords and workers with their guilds. The result was as one-sided as in the plebiscites in France. Piedmont's King Victor Emmanuel ruled from the Alps to Rimini on the Adriatic. To compensate Napoleon III, the province of Savoy and the city of Nice were turned over to France.

Moderate liberals had united half of Italy. Sputtering revolts in Sicily gave more democratic nationalists a chance to lead a different sort of risorgimento. Former Mazzinians, eager to promote a Sicilian uprising, gathered guns in Genoa and planned an expedition that Cavour dared neither support nor oppose. Its leader was Giuseppe Garibaldi, Italy's most popular hero. Exiled for his Mazzinian activity in the 1830s, Garibaldi had spent ten years fighting for democratic causes in South America, returning to Italy in time to take part in the wars of 1848. He had directed the heroic defense of the Roman Republic in 1849 and led the most effective corps of volunteers in 1859. In his greatest exploit of all, he set sail for Sicily one night in May 1860 with a thousand men, mainly middle-class youths from Lombardy, Venetia, and the Romagna.

Garibaldi Goes South

No event in the nineteenth century so captured the popular imagination as that daring venture. The Expedition of the Thousand was like some ancient epic come to life in an industrial age. Untrained men, wearing the red shirts Garibaldi had adopted in South America, fought with bravery and discipline, enthusiastically supported in the Sicilian countryside. Garibaldi's tactics confused and defeated the Neapolitan generals, despite their far larger and better-equipped forces. In two weeks the Red Shirts occupied Palermo and within two months almost all of Sicily. Volunteers flocked from all over Italy to join Garibaldi, and money was raised in his behalf in all the towns of northern Italy and from New York to Stockholm.

The epic continued when, against all odds, Garibaldi sailed across the strait and landed on the Italian mainland. He declared his goal to be Rome itself and not just Naples. That worried Cavour, who considered Garibaldi irresponsible and believed that an attack on Rome might lead Austria and France to intervene on behalf of the pope. So Cavour encouraged uprisings in the Papal States and then sent Piedmontese troops to preserve

The handshake of Victor Emmanuel and Garibaldi, which sealed the unification of Italy as their armies met in 1860, became a favorite subject for illustrations of the risorgimento. This engraving is English.
Culver Pictures, Inc.

MAP 24.2 THE UNIFICATION OF ITALY
Dreams of Italian unification began during the French revolutionary era, when "sister republics" were briefly established up and down the peninsula. What were the major obstacles to Italian unification? How was it that the Kingdom of Piedmont became the engine that drove the process to success?
◆ For an online version, go to www.mhhe.com/chambers9 > chapter 24 > book maps.

order. Carefully skirting the area around Rome, they moved south to meet Garibaldi. On September 18, between lines of suspicious men, Giuseppe Garibaldi and

Victor Emmanuel rode out to shake hands and unite Italy. Garibaldi added to his legend by thus giving way in the interests of union, and the Piedmontese took

A demonstration in Florence's historic Piazza della Signoria in 1866 for the annexation of Venetia to the new Kingdom of Italy.
Scala/Art Resource, NY

over. Plebiscites confirmed the union, and in March 1861 the Kingdom of Italy was proclaimed.

United Italy   The Kingdom of Italy included almost all of Italy except for Rome and Venetia. Catholics throughout the world opposed the annexation of Rome, which Napoleon III was pledged to protect, and Austrian troops were massed in Venetia. Italy acquired Venetia in 1866 as a by-product of war between Austria and Prussia. Austria offered it in return for Italy's neutrality; Prussia had promised it to Italy if Prussia defeated Austria with Italy's support. Italy kept its prior pledge to Prussia, went to war, fought poorly, but got Venetia following Prussia's rapid victory. Rome was annexed when French troops withdrew during the Franco-**Prussian War** of 1870; the new nation finally had its ancient capital.

More lasting problems remained. To many Italians, especially in the south, unification felt like a foreign occupation, and Italy's leaders were appalled at the poverty and corruption they could not overcome. Pius IX forbade Catholics to take part in national elections and rejected the indemnity and guarantees of protection the government offered. United Italy was poor and overwhelmingly agricultural. It had no coal or iron, and three-quarters of the population was illiterate. With liberal conviction, the Italian government assumed the debts of all the former governments and struggled to balance the annual budget. Despite taxes that were

among the highest in Europe, Italy continued to lag in schools, railways, and roads. The sale of Church lands failed to benefit peasants as much as hoped, and the lower Piedmontese tariffs brought instant distress to hundreds of small producers in the rest of the peninsula. It took years of sporadic fighting to enforce order in the south. For millions of artisans and peasants, few tangible benefits followed from replacing reactionary dukes with a liberal national state.

A New Nation: The Unification of Germany

German cultural identity had grown throughout the first half of the nineteenth century, from the battles against Napoleon to the statements of the Frankfurt Parliament. It was strengthened by achievements in philosophy, science, literature, and music that were seen as German accomplishments no matter what German kingdom, principality, or free city they occurred in. The open question was what the political expression of that identity should be. The German Confederation was ineffectual, none of the schemes for unification in 1848 had been adopted, and Austria had blocked Prussian plans for leadership in 1850. Yet it was Prussia that created modern Germany.

The Dominance of Prussia   Several factors account for Prussia's eventual dominance. One was economic.

The *Zollverein*, the tariff union Prussia led, continued to prosper with industrialization in the Rhineland and Prussia, and by 1853 every German state except Austria had joined it. Another factor was Austria's multinational preoccupations, and its vulnerability to nationalisms was highlighted by the campaign for the unification of Italy. Most important of all was the dynamism of Prussia itself. It was the largest German state, with a powerful army and an efficient administration, and Prussian politics began a new era in 1858 with the rule of William I.

After a long period of reaction, in which the press and public discussion were severely repressed, politics had become more open and livelier. The Prussian constitution of 1850 allowed universal male suffrage but avoided democracy by dividing voters into three classes according to the taxes they paid. Each of the three classes, though numerically unequal, elected an equal number of representatives, ensuring that those chosen by the two wealthier classes would be a majority. In addition, the king could veto any legislation and appoint the ministers of his choice.

Although designed to ensure conservative dominance, the three-class system had the unexpected effect of magnifying the voice of new industrial wealth, and the majority of the Landtag was now prepared to challenge the monarch. The military budget became their battleground. With William's support, his minister of war and his chief of staff proposed to double the army and add to its equipment. Although the proposal was defeated, the government went ahead with its plan. Liberals, who distrusted Prussian militarism and an army dominated by the Junkers, insisted the government must be responsible to the legislature; and the opposition gained in the elections of 1862. Convinced that royal authority was at stake, William called on God and conscience, threatened abdication, and named **Otto von Bismarck** his chief minister.

Bismarck's Leadership Bismarck was a member of the Junker class, better educated than many. His pride of caste and reactionary views were resented by liberals, while most conservatives considered him to be as erratic and dangerous as Napoleon III. An experienced diplomat familiar with Europe's major capitals, he stood out by reason of his cosmopolitan outlook as much as his enormous self-confidence. For thirty years officials and legislators would have to live with his stinging sarcasm, bruising contempt, and brilliance. Bismarck surprised conservatives with his appeal to nationalism, shrewdly used power wherever he found it, and made success in foreign policy his justification. He lectured the deputies: If Germans looked to Prussia, it was because of its powerful army, not because of any liberal institutions; and he added, in the most famous statement he ever uttered, "the great questions of the day will not be settled by speeches and majority decisions—that was the mistake of 1848 and 1849—but by blood and iron."

Bismarck dissolved the parliament and used heavy government pressure in the subsequent elections but with little effect. So Bismarck ignored parliament whenever he could and encouraged divisions within the legislature whenever possible. He closed opposition newspapers and manipulated the rest. Promotions in the civil service and judiciary went to those unquestionably loyal. Once confident of his position, Bismarck spent funds and collected taxes without parliamentary authorization.

In return he offered a remarkable string of foreign triumphs. While blocking Austria's efforts to lead the German Confederation, he courted Russian friendship. Bismarck used conflict over Schleswig and Holstein (see map 24.3) to assert leadership in German affairs. German nationalists were outraged at attempts by the king of Denmark to annex Schleswig and to extend his authority over Holstein, but Prussia persuaded Austria to join in war against Denmark in January 1864. Bismarck then foiled international negotiations until the Danes were defeated. Schleswig was placed under Prussian administration and Holstein, surrounded by Prussian troops, under Austrian control, in an awkward arrangement sure to breed contention between Austria and Prussia.

The Austro-Prussian War, 1866 Friction with the Habsburg Empire increased almost daily, and Bismarck prepared for war while ensuring Austria's diplomatic isolation. He dangled visions of territory along the Rhine before Napoleon III, won Italy's support by promising it Venetia, and gained Russia's assurance of neutrality. Both Austria and Prussia were already mobilizing when Prussian troops found an excuse to march into Holstein in June 1866. Initially, Austria had the support of most of the German Confederation, but Hanover surrendered to Prussia within two weeks. Three Prussian armies swept into Bohemia, and at the Battle of Sadowa, Austria suffered overwhelming defeat. The Austro-Prussian War lasted just seven weeks. Experts had predicted a long fight, but Prussia, well equipped and ready, applied the lessons of the American Civil War, using railroads and telegraph to move with a speed for which Austria was unprepared.

Many Prussian conservatives had been shocked at Bismarck's disrespectful and belligerent treatment of Austria, but now they were eager to take advantage of Austria's defeat and looked forward to significant territorial gains. Instead, Bismarck insisted on leniency, against the wishes of his king and generals. Austria surrendered no territory, but Prussia's gains elsewhere

Crowds cheer as Prussian troops parade through the Brandenburg Gate in Berlin in 1866, celebrating Prussia's victory over Austria and the formation of the North German Confederation.
AKG London

changed the face of Europe. It annexed several states that had sided with Austria, established a confederation of North German states under Prussian leadership (see map 24.3), and got the South German states to accept a military alliance with Prussia.

The North German Confederation   The North German Confederation was a Bismarckian structure that seemed to protect local interests and to point toward democracy yet ensured the dominance of Prussia. It left member states free to regulate their local affairs but joined them through a common army under Prussian officers and a bicameral federal parliament. The upper house, the Bundesrat, was composed of forty-three delegates sent in varying numbers from the separate states; Prussia's seventeen gave it more than the one-third necessary for a veto. The lower house, the Reichstag, was elected by universal male suffrage, but the king of Prussia appointed the chancellor, who was responsible to no one else.

After Prussia's victories, the Prussian Parliament retroactively legalized the taxes and expenditures Bismarck had imposed. No German nationalist believed Bismarck's federation to be a satisfactory or permanent

solution. Germany's unification, like Italy's, would be achieved in stages and through war and diplomacy. North Germany, Protestant and more industrial than the south, offered a sound foundation for the kind of Germany Bismarck envisioned, as different from the largely agricultural and Catholic south as northern Italy was from Naples. With their own cultural traditions and ancient dynasties, Germany's southern states still looked to Vienna as their traditional center, admired Paris, and remained suspicious of Berlin.

The Franco-Prussian War, 1870   More than elections and trade were necessary if Germany was to be quickly united, and war with France filled the need. Historians once hotly disputed who was to blame for that war and whether it was "necessary." New research and changing perspectives have lessened the controversy. The war was wanted by Bismarck but first declared by France, on both sides the result more of nationalism than of long-range calculation. It was provoked by competition over influence in Spain. Queen Isabella II had been forced to abdicate in 1868, and the provisional government there, seeking a replacement, picked a Hohenzollern prince. He declined, under heavy French

MAP 24.3 THE UNIFICATION OF GERMANY
This map makes clear the two-step process by which Prussia first unified the many separate states in the north of Germany, and then brought the southern states in as well. Austria was as "German" as Prussia, but still the unified German Reich of 1871 came into being without it. What accounts for this outcome?

◆ For an online version, go to www.mhhe.com/chambers9 > chapter 24 > book maps.

pressure; but a shaky French government, eager to curry popular favor at home, continued to press its case. In a famous interview at the western German spa of Ems, where William I was taking the baths, the French ambassador demanded a public guarantee that the Hohenzollern candidacy would not be put forward again. The king refused and telegraphed a report to Bismarck, who edited the Ems dispatch to make French demands seem more imperious and the king's refusal more abrupt, then released it to the press. Bismarck

correctly assumed that war would follow. The French government responded to the patriotic fury it had helped ignite and declared war on Prussia in July 1870.

France hoped for support from Italy and Austria but had failed to establish formal agreements, and these states remained neutral. The French army, more formidable than Austria's had been, possessed modern equipment in some respects superior to that of the Germans, but the Germans were better prepared and far more decisively led. In rapid movements German armies pushed through Alsace and encircled the French army at Metz. After heavy losses on both sides, another French force, attempting to relieve Metz, was defeated at Sedan in September. There Napoleon III surrendered and was taken prisoner. Major fighting was over, but French resistance continued. Paris, quickly surrounded by German troops, held out under a long siege, and a provisional French government kept an army in the field. An armistice came only at the end of January 1871, when Paris capitulated.

The brief war had profound effects. A German national state was created. In France the Second Empire fell, to be succeeded by the Third Republic after bitter internal conflict. France was required to pay an indemnity of 5 billion francs and to cede Alsace and Lorraine, harsh terms that established enmity between France and Germany as a central fact of European affairs.

The German Reich   The decision to annex Alsace-Lorraine was primarily a military one, intended to provide Germany with strong fortifications in case of future conflict with France. But it was also a response to the demands of German nationalists, whose support Bismarck still needed, for there were many Germans who did not welcome unification under Prussia. Well before the final French surrender, Bismarck began difficult negotiations with each of the South German states. They had joined in fighting France with a mixture of enthusiasm and fear, but it took threats, concessions, and secret funds to arrive at terms for a permanent union with North Germany. William I was then crowned German kaiser (emperor) in the Hall of Mirrors of the French palace of Versailles on January 18, 1871, the anniversary of the founding of the Prussian monarchy.

With modifications, the constitution of the North German Confederation was extended to all the new nation. Many domestic matters were reserved to the twenty-five states that made up the Reich. There was no doubt, however, that the great new nation would be dominated by Prussia. The Second Reich[3] was from its inception a powerful nation. Germany in 1871 was already more populous than France, and its rate of demographic growth was the fastest Europe had ever known. Germany's industrial production increased at an astounding rate. Because it had developed later than Great Britain and France, its industrial equipment was more modern, and the French indemnity added to the available capital. The German government made heavy investments in railroads and spurred industrialization with tax benefits, tariffs, and policies encouraging the formation of large combines, the famous German car-

tels. German universities led all others in the application of scientific methods to every discipline.

Such rapid growth fed tensions between powerful conservative circles, a growing but insecure middle class, and workers increasingly aware of their distinct interests. Nowhere were materialistic and urban values more intensely attacked than in industrial Germany. Bismarck, worried about internal threats to the new nation, chose to demonstrate the supremacy of the state by moving against two potential opponents: first the Catholic Church and then the socialist party.

Internal Conflict   Rather grandiosely named the *Kulturkampf* ("Struggle for Civilization"), the conflict with the Catholic Church centered on the state's right to approve appointments, restrict religious orders, and supervise seminaries. Many of these measures were common in much of Europe, but there was a harshness in the new state's execution of them and in the rhetoric surrounding them. Intended to ensure the "Germanization" of Alsace and the Polish parts of Prussia (both largely Catholic), the measures accentuated regional and ideological differences. Yet the Kulturkampf was not a success. It made martyrs of many a priest and nun, and Catholics rallied to their Church as a majority of bishops went into exile. The Catholic Center party steadily gained votes, and when the more flexible Leo XIII became pope in 1878, Bismarck sought an understanding with the Vatican. That battle of civilization subsided as Bismarck turned his sights on another growing movement.

Socialism did not offend Bismarck either in its criticism of laissez-faire economics or in its call for the state to be socially active, and he had gotten on well with the leading German socialist of the 1860s, Ferdinand Lassalle. But as socialists sought a mass following and in 1875 established the Social Democratic party, their attacks on autocracy, the military, and nationalism seemed dangerous. Using as justification two attempts in 1878 to assassinate the kaiser (neither by a socialist), Bismarck demanded laws repressing socialism. The Reichstag refused, and the election of 1878, in which conservatives and the Center party made some gains, was fought largely on that issue. Most socialist publications were banned and socialist meetings prohibited unless supervised by the police. The Social Democrats were, in effect, forced underground, although they were free to speak in the Reichstag, and their party gained support with every election.

The campaigns against Catholics and socialists were abandoned by the 1880s as no longer needed or effective, but they were part of a larger political realignment. The conservatives and Catholics who had resisted the new Germany came to accept it, while liberals, torn between Bismarck's accomplishments

---

[3] The old Holy Roman Empire was patriotically honored as having been the First Reich.

BISMARCK'S SOCIAL PROGRAM

Between 1883 and 1887 the German parliament passed three laws that created a new model for the role of the state in social legislation. Bismarck introduced the first of these (providing for sickness insurance) in April 1881 in a speech to the parliament that reflects the power of his personality as well as the clarity of his reasoning and of his prejudices.

"For the past fifty years we have been talking about the social question. Since the Socialist Law was passed, I have been repeatedly reminded, in high quarters as well as low, of the promise I then gave that something positive should be done to remove the causes of Socialism. . . . I do not believe that our sons, or even our grandsons, will be able finally to solve the question. Indeed, no political questions can ever be mathematically settled, as books are balanced in business; they crop up, have their time, and give way to other questions propounded by history. Organic development wills that it shall be so. I consider it my duty to take up these questions without party feeling or excitement, because I know not who is to do so, if not the imperial government.

"Deputy Richter has pointed out the responsibility of the state for what it is now doing. Well, Gentlemen, I feel that the state should also be responsible for what it leaves undone. I am not of the opinion that *laissez faire, laissez aller,* 'pure Manchester policy,' 'everybody takes care of himself,' 'the weakest must go the wall,' 'to him who hath shall be given, from him who hath not shall be taken even that which he hath,' can be practiced in a monarchically, patriarchically governed state. . . .

"An appropriate title for our enterprise would be 'practical Christianity,' but we do not want to feed poor people with figures of speech, but with something solid. Death costs nothing; but unless you will put your hands in your pockets and into the state Exchequer, you will not do much good. To saddle our industry with the whole affair—well, I don't know that it could bear the burden."

From Louis L. Snyder (ed.), *The Documents of German History,* New Brunswick: Rutgers University Press, 1958.

and their old principles, grew weaker. A more durable coalition was formed around the tariff of 1879. Its higher duties, a response to the economic problems caused by rapid growth and by a European agricultural depression, protected manufactured and agricultural goods, drawing together the most powerful interest groups in German society. Supported by Junker landlords, industrialists, the army and navy, and nationalists, the new tariff gave the conservative state and its powerful leaders their political base. In the 1880s Bismarck also established a system of national insurance to aid workers in times of illness and unemployment and to help provide for pensions upon retirement. Paid for by contributions from employers and workers, these measures became an influential model of modern social policy (see "Bismarck's Social Program," above). At home and abroad, Bismarck had mastered techniques for preserving conservative interests in a dynamic society.

Reshaping the Older Empires

In a Europe of industrial growth and national states, war more than ever stood as the ultimate test of the state's efficiency. The wars that made Italy and Germany were understood to require drastic political changes in the nations that lost—Russia in 1856, Austria in 1859 and 1866, and France in 1870.

Limited Reform in the Russian Empire   Of the 74 million people in Russia, some 47 million were serfs. Their emancipation began in 1861 by the tsar's decree. Intellectuals had argued against serfdom for generations, and peasants spoke through frequent uprisings. Serfdom was constricting economic development, and any major political reforms required its abolition. Defeat in the Crimean War added urgency, and Tsar Alexander II, who had assumed the throne in 1855, announced his commitment to modernization. Quietly he pressed the nobles to lead the way; but while secret committees drafted proposals for ending serfdom, most nobles dragged their feet.

Emancipation was thus imposed by edict, a daring step cautiously framed. More than 22 million serfs gained legal rights and were promised title to the land they worked or its equivalent. If they accepted one-quarter of that, they would owe no payments; otherwise they contracted a long-term debt to the state, which compensated the lord. In practice, the lord usually kept the best land for himself and often got an inflated price for the land he lost. Former serfs on the whole found themselves with less land than they

In this 1861 photograph a Russian official is reading to peasants on a Moscow estate the "Regulations Concerning the Peasantry," the decree that abolished serfdom.
Novosti/Sovfoto

needed to support families and make their payments. Although they were required to fulfill other obligations to their former masters for only two more years, they often remained dependent on those nobles for pasture and water rights and for the wage labor that had become a necessity. A few years later the government liberated the nearly 25 million state peasants, who worked on government-owned estates, granting them somewhat more favorable terms. Russia's peasants nevertheless remained a caste distinguishable in dress, speech, and customs, with special laws and punishments, including flogging, applicable only to them.

The law of 1861 also gave the *mir*, or village commune, new importance. It elected its own officials and held peasant land in common; the officials assigned plots to individuals, decided what would be planted, and assessed the taxes owed the state. The former serfs could not leave the commune or sell their land without permission. The *mir*, which came to be considered a characteristic Slavic institution, thus sustained traditional ways and served as the agent of the state at the same time that it provided peasants a voice in communal decisions.

Other reforms followed. In 1864 district councils (*zemstvos*, elected through a three-class system like Prussia's) were made responsible for local primary schools, roads, and welfare. These steps were part of a process that—along with increased schooling, relaxed censorship, and reduced military service[4]—made Russia more like other European nations. Each reform, however, accomplished less than hoped for and uncovered yet more that needed to be done. Leaders remained fearful. Concessions in Poland were followed by revolution in 1863. It was harshly quelled, and Poland's separate status ended. Repression increased in Russia, too, as censorship and police surveillance tightened. While pan-Slavists stressed Russia's special destiny and disdained liberal parliamentarianism as alien, an isolated intelligentsia was drawn to more radical ideas, and conspirators plotted more drastic remedies. Yet when a bomb killed Alexander II in 1881, his son smoothly succeeded him as Alexander III; tsarist Russia could survive an assassination.

Compromise to Preserve the Austro-Hungarian Empire

Following the revolutions of 1848, the Habsburg monarchy under the young Franz Joseph I had sought to create a modern, unitary state. For the first time in its history, the empire was subjected to uniform laws and taxes. But military defeats in Italy and then at the hands of Prussia plus mounting debts proved that more changes were needed. In 1860 Franz Joseph announced a new federal constitution, giving considerable authority to regional diets. Intended to reduce resentment against high-handed government, it was a failure from the start, opposed by liberals and bureaucrats alike while provoking dangerous arguments among the empire's diverse nationalities. So the emperor reversed himself the next year and established a bicameral parliament for the entire empire. Having stirred visions of local self-government and autonomous nationalities, he now wanted to subordinate local governments to rule from Vienna and to a parliament in which a lower house elected by a four-class system ensured the dominance of the German-speaking middle class.

Hungary in particular objected, led by the liberal nationalist Ferencz Deák, who had campaigned for Hungary's Constitution of 1848. Neither side was strong enough to have its way, and the war with Prussia finally brought a compromise. In 1867 Hungary became an autonomous state, joined to Austria only through the emperor, Franz Joseph, who became king of Hungary, and through common policies for defense and diplomacy, an arrangement known as the Dual

---

[4] The old military system, which required selected serfs to serve twenty-five years, was changed in 1874 to one of universal service, with generous exemptions and only six years of active duty. Those who completed primary school were liable for only four years of duty; those who finished secondary school, for two years; and those with university education, for just six months.

Most European cities boasted elegant theaters like this one in London.
The Mary Evans Picture Library

Monarchy. The emperor had kept his authority in foreign policy, which was what he cared about most, by conceding to one nationality what he denied to others. Within Hungary itself, domestic politics centered on conflict between the dominant Magyars and the non-Magyar majority and between the diverging interests of Austrian industry and Hungary's great landholders.

Within Austria's imperial parliament, the emperor turned for support first to the German liberals, who offended him by their anticlericalism, and then to the Czechs and Poles, who disturbed him with their nationalist demands. More fundamental reform proved difficult; and although ministers were now responsible to parliament, policy rested more on a conservative bureaucracy dominated by Germans. An awkward compromise, the Dual Monarchy gave power to wealthy landlords and merchants, and it rested on the dominance of Magyars (over Romanians, Croatians, and Serbs) and of Germans in cooperation with Czechs and Poles (over Slovenes, Slovaks, and Ruthenians). It lasted for fifty years as one of Europe's great powers, an empire of diversified peoples and cultures, threatened by nationalism, changing even while resisting change, with more freedom in practice than in principle, and sustained at its center by the graceful civilization of Vienna.

NINETEENTH-CENTURY CULTURE

Europe's cultural life was as dynamic as its economy and politics. In the nineteenth century the arts were understood to be national and urban rather than cen-tered in courts, salons, or villages, and they were remarkable for quantity as well as quality. There were more writers, artists, musicians, and scholars than ever before; and they reached larger audiences through expanding cultural institutions and markets.

The Organization of Culture

Before the nineteenth century, most paintings and musical compositions were commissioned for a particular place or occasion. Now music moved from palaces, churches, and private salons to public concert halls; artists sold their paintings to any purchaser and, by midcentury, in galleries created for that purpose; and writers found themselves engaged in commercial activity. Theaters ranged from the new music halls to the great stages and opera houses built (usually by the state) to rank with parliament buildings as monuments of national or civic pride. Most major cities supported choirs, bands, and symphony orchestras, which grew larger and technically more proficient. Conservatories and museums became national public institutions, maintaining official taste and considerably increasing Europe's stock of highly trained artists, musicians, and scholars. Whether in palaces once private or in imposing new structures, cultural institutions were treated as civic and national monuments. In Paris the Louvre became the model art museum that provided access to everyone and expressed the era's understanding of culture by displaying works of art by country of origin and in chronological order. This was an urban, bourgeois culture that sought to make the city itself a cultural statement.

Cultural life—associated with the state, tied to a market economy, and promulgating shared values and taste—helped to create national identity and to establish social status. The intended public was, for the most part, the same public that was active in politics, the professions, and business—or rather, such people and their wives. They bought tickets for concerts just as they frequented restaurants with famous chefs, enjoying in both cases pleasures once part of private society and now open to all who had the inclination and money. Participation in this exciting culture also set boundaries of decorum that distinguished the middle class from those below them and defined the distinctive roles thought appropriate to men and women. Some artists and intellectuals attacked a system that left an artist's fate dependent either on administrators or what would sell to the public. The tension between creative expression and market became a much lamented hallmark of modernity.

Reaching a Wider Public Public culture encompassed an expanded range of activities. For those who sought self-improvement, there were public lectures on political economy or the wonders of steam power or newer marvels like photography, which was widely used for portraits and recognized as the newest of the arts.[5] No cultural institution was more important than the press, and the newspaper became a major instrument of culture and politics. By 1830 there were more than two thousand European newspapers, and liberals everywhere fought the censorship, special taxes, and police measures with which governments sought to constrain so awesome a social force. The *Times* of London had a circulation of 5,000 in 1815 and of 50,000 by midcentury; two of the most popular French papers, the *Presse* and *Siècle*, reached a circulation of 70,000.

As newspapers came to rely more on advertising than on subscriptions for their revenue, they increased in size, published articles on a wider range of topics (including items on fashion and domestic concerns aimed at women), and attracted readers by serializing novels by writers as famous as Honoré de Balzac, Alexandre Dumas, and Charles Dickens. Technology aided these changes. Press services such as the Agence Havas and Reuters quickly adopted the telegraph. The *London Illustrated News* created the picture magazine in 1842, which was immediately copied in every large country. Satirical magazines made the cartoon a powerful political weapon, raised to art by Honoré Daumier's biting pictures of fat bankers and complacent bourgeois.

Honoré Daumier
FAT BANKER, LE CHARIVRAI, 1835
A typically devastating caricature of a banker by Honoré Daumier.
Photos12.com

The Cultural Professions Professionalization affected the arts as well as other occupations. The violinist Niccolò Paganini, who transformed violin technique, commanded huge fees and enormous crowds wherever he played; the soprano Jenny Lind was the rage of Europe, as was Franz Liszt, piano virtuoso and composer. Many a young man announced that he was a painter and proudly starved, in Paris if possible, out of loyalty to his career (there were 354 registered artists in Paris in 1789, 2,159 in 1838). A few, among them England's great landscape painter J. M. W. Turner, became wealthy.

The most popular writers—Balzac, Sir Walter Scott, Victor Hugo, Dickens—were able to live by their pen alone, among the most honored figures of their age. There were also many women novelists. Expected to write light romances, they generally were not taken seriously. To escape that prejudice, a number of women writers adopted masculine pen names. Still, the rising prestige of the professional writer enabled some extraordinary women, like George Eliot (Mary Evans Cross) and Elizabeth Gaskell in England and George

[5] Louis-Jacques-Mandé Daguerre announced his photographic process to the French Academy in 1839, which persuaded the government to purchase his rights and give the new technique to the world, unencumbered by royalties.

Sand in France, to be recognized as influential thinkers. For a middle-class public faced with so much new work to choose from, critics became important as professional intellectuals who guided taste much as the popular books on etiquette and gastronomy taught manners to people of new means.

The Content of Culture

Varied Forms   The most admired artistic works were valued for a moral seriousness and formality that distinguished them from popular culture. In painting, great historical scenes were the most admired, ranked considerably above genre painting or portraits. Music was increasingly treated as a kind of spiritual essay, to be heard reverentially in concerts suitable to its distinctive forms—symphony, concerto, quartet, and sonata. The novel's great popularity was related to the social panorama it presented. Balzac attempted in his novels to encompass all the "human comedy" (the phrase contrasted with Dante's divine concerns), showing the wealthy, the ambitious, and the poor in their roles as husbands, wives, soldiers, bankers, politicians, and writers. Novelists used social types to analyze society and challenge the public conscience, and no reformer was more influential than Dickens. Scott's swashbuckling stories of romance and chivalry in an earlier age probed the connection between personal character and social tension in a way that influenced writers throughout Europe. Theater and opera featured historical settings; and Hugo, Alexander Pushkin, and Alessandro Manzoni promulgated patriotism by connecting high ideals to the national past, painting in words monumental interpretations of historical events. The novel's most common theme, the conflict between personal feeling (especially romantic love) and social convention, explored critical contemporary issues of individualism and social change.

Conceptions of culture were also strongly gendered. Women were held to have qualities—including a natural sense of beauty and openness to emotion—that made them especially responsive to art. Women were thought to be the principal readers of novels, and novels presented women's lives in ways that underscored the inequities of their social subordination and ultimately enlarged the perception of women's abilities. Women were especially associated with the intimate side of middle-class culture, the popularity of poetry, lithographs, watercolor paintings, and piano music—all to be savored in the parlor, with the woman of the house at the center.

Changing Styles   In culture as in philosophy there was also a strong desire for synthesis, for ideas and forms that would tie everything together. In the arts

this urge gave lyric opera special resonance. Opera was first of all theater, combining popular appeal with aristocratic elegance. It featured elaborate plots, often in historical settings, flowery poetic texts, varied, tuneful, and complex music, the whole further enriched by ballet, colorful sets, and special effects. The two leading operatic composers of the period were Giuseppe Verdi and his exact contemporary Richard Wagner. Verdi, an Italian national hero, wrote compelling and often patriotic music that explored human emotion and character in diverse contexts, often historical ones explicitly about politics. Wagner carried the search for an artistic synthesis still further. He wrote his own texts and increasingly used Germanic myths with nationalist intent. In his operas recurrent musical themes were identified with major ideas and characters to create a whole in which voices, instruments, words, and visual experience moved inseparably to a powerful climax.

By the 1840s rapidly changing and competing artistic styles had become a characteristic of modern culture, a response to social change and new audiences but also an expression of the creative artist's sense of self. Some artists adapted Romanticism's emphasis on individual genius to claim that the merit of a piece of art was independent of any social or moral purpose and to adopt, therefore, the cry of "art for art's sake." For others, the goal of the artist should be to capture the essence of "modernity." By midcentury, **realism** was becoming the dominant style, as writers and painters reemphasized close observation in a socially concerned effort to portray ordinary people, sometimes with shocking directness, as in Gustave Flaubert's *Madame Bovary* (1857), an acid account of a young middle-class wife's aimless existence in a small French town, or J. F. Millet's paintings of rural workers and villages. Innovation was often taken for a sign of genius, and the belief that artists must be in an *avant-garde,* ahead of their duller public, became a cliché. Often disturbing to their audiences, the arts were never more honored nor artists more critical of their own society than in the nineteenth century.

Religious Thought   In some respects the nineteenth century was a very religious age, for thoughtful people cared greatly about religion. Protestant and Catholic missions campaigned with an intensity not seen since the seventeenth century, and the pious became more militant and turned to social action, preaching temperance, teaching reading, and establishing charities. This focus on the problems of modern life was connected, however, to the fear that religion was losing its social importance. Some intellectuals became bitter anticlericals, seeing in the church the barrier to progress. More typically, especially in England, stern morality and propriety were substituted for theology.

Jean Francois Miller
***THE GLEANERS*, 1857**
**Splendid example of realism in
nineteenth-century French
painting.**
Musée d'Orsay, Paris, France.
Réunion des Musées Nationaux/
Art Resource, NY

The impact of historical research on religion created a sensation across Europe when the Protestant David Strauss published his *Life of Jesus* in 1835, for it cast erudite doubt on the accuracy of the Gospels, frightening many with the apparent need to choose between scholarship and Christ. In Denmark the writings of Soren Kierkegaard starkly explored ethical dilemmas in a passionate search for faith; his intense, semiautobiographical essays that interweave biblical stories and personal symbols have continued to fascinate twentieth-century thinkers.

The Sense of History   Nineteenth-century intellectual life emphasized historical thinking. A romantic respect for the past, nationalists' claims, explanations of revolution, economic theory, and preoccupation with change all underscored the importance of history. Its systematic study became an admired profession. In England, France, and Germany, national projects were launched for publishing historical documents and for training scholars to interpret them. Some historians were as widely read as novelists, among them Jules Michelet, for whom French history was a dramatic story of the people's fight for freedom, and Thomas B. Macaulay, for whom the history of England was a record of progressive change through moderation and compromise. In each country certain events and themes—in England, the Glorious Revolution of 1688; in France, the Revolution; in Germany, the rise of Prussia—were favored as part of an intense search for national roots, heroes, and patterns of development significant for the present.

Summary

In 1848 a wave of revolutions, the most spontaneous and widespread Europe had ever known, brought new governments to power. Defeated before they could complete their democratic and egalitarian programs, these revolutionary regimes left important legacies not only in measures passed but lessons learned. In the future, radicals would not rely on middle-class support and political reform, while liberals would be more willing to sacrifice democracy for social order. In these circumstances the most effective governments of the 1850s were those that adopted parts of the revolutionaries' programs and some of their techniques for reaching a broader public while keeping the forces of order on their side. Thus, the Second Empire of Napoleon III was the principal guarantor of that social order and economic growth important to the propertied classes. Piedmont and Prussia, as the focus of nationalist movements, won significant followings and triumphed dramatically in creating national states in Italy and Germany. In this Europe of the modern national state, astute political leaders from England to Prussia found ways to undertake new social responsibilities, facilitate industrialization, and mobilize popular support without giving way to full democracy or radical programs. Closely associated with the nation, cultural institutions flourished, supporting a diverse and dynamic culture that was one of the great achievements of the age. By the 1870s, European nations had the means to generate unprecedented power and the will to spread their influence around the world.

QUESTIONS FOR FURTHER THOUGHT

1. What is the historical significance of revolutions in which the revolutionaries are defeated?
2. Why did nationalism become so important in the nineteenth century?
3. Nationalist ideologies have much in common, but what accounts for the important differences among them?
4. When you look at art, listen to music, or read works written in the nineteenth century, what characteristics do you identify with the period in which they were created?

RECOMMENDED READING

Sources

Marx, Karl. *The Class Struggles in France, 1848–1850* and *The Eighteenth Brumaire of Louis Napoleon.* Early and polemical applications of Marx's ideas to contemporary political events, the revolution of 1848 in France and Napoleon's coup d'état.

Treitschke, Heinrick. *History of Germany in the Nineteenth Century.* Written shortly after German unification, this vast work exemplifies the importance of history as nationalist propaganda.

Studies

*Agulhon, Maurice. *The Republican Experiment, 1848–1852.* Janel Lloyd (tr.). 1983. An authoritative study of politics and society during the Second French Republic, sensitive to popular attitudes and concerns.

*Alter, Peter. *Nationalism.* 1989. A valuable introduction to the different kinds of nationalism.

*Anderson, Benedict. *Imagined Communities: Reflections on the Origin and Spread of Nationalism.* 1983. An important analysis of modern nationalism worldwide, stressing its origins in European culture and capitalism.

*Beales, Derek. *The Risorgimento and the Unification of Italy.* 1982. Concise, skeptical introduction to the history of Italian unification.

*Chadwick, Owen. *The Secularization of the European Mind.* 1975. Perceptive, introduction to changing patterns of thought about religion.

Freifel, Alice. *Nationalism and the Crowd in Liberal Hungary, 1848–1914.* 2000. Demonstrates the unique aspects of Hungarian nationalism.

*Gellner, Ernest. *Nations and Nationalism.* 1983. An effort to build a theory by analyzing the relation of industrialization to nationalism.

Greenfield, Kent R. *Economics and Liberalism in the Risorgimento: A Study of Nationalism in Lombardy, 1814–1848.* 1978. A classic study of the connection between economic change and nationalism.

*Hamerow, Theodore S. *The Social and Economic Foundations of German Unification, 1858–1871.* 2 vols. 1969 and 1972. The politics and ideas of unification placed in the context of a developing economy.

Hemmings, F. W. J. *Culture and Society in France, 1789–1848.* 1987. *Culture and Society in France, 1848–1898.* 1971. A literary scholar's provocative and comprehensive analysis of the relationship between cultural styles and social context.

*Howard, Michael. *The Franco-Prussian War.* 1969. Exemplary study of how war reflects (and tests) an entire society.

*Jelavich, Barbara. *History of the Balkans.* 2 vols. 1983. A thorough survey of society and politics, from the eighteenth century to the present.

*Mack Smith, Denis. *Cavour.* 1985. An expert and well-written assessment of the personalities and policies that created an Italian nation.

*Mosse, George L. *The Nationalization of the Masses: Political Symbolism and Mass Movements in Germany from the Napoleonic Wars through the Third Reich.* 1975. One of the most complete efforts to find the roots of Nazism in popular nationalism.

Olsen, Donald J. *The City as a Work of Art: London, Paris, Vienna.* 1986. Combines an analysis of how ordinary people really lived with an appreciation of the aesthetics of the modern city and the economic and political realities behind it.

Pflanze, Otto. *Bismarck and the Development of Germany: The Period of Unification, 1815–1871.* 1963. Places each of Bismarck's actions in its larger context.

*Pinkney, David. *Napoleon III and the Rebuilding of Paris.* 1958. Studies the political background to one of the most extensive, influential, and successful examples of urban policy.

*Plessis, Alain. *The Rise and Fall of the Second Empire, 1852–1871.* Jonathan Mandelbaum (tr.). 1985. A balanced assessment of this important political experiment.

*Poovey, Mary. *Making a Social Body: British Cultural Formation, 1830–1864.* This study of how the public was conceived in literature and politics exposes the ways in which public institutions helped construct categories of gender and class.

*Read, Donald. *England 1868–1914: The Age of Urban Democracy.* 1979. Political change presented in terms of economic and social conditions.

Reardon, B. M. G. *Religion in the Age of Romanticism: Studies in Early Nineteenth-Century Thought.* 1985. An excellent introduction to the formation of one of the most important intellectual traditions of the century.

Rich, Norman. *Why the Crimean War? A Cautionary Tale.* 1985. A concise synthesis and engaging interpretation of the political and diplomatic problems involving the major powers.

Salvemini, Gaetano. *Mazzini.* 1957. Still the best introduction to Mazzini's thought and its relationship to his revolutionary activities.

*Sperber, Jonathan. *The European Revolutions, 1848–1851.* 1994. A fresh synthesis that pays attention to popular attitudes and symbolic actions as well as political and social conflict.

*Stearns, Peter N. *1848: The Revolutionary Tide in Europe.* 1974. Assesses conflicting interpretations in bringing together accounts of these diverse revolutions.

Wandycz, Piotyr S. *The Lands of Partitioned Poland, 1795–1918.* 1974. An excellent overview of the history of divided Poland.

*Available in paperback.

Ernst Ludwig Kirchner
STREET, DRESDEN, 1908
Kirchner's stark painting of Dresden's Königstrasse evokes the sensory barrage of modern urban life. In the midst of the crowd, the individual figures appear anguished and cut off from one another.
Digital Image © The Museum of Modern Art/Licensed by Scala/Art Resource, NY

Chapter Twenty-Five

PROGRESS AND ITS DISCONTENTS

ECONOMIC TRANSFORMATIONS • UNDERSTANDINGS OF NATURE AND SOCIETY •
THE BELLE EPOQUE • ATTACKS ON LIBERAL CIVILIZATION • DOMESTIC POLITICS

*I*n the second half of the nineteenth century, economic growth became an expectation for the first time in history. New technologies, large-scale industry, better communication, and greater capital investment made unprecedented productivity possible and seemingly self-sustaining, and these gains were in turn a triumph of social organization and new knowledge. Large-scale institutions—business corporations, government agencies, political parties, labor unions, national associations, and newspapers—became essential to a new society characterized by rapid economic growth and broader political participation. Most observers hailed this period as an age of progress, marked by a rising standard of living, greater democracy, new opportunities for education and employment, and greater leisure.

Yet as European power reached its peak, the weaknesses inherent in liberalism and capitalism began to show. Although millions shared in Europe's consumer culture, contemporaries worried about rampant materialism and its corrupting effects on moral standards, the erosion of community by widespread urbanization, and the poverty and hopelessness that persisted among the lower classes. Many organized movements, both radical and religious, stepped up their attacks on this confident society, and new intellectual currents questioned the basis for its optimism. Groups that felt most neglected or threatened—women, the lower classes, and those who feared political or economic change—sometimes turned to violence and revolution or encouraged racial hatred for political gain. Just as ominous were rising international tensions. Britain and France, historically the most powerful European nations, found themselves economically eclipsed by American and German industrial growth, and the expansionist ambitions of Germany and Japan threatened Britain's and Russia's global influence. An age that would be remembered for its optimism and peaceful prosperity was also a time of division and conflict.

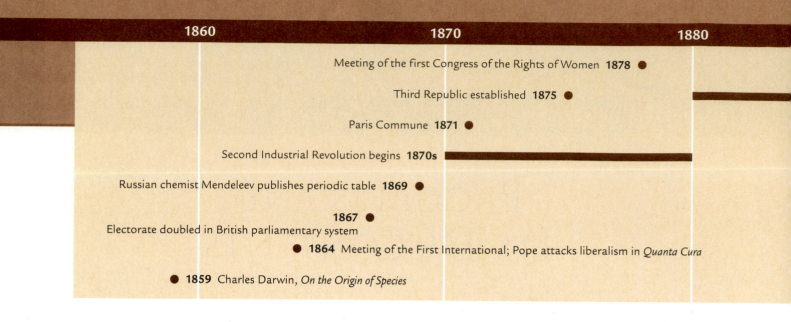

Meeting of the first Congress of the Rights of Women **1878** ●

Third Republic established **1875** ●

Paris Commune **1871** ●

Second Industrial Revolution begins **1870s** ▬▬▬▬▬▬

Russian chemist Mendeleev publishes periodic table **1869** ●

1867 ●
Electorate doubled in British parliamentary system

● **1864** Meeting of the First International; Pope attacks liberalism in *Quanta Cura*

● **1859** Charles Darwin, *On the Origin of Species*

ECONOMIC TRANSFORMATIONS

The dynamism of Europe's economy in the second half of the nineteenth century was unprecedented. As economic growth accelerated, it reached into sectors previously little affected and spread beyond Europe's industrial heartlands into most of the continent. While Europe's population grew more rapidly than ever before, the value of manufacturing went up three times as fast. Factories, especially those that produced steel and chemicals, coupled large-scale production with new technologies, like those connected to electricity. The impact of these developments was so great that historians often speak of this as the second industrial revolution. Distribution and marketing operated on a larger scale, too, and department stores used new techniques of merchandising to entice a wider public to higher levels of consumption.

The Second Industrial Revolution

New Technologies Exciting new inventions were adapted to commercial uses with striking speed. A whole new industry developed to produce and supply electricity. Thomas Edison's incandescent light bulb, developed in the 1870s, was quickly followed by central power stations to distribute power over a wide area, including public lighting in New York and London in 1882 and in Berlin a few years later. The steam turbine, shown in the 1880s to be more efficient than the steam engine, was soon widely employed in ships and factories, fueled by oil as well as coal. By 1900 the manufacture of generators, cables, and motors, an important new industry in itself, allowed greater and cheaper production in scores of other fields. The telephone, invented in 1876, became a business necessity and an established private convenience within a few

decades. New chemical processes and synthetics led to improved products ranging from dyes, textiles, and paints to fertilizers and explosives.

Inventions now affected people's everyday lives more than ever as the introduction of many new products into the consumer market responded to the growing purchasing power of the masses. Home sewing machines spread rapidly, first in the United States and then across Europe, the most important of many new labor-saving devices that allowed women to increase their contribution to the home economy

---

MAIL (MILLIONS OF PIECES)
Scholars use mail volume as an indicator of modernization because it reflects increased literacy, internal communication, and commercial activity. Notice the years in which a general spike in the volume of mail occurs.

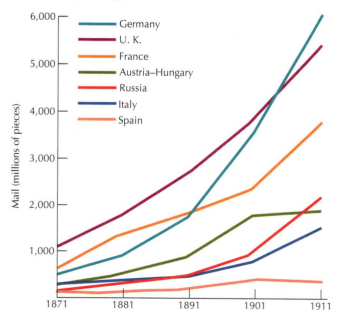

1880s–1890s
Anarchists bomb public places and assassinate heads of state

1885 Karl Marx, first volume of *Das Kapital*

Russo-Japanese War **1904** ●

Russian Revolution of 1905; parliamentary institutions created **1905** ●

Georges Sorel, *Reflections on Violence* **1908** ●

Britain grants Ireland home rule **1914** ●

The Bessemer process of removing impurities from molten iron, which revolutionized the industry, was based on English and American patents; but the Krupp steelworks installed these massive converters in 1862 and continued to lead in steel production in both size and efficiency when this photograph was taken in 1880.
Ullstein Bilderdienst

even when they also worked outside the home. The automobile in the 1890s, the airplane in the 1900s, and the radio a decade later were all greeted with en-thusiasm and heightened mass expectations that technological progress would continue to improve everyday life.

MAKING THE DEALS THAT CREATED A CARTEL

Cartels, strongest in Germany, existed in other countries too. Here, the general manager of an iron rolling mill that made rails describes how a cartel of rail producers came to be formed in Austria in 1878.

"In 1878 there were in Austria-Hungary nine rail rolling mills with an annual capacity of about 120,000 tons. A large part of these mills had been set up in the years 1869–73, that is to say in a period in which railway building flourished in Austria-Hungary as never before. . . . The picture changed in the course of 1873. The lines that had been started were being finished, but no new ones were being built. . . .

"I was then the general manager of one of these rail rolling mills. . . . If our works did not get an annual minimum quantity of orders of 10,000 tons, it would be faced with the impossibility of employing its work force. We should have had to close and face bankruptcy. . . . My task was therefore a simple one; to get orders at all costs.

"In 1878 . . . on the day when contracts were awarded [by the Kaiser Franz-Joseph Railway], the manager . . . told me: 'Yours was the lowest; but since two other works are also prepared to come down to our price, I shall divide the order into three parts. . . .' I tried to make representations; in vain, the decision stood. After I had left the office of the managing director, I met the managers of the other two works which had come down to my price. Because of the years of bitter competition, our personal relations had also suffered, but this time we shook hands, and the rail cartel, the first cartel in Austria, the model for other later cartels, also in Germany, was born. At the moment when it became clear that no works could succeed in getting sufficient orders to stay fully employed, each reached the conviction that there was nothing left but at last to attempt to get higher prices. The course of the tendering negotiations with the Franz-Joseph Railway had shown the way. We reached agreement to distribute the total demand according to certain ratios among all the works, and sought then to get the highest prices possible in the light of foreign competition, and the rates of freight and of customs duty."

From Karl Wittgensteing, "Kartelle in Österreich," in Gustav Schmoller (ed.), *Über wirtschaftliche, Kartelle in Deutschland und im Auslande*, Leipzig, 1894; as quoted in Carroll and Embree, *Readings in European History since 1814*, 1930.

By 1890 Europe was producing even more steel than iron. The Bessemer converter developed in the 1860s permitted far higher temperatures in smelter furnaces, and subsequent discoveries made it profitable to use lower-grade ores. British, German, and French maritime shipping, which doubled between 1870 and 1914, depended on faster and larger steamships.

Germany's Economic Growth The German economy, especially, expanded spectacularly following unification. Already rich in natural resources, Germany acquired more raw materials as well as factories with the annexation of Alsace-Lorraine. Its system of railroads provided excellent communications; its famous educational system produced ample numbers of the administrators and engineers the commercial sector now required. The government, which had played an active role in every facet of industrialization, continued to cooperate with business interests. Military needs stimulated basic industry, and a growing population provided an eager domestic market.

German factories, being newer than those of Britain or France, employed the latest and most efficient equipment, obtaining the necessary capital through a modern banking structure. By 1900 those plants were far bigger than anyone else's, and firms engaged in the various stages of production often combined in huge **cartels** that dominated an entire sector of industry, from raw material to finished product, as Germany became preeminent in new fields such as chemicals and electricity (see "Making the Deals That Created a Cartel," above). German salespeople appeared all over the world with catalogs in local languages and products suited to local conditions, selling with a drive and confidence British merchants resented as bad manners.

Older Industrial Economies The older industrial economies of Great Britain, Belgium, and France continued to grow but more slowly. By 1900 France's industrial production, despite the loss of important textile and iron centers in Alsace, had reached the level of Great Britain's a generation earlier, when Britain had led the world. French iron production more than doubled in the first twenty-five years of the Third Republic, and new processes made the nation's ore output second only to that of the United States. In value of production per capita, one measure of a nation's standard of living, France remained ahead of Germany, though behind England.

By the turn of the century, Great Britain, whose industrial superiority had seemed a fact of nature, was clearly being surpassed in some of the critical indices of production by both Germany and the United States. Although the British economy did continue to grow, the fear that it was falling behind became a serious issue in English public life. Several factors explain its relative decline. British plants and equipment were old, and owners hesitated to undertake the cost of modernizing or replacing them. Well-established firms often made it hard for new companies to get a start. Without technical secondary schools like those of Germany and France, English schooling remained weak in technical subjects and provided less opportunity for social mobility than on the Continent. Social attitudes also played a role. British industrialists were slow to appreciate the value of specialization and resistant to new ways. Even so, London remained the financial capital of the world.

The Spread of Industrialization   That world was increasingly industrialized. The industrial potential of the United States was apparent by the time of the Civil War, although few expected subsequent growth to be as dramatic as it was at the turn of the century. Rich in natural resources, America had a continent in which to expand, millions of immigrants eager to supply needed labor, schooling that sustained technological inventiveness, an openness and mobility that encouraged enterprise, and a democracy that pioneered in creating a consumer society.

But other nations were industrializing too, among them Italy and Japan, which had very limited natural resources, and Russia and Sweden, which had appeared rural, poor, and backward compared to industrialized Western Europe. Assumptions that related industrial progress to European values, Protestantism, or Anglo-Saxon institutions were belied by the changes in the nature of industrialization itself. It no longer depended so directly on the possession of critical resources like coal and iron ore but could be accomplished with foreign investment and imported technology.

Agriculture   Although greater prosperity and growing populations increased the demand for food, the percentage of the population that made its living in agriculture continued to decline, down to only 8 percent in Britain, 22 percent in Belgium, and 35 percent in Germany toward the end of the century. In France, the Netherlands, and Sweden, by contrast, agriculture

---

INDUSTRIAL PRODUCTION (THOUSANDS OF METRIC TONS) **Production of coal, pig iron, and crude steel indicates the rise of large-scale manufacturing and infrastructure using new technologies. Compare the industrial development of the United Kingdom and Germany.**

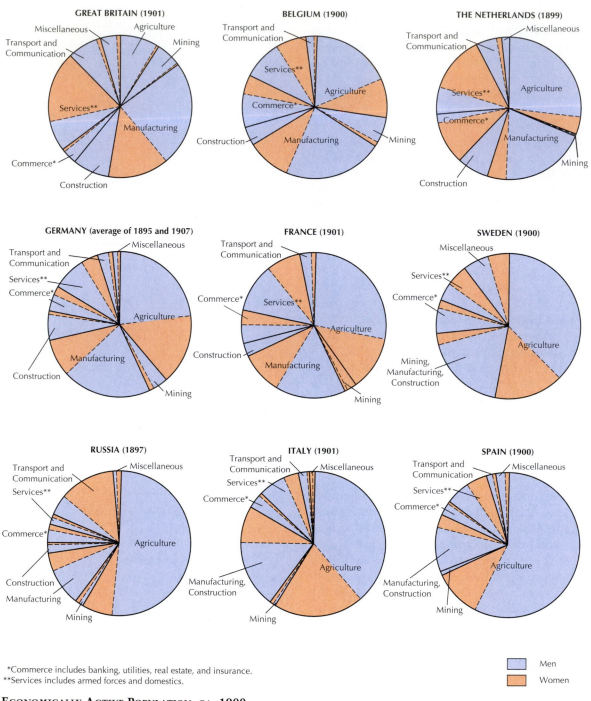

*Commerce includes banking, utilities, real estate, and insurance.
**Services includes armed forces and domestics.

Men
Women

ECONOMICALLY ACTIVE POPULATION, CA. 1900
The above charts track the pace of industrialization through the number of men and women employed in different economic sectors. What differences are noticeable among the economies of Great Britain, Russia, and Italy?
From P. Bairoch et al., *The Working Population and Its Structure*, Gordon V. Breach, 1968, p. 119.

continued to play a larger role in the economy. Everywhere, the wider use of machinery and chemical fertilizers increased the capital investment required for farming, and improved transportation intensified international competition. These factors encouraged much

greater specialization. A good example is Denmark, where agriculture began to center on a highly capitalized and profitable dairy industry.

Global connections were increasingly important. Civil war in the United States, which cut off Europe's supply of cotton from the southern states, caused unemployment in England's mills and created a boom for Egyptian cotton. After 1865, larger ships and improved railroads allowed cheaper grain from the Americas and Eastern Europe, especially Russia, to pour into Western Europe, driving prices down at a time when farmers needed cash for the improvements required to make farming profitable. Britain now imported almost all its grain, and Germany, a great deal. More young men abandoned the countryside, and landed interests pressed their governments for help in the face of recurrent agricultural crises. The most common response was protective **tariffs,** which were raised in France, Germany, Austria, Russia, Italy, and Spain. Initially applied primarily to agriculture, the new tariffs were soon extended to manufactured goods as well, reversing the trend toward liberal policies that had favored free trade from the 1830s to the 1870s.

The Long Depression   The trade barriers did not stop the general decline in prices. Strangely, the second industrial revolution occurred in one of the longest and most severe periods of deflation in European history. From the 1870s to 1896, prices, interest rates, and profits fell, with far-reaching effects. This situation, in which one part of the economy soared while another declined, was socially disruptive. Handicraft industries, which had survived side by side with mechanized manufacturing throughout Europe, were forced out of business. So were numerous smaller and less efficient industrial firms. The great boom in railroad building ended, and governments had to save socially or politically important lines deserted by bankrupt companies.

As competition sharpened, many industrialists welcomed the support governments could give through tariffs, state spending, and colonial policies. Economic demands became a central theme of politics as more and more of economic life centered on great factories owned by large corporations (and closely tied to banks and government) that employed hundreds or even thousands of workers who, in turn, increasingly organized into industrial labor unions.

Urbanization and Demographic Change

Europe's population continued to grow during the second industrial revolution and did so at an increasing rate. The 295 million Europeans of 1870 had become nearly 450 million by 1914, and the age distribution, or demographic profile, had changed completely.

The Demographic Transition: Declining Rates of Mortality and Fertility   Population increased despite the fact that in most of Europe birthrates had begun to decline, and it did so because mortality rates were falling

Department stores, like this one in Paris—a combination of theater and commercial display—were the seductive symbols of consumerism and prosperity.
Editions Tallandier

still more rapidly. This pattern of a declining birthrate accompanied by a more rapidly falling mortality rate, which is called the **demographic transition,** continues in our own time and has become one of the hallmarks of modernity.

Death rates initially declined because of lower infant mortality rates, a result of improved sanitation, better diet, and the virtual elimination of diseases such as cholera and typhus. By the turn of the century, improvements in medical care lowered mortality rates among adults as well. Thus, the population grew despite the declining birthrate.

Lower mortality rates reflected the benefits of industrial prosperity, but the declining birthrates marked a subtler change.[1] The number of children in a family was becoming more a matter of choice with the spread of contraception; where bourgeois values took root and

---

[1] *Birthrate* is used here as the more familiar term, but *fertility rate*—the ratio of the number of children born to the number of women of childbearing age—is the more precise term preferred by demographers.

child labor declined, workers followed the upper classes in the trend toward later marriage, fewer births, and smaller families.

UNDERSTANDINGS OF NATURE AND SOCIETY

Knowledge was expanding, too. Scientific discoveries underlay technological innovation far more directly than in the first industrial revolution, and science itself was becoming ever more the province of the expert. The field was increasingly organized into distinctive specialties and pursued by professional researchers (the term *scientist* was first used in the 1830s), freely exchanging ideas across national boundaries and working with precise methods and the logic of mathematics. Research demanded more systematic organization and larger and more expensive laboratories. The success of science stimulated a general expansion of secondary and higher education, and most of the academic disciplines that constitute the modern university achieved their separate identity in the late nineteenth century. The educated public could understand many of the new scientific theories, and scientific ideas were an important part of the general discourse about religion, progress, and ethics. The scientific establishment of the laws of nature rekindled hope that laws of social development might similarly be discovered and beneficially applied.

The Conquests of Science

Biology: The Darwinian Revolution A disturbing theory of human development emerged from Charles Darwin's *On the Origin of Species,* a milestone in the history of science published in 1859. He first formulated his concept of natural selection in 1838, but not until Alfred R. Wallace independently developed a similar theory could Darwin be persuaded to publish his findings.

Although Darwin's presentation was the more fully and carefully developed, the parallel theories of the two men suggest how much both owed to ideas already current. Darwin established that the variety of species is potentially infinite—rejecting the classical and Christian ideas of immutable forms in nature—and argued that there is an almost constant modification of species, each tested in the universal struggle for existence. He not only presented detailed evidence for **evolution** but described its mechanism: Only those well adapted to their environment survived to reproduce, as their progeny would after them. Over millions of years, through the process of natural selection, more complex

CHRONOLOGY
Scientific and Technological Advances

1830s–1840s	Michael Faraday discovers that changing magnetic fields induce electric currents, enabling creation of the electric generator.
1859	Charles Darwin publishes *On the Origin of Species,* elaborating theory of evolution.
1860s	Bessemer process for removing impurities from iron perfected, leading to more efficient steel production; Louis Pasteur develops pasteurization process as a means of eradicating germs; Gregor Mendel develops the gene-based theory of heredity.
1860–1880s	Internal combustion engine developed.
1869	Dmitry Mendeleev publishes periodic table of elements.
1870s	Thomas Alva Edison invents the light bulb.
1873	James Maxwell publishes a formal theory of electromagnetism.
1876	Alexander Graham Bell invents the telephone.

or "higher" forms of life emerged, each form proliferating as its environment dictated and as competition for food and survival permitted.

This scientific theory, expressed with caution and supported by massive evidence, almost instantly became the center of controversies that raged throughout Europe for a generation. Evolution, mutable species, survival determined by brute conflict rather than divine will—each of these theories challenged established assumptions in science and theology. Nor did Darwin hide his belief that the same laws apply to the development of human beings and beasts. This seemed to many a scandalous disregard of divine providence and Christian teaching. Nowadays, most theologians and scientists generally agree that there is no necessary conflict between the concept of evolving species and Christian doctrine, but such tolerance required a differentiation between the study of natural laws and religious tradition that few in the nineteenth century were willing to make.

Medicine   In the medical disciplines, the identification of germs and the realization that they were not spontaneously generated had immediate practical results. In the 1860s the discoveries of Louis Pasteur in France led to the techniques for destroying germs called pasteurization, which were of crucial importance to the wine, dairy, and silk industries. As a result of his work in immunology, Pasteur also developed a preventive vaccine against rabies. In England Joseph Lister discovered that germs could be killed by carbolic acid, and the application of that knowledge made surgery a reasonable remedy rather than a desperate gamble. A decade later Robert Koch in Germany showed that different diseases were caused by distinct microbes, discovered the microorganism responsible for tuberculosis, and opened the way to new techniques in bacteriology and in the battle against communicable diseases. Advances such as these not only improved agriculture and medicine but also stimulated the drive to make sanitation and public health into systematic sciences.

Physics and Chemistry   Advances in physics and chemistry gave a greater sense of a controllable and predictable universe. The fundamental generalizations of chemistry are contained in the periodic law and periodic table published by Dmitry Mendeleev in 1869. Mendeleev's table established a marvelous symmetry, so precise that the elements could all be charted by atomic weight, with similar elements occurring at regular intervals. This regularity even allowed for the prediction of unknown elements that would, when discovered, fill the gaps in the table.

Thermodynamics, the study of the relationship between heat and mechanical energy, became the core of nineteenth-century physics. The combined work of scientists in many countries culminated in the mathematical formulation of the two fundamental laws of thermodynamics. One states the principle of the conservation of energy: Energy can be transformed into heat or work but can be neither created nor destroyed, and heat or work can be transformed into energy. The other law declares that any closed physical system tends toward equilibrium, a system in which heat becomes uniformly distributed and which therefore cannot be used to produce work.[2]

The study of magnetism advanced in a similar way from the work of Michael Faraday. He had shown in the 1830s and 1840s that lines of magnetic force are analogous to gravity and that magnetic fields induce electric currents, allowing for creation of the electric generator. In 1873 James Clerk Maxwell published equations that described the behavior of electricity, magnetism, and light in terms of a single, universal system. By the end of the century, physics had established mathematical laws of theoretical beauty and practical power relating the forces of gravity, magnetism, electricity and light and extending from the universe to the atom. Thermodynamics led to the development of more efficient sources of power. Research on electricity led to the telegraph by midcentury and to electric lights and motors for many different uses a generation later.

Social Science and Ideas of Progress

In conjunction with the progress in science, theories of social change emphasized systematic improvement.

Auguste Comte   Philosopher Auguste Comte sought to erect a comprehensive philosophical system that would encompass all human knowledge. He was especially impressed, as were most contemporary intellectuals, by the social role of religion, the conquests of natural science, and the possibilities of human progress. For many years private secretary to Saint-Simon (see p. 680), Comte retained a confidence characteristic of the early socialists that society would soon be reorganized on rational principles.

He systematically elaborated his philosophy, which he called *positivism*, in ten volumes published between 1830 and 1845. These established positivism as an influential international movement.[3] The key to civilization, he argued, is humanity's understanding of the world, which has developed through three historical stages. In the first, the theological stage, humankind interpreted everything in terms of gods who lived in nature. In the second, or metaphysical stage, people learned through Christianity to think in more abstract terms. In the third, or positive stage, now dawning, human understanding was becoming scientific through objective and precise observation followed by generalization in the form of scientific laws. Every science, he argued, has already passed through the first two stages and into the third—astronomy first, then physics, chemistry, and biology. Now a new science, *sociology* (Comte coined the term), must crown the progression.

While thus honoring the role of established religion, Comte announced its demise, substituting a "religion of humanity" of his own invention. Comte's ideas contributed greatly to widespread acceptance of the view that civilization progresses with increased knowledge discovered through the scientific method and that the

---

[2] The measure of the energy available for work is called *entropy*, a term coined by the physicist Rudolf Clausius in 1865.

[3] Later, the term *positivism* came to refer not so much to Comte's specific theories as to a method he advocated: the construction of logical theories based on facts established through empirical research.

great need now was for the scientific study of society and of humankind itself. This creed inspired and shaped much of the rapid development of the social sciences—economics, political science, anthropology, sociology, and psychology—later in the century.

Georg Wilhelm Friedrich Hegel   Even more influential than Comte, Georg Wilhelm Friedrich Hegel set the tone for nineteenth-century intellectuals with a philosophy as comprehensive as that of Thomas Aquinas or Aristotle. He was determined to reconcile contradictions between science and faith, Christianity and the state, the ideal and the real, the eternal and the temporal. The key, he believed, lay in the meaning of history and the nature of the historical process. According to Hegel, that process is dialectical. The dialectical process works as follows: Society in any era constitutes an implicit statement about life and values expressed through social structure and actions, which can be thought of as its thesis. That thesis, however, is never adequate to every need, and its incompleteness generates contrary views, institutions, and practices—the antithesis. Thus, every society gives rise to conflict between thesis and antithesis until a new synthesis is born from that **dialectic.** This synthesis becomes, in turn, another thesis that generates a new antithesis. History moves by this dialectic in a steady unfolding of what Hegel called the World Spirit, toward greater human freedom and self-awareness. Hegel's influence increased after his death in 1831. By midcentury, it was a European habit to approach any question of society, culture, or politics in terms of historical change. Hegel also helped shape the most significant theory of social change in nineteenth- and twentieth-century Europe, for Marxism relied heavily on Hegelian philosophy.

Karl Marx   No theory about society and history has proved more influential than the work of Karl Marx. Trained in German philosophy, abreast of contemporary economics, and in touch with the currents of radical thought, Marx outlined his theory of history in a powerful, apocalyptic tone in the *Communist Manifesto*, written jointly with his friend Friedrich Engels, which was published just before the revolutions of 1848. Little noticed at first, it proved to be one of the greatest pieces of propaganda of all time, a specific program and a general call to action combined with a philosophy of history. Marx devoted the rest of his life—which he spent in poverty-stricken exile in London from 1849 to 1883—to the painstaking elaboration of his ideas in essays, letters, and the comprehensive treatise *Das Kapital.*

Marx's Theory of History   Marx wrote about contemporary affairs, but fundamentally he wanted, like so many thinkers of his time, to build a comprehensive

Something of the power of his personality shows through in this photograph of Karl Marx, bourgeois and scholar (with reading glass).
The Granger Collection, New York

philosophical system. Later in the century his followers would compare him with Darwin as the "discoverer" of the "law" of history: dialectical materialism. The dialectic came from Hegel and his followers. Marx kept the idea of a dialectic as the process of historical change but rejected Hegel's idealism—the view that the dialectic works through ideas that constitute the spirit of the age—and insisted instead that any society rests fundamentally on the organization of its economy, on its mode of production.

Political systems, Marx said, grow from these material underpinnings, and in each system the dominant social class expresses the needs, values, and interests associated with a particular mode of production. The agricultural economy of the Middle Ages required the feudal system with its particular social values and laws, upheld by the landowning aristocracy. That system produced its antithesis in the middle class. But the industrial society of capitalism, dominated by the middle class, was now producing a new antithesis embodied in the rising working class, or *proletariat.* Class conflict is the mechanism of historical progress, and the triumph of the proletariat will bring a new synthesis, a classless society.

By its own inevitable laws, history would thus lead to a new era, one similar to the future envisioned by other socialists. In the classless society, people would no longer be forced into the inequality that capitalist production requires. At present, the primary purpose of the state was to protect property and enforce inequality, but in the new era the state would wither away, unneeded. Revolutions thus mark the arrival to power of a new class. They are, however, more than mere transfers of power. A new class brings changes in law, religion, and customs, which it then maintains in its own interest. The advent of middle-class rule thus represented progress. But capitalism, despite all the ideologies and social institutions designed to shore it up, would fail through its own internal contradictions.

Marx's Analysis of Capitalism   Marx's detailed analysis of capitalism took much from the classical economists. The value of a product, he insisted somewhat obscurely, comes from the value of all the labor required to produce it, all the labor necessary to transform raw materials into manufactured goods. The capitalist makes a profit by keeping part of the value added by all this labor done by others, that is, by exploiting the working class. But capitalists must compete with each other, and to do so, they are forced to lower prices, which in turn reduces profits. This reduction in profits has two effects. First, the capitalist must exploit labor more harshly, cutting wages to the minimum required for subsistence. Second, the smaller producers will fail, which will lead to larger concentrations of capital and force more and more members of the middle class into the proletariat, the class of people who have nothing but their labor to sell. Thus, a shrinking capitalist class suffering from declining profits will face a growing proletariat. Capitalism, therefore, lays the basis for socialism by depriving all but a few of property. The contradictions will be resolved when the whole system fails.

The Appeal of Marxism   Although many of Marx's specific predictions were proven wrong, **Marxism** has deeply affected all modern thought, shaped the policies of all sorts of governments, and provided a core for some of the most powerful political movements of the last hundred years. Such impact requires explanation, and perhaps four points can capture something of the answer.

First, Marxism not only sees society as a whole and explains historical change but demands systematic and detailed analyses of the interrelationship among social values, institutions, politics, and economic conditions. It also suggests methods for conducting such analyses.

Second, Marxism accepts and indeed hails industrialization as inevitable and beneficial even while accepting most criticism of industrial society. Marx believed that the machine can free human beings from brute labor and that it can, through greater productivity, provide well-being for all. Industrialization could be made to provide solutions to the very problems it created. Thus, Marxism has special appeal for societies eager to modernize.

Third, the theory is rich in moral judgments without having to defend any ethical system. Although social values are considered relative, and those of his opponents are denounced as hypocritical, Marx's own rage at injustice rings out in a compelling call to generous sentiments that rejects sentimentality.

Finally, Marxism not only claims the prestige of science but offers the security of determinism. Knowing where destiny leads, Marxists can accept the uneven flow of change, confident that any defeats are temporary. Opponents are to be recognized and fought less for what they say or do than for what they represent—for their "objective" role in the structure of capitalism. Their concessions do not alter their destiny, and the Marxist is free to adopt whatever tactics will further the inevitable movement of history toward the victory of the proletariat. Just as Marx believed that small (quantitative) changes may lead to sudden qualitative ones, so Marxists can favor short-term reforms as well as revolution. The variety inherent in Marx's system has been a source of bitter division as well as strength among socialists, but it helped keep Marxism more vigorous and coherent than any other of the grand theories spawned in the nineteenth century.

Social Darwinism   Just as Marxists claimed scientific objectivity, so too did those who extended Darwin's principles to more current concerns, a tendency that came to be called **social Darwinism.** Social Darwinists tended to ignore the long time span in which Darwinian theory operated and saw the formal concept of species as loosely analogous to groups, classes, nations, or civilizations.

An invitingly tough-minded way to reason, social Darwinism was used to argue for opposing policies. Thomas Huxley, the greatest intellectual propagandist for Darwin's theories, held social Darwinism to be consonant with the teachings of Indian philosophy, Buddhism, ancient Greece, and Christianity (see "Huxley's Social Darwinism," p. 748). Some writers in Great Britain and the United States used the vocabulary of social Darwinism to argue that better education and social welfare constitute a higher stage of evolution and would help produce a superior species. But Darwinism was more commonly used to justify competition in the marketplace or between nations, as the mechanism of evolution in which

HUXLEY'S SOCIAL DARWINISM

"Evolution and Ethics," a much reprinted lecture that T. H. Huxley gave at Oxford in 1893, was perhaps the most famous statement of what can be called the gentle interpretation of the social implication of Darwin's theories.

"Man, the animal, in fact, has worked his way to the headship of the sentient world, and has become the superb animal which he is, in virtue of his success in the struggle for existence. The conditions having been of a certain order, man's organization has adjusted itself to them better than that of his competitors in the cosmic strife. In the case of mankind, the self-assertion, the unscrupulous seizing upon all that can be grasped, the tenacious holding of all that can be kept, which constitute the essence of the struggle for existence, have answered. For his successful progress, throughout the savage state, man has been largely indebted to those qualities which he shares with the ape and the tiger; his exceptional physical organization; his cunning, his sociability, his curiosity, and his imitativeness; his ruthless and ferocious destructiveness when his anger is roused by opposition.

"But, in proportion as men have passed from anarchy to social organization, and in proportion as civilization has grown in worth, these deeply ingrained serviceable qualities have become defects. . . . In fact, civilized man brands all these ape and tiger promptings with the name of sins, he punishes many of the acts which flow from them as crimes; and, in extreme cases, he does his best to put an end to the survival of the fittest of former days by axe and rope.

" . . . The history of civilization details the steps by which men have succeeded in building up an artificial world within the cosmos. Fragile reed as he may be, man, as Pascal says, is a thinking reed: there lies within him a fund of energy operating intelligently and so far akin to that which pervades the universe, that it is competent to influence and modify the cosmic process.

" . . . Moreover, the cosmic nature born with us and, to a large extent, necessary for our maintenance, is the outcome of millions of years of severe training, and it would be folly to imagine that a few centuries will suffice to subdue its masterfulness to purely ethical ends. Ethical nature may count upon having to reckon with a tenacious and powerful enemy as long as the world lasts. But, on the other hand, I see no limit to the extent to which intelligence and will, guided by sound principles of investigation, and organized in common effort, may modify the conditions of existence, for a period longer than that now covered by history. And much may be done to change the nature of man himself."

From Thomas H. Huxley, *Evolution and Ethics and Other Essays*, New York: D. Appleton and Company, 1916.

---

the fittest triumph. Such assumptions infiltrated many aspects of late-nineteenth-century social thought. Ideas of biological determinism were widespread. These ideas cropped up in loose talk about national characteristics and were used to rank races as superior or inferior, to discourage the unfit from breeding, to support traditional views of male dominance based on innate differences between men and women, and to identify criminal types by physiognomy.

Herbert Spencer One of the grandest statements of the laws of progress was the *Synthetic Philosophy* of Herbert Spencer, published in a series of studies that first appeared in the 1850s and continued to 1896. Spencer's ideas were closely tied to those of Comte and Darwin, and his contemporaries (especially in Great Britain and the United States) ranked him among the major philosophers of all time. Spencer's central principle, which made progress "not an accident, but a necessity," was the evolution of all things from simplicity to complexity, from homogeneity to diversity. With great erudition, he traced this process in physics and biology,

sociology and psychology, economics and ethics. Such comprehensiveness was part of his appeal, and he applied his theses to physical matter, to human understanding, and to social institutions. While he refused to worry about the metaphysical abstractions of traditional philosophy, Spencer maintained the assumptions of a narrow and rigid liberalism.

He argued that the marketplace is the true test of the fittest and that it must be uninhibited by state intervention even on behalf of welfare or public education. When he died in 1903, much of his work was already outmoded. Strict laissez-faire had been abandoned even by most liberals, and his sort of rationalism had come under heavy attack. His confidence that universal laws of development enshrined the values of middle-class English Protestants would soon seem quaint.

THE BELLE EPOQUE

With a touch of nostalgia, the thirty years or so before 1914 has come to be called the Belle Epoque, a phrase

Jean Béraud
OUTSIDE THE THEATRE DU VAUDEVILLE
The street life and vaudeville of Paris provided an international model, and all Europe's great cities delighted in an urban life that provided attractions for every class.
Christie's Images/Bridgeman Art Library/© 2005 Artists Rights Society (ARS), New York/ADAGP, Paris

evocative of the Paris of the 1890s, the city of lights where the Eiffel Tower was new, the grand boulevards were crowded with cafés, and great department stores were palaces of consumerism. In all the great cities of Europe, a sense of spectacle and dynamism accompanied the drearier realities of urban life as the industrial age fostered a culture of mass consumption.

The Culture of Capitalism

Mass Culture and the Business of Entertainment
Like the sciences, entertainment and sport became professions. Folk songs about work, the life of the soldier or sailor, and young love continued to be sung but more often now by paid singers in pubs or cafés or beer halls that featured singing and dancing. Music halls combined adaptations of opera, theater, and symphony with forms borrowed from the circus and vaudeville. The entertainments available in outdoor gardens (there were more than two hundred such places in London alone) and less expensive theaters also used elements of folk and high culture.

In the late nineteenth century, these entertainments became available to increasingly broader segments of society. First, laws restricting working hours all over Western Europe (for example, the adoption of the "English week," with Sundays and half of Saturdays off) provided workers with leisure time to fill. Second, the rise in real wages in the last quarter of the century meant that more people could afford entertainment. Leisure thus emerged as an important business, with a clientele that included families from the lower-middle and working classes. Performance designed to appeal to different social classes—revues, operettas, melodramas, and comedy routines (especially popular at the beach resorts now opening up to families from the lower-middle and working classes)—reached an ever larger part of the population. By the turn of the century, silent motion pictures won a still greater audience.

Women of all social classes also took part in the world of mass leisure. They were increasingly visible in a variety of new public venues, as consumers in department stores, spectators in dance and music halls, and cyclists in public parks. Their unprecedented freedom and mobility in the public sphere worried many contemporaries, who saw it as compromising women's ability to perform their primary domestic roles.

The world of sports epitomized the transformation of leisure. Its roughest forms (free-for-alls and animal baiting) had been banned and were replaced by more regulated activities; the Marquis of Queensberry rules for boxing, for instance, date from 1867. Many traditional games faded away, leaving a trace in ball games like cricket, soccer, and rugby. By midcentury, these ball games had become the sports of elite English secondary schools and had earned increasing notice in the press. Then teams formed in cities with players from the working classes, and the best of these teams began to be paid. Leagues were formed, and their matches became important communal events.

Professional soccer teams attracted huge, noisy, paying Sunday crowds, and the game spread across Europe. Most of the European professional teams famous today (like the older American baseball teams) were founded around the turn of the century. Their games became an important part of civic life, and teams depended on their ability to appeal to workers as well as to members of the middle class, while the upper-middle classes took to more individualistic games like golf and tennis.

Britain's elite schools had emphasized athletics, believing they inculcated the "manly virtues" of perseverance, sacrifice for the team, and playing by the rules. Sport, it was said, trained leaders (especially the sort of leaders empire required) and fostered religion, a "muscular Christianity" that was also embraced by schools in the United States, Canada, and Australia. But sports soon demonstrated the capacity to promote communal identity on a much broader civic and national scale. Athletic competition could invoke both individualism and nationalism, as it did in the modern Olympic games, established in 1896 through the efforts of Baron Pierre de Coubertin of France.

The Rise of Mass Media   Limited hours of work (and long tram rides home) left employees with time to read newspapers, and the papers quickly discovered ways to increase their circulation. Appealing to a broader public, several newspapers now approached daily sales of a million copies. The most popular of them gave more space to sensational accounts of crime and disasters and sought out colorful human-interest features.

Like the millions of popular novels, such writing candidly sought a wide audience rather than a learned one. For the first time in Western history, in the wealthier nations at least, a majority of the adult population was literate. By the 1880s governments almost everywhere, recognizing the importance of literacy to politics

and industry, had made education universal and compulsory and had reduced or eliminated school fees.

In 1850 Prussia was the only major nation in which a majority of the adult population could read and write. By 1900 more than 90 percent of the adult population of Germany, France, and Great Britain was literate, and the proportion elsewhere was climbing rapidly. Mass schooling was usually limited to a few years of the most elementary subjects, and the kind of education received became one of the clearest markers of class status. Nevertheless, the schooling available to everyone would be steadily extended, and access to secondary school, technical school, and university gradually increased.

Artistic Modernism

The creative arts continued to flourish, benefiting from ever larger and more sophisticated audiences. Yet the forms and styles employed grew so diverse that the arts hardly seemed to speak for a single civilization. One reason for the change (and the one most welcomed) was the trend toward national styles. The use of folk elements and distinct traditions gave an instantly recognizable national identity to English or Russian novels and French, German, or Russian music. Another reason for the variety of artistic styles was the tendency of artists to act as social critics, thereby bringing into the realm of aesthetics the issues of politics and values that troubled society. Thus, the tension between the individual and society, between the artist's personal perceptions and the unstable conventions of a world undergoing rapid change, remained a central theme of nineteenth-century art.

Divergent Schools   These concerns and then the reaction against them in favor of a "purer" art led to a bewildering variety of competing movements. "Naturalism," the "Pre-Raphaelites," "Impressionism," the "Decadents," "Symbolism"—such self-conscious labels for new artistic movements were frequently proclaimed with angry manifestos against previous art and present culture.

Naturalists claimed that the artist, like a scientist, should present life in objective detail after careful research. This aim was particularly suited to the novel, and Émile Zola, with his precise descriptions of industrial and Parisian life, was a master of the school. Determinism, the view that behavior was determined by social circumstance or blood inheritance, was a favorite theme in this Darwinian age. It proved especially effective on the stage, where the protagonist's destiny inexorably unfolded, and it gradually won new audiences to realistic drama in the plays of Henrik Ibsen of Norway, August Strindberg of Sweden, and Anton Chekhov of Russia.

Auguste Renoir
DANCE AT THE MOULIN DE LA GALETTE, **1876**
Renoir's festive scene of the outdoor Sunday dance at *Le Moulin de la Galette,* an outdoor café in Paris that catered to the working class and lower-middle class as well as to artists, is characteristic of the Impressionists' interest in urban life.
Musée d'Orsay, Paris, France. Erich Lessing/Art Resource, NY

The realistic painters of midcentury had turned to scenes from ordinary life. Like England's pre-Raphaelites, who took their name from the pious and simpler art of the early Renaissance, however, they tended to believe that much of a painting's importance lay in the message it conveyed and, therefore, in its subject matter. For them, art was supposed to be uplifting.

Toward a More Subjective Art   A new generation of painters called the **Impressionists** broke with this tradition to concentrate on capturing the effects of light and color, making the artist's brilliance in analyzing and re-creating such effects in itself a purpose of painting. Many of them, including Edgar Degas, August Renoir, Claude Monet, and the Postimpressionist Paul Cézanne were recognized in their own lifetimes as ranking among the great artists of Western history. Today their works remain the most reproduced and widely enjoyed of Western art. Yet painters only slightly younger, like Paul Gauguin and Vincent van

Gogh, quickly turned to still newer, more challenging, and more personal styles.

Poetry, like painting, became an increasingly private expression, indifferent to conventional morality, and constructed according to complex aesthetic doctrines. Decried as decadent for its fashionable fascination with death, languid despair, and obscure references, the Symbolist movement in poetry interpreted the things one sees and describes as signs of a deeper and more spiritual reality. Art was to be complexly understood on several levels of meaning at once, and individual style became a personal conquest, a private bridge between the artist's identity and external realities.

Architecture, as the most public and functional of the arts, was less able to address the tensions between individual and society. Only at the end of the century were the structural and aesthetic possibilities hidden in railroad sheds, bridges, and exhibit halls developed into a new architectural style that included the skyscraper. Even as that was happening, the international style

Vincent van Gogh
The Church at Auvers, France, June 1890
Much influenced by the Impressionists, Vincent van Gogh developed a style featuring vigorous strokes that made a dazzling, and often fervently mystical, personal statement. By 1890, when he painted this picture of a village church, Impressionism was being superseded.
Musée d'Orsay, Paris, France. Erich Lessing/Art Resource, NY

Edvard Munch
The Dance of Life, 1899–1900
In Norway Edvard Munch's use of Symbolism pointed the way to German Expressionism, using color and line to convey the anxiety underlying ordinary life, as in this bitter comment on the tragedy of the *Dance of Life.*
Nasjonalgalleriet, Oslo, Norway/Bridgeman Art Library/© 2005 The Munch Museum/The Munch-Ellingsen Group/Artists Rights Society (ARS), New York

known as Art Nouveau turned its back on the practical and efficient industrial world of the turn of the century and delighted in applying ornamental arabesques to everything from wrought iron to poster lettering and printed cloth.

ATTACKS ON LIBERAL CIVILIZATION

Although by the end of the century an increasingly prosperous and democratic Europe appeared to be fulfilling much of liberalism's promise, liberal civilization itself came under heavy attack during this period. Women agitated for greater political participation, radicals sought the end of the capitalist system, and conservatives and Christians mounted new attacks on liberal values. These attacks had their intellectual foundations in well-developed systems of thought, but

they had their greatest impact in organized movements that clamored for public attention and fought for political power.

Gender Wars in the Fin de Siècle

From the 1860s on, women everywhere had begun to organize on behalf of their own, distinctive interests. While they pressed for further change, the existence of these organizations also reflected important changes already taking place in the workplace, in social attitudes, and in the educational opportunities available to women.

Women's Movements   Often divided over goals and tactics, women's movements tended to separate themselves into three types. The first and largest were led by middle-class women and often reflected their experience in charitable work and education. The meeting of the International Congress of the Rights of Women on the occasion of the Paris exposition of 1878 brought together representatives from twelve countries, including the United States. Women's issues were becoming a regular part of the public agenda.

By the 1880s and 1890s, this growing awareness led to a second, politically more radical type of movement, less intent upon protecting women and more explicitly concerned with equal rights. Particularly in Germany, England, and France, these movements realized that their demands required fundamental social change, and they often looked toward the traditional left for support. But they met a mixed response. Working men, who were the strength of Britain's Labour party and the continental socialist parties, feared competition from women, who were traditionally paid less. And many feminist leaders worried that to seek special laws regulating women's work would tend to preserve paternalistic attitudes and close off new opportunities.

A third variant was the growing women's trade union movement, which was concerned primarily with the immediate problems of pay and working conditions. Yet employers' resistance, low pay, the nature of the jobs most working women were permitted, and a lack of sympathy from men's unions made it difficult to establish strong women's unions.

Working Women   The fact remained that in the late nineteenth century most women in industrial nations worked for wages from their early teens until they married and many continued to work afterward, once their children were no longer infants, making an often essential contribution to family income. The proportion of women who worked for pay was highest in France—about 40 percent—but the increase in the number of women workers was especially noticeable in countries in which industrialization was more recent, such as Germany, Italy, and the Scandinavian countries.

Jobs remained tightly tied to gender. More women in England and Germany were employed as domestic servants than in any other field. Many young women newly arrived in the city found jobs in the growing service sector, as laundresses or waitresses. Only about one-fifth were employed in factories and usually assigned tasks associated with domestic skills. In the textile industries the proportion of women workers steadily rose to become the majority everywhere. Women were less numerous in the burgeoning industries of the second industrial revolution than in more stagnant ones in which pay was lower; and far more women than men did piecework, fabricating buttons or cardboard boxes in shops or at home. The garrets of every city were filled with women living in tiny rooms where they worked late into the night making hats, artificial flowers, and lace; a measure establishing a minimum rate for piecework in England was an unusual protection, even in 1910.

New Opportunities   Some significant changes in women's employment were helpful to the women's movement generally. With the spread of elementary schooling, women slowly took over as bookkeepers, office clerks, and secretaries, occupations in which prestige, opportunities for advancement, and pay declined as they came to be women's work. Some professions also opened to women, especially nursing (primarily provided by nuns in Catholic countries) and teaching in elementary school. By the end of the century three-quarters of the elementary school teachers in England

Jens Ferdinand Willumsen
IN A FRENCH LAUNDRY, 1889
Middle-class women were the leaders in feminist movements, and efforts to organize women workers concentrated on industrial work; but far more women earned money in menial drudgery, like these women in a French laundry.
Göteborgs Konstmuseum, Sweden. Bridgeman Art Library/
© 2005 Artists Rights Society (ARS), New York

were women, as were more than half the teachers in Sweden and France and one-fifth of those in Germany.

The expanding field of social work began to pay women, often the sort of middle-class women whose earlier charitable work had pioneered in creating the field. Small shops and, more slowly, the great department stores also hired women as clerks, preferably women from the lower-middle class who were trained to speak and dress in the ways considered proper by a bourgeois clientele.

Public Policy   These developments, along with the women's movements and the formidable resistance to them, made "the woman question" a persistent topic of debate in newspapers, from pulpits, and in learned essays. The very awkwardness of the phrase suggested some embarrassment and confusion. Feminists found themselves combating custom and widespread attitudes as well as the prejudices of supposed experts: doctors who cited women's physical weakness and psychological instability and social Darwinists who declared that civilization required women to concentrate on their biological function. Nevertheless, dominant attitudes did begin to change.

Women's colleges were established at Oxford and Cambridge in the 1870s; and in Italy, where universities had never been closed to women, Marie Montessori's lectures at the end of the century on the "new woman" were widely hailed. Outstanding achievements by individual women in science, medicine,

This advertisement in a German magazine was typical in selling not just an inexpensive means of transport but the joys of youth, style, and a new freedom for women.
The Mary Evans Picture Library

education, literature, art, economics, and social reform challenged stereotypes; it became far less unusual for women to attend school beyond the elementary grades, to take part in demonstrations, and even to speak at public meetings.

As women lived longer and bore fewer children, legal and cultural constraints that assumed their lives would be circumscribed by marriage and motherhood became harder to defend. By 1910 most European nations had passed laws protecting women workers and increasing women's rights to dispose of property, to share in decisions affecting their children, and to take part in civic life. Wherever suffrage was universal for men, demands that women be allowed to vote were becoming louder.

Working-Class Movements

Although Marx had spent much of his career in the library of the British Museum, he and Engels aspired to lead an effective social movement. Their influence grew greatly toward the end of the century.

The First International   When in 1864 a group of English labor leaders called a small international conference in London, Marx readily agreed to attend as a representative of German workers. The International Working Men's Association, usually called the First International, was founded at that meeting, and Marx dominated it from the start. He did his best to replace traditional radical rhetoric about truth and justice with the hard language of Marxism. During the eight years the First International lasted, he gradually succeeded in expelling those who disagreed with him.

Socialist Parties and Trade Unions   As Marx gained ascendancy over the international workers' movement, socialist parties became an important part of political life in nearly every European country. Except in Great Britain, most socialist parties were at least formally

The nation was shocked when an anarchist bomb exploded in the French Chamber of Deputies in 1893, shown in this illustration in *Le Petit Journal*, France's most popular newspaper.
The Mary Evans Picture Library

Marxist. As they began to win elections, socialists disagreed over whether to follow a more moderate policy aimed at electoral success or to adhere rigidly to the teachings of Marx. The most common compromise combined moderate policies with flaming rhetoric, and the Second International, formed in 1889 with representatives from parties and unions in every country, sought to maintain doctrinal rigor and socialist unity. The Marxist critique of liberalism and capitalism was spread through print media, parliamentary debates, and election campaigns.

Labor organizations outside Germany were not often consistently Marxist, but trade unions everywhere were class conscious, frequently tempted by violent protest, and suspicious of politics. Their membership soared, with millions of workers paying dues in the industrialized countries, and the strike became the common expression of social protest. Skilled artisans, threatened by new modes of production yet strengthened by their own traditions of cooperation, often continued to be the leaders in militant action; but it was the successful organization of workers in larger factories that led to a great wave of larger, better organized strikes.

Anarchism Most people did not distinguish clearly among the various radical movements, and newspapers were quick to associate socialists and labor leaders with the anarchist "propaganda of the deed," violent acts that made headlines. In the 1880s and 1890s, bombs were thrown into parades, cafés, and theaters in cities all over Europe. Acting on their own, individual **anarchists** assassinated the president of France in 1894, the prime minister of Spain in 1897, the empress of Austria in 1898, the king of Italy in 1900, and the president of the United States in 1901. Such incidents were followed by the arrest of known radicals, spectacular trials, and denunciations of leftists.

But bomb throwers and assassins were only a tiny part of the broad anarchist movement. Anarchism's intellectual tradition was continuous from the time of the French Revolution. The Russian anarchist Mikhail Bakunin had established himself by 1848 as one of Europe's more flamboyant revolutionaries. Bakunin respected Marx, but his enthusiastic support of nationalism and his distrust of what he saw as a dangerous authoritarianism in Marxism led to his expulsion from the First International. Anarchism's most famous figure after Bakunin was Prince Peter Kropotkin, an exiled Russian aristocrat, who advocated for what he called anarcho-communism, but he was unable to unify the movement. Some anarchists stressed individualism, some pacifism, and some the abolition of private property. All rejected imposed authority and denounced the state as a repressive machine serving the interests of wealth.

They won their largest following among the poor who felt crushed by industrialization: immigrants to the United States, peasants in southern Spain, artisans and some industrial workers in Italy and France. Anarchism was an influential element in the opposition to bureaucratic centralization and to militarism. It appealed to artists and writers who shared the anarchists' contempt for bourgeois values, while it contributed heroes and martyrs to the growing mystique of the radical left.

Socialism, anarchism, and trade unions all fostered feelings of brotherhood and addressed the sense of justice and common interest that had developed within working-class life. Expressed in songs and speeches at meetings, demonstrations, and strikes, these shared values had developed over generations to be reinforced now by militant organizations but also by changes that made the conditions of labor in different industries more similar and by housing patterns that created working-class districts. One of the functions of radical movements was to sustain this solidarity by linking the immediate issues of the workplace to broad principles and to national politics. The result was a powerful challenge to the established system. Nevertheless, the left remained far from united. Different interests often divided skilled from unskilled workers, those in established trades from those employed in new industries, male from female workers, and labor unions from political parties.

The Christian Critique

While some Protestants felt a natural affinity for liberalism, it nevertheless was subject to a strong moral critique by the churches of Europe and the United States. Ministers and priests excoriated liberalism's tendency to mistake selfishness for individualism, moral indifference for toleration, and materialism for progress. Theories of evolution, positivism, and biblical criticism put defenders of traditional beliefs on the defensive and made them seem opponents of science. The expanding role of government, especially in matters of education and welfare, made conflicts between church and state a major theme of European life. Churches often found themselves opposing the growing claims of the state, and both Protestants and Catholics denounced the injustices of capitalist society as forcefully as socialists did.

Roman Catholic Opposition Since the French Revolution, the Roman Catholic Church found itself at odds with many modern trends, and it was particularly hostile to liberalism. In 1864 Pope Pius IX issued the encyclical *Quanta Cura*, which denounced total faith in human reason, the exclusive authority of the state, and attacks on traditional rights of the Church and stated that the pope had the option of opposing "progress, liberalism and modern civilization."

The Vatican Council of 1869–1870, the first council of the Church in three hundred years, confirmed the impression of intransigence, as prelates came from around the world to proclaim the dogma of papal infallibility. This belief had long been a tradition, and its elevation to dogma revealed increased centralization within the Church and affirmed the solidarity of Catholics in the face of new social and political dangers. Throughout Europe political leaders wondered whether Catholics who now followed an infallible pope could be reliable citizens of a secular state.

As chancellor of the new German state, Bismarck launched and then abandoned attacks on the Catholic Church as his government relied more and more on the Catholic Center party. The conflict between church and state was most open and bitter, however, in Spain, Italy, and France, where it was the central political division of the 1880s and 1890s. Generally, such church-state conflicts subsided somewhat after the turn of the century. Relatively secure states, having established the breadth of their authority, tended to become more tolerant; the churches, too, became more flexible, in the style of Pope Leo XIII (r. 1878–1903), who established an understanding with Bismarck and encouraged French Catholics to accept the Third Republic.

Social Action   At the same time, Christianity displayed renewed vigor. Christian political and social movements learned to mobilize enormous support and became more active in social work (the Protestant Salvation Army was founded in 1865). This engagement in charity, religious missions at home and overseas, education, labor unions, and hundreds of special projects not only strengthened Christian social influence but gave concreteness to religious denunciations of immoral and unjust conditions.

Pope Leo XIII added a powerful voice to the rising cry for social reform. The Catholic Church, he wrote, recognizes the right of workers to their own organizations and to "reasonable and frugal comfort"; but the state, he warned, should not favor any single class, and society must not consider human beings as merely a means to profit.

Strongest in rural areas and with more support among women than men, Christian churches knew a lot about those who had not necessarily benefited from modern social change. The churches now made more effort to reach workers and the middle class, urban groups whose special needs had often been overlooked in the past, and they spoke more readily for those discontented groups that tended not to rely on close ties to the state. By 1910 Christianity was more respectable among intellectuals, more active in society, and more prominent in politics than it had been since the early nineteenth century. Whether of the political left or right, Protestants and Catholics found in Christian teaching a whole arsenal of complaints against liberalism and industrial capitalism.

Beyond Reason

Until World War I, European political thought remained predominantly liberal, but some of its optimism was fading. Liberals themselves worried more about problems of community and social justice, and others questioned the power of human reason and argued for leadership by a small elite.

Georges Sorel and Henri Bergson   The Frenchman Georges Sorel shared the growing suspicion that public opinion owed more to prejudice than to reason. Like many intellectuals, he felt contempt for middle-class society, but he argued that its overthrow would not come in the way predicted by Marx. His most important book, *Reflections on Violence* (1908), postulated that historic changes occur when people are inspired by some great myth beyond the test of reason. As a myth for his times, Sorel proposed the general strike. Sorel thus contributed to the widespread **syndicalist** movement, which called on workers' organizations, or *syndicats*, to bring down bourgeois society. He rejected bourgeois rationalism in favor of violence as an expression of the will that could create powerful political movements, finding the energy for change in humanity's irrationality.[4]

Sorel's countryman, Henri Bergson, the most eloquent and revered philosopher of his day, expounded gentler, more abstract theories; yet he, too, pictured much of human understanding as arising not from reason but intuitively from subjective and unconscious feelings. Bergson was close to contemporary movements in the arts, psychology, and religion; and he believed society needed the new spirit of energy and common endeavor that could be achieved through spontaneity. That concern to translate feeling into action led away from liberalism's emphasis on the importance of law and formal procedures.

Friedrich Nietzsche   The revolutionary challenge that such ideas contained was clearest in the works of Friedrich Nietzsche. He, too, emphasized human will in a philosophy that lashed out at contemporary civilization. His disdain for ideas of equality and democ-

---

[4] Vilfredo Pareto and Sorel, both trained as engineers, are usually grouped together with Robert Michels as leading theorists of the new political "realism."

THE ARGUMENT OF ANTI-SEMITISM

Anti-Semitism became more organized and more vocal in most European countries in the 1880s. Despite important variations of tone and tactic in each nation, certain myths and themes were common to most of these movements. In 1883 a German publication calling itself The Journal for the Universal Rally for Combatting Jewdom *(Zeitschrift für die Allgemeine Vereinigung zur Bekämpfung des Judentums) repeated many of these themes. The article was presented in the form of a petition to Chancellor Bismarck, calling for a ban on Jews holding important offices and a restriction on their immigration.*

"Wherever Christian and Jew enter into social relations, we see the Jew as master and the native-born Christian population in a servile position. The Jew takes only a vanishingly small part in the hard work of the great mass of our people; in field and workshop, in mines and on scaffolding, in swamps and canals—everywhere it is only the calloused hand of the Christian that is active. But it is above all the Jew who harvests the fruits of this labor. By far the greatest portion of capital produced by national labor is concentrated in Jewish hands. Jewish real estate keeps pace with the growth of mobile capital. Not only the proudest palaces of our cities belong to the Jewish masters (whose fathers or grandfathers crossed the borders of our fatherland as peddlers and hawkers), but the rural estate—this highly significant and conserving basis of our state structure—is falling into Jewish hands with ever greater frequency.

"Truly, in view of these conditions and because of the massive penetration of the Semitic element into all positions affording power and influence, the following question seems justified on an ethical as well as national standpoint: *what future is left our fatherland if the Semitic element is allowed to make a conquest of our home ground for another generation as it has been allowed to do in the last two decades?* If the concept of 'fatherland' is not to be stripped of its ideal content, if the idea that it was our

fathers who tore this land from the wilderness and fertilized it with their blood in a thousand battles is not to be lost, if the inward connection between German custom and morality and the Christian outlook and tradition is to be maintained, then an alien tribe may never, ever rise to rule on German soil. This tribe, to whom our humane legislation extended the rights of hospitality and the rights of the native, stands further from us in thought and feeling than any other people in the entire Aryan world.

"The danger to our national way of life must naturally mount not only when the Jews succeed in not only encroaching upon the national and religious consciousness of our people by means of the *press,* but also when they succeed in obtaining state offices, the bearers of which are obliged to guard over the idealistic goods of our nation. We think above all of the professions of *teacher* and *judge.* Both were inaccessible to Jews until very recently, and both must again be closed if the concept of authority, the feeling for legality and fatherland, are not to become confused and doubted by the nation. Even now the Germanic ideals of honor, loyalty, and genuine piety begin to be displaced to make room for a cosmopolitan pseudoideal."

From Richard S. Levy (tr. and ed.), *Antisemitism in the Modern World,* D. C. Heath, 1991.

---

racy was balanced by his hatred of nationalism and militarism; he rejected his society not only for what it was but also for what it meant to be. The only hope for the future was the work of a few, the supermen who would discard the inhibitions of bourgeois society and the "slave morality" of Christianity. A deeply original thinker, Nietzsche would prove vastly influential for twentieth-century thought.

Anti-Semitism Like Nietzsche's philosophy, **anti-Semitism,** which he detested, was part of the rising current of opposition to liberal society. Anti-Semitism in the 1890s was remarkably widespread. Venomous assertions of Jewish avarice and lack of patriotism were used to discredit the entire republic in France and the opponents of imperial policy in Great Britain. Sixteen

deputies from anti-Semitic parties won seats in the German Reichstag in 1893, and Germany's prestigious Conservative party added anti-Semitism to its program (see "The Argument of Anti-Semitism," above). The Lord mayor of Vienna from 1895 to 1910 found anti-Semitism invaluable in his electoral victories, and anti-Semitism was an official policy of the Russian government from the terrible pogroms of 1881 on.

There is no simple explanation for the phenomenon, but scholars note that Jews were often perceived as a symbol of liberal, capitalist society. They first won their civil rights during the French Revolution, lived primarily in urban environments, and excelled in the expanding professions and businesses of the nineteenth century. Since nationalism, especially in Germany, stressed folk culture and race, conservatives attacked Jews as part of the liberal, capitalist world alien to national traditions. Conspiracy theories and racist distortions of Darwinism gave concrete and simple explanations for the baffling pace of social change, offering the hope that by circumscribing specific groups—and especially Jews—society could resist change itself.

Late-nineteenth-century anti-Semitism was no mere continuation of medieval prejudices. Social Darwinists of the era despised Jews not so much on the basis of religion as on their status as a biologically inferior "race." In Germany, Austria, and France, anti-Semitism emerged within a new politics of mass appeal; its prominence in France, where French Jews had long been recognized as equal citizens, was especially shocking. For Theodor Herzl, who became the leading spokesperson of Zionism, the lesson was clear: Jews must have a homeland of their own.

The Revival of the Right   Neither irrationalism nor anti-Semitism belongs inherently to a single political persuasion, but both were used primarily by the political right in the decades preceding World War I. Rightist movements revived notably in these years, building among those social groups that felt most harmed by the changes of the century: aristocrats, rural people, members of the lower-middle class whose status was threatened, and many Christians. A reinvigorated right also voiced concerns about the materialism of middle-class culture and the evils of unchecked capitalism. Right-wingers tried, frequently with success, to use patriotism and national strength as their battle cry, learning to make the effective mass appeal that had often eluded them in the past. Yet as critical as they were of liberal centrists, they saw socialists as their primary foes, declaring socialism the menace of the hour and the natural consequence of liberal error.

Thus, critics from the right and the left gained by addressing the discontents that liberalism tended to ignore and by criticizing the modern changes that most people still labeled progress. So many simultaneous assaults created grave political crises in many states. How those assaults were dealt with in each country reshaped the political system that would guide it through the challenges ahead.

DOMESTIC POLITICS

In many respects political systems were more similar at the end of the nineteenth century than they had been since before the French Revolution, and everywhere they faced many of the same issues. Yet each nation evolved its own distinctive response to the pressures for continuity and change.

Common Problems

There were certain issues that every political system confronted. One was who should participate in political life. The trend was to increase suffrage until every adult male had the right to vote, but extending that right to women became a divisive issue in many countries by the turn of the century. Each political system also found its own ways of constraining democracy, through royal prerogatives, a conservative second chamber, or limits on what legislatures could do.

The state was now a participant in social and economic life, but its precise role was often hotly contested, especially its responsibility for social welfare and its economic policies that affected banks, commerce, and labor unions. Powerful groups, such as the church, the military, or the aristocracy, sought to enlist the state on their side. Sometimes these competing interests could be balanced, but often these conflicts reinforced older ideological divisions that threatened to undermine the political system itself.

Large-Scale Organizations

These tensions emerged as states and social groups throughout Europe were increasingly represented by large bureaucracies. As governments took on increased responsibilities for public health, transportation, communications (the post and telegraph), their bureaucratic organization expanded, as did that of larger business companies. In response, smaller firms organized in associations that could represent their interests in dealings with government and with other lobbying groups.

Workers, too, were increasingly organized in national trade unions that negotiated for particular industries and mobilized major strikes in every industrial country from the 1880s. Political parties also adopted some form of national organization and a permanent staff, especially where universal male suffrage made such efforts worthwhile. The massive Marxist German Social Democratic party was the most impressive example of this.

New professional associations set standards, lobbied governments, and conferred prestige on the physicians, lawyers, engineers, and teachers that belonged to them. Like political parties, associations offered a means whereby scattered groups and new interests could make their presence felt in public life. This institutionalization of society was in many respects a source of stability, providing rapidly expanding occupations with norms, internal discipline, and a means for negotiating conflicts. But the very size of these organizations often promoted the growth of factions within them.

Nearly every country also struggled with the definition of national community and whether some groups—ethnic minorities, foreigners, Catholics, Jews, anarchists, or socialists—should be excluded as alien or of uncertain loyalty. The way each society responded to this challenge became an important test of its political system.

France: The Third Republic

In France political conflict revolved around the form of government following the fall of the Second Empire.

Monarchy or Republic   Shortly after Louis Napoleon surrendered in the Franco-Prussian War of 1870, Parisian crowds cheered the proclamation of a republic, and new leaders sought to mobilize the nation as an earlier republic had done in 1792. German forces quickly surrounded Paris, but French forces, strengthened by newly recruited peasants, still made some gains until, overmatched, they were pushed back in December.

Paris remained under German siege. Refusing to surrender, its citizens held out for four months. They cut down the trees of the boulevards for fuel, slaughtered pets, and emptied the zoo as a starving city continued to resist during a winter as severe as any on record. But heroism and patriotic fervor could not defeat a modern army, and at the end of January Paris capitulated.

France's newly elected assembly met at Versailles and quickly accepted peace on German terms. The assembly, divided between monarchists and republicans, could not agree, however, on the form of government. It compromised by naming Adolphe Thiers, a moderate politician who had been prominent in the July Monarchy thirty years earlier, as chief of the "Executive Power," thereby postponing the issue of whether France was to have a king or a president.

The Paris Commune   Thiers knew that his government must establish control of Paris, which had been cut off from the rest of France. As a first step, he decided to disarm the city's National Guard. When troops from Versailles tried to remove some cannons, however, they were confronted by an angry crowd. Shots were fired; by day's end, two generals lay dead. Faced with insurrection, Thiers withdrew his army, determined first to isolate the revolution and then to crush it. The municipal council of Paris, in another echo of the French Revolution of 1789, declared the city a self-governing commune and prepared to fight. The Paris Commune included moderate and radical republicans, militant socialists, and a few members of the Marxist First International. Its program, favoring democracy and federalism, was not very specific on other matters, and it had little time to experiment.

Scenes of the Paris Commune and the destruction that resulted were in great demand afterward. One dramatic moment was the execution of Generals Clément-Thomas and Lecomte by the communards on March 18, 1871. That scene was reconstructed a few months later in this composite photograph. Created for its commercial possibilities (in books and on postcards, for example), the image echoed traditional scenes of comparable historical episodes.
Roger-Viollet/Getty Images

Civil War   While German armies idly watched, the French engaged in civil war. The conservative assembly in Versailles sent its armies to assault the Paris Commune. The mutual hatred in this civil war was exacerbated by the recent anguish of siege and defeat as well as by the long-standing differences, ideological and social, between rural France and the capital. The two camps fought for competing visions of what the nation should become, and they fought with rising fury. On both sides, hostages were taken and prisoners shot. It took almost two months of bloodshed before government troops broke into the city in May.

Even then the fighting continued, barricade by barricade, into the working-class quarters, where the group commanded by the anarchist Louise Michel was among the last to fall. Among the most famous of hundreds of militant communards, she would later tell her captors, "I belong entirely to the Social Revolution." Solid citizens shuddered at revolutionary excess (and especially at the part played by women), but on the whole, the victors were more brutal. Tens of thousands of Parisians died in the streets, and summary court martials ordered execution, imprisonment, or deportation for tens of thousands more.

Throughout Europe, the Commune raised the specter of revolution. From the first, Marxists hailed it as a proletarian rising, the dawning of a new era, though Marx was indignant with the communard's lack of revolutionary daring and their respect for property and legality. Former communards became the heroes of socialist gatherings for the next generation, and to this day the cemetery where many of them were executed remains a shrine honored by socialists and communists.[5] Historians have been at great pains to show how little socialism, still less Marxism, there was in the Paris Commune (it respectfully left the Bank of Paris intact); yet myth has its historical importance, too. The Commune was indisputably a class conflict, and the rage on both sides was more significant than mere differences of program. After 1871 a proletarian revolution became a credible possibility to radical and conservative alike, and working-class movements across Europe pointed to the martyrs of the Commune as evidence of the cruelty of bourgeois rule.

The Founding of the Third Republic   Remarkably, a stable republic gradually emerged from this unpromising beginning. The administrative structure of the French state remained strong, and Thiers used it effectively. The loan needed to pay the indemnity to Germany was soon oversubscribed. As elections produced victories for moderate republicans, monarchists feared that their chance was slipping away. They ousted Thiers, put a monarchist in his place, and looked for a chance to restore the monarchy. They never found it.

The monarchists themselves were divided between the conservative supporters of the grandson of Charles X and those who favored the grandson of Louis Philippe. Meanwhile, moderate republicans continued to gain in popularity, and in 1875 the assembly passed a law declaring that "the president of the republic" should be elected by the two legislative houses. The Third Republic was thus quietly established as the government that, as Thiers put it, divided Frenchmen least.

There was a Chamber of Deputies, elected by direct universal male suffrage, and a Senate, indirectly elected by local officials. In elections the following year, republicans captured two-thirds of the seats in the Chamber and almost half those in the Senate. The presidency, which had been so strong under Thiers, was still in monarchist hands, but its authority continued to decline. That established a further precedent: The Republic would have a weak executive. Made acceptable by having crushed the Commune and by having a conservative Senate, this republic was a regime of compromise; it would last longer than any French regime since 1789.

Successive republican governments guaranteed political freedom and deferred to the middle class, while France's public institutions preserved the remarkable

---

[5] A century later a Russian sputnik proudly carried to the moon not only a Soviet flag but a red flag from the Commune of 1871.

CHRONOLOGY
Radicalism and Violent Protest in the Belle Epoque

1864–1872	First International.
1871	Paris Commune.
1887	Assassination of the prime minister of Spain.
1889	Strike of London dockworkers; formation of the Second International.
1894	Assassination of the president of France; Dreyfus affair.
1898	Assassination of the empress of Austria; left-wing riots in Milan.
1901	Assassination of the president of the United States.
1905	Russian Revolution of 1905.
1909	Left-wing riots in Barcelona.
1910–1914	Strikes in London.
1912	Social Democrats gain majority in Reichstag.

administrative continuity that had characterized them since 1800. For twenty years, from 1879 to 1899, the leading politicians were moderates who recognized unions and made elementary education in state schools compulsory but initiated few projects of public works or social welfare. Economic growth, less dramatic than in Great Britain or Germany, was also less disruptive. France found its own balance between the demand for order and the need for change.

Nevertheless, there were threats to the republic's moderate politics in the last years of the nineteenth century. In 1889, France escaped the threat of a coup d'etat by the authoritarian General Georges Boulanger, whose anti-German diatribes and speeches expressing concern for workers attracted public attention and support. Then the republic faced a scandal after companies financing a canal through Panama went bankrupt and investigations uncovered political graft. There followed a stormy campaign against republican politicians, liberal newspapers, and Jewish financiers. Only when the regime seemed close to toppling did its defenders pull together.

The Dreyfus Affair   The Third Republic's greatest trial came with the Dreyfus case. In 1894 a court-martial convicted Captain Alfred Dreyfus, a Jew and a member of the General Staff, of providing the German military attaché with secret French documents. Although the sensational press denounced Jewish treachery, the issue only became the center of public attention three years afterward, when evidence appeared implicating another officer as the guilty party.

The army's principal officers, refusing to reopen the case, spoke darkly of honor and state secrets, and the right-wing press hailed their patriotism. The controversy escalated with charges and countercharges in parliament and the press, a series of sensational trials, and huge public demonstrations. The nation was divided. The majority of Catholics, monarchists, and conservatives joined in patriotic indignation against Jews and socialists who were allegedly conspiring to sell out France and weaken a loyal army. The left—intellectuals, socialists, and republicans—came to view Dreyfus as the innocent victim of a plot against republican institutions.

Figures like the novelist Émile Zola, who was twice convicted of libel for his efforts, led in demanding a new trial. The military courts, however, were reluctant to admit past mistakes. A court-martial in 1898 instead acquitted the man who forged the principal evidence against Dreyfus, and a year later it convicted Dreyfus a second time but "with extenuating circumstances," a confusing ruling that led to a presidential pardon. The defenders of Dreyfus narrowly won the battle for public opinion,[6] yet that victory set the tone of subsequent French politics, cementing traditions of republican unity on the left and greatly reducing the political influence of the Church and monarchists.

A Stable Republic   From 1900 until World War I, government was in the hands of firm republicans who called themselves the Radical party. They purged the

---

[6] A few Dreyfusards continued collecting evidence and finally won acquittal in a civil trial in 1906. Dreyfus was then decorated and promoted to the rank of major.

At a mine entrance in the Ruhr in 1912, striking German mine workers read an official proclamation warning that the police are authorized to shoot.
Ullstein Bilderdienst

army of the most outspoken opponents of the republic and passed a law separating church and state in 1905. Yet these so-called radicals also solidified support for the republic through reform and conciliation, reaching out, for example, to small businessmen and peasant farmers, traditionally defenders of the status quo. At the same time, although the trade union movement doubled its membership during this period, frequent strikes never culminated in the revolutionary general strike so much talked about. On the eve of world war, France, prosperous and stable, appeared to have surmounted its most dangerous divisions.

Germany: The Reich

Bismarck had given Germany a constitution that established representative institutions but left power in the hands of a conservative monarchy, and throughout its history the Reich would be haunted by the question of whether this awkward system could hold together or must veer sharply toward autocracy or democracy. Until 1890 Bismarck dominated German public life with an authority few modern figures have equaled. Scornful of criticism, he made many enemies but remained untouchable until William II ascended the throne in 1888 and subsequently forced Bismarck's resignation.

The Army and the Conservative Leagues Bismarck's policies had allowed for great concentrations of political and economic power in a rapidly expanding society, one in which court, army, bureaucracy, and business were treated as semiautonomous interests. Holding the system together while balancing the demands of parliament and public opinion was a growing challenge, especially as the decline in agriculture

threatened the power base of the Junker ruling elite. Bismarck's successors tried to match his dazzling successes in foreign policy and followed him in attending to the army. Yet military appropriations were a constant, intense source of conflict between right and left, and each time the army expanded and government rhetoric grew more nationalistic, German society became increasingly divided.

Germany's conservatives had learned from Bismarck the value of appealing to the public, and they did so through the strident propaganda of political leagues—the Landlords', Peasants', Pan-German, Colonial, and Naval Leagues—organized in the 1890s. Well-financed by Prussian Junkers and some industrialists, these leagues campaigned for high tariffs, overseas empire, and the military, with attacks on socialists, Jews, and foreign enemies. As pressure groups, they won significant victories, including the naval bill of 1898, which proposed to create a fleet that could compete with Britain's. In addition to building railroads, roads, and schools, the government extended the comprehensive social welfare programs begun under Bismarck, and William II was hailed as "the Labor Emperor" for supporting social security, labor arbitration, the regulation of workers' hours, and provisions for their safety.

The Social Democrats But Bismarck's hope that such measures would weaken the socialists was not realized. The well-organized Social Democrats continued to gain in the 1890s, and they became the largest party in the Reichstag in 1912 (and the strongest socialist party in Europe) despite the distortions of the electoral system. Socialists also dominated Germany's vigorous labor unions, which had 2.5 million members by 1912, and the Social Democratic party sustained an influential subculture that had its own newspapers, libraries, and recreation centers.

In theory, at least, the Social Democrats remained firm revolutionaries, formally rejecting the revisionism of Eduard Bernstein, who in his book *Evolutionary Socialism* (1897), argued for less emphasis on economic determinism or revolution and a greater focus instead on improving working conditions and strengthening democracy. The subject of international debate, Bernstein's criticism of Marx and his alternative theory implied a less militant socialism willing to cooperate with other democratic parties, and it was an important moment in the history of socialism when Germany's powerful Social Democrats chose instead to make a rigorous Marxism their official policy.

The uncompromising stance of the left was matched in vigor and fury by conservatives. The royal court spoke openly of using the army against radicals. As the chancellor still remained responsible to the crown and not to the Reichstag, Germany's experiment with liberal institutions seemed to be coming to an end. Europe's other powers, facing economic competition from Germany, watched with anxiety as in the last years before World War I, its politicians emphasized militarism and risked imperial clashes with foreign powers to avoid facing political problems at home.

Italy: The Liberal Monarchy

Italy's liberal monarchy was committed to modernizing the nation while balancing the budget and steadily sponsoring modest reforms, but the political system in which only the well-to-do could vote and in which the government kept its parliamentary majority by means of political favors made it hard to win broad popular support.

The Crisis of the 1890s   As a hero of Italian unification and a former radical, Francesco Crispi, prime minister in the late 1880s and 1890s, tried to change that. His policies—which included anticlericalism, a trade war with France, and a disastrous imperial adventure in Ethiopia—proved divisive instead.

Domestic unrest increased both in the poverty-stricken agrarian south and in the rapidly industrializing north, where anarchist bombs, socialist demonstrations, and waves of strikes culminated in riots that reached revolutionary scale in Milan in 1898. The government restored order but at the cost of bloodshed, the suppression of scores of newspapers, and a ban on hundreds of socialist, republican, and Catholic organizations. Many conservatives argued for still firmer measures; yet the Chamber of Deputies, although frightened, refused further restriction of civil liberties, a stand supported in the elections of 1900. In Italy, as in France at the same time,

the political campaign of a revitalized right was defeated by parliament and public opinion.

Limited Liberalism   The political system acquired a broader base of support under Giovanni Giolitti, prime minister from 1903 to 1914. He acknowledged the right to strike, nationalized railroads and life insurance, sponsored public health measures, and in 1911 supported universal male suffrage. Giolitti also encouraged Catholics to enter the national politics they had boycotted since 1870. Like Crispi, he pursued imperial ambitions, waging war on the Ottomans for control of some of their Mediterranean holdings, including Tripoli in Libya. But in contrast to Crispi, whose military debacle in Ethiopia forced him from office, Giolitti's successful war earned his government fervent popular support. Although the economic problems of the south remained grave and the discontent of more and more militant workers went largely unappeased, the Italian economy, less developed than that of the great industrial powers, experienced the fastest growth rate in Europe during the decade ending in 1914. Italy appeared firmly set on a liberal, democratic course.

Russia: Defeat and Revolution

In Russia the pressures for political change were held in check for a generation by official policies that centered on a program of "Russification," meant to create a united nation. But defeat in war and the first stages of industrialization produced a revolution.

Reaction   Alexander III had become tsar in 1881 on his father's assassination, an event that he believed resulted from too much talk about further reform following the abolition of serfdom. He sought to achieve stability by using the Orthodox Church and the police to extend an official reactionary ideology through public life, and he gave nobles an increased role in regional councils, the *zemstvos*, and in rural administration. Local governors were authorized to use martial law, to restrict or ban the religions and languages of non-Russian peoples, and to persecute Jews.[7] These policies were continued with equal conviction but less energy by Tsar Nicholas II, who ascended the throne in 1894. As unrest increased in cities and in the countryside, many in the government searched for other ways of achieving the solidarity that repression had failed to create.

---

[7] One of history's famous forgeries, the *Protocols of the Elders of Zion*, was published (and written) by the Russian police in 1903. The protocols purported to be the secret minutes of a Jewish congress that revealed a conspiracy to control the world.

Umberto Boccioni
RIOT IN THE GALLERY, **1910**
Social tension in an era of prosperity: The excitement and uncertainty of a riot contrasts with the stable warmth of an elegant café.
Pinacoteca di Brera, Milan, Italy. Scala/Art Resource, NY

The Russo-Japanese War   War, and the patriotism it evokes, was thus welcomed in 1904, when Japan suddenly attacked the Russians at Port Arthur on the Yellow Sea. Russia had leased Port Arthur from China in 1898 as part of its expansion into East Asia and Manchuria. For years these moves had troubled the Japanese, and Russia had neither kept its promises to withdraw nor acknowledged Japan's proposals for establishing mutually acceptable spheres of influence. The war was a disaster for Russia. Surprise attack was followed by defeats in Manchuria, the fall of Port Arthur, and then the annihilation of a large Russian fleet. In the peace treaty, Russia ceded most of its recent gains and recognized Japanese interest in Korea.

The Revolution of 1905   So dramatic a defeat increased pressure for major reforms deep within Russian society. Peasant agitation had been on the rise since a terrible famine in 1891. Secret organizations were growing among the non-Russian nationalities, and workers drawn to St. Petersburg and Moscow by industrialization had begun to form unions. The Social Revolutionaries, a party combining the traditions of populism and terrorism, grew more active; the Marxist Social Democrats organized in exile and strengthened their ties within Russia.

In this atmosphere liberal members of the *zemstvos* held a national congress in 1904, though forbidden to by the government, and insisted on civil liberties. Then in January 1905 striking workers in St. Petersburg marched on the Winter Palace to petition the tsar for a national constitution and the recognition of labor unions. The workers carried religious icons and sang "God save the tsar," but the army opened fire, killing scores and wounding hundreds more.

"Bloody Sunday" led to agitation so widespread that in March the tsar promised to call an assembly of notables and announced immediate reforms: religious toleration, reduced restrictions on Jews and non-Russian nationals, and cancellation of part of the payments peasants owed for their land. Agitation for a constitution only grew stronger, expressed through urban strikes, peasant riots, and mutinies in both the army and navy. In August the tsar conceded more, declaring he would consult a national assembly, the Imperial Duma. A dissatisfied public responded with a wave of strikes.

On Bloody Sunday in January 1905, protesters, led by a priest and carrying a petition to the tsar, marched on the Winter Palace, where they were fired on by Russian soldiers. That bloodshed, following rising demands for a representative assembly, marked the beginning of the Revolution of 1905.
Sovfoto

A Russian Constitution   For the last ten days of October, Russia's economic life came to a halt in the most effective general strike Europe had ever seen. It won from the tsar the **October Manifesto,** which granted a constitution. Crowds danced in the streets, but proponents of change were divided. Those willing to work with this constitution, which guaranteed freedom of speech and assembly but was vague on much else, became known as Octobrists. Liberals who insisted on a constituent assembly and broader guarantees formed the Constitutional Democratic party, called Cadets for short. Further to the left, socialists and revolutionaries rejected compromise, and the St. Petersburg Soviet, a committee of trade union leaders and socialists, called another general strike. It was only partially successful, and an emboldened government arrested the leaders of the Soviet in December and bloodily defeated the Moscow workers who revolted in protest.

The Fundamental Laws, announced in May 1906, defined the limitations of the tsar's concessions. He would keep the power of veto, the right to name his ministers, and full command of the executive, the judiciary, and the armed forces; the national legislature would have an upper house in addition to the Duma, with half its members appointed by the tsar. Elections under this new system, however, brought the Cadets a large majority, which demanded representative government. Nicholas then disbanded the legislature and held new elections, but they produced an even more radical assembly; it, too, was disbanded. Only a new electoral law favoring the propertied classes ensured conservative majorities in subsequent legislatures.

The Revolution of 1905 had nevertheless brought important changes. Russia now had parliamentary institutions and organized parties, the power of the aristocracy had been greatly reduced, and the nation was clearly set on a modern course. The prime minister from 1906 to 1911, Peter Stolypin, reformed education and administration and strove to stimulate the economy by turning away from the *mir* system of communal lands in favor of the full private ownership of land. With the aid of foreign capital, the pace of industrialization rapidly increased. While discontent remained serious and radical movements were sternly repressed, the Cadets were finding it possible to work with the new system. Liberals throughout Europe rejoiced that the giant of the East had at last begun to follow the path of Western progress.

Austria-Hungary: The Delicate Balance

The political problems of Austria-Hungary were revealed not so much in crises as in stalemate. Creation of an autonomous regime in Hungary led to conflicts with the rest of the empire, and these political and nationalist issues were exacerbated by the divergent economic interests of the empire's industrializing and agrarian regions. The conservative instincts of the imperial court, the aristocracy, and the bureaucracy stymied further reforms.

Shifting Stalemates   Ruling elites settled on a cautious prime minister, Count Eduard von Taaffe, who held office from 1879 to 1893, but his parliamentary coalition was so divided that legislative inaction was the safest course. Social change brought further disagreements. In response to workers' agitation, Taaffe proposed welfare measures but repressed socialists, antagonizing both left and right. After his fall, governments came to rely more on decree powers and support from the crown than on parliament. After universal male suffrage was introduced in 1907, the Christian Socialists and the Social Democrats became the two largest parties, although neither was acceptable to the leaders of the empire. Kept from imperial office, they competed in the city of Vienna, where the Christian Socialists gained sway by combining social programs with demagogic anti-Semitism.

Within Hungary, Magyar notables maintained their dominance over other nationalities by requiring that the Magyar language be used in government and schools, by controlling the electoral system, and by subverting the bureaucracy through corruption. In 1903, when Hungary's leaders demanded greater autonomy for their own army, they touched on an issue about which Emperor Franz Joseph I cared too much to yield. He suspended the Hungarian constitution, ruled without parliament, and frightened the Magyars into submission by threatening to subject them, a minority in their own country, to universal male suffrage. Magyars and the empire needed each other; and Magyar politics, admired in the 1840s as a model of liberal nationalism, had turned by 1906 into the defensive strategy of a threatened aristocracy.

Spain: Instability and Loss of Empire

Spain developed a remarkable tradition of parliamentarism in which governments were careful to keep the support of the army, the Church, big business, and regional interests. By emphasizing the economy, a liberal coalition held power from 1854 to 1863, years in which Spain experienced on a smaller scale the waves of speculation, railroad building, economic growth, and ostentation associated with the Second Empire in France.

Revolution and Restoration This growth brought new demands that old alliances, palace intrigue, and electoral manipulation could not check. Rising discontent led in 1868 to the flight of the unpopular Queen Isabella II and to revolution. The leaders of the revolution were political moderates who quickly agreed on a constitutional monarchy with universal male suffrage, trial by jury, and freedom of religion and the press. It proved easier to adopt a new constitution, however, than to find a new king. The Italian prince who finally did accept the throne gave it up after three years in the face of rising opposition from left and right. The subsequent republic lasted only two years before

the military installed Isabella's son on the throne as Alfonso XII.

He began his reign in 1875 with a new constitution closer to the one in effect at midcentury than to the more democratic ones that had succeeded it. In a parliamentary system based on limited suffrage, the Conservative and Liberal parties alternated in power with little change in policy, a system that by keeping the state weak masked bitter social divisions. As in Russia and Austria, industrialization exacerbated these tensions. Unable to establish a consistent policy for its colonies, the government met unrest in Cuba with alternating policies of repression and laxity. Cuban resistance became guerrilla war, and in 1898 the United States entered the conflict with an imperialist enthusiasm of its own. As a result of the Spanish-American War, Spain was forced to withdraw from Cuba and to cede Puerto Rico, Guam, and the Philippine Islands to the United States.

Those losses led to a great deal of soul searching. A group of Spanish intellectuals known as the generation of 1898 brought new vitality to Spanish public life, but neither the caution of conservatives nor the mild reforms of liberals could stem the increasing dissension in which the Church denounced the liberals while growing anarchist and socialist movements attacked the whole establishment. In 1909 these conflicts burst forth in a week of violence in Barcelona during which churches were burned and looted and private citizens were murdered. Yet the authorities soon restored order. Spain's unadmired moderate regime remained less divisive than the alternatives.

Great Britain: Edging toward Democracy

From Russia to Spain, European nations adopted parliamentary systems, and until the end of the century, Britain provided the model of how such a system was supposed to work. In Britain, Parliament gradually reduced legal inequalities, opening the civil service to those who passed competitive examinations, removing the legal disabilities of Jews, and eliminating special taxes on behalf of the Church of England. At the same time, order was maintained through respect for law, toleration, and social deference. There were serious domestic tensions, but they were attenuated by a thriving two-party system.

The Liberal and Conservative Parties The creation of modern political parties led by two brilliant leaders facilitated Britain's adaptation to change. William Gladstone was instrumental in transforming the Whigs into the Liberal party, and Benjamin Disraeli led in making the Tories into the modern Conservative party. Gladstone was a skilled parliamentary tactician sympathetic to liberal reformers and even radicals, for whom political liberalism was a moral cause. Somewhat hesitantly, he made increased suffrage a central plank, but his complicated bill was defeated in Parliament.

Instead, Disraeli persuaded his startled party to support a simpler, more generous reform, which passed in 1867. It doubled the electorate by extending the right to vote to all men who paid property taxes directly or indirectly through rent (about one adult male in three). Equally important, imperial policies and major programs of reform now became a regular part of the competition for popular favor.

Political Reforms   The enlarged electorate after the 1867 reform gave the Liberals a great victory, and for six years Gladstone's first ministry fundamentally altered the relations between government and society. State aid to elementary schools, both religious and secular, brought Britain closer to universal education. The Liberals also reformed the army and disestablished the Anglican Church of Ireland (so that an overwhelmingly Catholic population no longer paid taxes to support a Protestant church). Recognizing the festering poverty and discontent in Ireland, new laws restricted the abuses of absentee landlords and provided peasants some protection against eviction.

The Conservatives, returned to power in the elections of 1874, were more willing than the Liberals to expand the authority of the state. A public health act established a national code for housing and urban sanitation, and new measures allowed striking workers to picket, making unions more effective. These social concerns, which offered a British parallel to the policies of Bismarck and Napoleon III, became the cornerstone of the revived Conservative party.

Gladstone, in turn, adopted the principle of universal male suffrage, which became law in 1885. Men with an independent place of residence could now vote, but this one requirement excluded roughly one-third of all adult males. Gladstone's perpetual compromises, moreover, were losing their appeal. His renewed efforts on behalf of Irish peasants failed to satisfy Irish nationalists who wanted an independent parliament of their own, and when Gladstone acquiesced to Irish home rule in 1886, his party split. A group of Liberals led by Joseph Chamberlain allied with the Conservatives. A radical in domestic social policy, Chamberlain was also an ardent imperialist, a stance which would help the Conservatives stay in office for sixteen of the nineteen years between 1886 and 1905.

Rising Social Tensions   While projecting British power around the world, Conservative governments remained active at home. They extended the reforms of the civil service and, in an act of 1902, established a national education system that for the first time included secondary schooling. Yet these important changes did not address the needs of the working class, whose rising dissatisfaction was marked by the dramatic strikes of London match girls in 1888 and dockworkers the

EMMELINE PANKHURST ON WOMEN'S RIGHTS

Emmeline Pankhurst founded the Women's Social and Political Union in 1903. As the militant leader of the British suffragettes, she won headlines and eventually significant support for her cause with her disruptive tactics and powerful speeches. Her fame was international by the time she went on a speaking tour in Canada in 1912, where on January 14 she gave a long speech from which this passage is taken. Delighting her audience with stories of the resistance she had met, she focused on the right to vote but made clear that her vision of women's roles was much broader.

"There has been a great deal of talk lately of new legislation for those who are about to enter into marriage. Women should have a say as one of the contracting parties. There are the questions of divorce and of the training of children. Who knows better of these matters than do women? There are also the trades and professions which are at the present time open to women. It is only right that we should have some say in the legislation concerning us. We have heard much of the English divorce law. It is a disgrace to any civilized country. The only redeeming feature of the matter is that the bulk of men are better than the law allows. But there is the minority, and the law should be severe for them. They are as bad as the law allows them to be. If woman only had weight in politics this would be rectified soon. She will serve to call more attention to such questions of national welfare. If we are to have any divorce law at all, and that is a much-debated question, it should be a law that is equal both for man and woman. Unless women get the vote we have no guarantee that it will be so.

" . . . Men are responsible if they allow the present condition of things to continue. Women have the power to work out their own salvation. But as it is, if a woman is ruined, if a child is injured, man is responsible for it all. It is a responsibility I would not care to have, and, as things are, I would not be a man for all the world. If women fail as men have failed, then they will bear the burden with them. But since men cannot protect and shield us, let us share the duty with them, let us use our power so that woman may be a participant, not to tyrannize over man but to take a share in the responsibilities of ruling, without which there is no real representative government. What we really are interested in in this fight is the uplifting of the sex and better conditions of humanity than men can secure. In the legal home there is but the man. What we want is the combined intelligence of man and woman working for the salvation of the children of the race. This will make for the world a better time than ever before in its history. It will raise mankind to heights of which now it has little conception. We must only make this last fight for human freedom that as the class distinction disappeared so that sex distinction may pass, and then you will get better things than men can by themselves secure."

From Emmeline Pankhurst, "The Last Fight for Human Freedom," speech given in Canada in 1912, in Brian MacArthur, *Twentieth-Century Speeches*, New York: Viking, 1992.

next year. The strikes, which won public sympathy, were part of a "new unionism" that included unskilled workers in a more militant labor movement.

In 1900 a combination of union representatives and some prominent intellectuals formed the Labour party on a platform of democratic socialism. Both the Labour and Liberal parties campaigned for social programs that the Conservatives resisted, relying instead on the popular appeal of empire to keep them in power. In 1906 the Liberals won the most one-sided electoral victory since 1832. They immediately established systems of worker's compensation, old-age pensions, and urban planning. These measures—and the expanding arms race—required new revenues, and in 1909 David Lloyd George, the Chancellor of the Exchequer, proposed a "people's budget." A skilled orator who delighted in the rhetoric of class conflict, he promised to place the costs of social welfare squarely on the rich.

Constitutional Crisis An irate House of Lords rejected Lloyd George's budget, an unprecedented act that forced a constitutional crisis and new elections. The king's threat to appoint hundreds of additional peers finally forced the upper house to accept not only the hated budget but also a major change in the constitution. By law, the Lords could no longer veto money bills or any measure that passed the Commons in three successive sessions.

The peers' intemperate outburst, which cost them so much, was part of a general rise in social tension. From 1910 to 1914 strikes increased in frequency, size, and violence; a general strike became a real and much-talked-of threat. Women campaigning for the right to vote interrupted public meetings, invaded Parliament itself, smashed windows, and planted bombs. Arrested, they went on hunger strikes until baffled statesmen ordered their release. As the movement gained strength, recruiting women (and some men) from every social class, its outraged attack on smug male assumptions reinforced the rising challenge to a whole social order (see "Emmeline Pankhurst on Women's Rights," p. 768).

Nor was the threat of violence limited to the left. In 1914 the Commons for the third time passed a bill granting Irish home rule, which made it immune to a veto in the House of Lords. The Protestants of northern Ireland openly threatened civil war. Squads began drilling, and the British officer corps seemed ready to mutiny rather than fight to impose home rule on Protestant loyalists.

Only the outbreak of world war generated the national unity that neither imperialism nor social reform had been able to achieve.

Summary

In the period from 1870 to 1914 every European nation faced major political crises; yet as political systems worked to diminish class conflict and balance clashing interests, the trend toward greater democracy and large-scale organization seemed undeniable. There were fewer major upheavals, save in backward Russia, and no European war, facts that contemporaries often cited as proof of progress. In most countries there was greater freedom of expression, more political participation, more leisure, increased literacy and education, and better health care than in the past. In general, productivity and prosperity, already at levels never achieved before, continued to rise. Science and technology promised still greater wonders. Even in retrospect, the level of creativity in the arts and scholarship and the growth of knowledge and professional standards in every field remain impressive.

Yet the civilization that achieved all this was bitterly denounced not only for its manifest injustices, which stood out in contrast to its achievements, but more fundamentally for its lack of coherent values, for its materialism, for the ugliness of industrial society, and for the privileged position of a middle class portrayed as self-serving and philistine. Perhaps European society was evolving toward solutions of these deficiencies, as many believed. Or maybe the positive trends were less significant than the effects of imperialism, domestic social conflict, and the arms race. In 1914 the very compromises that had held society together and kept the peace exploded—not in revolution, but in total war.

QUESTIONS FOR FURTHER THOUGHT

1. How did the second industrial revolution differ from previous examples of economic growth? Was its social impact equally unprecedented?
2. In what respects did discoveries in the natural sciences influence developments in the social sciences?
3. In what ways did the nineteenth-century women's movement reflect economic and social change?
4. How could an era widely proclaimed as an age of progress produce such powerful and diverse criticism?

RECOMMENDED READING

Sources

*Dangerfield, George. *The Strange Death of Liberal England.* 1935. Skillfully crafted, contentious account of a society in crisis that has influenced subsequent interpretations of the period.

*Hélias, Pierre-Jackez. *The Horse of Pride: Life in a Breton Village.* June Guicharnaud (tr.). 1980. A compelling memoir of a preindustrial society about to be transformed at the turn of the century.

Snyder, Louis L. *The Dreyfus Case: A Documentary History.* 1973. These well-edited documents convey the passions that this famous affair stirred and the broad implications that all sides saw in it.

Weintraub, Stanley. *The Yellow Book: Quintessence of the Nineties.* 1964. The stories and articles in this collection are all taken from the most daring literary quarterly of the day; nearly every piece is an exercise in the rejection of Victorian properties and, in that respect, characteristic of the new movements in the arts.

Studies

Abrams, Lynn. *The Making of Modern Woman: Europe 1789–1918.* 2002. Provides a thorough and wide-ranging examination of both the changing role of women throughout the nineteenth century and the extensive historiography on this subject.

Agulhon, Maurice. *The French Republic 1879–1992.* Antonia Nevill (tr.). 1993. The first part of this comprehensive history of France discusses the Third Republic, with special emphasis paid to political developments.

*Avineri, Shlomo. *The Social and Political Thought of Karl Marx.* 1971. There are dozens of excellent introductions to Marx's thought; this one stands out for its clarity and freshness.

Berghahn, Volker R. *Germany, 1871–1914: Economy, Society, Culture, and Politics.* 1993. A thematic survey unusual in its breadth, particularly attentive to public culture and social structure.

Berlanstein, Lenard R. *The Working People of Paris, 1871–1914.* 1984. Looks at the important changes in the lives of wage earners, in the nature of work, and in the workplace, as well as their impact on working-class movements.

Bowler, P. *Evolution: The History of an Idea.* 1989. Combining recent work in the history of science with more general intellectual history, this book traces the various conceptions of evolution in different fields.

Canning, Kathleen. *Languages of Labor and Gender: Female Factory Work in Germany, 1850–1914.* 1996. Connects social changes in the nature of work to changes in women's lives and to the shifting discourse on gender.

Derfler, Leslie. *Socialism since Marx: A Century of the European Left.* 1973. Thoughtful discussion of the movements that stemmed from Marx, showing their variety, creativity, and contradictions.

Evans, Richard J. (ed.). *Society and Politics in Wilhelmine Germany.* 1979. An important collection of essays applying the "history from below" approach to the study of German history and society.

*Gullickson, Gay L. *Unruly Women of Paris: Images of the Commune.* 1997. A richly illustrated study of the newspaper accounts of the role of women in the Commune.

Hughes, H. Stuart. *Consciousness and Society: The Reorientation of European Social Thought, 1890–1930.* 1958. A gracefully written and indispensable analysis of the currents of modern thought in this time of transition from midcentury certitudes.

Johnson, Douglas. *France and the Dreyfus Affair.* 1966. A cogent account of the affair that explains its extraordinary impact.

*Joll, James. *The Second International, 1889–1914.* 1966. A general history of the socialist movement in this period, with striking portraits of the major figures.

Kaplan, Marion. *The Making of the Jewish Middle Class: Women, Family, and Identity in Imperial Germany.* 1991. An engaging analysis of the position and priorities of Jewish women in late-nineteenth-century Germany.

Kennedy, Paul. *The Rise of the Anglo-German Antagonism, 1860–1914.* 1980. This massive study of international relations includes economic and political rivalry as well as imperialism in accounting for the rising tension between the two nations.

Kocka, Jürgen, and Allan Mitchell (eds.). *Bourgeois Society in Nineteenth-Century Europe.* 1993. A collection of essays examining and comparing the rise of the middle class in Britain, France, Germany, and Italy.

Lidtke, Vernon. *The Alternative Culture: Socialist Labor in Imperial Germany.* 1985. A significant analysis of how German socialists created Europe's best-organized working-class subculture.

*Löwith, Karl. *From Hegel to Nietzsche: The Revolution in Nineteenth-Century Thought.* 1964. A sober essay on the pessimistic and irrationalist transformations in modern thought and the powerful insights that resulted.

McLellan, David. *Karl Marx: His Life and Thought.* 1977. Considers the more youthful writings as well as *Das Kapital,* bringing out their essential unity.

Milward, Alan S., and S. B. Saul. *The Development of the Economies of Continental Europe, 1850–1914.* 1977. A study of the second great wave of industrialization, which underscores the difference between this later continental experience and the earlier English one.

Moses, Claire. *French Feminism in the Nineteenth Century.* 1984. Reveals the vigor of a feminist movement quite different from its British and German counterparts.

*Mosse, George L. *The Crisis of German Ideology.* 1964. Looks for the currents of Nazi ideology in the views of nation and race embodied in the popular ideas and movements of the late nineteenth century.

Nord, Philip. *Paris Shopkeepers and the Politics of Resentment.* 1986. Explores the antimodern militancy of lower-middle-class shopkeepers seen in response to the rise of mass-produced goods and the prominence of the department store.

Paret, Peter. *The Berlin Secession: Modernism and Its Enemies in Imperial Germany.* 1980. Examines the Berlin Secessionist movement, which was a major cultural force in German politics and culture between 1898 and 1918.

Pick, Daniel. *Faces of Degeneration: A European Disorder, c. 1848–1918.* 1989. Comparative study of the cultural preoccupation with "degeneration" in Great Britain, Italy, and France in the decades before the First World War.

Ralston, David B. *The Army of the Republic, 1871–1914.* 1967. Treats the role of the military in France both before and after the Dreyfus affair.

Reddy, William M. *Money and Liberty in Modern Europe: A Critique of Historical Understanding.* 1987. A critical look at the social impact of the expansion of capitalism in England, France, and Germany, probing the nature of the inequality that resulted.

Schivelbusch, Wolfgang. *The Railway Journey: The Industrialization of Time and Space in the 19th Century.* 1986. Explores the psychological and technological impact of the introduction and expansion of rail travel throughout later nineteenth-century Europe.

*Schorske, Carl E. *Fin-de-Siècle Vienna: Politics and Culture.* 1980. Sensitive and imaginative assessment of one of the important moments in European cultural history.

Seton-Watson, Christopher. *Italy from Liberalism to Fascism.* 1967. A general political account of Italy in its first period of rapid industrialization.

Sheehan, James J. *German Liberalism in the Nineteenth Century.* 1978. A detailed assessment of a much disputed and critical issue, the place of liberalism in German intellectual and political life.

Showalter, Elaine. *Sexual Anarchy: Gender and Culture at the Fin de Siècle.* 1990. Analyzes the myths and images of sexual crisis that were dominant in both Europe and the United States at this time.

Smith, Helmut Walser, *The Butcher's Tale: Murder and Anti-Semitism in a German Town.* 2002. Engaging analysis of an unsolved murder, committed in 1900 in the easternmost part of the German empire, that testifies to both the strength and irrationality of European anti-Semitism at the turn of the century.

*Weber, Eugen. *Peasants into Frenchmen: The Modernization of Rural France, 1880–1914.* 1976. A provocative treatment stressing how resistance in rural France to pressures for change delayed modernization efforts.

*Available in paperback.

Thomas Jones Barker
THE SECRET OF ENGLAND'S GREATNESS, CA. 1863
Painted by Thomas Jones Barker in 1863, this painting, entitled *The Secret of England's Greatness*, epitomizes the nineteenth-century liberal conception of empire. Prince Albert and the statesmen Lord Palmerston and Lord John Russell look on as Queen Victoria gives a Bible to a kneeling African. The queen represents empire as a benevolent, paternalist force, bestowing European civilization and Christianity on the colonies. The African symbolizes the colonial subject, who embraces his subordinate position and gratefully receives these gifts.
The National Portrait Gallery, London

NINETEENTH-CENTURY EMPIRES

Since the first invasions of the Spanish conquistadors in the early sixteenth century, Europeans had amassed a vast New World empire. A flourishing plantation economy, sustained by African slave labor, formed the economic base of this world, the hub of which was the prosperous sugar colonies of the West Indies. The New World colonies served the mercantilist goal to enrich the monarchical state through the creation of advantageous trade monopolies with its colonies and found moral justification in the religious mission of saving the immortal souls of "heathens."

In the early nineteenth century, a new liberal empire supplanted this older religious-mercantilist colonial regime. Abandoning the New World, European entrepreneurs, merchants, missionaries, and explorers staked claims in Asia and Africa. European governments frequently followed in their wake, carving out spheres of influence to protect their interests and activities. Operating increasingly within the context of a market economy, nineteenth-century Europeans perceived the non-Western world as untapped markets for European manufactures and capital investment and as sources of raw materials for Europe's burgeoning industries. Steeped in the culture of the Enlightenment and principles of liberal universalism, moreover, Europeans saw empire not just as a means of benefiting themselves, but as an opportunity to bring the fruits of European civilization to the non-Western world.

In the late nineteenth century, empire's foundations shifted once more. The "new imperialism" of this period was characterized by the aggressive expansionism of competing European nation-states. In the space of a few decades, Europeans conquered and colonized virtually all of Africa and vast regions of Asia. European attitudes toward colonial subjects changed as well, shaped by anticolonial insurgence and, after Darwin, the ascendancy of biological determinism in thinking about culture and race. These developments undermined the liberal aims of the early nineteenth century, raising new doubts about both the desirability and the feasibility of Europeanizing non-European peoples. The turn of the century was thus a moment of intense contradictions: the peak moment of Europe's global power, but also one in which Europeans began to rethink the scope and future of empire.

THE BIRTH OF THE LIBERAL EMPIRE

In the nineteenth century, Europeans lost their Atlantic empires and built new ones in Asia and Africa. Although the first two-thirds of the century saw little outright colonization, Europeans steadily expanded their influence overseas. As European merchants, missionaries, explorers, and settlers penetrated different parts of the world, European governments provided them with support and, in so doing, became increasingly involved in the affairs of foreign polities. The expansionism of this period had its economic foundation in the growth of a capitalist market economy and its philosophical roots in the Enlightenment culture of liberal universalism. Europeans thus saw the acquisition of overseas spheres of influence as a way to secure new sources of raw materials and new markets for their industrial manufacturers and, equally important, as an opportunity to "civilize" the non-Western world by making it over in the European image.

The Decline of the Mercantile Colonial World

The mercantile colonial world sustained an unprecedented series of external and internal challenges during the late eighteenth and early nineteenth centuries. Outside of Europe, the threat to empire came primarily in the form of independence movements and slave revolts. Simultaneously, within Europe, the gradual rise of a market economy and the cultural revolution sparked by the Enlightenment undermined the foundations of the old empire.

External Challenges   Independence movements, starting with the American Revolution of 1776, drove European colonial powers from much of the New World at the turn of the nineteenth century. From 1804 to 1824, France lost control of Haiti (then known as Saint-Domingue); Portugal of Brazil; and Spain the rest of Latin America except for Cuba and Puerto Rico (see chapter 21). Led by landed Creole elites (American-born people of European descent), Latin American independence movements were influenced by Enlightenment thought and the examples of the French and American Revolutions.

Slave agitation constituted a central part of the assault on the mercantile colonial world. From the late eighteenth through the early nineteenth centuries, runaway slaves called *Maroons*, living in outlaw societies behind the lines of colonial settlement in South America, the Caribbean, and Spanish Florida, waged sporadic guerilla attacks against local plantations, a phenomenon known as the Maroon Wars. Simultaneously, a series of increasingly well-planned and militant slave revolts from Dutch Surinam to British Jamaica erupted in the second half of the eighteenth century, culminating in the Haitian Revolution in the French colony of Sainte-Domingue in 1791 (see "The Fight for Liberty and Equality in Saint-Domingue," p. 598).

The Antislavery Movement in Europe   A rapidly expanding European movement to end slavery further threatened the Atlantic colonial system during the late eighteenth century. Although abolitionists organized in the Netherlands and France as well, the British campaign was by far the strongest and most effective.

Religious antislavery sentiment served as the catalyst to abolitionism. In spite of the fact that most world religions had historically sanctioned slavery, by the eighteenth century newer forms of Protestantism—Quakerism among them—condemned slavery as a sin antithetical to religious tenets of brotherly love and

1898 Fashoda Crisis

1900 Boxer Rebellion in China

1859 Darwin, *On the Origin of Species*

1899–1902
Boer War in southern Africa

1904–1905
Russo-Japanese War

1869 Opening of the Suez Canal

1884–1885 Berlin Conference

1885 Indian National Congress established

1894–1895 Sino-Japanese War

1896 Ethiopian defeat of the Italians at Adowa

spiritual equality. These religious dissenters sparked the movement and established its emotive tone and ethic of benevolence, but antislavery soon spread from there to the religious mainstream, including well-connected Evangelicals, such as the parliamentary member William Wilberforce.

The Influence of the Enlightenment   Secular reformers joined forces with religious abolitionists. Although philosophers had debated the morality of slavery well before sustained Christian opposition to slavery burgeoned, most had found ways to justify slavery as a rational and efficient economic and social system. Such justifications became more difficult to make in the humanist intellectual climate of the Enlightenment. Thus, while the seventeenth-century political theorist John Locke himself condoned slavery, his ideas—in particular, his critique of arbitrary power, appeal to rule by reason, and championing of natural and universal human rights—shaped arguments mounted against slavery by Enlightenment humanists such as Baron Montesquieu and Denis Diderot a century later.

Most fundamentally, Enlightenment universalism, or belief in the basic sameness of all humans, undermined the acceptance of slavery and allowed eighteenth-century thinkers to link oppressed Africans to the disenfranchised poor of Europe. Values and principles rooted in this universalist framework, including belief in the individual's natural and inalienable right to freedom, ownership of one's self and labor, and equality before the law, also clashed deeply with the concept of human bondage. Finally, the Enlightenment's optimism and emphasis on the inner goodness and malleability of human beings made it difficult to defend slavery as a necessary evil for less "civilized" peoples. This view was perhaps best encapsulated in Rousseau's cult of the noble savage, which contrasted the natural

Illustration from a nineteenth-century British children's book of a slave being flogged. Part of the abolitionist campaign against British slavery, the image was intended to stir compassion for the slaves' suffering in young readers. The British Library, London

virtues of the so-called primitive with the moral flaws of civilized Europeans and further fostered popular sympathy for enslaved Africans. Taken together, these ideas persuaded Enlightenment thinkers across Europe to soundly reject slavery as an unreasonable, unnatural, and immoral system.

Enlightened philosophical and religious arguments also influenced a romantically oriented popular culture of feeling in the late eighteenth century. This helped make antislavery a pervasive, even fashionable, position among the European elite, especially among well-to-do women, who came to play a pivotal role in the British movement. Religious emphasis on the goodness of humans and the importance of compassion fit with a secular, sentimental worldview that cast the slave as innocent victim and the civilized European as heroic savior. Similarly, Enlightenment universalism and recognition of the decadence of European civilization fed educated European outrage against slavery as a barbaric system that not only violated the rights of slaves, but also impeded Europe's own moral progress. Popular primitivism in the wake of Rousseau also elevated the status of the African slave in the public eye, while acclaimed Romantic poets such as William Wordsworth, Percy Bysshe Shelley, and Robert Burns fashioned their own poetic attacks on tyranny and human bondage, making antislavery ever more modish. All over Western Europe, and especially in Britain, elite women and men of the late eighteenth and early nineteenth century inspired by these trends joined abolitionist circles, signed antislavery petitions, and circulated tracts and images that exposed the cruelties of human bondage.

The Free-Trade Lobby   By themselves these intellectual and cultural developments probably would not have had the force to abolish slavery. However, antislavery sentiment was strongly reinforced by merchants and industrialists seeking to replace the mercantile colonial system—and its system of protective tariffs intended to privilege trade between colony and mother country—with free trade. By the early nineteenth century, European manufacturers objected increasingly to the protective tariffs levied on foreign imports in the mercantile marketplace. These tariffs effectively prevented domestic manufacturers and consumers from buying cheaper foreign goods, compelling them instead to purchase goods exclusively from domestic producers, at home or in the colonies. British sugar refiners, for example, felt exploited by a system that forced them to buy high-priced raw sugar from Jamaica, while shielding Jamaican sugar producers from competition from French sugar producers in Sainte-Domingue and Spanish sugar producers in Cuba.

Capitalists in favor of free trade based their arguments on both theory and real-world experience. For theoretical support, they drew on critiques of **mercantilism** and the slave economy elaborated by Enlightenment classical economists such as Adam Smith and David Ricardo. Smith and Ricardo contended that the mercantile colonial economy was an inefficient, irrational system that flouted the natural law of rational utility by preventing most people from pursuing their economic self-interest. In contrast, they argued, market competition was both natural and rational because it afforded economic liberty to individuals and benefited the majority by generating lower prices all around. Smith also censured the built-in inefficiency and inflexibility of the slave economy, pointing out that slaves, unlike wage laborers, lacked the incentive to

work hard and could not be laid off in the event of an economic slump.

For those unconvinced by arguments based on utility or natural law, the rapid deterioration of Haiti and Jamaica in the closing years of the eighteenth century offered compelling evidence that the mercantile slave economy was economically retrograde. By the turn of the nineteenth century, economic troubles in the West Indies, combined with the growing wealth and influence of industrial and merchant capitalists in Europe, made the claims of the free traders more convincing.

The End of European Slavery   In the early years of the nineteenth century, the convergence of religious and humanitarian sentiment and economic support for free market competition led to the abolition of the European slave trade. Denmark outlawed the Atlantic slave trade first in 1803, followed by Britain and the United States in 1807. Although Spain, Portugal, France, and the Netherlands agreed to abolish the slave trade in 1815, they did little to eliminate it. Britain, by contrast, embarked on a zealous antislaving mission, searching ships in the Atlantic suspected of carrying slave cargo and rescuing slaves along the West African coast. They provided the latter with passage to Liberia, an African settlement created for and partly by freed American slaves in 1821. By 1850 the European slave trade had essentially ended.

Britain abolished slavery itself in 1834, emancipating the remaining 780,000 British-owned slaves in the West Indies. The British government paid £20 million to slave owners to compensate them for their loss of property. While France and Denmark followed suit in 1848, slavery continued until 1863 in the Dutch New World colonies, 1865 in the United States, 1886 in Spanish Cuba, and 1888 in Brazil. These dates often mattered more to Europeans than to freed slaves, however, who in some cases continued to be treated as slaves for several decades after emancipation.

New Sources of Colonial Legitimacy

Just as the economic, religious, and intellectual forces of the Enlightenment undermined the mercantile colonial world, they also built the new liberal empire that replaced it.

The Growth of the Market Economy   The continued growth of industrial capitalism and the market economy brought a new economic rationale to empire. Free-trade advocates in the business world became richer and more influential during the early nineteenth century. By the 1830s, their belief in the individual pursuit of profit in a free, self-regulating market as efficient, natural, and moral was considered common sense. Yet, while free market competition was the mantra of early-to-mid-nineteenth-century capitalists, economic practice sometimes contradicted imperial rhetoric. From 1830 to 1870—the peak era of economic liberalism—European nation-states competed with one another for spheres of economic influence abroad. Europeans were quick to abandon free trade, in other words, when they perceived their own economic interests to be threatened by indigenous and other European competitors.

Enlightenment Universalism   The liberal empire's philosophical underpinnings also differed fundamentally from those of early modern empire. Liberal empire had roots in Enlightenment theories of human biological and cultural sameness and belief in human improvement through the application of reason to social reform. While pre-Enlightenment Europeans had emphasized the irreconcilable, permanent gap between themselves and others, eighteenth-century philosophers from Montesquieu to Voltaire claimed the similarities between human societies to be far more significant than the differences. Likewise, although Enlightenment natural scientists like the Swede Carolus Linnaeus or the Frenchman Georges-Louis Leclerc de Buffon sought to classify the varieties of human physical types, they assumed that the "races" of man belonged to a single species. Enlightened Europeans posited that, while different societies had attained different levels of civilization, all of them occupied positions along a common developmental path. This belief meant not only that change was possible, but that the process of development could be guided and accelerated through reasoned social intervention.

Cultural Relativism   Europeans at the turn of the nineteenth century were also less firmly convinced of their own superiority and more critical about the colonial enterprise than their forebears. The universalist framework of the eighteenth century allowed for a new cultural relativism that recognized the value and achievements of other societies. Voltaire's respect for ancient Chinese and Islamic civilizations and the English historian Edward Gibbon's admiration for Islam exemplify this trend, as does the rhetoric of Christian brotherhood preached by evangelical missionaries. Similarly, cultural relativism permitted Rousseau and his followers to exalt New World societies as models of virtue and freedom for a decadent Europe. In the main, however, European cultural relativists still insisted on their own supremacy, even while acknowledging the achievements of other cultures.

These Enlightenment ideas had radical implications for the colonial project. During the sixteenth and seventeenth centuries, colonizers had concerned themselves primarily with the "heathen" nature of "savage" societies and the future of their immortal souls. Assim-

ilation to a European way of life had occurred largely as an unintended consequence of missionary efforts to impart Christian faith to New World peoples. By the turn of the nineteenth century, in contrast, universalism had humanized the colonial subject, and assimilation, rather than exclusion or outright exploitation, emerged as the dominant model for confronting the difference of the non-European. The majority of Europeans, both secular and religious, saw the assimilation of other peoples to European political, economic, and cultural models as a moral imperative and colonial domination as the ideal means to achieve this end. At the same time, a powerful new sense of instrumentality—of the ability of humans to shape the world around them—lent confidence to their civilizing endeavors.

The Case of Captain Cook   The new ideological underpinnings of the emergent liberal empire were exemplified by Captain James Cook's expeditions to the South Pacific. The prototypical colonialist of the Enlightenment, Cook's explicit goals were not merely commercial but also scientific: his voyage was part of a series of eighteenth-century expeditions to explore this region, the last maritime frontier for Europeans, and, in particular, to locate the missing continent, known as *Terra Australis*. Toward this end, a team of more than twenty ethnographers, geographers, botanists, and other scientific experts, accompanied Cook on his South Seas voyages.

Cook's voyages to the South Pacific also bore traces of Europeans' new moral scruples in their interactions with non-Europeans. Unlike earlier generations of colonizers, Cook and his contemporaries were self-conscious about the delicate nature of their enterprise and sought to justify their intrusion with the lofty goals of advancing science and spreading civilization. As universalists, they accorded rights to non-Europeans; as cultural relativists, they ascribed value to cultural difference. In practical terms, this meant that King George III authorized Cook to establish British authority in Hawaii in 1779, for example, but cautioned him to do so only with the express consent of the natives; similarly, the Royal Scientific Society, one of the chief backers of the voyage, instructed Cook to treat the local customs and culture with the utmost respect. In ways such as these, late-eighteenth-century colonizers sought not only to legitimize their role as civilizers in the eyes of the colonized but to reinforce their own identities as the civilized by divorcing themselves from the brutality of their imperial precursors.

The Civilizing Mission in India   In the early nineteenth century, India was the laboratory in which Britain conducted its most ambitious civilizing experiments. While evangelical missionaries such as Charles Grant

Johann Zoffany
THE DEATH OF CAPTAIN JAMES COOK, 1779
Zoffany's painting depicts the prototypical explorer-scientist of the Enlightenment, Captain James Cook (lying on the ground in the center of the image), and his men being attacked by angry, armed Hawaiians in Kealakekua Bay in 1779. Cook was killed in the fracas. His death helped call into question the popular myth of the noble savage, marking a turning point in European views of "primitive" people.
National Maritime Museum, Greenwich, London

Thomas Rowlands
THE BURNING SYSTEM, 1815
This engraving shows an Indian woman committing sati, or burning herself on the funeral pyre of her dead husband. On one side are native musicians. On the other, Englishmen debate the pros and cons of abolishing sati, the practice of which was considered a sign of India's backwardness.
The British Library, London

and William Wilberforce sought to bring religious enlightenment and to stamp out Indian "superstition," secular liberal reformers like Jeremy Bentham, James Mill, his son, John Stuart Mill, and Thomas Macaulay determined to rid India of "Oriental despotism" by eradicating "barbaric" Indian laws and customs and introducing a British-style educational system (see "Macaulay's Minute on Indian Education," p. 779). Macaulay claimed that the "entire native literature of India and Arabia" was not worth "a single shelf of a good European library," asserting that a British model of education was

needed to produce "a class of persons Indian in blood and color, but English in taste, in opinions, in morals and intellect." The potent triad of law, education, and free trade, British reformers believed, would bring the hopelessly backward Indians into the modern world.

Liberal reformers sought to apply liberal ideas to eliminate the barriers of custom and tradition and managed to bring about several important policy changes in India. One of the controversial reforms was to prohibit *sati*, the practice of the widow burning herself to death on the funeral pyre of her dead husband.

MACAULAY'S MINUTE ON INDIAN EDUCATION

Thomas Macaulay (1800–1859) was the Law Member of the Governor General's Council and an important example of the British liberal voice in India. He believed that "backward" societies like India's could be transformed through the introduction of law, free trade, and education. In the early part of the nineteenth century, Orientalist scholars and administrators felt that India should be ruled through its own laws and through indigenous institutions and languages. British liberals like Macaulay thought otherwise. In 1835 a major debate took place as to what kind of education the British should promote and finance. Macaulay argued that Indians should be taught Western subjects and the English language instead of Arabic and Sanskrit. This was seen as imperative to disseminate moral values as well as maintain and strengthen British rule in India. On Macaulay's advice, English was made the medium of education in secondary schools established in major cities across India.

"How, then, stands the case? We have to educate a people who cannot at present be educated by means of their mother-tongue. We must teach them some foreign language. The claims of our own language it is hardly necessary to recapitulate. It stands pre-eminent even among the languages of the west. It abounds with works of imagination not inferior to the noblest which Greece has bequeathed to us; with models of every species of eloquence; with historical compositions, which, considered merely as narratives, have seldom been surpassed, and which, considered as vehicles of ethical and political instruction, have never been equalled; with just and lively representations of human life and human nature; with the most profound speculations on metaphysics, morals, government, jurisprudence, and trade; with full and correct information respecting every experimental science which tends to preserve the health, to increase the comfort, or to expand the intellect of man. Whoever knows that language has ready access to all the vast intellectual wealth, which all the wisest nations of the earth have created and hoarded in the course of ninety generations. It may safely be said, that the literature now extant in that language is of far greater value than all the literature which three hundred years ago was extant in all the languages of the world together. Nor is this all. In India, English is the language spoken by the ruling class. It is spoken by the higher class of natives at the seats of Government. It is likely to become the language of commerce throughout the seas of the East. It is the language of two great European communities which are rising, the one in the south of Africa, the other in Australasia; communities which are every year becoming more important, and more closely connected with our Indian empire. Whether we look at the intrinsic value of our literature, or at the particular situation of this country, we shall see the strongest reason to think that, of all foreign tongues, the English tongue is, that which would be the most useful to our native subjects. . . .

"To sum up what I have said, I think it clear that we are not fettered by the Act of Parliament of 1813; that we are not fettered by any pledge expressed or implied; that we are free to employ our funds as we choose; that we ought to employ them in teaching what is best worth knowing; that English is better worth knowing than Sanscrit or Arabic; that the natives are desirous to be taught English, and are not desirous to be taught Sanscrit or Arabic; that neither as the languages of law, nor as the languages of religion, have the Sanscrit and Arabic any peculiar claim to our engagement; that it is possible to make natives of this country thoroughly good English scholars, and that to this end our efforts ought to be directed.

"In one point I fully agree with the gentlemen to whose general views I am opposed. I feel with them, that it is impossible for us, with our limited means, to attempt to educate the body of the people. We must at present do our best to form a class who may be interpreters between us and the millions whom we govern; a class of persons, Indian in blood and colour, but English in taste, in opinions, in morals, and in intellect. To that class we may leave it to refine the vernacular dialects of the country, to enrich those dialects with terms of science borrowed from the Western nomenclature, and to render them by degrees fit vehicles for conveying knowledge to the great mass of the population."

G. M. Young (ed.), *Speeches by Lord Macauley with His Minute on Indian Education*, Oxford University Press, 1935.

For the British, *sati* epitomized both the moral weakness of Indian men, who degraded rather than protected their women, and the general backwardness of Indian civilization as a whole. Although *sati* became a key public symbol of the liberal reform agenda, it was not, in fact, a widespread practice, but was actually limited only to certain groups of upper-caste Hindus.

British civilizing efforts came to an abrupt halt, however, with the Indian Rebellion of 1857 (see "The Indian Rebellion of 1857," pp. 800–802). Hereafter, British officials ceded issues of Indian reform to Indian social reformers, since they saw their interference in Indian religion and ritual as one of the key causes of the discontent that had sparked the rebellion.

EUROPEAN EXPANSION IN THE MIDCENTURY

During the first two-thirds of the nineteenth century, European commercial involvements in Africa and Asia intensified, and Europeans acted to protect their economic interests in new, more assertive ways. This intensification was driven primarily by industrialization in Britain and, with that, the rise of British economic, military, and technological might. Although other Western European nations behaved similarly, it was the British who took the initiative in aggressively developing and safeguarding overseas commercial contacts during this period.

India and the Rise of British Sovereignty

The economic penetration of Asia in the nineteenth century exploited commercial ties between Europe and the East cultivated over the course of several centuries. From the seventeenth century on, joint stock companies—the Dutch, the French, and the English East India companies—were the chief players in a European-Asian trade based on the exchange of Asian spices, silks, and other luxury goods for European specie. By the early eighteenth century, Europeans, including the representatives of the East India Companies, clustered in what were known as "factories"—trading posts—along the coasts from India to Java, the Philippines, and China, in ports such as Bombay, Batavia, and Canton. Although traders and trading companies of several nationalities could be found in any of these locations, different nations dominated the Asian trade in periods. The Portuguese were leaders in the sixteenth- and seventeenth-century trade with Asia, superseded by the Dutch in the late seventeenth century and by the French and British in the early eighteenth century.

The British East India Company   Until the middle of the eighteenth century, nothing distinguished the British East India Company from the other companies in Asia. This state of affairs changed dramatically in 1757, when the decisive victory over the nawab of Bengal in the Battle of Plassey catapulted the British to ascendancy in Asia and, indeed, the world (see Chapter 18). Plassey's significance was both economic and symbolic: it dealt a crushing blow to the already weak Mughal Empire, fortified the British East India Company as a political power within the subcontinent, and gave Britain access to enormous Indian wealth. The capture of Bengal thus gave the British East India Company a firm base for territorial expansion in India over the course of the next century.

The conquest brought economic disaster to Bengal, until then a flourishing center of Indian commerce and industry (and the source of 75 percent of the British East India Company's trade). Before 1757, the British had paid for Bengali textiles, metal goods, and spices in silver bullion from the New World. With the conquest secured, the British used Bengali land revenues to pay for Bengali goods and assumed direct control of Bengal's external trade. As the British expanded out of Bengal, this same pattern repeated itself all over India. The British conquest thus transformed the Indian economy into a closed system, forcing India through taxation to effectively give away its exports to Britain and severing its independent trade connections with the outside world.

British rule in India also irrevocably altered the structure and orientation of the Indian economy. As it industrialized at the turn of nineteenth century, Britain stopped importing Indian calicoes and other textiles, transforming India into a supplier of raw materials (especially cotton and indigo) for British textile mills as well as a major market for British manufactures. As a consequence, Indian manufacturing went into decline, with British imports accounting for more than half of India's textile consumption by the 1840s. In addition, the commercialization of Indian agriculture led to the abandonment of subsistence farming, leaving the Indian peasantry more vulnerable than ever to famine.

Further British Expansion in Asia   The British East India Company's conquest of India also promoted British expansionism elsewhere in central Asia, as the company sought to extend its power and influence in neighboring territories to protect its Indian empire. Their chief adversary was Russia, which harbored imperial ambitions in the region. In the 1840s Britain annexed Punjab and Sind, to the west of India, as buffer zones against the Russians. When the British tried to do the same to Afghanistan, they met with stubborn resistance in the Afghan Wars of 1839–1842 and 1878–1880. Although the British never formally colonized Afghanistan, it became, for all practical purposes, a client state by the 1880s. Simultaneously, the fiercely independent kingdom of Burma (Myanmar) harassed the British on the northeastern frontier of the Indian Empire. After a series of Anglo-Burmese wars fought in 1826, 1852, and 1886, the British annexed Burma.

The "Sick Men": The Ottoman Empire and China

While the British tightened their territorial stranglehold over Mughal India, Europeans took a fundamentally different approach to the other two major non-Western empires, that of the Ottomans and Qing China. Labeled respectively the "Sick Man of Europe" and the "Sick Man of the East," the Ottoman Empire and Qing China were perceived as ailing polities. But in contrast to the military conquest and direct rule of Mughal India, Europeans exploited the Chinese and Ottoman empires through financial subjugation and political maneuvering. This strategy avoided the costs of direct rule, which promised to be especially high since the Qing and the Ottomans were relatively successful at holding their empires together. It also allowed Europeans to use the empires as buffers against Russian and Japanese expansionism.

The Ottoman Empire   The Ottoman Empire was ripe for this kind of infiltration by the nineteenth century. The empire was still vast, stretching from Algeria in the west to the borders of Persia and Arabia in the east and from the Balkans in the north to Egypt and Sudan in the south, but its power had declined sharply from its peak point in the sixteenth century. While the predominantly Muslim identity of Ottoman subjects gave the empire some political and cultural cohesion, the ambitions of provincial governors were challenging the authority of the Sultan, Mahmud II.

Hoping to rejuvenate the empire, the sultan himself attempted to initiate a program of administrative, legal, and technological Westernization known as the *Tanzimat* (reorganization) reforms in the 1830s. Although he faced strong resistance to his efforts on the part of the Muslim military and clerics who feared the pollution of Islamic culture by the West, the European powers, especially the British, supported his efforts for their own diplomatic and political reasons. This support turned into Ottoman dependency on Britain in 1838, when the sultan asked the British to intervene militarily to restore Ottoman control in Syria, which had been seized by the breakaway Ottoman province of Egypt in 1831. In return for military assistance, the British and French demanded the full implementation of Tanzimat, along with trade privileges and extraterritorial judicial rights for themselves.

By the early 1840s, the sultan's efforts to check the burgeoning power of the Europeans faltered and the Ottoman Empire became a de facto economic colony of the British, forced to export raw materials (cotton, cereals, opium) to Britain and to import British manufactures (textiles, machinery) in large quantities. These new arrangements dealt a near-fatal blow to local Ottoman handicraft industries, especially textile production. Economic dependence turned into subjugation during the Crimean War (1852–1854) (see chapter 24), when the Ottoman government borrowed money on extremely unfavorable terms from the French and the British to subsidize its military mobilization. The formation of the Ottoman Public Debt Commission in 1881 formalized British and French control of the bankrupt Ottoman economy, including taxation, tariffs, and the provincial tribute system.

European financial involvement was not without social and cultural repercussions. The once culturally cohesive Ottoman Empire fragmented across ethnic and religious lines as the British and the French sought to align themselves with non-Muslim Ottoman minorities. Local Christian and Jewish intermediaries who facilitated the economic transactions of British and French merchants were permitted to buy European passports, which qualified them for the same judicial immunity granted to Europeans. Economic considerations only partially motivated the Europeans, who also saw themselves as the civilizers of a degenerate "Oriental" empire, shoring up Christianity and rooting out all traces of "despotism." Overall, internal discord within the empire grew as privileged groups profited from a European presence that brought extensive suffering to peasants and artisans.

China   The narrative of imperial domination was roughly similar in China. At the turn of the nineteenth century, the ruling Qing Dynasty, members of the foreign Manchu minority who had ruled China since the mid-seventeenth century, enjoyed considerable economic prosperity and sought to extend the boundaries of the empire in Asia. However, they remained resolutely isolated from and indifferent to Europe. Not only did the Chinese remain unaware of the culture of Enlightenment influencing elites in Europe, North America, and South America, but they also exhibited no interest in European manufactures. By contrast, Europeans long had been eager consumers of Chinese tea, silk, porcelain, and paper, among other goods.

This imbalance was dramatically reversed in the late eighteenth century, when opium smoking became an entrenched practice at all levels of Chinese society. Despite an official ban on opium imports, the Chinese demand for opium skyrocketed as the British East India Company, followed by other European merchants, flooded the Chinese market with cheap Indian-produced opium, which they used to pay for Chinese goods, especially tea. By the turn of the nineteenth century, this situation had wreaked economic and social havoc. Not only did the Chinese experience huge silver shortages as Europeans stopped paying for Chinese imports with metal specie, but opium addiction was debilitating large segments of Chinese society. In 1840, when the emperor tried to gain control of the situation by blockading the port of Canton and seizing the opium supplies of foreign merchants, the British sent a naval force to defy him. The Opium War of 1840–1842 ended in Chinese defeat. The Treaty of Nanjing ceded Hong Kong to Britain, gave the British trading rights in five ports, and forced the Chinese to pay an indemnity for the war. A second Opium War (1856–1858), fought over the same issues, also ended in Chinese defeat and

In this American newspaper cartoon of 1864, England, personified by John Bull, forces China to accept opium at gunpoint. The Opium Wars, which erupted when the Chinese attempted to restrict the opium trade in the mid-century, ended in Chinese defeat and in treaties conferring extraordinary economic and legal privileges on the European victors. How did European encroachment in China differ from the European penetration of Africa?

The Granger Collection, NY

the ceding of extraterritorial rights, trading privileges, and missionary protection to Britain, France, the United States, and Russia. When the Qing emperor refused to ratify the peace treaties, British and French forces occupied Peking in 1860 and burned the emperor's imperial gardens at the Summer Palace, while Russia obtained Vladivostock.

Fomented by the economic hardships and political humiliation brought by the Opium War, the bloody Taiping Rebellion of 1850–1864 further destabilized Chinese politics and society. A millenarian peasant movement to overthrow the European-dominated Qing regime and establish a harmonious, egalitarian society, the rebellion ravaged the Chinese countryside, with a staggering death toll of twenty million. In the mid-1850s, the European powers intervened militarily in the conflict, acting to safeguard their trading privileges. By 1864, the Western-trained "Ever-Victorious Army," under the leadership of General Charles "Chinese" Gordon, definitively quashed the rebellion, although sporadic resistance continued in parts of the country until 1868. The European role in rescuing the floundering Qing Dynasty greatly strengthened European commercial interests in China.

Although the British constructed an economically exploitative relationship with China during the nineteenth

century, they never formally colonized it (except for Hong Kong). Moreover, since European traders remained clustered in port cites, foreigners did not penetrate Chinese society to the extent that they did elsewhere. Even so, British-Chinese relations had deeply colonial overtones. From the British point of view, China's economic subjugation was part of a larger plan to make empire self-financing. India was at the center of this system, both as a model of economic exploitation and as a source of cheaply obtained goods that the British used to trade with others. By the turn of the nineteenth century, the British had incorporated the Chinese into this arrangement; since the British bought opium at a mere pittance from Indian producers, they effectively forced India to finance Britain's trade with China. Like India, China lost access to the silver bullion that the British formerly had used to buy its goods, but China also squandered its metal reserves to sustain its debilitating opium habit. In both cases, overtaxed peasants bore the brunt of lost government revenues, fomenting political unrest in the countryside.

Expansion in Southeast Asia and the Pacific Rim

European engagement in India and China led to further expansion in Southeast Asia. In Australia and New Zealand, Europeans established settler colonies in this period, while in Japan, their attempts to exert influence met with failure for the first time.

Southeast Asia   To safeguard the critical trade route between India and China, the British East India Company sought to establish fortified settlements in Southeast Asia from the 1780s on. They seized the opportunity to consolidate their position when the Dutch—the most important European power in the area—asked the British to oversee their Southeast Asian holdings during the French revolutionary occupation of the Netherlands starting in 1795. Although the Dutch resumed control of these holdings in 1808, the episode provided the British with additional territory and whetted their appetite for greater involvement in the region. By the 1820s, they had emerged as the preeminent European commercial presence in Southeast Asia, in possession of the valuable ports of Penang, Malacca, and Singapore (known collectively as the Straits Settlements).

This flourishing British-dominated trade economy, however, soon came to an abrupt halt. With the passage of the Charter Act of 1833, the British East India Company lost its monopoly of the China trade and the company's interest in the India-China trade route waned sharply. While the British no longer valued Southeast Asia as a trade depot, they did develop an interest in the region as a source of raw materials, investing in tin mining and rubber production. In this way, Southeast Asia entered into the classic colonial economic arrangement, producing raw materials for industrial production in Europe.

Meanwhile, kingdoms and chiefdoms outside of the British sphere of interest were also being gradually drawn into the European orbit. Even Siam (Thailand), often touted as the exception to the rule, ultimately lost its political and cultural sovereignty, if not its formal political independence, to the British. The process began in the 1820s and 1830s, when the Siamese monarch abandoned a century-long isolationist policy and resumed relations with Europe, negotiating trade treaties and relinquishing some of Siam's border territories in the interests of maintaining the kingdom's political independence. While he managed to fend off direct conquest, he did so in part by launching an ambitious program of Westernization, including the implementation of a European-style educational system and the appointment of foreign advisors to the government. While the fiction of independence was maintained, Siamese policy decisions were essentially dictated by foreign advisors or made within the context of the competing European interests in the region. Following a pattern emerging in many parts of the world, the Siamese king's decision to modernize along Western lines constituted a form of implicit colonization.

The Pacific Rim   There were a few notable exceptions to the European pattern of implicit colonization in the Pacific Rim. The conquest of Australia and New Zealand and establishment of settler colonies there deviated sharply from the ideology of liberal paternalism and practices of economic imperialism that characterized European ventures abroad during the early nineteenth century. The narrative of settlement in Australasia instead mirrored the conquest of the Americas in the seventeenth and eighteenth centuries in its strident frontier mentality, thirst for land, and unapologetic decimation of indigenous populations.

Although the British government claimed Australia as a penal colony—and a humane alternative to capital punishment—in 1788, the government nonetheless opposed the emigration of free labor there as a drain on British manpower. Land-hungry settlers came anyway, in pursuit of economic opportunity. British settlement in Australia increased in the 1840s as the first generations of free settlers offered cash incentives to try to induce more and more affluent Britons to emigrate. Emigration soared after the Australian Gold Rush of 1851. New Zealand followed a similar path. British settlers began to arrive in 1839, enticed by the foundation of the New Zealand Trading Company, even though the British government actively discouraged emigration.

As increasing numbers of settlers poured in—over a million British citizens emigrated in the 1850s alone,

most of them to Australia—the British government grew more psychologically invested in its settler colonies and came to perceive emigration as a demographic and economic necessity. The preponderance of British-descended settlers in these colonies, known as "the White Dominions," naturally afforded them a uniquely privileged position in the colonial hierarchy. Over time British settlers began to self-identify as natives of the region and, as that happened, to press for self-government. They achieved that status incrementally. In the 1850s, Britain granted New Zealand and Australia limited autonomy. It conferred Dominion status—a classification that offered domestic autonomy to the settler colonies but retained British control over foreign policy and trade—first on Canada in 1867, then on Australia in 1901, New Zealand in 1907, and South Africa in 1910.

White settlement in Australasia devastated indigenous populations and destroyed existing economies, just as it had in North and South America. European diseases killed most of the local inhabitants. Of those who survived, most were forced off their land by expropriating settlers. They also lost major food sources as entire ecosystems were destroyed by settlers seeking to turn forest and prairie into farmland. The British government offered crucial military support for settlers and made the displacement of local peoples a violent affair. In New Zealand, for example, both the settlers and the British government signed the Waitangi Treaty in 1840 promising indigenous Maoris protection of their land rights, but the settlers quickly reneged on their promises. When the Maoris fought back and the settlers were drawn into armed conflict with them, the British government ultimately intervened to savagely crush Maori resistance during the 1860s.

Japan   Only Japan managed to escape European rule, implicit or explicit, in nineteenth-century Asia. Nonetheless, during the first two-thirds of the century, it appeared that Japan would follow in China's footsteps. Starting with Russian interference in the late eighteenth century, Europeans and Americans tried to end Japanese isolationism and foster trading contacts. Once the American naval commander Commodore Matthew Perry induced the Japanese Tokugawa government to sign a treaty opening some of its ports to Western trade in 1854, other major European nations soon followed suit. By midcentury, the European penetration of Japan was under way, although on a considerably smaller scale than in China.

But Japan was to radically shift course with the downfall of the Tokugawa regime and the advent of the revolutionary Meiji Restoration in 1868. Meiji leaders dismantled an essentially feudal system that had lasted for seven centuries by promoting rapid-fire industrialization of the economy and Westernizing key

At the turn of the nineteenth century, the Scottish explorer Mungo Park led two ill-fated expeditions to west Africa to explore the course of the Niger River. This drawing, the frontispiece of his book, *Travels in the Interior of Africa,* shows him, assisted by local guides, as he locates the Niger for the first time. Explorers' accounts such as Park's were enormously popular reading and helped stoke public interest in Africa.

aspects of the government and educational system. Industrialization rapidly catapulted Japan to the status of a global economic competitor. It also made Japan strong enough to retain control of the Westernization process, thus preempting the kind of covert European colonialism experienced elsewhere in Asia. Instead, Japan was able not only to revise the unequal trade treaties it had signed with the West at midcentury, but to emerge as a world political player and an imperialist nation in its own right, forcing trade concessions from Korea and extending its influence there starting in 1873.

The European Awakening to Africa

Perhaps the greatest imperial shift of the nineteenth century was in the European stance toward Africa. Before the late eighteenth century, the vast majority of Europeans had paltry knowledge of Africa and, in marked contrast to the New World and the South Seas, scant interest in it. In maps, writings, and visual imagery, Europeans tended to imagine Africa as outside the bounds of civilization: a hostile natural terrain whose few human inhabitants were savage brutes bereft of civilization. The fact that Africans had constituted the primary labor source for the Atlantic slave economy for four centuries only reinforced this notion of Africa as beyond the human pale.

New Interest in Africa   In large measure, European ignorance and indifference stemmed from a lack of con-

tact with Africa. Apart from Portuguese slave traders, who settled along the west African coast (Angola), French traders in the Senegambia region (Senegal), and Dutch and English settlers on the Cape of Good Hope at the southern tip of Africa, Europeans had little experience of Africa.

This pattern of negligible contact changed at the turn of the nineteenth century. As a capitalist economy based on free enterprise took shape in Western Europe, Africa came into focus as a potential marketplace. For the first time, Europeans perceived Africa both as a source of raw materials to feed its industrial economy (peanut and palm oil from West Africa, for example, were used to lubricate industrial machinery) and as an outlet for its new manufactures. Thinking about Africa's economic potential in this way meant imagining it as a site of civilization in a way Europeans had never before done: an Africa that could be a European trading partner was an Africa that had states, cities, and markets of its own. The late-eighteenth-century formation of the African Association, dedicated to British commercial expansion in Africa, reflected this sudden surge of awareness of Africa's commercial potential. The best known of the Association's agents was the explorer Mungo Park, whose expeditions up the Niger River in West Central Africa in 1795 and 1805 brought him into contact with the sophisticated Fulani and Bambara states, confirming hopes that Africa possessed the commercial infrastructure to become a significant British trading partner.

But if Park's expeditions exemplified the new interest in Africa, they also demonstrated the obstacles to European penetration in the early nineteenth century. The devastation of both his expeditions by illness curbed the enthusiasm of would-be explorers. Disease posed a formidable barrier to the European pursuit of African commercial ties until the middle of the nineteenth century. Unlike the New World, where European strains of disease virtually obliterated indigenous peoples, in Africa it was the local inhabitants who had the advantage. Dysentery, yellow fever, typhoid, and, above all, malaria decimated European visitors so predictably that nineteenth-century Africa became widely known by the epithet "The White Man's Grave." Standard remedies for malaria were either ineffective or—as in the case of dosing with mercury—lethal. Not until the 1820s did European chemists discover that quinine, a substance from the bark of the South American cinchona tree, could treat malaria. By the 1850s, Europeans realized that the prophylactic use of quinine prevented the contraction of the disease. Yet, even though improvements in the treatment and prevention of malaria and other tropical diseases by midcentury made European infiltration of Africa possible, death rates from disease remained so high that, as late as the 1870s, more European soldiers involved in African military campaigns died from disease than from warfare.

Africa's topography, with its jungles, deserts, and complex river systems, also impeded European access to the continent. The early-nineteenth-century advent of the steamboat, which applied James Watt's steam engine to boat travel, greatly facilitated the exploration of continental interiors by river in Africa, as well as in Asia and Australia. Not only could steamboats navigate independent of wind conditions, but the power of the steam engine allowed them to travel against the current at high speeds. Once steamboats were in use, Europeans were able to gain access to virtually every region in Africa, with the notable exception of areas lacking navigable waterways such as the Horn of Africa (these areas, not incidentally, were among the last to be colonized). Even so, steamboat exploration in Africa remained difficult for some time, in part because steamboats had to be dismantled, carried in sections around rapids, and then reassembled.

Missionaries and Explorers By the middle of the nineteenth century, many of the obstacles preventing European expansion into Africa thus had been removed. Missionaries, many of them abolitionist evangelicals seeking to end slavery in Africa, often ventured first into the African interior. They strove not merely to save souls, as their early modern predecessors had, but to Europeanize native subjects whom they now saw as more primitive brethren. Likewise, they saw the cultivation of commerce and the conversion to Christianity as mutually reinforcing goals, since both were part of the overall civilizing process that would ultimately elevate non-Europeans to the level of Europeans. Mission stations in the African interior quickly attracted other Europeans, in particular traders, who made use of missionary expertise and contacts with the local population for commercial ends. In seeking government backing and protection, moreover, missionaries also promoted European political involvement in Africa.

Following in the footsteps of missionaries, explorers raised public interest in Africa to a fever pitch by midcentury. Most explorers were unknown adventurers who publicized their exploits in book form and on lecture tours in the hope of raising money for their expeditions from the government, scientific authorities, and the general public. The most successful were often the most skilled speakers and rhetoricians, able to dramatize their experiences and aggrandize their contributions. Many of these became national icons. Among the best known was David Livingstone, a missionary-explorer who described his dual quest to open central Africa to commerce and religion in his book *Missionary Travels* (1857). A distinctly different model of the explorer as adventurer and entrepreneur was represented by Henry Stanley, an Anglo-American hired by the *New York Herald* to find Livingstone when the latter was thought to be missing in the Central Congo. Stanley became an overnight celebrity with the publication of his great scoop, *How I Found Livingstone,* in 1872.

While explorers' encounters brought Africa to life for European audiences, they also provided Europeans with extensive misinformation and helped to fashion an increasingly negative portrait of African cultures and societies. Henry Stanley's writings, for example, influenced Europeans in their association of darkness—defined variously as savagery, irrationality, and immorality—with Africa. Stanley's exploits captured the imagination of writers and intellectuals, including the American novelist Edgar Rice Burroughs (*Tarzan of the Apes*, [1912]) and the Polish-English novelist Joseph Conrad (*Heart of Darkness* [1902]).

Expansion into the Interior European traders and settlers on the African coast also began to spread out of established enclaves into new areas in the interior during this period. In the southwest, the Portuguese extended their holdings in present-day Angola. In the northwest, the French moved inland from the coastal city of Saint Louis into modern-day Senegal. They also expanded from Algiers—conquered in a military invasion in 1830—into the Algerian interior. French troops spent the better part of the 1840s and 1850s trying to consolidate their holdings in Algeria, fighting a costly and difficult war with well-armed Algerian guerrillas under the leadership of Abdelkader. By 1869 France claimed Algeria as a colony.

MAP 26.1 SOUTHERN AFRICA IN THE NINETEENTH CENTURY
Friction between Afrikaner and British settlers in southern Africa sparked Afrikaner emigration from the Cape Colony during the 1830s and 1840s (the Great Trek) and led to the establishment of independent Afrikaner republics. British expansionist aspirations, intensified by the discovery of diamond and gold in Afrikaner territory in the late nineteenth century, threatened the long-term survival of the republics. They were absorbed into British South Africa after the Boer War of 1889–1902. How did conflict between Europeans and Africans in the region affect the intra-European conflict?
◆ For an online version, go to www.mhhe.com/chambers9 > chapter 26 > book maps

In southern Africa, fifteen thousand Afrikaners migrated north of the Orange River in the Great Trek of 1835–1845, fleeing British control and seeking land of their own. Despite ongoing battles over territory with Bantus, in particular the Zulus (a southern Bantu people), the Afrikaners flourished as cattle ranchers and, by the late 1830s, had established independent Afrikaner republics in the Natal, the Orange Free State, and the Transvaal. For the British, however, Afrikaner expansionism threatened their own sovereignty and plans for further expansion in southern Africa. To cut the Afrikaners off from strategic coastal access, they annexed the Natal province outright in 1843 and, although the British eventually recognized the sovereignty of the Orange Free State and the Transvaal in 1854, they meddled continually in Bantu-Afrikaner conflicts.

Clashes with African Powers   These European incursions did not meet with a passive, quiescent Africa. Parallel to the European infiltration of Africa, widespread

internal war and conquest destabilized African politics and economic life in large parts of the continent during the early to mid-nineteenth century. In particular, Zulu political ambitions in southern Africa and the theocratic aims of Islamic jihad states in West Africa during this period created political and economic upheaval across broad swathes of Africa. In many cases, African polities on the move collided with expansionist Europeans, often ending in violent confrontation.

The sudden ascendancy of the Zulus in South Africa in the early nineteenth century was a case in point. In the 1820s, the military genius Shaka Zulu built a powerful and extensive Zulu empire in the Natal region, sparking major disturbances in Southern Africa. Although many inhabitants of the area capitulated outright to Shaka's dominion, his raiding armies also drove many other Bantu peoples, including the Ndebele, to seek refuge elsewhere. As huge numbers of Bantus fled the Zulus south into British territory and north into the Afrikaner republics, Bantus and Afrikaners warred continually over land. The Zulus themselves also battled Afrikaners who migrated north into Zulu dominions in 1837–1838, as well as the British, most notably in the Anglo-Zulu War of 1878–1879. Although the latter marked the first defeat of a European power by an African force in the Battle of Isandhlwana, the British ultimately crushed the Zulus.

The expansion of Islam in Africa during this period also triggered great turmoil. In the late eighteenth century and early nineteenth century, a fundamentalist Islamic revival emerged among the Fulani people in West Africa. The Fulani reviled indigenous religious beliefs and practices as well as European Christianity as threats to the purity of Islam. Overthrowing the local Hausa chieftains, the Fulani established an enduring decentralized state structure known as the Sokoto caliphate in 1809, which waged *jihad*—holy war—to impose Islam throughout the region. By midcentury, expansionist Fulani jihadists came into conflict with French colonizers moving east out of Senegal.

European Encroachment in Egypt   Europeans sought control of Egypt, an Ottoman province since the sixteenth century, because of its strategic location on the Red Sea en route to India. When Ottoman control wavered in the late eighteenth century, Napoleon seized the opportunity to invade Egypt in 1798, although British forces, backed by Ottoman Turks, ultimately destroyed his fleet in the Battle of the Nile. Although the Ottomans regained nominal rule of the province, the Sultan lost control when Mohammed Ali, an Al-

banian officer in the Ottoman army of reoccupation, seized power. Mohammed Ali's efforts to establish Egyptian autonomy were thwarted, however, by the Sultan's continued resistance and British and French commercial interests in Egypt. By midcentury, Europeans controlled a large portion of Egypt's trade and European bankers were financing modernization projects. These included constructing an Egyptian railway system from Alexandria to Cairo and building the Suez Canal connecting the Red Sea to the Mediterranean Sea under Ferdinand Lesseps's direction from 1859 to 1869.

THE NEW IMPERIALISM, 1870–1914

In the closing decades of the nineteenth century, Europeans remapped the contours of empire. By the 1870s, the piecemeal expansionism of the earlier part of the century gave way to a systematic campaign of explicit conquest and occupation of much of Africa and Asia. This global conquest is often described as the "new imperialism" to differentiate it from earlier forms of empire. Indeed, while late-nineteenth-century imperialism was built on many of the same ideological foundations as the midcentury empire and endorsed the liberal civilizing mission at the outset, it soon metamorphosed into a distinctive intellectual and material enterprise.

Four features of the new imperialism stand out as novel. First, late-nineteenth-century European nations adopted imperialism as an official policy for the first

In 1897, the British troops attacked and looted the Edo capital of Benin, in present-day southern Nigeria. The Benin expedition was a punitive one, responding to the ambush of a British military party sent to force trade concessions from the Edo king a year earlier. This photograph shows British officers of the expedition surrounded by booty, including the famed Benin bronzes, seized from the royal compound. The plundered objects ended up in European and American art museums.
Courtesy of the Trustees of The British Museum

time, replacing empires governed largely by traders with those ruled by expansionist states. Although European nation-states had sponsored imperial expansion earlier in the century, they had most often done so after the fact, in an effort to protect and promote the activities of their missionaries and merchants overseas; now it was the state that took the imperial initiative. Second, the entrance of a new group of nations into the race for territory during this period changed the rules of the imperial game. In Europe, Germany, Belgium, and Italy appeared on the imperial scene, while outside Europe, the United States and Japan emerged as major imperial powers. As multiple players competed aggressively for territory and power, Britain's longstanding global sovereignty began to fade. Third, the more competitive imperial climate changed the political objectives of imperial nations. No longer content with informal influence, they now sought explicit territorial occupation and political conquest. Finally, the new imperialism defined its own distinctive ideological mission, gradually abandoning the universalist premise of the liberal empire for a belief in the unbreachable gap between Europe and its colonial subjects. As that happened, Europeans began to retreat from the civilizing goals of the early to midcentury and to seek increasingly to secure and consolidate imperial rule through force. Unfettered by the moral constraints of early nineteenth-century colonizers, the new imperialism brought Europe to the peak of its power.

Europe Transformed: Explaining the New Imperialism

No single factor can explain the new imperialism. Rather, it emerged out of a number of significant changes that occurred in Europe during the second half of the nineteenth century.

Technology   By the late nineteenth century, Europeans had access to new and astonishingly efficient technologies that would change the course of colonial conquest and domination. To be sure, technology had played a major role in spreading European influence abroad throughout the nineteenth century and earlier; steamships, industrial weaponry, and the use of quinine to treat malaria had allowed Europeans to penetrate continental Africa, and the arrival of gunboats—armed steamboats—had played decisive roles, for example, in the conquest of Burma and the opening of China. Nevertheless, the advent of the second industrial revolution (see chapter 25) in the late nineteenth century made technology an even more important factor in the speed, extent, and vigor of the conquests. Ironclad warships with steam turbines now spread the power of far more advanced and

deadly European weaponry overseas, while the invention of the telegraph radically simplified the logistics of military mobilization from afar. After conquest, dynamite lessened the difficulty of building roads, and modern medicine significantly reduced the dangers of fighting and living in the tropics.

Nationalism   While turn-of-the-century technologies made possible conquest on a global scale, they did not create new incentives to conquer. Most historians would agree that it was nationalism—understood in the broadest sense of the term—that propelled the new imperialism forward. Although nationalism was hardly new, it developed in strikingly new ways during this period. The ideological tenor of nationalism changed, moving away from its early-nineteenth-century romantic and liberal origins and tilting toward a more strident, aggressive, and exclusionary variant. Nationalism was transformed, in other words, from a phenomenon associated with the democratic and liberal left to one linked to the emergence of a new mass politics on the right. Based on emotional appeals to community and history, the new nationalism challenged the liberal politics of the midcentury based on the rational individual and the possibilities of societal progress. Imperial domination, in this context, was seen as a sign of national vigor and a marker of prestige.

Nationalism also played an integral role in the rise of a new political and economic order of nation-states in this period. Germany's national unification transformed it overnight into one of the foremost continental powers. Its meteoric economic and political ascent, along with the emergence of Japan and the United States as industrial giants, fundamentally reconfigured the global balance of power and in so doing changed the stakes of empire. The new order sharply challenged British global sovereignty, unrivaled since the late eighteenth century, and demoted Britain's lagging rival, France, to a third-rate power. On the economic and political defensive, Britain and France sought to expand their empires to compensate for their loss of economic primacy and political prestige. Germany, Japan, and the United States responded in turn by carving out their own colonial empires.

Economic Factors   Within this charged nationalist framework, economic, political, and cultural forces each played their role in promoting the imperial scramble. Economic factors were critical. As they had done earlier in the century, turn-of-the-century imperial nations viewed their colonies as vital markets for selling European industrial goods, buying raw materials and cash crops, and investing surplus capital. But now the economic context had changed. One new factor was the presence of Germany and the United States as leading industrial powers. By 1890 both Germany and the United States had surpassed British steel and iron production and Germany was outselling the British in certain overseas markets (Latin America, China, and the Ottoman Empire). A lengthy industrial depression from 1873 to the early 1890s played a significant role as well. This unstable economic context promoted the view that colonial markets could act as buffers against the fluctuations of global commerce. As a consequence, the Western European nations started to abandon the rhetoric of free trade in the 1880s and 1890s, once again endorsing mercantilist policies that—in addition to raising trade barriers in the domestic market—explicitly demarcated the colonies as protected economic spheres. Finally, the advent of a new, more advanced phase of industrial capitalism in the late nineteenth century brought with it fears of saturation of the domestic market and, with that, industrial overproduction. In this context, many Europeans came to view empire as an essential outlet for surpluses of goods and capital.

As scholars of empire have pointed out, however, economic incentives alone cannot account for the new imperialism, and nation-states often pursued imperial objectives even when their economic costs appeared to outweigh their benefits. Undoubtedly, the colonies furnished attractive markets for Europe's industrial manufactures in the late nineteenth century; in 1890 Britain exported one-third of its industrial goods and one-quarter of its investment capital to India. However, strictly in terms of trade volume, European nations traded far more with other independent countries, including their European neighbors, than they did with their colonies. Britain, the largest overseas investor and trader, traded more with Latin America and the United States, for example, than with its African or even its Asian colonies. Moreover, it was not always the most industrialized, economically powerful nations that took the imperial initiative. Although France lagged far behind Germany as an industrial producer, for example, it was the French who amassed the world's second largest empire.

Political Motives   The primacy of the nation-state during this period also put strategic and territorial ambitions at center stage. The actions of European nations within the imperial arena were taken as much to jockey for political power and to preempt the territorial claims of other nations as they were to pursue economic gain. For Kaiser Wilhelm II, the German ruler from 1888 to 1918, for example, a central motivation for building up a strong German navy was to contest Britain's global power, so dependent on its naval strength, in North Africa, China, and the Ottoman Empire. The new nation of Italy likewise sought a colonial empire in North and East Africa as part of its quest to achieve great-power status.

Cultural Incentives   In the cultural realm, too, late-nineteenth-century nation-states mobilized imperialism to assist with internal processes of state-building. Newly unified nation-states, in particular, but older and established ones as well, actively sought to fully unify their citizens, in large part by inducing them to transfer their primary loyalties from their local community to the far more abstract, "imagined" community of the nation. This process met with significant resistance, particularly since it entailed a loss of regional identity, and national leaders used the attractions of empire as one means of appealing to its citizens. Empire was presented as the shared symbolic property of the nation, an asset that in theory (but not in practice) transcended social class and allowed peasants and workers—as much as members of the upper classes—to cast themselves as superior to the nation's colonial subjects. Governments also encouraged their citizens to conceive of empire as a measure of the nation's virile masculinity, seen in favorable contrast to the supposedly weak, "effeminate" colony. Imperialism and, more specifically, imperial racism helped to consolidate the nation-state, in other words, by substituting race hierarchies for the hierarchies of class.

The Scramble for Africa

The Scramble for Africa constituted by far the most remarkable chapter of the European expansion of the late nineteenth century. Between 1880 and 1912, seven European states partitioned most of the African continent, leaving only Abyssinia (Ethiopia) and Liberia independent.

The Berlin Conference   By the mid-1880s, a number of European governments had begun to object to the haphazardness with which conflicts over African territory were being settled. The Berlin Conference of 1884–1885, presided over by the German Prime Minister Otto von Bismarck, was convened to sort out the conflict between the Portuguese and the Belgians over control of the Congo River in particular and, more generally, to lay the ground rules for colonization. A watershed in European diplomacy, the conference brokered conflicting claims without recourse to intra-European violence, even as it came to inflict bloodshed and suffering on Africa. European cooperation at Berlin owed a great deal to Bismarck's diplomatic shrewdness. Seeking to compensate France and Britain for their loss of power in the European arena and, at the same time, to fuel Franco-British imperial rivalry, he conceded the bulk of African territories to Britain and

This is an image of a popular French children's board game from the late nineteenth century, the objective of which was to conquer Africa. Popular culture proved a powerful tool for propagating ideas about the "natural inferiority" of Africans and the legitimacy of the European conquest.

France. Despite its small number of African colonies, Germany's foreign policy thus decisively influenced the Scramble.

Since the lines of partition had been drawn long before the Berlin Conference, its main role was to formally ratify the principle that coastal settlement by a European nation also gave it claim to the hinterlands beyond as long as it could establish authority in the region. Although the Berlin participants legitimized some new claims in central Africa—such as those of Belgium's King Leopold II in the Congo—in the main, the African partition extended European control from older coastal enclaves into the interior of the continent.

For Africans, the carving up of the continent redrew the African map in ways that consolidated previously separate polities and ethnic groups in new, European-made units—a single new colony, for example, could comprise three hundred smaller political units. The Berlin Conference thus centralized power in a previously decentralized political landscape. In addition, by using the artificial entity of the "tribe" to designate previously distinct groups of the same region, it permanently reconfigured ethnic and cultural identities in African society. While colonial rule and the work of Christian missionaries in standardizing related language dialects ultimately strengthened the cultural bonds between disparate groups, many of the African "tribes" of the present day are at least partial inventions of the Berlin Conference.

The Berlin Conference also extended the European abolition of slavery and the slave trade to Africa. Missionaries such as David Livingstone had campaigned ardently against the slave trade in East Africa since midcentury without making much headway. As formal colonizers, however, Europeans could enforce abolitionism to a much greater extent than before. Their desire to abolish African slavery emerged both from a genuine humanitarianism and from the understanding that it was politically expedient as a justification for conquest. In spite of partial successes, clandestine slav-

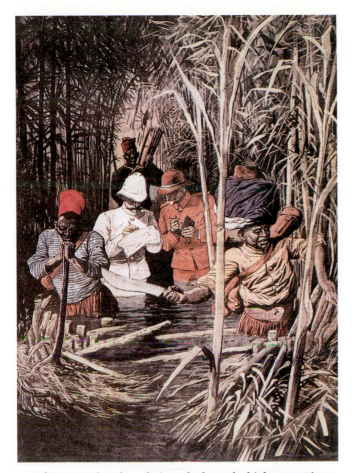

As African guides clear their path through thick vegetation, French and German negotiators consult their maps and renegotiate the boundaries of French Equatorial Africa and German Cameroon. European powers frequently came into conflict with one another on African soil, but for the most part were able to resolve their differences peacefully.

ery and slave trading in Africa continued into the early twentieth century and new forms of forced labor, heavily relied upon by European colonizers themselves, also replaced slavery in many regions.

The Wars of Conquest   In the aftermath of the Berlin Conference, the conquest of Africa unfolded in a series of bloody wars that took place between the 1880s and the first decade of the twentieth century. Although European powers faced fierce African resistance, they enjoyed several advantages in these conflicts. Their footholds on the African coast and, in many cases, longstanding commercial connections with coastal communities provided them with a base of operations and a ready source of supplies. Europeans also benefited from, and sometimes ruthlessly exploited, the divi-

sions between local communities. In their expansion into West Africa (Nigeria) in the 1890s, for example, the British profited from local enmity by mobilizing the subjugated Nupe against their Fulani overlords, only to conquer the Nupe soon afterward.

Most important in facilitating the conquest was the immense and growing technological advantage enjoyed by the Europeans, especially in weaponry. To be sure, the weapons gap was nothing new. But the new military equipment produced by the second industrial revolution magnified the inequality between African and European forces. By the time Africans acquired rifles in the late nineteenth century, Europeans were deploying, first, rapid-firing breechloaders (repeating rifles) and, later, machine guns. In fact, most of the new weaponry of the First World War was first tested in the laboratory of late-nineteenth-century colonial warfare. One example of the devastation wrought by these new technologies was in the Battle of Omdurman in Sudan in 1898, where field artillery and hand-driven Gatling machine guns allowed Anglo-Egyptian forces to kill 11,000 and wound 16,000 Sudanese soldiers, with only 49 dead and 382 wounded among their own ranks. In the few cases where Africans had access to equally advanced technology, they were often able to thwart conquest. In part of French West Africa (Mali), for example, the troops of Islamic Malinké ruler Samori Touré, armed with up-to-date European weaponry, staved off French conquest from the mid-1880s to the late 1890s. These exceptions further underscore how critical advanced weaponry was to the European conquest.

New Imperial Nations   While France and Britain dominated the conquest, other European nations carved out significant African territories as well. After the Berlin Conference had recognized King Leopold II's claims in the Congo in exchange for free trading and shipping rights in the region for other European states, Belgium emerged as a major African power. The full-scale subjugation of the massive Congo Free State (Democratic Republic of the Congo)—76 times as large as Belgium—took over ten years and met with continued insurgence, particularly from Arab slave traders of the Lualaba River region.

Germany also played a central role in the Scramble. At Berlin, Bismarck had ceded dominance in Africa to Britain and France, claiming a few protectorates in the areas where German traders and missionaries were most active, such as Togoland (Togo), Cameroon, South West Africa (Namibia), and East Africa (Tanzania). In 1888, however, the accession of Wilhelm II to the German throne and the subsequent dismissal of Bismarck ushered in a new era of aggression in German foreign policy. Thereafter, Germany posed an active threat to

CHRONOLOGY
Scramble for Africa

1881	French occupy Tunisia.
1882	Revolt in Egypt (against British and French financial influence by Arabi Pasha) prompts occupation by British.
1883	Start of French conquest of Madagascar.
1884	Germany acquires South West Africa, Togo, Cameroon. Berlin Conference.
1885	King Leopold II of Belgium acquires Congo.
1886	Germany and Britain divide East Africa.
	Discovery of gold in South Africa.
1889	Italy establishes colonies in Eritrea and Somaliland.
	Cecil Rhodes's British South Africa Company begins colonization of Rhodesia.
1894	Britain occupies Uganda.
1896	Abyssinian (Ethiopian) army defeats invading Italian army.
1898	Fashoda Crisis.
1899–1902	Boer War.
1905–1906; 1911	Morocco Crises.

France and Britain in the imperial arena. The Moroccan Crisis of 1905–1906 developed, for example, when Germany protested against the Franco-Spanish division of power in the region and demanded a sphere of its own. A second crisis, the Agadir Incident of 1911, erupted when the Kaiser sent a gunboat to the Moroccan port of Agadir in a display of German power meant to intimidate the French. Although both crises were resolved diplomatically, with France retaining effective control of Morocco, episodes like these signal the belligerent diplomatic stance of post-Bismarckian Germany and the consequent heightening of imperial competition.

Worried about Belgian and German encroachment on its colonial borders, Portugal managed to enlarge its Angolan holdings on the West African coast and to establish Portuguese East Africa (Mozambique) on the southeastern coast of Africa. These incursions sparked extended wars of resistance, especially in the Zambezi Valley. Meanwhile, the new nation-state of Italy, seeking to enhance its international standing by staking out terrain in East Africa, faced the unique humiliation of being defeated by an African polity. On the Horn of Africa, Italy seized Eritrea and Somaliland (Somalia) as colonies

in 1889, but failed to conquer Abyssinia (Ethiopia), when King Menelik II's troops—about 100,000 soldiers armed with European breechloaders, a few machine guns, and field artillery—soundly defeated an Italian force of 14,500, equipped with inaccurate maps, at the Battle of Adowa in 1896. Italy fared better in Tripoli (Libya), declaring a protectorate there in 1912.

France French and British expansion in Africa overshadowed that of all other powers. Although the British denigrated the French Empire as a large "sandbox," France clearly dominated West Africa and North Africa. From Algeria, where they had been entrenched since 1830, France expanded in virtually every direction. To the east, it squeezed out Italian and British interests, using the growing indebtedness of the ruling bey as the pretext for making Tunisia a French protectorate in 1881. To the west, France moved on Morocco, thwarting German interests and appeasing Spain with a small zone of control. By 1895 they dominated an enormous swath of sub-Saharan territories known as French West Africa (Ivory Coast, Senegal, Guinea, Mali). In 1897, France seized the French Congo in central Africa (Republic of the Congo) and, three years later, invaded the Lake Chad region, thereby linking up its possessions in the west and the north with those in central Africa. In 1911 it combined Chad and French Congo to form French Equatorial Africa. On the east coast, the French also claimed part of Somaliland and, in 1896, conquered the island of Madagascar, where they established a prosperous sugar plantation economy based on the forced labor of the local population.

Britain and the Boer War British imperialists envisioned a railway from Capetown to Cairo that would span their African Empire. Starting in the 1880s, Britain moved to consolidate its hold on Egypt and Sudan. Although Britain had shared financial control with France over an increasingly bankrupted Egypt during the late nineteenth century and the French had financed the construction of the Suez Canal, the British finally edged the French out of Egypt in the 1870s and 1880s, claiming it as a protectorate in 1882 (see "The Earl of Cromer: Why Britain Acquired Egypt," p. 794).

Once entrenched in Egypt, the British moved to extend their power south into Turco-Egyptian-controlled Sudan. There they clashed with the millenarian jihadist Mahdist state, which had sought repeatedly to overthrow Egyptian rule during the 1880s. In 1885, the armies of the Mahdi (the Guided One) attacked Khartoum, the Egyptian capital of Sudan and, after a ten-month siege, annihilated Anglo-Egyptian troops led by General Charles Gordon (known as "Chinese" Gordon because of his role in suppressing the Taiping Rebellion). At nearby Omdurman, the Mahdi established an Islamic

Image of the Battle of Adowa of 1896, in which the troops of Menelik II, armed with European weaponry, routed the Italian army and effectively saved Abyssinia (Ethiopia) from colonial conquest.
The Mary Evans Picture Libary

state, which thrived for the next twelve years. But the British did not forget the defeat at Khartoum and in 1896 launched a new campaign to take the Sudan. In 1898 British troops led by Lord Kitchener handed the Mahdist State a fatal defeat at the battle of Omdurman.

The expansion into Sudan allowed Britain to link up Egypt with its territories to the southeast, British East Africa (Kenya) and Buganda (Uganda), seized in 1888 and 1894, respectively. At the same time, in West Africa, the British expanded from trading forts along the Gold Coast, purchased earlier from the Dutch and the Danes, and defeated the Asante to colonize Ghana. In an effort to protect the commercial interests of British palm oil merchants in the Niger River delta, the British-chartered Royal Niger Company, under the leadership of George Goldie, also expanded into Nigeria between 1886 and 1899.

Pressing north from the British Cape Colony, the British fought the Zulus in the Anglo-Zulu War of 1878–1879. Led by the archetypal expansionist Cecil Rhodes, they took Bechuanaland (Botswana) in 1885, Rhodesia (Zimbabwe) in 1889, and Nyasaland (Malawi) in 1893. In so doing, the British managed to create a wedge separating German South West Africa (Namibia) and German East Africa (Rwanda, Burundi, continental Tanzania, part of Mozambique) and to approach the southern border of the Congo Free State. More importantly, this expansion threatened the independent Afrikaner republics north of the Cape Colony, a conflict that ultimately led to the Boer War of 1899–1902, in which approximately 75,000 lives were lost.

The British encroachment on the Afrikaner republics had been fueled by the discovery there of diamonds in the 1860s and gold in the 1880s. By 1890 the Afrikaner republics were overrun by British citizens and surrounded by British colonies. Conflicts between the two groups grew more heated, and in 1899 the Afrikaners declared war. British forces rapidly occupied

THE EARL OF CROMER: WHY BRITAIN ACQUIRED EGYPT

Evelyn Baring (1871–1917), First Earl of Cromer, was the first British Commissioner of the Egyptian Public Debt Office and then British Agent and Consul General after Egypt became a British colony in 1882. Ruling Egypt with an iron hand, Cromer reorganized its financial, judicial, and administrative system as well as defended it from the incursions of other European powers. Although he brought about important changes in Egypt and virtually rescued it from bankruptcy, the Egyptians disliked his autocratic ways and his willingness to subordinate the interests of Egypt to that of Britain. He ignored demands by middle-class Egyptians for higher education, for instance, for fear that it would lead to the emergence of nationalist sentiment, as it had in India. Likewise, the primary objective of his successful agricultural experiments to promote the growth of Egyptian cotton was to provide British industries with raw materials. Still, Cromer was greatly admired in the West. When he died in 1917, the London Times called him the "Maker of Modern Egypt." In this excerpt, Cromer explains why the British and not any other European power could—and did—take over Egypt.

"History, indeed, records some very radical changes in the forms of government to which a state has been subjected without its interests being absolutely and permanently shipwrecked. But it may be doubted whether any instance can be quoted of a sudden transfer of power in any civilized or semi-civilized community to a class so ignorant as the pure Egyptians, such as they were in the year 1882. These latter have, for centuries past, been a subject race. Persians, Greeks, Romans, Arabs from Arabia and Baghdad, Circassians, and finally, Ottoman Turks, have successively ruled over Egypt, but we have to go back to the doubtful and obscure precedents of Pharaonic times to find an epoch when, possibly, Egypt was ruled by Egyptians. Neither, for the present, do they appear to possess the qualities which would render it desirable, either in their own interests, or in those of the civilized world in general, to raise them at a bound to the category of autonomous rulers with full rights of internal sovereignty.

"If, however, a foreign occupation was inevitable or nearly inevitable, it remains to be considered whether a British occupation was preferable to any other. From the purely Egyptian point of view, the answer to this question cannot be doubtful. The intervention of any European power was preferable to that of Turkey. The intervention of one European power was preferable to international intervention. The special aptitude shown by Englishmen in the government of Oriental races pointed to England as the most effective and beneficent instrument for the gradual introduction of European civilization into Egypt. An Anglo-French, or an Anglo-Italian occupation, from both of which we narrowly and also accidentally escaped, would

have been detrimental to Egyptian interests and would ultimately have caused friction, if not serious dissension, between England on the one side and France or Italy on the other. The only thing to be said in favor of Turkish intervention is that it would have relieved England from the responsibility of intervening.

"By the process of exhausting all other expedients, we arrive at the conclusion that armed British intervention was, under the special circumstances of the case, the only possible solution of the difficulties, which existed in 1882. Probably also it was the best solution. The arguments against British intervention, indeed, were sufficiently obvious. It was easy to foresee that, with a British garrison in Egypt, it would be difficult that the relations of England either with France or Turkey should be cordial. With France, especially, there would be a danger that our relations might become seriously strained. Moreover, we lost the advantages of our insular position. The occupation of Egypt necessarily dragged England to a certain extent within the arena of Continental politics. In the event of war, the presence of a British garrison in Egypt would possibly be a source of weakness rather than of strength. Our position in Egypt placed us in a disadvantageous diplomatic position, for any power, with whom we had a difference of opinion about some non-Egyptian question, was at one time able to retaliate by opposing our Egyptian policy. The complicated rights and privileges possessed by the various powers of Europe in Egypt facilitated action of this nature."

From The Earl of Cromer, *Modern Egypt*, vol. 1, New York: Macmillan, 1908, pp. xvii–xviii.

the major cities of the Afrikaner republics, but it took two years to subdue the Afrikaners' skillful guerrilla resistance. The rest of Europe watched Britain's slow progress with surprise and then shock as farmhouses were destroyed and homeless Afrikaners herded together in guarded areas called concentration camps, where disease and starvation killed at least 20,000 of

them. In Great Britain, the Boer War initially produced patriotic fervor, but politicians and the public alike grew disillusioned as the war dragged on. British victory allowed the establishment in 1910 of the Union of South Africa, a partial fulfillment of Rhodes's ambitions. To appease the disaffected Afrikaner minorities, British leaders implemented Afrikaner policies of

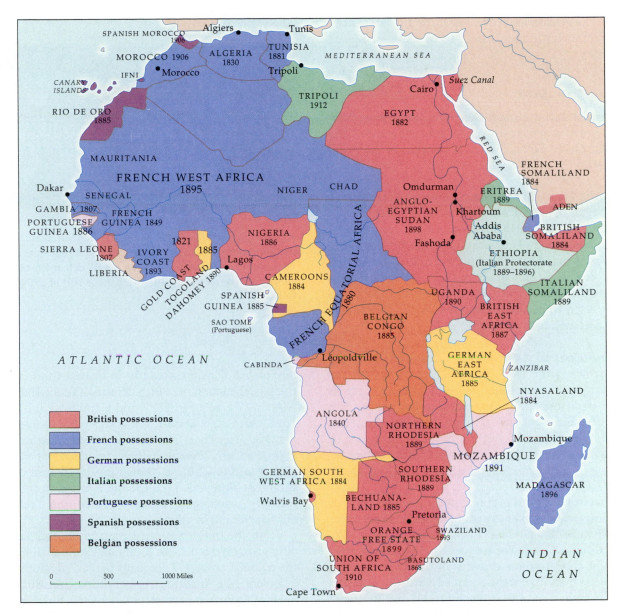

MAP 26.2 AFRICA, 1914
This map shows the European partition of Africa. Only Liberia and Ethiopia were independent after the turn of the century. Notice how the west-east axis of French territories runs into the north-south axis of British holdings. How were the European powers able to overrun an entire continent in such a short period of time?
◆ For an online version, go to www.mhhe.com/chambers9 > chapter 26 > book maps

Apartheid, and the legal segregation of white and black Africans became the law of the land.

Intra-European Conflict in Africa   By the turn of the century, the extent of European expansion, compounded by the heightened tension within Europe, led to a growing number of intra-European imperial clashes. The Boer War, in which Afrikaners were armed with German weapons, was one of these. Another important confrontation occurred between Britain and

France at Fashoda, on the Nile, in 1898. With the French driving inland across Africa from west to east and the British expanding south from Egypt and north from the Cape Colony, such conflict was inevitable. At Fashoda, British troops marching south from Omdurman met French expeditionary forces advancing east from the Congo. Both sides declared that their national honor was at stake, but after several weeks of threats the French government backed down, distracted by the Dreyfus affair at home. After the French retreat from

Fashoda, the French agreed to recognize British control of the Nile in return for British recognition of French West Africa.

Conquest in Asia

While Africa was the main theater of late-nineteenth-century imperial expansion, Asia was the second key site of aggressive expansionism at the turn of the twentieth century.

The Middle East　In the late nineteenth century, the British began to withdraw their support from the Ottoman Empire. Although the empire had been strategically and commercially important to the British as the gateway to Asia, it no longer played that role after the opening of the Suez Canal in 1869. Bankrupted, in commercial decline, and riven by internal dissent, the empire ceased to be the attractive ally the British had made use of earlier in the century.

South and Central Asia　India, ruled directly by the British crown after 1857, remained the jewel of the British Empire. It continued to be invaluable, both in terms of trade and capital investment. During the last quarter of the nineteenth century, London financiers invested more than £2.5 million in India, most of it in railways. By the eve of the First World War, India also had emerged as the chief export market for British industrial goods.

The security of India continued to obsess British politicians, who sought to protect her borders from other expansionist powers, in particular Russia. The British, allied with the French and the Ottoman Turks, had fought the Russians directly in the Crimean War (1854–1856) but otherwise grappled with the Russian threat through a combination of formal and informal diplomacy known as the "Great Game." The political maneuverings of the Great Game finally ended with the Anglo-Russian Entente of 1907, which resolved British and Russian differences over Persia, Tibet, and Afghanistan, dividing Persia into British and Russian spheres of influence and effectively consolidating Russian power in Central Asia.

Southeast Asia and the South Pacific　In Southeast Asia, the Dutch strengthened their hold over the Dutch East Indies (Indonesia), including Sumatra, Java, Borneo, and the western half of New Guinea, and continued to prosper from a colonial plantation economy based largely on rubber and coffee. The British, meanwhile, expanded their territories in Southeast Asia, annexing upper Burma in 1886 and a part of Malaya (Malaysia) in 1896. The French, who had established commercial interests in Indochina at the turn of the

Russian postcard (ca. 1902), showing the United States and Britain pushing Japan, the only imperial Asian state, into a confrontation with Russia. Japan would defeat Russia shortly thereafter in the Russo-Japanese War of 1904–1905.
© British Museum

nineteenth century, steadily increased their holdings there in the late nineteenth century, taking Tonkin and Annam (Vietnam) in 1883 and Cambodia and Laos in 1893. Although a militant and well-organized Vietnamese resistance movement, known as the "Black Flags," fought French infiltration (even appealing for help from the Chinese, their former colonial masters) the French prevailed. Following a series of protracted military campaigns, France formed the French Indochina Union in 1894.

From the mid-nineteenth century on, the South Pacific also emerged as an arena for competition among the colonial powers. Europeans perceived South Pacific Islanders, like Africans, to be childlike "primitives," in need of European protection and divided the many islands of the region among themselves. While Britain and Germany split the western half of New Guinea, France seized New Caledonia and Tahiti. Germany also acquired the Marshall Islands, and the British took Fiji and Tonga. The Germans, British, and Americans fought for dominance in Samoa, resulting in a split between German and American Samoa, while the Germans and the British divided up the Solomon Islands. In addition to a highly prosperous sugar economy centered in Fiji, the region also provided cheap labor for Australian sugar plantations.

As the European powers snatched up Pacific islands, the generally isolationist United States became involved in the imperial politics of the region. In 1898 it annexed Hawaii, a strategic Pacific naval base and a profitable sugar cane and pineapple producer. After defeating Spain in the Spanish-American War, ignited by conflict over the control of Cuba, the United States re-

楊村大戰

Chinese woodblock print showing Western soldiers being humiliated in a battle during the Boxer Rebellion of 1900 directed against Western exploitation of China. Although China was battered by the Rebellion and the Western powers emerged with still more influence over Chinese affairs, the Rebellion influenced the establishment of the first Chinese nationalist movement, led by Sun Yat-sen.
The British Library, London

ceived a number of Spanish territories, including the Philippines, Cuba, Puerto Rico, and Guam. In the Philippines, the Americans faced a fierce indigenous resistance movement that sought Filipino independence, but after three years of fighting and the capture of the insurrection leader, Emilio Aguinaldo, the United States declared the Philippines its territory. These conquests, combined with growing American influence and economic power in Latin America during this period, transformed the United States into a formidable global power.

East Asia   The continued decline of China and rise of Japan were the central developments in East Asia during the late nineteenth century. Although some Chinese reformers favored economic and technological modernization, including the building of railways, as a way to strengthen the nation, considerable conservative opposition to the process existed. The pattern of the midcentury thus continued unabated, with the European powers and the United States forcing trade concessions, annexing territory, and lending money to the

Chinese government on disadvantageous terms. In the aftermath of the Sino-Japanese War of 1894–1895, fought over control of Korea, the Chinese were forced to borrow money from Europe to pay a war indemnity to Japan and, in return, the Europeans exacted more trade privileges and concessions to build railways. The 1897 murder of two German missionaries in China led to further concessions. The Germans received a lease of the port of Quingdao and the right to build railways in Shandong Province, the Russians took Port Arthur, and the French acquired a lease on Canton Bay and a sphere of influence in southern China. To prevent the further partitioning of China, the United States initiated the Open Door policy in 1898, agreed upon by all colonizing nations with the exception of Japan. Allowing all nations equal trading rights in all parts of China, the Open Door policy also protected China's territorial integrity.

Foreign encroachment and exploitation sparked the Boxer Rebellion in 1900. A clandestine society called the "Patriotic Harmonious Fists"—known as Boxers because of the martial arts training of its members—

MAP 26.3 IMPERIALISM IN ASIA, 1900
This map shows the European colonies in Asia. Notice British dominance in this part of the world, centered largely on India. How did the entry of Japan and the United States into the Asian imperial arena change the power balance in the region?

◆ For an online version, go to www.mhhe.com/chambers9 > chapter 26 > book maps

organized to protest the corrupting influence of "foreign devils," including missionaries, traders, and soldiers. The Boxer Rebellion erupted in northern China, where Boxers attacked European, American, and Chinese Christians in Shandong Province, sabotaged rail lines, and besieged foreign embassies in Beijing for almost two months. A force of twenty thousand British, French, German, Russian, Italian, American, and Japanese troops viciously suppressed the Boxer Rebellion and imposed a huge indemnity on the Qing regime. Continued degradation and economic exploitation at the hands of the Europeans, Americans, and Japanese (often in the form of disadvantageous railway leases) fueled the Chinese nationalist movement led by Sun Yat-sen, which finally overthrew the beleaguered Qing Dynasty in 1911.

Japan's fate differed dramatically from that of China. An industrial giant after the Meiji Restoration of 1868, Japan sought an empire to reflect its global

standing. A Korean insurrection against Chinese influence in 1894 offered the Japanese an opportunity to establish a foothold in Korea. The ensuing Sino-Japanese War of 1894–1895 ended in Chinese defeat, the Japanese annexation of Taiwan, and increased Japanese trade privileges and political influence in Korea. Japan's expansionist ambitions brought it into direct conflict not only with China, but also with Russia. Its victory in the Russo-Japanese War of 1904–1905 stunned the world. A clash over influence in Chinese-held Manchuria and Korea, the war broke out following Russian maneuvers to take the Chinese province of Liaotung (and, in particular, the ice-free harbor of Port Arthur), controlled by the Japanese since the Sino-Japanese War. Japan not only kept Liaotung after victory, but took over the Russian sphere of influence in Chinese Manchuria, as well as half of Sakhalin Island, and seized Russian-controlled railways in Manchuria. The Japanese triumph over Russia marked a turning point for both European imperialists, who suddenly perceived the limits to their power, and for colonial subjects from Bombay to Cairo, who rejoiced and found hope in the European defeat. Undermining the credibility of Tsar Nicholas' regime, it also contributed to the failed first Russian Revolution of 1905. In 1910 a triumphant Japan annexed Korea.

The New Imperial Mission

New ideological foundations also distinguished the new imperialism from the liberal empire. Responding to anticolonial insurgency in India and to the Darwinian revolution at home, Europeans reconsidered the nature of their political, cultural, and biological relationship to subject peoples.

The Failure of the Liberal Vision   Europeans at the end of the nineteenth century confronted their vast global empire with a transformed sense of mission. Gradually abandoning the liberal conceit of Europeanizing the non-Western world for the more modest goal of improving the "natives" within their own cultural context, Europeans increasingly replaced paternalist justifications of empire with the unabashed consolidation of imperial rule by force. The new mission did not appear overnight. In fact, the self-critical attitude and eagerness to legitimize Europe's imperial presence characteristic of colonial encounters of the late eighteenth and early nineteenth centuries were already fading by midcentury, supplanted by a growing intolerance of cultural difference.

By the late nineteenth century, attitudes had further hardened. Europeans still believed in the flagrant inferiority of subject peoples, but, unlike previous generations of colonizers, they were far more inclined to see this inferiority as biological and, therefore, irremediable. While they continued to vaunt their own superiority as the justification for empire, Europeans thus increasingly questioned the extent of their responsibilities as civilizers and the likelihood that such efforts would succeed. The concrete experience of imperial rule contributed significantly to the new cynicism. In the case of Britain, for example, the Indian Rebellion of 1857 (see p. 800–802) irrevocably changed not only the conception of imperial duty but British expectations of their colonial subjects.

By the end of the century, many took the pessimistic view of the British poet Rudyard Kipling, captured in his poem of 1898, "The White Man's Burden." In it Kipling described the unrewarding task of bringing civilization to "new-caught, sullen peoples," whose response to European benevolence was not gratitude but intransigent hostility:

Take up the White Man's burden—
And reap his old reward:
The blame of those ye better,
The hate of those ye guard—

In Kipling's depiction, the civilizing mission was not only thankless, but futile, because subject peoples inevitably backslid into barbarism:

And when your goal is nearest
The end for others sought,
Watch sloth and heathen Folly
Bring all your hopes to nought

Darwinian Challenges to the Enlightenment   Even more than the politics of imperial rule, ideological developments within Europe profoundly influenced the civilizing mission. The Darwinian revolution of the late nineteenth century irrevocably changed what it meant to be human and, therefore, to be European. Although decades of nineteenth-century scientific research on race difference and racial development had seriously weakened the Enlightenment conception of a single human species developing largely through environmental influence, it was Darwin's particular formulation of the theory of evolution—and its distortion by social Darwinists (see chapter 25) to explain cultural difference—that most affected late-nineteenth-century European views about the capacity of "primitives" to become civilized.

Darwinian theory undermined several key tenets of liberal Enlightenment thought. First, in linking humans to a common ape ancestor, Darwin raised the specter of the animal nature—and thus, the fundamental primitivity—of all humans. Scandalized Europeans responded by accentuating the gap between their own civilized nature and the primitive nature of other "races." Although they disagreed intensely as to whether the gap was wide enough to warrant the classification of other races as separate species (and Darwin himself favored the idea of a single species), most came to view the differences between the races as more significant than the similarities. As a consequence, some abandoned the Enlightenment notion of a single human trajectory along which all cultures developed at varied paces and came to believe in the separate and incommensurable developmental paths of different cultures. Social Darwinian thought thus dealt the liberal universalism of the Enlightenment a serious blow.

Second, Darwin's theory of **natural selection,** which held that the natural selection of traits best adapted to survival served as the prime motor of human development, also challenged European understandings of human agency. In contrast to Europeans of the Enlightenment, who believed that environment—both natural and social—shaped culture, their late-nineteenth-century

Global Moment

THE INDIAN REBELLION OF 1857

The Rebellion of 1857 was an event of immense significance, not just for modern South Asia but also for British colonialism in general. Sparked off by a military mutiny, the rebellion spread through North India, nearly overthrowing the rule of the British East India Company. Although distinctly local in character, the Rebellion of 1857 had dramatic global repercussions, fundamentally shaping the ways in which British colonies were henceforth viewed and governed by their colonial masters.

In the summer of 1857, rumors spread in the military camps in the town of Meerut that the cartridges for the new English rifles used by Indian soldiers or "sepoys" were greased with cow and pig fat. This practice offended the religious sensibilities of both Hindus and Muslims, and on May 9, the sepoys violently revolted against their British officers, who were caught unawares. Many officers were killed in the fracas that followed.

While the issue of the greased cartridges triggered the rebellion, the causes for dissatisfaction with British rule went far deeper. The rebel sepoys were largely recruited from the peasantry in the princely state of Awadh in Northwestern India. Under the British, peasants in places such as Awadh were forced to pay exorbitant taxes. In addition, the British Governor-General Lord Dalhousie had recently conquered Awadh, disregarding his treaty obligations to its ruler, Nawab Wajid Ali Shah. The peasants of Awadh now faced both financial hardship and the humiliation of having their king treated with indignity. Led by the former elites of the Awadh court, the peasantry joined the sepoys and rose in protest against their colonial masters, attacking institutions representative of British rule, such as courts, police stations, and revenue offices. They marched on the capital, Delhi, to reinstate the old and decrepit Mughal emperor, Bahadur Shah Zafar, as their rightful and legitimate ruler. Many similar rebellions in support of local rulers occurred in other parts of India, such as Jhansi and Gwalior in Northern India and the territories ruled by the Maratha chieftains of Central India.

Although the rebels of 1857 toppled British administration in many towns, the British army ultimately suppressed the uprising with great brutality. Despite widespread support for the rebellion among the peasantry and the artisanal classes, it was limited to northern and central India alone. Furthermore, the middle-class intelligentsia as well as many Indian princes loyal to the British refused to participate in the movement, seriously weakening its potency. Both factors contributed to British success in regaining control over the rebellious regions.

The East India Company refused to acknowledge that the rebellion was in any way a result of its own conduct, casting it instead as an unprovoked betrayal on the part of ungrateful subjects. Determined to teach the rebelling Indians a lesson and to inspire enough fear to prevent another rebellion, it torched villages, capturing and executing rebels, some of whom were blown to bits from the mouths of cannons. It also exiled the Mughal emperor, Bahadur Shah Zafar, to Burma and killed his sons.

The British Parliament was less than convinced that mistakes on the part of the East India Company had not contributed to sparking the rebellion. As a result, Parliament transferred the right to rule India from the Company to the Crown on August 2, 1858. The supreme authority in India was to be the "Viceroy"; Queen Victoria became the empress of India and, instead of the board of governors of the East India Company in London, a secretary of state for India who belonged to the British cabinet exercised decision-making and control over Indian affairs.

The British government was now determined that none of the administrative errors of the past would ever be repeated. Since many commentators perceived that British interference in Indian religion and customs had fostered the widespread resentment that had led to the uprising, British rule after the rebellion claimed explic-

When the Indian rebellion erupted in 1857, the rebels besieged the city of Lucknow, the capital of Oudh (in northwestern India), for two months. British troops rescued the British inhabitants of the city and took revenge on the local population. This photograph, taken a few months after the British attack, shows the courtyard of the Sikander Bagh, the royal garden and summer estate of the Nawab of Oudh, littered with the skulls and bones (only one skeleton is complete) of about two thousand Indian insurgents killed there.
Hulton Archive/Getty Images

itly to avoid involvement in the religious and customary practices of Indians. In this context, Queen Victoria's Proclamation in 1858 proclaimed grandly that the government would respect the "ancient rites, usages and customs of India."

Postrebellion British rule in India therefore moved away from the liberal civilizing mission of the early nineteenth century to the idea that India could be efficiently ruled only through its own institutions. This shift, however, often had unfortunate repercussions since the government's identification of certain practices and ideas as "customary" was often flawed and inaccurate, in part because it relied on the advice of upper-caste elites who propagated their own biased views. As a result, the British codified, systematized, and made rigid everyday practices that had been flexible for centuries. This change in ruling ideology and practice affected not just India, but other colonies as well, in particular those in Africa, which were colonized in the late nineteenth century and governed on the Indian model.

Racism also increased alarmingly in the years after the rebellion as the British grappled with feelings of outrage and fear of their subject population. More and more, British and Indians began to live and socialize separately. Furthermore, as social Darwinism became influential in Europe, the British began to see Indians in increasingly racialized ways, often stereotyping groups of people. The British also conferred special privileges on certain segments of the population, such

continued

as rulers who had remained loyal to them during the re-volt, while treating those who had been active in the rebellion as traitors, including many Muslims. By deepening the divisions in Indian society, these policies helped the British maintain control over Indian subjects and prevent future uprisings.

Antagonistic feelings toward Indians ran high not just among the British in India, but in Britain itself. In spite of the extreme brutality with which the rebellion had been suppressed, the popular press and literature depicted British rule as a noble and benign one that had been attacked by savages. Particularly offensive to the British imagination was the idea that Englishwomen had been "defiled" by the rebels, and Victorian paintings and mass market novels were filled with lurid accounts and images of white women being raped and mutilated by Indians. Such images contributed to an enduring British view of the Indian as barbaric and uncivilized.

In the final analysis, how does one judge the Rebellion of 1857? Depending on the perspective, the Rebellion of 1857 has been regarded as a "Mutiny" or the "First War of Indian Independence." As we have seen, British colonial officials perceived the uprising as mindless violence by an ungrateful native population. Indian nationalist leaders and historians have glorified the rebellion as representing the first stirrings of nationalist sentiment in India. Most modern historians, however, emphasize that it is somewhat anachronistic to see the Rebellion of 1857 in terms of the emergence of Indian nationalism. No sense of a shared mission united the local rulers who rose up in rebellion against the British. The loyalty of these rulers was to their own kingdoms, not to the Indian nation. Even the Mughal emperor was seen as the supreme head of a feudal system, not as a representative of a modern state. In their turn, peasants did not always understand that many of their difficulties emerged out of colonial exploitation and attacked the most visible manifestations of oppression such as local landlords and moneylenders. In fact, peasant nationalism was not to emerge in India until the twentieth century.

In spite of its ultimate failure, however, the Rebellion of 1857 remains extremely important for many reasons. It was certainly the largest anticolonial movement that had taken place so far in British India. Moreover, its emphasis on Hindu-Muslim unity made it a powerful symbol for later nationalist leaders. Although many Muslims felt the end of Mughal rule meant that their fortunes and prestige would be under threat, there was also a real recognition that Muslims and Hindus suffered together under British oppression, and in many places they fought side by side against what they perceived as a common foreign enemy. In addition, although led by the landed elite and feudal chieftains, the rebellion saw the participation of different classes, including tribal peoples and low castes. In many ways, therefore, the rebellion marked a crucial turning point in the history of colonial India. Perhaps its greatest legacy is that it served as an inspiration to anticolonial movements, not just in India, but also in Asia and Africa in the late nineteenth and twentieth centuries.

counterparts took Darwin's theory to mean that biology determined culture. Darwin's influence thus undercut the liberal Enlightenment belief in the human mastery of nature and the possibility of socially engineered progress.

Finally, whereas Enlightenment thinkers stressed the mutability of human beings, Darwin's theory of race differentiation lent itself to belief in the permanence of racial traits. Unlike all other human traits, which evolved continually under the pressures of natural selection, Darwin argued, the superficial physical distinctions between the races emerged early in human history through the process of **sexual selection,** preferences marked out in the sexual competition for mates. Because these sexually selected traits—such as hair texture or skin color—provided no benefit for survival, moreover, they tended either not to change or to evolve much more slowly than other traits. While Darwin himself never said that racial traits were fixed, many race scientists of the late nineteenth century made that mental leap themselves and erroneously used Darwin to assert that racial difference was permanent. Social Darwinian misinterpretations of Darwin in this way eroded the liberal Enlightenment belief in mutability and progress.

Popular Views of Race   Darwinian and social Darwinian ideas had an astonishingly broad impact on European conceptions of race and empire. Racist tracts influenced by Darwin, in tandem with newspapers, periodicals, and imperial adventure novels, shaped popular conceptions of the colonial "native," inculcating the widespread belief that non-Western peoples were biologically—and not simply culturally—retrograde and lacked the capacity to improve. Although racist propagandists had been disseminating their ideas for decades (two of the most influential racist writers of the nineteenth century, Count Gobineau and Robert Knox, published their works almost ten years before Darwin), Darwinian theory seemed to many to grant them new legitimacy and authority.

Africa and black Africans occupied a special place in post-Darwinian racist hierarchies because of their presumed proximity to apes. While these links had been made much earlier, they were now widely regarded as having been verified by scientific inquiry and therefore to constitute a sound basis for imperial policy. Some of the most extreme arguments—like those made by social Darwinist imperialist propagandists such as Benjamin Kidd, author of *Social Evolution* (1894)—cast Africans as biologically defective and asserted the inevitability of black extinction and white rule in Africa. Similarly, the ideas of social Darwinist Herbert Spencer propagated the notion that the domination and ultimate biological elimination of less fit African societies was the natural—and therefore evolutionarily desirable—outcome of the struggle for survival of the fittest. While Europeans had viewed African blacks as lesser beings for centuries, for many blackness now became the mark of innate and unchanging biological inferiority.

Race Science and Eugenics   Darwin's work decisively influenced scholarly views of the "native" as well. Race scientists, for example, used—and distorted—his ideas to support theories of race hierarchy. Like Darwin, the race scientists of the late nineteenth century believed in the animal nature of humans and the biological, rather than social, determinants of civilization. Unlike Darwin, however, they believed in the permanent character of race traits and in the unbreachable gap between different race-culture groups. These theories were far from new. Polygenism, or the belief in many human species, had been on the rise in the scientific community since 1800 and dominant since 1850.

This photograph was taken around the turn of the twentieth century by Harry Hamilton Johnson (1858–1927), a colonial administrator, geographer, and naturalist. Like many contemporaries, Johnston was preoccupied with the "racial" classification of colonial subjects and used anthropometry, the measurement of differences in the body types of the human "races," as a tool toward this end.
Royal Geographical Society, London

But Darwin's work lent new conviction and credibility to this theoretical foundation for race science.

The new field of **eugenics** was also an outgrowth of Darwin's influence. Both a science of human heredity and a social program of selective breeding, eugenics was founded in 1883 by Darwin's cousin, Francis Galton, and Galton's colleague, Karl Pearson. Believing that biological differences between races and individuals determined the social order, eugenicists sought to control the process of natural selection and, thereby, to engineer the production of a fitter race. Using the techniques of **biometry,** early eugenicists such as Pearson and Galton tried to apply statistical analysis to identify the salient traits of the races. But Galton soon realized that the eugenicist project required more research into the laws of heredity. That recognition led to the acceptance of the new science of genetics, which identified the gene as the unit of inheritance. Although the Austrian scientist Gregor Mendel had first elaborated the gene-based theory of heredity in the 1860s, it was not until Galton and Pearson made use of Mendelian genetics around 1900 that genetic theory gained scientific respectability.

By the turn of the century, the eugenics movement was a highly prestigious scientific movement in Europe, the United States, and Japan. As such, it influenced public policy, including the forced sterilization of "unfit" groups (people with mental impairment, for example) and the introduction of immigration quotas limiting the influx of "racial undesirables." Despite the nefarious connotations of the movement, especially in the aftermath of Hitler, the eugenicists of the early twentieth century were a motley political group. While Galton himself was a Victorian liberal committed to human progress, for example, Pearson embraced social Darwinist views and argued in his work *National Life from the Standpoint of Science* (1901) that Africans must be eliminated from British South Africa for the biological and moral purification of the colony (see "Karl Pearson on National Life from the Standpoint of Science," p. 805).

The Rise of Anthropology Darwinian theory also had a formative impact on the view of the "native" adopted by the new field of anthropology, which emerged as a formal academic discipline in the late nineteenth century to chart the stages of human cultural evolution and to identify the universal cultural traits of humankind through the comparative study of cultures. Anthropologists and archaeologists of the period fiercely debated whether contemporary "savages" were remnants of the European past, whether they had degenerated from a higher level of civilization, and whether they had the capacity to improve. A dominant model was expounded by the social evolutionary anthropologist Edward Burnett Tylor. His **doctrine of survivals** argued that contemporary "savages" were evolutionary atavisms whose cultural life provided a window onto the European past. A liberal universalist and relativist himself, Tylor admired many of the moral traits he observed in "savage" culture and acknowledged certain defects in European society. Nevertheless, his social evolutionary paradigm reinforced the view that contemporary "savage" culture—especially that of black Africans—had developed outside of the evolutionary mainstream and, therefore, would always remain inferior to European civilization.

If nineteenth-century anthropology created images of innate or cultural primitivity that seemed to invite European domination, European colonizers also made use of anthropological study to implement imperial rule. Believing that knowledge of "primitive culture" was the key to the consolidation of colonial rule, European governments were frequently the sponsors of ethnographic research in the late nineteenth century. They had also done this earlier, of course, and the late-nineteenth-century application of scientific study to political control was in a sense merely a continuation of the Enlightenment project of systematically studying the world in order to master it; Captain James Cook's scientific voyages to the Pacific had embodied this project, as had Mungo Park's African expeditions. Two key ideas, however, frequently distinguished the project in the late nineteenth century: first, the conviction that European cultural superiority stemmed from biological roots and, second, that this superiority—and with it the mandate to rule the world—was a permanent feature of the global order.

IMPERIALISM AT ITS PEAK

By the turn of the century, Europeans had transformed the constructed environment, the economic life, the social order, and the cultural practices of their colonial subjects. The emergence of the first anticolonial nationalist movements in this period responded to this upheaval. At the same time, ordinary Europeans were becoming more aware of the empire. By the eve of the First World War, the colonies permeated European consciousness and culture as never before. Just as empire imposed European culture on the non-Western world, it brought that world into the heart of Europe.

The Reordering of Colonial Life

Once Europeans had secured control over their colonies, they moved to consolidate and exploit that power to its fullest. In so doing, they transformed every aspect of colonial life, from building colonial cities and establishing a cash crop economy to introducing Western education and remapping indigenous social hierarchies.

Building Colonial Infrastructure With the global conquest completed by the turn of the twentieth century, European colonizers embarked on the massive enterprise of building colonial infrastructure and implementing colonial administration. In less urbanized parts of the empire they erected colonial cities, towns, and ports, and in them schools, hospitals, clock towers, and ceremonial gateways. In places where cities and ports existed, such as Cairo, Lagos, Singapore, and Bombay, Europeans undertook ambitious modernization projects, including clearing slums and

KARL PEARSON ON NATIONAL LIFE FROM THE STANDPOINT OF SCIENCE

Karl Pearson (1857–1936) was an English, Cambridge-educated mathematician who also studied law and social and political philosophy. He held the first chair of eugenics at University College, London, and became the director of the eugenics laboratory there. He was a disciple of Francis Galton, the founder of eugenics, which sought to improve the human race through selective breeding. Pearson, in his turn, applied statistical methods to the study of biological problems, especially evolution and heredity, a science he called biometrics. Pearson's views on eugenics are seen as deeply problematic and racist today. He claimed that he was a socialist, committed to uplifting the masses, but in fact, his "scientific" view of a nation, as presented in National Life from the Standpoint of Science, *claimed that a country's progress and well-being depended on constantly replenishing its "better" stock at the expense of its "inferior races." The twentieth century was to see many undesirable applications of the principles of eugenics in the Western world, including the mass exterminations carried out by Nazi Germany.*

"History shows me one way, and one way only, in which a high state of civilization has been produced, namely, the struggle of race with race, and the survival of the physically and mentally fitter race. . . . The struggle means suffering, intense suffering, while it is in progress; but that struggle and that suffering have been the stages by which the white man has reached his present stage of development, and they account for the fact that he no longer lives in caves and feeds on roots and nuts. This dependence of progress on the survival of the fitter race, terribly black as it may seem to some of you, gives the struggle for existence its redeeming features; it is the fiery crucible out of which comes the finer metal. You may hope for a time when the sword shall be turned into the plowshare, when American and German and English traders shall no longer compete in the markets of the world for their raw material and for their food supply, when the white man and the dark shall share the soil between them, and each till it as he lists. But, believe me, when that day comes mankind will no longer progress; there will be nothing to check the fertility of inferior stock; the relentless law of heredity will not be controlled and guided by natural selection. Man will stagnate; and unless he ceases to multiply, the catastrophe will come again; famine and pestilence, as we see them in the East, physical selection instead of the struggle of race against race, will do the work more relentlessly, and, to judge from India and China, far less efficiently than of old. . . .

"There is a struggle of race against race and of nation against nation. In the early days of that struggle it was a blind, unconscious struggle of barbaric tribes. At the present day, in the case of the civilized white man, it has become more and more the conscious, carefully directed attempt of the nation to fit itself to a continuously changing environment. The nation has to foresee how and where the struggle will be carried on; the maintenance of national position is becoming more and more a conscious preparation for changing conditions, an insight into the needs of coming environments.

"We have to remember that man is subject to the universal law of inheritance, and that a dearth of capacity may arise if we recruit our society from the inferior and not the better stock. If any social opinions or class prejudices tamper with the fertility of the better stocks, then the national character will take but a few generations to be seriously modified. . . . You will see that my view—and I think it may be called the scientific view of a nation—is that of an organized whole, kept up to a high pitch of internal efficiency by insuring that its numbers are substantially recruited from the better stocks, and kept up to a high pitch of external efficiency by contest, chiefly by way of war with inferior races, and with equal races by the struggle for trade-routes and for the sources of raw material and of food supply. This is the natural history view of mankind, and I do not think you can in its main features subvert it."

From Karl Pearson, National Life from the Standpoint of Science, *1900, available at housatonic.net/Documents/333.htm.*

constructing new housing and roadways. They also brought new modes of transportation to their empires, in the form of highway systems, bridges, canals, and railway networks, as well as new systems of communication, notably the telegraph. By 1865 telegraph lines connected India to Europe; by 1871 a cable ran from Vladivostok to Shanghai, Hong Kong, and Singapore. In addition to constructing a new built environment, colonial rulers imposed European models of administration in many spheres of colonial life. Colonial administrators reorganized the police, army, judiciary, and postal service along European lines and, to varying degrees, introduced European models of education—including European language instruction—and Western-style medicine.

Europeans regarded these projects as central to the task of colonial rule. The use of grid layouts in colonial cities and ports and the laying of railway lines were intended to efficiently transport goods to both domestic and metropolitan markets and thus to facilitate

With the conquest of much of the world complete by the turn of the twentieth century, Europeans turned their attention to the introduction of European technologies and communications in their colonies. Using local and imported colonial labor, they built extensive road and rail networks in many parts of Africa and Asia. This photograph of 1891 shows workers clearing the ground for a railway in rural Kenya. What strategic and economic objectives motivated European colonizers to undertake these projects?
Hulton Archive/Getty Images

European commercial exploitation of the colonies. This infrastructure also had military and strategic importance. Railways and telegraphs allowed for the rapid mobilization of European troops, while urban street grids permitted the policing and surveillance of local populations. The construction of colonial cities and towns also revealed the European agenda to regulate race relations in this period through the spatial separation of "natives" and Europeans. Colonizers built better ventilated, more sanitary residential areas for themselves—for security reasons, often near military cantonments—where they re-created European-style institutions, including clubs, polo fields, and churches, leaving "natives" to cluster in what they saw as crowded and unhealthy urban spaces. The British, for example, successfully segregated colonial Madras into European and Indian quarters and labeled them, respectively, "White Town" and "Black Town."

The New Colonial Economy Explicit colonial rule also triggered major economic transformations. Although the global terms of trade had long worked against Asia and Africa, the European conquest, along with increased industrial development in Europe, further widened the gap between **metropole** and colony in the late century. As they had done earlier, the industrial economies of Europe exported manufactured goods to their colonies and imported raw materials, especially cash crops, from them. By the late nineteenth century, however, more countries were flooding colonial markets with industrial goods, while the European adoption of neomercantilist trade policies from the

1880s on prevented the colonies from pursuing trade relationships outside the metropole.

Above all, the conquests of the late nineteenth century ensured that European colonists could use coercion to install and support new agricultural and labor regimes. The advent of a cash-based agricultural economy meant that many peasants no longer primarily relied on subsistence farming, turning instead to the production of crops required as raw materials to feed industrial production in Europe or to wage labor, both on small farms and big European-run plantations. British India, for instance, became a major producer of opium, rice, indigo, tea, and, above all, cotton during this period. While some peasants prospered from cash-crop production, many paid an exorbitant price for the abrupt transition to a new agricultural economy. Their abandonment of subsistence farming based on food grain production made them much more vulnerable to famine and also exposed them to the fluctuations of international commerce. Thus, for example, the invention of synthetic dyes in the early twentieth century rendered Indian indigo, long a staple of the British textile industry, obsolete, leaving thousands of Indian indigo farmers bankrupted. Despite the weakened economic position of peasants, taxes remained high, thus forcing rural populations to migrate to cities and towns in search of work as urban laborers.

Another distinctive feature of the late-nineteenth-century colonial economy was the global migration of labor. The advent of modern transportation allowed Europeans to dispatch millions of indentured laborers to build irrigation systems and railroads and to work on plantations and in mines in regions far from their homes. This diaspora of migrant labor divided families and created local demographic imbalances. Cochin-Chinese (Vietnamese) laborers worked the plantations of French Cambodia, for example, while tens of thousands of Indian and Chinese laborers, known as "coolies," migrated to work in British possessions, including South Africa, East Africa, Ceylon (Sri Lanka), the West Indies, Burma, Malaya, Fiji, and Australia. In certain cases, indentured labor from existing colonies facilitated the colonization of other regions. The construction of a vast railway network by indentured laborers from India, for example, made possible the British settlement of East Africa.

The Cultural Dimensions of Colonial Rule   Europeans conquered the globe not merely by military, diplomatic, and economic means, but by cultural domination as well. This Western cultural influence reached far and wide—including education, the maintenance of law and order, relations between different groups in society, language use, and dress codes—and often fundamentally transformed and restructured the existing social fabric. In fact, few aspects of everyday life in postcolonial societies are untouched by the colonial encounter, from the architecture in towns like Dakar and Delhi and the vast networks of railroads across Asia and Africa to the immense popularity of cricket in the West Indies and South Asia and the addition of the blouse to the sari at the behest of prudish missionaries in India.

One important effect of European dominance was to create new hierarchies and divisions within colonial society. The establishment of Western-style schools and universities throughout the European empires, for example, served the purpose of producing a Western-educated colonial elite. European colonizers hoped in this way to create loyal subjects who would serve their imperial rulers in the lower levels of the local colonial administration and, to some extent, bridge the gap between colonizers and colonized. However, this vision was only partially fulfilled. In many situations, European colonizers favored traditional elites at the expense of the newly educated professional classes, believing the former to be more reliable supporters of colonial rule. Indeed, Western-educated colonial subjects found themselves doubly marginalized, by Europeans who continued to condescend to them and to exclude them from positions of power, and by their own alienation from the indigenous masses. As one example of this kind of cultural displacement, educated Algerians refused to speak Arabic, favoring French, the language of their colonial masters, instead.

As they sought to understand and classify native societies, European colonial rulers also emphasized particular social identities of the colonized, thus fueling social conflict between different indigenous groups. In late-nineteenth-century British India, for example, colonial administrators and politicians reinforced divisions of caste (the hierarchical division of society based on birth). Following the questionable advice of upper-caste Indian scholars, the British declared caste to be the foundation of traditional Indian society, even though it had been only one of several such social markers in precolonial India. British authorities relied increasingly on caste stereotypes. They labeled the Gurkhas and the Sikhs, for example, as "martial" and considered them to be good recruits for the British army, while they classified others, such as the Kallars, as intrinsically "criminal" and treated them with deep disdain and suspicion. With time, these classifications became increasingly fixed, leading to the hardening of social boundaries within Indian society.

Methods of Governance

How did Europeans govern the vast empire of the late nineteenth and early twentieth centuries? Virtually everywhere, the new imperial mission of the period translated into transformed models of colonial governance, although these models—and their implementation—varied widely from empire to empire and, within each empire, from colony to colony.

Brute Force: Exploitation in the Belgian Congo   In some places, Europeans ruled by brute force. Perhaps the most egregious example of domination through ruthless violence was the Belgian King Leopold II's Congo Free State. There, the increasingly cynical and racist European view of the colonial "native" was taken to its logical conclusion. Between 1898 and 1905, Leopold's troops impressed Congolese men into hard labor at gunpoint. Some were used to build roads, while others served long periods in the army and, after discharge, in the rural police. This indigenous police force, in turn, compelled the rest of the population to abandon subsistence farming and instead produce rubber for the state. When the police encountered resistance to these arrangements, they responded by shooting recalcitrants, turning over baskets of severed hands from the corpses—as well as from the living—to the Belgian authorities as proof that punishment had been carried out.

Although Leopold's methods saved him from bankruptcy, other European powers condemned his de facto enslavement, murder, and maiming of his subjects as a moral outrage. In 1908 the Belgian Parliament assumed control of the colony as a direct consequence of this international outcry. An official inquiry mounted by a Belgian commission reported in 1919 that Leopold's methods had reduced the population of the Congo by

Photograph of mutilated workers from the Belgian Congo from the late nineteenth century. Under the rule of King Leopold II, Africans were forced into rubber cultivation at gunpoint. Those that did not meet their production quotas were either killed or had their hands cut off. The forced labor regime of rubber production in Leopold's Congo was one of the most atrocious chapters in the history of the European colonization of Africa.
Courtesy of Auti-Slavery International

half. Most recent scholarly assessments have been even grimmer, estimating that the population of the Congo Free State shrank from between 20 and 30 million to 8 million during Leopold's rule.

Indirect Rule in the British Empire More than any other ruling power, Britain took the lessons of empire to heart in elaborating a new system of "indirect rule." Interpreting the Indian Rebellion as evidence of the futility and folly of direct colonial involvement, British administrators devised a relatively hands-off policy that largely delegated power to traditional chiefs, kings, and princes. These traditional leaders, in turn, were expected to carry out the dictates of colonial officials. The system was implemented in its fullest form in colonial Africa.

The British favored indirect rule for a variety of reasons. Because it relied largely on local people, it was far less expensive than other methods of rule. Furthermore, by using indigenous leaders and thus attaching themselves to "tradition," the British sought to gain legitimacy among subject peoples. This legitimacy, it was hoped, would make British colonial administration more stable and better able to withstand colonial insurgence.

Indirect rule had several negative consequences for the colonies. First, although the British made much of the fact that indirect rule left indigenous cultures essentially intact, this was not the case. In the African context, for example, indirect rule removed traditional limitations on the power of the local chieftain. Required to obey the British authorities alone, he was no longer accountable to his subjects or to other political leaders in the community. By thus granting unfettered power to traditional leaders, the British cleared the way for the establishment of despotic regimes. The Fulani Emirs who acted as British agents in Nigeria, for example, were effectively dictators. Second, by casting themselves as the benevolent guardians of African "custom" and "tribal" practice, the British promoted the tribal identity at the expense of other social affiliations and loyalties in colonial society. Indirect rule thus fomented division and conflict along "tribal" or ethnic lines. Finally, in emphasizing African "tradition," indirect rule tended to neglect the higher education of colonial subjects, at the same time marginalizing Western-educated Africans perceived as threatening to British rule.

Sustaining the Civilizing Mission in the French Empire While the Germans and Dutch adopted some variant of the British model of indirect rule and the Portuguese and the Belgians ruled by unadorned coercion and violence, the French developed an alternative model of governance. In many (although not all) parts of the French Empire, they implemented a system of "direct rule" that unequivocally repudiated the authority of existing leaders and political institutions in favor of that of French officials, laws, and codes. The method of direct colonial rule reflected the French *mission civilisatrice*, its civilizing mission to assimilate the "native" to French culture. The French thus retained the ideal of assimilationism even after other nations had begun to move away from it.

In part, this can be explained as an outgrowth of French chauvinism and the sense that France had been the guardian of "civilization" in Europe for centuries. But there were other reasons as well. Although the *mission civilisatrice* was simply a variant of the liberal civilizing mission, with its origins in Enlightenment universalism and principles of universal equality and rationality, the French tradition of republicanism made these beliefs more central to French political identity

This photograph shows the Lieutenant-General of the Punjab, in northwestern India, surrounded by the chieftains and rulers of various Indian states in traditional regal garb. Although British authority over their kingdoms was unquestioned, the colonial administration often allowed local rulers nominally to remain in power. In return these Indian rulers were often the staunchest supporters of British rule in India.
Popperfoto

and culture than they were elsewhere in Europe. Also, because French philosophical and scientific tradition tended to emphasize the importance of environment in determining human development, Darwin's influence and that of biological determinism came later to France and carried less weight there than in other European nations.

The French method of governance had contradictory effects. On the one hand, the French policy destroyed indigenous political and cultural institutions even more than the British policy did. On the other hand, "natives" were in principle seen as potential Frenchmen, with the implication that, once civilized, they could be granted the rights of French citizens. In some instances, France conferred citizenship rights on colonial subjects. For example, in 1848 African males from the coastal region of Senegal were granted voting rights and sent a Senegalese representative, Durand Valentin, to the French legislature. However, even the promise of French citizenship was double-edged, connoting greater dependence on and integration with colonial masters, rather than greater self-determination and autonomy. In practice, moreover, intense racism and violent subjugation undermined lofty French ideals of republicanism and democracy. In places like West Africa, for example, the exclusion of Africans from administrative posts and the denial of their right to elect their own representatives tarnished the rhetoric of full citizenship.

Comparing French and British Rule   Despite these important ideological distinctions, the difference between French and British forms of governance should not be exaggerated. In practice, both Britain and France relied on a combination of direct rule through a European official and indirect rule through local collaborators and paid agents. The French also focused their assimilationist efforts on those colonies—like Algeria—which they

felt had the greatest potential for Europeanization. Elsewhere—as in Indochina, Madagascar, and Morocco—they settled for improving "natives" within the context of their own cultures. Moreover, as Darwinian ideas grew stronger in France, the debate over whether the cultural assimilation of colonial subjects was possible or even desirable intensified, leading to the abandonment of the *mission civilisatrice* as official policy after the First World War. French and British rule thus differed more in theory than they did in practice.

Non-Western Nationalisms

The mid-to-late nineteenth century witnessed the emergence and growth of nationalist sentiments not only in Europe, but in its colonies in Asia and Africa as well.

Characteristics of Colonial Nationalism   In the late nineteenth century, notions of the nation and nationhood in the colonial world shared important features with their European counterparts. Nationalisms in Asia and Africa thus typically centered on the belief in a shared—sometimes fabricated—history and culture. For Chinese nationalists like Sun Yat-sen, the splendors of the Chinese past rendered the present-day subjugation of the Chinese under the Qing and the European powers unnatural and unacceptable. Likewise, the Pan African movement appealed to an imagined precolonial past in which harmony between African polities and ethnicities prevailed.

Like late-nineteenth-century European nationalism, non-Western nationalisms also frequently defined themselves in racial, ethnic, and religious terms. Chinese nationalists, for example, privileged the majority Han as the "true" Chinese and denied equal status to other ethnic groups, such as the Tibetans and Mongols. Exclusion along religious or cultural lines was also

MAP 26.4 RESISTANCE TO IMPERIALISM, 1880–1920
This map reveals widespread opposition to colonial rule at the turn of the twentieth century. Although strategic and technological advantages allowed the European nations to conquer much of Africa and Asia in this period, indigenous resistance made the full-scale pacification of the colonies a longer, more difficult process. How did European methods of colonial governance attempt to thwart rebellion?
◆ For an online version, go to www.mhhe.com/chambers9 > chapter 26 > book maps

common. In India, a Hindu branch of nationalism claimed Indian history as Hindu history, labeling the long periods of Muslim rule in India as the dark years of foreign invasion. With the substantial Muslim population in India thus excluded from Indian nationalism, some Muslim leaders pledged loyalty to the British while others demanded a separate Muslim nation.

Some nationalist movements, notably those in China and the Ottoman Empire, saw the indigenous regime that had allowed European encroachment as the primary enemy. Under the leadership of Sun Yat-sen, Chinese nationalists attacked and, in 1911, ultimately overthrew the declining Qing Dynasty, which they condemned as both inefficient and illegitimate. Likewise, a group of nationalist reformers known as the Young Turks revolted against Ottoman rule in 1908, blaming both Sultan Abdul Hamid's authoritarian regime and European intervention for the decline of Ot-

toman power. Seeking to introduce Western-style political and administrative reforms independent of European interference, the Young Turks succeeded, for a brief period, in establishing a constitutional government with secular institutions.

Non-Western nationalist movements at the turn of the century differed sharply from other forms of anti-colonial insurgence. The latter tended to be local in character and aimed against the direct oppressor, rather than at colonial rule. The Indian Rebellion of 1857, for example, targeted local Indian landholders and moneylenders and local colonial magistrates and police, rather than the British government in India. Similarly, in the Maji Rebellion of 1906–1907 in German East Africa, traditional religious leaders led angry peasants in fighting the imposition of cotton cultivation by the Germans, targeting African as well as German overseers. Non-Western nationalist movements, by contrast, clearly articulated their struggle as one against foreign rule, with the long-range political goal of introducing modern constitutional forms of government. The fact that anticolonial insurgence persisted in the late nineteenth century reveals that African and Asian nationalisms of the period remained largely elitist movements that often failed to address the more immediate, acute grievances of the colonial masses.

Causes of Colonial Nationalism   Ironically, the colonial state itself in many ways facilitated the rise of colonial nationalism. First, colonial educational institutions, courts of law, and railways that crisscrossed vast countries like India brought people from faraway regions together in ways that had simply not been feasible in the past. Furthermore, as European colonists drew disparate regions together into a common, exploitative economic system, nationalists could appeal to a sense of shared fate.

Second, most leaders of nationalist movements in Asia and Africa received liberal educations in Western-style institutions and often became professionals, such as doctors and lawyers. This made them well-equipped to lead efforts to modernize their administrations and economies along Western lines, as was the case in Egypt and Turkey. Hence, the colonial rulers' efforts to produce a local elite through the promotion of Western education often backfired, as some of these intended allies used European concepts of universalism and democracy to question their own subjection to foreign rule.

The emergence of the mass press and, with that, the growth of a politically informed civic public also contributed to the growth of colonial nationalisms. Print media, including newspapers, journals, books, and pamphlets, that addressed nationalist issues now circulated among a much larger literate audience. This literature appeared not just in the languages of the colonizer but in local languages that had become systematized and standardized with their own formal grammars in this period, both by educated natives and by colonial administrators and missionaries seeking to modernize and master languages unfamiliar to them. The formation of a broad range of indigenous voluntary associations also created a new arena in which the educated public came together to discuss the pertinent issues of the day. Nationalist organizations, such as the Indian National Congress (founded in 1885), often took shape in this setting.

Debating Empire: Imperial Politics in the Metropole

While a common cultural framework informed European attitudes toward empire in the nineteenth century, a range of different views and voices nevertheless existed. In fact, in the late nineteenth century, with Western global domination at its peak and European racism and cultural arrogance on the rise, more Europeans debated the nature and scope of empire than ever before. There were several reasons for this. In part, the efforts of nineteenth-century nation-states to engage the masses in issues of empire explain the reach of the debate. Better educated, more literate Europeans now learned about empire in state-supported primary schools and from reading the mass press. With the broadening of the electorate, moreover, many more Europeans had voting rights and, thus, a stake in the nation's imperial politics than ever before. The vast scale of empire in this period also drew many more Europeans directly into the empire, whether as soldiers fighting in colonial wars, as civil servants sent to govern the empire, as emigrants to the settlement colonies, or as relatives of Europeans abroad.

Imperialist Politicians and Parties   No one political party, but rather groups within all parties, waved the imperial banner. Nonetheless, almost everywhere in Europe, imperialism aided the political resurgence of the right, especially in Great Britain and Germany. Indeed, imperialism allowed conservative groups with their traditional base in the army, the Church, and the aristocracy to ally themselves with commercial interests in a program of popular appeal that promised prosperity and national glory. In Britain, for example, the Conservative party, led by Prime Minister Benjamin Disraeli (1868; 1874–1880), embraced empire in principle as well as in practice. In 1875 Disraeli snatched up shares in the Suez Canal in 1875 from the indebted Khedive in a successful attempt to outmaneuver the French and secure British control over Egypt. In 1876 he conferred the title Empress of India on Queen Victoria, a gesture that captured the popular imagination.

Liberals and centrists took the imperial initiative elsewhere. In France, republicans like Jules Ferry and Leon Gambetta, backed by a group of former colonial administrators and military men in the parliament, promoted expansionism in an effort to bolster national prestige after the demoralizing defeat in the Franco-Prussian War of 1870–1871. Likewise, Italian liberals such as Francesco Crispi and Giovanni Giolitti pursued imperial ventures in the hope of fostering Italian nationalist sentiment.

Critics of Empire   Outspoken critics of empire could be found, however, in almost all political camps. In Belgium, the king's sponsorship of empire met with political opposition from the entire Belgian parliament. Some on the political right also disapproved of empire as a dangerous distraction from domestic issues. According to French rightists, for example, empire diverted attention from the nation's mission to take back Alsace-Lorraine, seized by the Germans in 1871. In

HOBSON'S INTERPRETATION OF IMPERIALISM

Debate on the interpretation of imperialism has not ceased since the publication of J. A. Hobson's Imperialism: A Study *in 1902. The work went through many editions and remains worth reading today. Hobson was a highly respected British economist and social scientist, and his study is filled with statistics and careful argument. His conclusions capture some of the essence and polemic tone of the case he made.*

"If Imperialism may no longer be regarded as a blind inevitable destiny, is it certain that imperial expansion as a deliberately chosen line of public policy can be stopped?

"We have seen that it is motivated, not by the interests of the nation as a whole, but by those of certain classes, who impose the policy upon the nation for their own advantage. . . . The essentially illicit nature of this use of the public resources of the nation to safeguard and improve private investments should be clearly recognized.

". . . Analysis of Imperialism, with its nature supports, militarism, oligarchy, bureaucracy, protection, concentration of capital and violent trade fluctuations, has marked it out as the supreme danger of modern national States. The power of the imperialist forces within the nation to use the national resources for their private gain, by operating the instrument of the States, can only be overthrown by the establishment of a genuine democracy."

Britain, the liberals largely opposed further imperial expansion, particularly after the Indian Rebellion of 1857. Liberals also rejected many of the techniques of imperial expansion, including the use of ambiguous treaties and the hasty reliance on force. The liberal leader William Gladstone (1868–1874; 1880–1885; 1886; 1892–1894) won the election of 1880 after campaigning against the immoral and un-Christian imperialist policies of the Conservatives and only supported imperial rule in the most lukewarm fashion. Even so, many liberal imperialists joined the conservative Tories because of Gladstone's "betrayal" and, ultimately, the Liberal party hatched its own imperial wing.

Across Europe, the radical left, especially socialists, presented the most consistent and vocal opposition to imperialism. Anatole France, one of France's most popular authors, told a protest meeting in 1906, "Whites do not communicate with blacks or yellow people except to enserf or massacre them. The people whom we call barbarians know us only through our own crimes." Socialists, radicals, and labor leaders likened the suppression of strikers and radical agitators to the brutality of imperial repression and protested the living conditions of European workers and peasants by comparing their subordination to that of colonial subjects.

The opposition of leftists to empire emerged not only out of feelings of solidarity with oppressed peoples but also out of their fundamental ideological antagonism toward capitalism, which they saw as inextricably entwined with imperialism. Leftist thinkers, in fact, wrote some of the first and most influential (if inaccurate) analyses of the causes and consequences of empire at the turn of the nineteenth century. In *Imperialism: A Study* (1902), the British left liberal econo-

mist J. A. Hobson argued that imperialism emerged out of the inherent logic of industrial capitalism and its fundamentally unequal distribution of wealth (see "Hobson's Interpretation of Imperialism," above). Underconsumption caused by the low wages of industrial workers and the excess savings of the wealthy created insufficient aggregate demand in the domestic economy, and profit-seeking capitalists therefore turned to new markets overseas as a more profitable setting in which to invest their surplus capital. Imperialism thus stemmed from capitalist exploitation of the European working classes and fostered still greater injustice in its exploitation of the colonial masses.

Hobson inspired the even more scathing critique of imperialism's exploitation of the global masses of the Russian Marxist leader V. I. Lenin. In *Imperialism: The Last Stage of Capitalism* (1916), Lenin elaborated on Hobson's analysis, linking imperialism specifically to the advent of monopoly capitalism, a new and more advanced phase of capitalist development in which financial, rather than industrial, capital propelled the European economy. In his view, the new imperialism was fomented by competition between an ever-smaller number of monopoly capitalists—large firms—for domination of global investment and raw material markets. For Lenin, imperialism represented capitalism in its highest and most parasitic stage.

Popular Attitudes toward Imperialism   While imperial support cut across class divisions, certain social groups nevertheless tended to identify more with the imperial mission than others.

Imperial rule had particular meaning, for example, for members of the aristocracy, especially in Britain

Although missionaries confronted great obstacles—including little success in converting Africans and colonial administrators who regarded Christian conversion as a potential threat to the status quo—they continued to come to Africa in large numbers. In this photograph, from late-nineteenth-century French Equatorial Africa, the missionary's evident satisfaction in his paternalistic role provides a stark contrast to the sullenness of his flock.

and France. Aristocrats, after all, expected to feel distant from the people they ruled and were comfortable with a language of subordination applicable to both European and colonial societies. In Britain, the younger sons of aristocratic families had a long tradition of government and military service. With democratization and the rise of a civil service, their best chances for the experience of governing or of military command were in the empire. In France, where the Republic turned anticlerical after 1875, Catholic and monarchist nobles were largely excluded from public positions at home but could still find them in the colonies.

The European working classes were divided on the issue. In Britain and Germany, they tended to support empire more often than not. In Britain, the popularity of proimperialists skits and songs in music halls and pubs attests to the **jingoism** of working-class audiences. In Germany, the government's dedication to militarism and nationalism promoted popular support of the German Empire. By contrast, large segments of the French and Italian masses opposed colonialism, even during the zenith of expansion in the late nineteenth century, and protested conscription to fight in colonial wars. Ill-fated imperial ventures, in fact, swept both the French leader Jules Ferry (1885) and the Italian leader Francesco Crispi (1896) from office.

The Effects of Imperialism on European Society

Although empire did not necessarily constitute the central political or social issue of the late nineteenth century, it nevertheless touched the lives of ordinary Europeans more than ever before. This new reach reflected the scope of empire itself, which attracted increasing numbers of Europeans overseas. Growing awareness of and involvement in empire may also be traced to the rise of a new commercial culture, exposing Europeans to a flood of imperial imagery and goods. Finally, as empire became closely identified with new European gender roles, it became further integrated into the mainstream of European culture.

Europeans in the Empire   Although European manpower was scarce almost everywhere outside the few colonies where Europeans had settled, European soldiers, administrators, and missionaries came to the empire in growing numbers. European conscripts fought not only in wars of conquest but in the ongoing repression of anticolonial insurgence as well. For officials at every level of the expanding colonial administration, employment in the colonial service conferred a degree of prestige and power that an analogous position in Europe simply could not bring. Peasants and villagers revered the District Collector (tax collector) in India, for example, as a minor *raja* or deity. Missionaries also continued to flock to the empire, where they confronted new challenges, including the advance of Islam and the erosion of their authority in the form of breakaway "Africanized" Christian churches. They also faced the obstructionism of colonial administrators who feared that conversion efforts would spark indigenous unrest.

With the opening of the Suez Canal (which cut the distance by boat from England to India almost in half), the introduction of faster steamships, and the expansion of colonial railway networks, European women also appeared on the imperial scene in new numbers. In addition to married women who joined their husbands in the army or the colonial administration, a substantial number of single women emigrated to the colonies during the late nineteenth century in search of employment or marriage opportunities unavailable at home. Many of them failed to find suitable jobs, suffering downward economic mobility and a loss of social status.

In addition, European migration to the settlement colonies peaked in this period, although it never approached the numbers of Europeans emigrating to the United States. The French emigrated primarily to Algeria in the late nineteenth century, where they ultimately constituted 10 percent of the Algerian population. British emigration to Canada, Australia, and New Zealand also increased substantially. Between 1896 and 1914, for example, 150,000 British citizens resettled in Canada. By the end of the century, many French and British citizens had friends or relatives who lived in or had completed a stint in the colonies.

Representing the Empire   In the late nineteenth century, Europeans absorbed information about and images of the empire in myriad new ways. To begin with, a more literate European public, educated in state-supported primary schools, now could read about empire in a variety of print venues. The most important of these was the mass press. European governments were quick to recognize the political potential of the press and to use it to mobilize public opinion in favor of empire at key moments. When British metropolitan support for the Boer War was at low ebb, for example, the *London Times* played a critical role in drumming up anti-Afrikaner sentiment. Europeans also avidly read the memoirs of explorers and missionaries and devoured imperial adventure novels during this period. H. Rider Haggard's best-selling novel, *King Solomon's Mines* (1885), detailing the exploits of British heroes as they penetrate a remote African region, encounter savages, and discover the riches of a vanished civilization, exemplifies the genre.

Beyond the world of print media, the empire was on visual display, often in spectacular form, at the turn of the century. Unlike earlier periods, when elite boutiques sold luxury goods from the empire to the rich, the emergence of the department store meant that middle-class consumers could purchase an array of moderately priced imperial exotica, ranging from Persian rugs to shawls from India. From the 1880s on, department stores catered to the middle-class European taste for Japanese and Chinese ornaments—screens, fans, and porcelain, for example—in household decor. By the 1890s, some department stores featured fashions designated specifically for the colonies, often with a rugged or military look, to outfit the fashionable European elite overseas.

This advertisement from the *Illustrated London News* in 1897 depicts a group of Sudanese warriors dumbfounded at the sight of the Pears' soap slogan carved into a cliff-side. Pears had no intention of selling soap to the Sudanese. Instead, its product was being presented to British consumers as a symbol of the superiority of British civilization and its imperative to dominate others.
The Mary Evans Picture Libarary

The budding advertising industry also exploited imperial imagery in magazines, on city billboards and posters, and in product brochures. Advertisers exploited the appeal of empire to market products with no imperial connection, plastering likenesses of the popular explorer of Africa, Henry Stanley, for example, on advertisements for Bovril bouillon and Congo Soap. Some advertisements seemed to serve as much as imperial propaganda as they did marketing tools. In a striking example, an advertisement for Pears' Soap linked themes of cleanliness, civilization, and hygiene by depicting awed Sudanese "savages" genuflecting before a cliff etched with the words "PEARS' SOAP IS THE BEST" (see above).

From the 1860s on, Europeans began to exhibit their empires in the setting of world's fairs. Mounted in different European and American cities about once every decade, the fairs displayed the industrial prowess of participating nations to vast audiences. By the 1890s, no world's fair was complete without its own ethnographic displays of colonial peoples, often located, significantly, next to the animal displays. Grouped in reconstructed colonial villages, between fifty and two hundred men, women, and children lived for months at a time on the fairgrounds. There they carried out "exotic" rituals, such as indigenous dancing, along with the mundane activities of daily life, in effect performing the role of "primitive" before rapt European audiences. The most popular exhibits were often those of peoples deemed to be most "savage," such as villagers from Dahomey (Benin).

In addition to the imaginary travel enabled by the world's fairs, middle- and upper-class Europeans began to visit parts of the empire as tourists in the late nineteenth century. While the tourist industry itself was new and still developing largely around seaside and spa resorts within Europe, improved steamships and the development of railway networks in many parts of the world made it possible to travel farther afield. Starting in the 1850s, the British entrepreneur Thomas Cook organized the first commercial tours to North Africa and the Middle East. Algeria and Egypt quickly emerged as popular destinations. Relying on Baedeker and other guidebooks to provide insight into the exotic, British, German, French, and American tourists admired indigenous architecture, purchased "native" handicrafts, and gawked at the local populations.

Empire also influenced the development of high art in the late nineteenth century, in particular the birth of artistic modernism. Imperial expansion fueled new interest in the "primitive" as a subject of art, as in the case of the French artist Paul Gauguin, who left Europe to relocate to Oceania, where he took a series of indigenous wives and embarked on a career of painting unspoiled and sensual "noble savages." By the turn of the century, "primitive" art itself soon came to influence the artistic vanguard in Europe. As invading Europeans conquered new terrain, plundered art and artifacts from Africa and Oceania began to surface as curios in European flea markets and as parts of ethnographic exhibits in natural history museums. Avant-garde artists in Dresden, Berlin, and Paris (including Wassily Kandinsky, Henri Matisse, and Pablo Picasso) quickly "discovered" them and sought to incorporate "primitive" elements into their own art. For Picasso, for example, the simple geometric abstractions of African masks could convey powerful emotions with an immediacy and directness lacking in European representational

This illustration of 1900 shows French tourists in Biskra, Algeria, visiting the Ouled Naïls, a nomadic tribe well known for its dancing women. The man consults his Baedeker guide while the woman inspects the Ouled Naïls women through her lorgnette, almost as if the women were animals or inanimate objects.

art. His efforts to reproduce this effect by fusing features of African art with elements of ancient Iberian sculpture gave rise to **Cubism,** one of the first European forays into abstraction.

Gender and Empire   With a European population comprising mainly male colonial administrators, soldiers, and missionaries, empire emerged as a male-dominated sphere early in the nineteenth century. This male ethos became even more pronounced in the latter part of the century, as the empire became closely associated with a new model of masculinity. Under the influence of Darwinian theory, a substantial number of Europeans came to fear that "overcivilization"—the loss of instinct and physical fitness due to urbanization and industrialization—was promoting the "degeneration" of the white race. They targeted modern men, in particular, as the passive, enfeebled, unmanly products of the machine age, urging participation in the competitive arenas of nature, war, and empire as the cure. In effect, the new masculinity cast off what were seen as the "soft" female characteristics of midcentury manhood, such as sensitivity and dependency, and embraced "hard" masculine values of instinct, aggression, virility, and self-reliance. In European primary schools, in popular books and magazines, and in a slew of new scouting, hiking, gymnastics, and hunting organizations designed to toughen boys and young men, a whole generation learned to celebrate empire as a proving ground for masculinity. Enthusiasts applied the same formula to the nation: Just as competition and the struggle for domination could make men out of boys, so would imperial conquest empower weak and degenerate nations.

The imperial experience also shaped feminine gender ideals, both in the metropole and abroad. Earlier in the century, Victorian domestic ideology had established women's special mission to be that of safeguarding civilized values and morally and spiritually elevating those around them. For British women, this mission found particular expression in their intense involvement in the antislavery movement. Europeans still assigned this moralizing role to women in the late nineteenth century but imbued it, in the aftermath of Darwin, with new racial significance. As women took their place in the empire, their charge was not merely to protect European standards of morality but to defend the biological purity of the white race.

European women were to fulfill these responsibilities in several ways. They were expected both to produce white offspring and to deter European men from having sexual relations with indigenous women, thereby preventing interbreeding between "natives" and Europeans, said to contaminate whiteness and lead to the degeneration of the race. They were also in-

tended to police the cultural and social boundaries between Europeans and subject peoples, in large part by implementing the rules of European etiquette. By insisting that Indian subjects appear before the British without shoes, for example, British women clearly demarcated the social distance between ruler and ruled. After the arrival of women, the British club also became a much more exclusive institution, where the social rituals of British life—dances, card-playing, teas—were meticulously reproduced. Because women's presence in the empire exposed them to the supposed lechery of barbarous natives, moreover, the lines between white and nonwhite societies furthered hardened, as European males felt that the virtue of their women had to be protected at all costs. Acting out of those beliefs, colonial administrators subjected colonized men to new surveillance and, if suspected of any infraction, to draconian punishments.

The presence of women in the colonies thus tended to exacerbate tensions between Europeans and indigenous populations. The most extreme example of this was the role played by the British woman in India, the detested **memsahib,** in part a caricature, in part a real social type. Pampered and spoiled, blatantly racist and contemptuous of all things Indian, the *memsahib* quickly earned the hatred of her colonial subjects. British men, as well, often blamed her for deteriorating relations between Indians and British, conveniently ignoring the fact that economic changes—including the intensified expropriation of peasant lands, political mobilization by Indian nationalists, and the more general rise in European racism—were clearly at fault. Moreover, while the *memsahib* did indeed accentuate the boundaries between the colonizer and the colonized, in doing so she merely carried out the imperial duty that had been assigned to her.

Summary

Europeans conquered much of the world during the nineteenth century. During the first two-thirds of the century, Europeans built their empire gradually and implicitly, as governments intervened politically and militarily to protect commercial interests overseas. They legitimized their growing global presence through the liberal mission of "civilizing" the non-European world. In the last quarter of the century, all this changed. European nation-states now took the imperial lead, competing with one another in an intense race for colonial territory. Influenced by Darwinian biological determinism and disillusioned by anticolonial insurgency, moreover, Europeans increasingly scaled back their civilizing ambitions, often exchanging the exercise of paternalistic authority for that of unapologetic domination.

The European conquest fundamentally altered life both in the colonies and in Europe itself. For colonial subjects, European intervention meant the destruction of indigenous economic, political, and cultural arrangements. The fierce resentment provoked by European rule manifested itself in anticolonial violence and in nationalist movements to end colonial rule. European colonial domination also profoundly influenced European society and culture in this period, affecting everything from gender roles and national identity to popular culture and art.

QUESTIONS FOR FURTHER THOUGHT

1. European colonial rule changed the face of much of the non-Western world during the nineteenth century. How did the imperial experience affect European identity?

2. European colonialism caused immense suffering among subject peoples. Did any segments of colonized societies benefit from colonial rule?
3. In what ways did Europeans themselves contribute to the eventual downfall of their empires?

RECOMMENDED READING

Studies

*Adas, Michael. *Machines as a Measure of Man: Science, Technology, and the Ideology of Western Dominance.* 1989. Argues that the formation of imperial ideology in Africa and Asia was linked to notions of scientific progress prevalent in Europe.

*Anderson, Benedict. *Imagined Communities: Reflections on the Origin and Spread of Nationalism.* 1983. Classic on the creation and global spread of national identity in the nineteenth century.

*Bayly, C. A. *Imperial Meridian: The British Empire and the World, 1780–1830.* 1989. Comprehensive analysis of the expansion of the British Empire in the late eighteenth and early nineteenth century.

*Betts, Raymond, ed. *Scramble for Africa: Causes and Dimensions of Empire.* 1966. Early, seminal work on European expansion in Africa.

*———. *Assimilation and Integration in French Colonial Theory.* 1961. The now classic study of the shift in the governing ideology of French colonialism from the conversion of the colonized into French citizens to a rejection of this universalism in the years after the First World War.

*Boahen, Adu. *African Perspectives on Colonialism.* 1989. Views on the colonial encounter in Africa by a well-known historian from Ghana.

*Brantlinger, Patrick. *Rule of Darkness: British Literature and Imperialism, 1830–1914.* 1988. Important exploration of the ways in which imperialist assumptions pervaded Victorian literature.

*Brion Davis, David. *The Problem of Slavery in the Age of Revolution.* 1999. A classic on the different factors that influenced opinions on slavery in late-eighteenth- and early-nineteenth-century England and America.

*Burton, Antoinette. *Burdens of History: British Feminists, Indian Women, and Imperial Culture, 1865–1915.* 1994. Analysis of the role of imperial ideology in shaping British feminism in the late nineteenth century.

*Chaudhuri, Nupur, and Margaret Strobel (eds.). *Western Women and Imperialism: Complicity and Resistance.* 1992. Important collection of essays that analyzes the complex and sometimes contradictory relationship between European women in the colonies and imperial ideology and practice.

*Cohn, Bernard. *Colonialism and Its Forms of Knowledge: The British in India.* 1996. Landmark book that argues that imperialism was a project of cultural and not merely military or diplomatic control.

*Conklin, Alice. *A Mission to Civilize: The Republican Idea of Empire in France and West Africa, 1895–1930.* 1997. Argues that the democratic assimilationist ideology of the French Third Republic in its colonies was deeply hierarchical and racist.

*Coombs, Annie. *Reinventing Africa: Museums, Material Culture, and Popular Culture in Late Victorian and Edwardian England.* 1994. Discusses how the representation of Africa in exhibits and displays in nineteenth-century Europe served to shape notions of African "otherness" and European superiority.

*Cooper, Frederick. *Africa since 1940: The Past of the Present.* 2002. History of decolonization and independence in Africa that links developments in the processes of nation and state building by contemporary African leaders to its colonial history.

*Cooper, Frederick, and Ann Laura Stoler. *Tensions of Empire: Colonial Cultures in a Bourgeois World.* 1997. Important collection of essays on the ways in which imperialism shaped both metropolitan and colonial cultures.

*Curtin, Philip D. *The World and the West: The European Challenge and the Overseas Response in *the Age of Empire*. 2000. An overview of the response of the colonized parts of the world to European expansion.

*Duus, Peter. *The Abacus and the Sword: The Japanese Penetration of Korea, 1895–1910*. 1995. Discusses the Japanese expansion into Korea in the heyday of Meiji-era imperialism.

*Fieldhouse, David Kenneth. *The Colonial Empires: A Comparative Survey from the Eighteenth Century*. 1982. Classic on the subject from a comparative perspective.

*Hall, Catherine. *Civilising Subjects: Colony and Metropole in the English Imagination, 1830–1867*. 1992. Using the example of Jamaica, this seminal work argues that the idea of empire was at the heart of the self-imagining of Britain by the middle of the nineteenth century.

*Headrick, Daniel R. *The Tools of Empire: Technology and European Imperialism in the Nineteenth Century*. 1981. Argues convincingly for the importance of technology for various aspects of European imperialism.

*Hobsbawm, E. J. *Age of Empire: 1875–1914*. 1987. Discusses the role of imperialism in shaping political and social life in the metropole.

*Hochschild, Adam. *King Leopold's Ghost: A Story of Greed, Terror, and Heroism in Colonial Africa*. 1998. The story of the ruthless plundering of the Belgian Congo by King Leopold II of Belgium in the early nineteenth century and the battles against him both by African rebel leaders and by other Europeans.

*Mamdani, Mahmood. *Citizen and Subject: Contemporary Africa and the Legacy of Late Colonialism*. 1996. Bold, insightful analysis of how British indirect rule in colonial Africa reproduced racial and ethnic divisions that have stood in the way of democratic reforms in contemporary times.

*Metcalf, Thomas. *Ideologies of the Raj*. 1995. Examines the transformation in British rule in India after the Rebellion of 1857.

*Owen, Roger, and Bob Sutcliffe. (eds.). *Studies in the Theory of Imperialism*. 1972. Seminal collection of Marxist and non-Marxist essays on theories of imperialism.

Pitts, Jennifer. *A Turn to Empire: The Rise of Imperial Liberalism in Britain and France*. 2005. Looks at the changes in nineteenth-century liberal thought from a critique of empire to its justification by men like John Stuart Mill and Alexis de Tocqueville.

*Richards, Thomas. *The Commodity Culture of Victorian England: Advertising Spectacle 1851–1914*. 1990. Examines how capitalism and empire influenced consumerism in Victorian England.

*Said, Edward. *Culture and Imperialism*. 1993. This landmark books draws connections between imperialism and Western literature in the nineteenth and twentieth centuries.

*Stocking, George. *Race, Culture, and Evolution: Essays on the History of Anthropology*. 1968. Classic on the history of the discipline of anthropology, focusing on the shifts in the approach to the issue of race.

*Stokes, Eric. *English Utilitarians in India*. 1959. Classic study of liberal thinkers and British administrators in India.

*Available in paperback.

Henry Tonks
AN ADVANCED DRESSING STATION IN FRANCE, 1917
A British surgeon and painter, Henry Tonks, was sent to the front in 1917 to paint this scene of a dressing station at the Somme, where officers classify the wounded while the artillery barrages go on.
Imperial War Museum, London

Chapter Twenty-Seven

WORLD WAR I AND THE WORLD IT CREATED

THE COMING OF WORLD WAR • THE COURSE OF THE WAR •
THE PEACE • POSTWAR DEMOCRACY

In 1914 Germany, Russia, Austria-Hungary, France, and Great Britain were suddenly at war—a war different from any that had gone before, a war that permanently altered society and politics, and a war that even in retrospect stands as the dividing point between two eras. Interpreting its origins is thus crucial to any understanding of modern history and is still the subject of controversy. Historians have given few subjects closer study than the system of alliances and the diplomatic moves that led to World War I. We understand the role of events, the arms race, and strident nationalism in leading to catastrophe.

The larger question is whether these fatal steps were themselves a result of long-term trends—economic expansion, imperialism, social divisions, ideological conflicts, and democratic politics. Once it came, the war strained every resource of the belligerents and mobilized civilian life as never before. As it ended, the victors were shaken, their societies and politics different. The losing states crumbled, opening the way to still more dramatic political changes. The complicated peace settlement, which changed the map of Europe and tried to make democracy universal, was meant above all to ensure that there would not be another world war.

● **1890** French-Russian Alliance

● **1882** Triple Alliance between Germany, Austria-Hungary, and Italy

● **1878** Berlin Congress awards Bosnia-Herzogovina to Austria-Hungary

● **1871** German Empire founded under Emperor William I and Chancellor Bismarck

THE COMING OF WORLD WAR

International relations held center stage in the period from 1870 to World War I for a variety of reasons. The balance of power established at the Congress of Vienna in 1815 had been overturned by the unification of Italy and Germany and by Prussia's defeat of Austria in 1866 and of France in 1870. The heightened sense of insecurity that followed led to an intricate web of alliances requiring constant attention. At the same time, imperialism, economic competition, and an escalating arms race multiplied the arenas in which national interests might clash. In addition, every threat, insult, or setback was magnified in daily journalism and domestic politics, for nationalism sold newspapers and made political careers. Foreign ministries worked to keep these conflicting pressures under control through diplomacy conducted by gentlemen, largely in secret and according to elaborate rules.

Bismarck dominated the Congress of Berlin in 1878 much as he dominates this portrait, which shows him being congratulated by the Russian delegate, with Count Andrassy of Austria-Hungary on the left.
AKG London

Bismarck's System of Alliances

From the 1860s to 1890, Bismarck dominated international relations. His diplomacy was essential to the creation of the Second Reich, and he led Europe's major nations in addressing a series of long-term issues, particularly the decline of Ottoman power, the resulting power vacuum in the Balkans, and competing Russian and Austrian ambitions there. His first concern was to make the new German nation secure from any potential foreign threat. Although intended to increase security, the treaties Bismarck fostered ultimately stimulated a dangerous arms race.

The Congress of Berlin, 1878 Bismarck established his mastery at the Congress of Berlin in 1878. Once again, as at the time of the Crimean War twenty years

earlier, Russia had expanded its influence in the Balkans by defeating Turkey in war and by forcing the sultan to cede territory across the Caucasus Mountains to Russia, to allow creation of an enlarged Montenegro and Serbia, and to grant full independence to a large and autonomous Bulgaria, which everyone believed would be a Russian puppet. This was more than the other European powers would allow. The aim of the Congress was to restrain Russian ambitions while finding a response to Balkan nationalism and Ottoman weakness that avoided further war.

With few German interests directly involved, Bismarck presented himself as an "honest broker" and skillfully orchestrated agreements in which everyone got something. The settlement granted autonomy to a

1910   1920   1930

1905–1911 Series of diplomatic crises between France, Germany, and Austria-Hungary over control of North Africa and the Balkans

● **1912** Bulgaria, Serbia, and Greece defeat Turkey in the First Balkan War

1904
Anglo-French
Entente Cordial

● **1913** Serbia, Greece, Romania, and Turkey defeat Bulgaria in the Second Balkan War

● **1914** Assassination of Austrian Archduke Franz Ferdinand in June leads to beginning of World War One

● **1915** Italy changes sides, entering war on side of Entente Powers

● **1932** League of Nations General Disarmament Conference

Russian Revolution begins; **1917** ●
U.S. enters the war on side of Entente

● **1920** League of Nations established

Early in year, Russia signs Treaty of Brest Litovsk **1918** ●
with Central Powers; war ends in November

● **1925** Locarno Pact between Germany, Belgium, France, Great Britain, and Italy

Paris Peace Treaties **1919** ●

● **1928** Kellogg-Briand Pact renounces war as instrument of national policy

greatly reduced Bulgaria (thus lessening Russia's gains) and recognized the independence of Serbia, Romania, and Montenegro (acknowledging rising nationalism).[1] Austria-Hungary, nervous about a challenge from new and nationalist Balkan states, was authorized in compensation to occupy Bosnia and Herzegovina, which nevertheless remained formally under Ottoman rule. In addition Britain's occupation of Cyprus was confirmed, and Tunis was in effect promised to France. The balance the Congress of Berlin achieved among competing nations had come at the expense of a weakening Ottoman Empire and by extending the dominion of the major powers—a pattern characteristic of imperialism.

Germany's Alliances Fresh from this triumph, Bismarck persuaded Austria-Hungary to a mutual defense pact. Austria was worried by Russia's ambitions and grateful for Germany's support at the Congress, and the secret pact became the foundation of German foreign policy. The two nations promised that should either be attacked by Russia the other would come to its defense. But Bismarck sought further insurance, and so in 1881 he audaciously persuaded Russia (eager to escape diplomatic isolation) to join Germany and Austria-Hungary in promising to remain neutral in the event of war between any of them and a fourth power. To these understandings, Bismarck then added a third, the Triple Alliance of Italy, Germany, and Austria-Hungary. This renewable, five-year pact was first signed in 1882. In creating this treaty, Bismarck took advantage of Italy's

[1] The tsar's nephew was elected to the Bulgarian throne. Rumelia, the southern part of Bulgaria, remained under Turkish rule as a separate province. The provinces of Wallachia and Moldavia had been joined in 1862 to form Romania and received their own prince two years later. A Hohenzollern, he became King Carol in 1881.

resentment of France for occupying Tunis in 1881. While imperial competition worked in his favor, Bismarck's goal was the diplomatic isolation of France, for he feared the continuing bitterness in France over the loss of Alsace-Lorraine to Germany in 1870.

Formally, these treaties were defensive, although the secrecy surrounding them fostered a sense of insecurity (see "The Terms of the Triple Alliance," p. 824). They gave Germany an international influence rare in peacetime, but holding them together took great skill. Italy and Russia had more reasons for conflict with Austria-Hungary than with any other nation, and it was hard to keep them tied to Germany. In fact, Russia and Austria-Hungary let their alliance lapse in 1887 because of their disagreements in the Balkans, and Bismarck could only partially repair the damage through a separate Reinsurance Treaty in which Germany and Russia promised to remain neutral toward each other if one of them was at war. For Italy, Austria-Hungary was not only the traditional enemy Italy had fought to achieve unification but the occupier of Italian-speaking lands in the region of Trieste. To persuade Italy to renew the Triple Alliance in 1887, Bismarck had to recognize a range of Italian ambitions in the Balkans, Africa, and elsewhere.

The Shifting Balance

Germany's system of alliances was already showing strains when the Kaiser dismissed Bismarck from office in 1890. Without him, that system disintegrated and German diplomacy became erratic and even abrasive.

German Diplomacy after Bismarck Bismarck's successors understood the importance of Germany's alliances but tended to overlook the new factor that could draw other nations together: common fear of Germany. When Germany's new leaders let the Reinsurance

823

THE TERMS OF THE TRIPLE ALLIANCE

These articles are from the treaty of 1912 in which Austria-Hungary, Germany, and Italy renewed the Triple Alliance for the fifth time since 1882. This version essentially continued earlier ones, except for articles VI through XI, not printed here, which dealt rather vaguely with the Balkans, Ottoman territories, Egypt, and North Africa. With respect to those regions, the signatories reassured each other that they preferred to maintain the status quo but promised mutual understanding and even support if Austria-Hungary or Italy found it necessary temporarily to occupy territory in the Balkans or if Italy had to take measures against French expansion in North Africa. The promises of support to Italy indicated the higher price now required to keep Italy in the Alliance.

"Article I. The High Contracting Parties mutually promise peace and friendship, and will enter into no alliance or engagement directed against any one of their States.

"They engage to proceed to an exchange of ideas on political and economic questions of a general nature which may arise, and they further promise one another mutual support within the limits of their own interests.

"Article II. In case Italy, without direct provocation on her part, should be attacked by France for any reason whatsoever, the two other Contracting Parties shall be bound to lend help and assistance with all their forces to the Party attacked.

"This same obligation shall devolve upon Italy in case of any aggression without direct provocation by France against Germany.

"Article III. If one, or two, of the High Contracting Parties, without direct provocation on their part, should chance to be attacked and to be engaged in a war with two or more Great Powers nonsignatory to the present Treaty, the *casus foederis* will arise simultaneously for all the High Contracting Parties.

"Article IV. In case a Great Power nonsignatory to the present Treaty should threaten the security of the states of one of the High Contracting Parties, and the threatened Party should find itself forced on that account to make war against it, the two others bind themselves to observe towards their Ally a benevolent neutrality. Each of them reserves to itself, in this case, the right to take part in the war, if it should see fit, to make common cause with its Ally.

"Article V. If the peace of one of the High Contracting Parties should chance to be threatened under the circumstances foreseen by the preceding Articles, the High Contracting Parties shall take counsel together in ample time as to the military measures to be taken with a view to eventual cooperation.

"They engage, henceforth, in all cases of common participation in a war, to conclude neither armistice, nor peace, nor treaty, except by common agreement among themselves.

"Article XII. The High Contracting Parties mutually promise secrecy as to the contents of the present Treaty."

From Sidney Bradshaw Fay, *The Origins of the World War,* Macmillan, 1930.

Treaty with Russia lapse, France pressed Russia for an understanding. By 1894 that became a full alliance. France and Russia promised that each would support the other if either were attacked by Germany or by another member of the Triple Alliance that was aided by Germany. Such an accord between the Russian autocracy and the French Republic had seemed politically impossible, despite Russia's having already turned to France for loans and arms purchases. Now the tsar greeted French delegates while a band played the "Marseillaise," previously outlawed in Russia as a song of revolution.

In response, German diplomats were determined to reassert Germany's importance in world affairs. They did so in inconsistent, even contradictory, ways. On the one hand, the Kaiser attempted to reach some understanding with Great Britain and spoke of a "natural" alliance between the Teutonic and Anglo-Saxon races. On the other hand, the Germans antagonized and alienated the British. When, in 1896, the South African Boers foiled an attack on the republic of the Transvaal mounted by the British Cape Colony (the Jameson Raid), Kaiser William II sent a telegram congratulating the president of the Boer republic (the Kruger telegram). The British public responded with anger. The Kaiser also explored the possibility of organizing a continental coalition against Great Britain. Above all, the massive expansion of the German navy, vigorously lobbied for by the German Navy League, roused the hostility of the British.

Anglo-French Understanding Relations between Great Britain and France had centered on their colonial competition, in which they had seemed ready to risk war. Instead, they settled for defined spheres of influence. Following the confrontation at Fashoda in 1898, the French set about turning humiliation into good relations. They accepted British domination in Egypt in return for Britain's recognition of French interests in North Africa, particularly Morocco. Further understandings followed, culminating in the Anglo-French Entente Cordiale of 1904, in which France and Great Britain eliminated their major issues of imperial conflict. Those issues stretched from Asia to the Atlantic (from Siam to Newfoundland) and across the African continent (from the Niger River to North Africa). Formally a mere understanding, the Entente implied much more, as the exchange of public visits between Edward VII and the president of France was meant to demonstrate.

Germany's diplomatic position remained strong, and German leaders reasoned that an assertive foreign policy would demonstrate that strength. But the tenor of international relations was changing. As armaments increased and treaties proliferated, each power became more obsessed with its own security, and public opinion grew more sensitive to questions of national honor.

Testing Alliances: Three International Crises   From 1905 to 1911 three diplomatic crises—each of which initially seemed a German victory—in fact drew Germany's opponents closer together. The first of these crises arose over Morocco. France, with well-known designs on Morocco, had carefully won acquiescence from the powers except for Germany. The German chancellor, Bernhard von Blow, demanded that an international conference settle Morocco's future. He aimed to demonstrate that France was isolated, and in fact his warnings forced the resignation of Théophile Delcassé, France's foreign minister and the architect of French policy. When in 1906 the conference met at Algeciras, it confirmed that Morocco had special international status but recognized the primacy of French interests. The crisis was a disaster for German diplomacy. Only Austria-Hungary loyally voted with its ally. Italy, Russia, Great Britain, and the United States (now a regular participant in such international agreements) supported France, and Germany's threatening tactics led French and British officials to begin talks about their mutual military interests.

The second crisis arose over the Balkans. Austria was concerned that Serbia, led by a new king and a radical nationalist government, had become a dangerous antagonist. Austria also feared that Turkey's influence in the Balkans would grow following the 1908 revolution in Turkey—led by a group known as the Young Turks, who were determined to modernize their nation. In response, Austria-Hungary decided to annex Bosnia and Herzegovina. That move, which threatened Serbia, in turn outraged Russian Slavophiles. They were nationalists who believed that Russia should defend the interests of Slavs everywhere, and they demanded an international conference. Britain and France agreed. Germany supported Austria-Hungary, although angered by the sudden annexation.

Diplomatic crises were becoming tests of alliances (and significantly, Italy expressed resentment at not being consulted by Austria-Hungary rather than loyalty to the Triple Alliance). There had been earlier signs that Italy might drift away. In 1902 France recognized Italian ambitions in Libya, and France and Italy pledged neutrality if either was attacked by a third power (i.e., Germany). Although the Triple Alliance was renewed in the same year, Italy now sat on the fence between the Franco-Russian and the Austro-German alliances. Only time would tell on which side Italy might end up.

The third major crisis once again involved Morocco, which France now wanted to annex. It had consulted all the European powers, and talks with Germany seemed to be going well when suddenly in 1911 the Germans sent the gunboat *Panther* to the Moroccan port of Agadir (a show of power and a classic imperialist gesture) and then asked for all of the French Congo as the price for accepting France's annexation of Morocco. Both the demands and the method seemed excessive, and in Great Britain David Lloyd George publicly denounced them. Once again, eventual compromise (France would cede parts of its Congo lands and bits of its other African territories adjacent to German colonies) counted for less than the rising tension and growing international distrust of the Germans.

The Arms Race   The standing armies of France and Germany doubled between 1870 and 1914, and all able-bodied men had some military responsibilities from the age of twenty to their late fifties. In 1889 Great Britain adopted the principle that its navy must equal in size the two next-largest fleets combined, and in 1906 it had launched the *Dreadnought*, the first battleship armed entirely with big guns. By 1914 Britain had twenty-nine ships of this class afloat and thirteen under construction. The German navy had eighteen, with nine being built. With the dangers of a European arms race ever more apparent, especially the growing naval competition between Britain and Germany, the major powers agreed to two great conferences on disarmament and compulsory arbitration. The conferences met at The Hague in 1899 and again in 1907, but no country was willing to sacrifice any of its strength. At the second conference German delegates bluntly rejected any limitation on their sovereign right to make war, while at that very moment Kaiser William complained to the British press that England should be grateful to Germany for having remained neutral in the Boer War. This time, British recriminations against the outspoken Kaiser reflected an important shift in policy as well as anger.

The Triple Entente   In 1902 Britain ended its long tradition of refusing peacetime alliances and did so by signing a treaty with Japan, the rising power in the East. It was a first step toward reducing conflicts over

MAP 27.1 THE BALKANS, 1878–1914
These two maps of southeastern Europe show the new nations created in the period between the Congress of Berlin in 1878 and the beginning of the First World War. Notice which of these nations had gained considerable territory by the end of this period. What developments and events led to such geographical changes in the region, and which of these new countries do you suppose were most aggrieved by these various settlements?
◆ For an online version, go to www.mhhe.com/chambers9 > chapter 27 > book maps

imperial claims. That agreement was followed in 1907 by an accord among France, Russia, and Japan. It delimited each nation's areas of interest and, by guaranteeing the integrity of China, sought to reduce their competition there. Such understandings opened the way for further agreement between Great Britain and Russia, old imperial antagonists. They resolved points of contention reaching from the Black Sea to Persia, Afghanistan, and Tibet. The treaty between Britain and Russia, each already allied with France, brought into being the Triple Entente as an informal coalition of France, Russia, and Britain. It was clearly intended to counterbalance the Triple Alliance of Germany, Austria, and Italy, and its implications became clear when Britain decided in 1912 to withdraw its battleships from the Mediterranean, leaving the French navy to defend Britain's interests there while the British fleet concentrated on the German threat in the North Sea.

The Outbreak of World War

The Triple Alliance and the Triple Entente glared menacingly at each other, increasing their armament and measuring every international event as a gain or loss for their side.

The Balkan Threat   Turmoil in the Balkans became a test of strength for the two sides. The ferment there of nationalism, modernization, militarism, and shaky parliamentarism echoed Europe-wide trends, but it was complicated by centuries of oppression, by disputed boundaries (most of recent invention), and by social, ethnic, and religious rivalries. The privileged role of Hungarians in Austria-Hungary and the Hungarian policy of enforced "Magyarization"—both consequences of the Compromise of 1867 (see chapter 24) fostered resentment and stoked nationalist aspirations among other ethnic groups living in the Habsburg Empire. The competition between Russia and Austria-Hungary quickly became enmeshed in these conflicts, and so did the Balkan ambitions of Germany (with railway and economic interests in the peninsula) and of Italy.

Italy's defeat of Turkey in 1912, when Italy gained Libya and important Mediterranean islands, triggered what came to be known as the first Balkan War. In the fall of that year Bulgaria, Serbia, and Greece also declared war on Turkey. In a few months they drove the Ottomans from all their remaining holdings in Europe except Constantinople. After a partial truce and months of border skirmishes, the great powers hammered out the terms of peace at the end of May 1913.

One month later Serbia and Greece, quickly joined by Romania and Turkey, declared war on Bulgaria, the big winner in the previous war. This conflict ended in a few weeks, but local anger and international concern did not. The great powers pressured the belligerents to accept peace, but they were watching each other more closely still.

The Assassination of an Austrian Archduke   In this atmosphere of growing distrust, tension between Austria-Hungary and Serbia increased. Groups of Serbian nationalists scattered throughout the Balkan region agitated on behalf of their fellow Slavs living under Austrian rule in Bosnia and Herzegovina, and Austria threatened to use force against Serbia if it did not abandon some of its nationalist claims. Against this background, Archduke Francis Ferdinand, the heir to the Austrian and Hungarian thrones, chose to parade in Sarajevo, the capital of Bosnia, on June 28, 1914. If the archduke wished to display Habsburg authority, others were eager to demonstrate against Austria. As the archduke's car moved down the street, a bomb just missed him. Then other conspirators lost their courage and failed to fire as his car passed by. At that point his driver made a wrong turn, started to back up, and yet another young Bosnian revolutionary fired point-blank, killing both the archduke and his wife.

The leaders of Austria-Hungary, convinced that the Serbian government was involved, believed it essential to respond strongly. They dispatched a special emissary to Berlin, where he was promised Germany's full support, and on July 23 Austria sent an ultimatum to Serbia. Meant to be unacceptable, it gave Serbia forty-eight hours in which to apologize, ban all anti-Austrian propaganda, and accept Austria-Hungary's participation in investigations of the plot against Francis Ferdinand.

Serbia replied with great tact, accepting all terms except those that diminished its sovereignty and offering to submit even these to arbitration. Great Britain proposed an international conference, to which France and Russia reluctantly agreed, and Germany hinted that Serbia and Austria-Hungary alone should settle the

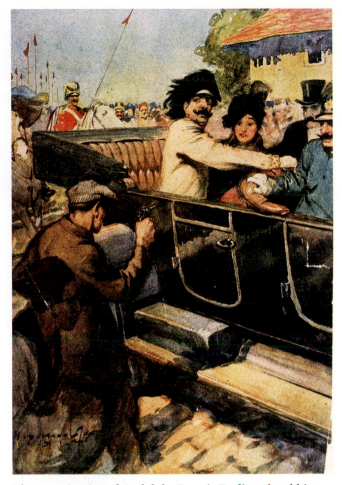

The assassination of Archduke Francis Ferdinand and his wife in Sarajevo, painted as a dramatic moment when a single act affected the course of history.
Bettmann/Corbis

matter. Another crisis seemed about to pass when, on July 28, Austria-Hungary declared war on Serbia.

Stumbling into War   The system of alliances, increasing armament, bluster, and compromise had become a trap. Austria-Hungary was in reality not yet ready to fight. Germany and Great Britain still hoped the Austrians would limit themselves to occupying Belgrade, the Serbian capital, and then agree to an international conference. But Russia could not appear to abandon its role as protector of the Slavs nor let Austria-Hungary unilaterally extend its sway in the Balkans.

On July 29 Russia ordered partial mobilization, making clear that its move was aimed at Austria-Hungary only. The following day, however, the Russians discovered they lacked the organization for a partial call-up and so announced a general mobilization instead. On

By 1912 this Krupp factory at Essen was devoted to the arms race that was consuming an increasing proportion of Europe's energy and wealth.
AKG London

July 31 Germany proclaimed a state of readiness, sent Russia an ultimatum demanding demobilization within twelve hours, and requested France to declare what it would do in case of a Russo-German war.

France answered that it would act in its own interests and then mobilized but held its troops ten kilometers (about six miles) from the German frontier to prevent any incidents. The Germans, who had planned next to demand that France guarantee its neutrality by surrendering its border fortresses, were unsatisfied.

On August 1 Germany mobilized and declared war on Russia. Convinced this step meant war on the Western front as well, Germany also invaded Luxembourg and sent an ultimatum to the Belgians demanding the unobstructed passage of German troops. On August 3 Germany declared war on France and invaded Belgium. The following day Great Britain declared war on Germany. Of Europe's six major powers, only Italy remained neutral. Within forty-eight hours, each belligerent had 2 million soldiers under orders. World War I had begun.

The Origins of World War

The question of what caused the Great War—or, more simply, who was to blame—would become an important issue in European affairs. Four years later the victors in that war blamed Germany so insistently that they would write its guilt into the peace treaty. Most historians have considered that assessment to be one-sided. German scholars rejected it with special force, which explains the furor some forty years later (after

another world war) that greeted the research of the German historian Fritz Fischer. He found evidence that Germany's leaders had, in fact, looked forward to war and nurtured almost boundless ambitions for military dominance. But the question remains without a final answer, for the causes adduced depend very much on how long-range a view one takes.

The Response to an Assassination The immediate cause, the assassination of the archduke, almost did not happen. The tensions that made it so significant had deeper roots, however: in Balkan struggles for independence, in Austria-Hungary's declining power, and in each nation's fears for its safety. Human judgment was also involved, and individual leaders and governments can be blamed for Austria-Hungary's untoward haste in attacking Serbia, Germany's irresponsible support of Austria-Hungary, Russia's clumsy and confused diplomacy, and France's eagerness to prove loyalty to the Russians. British leaders were at fault as well. Not wanting to admit that they were already attached to one side, they failed to warn the Germans that an attack on France meant war with Britain.

The Limits of Diplomacy Such an analysis, however, may make statesmen seem to have been more autonomous and therefore more to blame than they were. The system of alliances that was intended to achieve security had been hardened by habit, military imperatives, and domestic politics. The fears that cemented these commitments were reflected in: Britain's conviction that empire required supremacy at sea; France's ea-

Summer hats in the air, an August crowd in London's Trafalgar Square cheers the declaration of war on Austria, as it had a week earlier the announcement of war with Germany. Similar scenes occurred throughout that week of 1914 in France and Germany.
Bettmann/Corbis

In Berlin during August 1914, German volunteers march down the street hailing their good fortune; they will soon fight for their country.
Ullstein Bilderdienst

gerness to revenge the defeat of 1870 and regain Alsace-Lorraine; Russia's 150 years of territorial expansion; Italy's need to show itself a great power; Austria's dependence, since Metternich, on foreign policy to sustain a shaky regime; and Germany's fear of encirclement and use of prestige abroad to reduce conflict at home.

The arms race itself contributed to the outbreak of war. Strategy was a factor, too. Germany's victory over France in 1870 had been understood to prove the supe-riority of the Prussian system of universal conscription, large reserves, and detailed military planning.

Military mobilization, which in the eyes of some diplomats was a cumbersome but effective show of resolve, was considered by military men in each country to be an essential act of self-defense. Even slight disadvantages in numbers, weapons, speed, or tactics might prove fatal. Thus, each increase in personnel and weapons was quickly matched, often with enormous effort; France, for example, had only 60 percent of

Germany's potential manpower and yet equaled its rival through more burdensome conscription. The arms race, justified by the fear that it was meant to allay, fed on itself.

Public Opinion   Because such large military expenditures had to be justified to parliaments and the public, there was a heavy political investment in the build-up to war. In every country, those who feared socialism or had military and imperial interests at stake used flag-waving to win votes and nationalism to overcome domestic divisions. This push by conservative forces was especially strong in Germany, where economic growth and social change threatened Prussian dominance and the Junker ruling elite and where militaristic interests groups such as the Pan-German League had been manipulating public opinion since the 1890s.

Throughout Europe, the press added its voice to other pro-war forces. Warmongering appealed most to upper- and middle-class young men who were imbued with the "manly virtues" of perseverance and heroic sacrifice in public schools and universities—but others were not so quick to celebrate. Although many in the working class ended strikes and antiwar protests when war was declared, their response was hardly enthusiastic. For farmers, the coming conflict meant the requisition of their horses and wagons and the drafting of their farmhands. Some historians assert that even among the cheering crowds in the capitals of Europe, exuberance

was short-lived and that most people exhibited solemn resignation at the prospect of war.

THE COURSE OF THE WAR

For decades European military staffs had prepared detailed plans for the situation they now faced. The French intended to drive into Alsace and Lorraine in coordinated dashes that reflected their almost mystic belief in the spirit of a patriotic offensive. German strategy began from the desire to avoid fighting on two fronts simultaneously: A detailed plan adopted years earlier called for assigning minimal forces to hold the Russians in the East and to slow the expected French attack in Alsace. Then Germany's main armies would pour through Belgium and on to Paris. The German aim was to knock France out of the war before Russia could bring its massive armies into play and before British aid could make a difference. That strategy envisioned the German army as a coiled spring to be released the moment war began, and it required the invasion of neutral Belgium, further labeled Germany as the aggressor, and determined Britain's entry into the war. Both sides believed they were ready. The Triple Alliance was reduced to two, Germany and Austria-Hungary, referred to as the **Central Powers.** Italy announced its neutrality when war broke out, declaring the attack on Serbia an offensive action that did not meet the terms of the Triple Alliance. Against the Central Powers stood Britain, France, and Russia, referred to as the **Entente Powers** or the Allies.

The Surprises of the First Two Years

In 1914 the belligerents all assumed the war could not last long. It was thought that modern economies, intricately connected by trade, would be unable to sustain a long conflict and that modern weapons would make for brief wars of rapid movement (as in 1870). But in a few months it began to be clear that the war being fought was not the one planned, though commanders were slow to admit it. Increased firepower gave defensive forces unexpected strength. Cavalry was ineffectual, for rifles could now hit horses from great distances; infantry, loaded down with equipment, could not go far very rapidly; and the common soldier proved able to absorb more punishment than anyone had thought possible.

The German Offensive   In their western advance, German commanders had originally sought to implement a set of elaborate plans, first drawn up by Count Alfred von Schlieffen in 1891 and regularly modified thereafter. The plan called for the German armies to advance in a northern arc through France, capture Paris, and thus definitively defeat France. For such a victory, the general staff was willing to violate Belgian and Dutch neutrality and leave the Eastern front largely to Austrian forces, for which they had little respect. The **Schlieffen Plan** was based on a series of assumptions: that there was no decisive strategic objective on the Eastern front (which proved true), that Russia would be slow to mobilize (less true than expected), and that modest German forces therefore would be sufficient to hold off the Russians while Germany, employing two-thirds of its forces against the French, would gain an overwhelming advantage on the Western front.

Despite initial successes, the Germans did not achieve the great victory they had hoped for. Belgium offered unexpected resistance, thus delaying the German advance through the formerly neutral country (Germany ultimately did not invade the Netherlands, which remained neutral for the duration of the war). Then, when a small British force arrived sooner than expected and Russian armies made unexpected advances on the Eastern front, the indecisive if not unstable German chief of staff, Helmuth von Moltke (nephew of the field marshal who had led the Prussians to victory in 1866 and 1870 over France and Austria), modified the Schlieffen Plan. He ordered troops intended for the Western front to the East and sent extra forces to Alsace in hope of a breakthrough there. The French, for their part, saw their offensive halted in Al-

MAP 27.2 WORLD WAR I, THE WESTERN FRONT
This map illustrates both the initial German assault on France and Belgium and subsequent Allied offensives. For the remainder of the war, the battle lines on the Western front would be drawn around these areas. How did this German assault of the first few months of the war differ from the original Schlieffen Plan?
◆ For an online version, go to www.mhhe.com/chambers9 > chapter 27 > book maps

sace, where both German and French forces suffered heavy losses. The French command had underestimated by half the forces they would face at the outbreak of war, and in the first weeks the Germans drove to within thirty miles of Paris. However, with von Moltke's change in plans, the Germans halted their advance east of Paris. The German army soon found itself as battered as its opponents, its casualties as high, and its lines of communication and supply dangerously stretched. After each bloody encounter, the enemies retreated but were not routed, and German officers were surprised they took so few prisoners. This pattern of small initial advances followed by long periods of attrition would remain in place on the Western front for the duration of the war.

French and Russian Offensives   On the other side, the French commander in chief, Joseph Joffre, remained imperturbably confident of the ultimate success of a great

CHRONOLOGY
The Western Front

August 1914	Germany invades Belgium.
September 1914	Battle of the Marne ends in stalemate.
December 1914	Battle lines for rest of the war established.
April–May 1915	Germans introduce chlorine gas during Second Battle of Ypres and make slight gains.
May–June 1915	Second Battle of Artois, with some gains for French.
February–July 1916	Battle of Verdun results in nearly 350,000 casualties for each side.
July–November 1916	Battle of the Somme: British lose 400,000 men; French lose 200,000; Germans lose nearly 500,000.
April 1917	United States declares war on Germany and enters the war.
May 1917	Mutinies in the French Army.
July–November 1917	British-led offensive in Flanders; Battle of Passchendaele results in 300,000 dead or wounded British soldiers.
March–June 1918	German offensive makes major gains but is then checked.
May 1918	First major engagement of American troops at the Third Battle of the Aisne.
July–August 1918	Second Battle of the Marne; Germans forced back over Marne.
September 1918	Battle of Argonne and Fourth Battle of Ypres, with slow Allied advance.
November 11, 1918	Armistice.

French drive. In September the French launched a counteroffensive along the Marne River that saved Paris and hurled the Germans back to the natural defenses of the Aisne River. There, despite repeated Allied attacks, the Germans held. In the next few months the armies tried to outflank each other but succeeded only in extending the front northward to the sea. With changes of only a few miles, the battle lines that were established at the end of 1914 would remain those of the Western front for the next four years. France had not been knocked out of the war, but Germany held the important industrial and agricultural area of northeastern France, a tenth of its territory, and nearly all of Belgium.

On the Eastern front, Russian armies scored important gains in early August, taking eastern Galicia from Austria-Hungary and beginning an invasion of eastern Prussia in the north. Moltke talked in panic of a general retreat until the battle of Tannenberg late in August. There generals Paul von Hindenburg and Erich Ludendorff, who became Germany's greatest war heroes, surrounded and destroyed a Russian army and then pushed on almost to Warsaw before being stopped.

In the south, Austria-Hungary halted the Russian advance with German aid and took Belgrade despite the strong resistance of the Serbian army. By the end of 1914, Germany and Austria-Hungary had made impressive gains at every hand. They had also gained from Turkey's entry into the war in late October on the side of the Central Powers (and against its old enemy, Russia), which threatened Britain and France through the Eastern Mediterranean all the way to Suez.

Trench Warfare   After the first month, it became clear that new military technology and mass transport had changed the manner in which war would be conducted, with terrifying results. The Eastern front experienced the traditional warfare of mobile armies and shifting battlefields, but the great armies on the Western front soon found themselves bogged down in siege conditions. Transport by trains allowed for a nearly endless supply of soldiers and material to a front in which the new machine guns, mass shelling by artillery, and fields of barbed wire made advance practically impossible. Both sides dug trenches stretching thousands of miles across France, dotted with concrete huts called pillboxes and lined with communication cables. From these trenches, the Allied armies repeatedly mounted offensives, only to be stopped when German reinforcements arrived. Battles were now numbered—the Second Battle of Ypres (April–May 1915), the Second Battle of Artois (May–June), the Second Battle of Champagne (September–November), the Third Battle of Artois (September–October)—and after a year's bloodshed, the Western front remained essentially the same, though hundreds of thousands of men had lost their lives.

Within the trenches, morale declined as the soldiers waited for months, suffering through ice, wind, rain, mud, lice, and vermin, while facing interminable boredom and the threat of death. Attempts by the British and the Germans to break the stalemate by using poison gas added to the horror, but neither side was able to capitalize on the momentary gains this new weapon provided. Among many on the front lines, the constant shelling and specter of death led to psychic distress called **shell shock.** Its widespread diagnosis was a testament to the enormous strain **trench warfare** placed on soldiers, many of whom had envisioned a quick and heroic war.

Italy Joins the Allies   Nothing broke the stalemate, neither desperate new offensives nor Italy's entry into the war. Both sides had been negotiating with Italy; Britain and France could make the better offer. In April 1915 Italy signed a secret agreement, the Treaty of London, and committed itself to the Allies. In return Italy was promised considerable territory along its border with Austria-Hungary, important Dalmatian islands, and expansion of its colonial holdings. Italy declared war in May and soon advanced to a line along the Isonzo River. Eleven battles would be fought along that line in the next two years.

Costly Offensives   Early in 1916 the Germans launched another all-out offensive to knock France out of the war. They stormed the fortifications at Verdun. Their aim, knowing the French would be determined to hold, was more to bleed the enemy than to take territory. For days shells poured down, and then the Germans attacked in overwhelming numbers. From February to July 1916 the fighting continued at full pitch. German forces captured two outlying forts, but the French managed a brief counterattack. Verdun held; and though the French losses, more than 300,000 men, weakened the subsequent Allied offensive, Germany casualties were only slightly less.

Massive German forces cross the Schara River, the opening of the drive into Galicia in May 1915 that would carry the Central Powers into Russia.
AKG London

The Allied attack in the Battle of the Somme, from July to November, brought still heavier casualties and a maximum advance of seven miles. The doctrine of the offensive, like general morale, was sinking in mud and gore. If tactics could not guarantee victory, then attrition, systematically exhausting men and resources, was the alternative.

There was more movement on the Eastern front but no decisive result. The Central Powers (Germany,

Austria-Hungary, and the countries on their side) launched an offensive through Galicia in May 1915, drove forward a hundred miles, and followed that with a general offensive in July. By late September—while their new ally, Bulgaria, pushed into Serbia—the Central Powers were massed on a line from Riga in the north to the easternmost part of Hungary. Russia lost Poland and Lithuania.

The following year, however, in one of the few really well-conducted Russian campaigns, General Alexis Brusilov regained a large part of those losses. The effort cost Russia a million men and used up the capacity to do more. Although the Russian offensive brought Romania into the war on the Allied side, Austria-Hungary took Bucharest at the end of the year.

The Naval War Naval strength, so significant to the arms race, proved more important in terms of supply lines than combat. The single large-scale attack by sea, the dramatic landing of Allied forces on the Gallipoli peninsula in April 1915, was a failure. The Allies were grateful to withdraw in December without having either opened the Dardanelles as a pipeline to Russia or forced the Ottomans out of the war.

Britain's naval blockade of Germany was more effective. As the blockade began to hurt, Germany countered in 1915 by announcing a submarine blockade of Britain; but the angry reaction of neutrals, led by the United States, forced Germany to abandon the tactic. The sinking of passenger ships—most sensationally the *Lusitania*, killing more than a thousand civilians—gave way in 1916 to attacks on armed merchant ships and then, in the face of American warnings, to the renunciation of "unlimited" submarine warfare. The one great naval battle of the war, at Jutland in May 1916, was indecisive. British and German fleets lost the same number of ships, though three British battle cruisers were sunk to only one German capital ship. The British retained a two-to-one naval superiority, however, and after Jutland the feared German fleet stayed in its harbors.

Adjustment to Total War

In contrast to nineteenth-century conflicts, the First World War was conducted on a massive scale, affecting not only soldiers in the battlefield, but also radically disrupting the lives of civilians at home.

Domestic Mobilization Across Europe, the first domestic response to the war was national unity. The German public was convinced that theirs was a just and defensive war, and the parliament unanimously approved funding for the war. The French hailed their "sacred union," and a leading socialist joined the cabinet. In Great Britain the Liberal government soon gave

CHRONOLOGY
The Eastern Front

August 1914	German victory over Russia at the Battle of Tannenberg; General von Hindenberg is proclaimed the "Hero of Tannenberg."
October 1914	Turkey enters war on the side of the Central Powers.
January 1915	German and Austrian forces launch attack in Galicia; they break through Russian lines in May.
May 1915	Italian forces tie down Austrian and German troops in the Tyrol.
September 1915	Bulgaria joins war on side of Central Powers.
October 1915	Austro-Hungarian army, with Bulgarian support, defeats and occupies Serbia.
August 1916	Romania enters the war on the side of the Entente and declares war on Austria.
February–March 1917	Russian Czar Nicholas II abdicates; Russian Revolution begins.
October–November 1917	Bolshevik regime created.
February 1918	Russians sign Treaty of Brest-Litovsk with Central Powers, although treaty is then annulled in November; Russians withdraw from the war.
September 1918	Bulgaria surrenders and signs armistice.
October 1918	Austro-Hungarian armies defeated in Italy; other Southern fronts of the Central Powers collapse; Czechoslovakia and Yugoslavia declare their independence from the Austro-Hungarian Empire.
November 3, 1918	Austria signs armistice.
November 11, 1918	German armistice.

way to a coalition that included Conservatives, and in Russia the czar's government seemed almost popular. In the warring countries of Western Europe, military leaders assumed a leading if not dominant role within society, particularly for the first year of the war. French General Joseph Joffre exercised virtually dictatorial powers and censorship was severe. Nevertheless, in France and Great Britain, civilian authority began to reassert itself by 1915.

Despite the initial surge of patriotism, Europeans soon began to feel the effects of the war at home. At first, factories closed and unemployment rose despite conscription; a labor shortage followed as war production became crucial. Everywhere, agricultural output dropped, contributing to the food shortages of subsequent years. Prices rose rapidly, and consumer hoarding further strained faltering systems of distribution. Just as the rules of warfare were bent or shattered by unlimited submarine warfare, poison gas, and a blockade that included consumer goods, so governments expanded their powers to move workers, censor the press, control railroads and shipping, and direct the economy. Unprepared for the ever greater amounts of ammunition and supplies required by the war, governments quickly learned to use paper money, rationing, and central planning.

In the first weeks of German advances, France lost half of its iron ore and coal fields and more than half its heavy industry; yet as commissions established quotas and allocated supplies, production steadily increased. Similarly, in Great Britain the government requisitioned supplies and forced industry to new efficiency. Despite voluntary enlistments that raised the largest army in British history, it had to adopt conscription in 1916, a step Winston Churchill would call "the greatest revolution in our system since the institution of feudalism under William the Conqueror." Rebellion in Ireland that Easter was quickly put down; yet it was a serious diversion for British troops and a disturbing reminder of how cruelly war tested every weakness in the social structure.

Germany, deprived of critical raw materials, developed the most fully controlled economy of any of the combatants, under the brilliant direction of Walther Rathenau. Private firms were organized into sectors of production so that the most important could be favored, inefficient firms closed, and national planning enforced. The chemical industry created rubber substitutes, culled aluminum from local clays, manufactured fertilizers from nitrates in the air, and made textiles from wood pulp. Substitutes, which made *ersatz* an international word, included chestnut flour and clover meal used in the "war bread" that, like meatless days and conscription, soon made civilians feel the burden of all-out war. German officials were less sensitive to civilian needs, and far less efficient in meeting them, than Allied leaders.

Great Britain, France, and Germany adjusted effectively to the new challenge of fielding vast armies while increasing industrial production and maintaining intricate logistical networks. The Austro-Hungarian and Russian empires could not match these feats. Their industries were less well developed; supplies and trained personnel were often lacking. Equally important, neither government knew how nor dared try to squeeze from the economy the quantities of food, ammunition, and clothing that war required. Russian armies increasingly showed the effects of fighting ill-fed and ill-shod, with inadequate weapons and ammunition, and without good communication. (Orders to Russian troops were broadcast uncoded, and the German ability to intercept them contributed to Ludendorff's reputation as a great tactician.) In adversity, Austria-Hungary could not rely on the continued loyalty of subject peoples, and soldiers were carefully dispatched to zones far from their native lands so as not to be fighting against people who spoke their own language. Poles, for example, found themselves fighting for both sides, as they served in the respective armies of the Austro-Hungarians, the Germans, and the Russians.

Social Effects   By the winter of 1916–1917, the strains were visible to all. Everywhere on the bloodied continent, Europeans were thinner, more shabbily dressed, overworked, and grieved by the endless losses of husbands, sons, and homes. Poor crops and overloaded transportation systems further reduced the diet; this winter was Germany's "turnip winter," when the best prepared of the domestic war economies could barely keep its people healthy. Society itself was subtly altered from the first month, when Belgian refugees poured into France, until years after the war. The strains of war were changing society. As the queue became a kind of public rite and rationing a way of life, distinctions of social class blurred. Each government awkwardly tried to restrict the consumption of alcohol and worried about rising rates of illegitimacy.

Women on the Home Front   While men fought on the battlefront, women were essential in sustaining what was now called the **home front,** and even most feminists—at odds with their governments over the issue of female suffrage—rallied to support the war effort. In every country, women left home and domestic service to work in industry, transportation, and business. Such employment was often divided by class. In Great Britain, two million upper- and middle-class women worked without pay in medical, paramilitary, and aid organizations, while their working-class compatriots often found employment in army auxiliary corps or in industry. In the latter area especially, women's involvement represented a dramatic shift in employment. Many found jobs in the new munitions factories and other war-related industries that previously had employed only men. In Great Britain's munitions industries, the number of women workers rose

At a Vickers factory in England, women labored with patriotic seriousness at the task of preparing artillery shells.
© Hulton-Deutsch Collection/Corbis

steadily to become one-third or more of the total. Women also ran farms, became firefighters and bus conductors, and worked in offices. On the front, they served as nurses.

The feminization of the workforce, however, was not accompanied by new enlightened attitudes toward women. War propaganda reinforced traditional gender stereotypes by emphasizing the enemy's brutality toward women and the maternal care that nurses provided the wounded. In Britain the first women who volunteered for the war effort were rejected, and only the pressures of war pushed the government to encourage women to go to work with the Munitions Act of 1915. Such employment was supposed to be temporary: Women first entered the workforce to replace conscripted male relatives until their return from the front. In France women were not allowed to provide military support services at all for two years. However, the need for their contribution overrode qualms about allowing the "weaker sex" to hold jobs previously reserved for men. By 1917 the British government denied contracts to employers unwilling to hire women (see "Meet the 'Khaki Girls,'" p. 837). The French government forbade hiring men for jobs that women could do; and in Germany the Krupp steelworks, which had no women employees in 1914, counted twelve thousand by 1917.

Women's contributions outside the home were publicly acknowledged as loyal service to the nation, and for some women wartime activities brought increased independence. They were more likely to live on their own and go out in public alone. For most women, how-

ever, income provided the greatest compensation for the danger and drudgery of the work. Lower-class women often worked 60 to 70 hours a week and still endured poor living conditions outside the factory. Inevitably, questions arose about unequal pay and whether men might be permanently displaced, and there was debate over the proper role of women, echoing the issues raised by the suffrage movement before the war.

As a result, women's roles in the workplace created as much criticism as praise, especially among the men on the front lines. Women were attacked for spending money, or even for benefiting from the war as their husbands, sons, and brothers paid the ultimate sacrifice. Women in Britain and France also had to defend themselves from accusations that their work outside the home was motivated by their desire to win the right to vote rather than by patriotism.

Nevertheless, women in the workforce stood to benefit from a general wartime trend toward a more democratic, inclusive conception of national politics. Trade unions were treated with new respect, and officials began to talk of the benefits to be granted after the war. Even the Kaiser spoke of ending the three-class voting system in Prussia and hinted at a government that would be responsible to parliament, while the House of Commons, in a notable reversal, declared its support in principle for women's suffrage.

Changes on the Battlefield   While economic pressures brought rapid social change at home, the men on the front felt increasingly cut off from their families

MEET THE "KHAKI GIRLS"

The two women who wrote this brief article, published in June 1917 in The Englishwoman, *a women's magazine, present it as an upbeat account of the dedication of women workers, but it is also a document about class distinctions.*

"We got out of the tram and walked up the short, muddy path, past the sentry, who with fixed bayonet guards the entrance to A_3, the 'shop' in which we work. It was twenty minutes past two—ten minutes before the hour for the shift to begin—so there were plenty of our fellow-workers passing through the door. Among the three hundred girls employed on this shift there are not more than four or five lady-workers, so the crowd was made up of 'khaki girls', the colloquial name given to the industrial hands, originating from the fact that when women were admitted last July to the munition shops they wore khaki overalls, which since have been replaced for economical reasons by those made of black material.

"We had grown accustomed to the sight of the endless procession of girls pouring into the factory . . . all of the same type, rather wild, yet in their quieter moods giving an impression of sullen defiance, ready to answer you back if you should happen to tread on their very tender corns. So long, though, as you keep off those corns, and do not let these wayward creatures feel you are intruding nor provide yourself with anything which they have not, even though it be merely a newspaper to sit upon in preference to a dusty board, they will show their good nature to you—and they have plenty. Then there is their good humour and their gay spirits. No matter how strenuous the work, nor how wearing the hardships, they will always give out from this wonderful gaiety of spirits, and keep the ball rolling with their sense of humour—obvious and childlike—running as it does mostly to nicknaming, pelting the me-chanics with orange peel, or skipping with a rope of steel shavings cut from the shell on the lathe.

"Every one of them carries a brown or green despatch-case. Most of them are flashily dressed: a cherry-coloured coat, a black-and-white check skirt, a satin blouse trimmed with swansdown, a hat, small in shape but too large to fit, so it drops over one eye, and down-trodden boots, is typical of what they wear. Some of them are exceedingly pretty; they are all heavily powdered, and in some cases rouged. Their hair is dressed with great care, and even if it does fall about their eyes it is not untidiness, but an effect purposely arranged by the aid of the small mirror—often a beautiful thing to look upon, either encrusted with shells or mounted on scarlet plush—carried in that despatch-case which is the essential part of a khaki girl's equipment, since it contains the food with which she is obliged to provide herself.

"We stood in the doorway a moment looking at the sun shining down upon the river. 'Do you think the Zeppelins will come tonight?' one of us said to the other. 'It will be a good night for them.' 'There's no moon.' 'Nor wind—and they were at Paris last night.'

"Then we went to our work, and the absorption of screwing plugs into shells, turning them on the lathe, taking them out and gauging them, working to exceed the standard number, swallowed up every other thought."

From Brenda Girvin and Monica Coxens, "Meet the 'Khaki Girls,' " *The Englishwoman,* 1917.

---

and countries. The reality of the trenches led many to express contempt for and alienation from what the poet Siegfried Sassoon described as the "callous complacency" of the civilian view of the war.[2] Mired in the trenches, facing death every day, soldiers soon relinquished their ideas of war as a heroic or patriotic duty and instead sustained themselves through close relationships with those who shared their battlefield experiences and the memories of dead comrades.

Meanwhile, the continuation of the war brought changes in the high command. In France Joffre's intolerance of civilian leaders brought his downfall in December 1916; he was replaced by the tactful and dashing General Robert Georges Nivelle, who planned a massive new offensive. This one, he promised, would break through German defenses.

In Germany two heroes of the Eastern front had been promoted. Hindenburg received overall command and with Ludendorff took charge of campaigns in the West in the fall of 1916. To destroy the shipping on which Britain depended, Germany returned to unlimited submarine warfare in January 1917. Aware that such a step might bring the United States into the war, the Germans calculated that Britain would have to sue for peace before American power could make a difference.

Political Changes In Great Britain, Lloyd George, made minister of war in June 1916, became prime minister in December. Eloquent and energetic, once a

[2] Robert Giddings, *The War Poets* (Bloomsbury, 1990), p. 111.

Illustration of Indian soldiers, supported by a British grenade thrower, engaged in hand-to-hand combat with Germans on the Western front, from the *Illustrated London News*, March 27, 1915. Such images were used to demonstrate to the British public the bravery and devotion of the imperial troops.
The Illustrated London New Picture Library

radical orator who had terrified the upper classes, he now seemed the kind of popular and decisive leader who could galvanize the British war effort. After French morale hit a dangerous low, that country made the fiery Clemenceau premier again in November 1917.

Change came to Russia too—through revolution. In March 1917 popular protest forced the tsar to abdicate (see "Revolution in Russia," p. 862), and a new provisional government proclaimed sweeping democratic reforms while promising to continue the war. At the same time, however, physical conditions on the Russian military and home fronts were rapidly deteriorating. For the Allies these changes in Russia gave the war itself new meaning. Now democracies, led by politicians with ties to the left, were fighting together against authoritarian governments. A war that involved the people more fully than any before took on an ideological meaning. The Allies' sense of democratic purpose was strengthened in April when the United States—resentful that Germany was sinking its ships and making overtures to Mexico that included prom-ises of the return of former Mexican lands now part of the United States—declared war on Germany.

The Armenian Genocide The most extreme example of civilian involvement in the First World War was the Armenian Massacre of 1915, in which civilians themselves became the targets of violence. For decades before the outbreak of the First World War, the large Armenian minority living in the Ottoman Empire had been subject to repression and violence. In the late nineteenth century, about 200,000 Armenians living in Eastern Anatolia were killed, with government authorities citing their nationalist ambitions and cooperation with Russia. The position of the Armenians further deteriorated after they refused to support the Ottoman Empire during the Balkan Wars. In February 1914, as a result of international and especially Russian pressure, the Ottoman government agreed to allow international monitors into the empire, who were to ensure that Armenian minority rights would be protected. With the outbreak of war, however, the Ottoman government renounced this agreement and instead formulated a plan

In March 1917 women demonstrated in Petrograd, demanding that the rations for soldiers' families be increased.
Sovfoto

for the forced relocation of Armenians, ostensibly to protect them from the Russians. Beginning in March 1915, the Ottoman government deported 1,750,000 Armenians to the deserts of Syria and Mesopotamia. At least 800,000 Armenians died during this expulsion from their homes, and thousands more were killed before reaching the desert. This calculated large-scale massacre both demonstrates the nature of **total war** and its effects upon civilians and foreshadows the kind of mass murder later seen during the Second World War.

The Empire at War   World War One was a total war in yet another crucial sense. Although fought mainly in Europe, imperialism transformed the conflict into a global one. All the major European powers saw the war as an opportunity to gain more territory overseas. Britain and France both hoped to gain dominance over the weakening Ottoman Empire, and Germany drew up plans for imperial control of parts of Eastern Europe as well as most of Southern Africa.

As a result, the war spread to colonial areas and involved peoples from countries where Europe had imperial aspirations. Battles between the Allies and German-led forces took place throughout the Ottoman Empire, most notably in Gallipoli, Baghdad, Jerusalem, Syria, and Beirut. Fighting also spread to West Africa and German-held areas of Southwest Africa. Thousands of individuals from European colonies were recruited or conscripted to fight in Europe itself: 62,000 Indian soldiers died fighting alongside the British;

30,000 Senegalese lost their lives for France; and over 400,000 Africans served the Allies by transporting supplies and the wounded. On the home front, colonial recruits manned factories necessary for war production; in France alone, 250,000 workers were from its overseas colonies. Many of those who came voluntarily to assist the war effort expected new rights or even full independence for their home countries and would assert their claims at the end of the war. Instead of reinforcing imperialism, the involvement of the colonies threatened to undermine Europe's global power.

The Great Trials of 1917–1918

In the fighting itself, neither new leaders nor shared ideals seemed to make much difference (see "Wilfred Owen Describes Trench Warfare," p. 840). Relentlessly, the war went on. Russia's collapse aided the Central Powers; American entry into the war was a gain for the Allies. Not until late in the summer of 1918 did the outcome begin to be clear.

Fighting in the West   On the Western front, French general Robert Georges Nivelle launched his great offensive in April and May 1917 despite multiple handicaps. The Germans had strengthened their defenses; disagreements arose between the British and French commands; and some French troops, dispirited by two years of endless death on the same desolate terrain, mutinied, refusing to fight. The Second Battle of the

WILFRED OWEN DESCRIBES TRENCH WARFARE

Wilfred Owen's moving poems about World War I were published after he was killed in action in 1918, and they continue to be widely read. His first tour of duty had ended when he was sent home suffering from "shell shock." Some months later, he was back in France. On January 4, 1917, he wrote his mother that "on all the officers' faces there is a harassed look that I have never seen before," adding, "I censored hundreds of letters yesterday, and the hope of peace was in every one of them." He was back in the fighting a few days later, when he wrote her this letter.

Tuesday, 16 January 1917
[2nd Manchester Regt, B.E.F.]

"My own sweet Mother,

" . . . I can see no excuse for deceiving you about these last 4 days. I have suffered seventh hell.

"I have not been at the front.

"I have been in front of it.

"I held an advanced post, that is, a 'dug-out' in the middle of No Man's Land.

"We had a march of 3 miles over shelled road then nearly 3 along a flooded trench. After that we came to where the trenches had been blown flat out and had to go over the top. It was of course dark, too dark, and the ground was not mud, not sloppy mud; but an octopus of sucking clay, 3, 4, and 5 feet deep, relieved only by craters full of water. Men have been known to drown in them. Many stuck in the mud & only got on by leaving their waders, equipment, and in some cases their clothes.

"High explosives were dropping all around us, and machine-guns spluttered every few minutes. But it was so dark that even the German flares did not reveal us.

"Three quarters dead, I mean each of us 3/4 dead, we reached the dug-out, and relieved the wretches therein. I then had to go forth and find another dug-out for a still more advanced post where I left 18 bombers. I was responsible for other posts on the left but there was a junior officer in charge.

"My dug-out held 25 men tight packed. Water filled it to a depth of 1 or 2 feet, leaving say 4 feet of air.

"One entrance had been blown in & blocked.

"So far, the other remained.

"The Germans knew we were staying there and decided we shouldn't.

"Those fifty hours were the agony of my happy life.

"Every ten minutes on Sunday afternoon seemed an hour.

"I nearly broke down and let myself drown in the water that was now slowly rising over my knees.

"Towards 6 o'clock, when, I suppose, you would be going to church, the shelling grew less intense and less accurate: so that I was mercifully helped to do my duty and crawl, wade, climb and flounder over No Man's Land to visit my other post. It took me half an hour to move about 150 yards.

"I was chiefly annoyed by our own machine-guns from behind. The seeng-seeng-seeng of the bullets reminded me of Mary's canary. On the whole I can support the canary better.

"In the Platoon on my left the sentries over the dug-out were blown to nothing. One of these poor fellows was my first servant whom I rejected. If I had kept him he would have lived, for servants don't do Sentry Duty."

From Harold Owen and John Bell (eds.), *Wilfred Owen: The Collected Letters*, Oxford University Press, 1967.

Aisne and the Third Battle of Champagne took a toll as great as their predecessors and made even slighter gains. Nivelle was replaced by General Henri Philippe Pétain, the hero of Verdun, who began a concerted effort to raise morale, but it would be months before France dared another offensive.

The British went ahead with plans for an attack in the north, spurred by the desperate need to knock out at least some of the submarine bases from which German U-boats were sinking such enormous tonnages that the Admiralty openly wondered how many months Great Britain could last. The noise of battle could be heard in England, and hundreds of thousands of men fell, but the British fared no better in the Third Battle of Ypres (July–November) than the French had in

their spring offensive. British morale, too, was shaken; yet stalemate continued. Germany's submarine warfare had come close to its goal, but Allied losses dropped to a tolerable level in mid-1917 with the development of the convoy, in which fleets of armed ships accompanied merchant vessels across the ocean. With America's entry into the war, the tonnage those convoys delivered grew still greater.

Allied Defeats: Russia and Italy Elsewhere, the picture was different. On the Eastern front, Russian advances in July soon turned into almost constant retreat, and Russian troops suffered from shortages in essential supplies and equipment. In November, the communists gained control of the government. They invited

Desolation surrounded weary Allied soldiers as they made their way across the mud on the battlefield at Ypres.
Imperial War Museum, London

all nations to join in peace without annexations or indemnities, then entered into independent negotiations with the Central Powers. The most populous of the Allies had been defeated.

Able now to engage more troops on the Italian front, Germany and Austria-Hungary launched a concentrated attack there in October, scoring an overwhelming victory at the Battle of Caporetto. Italy's armies collapsed as tens of thousands died, surrendered, or deserted. But the Italians regrouped along the Piave River; Britain and France rushed in reinforcements, and the Austro-German onslaught was slowed and then stopped.

The Last Year Although the Russians stopped fighting in February 1918, the Central Powers did not. They continued their eastward march until Russia signed the Treaty of Brest Litovsk in March. Russia surrendered Russian Poland, the Baltic provinces, the Ukraine, and Transcaucasia. Germany had acquired invaluable wheat and oil when it most needed them and a respite on one front. But merely safeguarding such immense gains required substantial numbers of troops badly needed elsewhere, especially since the incredibly harsh terms of the Brest Litovsk Treaty intensified the Allies' determination to win the war.

On the Western front, the Germans, their reserves of personnel and resources nearing exhaustion, opened a great offensive. Attacking sector after sector from March through June, they made the greatest advances seen there in four years. It was a triumph of careful strategy, improved tactics, heavy artillery, and gas. To correct the weakness of divided command, the Allies

named General Ferdinand Foch supreme commander of all their forces; and they retained their reserves while the Germans exhausted theirs. Enemy guns once more bombarded Paris before the Allied counteroffensive began in July. Slowly, then faster, the Germans were driven back over the familiar and devastated landscape. By the end of August, German armies had retreated to the Hindenburg line, a defensive position established at the beginning of 1917. The Allies continued their push in battles of the Argonne and Ypres in September and October, gaining inexorably—even if less rapidly than hoped or expected.

The Collapse of the Central Powers On other fronts the Central Powers collapsed dramatically. In the Middle East, Turkish and German troops were defeated by British and Arab forces led by T. E. Lawrence, whose exploits in mobilizing Arab opposition to Turkey became part of the romantic lore in which this war was poorer than most. In October the sultan was deposed, and a new government sued for peace. Combined Serbian, French, British, and Greek forces under French leadership drove up the Balkan Peninsula. Bulgaria surrendered at the end of September, and the Allies moved toward Romania.

The Austro-Hungarian Empire was disintegrating. Czech, Yugoslav, Romanian, and Polish movements for independence, encouraged by the Allies, gained strength throughout 1918. Austria-Hungary attacked once more on the Italian front but withdrew after heavy losses. Its armies, defeated at Vittorio Veneto at the end of October, began simply to dissolve as the various nationalities left for home and revolution. Czechoslovakia and the kingdom later called Yugoslavia both declared their independence. In November Austria-Hungary surrendered unconditionally to the Italians.

At the end of September, Ludendorff had demanded that Germany seek an armistice, but that required political changes as well. Twice in 1917 Kaiser William II had promised to make his cabinet subject to a majority in the Reichstag; and in October 1918 he appointed Prince Max of Baden as chancellor to begin this transformation from above. Ludendorff resigned his command at the end of October, and Germany asked for peace on the general terms set forth by President Woodrow Wilson. But Wilson now insisted on the evacuation of occupied territories and a democratic German government with which to negotiate.

The German Republic Accepts an Armistice While German leaders hesitated, they faced the threat of revolution at home. A liberal believer in parliamentary government, Prince Max represented a compromise that might have worked earlier but now could not in the face of uprisings in the name of peace, democracy, and

MAP 27.3　TERRITORIAL GAINS, 1914–1919
This map illustrates the vast expanses of territory held by the Allied powers during the war, as well as the considerable part of Eastern Europe occupied by the Central Powers. At what point in the war were these Central Power advances repelled by the Allied powers?

◆ For an online version, go to www.mhhe.com/chambers9 > chapter 27 > book maps

socialism. Germany threatened to break apart. Prince Max pleaded with William to abdicate and, when revolt spread to Berlin, simply announced that the kaiser had done so. William II abdicated on November 9 after a mutiny in the German fleet and revolution in Munich. The government was handed over to Friedrich Ebert, the leader of the Social Democrats; a German Republic was proclaimed and an armistice commission sent to meet with Foch. The commission agreed to terms on November 11. By then Allied troops were approaching German borders in the West and had crossed the Danube in the East, taken Trieste on the Adriatic, and sailed through the Dardanelles. In the meantime, revolution was sweeping across central Europe.

THE PEACE

From the Rhine to Russia so many governments were new and so many boundaries undecided that, by default as well as victory, the Allies seemed free to construct the new Europe of peaceful democracies their wartime statements had foreshadowed. Instead, the diplomats assembled at the Peace Conference in Paris found their task complicated by the very extent of victory and beset by more interests than they could satisfy. So great an opportunity and so grand an undertaking fed the extremes, first of hope, then of disillusionment. Meanwhile, away from Paris, more direct means were being used to shape the postwar world.

The Effects of World War I

The war itself had some of the effects of revolution. Among the defeated nations, governments were overturned and shaky new ones established. Even among the Allies, war had created so much that no one could be sure what the postwar world would be like. Society had to be put together again.

The New State of Affairs   Throughout central Europe, political conflict adopted the techniques of force. In Germany radical groups staged a number of local revolts, creating an air of instability sustained by ***Freikorps*** ("free corps"), mercenary squads made up of former soldiers available to any movement that could pay them for street fighting and marauding. To the east of Germany, new regimes and sometimes whole new nations replaced the defeated states.

The victorious governments, having shown the capacity to mobilize society for war, would now be held more responsible than in the past for society's peacetime needs, as evidenced in a spate of postwar legislation on housing, education, and pensions. Clemenceau, Lloyd George, and Wilson, the spokesmen of victory, had all been vigorous reformers, but now they watched with apprehension the revival of the radical left.

Life in wartime had affected social classes differently. Even where there was no open revolution, the aristocracy and other traditional elites had been weakened by the general democratization of political life and by the decline in purchasing power that resulted from inflation, reduction in the value of land, and increased taxes (especially in England). A middle class confident in 1914 found itself exposed and vulnerable after the war, its savings threatened, its possibilities limited, its values challenged. Those on salary or fixed income suffered more from inflation than those on workers' wages; middle-class life became less lavish, and there were fewer servants (some 400,000 English women left domestic service in the course of the war). Workers, particularly the skilled, were on the whole relatively well off. Although rates of pay usually lagged behind inflation, the years of full employment and more jobs for women had increased family income; and trade unions used their greater influence to maintain shorter hours and higher pay. Peasants, though declining in number, were also often better off, helped by the demand for food and by inflation, which made it easier to pay off their debts.

The Change in Social Mores   Even ordinary manners and dress were different. Gentlemen, forced to use public transportation, had abandoned their top hats; women's clothes grew simpler and their skirts shorter. Women of the working class took to wearing cosmetics and high-heeled shoes and smoking and drinking in

It would take years to recover from the damage to roads and bridges and private housing in Belgium and northeastern France. The French village of Craonne, where Napoleon once won a battle and which was the scene of fighting in 1917 and 1918, looked like this in 1919.
Roger-Viollet/Getty Images

public, as did their middle-class sisters. Such changes in customs, even more than the increase in violent crime and juvenile delinquency, shocked moralists, who associated them with casual encounters between the sexes, increased illegitimacy, and the popularity of dance halls.

Public appearance thus added to the economic and political disruptions of wartime in suggesting a new openness and uncertainty, a more fluid society in which old standards could not be recaptured. Millions of refugees constituted more tangible displacement, and millions of other Europeans (especially peasants and women) were not eager to return to their old way of life. Of course most people more or less did, and by the 1920s prewar constraints of class and gender were largely back in place, despite some relaxation.

The psychological impact of war, harder to demonstrate than the social changes, may have been just as important. Throughout society, there was a tendency following the war to expect instability. Intellectuals suffered what one historian has called "minds scorched by war"; and among the populace, a cynical distrust of leaders and institutions seems to have spread after years of wartime promises. There was a cleavage, too, between those who had fought and those who stayed home, those whose lives were transformed and those who had more nearly maintained business as usual. Bitterness about these inequalities of sacrifice surfaced in public denunciations of war profiteers and in a more inflammatory political rhetoric. At the same time, with a kind of selective nostalgia, many regretted the loss of that sense of common purpose and national unity that war had brought, and some even yearned again for the thrill of combat.

Economic Effects Military needs had stimulated the rapid development of certain technologies. When World War I began, the cavalry was a major element of every army, pack horses and horse-drawn wagons the principal form of transport from rail lines to the front. By war's end, the practical importance of automobiles and airplanes, radio, and the chemical industry had become clear to all. In many factories the effort to speed up industrial production altered the nature of work as tasks were reorganized in ways thought to be more rational and efficient but that workers found increasingly impersonal and demanding.

Although some sectors of the economy gained from their wartime importance, the overall losses were dramatic. World trade had been disrupted and Europe's place in it transformed. In 1914 Europe was the world's greatest lender of money; in 1918 its nations were debtors. The physical destruction of property, aside from the billions lost in war matériel, was greatest in Belgium and France. In France alone, thousands of bridges and factories as well as a million buildings were destroyed. Total European production in the 1920s would fall below the level of 1913.

The Dead and the Culture of Mourning The greatest change in postwar Europe resulted directly from the war: the deaths of 10 to 13 million people, perhaps one-third of them civilians. Among the armed forces, casualties ran about 50 percent for the major combatants except France, which suffered higher losses. In each country whole classes from the elite schools were virtually wiped out. For France, with its older population and low birthrate, the war was a demographic catastrophe in which 10 percent of the adult population—one out of every two Frenchmen between the ages of 20 and 32—disappeared on the Western front. Moreover, for every soldier who died, two or three were wounded, and millions were maimed for life.

The stupefying death toll not only affected the economy through manpower losses, but it placed a heavy burden on European governments. Throughout Europe, the one-armed, the one-legged, and the blind would live on, supported by pensions and performing menial tasks, in silent testimony to the cost of total war. Millions of widows with young children also relied on the state, though often the income was meager, especially as inflation increased in the postwar years.

As divided as Europe had been in war, it was now united in grieving and remembrance. Associations such as the Red Cross and informal groups offered consolation for those most directly affected and helped to mend social dislocation by creating bonds between widows, former soldiers, and others whose lives were disrupted. Memorials sprang up throughout Europe, especially on sites that witnessed the most carnage in Belgium and France. These often became the focus of pilgrimages through which the public could express its collective grief. Publicly commemorating the dead took perhaps its most concrete form in tombs of "unknown soldiers" erected in Europe's capitals, and the ceremonies surrounding Armistice Day became a central experience of interwar life.

Faced with such loss, the leaders of exhausted nations sat down to make a lasting peace, one that would end

MILITARY FATALITIES IN WORLD WAR I (MAJOR POWERS)	
Germany	1,900,000
Russia	1,700,000
France	1,400,000
Austria-Hungary	1,200,000
British Empire	900,000
Ottoman Empire	700,000
Italy	600,000
United States	100,000

the secret diplomacy that juggled spheres of influence and national interests without regard for public opinion. With Wilson as its greatest advocate, democracy—meaning popular participation in public life—seemed to the Allies the best guarantee against future conflict.

The Revolutionary Situation

The Russian Revolution, while clearly the most dramatic, was not the only political upheaval conceived in war. Disruptions of normal life, including mass migrations, military desertions, and mutinies, posed acute threats to the established authorities. The war weakened many European states, giving radicals on the left and right new opportunities to claim power.

New Nations in Eastern Europe   The peoples suddenly released from Habsburg and Russian rule fought to define the boundaries of their new nations. In the Baltic lands, Lithuanian, Estonian, and Latvian republics marked their independence by war with Russia. Lithuania was also at odds with the new republic of Poland; and Poland faced conflict on all its other borders—against Russians, Ukranians, Czechs, and Germans. The creation of Czechoslovakia and the new kingdom of Yugoslavia led to renewed warfare as Hungary attacked Czechoslovakia, while in the Balkans Romania attacked both Hungary and Yugoslavia—just the kind of hostility that had preceded World War I.

Leftist Militancy   Russia's communists had good reason to hope that revolution would sweep from East to West, and Marxists throughout Europe looked to the miraculous events in Russia as the beginning of the socialist future they had so long imagined. In March 1919 delegates from a score of countries met in Moscow to establish the Third International. Communists were active in the Baltic states, and in 1919 Lenin's friend Béla Kun led a communist government in Hungary until Romanian armies ended his brief reign. There was also communist agitation in Vienna, where the provisional government of truncated Austria, all that was left of the Habsburg Empire, looked forward to union with the new German republic. Such an alliance, however, was forbidden by the Allies and embodied in the Paris Peace Treaty Austria was made to sign.

Marxists, however, had long set their eyes on highly industrialized Germany, finding revolutionary promise in its class tensions and strong socialist movement. Germany's defeat and a shaky new German republic appeared to fulfill old portents. In January 1919 a communist revolt broke out in Berlin, and the following spring another uprising managed for a few weeks to make Bavaria a Soviet republic. Both were quickly defeated by remnants of the German army. Russia remained the center of the communist world.

The Peace Treaties

President Wilson's Fourteen Points had won acceptance as a basis for defining a new European order. The points dealt mainly with territorial adjustments but idealistically proclaimed the self-determination of peoples to be the governing principle of the peace. Wilson's

When Woodrow Wilson paraded through the streets, Parisians cheered the representative of a new democratic era as well as an ally in victory.
The Granger Collection, New York

call for free trade and open seas had long been part of the liberal canon. His attention to the dangers of colonial warfare, the need for disarmament, and the benefits of open diplomacy was more radical but echoed the common belief that such policies would have averted world war. Wilson's final point, and the one closest to his heart, called for a **League of Nations** to guarantee the safety of all. The American president's talk of "impartial justice," a "peace that will be permanent," and covenants that will be "sacredly observed" caught the imagination of the world.

The Paris Conference At the Paris Peace Conference, which opened in January 1919, all parties agreed not to repeat the mistakes of the Congress of Vienna a century earlier. No defeated nations would take part in the early discussions; no German Talleyrand would divide the Allies. The atmosphere was one of sober business, organized around commissions of expert advisers. Thirty nations had joined the Allies, at least formally,[3] but the major decisions would be taken by the five big powers: France, the United Kingdom, Italy, Japan, and the United States.

Although Japan was a colonial power in its own right, primary authority resided in four men: Clemenceau, Lloyd George, Premier Vittorio Orlando, and Wilson. Disagreements among the Big Four soon became the center around which the negotiations turned. All were elected leaders, sensitive to public opinion, faced with grave domestic problems, and worried by the turmoil in Central and Eastern Europe. Experienced politicians, they knew they had to hurry.

The Treaty with Germany To settle by May the complicated terms for peace with Germany was a remarkable achievement. Haste itself probably made the treaty more severe than it might otherwise have been. Commissions, assuming their proposals would be subject to later bargaining, tended to begin with maximum terms, but these were often simply written into the treaty itself.

Germany lost its overseas territories in Africa and the Pacific, which were assigned by the League of Nations to the various Allied powers to be administered as mandates. It also lost territory much closer to home, such as Alsace-Lorraine, but was still able to remain a powerful state. Germany's new boundaries in Europe continued to be a source of problems. France was satisfied with the return of Alsace-Lorraine, but it did not receive the left bank of the Rhine, as it had wanted. Instead, the Allies were to occupy the Rhineland for fif-

teen years; and the coal-producing regions along the Saar River, while remaining under German sovereignty, would be supervised by France until a later plebiscite by universal suffrage determined the final disposition. Plebiscites would also decide whether Germany surrendered part of Schleswig to Denmark and part of upper Silesia to Poland.

The Polish provinces of eastern Prussia, where Germans formed about 40 percent of the population, were immediately ceded to Poland. That created the controversial Polish corridor to the sea, which awkwardly separated eastern Prussia from the rest of Germany. Although a majority of the population within the corridor was Polish, its outlet was the German port city of Danzig, restored to its ancient status as a free city. Poland would always feel insecure with an arrangement the Germans never accepted.

Germany was to have no large artillery, submarines, or military air force, and no more than 100,000 men under arms—requirements that were intended to lead to a general disarmament. The lists of items Germany had to deliver to the Allies were more punitive: horses and railway carriages, quantities of coal, most of its present ships, and some new vessels to be specially built.

Reparations The required reparations were more burdensome still. Despite fine talk of not requiring an indemnity, the Allies decided that Germany should pay for civilian damages. The claims of Belgium, a neutral attacked without warning, were easily justified; and Clemenceau could argue that the most destructive fighting had occurred in Belgium and France. But Lloyd George had campaigned on a platform of making Germany pay. He insisted, over American objections, on including Allied military pensions as civilian costs—a demand that made Germany liable for sums unspecified and without foreseeable end. Germany was required to accept Article 231 of the Versailles Treaty, which was known as the **war guilt clause.** This clause required Germany to accept "responsibility" for losses from a war "imposed . . . by the aggression of Germany and her allies." The war guilt clause became a subject of controversy in every country and a source of bitter resentment, official and private, in every part of Germany.

In German eyes, the treaty was an intolerable *Diktat* that German delegates had no chance to discuss until it was already drafted, when only minor revisions could be made. Faced with these terms, the German government resigned, and the parliament at first rejected the treaty's stipulation of German guilt. But when the Allies held firm, parliament angrily acquiesced. The treaty was signed on June 28, 1919, the fifth anniversary of the assassination at Sarajevo, in the Hall of Mirrors at Versailles, where Bismarck and Kaiser Wilhelm I had announced the founding of the German

---

[3] The newly created nations of Yugoslavia, Czechoslovakia, and Poland were treated as Allies; the new republics of Austria, Hungary, and Germany as the defeated Central Powers.

John Christen Johansen
SIGNING OF THE TREATY OF VERSAILLES, 1919
The Treaty of Versailles was signed by elected political leaders in the Hall of Mirrors at Versailles and presented as a great public event, in self-conscious contrast to the Congress of Vienna a century earlier.
National Portrait Gallery, Smithsonian Institution, Washington/Art Resource, NY. Gift of an anonymous donor through Mrs. Elizabeth Rogerson, 192

Empire forty-eight years before. The symbolism was complete.

Italian Aims For the Big Four, Italy's expectations were especially difficult, and Italian insistence on them particularly irksome. The Treaty of London of 1915 had promised Italy much of the Slavic-speaking lands of the Dalmatian coast, and the Italian delegates expected to get them. Wilson was determined to prevent further violations of the principle of nationality beyond allowing Italy, for strategic reasons, to have the Tyrol south of the Brenner Pass through the Alps, although that former Austrian land was German-speaking.

Using a press interview, Wilson in effect spoke directly to the Italian people, asking them to reject the position taken by their representatives at the conference. The Italian delegation withdrew in protest, to a great outpouring of nationalist feeling at home. Eventually, Italy was given the Istrian Peninsula and some islands but not Dalmatia. For years to come, resentment over the promises not kept at Paris would be a disruptive issue in Italian domestic politics.

The Other Treaties With the signing of the Treaty of Versailles, the Big Four dispersed, leaving the details of the remaining settlements to their foreign offices. The treaty with Austria in September was closely modeled on the treaty with Germany, but reparations and demilitarization, including naval restrictions, hardly seemed appropriate for the shaky little landlocked Austrian republic. Boundaries for the other new states were settled on the basis of nationality in some cases and strategic needs in others.

Treaties with Bulgaria in November and with Hungary in June 1920 gave Bohemia to Czechoslovakia on historical grounds, while Hungarian claims to a larger historical kingdom were largely ignored. Hungary lost almost three-quarters of its former lands. Although Bulgaria surrendered relatively little territory to Greece, Romania, and Yugoslavia, it greatly resented its new borders. Romania, by contrast, emerged as the territorial winner, gaining land not only from Bulgaria, but from Austria, Hungary, and the Soviet Union. Every state in Eastern Europe, it seemed, lay claim to territory based on history, culture, or religion, so that existing railways, economic ties, and more "natural" boundaries such as rivers and mountain ranges simply did not coincide with the borders established at Paris. It would fall to the new League of Nations to make these arrangements work.

MAP 27.4   TERRITORIAL SETTLEMENTS, 1919–1926
This map shows the national boundaries of Europe as they were decided upon after the First World War; they would remain in existence for nearly thirty years. Note the new nations that emerged out of the former Russian, Austro-Hungarian, and Ottoman Empires. Notice, too, the areas where national affiliations were to be decided by local plebiscites. Why do you suppose the representatives at Paris decided to hold these plebiscites?
◆ For an online version, go to www.mhhe.com/chambers9 > chapter 27 > book maps

Much remained to negotiate. The fate of many territories was determined later, sometimes by plebiscite. Moreover, some peace arrangements engendered great hostility or were simply untenable. One example was the Minorities Protection Treaty, promising just treatment for minorities such as Jews and other ethnic and national minorities, which the nations of Eastern Europe took as an affront to their new-found sovereignty.

One of the great tensions created by the peace treaty—although the European powers did not realize it at the time—was over the scope of self-determination. African and Asian colonial subjects interpreted the Wilsonian principle of national sovereignty as applicable to their own situations, particularly in light of the massive colonial contribution to the war effort. Yet European leaders had no intention of extending self-determination to their colonies, and their failure to recognize the rights of colonial subjects fostered great bitterness, spurring the growth of colonial nationalism.

The Unstable Settlement in the Middle East

The final treaty, with Turkey, was not signed until August 1920, and much of it never went into effect. The Allies' aims had been contradictory all along, and the postwar situation spawned indigenous movements in the former Ottoman Empire as complex and uncontrollable as those in Eastern Europe. The Russian and Habsburg empires no longer competed for influence there, and the Soviet government's release of earlier secret Allied plans for partitioning the Ottoman Empire reinforced suspicions that Britain and France were more committed to an old imperialism than to any new arrangements.

A nationalist revolt in Turkey had brought the reforming Mustafa Kemal (Atatúrk) to power, and he succeeded in ensuring Turkey's territorial integrity. Arabia's independence was also recognized, although internal conflict there created further opportunities for European influence. The pressing need to create political order on the eastern shores of the Mediterranean was met by a solution defined as temporary. France was to have a supervisory authority in Syria, and a vaguely defined area—carved from Palestine, Trans-Jordan, and Iraq—would be subject to British authority. Aside from recognizing the presence of Britain and France in the Middle East, the treaty settled little, and lasting boundaries would be determined only through the conflicts and diplomacy of the next few years.

British intentions in separating Palestine from Trans-Jordan were especially confusing. Anti-imperialist sentiment was strong in the Middle East, where it was often connected to Islam. During the war, the European powers had competed with each other in showing sympathy for the region's nationalist movements; and the Allies had encouraged Arab nationalism. In 1917 the British foreign secretary, Arthur Balfour, had also promised that a "national home" for Jews would be created in Palestine. In accord with the propaganda and humanitarian concern of that difficult year, the Balfour Declaration also guaranteed the rights of Muslims. In short, British intentions for Palestine remained uncertain, and their subsequent statements provided little clarification.

Colonial Mandates

The peace settlements also saw an important innovation, established in part to safeguard British and French imperial interests. Under the new arrangements, German and Ottoman colonial territories were declared "mandates" of the League of Nations and assigned to "classes." Under the auspices of the League, Britain, France, South Africa, Australia, and New Zealand all served as administrators for these **colonial mandates.** The parts of the Ottoman Empire newly placed under British or French rule were Class A mandates, states considered on the verge of self-government. Most of the reassigned African territories were Class B mandates. The League of Nations restricted European authority in these mandates in ways intended to protect the rights of the indigenous population. For example, Europeans were prohibited from subjecting mandate subjects to military training and were forced to grant them religious freedom. Class C mandates were primarily Pacific islands, to be ruled essentially as colonies.

In every case, the mandate power had to submit annual reports to the League of Nations for review. Like much else in the treaties, the system of mandates can be seen both as an expression of conscience toward the rest of the world and as a device for absorbing former German colonies while legitimating continued European dominance.

Europe's Diminished Position

Taken together, all these arrangements confirmed Europe's importance in world affairs and the dominance of Britain and France among the European powers. Yet these provisions also reflected changes in Europe's position. The French and British could take pride in the contributions of wealth and people they had received from their empires, but imperialism was weakened by the war. Its assumptions and ideals were challenged around the world; in fact, the mandate system itself was a response to widespread criticism of European rule. During the war, China and Siam (Thailand) eliminated many of the treaties that granted special rights to European states. In India, South Africa, Madagascar, and Egypt, powerful new nationalist groups began to demand self-government, and the African and African-American leaders meetings at the Pan-African Congress in February 1919 launched claims for better treatment from the colonial powers. Yet Europe was still reeling from the effects of war, and those within the imperial nations who might support colonial reforms were distracted by domestic and economic issues. When European nations did not respond to colonial concerns after the war, many nationalist movements began to abandon their moderate plans for the more militant objective of complete independence from the European powers.

Economically, while Europe had been enormously weakened, its suppliers (including countries with a single valuable crop, like Chile or Cuba) had prospered. The two that benefited most were Japan and the United States. Japan sold munitions and weapons to the belligerents, especially Russia, and quickly replaced German traders throughout East Asia. American production reached new heights in sector after sector (steel production doubled), and by war's end the United States had a huge new merchant fleet. The United States, increasingly willing to intervene in South America, economically, politically, and militarily, now dominated that continent, while its financiers directed the flow of world capital.

In the conflict everyone called "The Great War," the battles that mattered most had all taken place in Europe, but it had been a world war in the sense that its effects were felt around a globe that was getting smaller. The improved communications that carried supplies more rapidly across the seas (the Panama Canal opened in 1914) and on railroads from Japan to Russia and across Africa (the railroad from the Cape of Good Hope to Cairo was completed in 1918) also opened the possibility of communications and trade independent of Europe.

Disillusionment Not since 1848 had liberal conceptions so thoroughly dominated European politics. There was much to hope for in the call for self-determination and plebiscites, the League of Nations, the system of colonial mandates, and the establishment of representative regimes throughout Central Europe. By 1920, however, the limitations of what had been accomplished at Paris were all too apparent. Although the Allies had endorsed high principles in Paris, many of the agreements reached there actually reflected a cold assertion of national interest and a realistic appraisal of power.

Living in a time of revolutionary changes that they themselves had advocated, the leaders who forged the peace were not revolutionaries. They never managed to find a place for Russia at the conference. They took little account of the social and economic complexities of Eastern Europe. Believers in democracy, they were baffled by the turmoil it created. They stimulated nationalist movements but recognized the dangers of nationalism. Slogans that sounded radical in November 1918 gave way to frightened insistence on order a few months later. None of the leaders of democracy yet fully understood how much had changed.

Disillusionment came quickly. Having claimed moral leadership, America would in the end fail to assume the role. In March 1920 the United States Congress, again adopting an isolationist stance, refused to approve American membership in the League of Nations. This alienated the French, who had dropped demands to weaken Germany in return for the promise of American and British protection from future German

aggression. Meanwhile, China refused to sign the treaties because of terms that gave Japan, in addition to other gains, extensive rights in China. Japan was offended by the conference's rejection of a formal declaration that all races are equal.

The reparations were denounced in a brilliant and influential pamphlet in which the English economist John Maynard Keynes castigated the Carthaginian peace the victors had exacted.[4] He argued that the Allies owed one another more money than Germany could pay and that reparations would merely slow Europe's economic recovery. His analysis helped undermine confidence in the terms of peace, but his prescriptions—cancellation of international war debts and recognition that the international economic system was essentially artificial—were as utopian in their way as any of Woodrow Wilson's points. Keynes's criticisms, like those that for decades would ring from party platforms in every country, tended to exaggerate how much of the postwar world could be shaped by worried statesmen quarreling in Paris.

POSTWAR DEMOCRACY

From Finland to the Balkans, most of the states of Eastern Europe were new, and most of them had democratic constitutions. The disappearance of the Russian, Austrian, and Ottoman empires opened the way for systematic modernization using the administrative institutions and practices they left behind. There were some hopeful signs. Schools, for example, were built by the thousands and functioned fairly effectively despite issues of language and nationality. But stability was threatened by economic, social, and ethnic conflict.

The New Governments

Economic Underdevelopment and Ethnic Conflict The newly independent states of Central and Eastern Europe had to construct a reliable administrative system while dealing with the destruction and dislocation left by war. In addition, their economies were hampered by national tariffs intended to protect local producers but that made conditions worse by impeding the prewar flow of goods.

Extensive help from the new League of Nations proved essential as growing populations, widespread illiteracy, and lack of capital plagued economic develop-

---

[4] John Maynard Keynes, *The Economic Consequences of the Peace*, 1920; and the famous rebuttal, Etienne Mantoux, *The Carthaginian Peace: Or the Economic Consequences of Mr. Keynes*, 1946. The reference is to the harsh peace terms that Roman senators demanded upon the defeat of Carthage in the Third Punic War, 149–146 B.C.

Friedrich Ebert took the oath of office as provisional president of Germany in February 1919; note the absence of men in uniform.
Ullstein Bilderdienst

ment. Only Austria and Czechoslovakia had advanced industries that could compete in European markets. Elsewhere, land remained the central economic issue, as many countries remained primarily agricultural.

Independence brought the eviction of "foreign" landlords, the breakup of large estates in the Baltic countries, and land reform in Bulgaria, Romania, and Czechoslovakia. These measures, less effective than expected, fostered accusations in each region of special treatment for favored nationalities. In Poland and still more in Hungary, the great estate owners of the aristocracy succeeded in protecting their interests.

These resentments favored peasant parties, which combined agrarian radicalism with more modern populism; these parties soon dominated most of Eastern Europe. In this environment, economic and social conflicts were reinforced by ethnic and religious differences. German minorities in Poland, Czechoslovakia, Hungary, and Bulgaria were resented; the rural Slovaks were at odds with the Czechs of industrialized western Czechoslovakia; and anti-Semitism was especially virulent in Poland and Romania, where it was partly an expression of rural hostility toward village moneylenders and urban values. In Yugoslavia the claims of Greek Orthodox Serbians to be the "national" people angered the Roman Catholic Croatians and Slovenes. Macedonians— their homeland divided among Yugoslavia, Greece, and Bulgaria—agitated in all three countries and staged an insurrection in Bulgaria from 1923 to 1925.

Such circumstances encouraged military intervention in politics, as in the new Greek republic and in Hungary. But most of the governments of Eastern Europe worked more or less within their constitutions; Czechoslovakia, under President Tomáš Masaryk and Foreign Minister Edvard Beneš, became a model of the order, freedom, and prosperity that democracy was supposed to bring.

The Weimar Republic   The German provisional government was established just in time to sign the armistice. Its officials referred proudly to the German "revolution" and promulgated decrees promising democracy, freedom of speech, a return to the eight-hour workday, and improvements in social security. Frightened of a communist revolution, the government quickly reached an accommodation with the army, which was already encouraging the legend that it had not lost the war but had been stabbed in the back by politicians and radicals at home. General Wilhelm Groener, who replaced Ludendorff as Hindenburg's principal aide, promised to assist the government provided it would not meddle in the army's affairs.

President Ebert accepted those terms, and when the Spartacists, a group of left-wing Marxists, gained control of most of Berlin in January 1919, the army, supported by the paramilitary Freikorps, crushed the revolt and shot its leaders. Lenin's best hope for a communist revolution in Germany died with them. One of those murdered was Rosa Luxemburg, who had drafted the Spartacist platform calling for a proletarian revolution. An effective leader and impressive intellectual, she had urged the Spartacists to avoid useless violence and had recognized that most workers remained loyal to Ebert's Social Democratic government. But she would not abandon her party when hotter heads chose armed conflict. Her death was a lasting blow to the radical left, the government's reliance on the army a blow to Germany's new democracy.

Nevertheless, Germany's new leaders held elections in January 1919 for a constituent assembly. It met in Weimar, with nearly three-quarters of the delegates intent on installing a republic. They wrote a thoroughly democratic constitution that joined proportional representation to universal suffrage. The

By November 1923 German children could play with their nation's worthless paper money.
AKG London

president, directly elected for a seven-year term, would nominate the chancellor, or prime minister, who would have to be approved by the Reichstag. The Reichsrat, the upper house, would still represent the individual states but with reduced powers. In the new Germany, government would be responsible to parliament, minorities would be fairly represented, the aristocracy would hold no political privilege, and civil rights and private property would be guaranteed. With women voting, the Social Democrats in power, and a broad spectrum of parties, German politics was launched on a new course.

German Inflation   The gravest problem of these years was inflation. Early in 1923 French and Belgian forces occupied the Ruhr district of Germany, after it failed to make the coal deliveries required as reparations. The local population, encouraged by the German government, responded with passive resistance, a kind of general strike that made the occupation fruitless. The resulting dislocation and scarcity drastically

accelerated the already serious inflation. The German government, which from 1920 on found it easier to print more money than to raise taxes, continued that practice in 1923 as its expenses rose and its revenues declined.

The German mark, valued at 4 marks to 1 U.S. dollar in 1914 and 9 to 1 in 1919, was exchanged at 500 to 1 by 1922. Its subsequent fall was cataclysmic. One dollar was worth 18,000 marks in January 1923, 350,000 marks in July, and nearly 5,000,000 in August. New money was run off the presses at top speed, and old notes with additional zeros printed on them were rushed to the banks before they, too, became valueless. Prices changed within hours, always upward. By November a newspaper could sell for nearly 100 billion marks (see "German Inflation," p. 853).

By the end of the year a restructuring was begun. The government imposed stringent new financial measures, a moratorium on reparations, and subsequently a new schedule of payments. Some fortunes had been made during the inflation, especially by speculators and financiers; many large industries and property owners had fared quite well. Small businesses were more often hurt, as were nearly all wage earners. Savings held in cash had been wiped out. Although a slow recovery began, it did not last very long and the same pattern emerged once again in the late 1920s.

Domestic Conflict   At the height of the Ruhr crisis, a little-known man named Adolf Hitler led a nationalist *putsch*, or coup, in Munich. Notable for Ludendorff's participation, it was quickly defeated, and the plotters' punishment was ludicrously light. Ludendorff was acquitted, and Hitler was given a five-year sentence in comfortable prison quarters, where he composed *Mein Kampf (My Struggle)* during the thirteen months he actually served. Such attacks on the new government were becoming less frequent, however. Its moderate policies and general prosperity brought relief from the assassinations and revolts of the earlier years, and it was reasonable to believe in 1924 that Germany was on the road to stability.

But the divisions in German society were sharpening, and there was no significant group with primary loyalty to the existing regime. The leading statesman was Gustav Stresemann, who sat in every cabinet, usually as foreign minister, from 1923 to his death in 1929. A nationalist of the center-right, he acquiesced in the army's violations of the disarmament clauses, but the right denounced him for his conciliatory tone toward former enemies and for bringing Germany into the League of Nations. German workers felt little was being done for them. The middle class could not forgive the inflation. The political extremes were growing at the expense of the center. When President Ebert died in

GERMAN INFLATION

The German statistical office published this description of the effects of inflation in 1923. Obviously concerned that foreigners did not understand how bad the effects of inflation were, the account also expresses the rising insecurity of the middle class.

"The greater part of the population has been forced down far below their old standard of living, even with regard to the most important necessities of life.

"Consequently the foreigner, for example, who has visited Germany since the war, would do well to ask himself whether, in the overcrowded first-class railway carriages, he has found many Germans, or whether in the best seats at the theatre Germans are in the majority. He would do well to inquire whether in fashionable places of entertainment the German or the foreign public predominates, and if he does see Germans present spending their money for light entertainment, let him consider whether these are the majority of the German people. He must not forget either that many people today are influenced by the psychological fact that saving is no longer of any use: 100 marks today will perhaps be only 50 marks tomorrow. He who before the war, for example, had saved 5,500 marks could purchase for that amount furniture for a middle-class flat of three rooms as well as clothing, for a married couple with two children. In the middle of February 1923 (with an average dollar rate of 27,819 for February) the same person, for the same articles, would have had to spend 26.3 million marks in paper money. The man who did not spend the 5,500 marks, but preferred to save it together with the interest thereon might have over 7,000 marks today, with which, however, he cannot even buy a shirt! Who would care to 'save' under such conditions? Does the stranger realize, moreover, that such violent changes in the valuation of German money have meant for many thousands of German savers the annihilation of their savings? Does the stranger see the formerly well-to-do men and women of the middle class who today with a heavy heart carry their old family jewellery to the dealer, in order to prolong their physical existence a little longer? He who before the war could spend the interest on 1 million marks was a rich man, even up to 1919 he could still live upon it with reasonable comfort; today he is poor, for with his 50,000 marks interest he can today barely provide his own person with the necessities of life for a week! Does the stranger see the women and girls from the higher circles, even up to the highest, who are compelled to take up some occupation or who help to eke out the family income by working in their homes for a miserable wage? Does the stranger see the 1½ millions of war cripples, who are struggling desperately to earn their living, because the pensions that the State can afford to pay them are utterly inadequate?"

From Sidney Pollard and Colin Holmes (eds.), *Documents of European Economic History*, Vol. 3: *The End of Old Europe, 1914–1939*, St. Martin's Press, 1972.

1925, a rightist coalition elected General von Hindenburg as his successor, defeating the candidate supported by both the Center and the Social Democratic parties.

The Established Democracies

Except for Italy, where Fascism came to power in 1922, democracy at first fared rather well in the postwar years. Belgium recaptured its place among Europe's most prosperous and freest countries. The Netherlands faced nationalist unrest in its colony of the Dutch East Indies, but such problems hardly threatened democratic institutions at home. The Scandinavian countries, while often at odds among themselves, sustained effective democracies.

Social Changes   In every country the most militant Marxists felt strengthened by the presence of the Soviet Union as an international homeland for the proletariat. Nevertheless, the founding of Communist parties and allegiance to the Soviet Union split and weakened the left in domestic affairs. Economic recovery, though slower than expected, brought a general prosperity by the mid-1920s that contributed to the electoral victories of moderate and conservative parties. Constitutional democracy was the European norm, and many were convinced that even the Soviet Union and Italy would in time return to that standard.

Generally, the central government now spent a higher proportion of national wealth; although most of that went to the military, the national debt, and to pensions, some of it was used to lay the basis for broader measures of social security for all. Politically, both business interests and labor unions exercised a more direct influence, supporting efforts to achieve economic stability. Yet despite periods of prosperity and a genuine boom in certain industries, the 1920s did not provide the steady growth of the prewar decade. Economic uncertainty, increased by inflation and unemployment, tended, like the disillusionment over reparations or the specter of Bolshevism, to favor caution.

Changes in Women's Lives Women's suffrage, once hotly debated, had been adopted in the Scandinavian countries (Finland, 1906; Norway, 1907; Denmark, 1917; Sweden, 1919) and in Great Britain (1918) and was part of the new constitutions of Austria and Germany. The effects on public life were less dramatic than either advocates or opponents had predicted, but there was significance in the growing sense that for women to vote was a natural extension of democracy.

The most fundamental social changes of the period were usually not the result of deliberate policy. Employment in services such as sales and office work increased more rapidly than in industry, and the number of domestic servants continued to decline. These changes affected unmarried women especially. In most countries more women were gainfully employed than before the war despite a sharp decline from the wartime peak and despite the strong tendency for women to leave work upon marriage. Everywhere, women received more years of schooling than before, and the number of middle-class male youths enrolled in universities increased sharply. A rising standard of living and the automobile began to alter middle-class life.

Limited Recovery in France Life in France quickly returned to prewar patterns. The nation had become par excellence the land of the middle class, the artisan, and the peasant proprietor fiercely attached to a tiny plot of land. Though the expected cornucopia of reparations never materialized, ordinary people accomplished miracles of reconstruction, carefully making their new buildings look as much as possible like those destroyed. The Chamber of Deputies elected in 1919 at the height of patriotic pride in victory was the most conservative since the founding of the Third Republic; and politics, too, focused on restoration.

The depreciation of the franc, for a century one of the world's most stable currencies, was the principal concern of President Raymond Poincaré's conservative program. Inadequate taxation during the war lay at the root of the problem, and budgetary contraction was the preferred solution. The rigid focus on a stable franc and military security reflected the psychological as well as the economic and demographic costs of war.

In the subsequent prosperity, competent leaders presided over governments content with policies that permitted domestic stagnation and encouraged inflexibility in foreign affairs. Poincaré's concern for national honor and a stable currency appealed to a cautious middle class but avoided more difficult long-term issues of working conditions, social inequality, cultural change, or international peace.

The Altered Circumstances of the United Kingdom
In the United Kingdom, also, the elections of 1919—the first in which women were allowed to vote—produced an overwhelming victory for leaders who promised to extract enough from Germany to make winning the war worthwhile. Lloyd George remained prime minister, but his government was essentially conservative. The breakup of the wartime coalition exposed the Liberal party's decline, and in 1924 new elections brought the Labour party briefly to power. Except for recognizing the Soviet Union, Labour did little to recall its leftist origins. For most of that decade, Britain was led with dull caution by the Conservatives and Stanley Baldwin, who inherited problems of unemployment, Irish nationalism, and a changing empire.

A crisis in the coal industry led to a ten-day general strike in 1926 that became a lightning rod for social division. Frightened by the bitter class conflict, many of the well-to-do volunteered in maintaining essential services, thus helping to break the strike. That response and the antilabor legislation that followed did much to deepen the resentments of British workers and heighten the angry rhetoric of public life.

Irish Independence The Irish question was equally explosive. The promise of home rule had been suspended during the war, and the Easter Rebellion of 1916 had been firmly suppressed. In 1919, however, the most militant Irish nationalists, led by the Sinn Fein

Demonstrations and parades were banned in Dublin and Belfast, where an armored car stands ready to put down any trouble; violence had become an expected part of political struggle in Ireland.
Bettmann/Corbis

(meaning "We Ourselves") party, refused to take their seats in the House of Commons and met instead at Dublin in a parliament of their own, the Dail Eireann. There, they declared Ireland an independent nation.

To this defiance the London government responded slowly and ineptly, finally choosing to suppress the Sinn Fein party and with it Irish independence. The government then sent armed reinforcements in numbers sufficient to spread the fighting without ending it, troops that soon became the most hated symbol of British repression. Violent civilian resisters called themselves the Irish Republican Army. By the 1920s the two sides were fighting a bloody war.

With pressure mounting at home and abroad for some settlement, the British government in 1920 passed the Ireland Act, creating two Irish parliaments, one in the predominantly Catholic areas of the south and west, and the other in the predominantly Protestant counties of the northeast. Sinn Fein warred against this division of the island during almost two more years of fighting. Nevertheless, in December 1922 the Irish parliament sitting in Dublin in the Catholic south proclaimed, with British acquiescence, the existence of the Irish Free State, which included all Ireland except the six northern counties of Ulster. As Northern Ireland, these counties maintained the traditional union with Great Britain in an uneasy peace.

The British Commonwealth   Only in imperial affairs did flexible compromise still seem to work. Canadian complaints led the Imperial Conference of 1926 to a significant new definition of all dominions as "autonomous communities . . . equal in status . . . united by a common allegiance to the crown and freely associated as members of the British Commonwealth of Nations." Autonomous in all domestic and foreign affairs, dominions accepted ties to the British crown as the expression of their common traditions and loyalties. Given legal sanction by the Statute of Westminster in 1931, this conception of empire proved a skillful adaptation to new conditions crowned by the stability, prosperity, and loyalty of dominions such as Canada, New Zealand, and Australia.

International Relations

From 1924 to 1930 the conduct of international relations reflected some of the idealism of the Paris Peace Conference. The League of Nations, formally established in 1920, successfully resolved a number of disputes, despite the absence of the United States, Britain's greater concern for its empire, and France's tendency to use the League for its own security. The League's special commissions helped restructure the disjointed economies of new states, aided refugees, and set international standards for public health and working conditions. To further the rule of law, the League also established the Permanent Court of International Justice in The Hague, and in the late 1920s its decisions were treated with great respect.

Debt Payments   Crises over debt payments were dealt with directly by the major powers. As Germany fell behind in its payments, the Allies took the position that they, in turn, could not pay their war debts to the United States. Some compromise was essential, and in 1924 the nations involved accepted the proposals of an international commission of financial experts, headed by the American banker Charles G. Dawes. The Dawes Plan fixed Germany's reparations payments on a regular scale, established an orderly mode of collection, and provided loans to Germany equal to 80 percent of the reparations payment Germany owed in the first year of the plan.

The Dawes Plan did not admit any connection between Allied debts to the United States and German reparations to the European victors, but it did end the worst of the chaos. For the next six years, Germany, fed by loans largely from the United States, made its reparations payments on schedule. The issue seemed forever resolved with the adoption of the Young Plan in 1929, which finally set a limit to Germany's obligations, reduced annual payments, and ended foreign occupation of the Rhineland. Under the leadership of American bankers, the interests of international capital had come to shape policy.

The Locarno Era   International efforts to outlaw war led to a series of treaties in 1925 known as the Locarno Pact. In the major agreement—entered into by Germany, Belgium, France, Great Britain, and Italy—all parties accepted Germany's western frontier as defined by the Versailles Treaty and promised to arbitrate their disagreements. In addition, France pursued a more traditional diplomacy, signing a mutual-defense alliance with Poland and Czechoslovakia. A continental war caused by German aggression now seemed impossible.

The optimism of the Locarno era was capped by the Kellogg-Briand pact of 1928. The French had suggested that the American entry into World War I be commemorated by a friendship pact, and the Americans proposed to include others as well. More than a score of nations signed the pact, which, though unenforceable, renounced war "as an instrument of national policy."

Disarmament   From 1921 on, some League commission was always studying the problem of disarmament. Given the enormous cost of capital ships, naval disarmament seemed especially promising. At the Washington Conference of 1921–1922, the United States, Great

Britain, Japan, France, and Italy agreed after some difficulty to fix their relative strength in capital ships at current levels,[5] not to expand their naval bases, and even to scrap some of their larger vessels. Never again did discussions of naval disarmament prove so fruitful. At Geneva in 1927 and London in 1930, Italy and France refused to accept a treaty. By 1935 Japan would reject even the Washington accord.

Attempts to limit land and air arms were even less successful. League commissions could not agree on the definition of offensive weapons, whether a professional army was comparable to a reserve force, and on whether limitations should be expressed in terms of budgets, weapons, or personnel. German and Russian proposals that their own military weakness be made the standard for other nations only aroused suspicion. After much preparation, these League commissions called a conference on general disarmament in 1932. Before agreements could be reached, however, Hitler had come to power in Germany, and a new arms race ensued.

The Beginning of a New Era To contemporaries, and for historians since, World War I was the beginning of a new era. The war itself was understood to have resulted from a dangerous system of alliances, secret diplomacy, and the arms race. Creation of the League of Nations, agreements like the Locarno treaties, and conferences on disarmament were unusual examples of an extensive effort to learn from history and to correct the errors of the past. Postwar international relations differed in other respects, too; the nations of Europe were now deeply in debt, and their hold on empire was weakened.

Multiple new states with contested boundaries, in which nationalism was often the strongest communal bond, wrestled with the unfamiliar complications of democracy. In those countries and in the established democracies, the relationship between politics and the general public had changed. Old elites were less trusted, the techniques of mass mobilization now more familiar and available to every party, and groups once treated as peripheral (such as workers, farmers, women, and veterans) were more assertive. Disillusionment with politics was deep after years of propaganda; yet more was expected of government. Revolutionary new political movements on both the right and the left threatened to change the rules of politics altogether.

Economic conditions were different, too. The war and the terms of peace left enormous problems of physical destruction, burdens of debt, and broken trade patterns. The flood of former soldiers seeking jobs while war industries shrank was followed by long-term changes involving new technologies and the reorganization of production to incorporate American techniques of mass production for mass markets.

In these circumstances the radical ideas and shocking cultural movements of the 1890s had new relevance. Nearly all Europeans had personal experience of lives disrupted—families broken up, women adding new roles to demanding old ones, jobs gained and suddenly lost, savings wiped out, property destroyed, invading armies, civil war, or sickness and death. All these changes at once, from the international to the personal, marked the advent of a new era.

[5] The current level was defined as parity between the United States and Great Britain at 525,000 tons apiece in capital ships, 315,000 tons for Japan, and 175,000 tons each for France and Italy.

Summary

In 1914 the nations of Europe stumbled into the most destructive war in their history. Machine guns and poison gas created unforeseen carnage on the battlefield. The subsequent drain on each nation's resources disrupted civilian life, eliminated the German, Austro-Hungarian, and Russian empires, and left the victors only marginally better off than the losers. Countries were forced to change their political systems or face dangerous political unrest and to rely on new segments of the population, especially women and colonial peoples, for economic and military support. After the war, the Allies promulgated democratic values and created, through the League of Nations and diplomatic agreements, a short-lived era of international cooperation. While these values never overcame national rivalries, the war gave rise to more democratic social structures and greater gender equality. The response of this reconstructed Europe to the new challenges arising in the postwar world would determine the chances for domestic and international peace.

QUESTIONS FOR FURTHER THOUGHT

1. What factors led to the outbreak of World War I?
2. The First World War is often referred to as the "first modern war." What made this war particularly modern, and did new technology alone win the war for the Allies?

3. How did the war disrupt and permanently change life on the home front? What tensions arose from such changes?

RECOMMENDED READING

Sources

*Brittain, Vera. *Testament of Youth: An Autobiographical Study of the Years 1900–1925.* 1933. Memoir written by a young upper-middle-class British woman containing reflections on her wartime work as a nurse and her return to a changed Europe.

*Junger, Ernst. *Storm of Steel.* 1920. Details the author's wartime experiences as a company commander in the German army; glorifies the behavior of soldiers and the significance of war in modern life.

*Nicholson, Harold. *Peacemaking, 1919.* 1965. The retrospective analysis of an experienced diplomat who was a disillusioned participant at the Versailles Conference.

*Remarque, Erich Maria. *All Quiet on the Western Front.* First published in Germany in 1928, this novel with its realistic (and antinationalist) depiction of the war became the subject of great controversy there. Its moving rejection of modern warfare made it a best-seller throughout Europe and in the United States.

*Sassoon, Siegfried. *Memoirs of a Fox-Hunting Man; Memoirs of an Infantry Officer; Sherston's Progress.* Series of pseudo-autobiographical works written by the British poet, novelist, and former trench soldier, which were collected and published in the 1930s.

Studies

*Becker, Jean-Jacques. *The Great War and the French People.* 1985. Shows the multiple ways in which the war was a turning point in French life.

Culleton, Claire A. *Working-Class Culture, Women, and Britain, 1914–1921.* 1999. Uses oral history collections to demonstrate that, despite their wartime contributions, the position of women workers within British society remained largely the same after the war.

*Feldman, Gerald D. *Army, Industry, and Labor in Germany, 1914–1918.* 1966. A fundamental analysis of the war's effects on institutions and power in Germany.

*Ferguson, Niall. *The Pity of War: Explaining World War One.* 1999. A controversial work. The author refutes conventional explanations for the origins, events, and aftermath of the First World War and argues that

Britain's involvement created a world war out of a localized conflict.

*Fischer, Fritz. *Germany's Aims in the First World War.* 1967. The reassessment that became a center of controversy among German historians.

*Fussell, Paul. *The Great War and Modern Memory.* 1975. An important study of the cultural impact of the war, as seen by soldier poets and writers.

*Grayzel, Susan. *Women's Identities at War: Gender, Motherhood, and Politics in Britain and France during the First World War.* 1999. Shows how the war challenged conventional views of women and describes the backlash against those challenges in the postwar period.

*Hermann, David G. *The Arming of Europe and the Making of the First World War.* 1997. Uses new archival evidence to show the importance of military considerations in the diplomacy that led to world war.

*Horne, John N., and Alan Kramer. *German Atrocities, 1914: A History of Denial.* 2001. The authors recount the atrocities committed by German troops as they advanced through Belgium and France and explore how the stories of these atrocities became national, if often fabricated, legends in Belgium.

*Joll, James. *The Origins of the First World War.* 1987. A synthesis of the vast literature on this controversial topic that takes a balanced perspective on the question.

*Keegan, John. *The First World War.* 1998. Standard and comprehensive account of the war's military developments, concentrating on the Western front.

*Kennedy, Paul (ed.). *The War Plans of the Great Powers, 1880–1914.* 1979. Places the arms race in the context of imperialist and political rivalries in the prewar era.

Kocka, Jürgen. *Facing Total War: German Society, 1914–1918.* Barbara Weinberger (tr.). 1984. A leading social historian's assessment of the impact of the war on the German home front.

*Marwick, Arthur. *War and Social Change in the Twentieth Century: A Comparative Study of Britain, France, Germany, Russia, and the United States.* 1975. Develops the case for the revolutionary effects of World War I and World War II on the domestic economies of modern Western society.

*Miller, S. (ed.). *Military Strategy and the Origins of the First World War.* 1985. Collection of essays assessing the role of the military in the decisions that led to war.

*Smith, Leonard V., Stéphane Audoin-Rouzeau, and Annette Becker. *France and the Great War, 1914–1918.* Synthesizes decades of scholarship examining France's wartime experiences on the battlefront and the home front, as well as postwar issues facing the French national community.

*Stone, Norman. *Eastern Front, 1914–1917.* 1975. The leading account of the war's other military theater, concluding with the Russian Revolution and the Treaty of Brest Litovsk.

*Verhey, Jeffrey. *The Spirit of 1914: Militarism, Myth, and Mobilization in Germany.* 2000. Uses an array of contemporary sources to refute "The Myth of 1914," which proclaimed that the German public responded to the outbreak of war with unqualified enthusiasm.

*Williamson, Samuel R. *Austria-Hungary and the Origins of the First World War.* 1991. Examines how Austria-Hungary's involvement in the war was motivated by its leaders' fears of domestic disorder and willingness to risk a general war to settle a local conflict.

*Winter, J. M., and R. M. Wall, eds. *The Upheaval of War: Family, Work, and Welfare in Europe, 1914–1918.* 1988. An insightful assessment of the effects of the war on domestic society.

*Winter, Jay. *Sites of Memory, Sites of Mourning.* 1996. A powerful study of the impact of the war on European culture.

*Available in paperbacks.

This idealized image of Lenin addressing the people conveys the power of Lenin's oratory skills and the sense that his leadership began a new era. The portrait of impassioned workers, soldiers and sailors, men and women—all inspired by their leader—and the careful placement of Stalin just behind Lenin reveal the painting as the subsequent official view of the Soviet government. One of the marks of the new era in Europe was, in fact, the effective propaganda of single-party states.

Sovfoto

Chapter Twenty-Eight

THE GREAT TWENTIETH-CENTURY CRISIS

TWO SUCCESSFUL REVOLUTIONS • THE DISTINCTIVE CULTURE OF THE TWENTIETH CENTURY • THE GREAT DEPRESSION AND THE RETREAT FROM DEMOCRACY • NAZI GERMANY AND THE USSR • THE DEMOCRACIES' WEAK RESPONSE

The 1920s and 1930s opened an era of intense hope and great fear. As the prosperity and consumerism of the 1920s gave way to economic depression, Europe's liberal governments had difficulty responding. Domestic divisions grew sharper, reinforced by the example of radical alternatives; for, although most of the revolutions in the aftermath of World War I had failed, new political systems emerged in Communist Russia and Fascist Italy. Relatively isolated at first, these new regimes became influential models. The possibility of communist revolution and the potential of fascist nationalism reshaped political life throughout Europe.

Cultural life was unsettling, too. A flourishing popular culture, flippant and commercial, undermined nineteenth-century standards of propriety (and the confidence that went with them). Europe's most interesting artists and intellectuals disdained the prosperity of the 1920s, and provocative theories, in both the physical and social sciences, invited skepticism about absolute truths and traditional values. Politics and culture both struggled with questions about the nature of modern mass society.

There were also immediate reasons for discontent among workers who had expected the postwar world to bring greater improvements in their way of life, among peasants who found it hard to make a living from small but often inefficient holdings, among ethnic groups resentful of sudden minority status as a result of the boundary changes in Eastern Europe, among nationalists angry that their new states had not gained more territory, and among all those who disliked the altered lifestyle of the postwar era. Then economic depression drove home the failures of capitalism, the limitations of liberalism, and the weaknesses of democracy.

Two nations seemed to rise above the economic crisis: Communist Russia under Stalin and Nazi Germany under Hitler. Their apparent escape from the Great Depression, their capacity to mobilize popular support, and their brutal use of force contrasted with the hesitant compromises of more democratic governments. In the 1930s that contrast sharpened as they began asserting their authority in international relations.

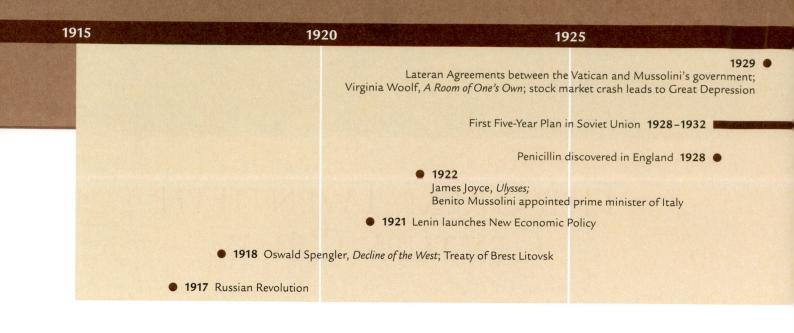

1929 ●
Lateran Agreements between the Vatican and Mussolini's government;
Virginia Woolf, *A Room of One's Own*; stock market crash leads to Great Depression

First Five-Year Plan in Soviet Union **1928–1932**

Penicillin discovered in England **1928** ●

● **1922**
James Joyce, *Ulysses*;
Benito Mussolini appointed prime minister of Italy

● **1921** Lenin launches New Economic Policy

● **1918** Oswald Spengler, *Decline of the West*; Treaty of Brest Litovsk

● **1917** Russian Revolution

TWO SUCCESSFUL REVOLUTIONS

In Russia and in Italy the aftermath of war was revolution. Both nations had begun rapid industrialization in the 1890s, and both were sorely tested in the world war that followed. Revolution in Russia began while the war was still going on, and it continued for several years before the outcome was certain. Revolution in Italy occurred quickly a few years after the war. Each resulted in a new kind of political regime, and only gradually did it become clear that Russian communism and Italian fascism might change the face of Europe.

Revolution in Russia

When world war broke out in 1914, Russia's parliament (the Duma) and local councils (or *zemstvos*) helped coordinate the war effort. But when the Cadet party maintained its insistence on further liberal reforms, the tsar suspended the Duma. Resentful that political aims should be pursued in wartime—they still did not see that a more representative government could strengthen the war effort—the tsar and his officials grew increasingly isolated from the country. More comfortable as a military strategist than as a head of state, Tsar Nicholas II grandly departed to command his army, leaving Tsarina Alexandra and those closest to her to oppose any program for reform. Her chief confidant was Grigori Rasputin, an ignorant and corrupt mystic whose influence symbolized the decadence of this regime.

The February Revolution Throughout 1916 signs of Russia's failures accumulated. Production and transportation were undependable, war refugees filled the roads, inflation soared, and food shortages became critical. All this came on top of years of rising anger among peasants eager for land and workers determined to change their lot. Without realizing the depth of this social strife, officials were well aware of how serious the situation was. Even in the highest circles, there was talk of deposing the tsar. In November in the reconvened Duma, Pavel Milyukov, a noted historian and the leader of the liberal Cadets, courageously delivered a biting attack on the government. In December a group of nobles murdered Rasputin. Strikes spread, and in March 1917, when strikers filled the streets of Petrograd,[1] their economic demands quickly broadened to include political issues. The army could not be relied on to oppose them. Once again, much as in 1905, a soviet of workers (now called the Soviet of Workers' and Soldiers' Deputies) became the voice of revolution, and they joined with a Duma committee in seeking a provisional government. They prepared to resist any tsarist force that might be sent against them. None came. The military situation was desperate, the government in disarray, and the tsar unpopular. With nowhere to turn, Nicholas II abdicated, and the February Revolution[2] was hailed with joy and relief throughout the country.

The provisional government's central figure was Milyukov; its only socialist was Aleksandr Kerensky, a member of the Social Revolutionary party and vice-

[1] St. Petersburg was a Germanic name, and in 1914 Nicholas had changed it to the Russian *Petrograd*. The capital until 1918, the city would become Leningrad in 1924 and St. Petersburg again in 1991.

[2] These events occurred on March 8–12 according to the Gregorian calendar used throughout the West. Russia, however, had never abandoned the older Julian calendar (which continues to be the calendar of the Orthodox Church). The revolutions of March 8–12 and November 7, 1917, according to the Gregorian system, were dated thirteen days earlier according to the Julian, and they continue to be called the February and October revolutions.

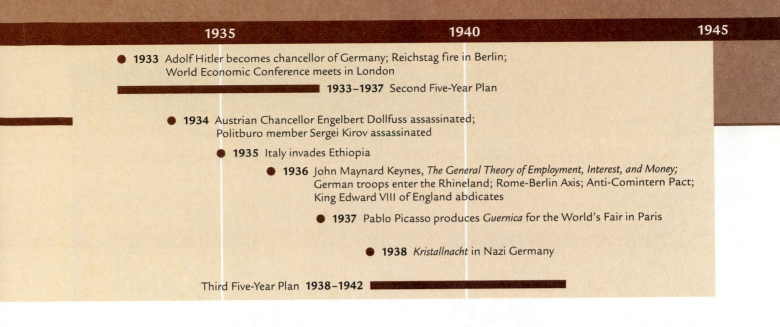

- **1933** Adolf Hitler becomes chancellor of Germany; Reichstag fire in Berlin; World Economic Conference meets in London

1933–1937 Second Five-Year Plan

- **1934** Austrian Chancellor Engelbert Dollfuss assassinated; Politburo member Sergei Kirov assassinated
- **1935** Italy invades Ethiopia
- **1936** John Maynard Keynes, *The General Theory of Employment, Interest, and Money;* German troops enter the Rhineland; Rome-Berlin Axis; Anti-Comintern Pact; King Edward VIII of England abdicates
- **1937** Pablo Picasso produces *Guernica* for the World's Fair in Paris
- **1938** *Kristallnacht* in Nazi Germany

Third Five-Year Plan **1938–1942**

chairman of the Petrograd soviet. The new government quickly established broad civil liberties, an amnesty for political prisoners, and the end of religious persecution. It also proposed granting a constitution to Finland, which Russia ruled, and independence to Russian Poland. Declaring its support for an eight-hour work-day and for the abolition of class privileges, it left most other social issues to a constituent assembly, which it promised to call soon.

In fact, the parties of revolution sharply disagreed on these issues. The Cadets, who dominated the provisional government, came to accept the idea of a republic, political democracy, and distribution of land with compensation to former owners. To their left, the Social Revolutionary party and the Menshevik wing of the Social Democratic party, which was especially strong in the soviets forming across the nation, demanded more drastic reforms. These parties were divided, too, however. Some of their members were willing to postpone these further reforms until after the war, which, like the Cadets, they still meant to win. The more radical of them stressed an early end to the war, without yet advocating an immediate armistice. For the time being, the soviets, watching from the outside and ever ready to criticize, allowed the provisional government its chance. To the left of all these factions stood a small group known as the Bolsheviks.

The Bolsheviks   In 1898 Russian Marxists had secretly formed the Social Democratic party, which functioned mainly in the conspiratorial world of exile. At the party's second congress, held in Brussels and London in 1903, it had split into two groups, called the **Bolsheviks** (majority) and Mensheviks (minority); in fact, the Bolsheviks rarely had a majority, but these nicknames stuck. Their differences were theoretical, organizational, and personal. The theoretical issues, which

engaged Marxists everywhere, were fought with the special intensity of revolutionaries far from home and power. On the whole, the Mensheviks placed greater emphasis on popular support and parliamentary institutions, which implied cooperation with other parties. The Bolsheviks stressed instead the need for a disciplined revolutionary party to instruct and lead the masses, which might otherwise be likely to settle for immediate gains rather than the European revolution that would bring about socialism. Led by Georgi Plekhanov and V. I. Lenin, the Bolsheviks denounced as enemies all who did not join them. Only later would these party battles waged in foreign cities prove significant for Russian history.

The ideas of socialism that spread in Russia after 1905 were not so much those of the Bolsheviks as those of the Mensheviks and the Social Revolutionaries, who were less consistently Marxist and were closer to the peasants. Although Plekhanov tried on his own to heal the breach in the Social Democratic party, Lenin's conception of iron discipline allowed little room for compromise; and he soon consigned Plekhanov to the Mensheviks.

Lenin's Tactics   Removed from events in Russia, Lenin continued from Switzerland to organize selected followers, denounce the heresies of others, and develop his theoretical view of the special role a militant party should play in a country that, like Russia, was just achieving modern capitalism. The party could achieve its aims, he argued, only by recognizing the revolutionary potential in the peasants' hunger for land (most Marxists considered the peasantry a socially backward class and believed land ownership was opposed to socialism). Thus, the Bolsheviks, although they lacked a large following in Russia, had a theory of how to make a revolution.

The armed civilians in the foreground are Red Guards, demonstrating their might and protecting the Bolshevik leaders addressing a large crowd of workers.
Sovfoto

Lenin considered World War I a civil war among capitalists, and in a sense that theoretical stand gave Lenin his chance, for it suggested to the Germans that his presence in Russia as an agitator might be useful in undermining the Russian war effort. In April 1917 the Germans arranged to send Lenin by sealed train through Germany and Scandinavia to Russia. Lenin, however, had something grander than mere agitation in mind.

Marxists were ambivalent in their attitude toward the February Revolution, which they welcomed as progressive but tended to disdain as a bourgeois revolution and not a victory of the proletariat. Lenin offered another interpretation: Revolution in Russia was part of a larger revolution about to sweep all of Europe. Socialists had no interest in the capitalist war, which Russia's provisional government continued to support, but Bolsheviks could seize the chance to push the revolution beyond its bourgeois phase to a "second stage" in which the soviets would be the true representatives of the proletariat. That in turn dictated the tactics the Bolsheviks should follow: They must gain the leadership of the soviets, and then Russia could join in the international revolution that was imminent. Historians have emphasized Lenin's tactical flexibility, but in

April his views seemed impossibly dogmatic even to radicals. It was the force of his personality, his political skill, and his oratory that kept him leader of the Bolsheviks.

Summer Crisis While the soviets were building a national organization that claimed authority over railroads, telegraph lines, and troops, the provisional government was falling apart. Its members disagreed over war policy and land reform; its police and officials were abandoning their posts. Workers continued to strike, and nationalist movements erupted in Latvia, Georgia, and the Ukraine. Milyukov resigned, four more socialists joined the cabinet, and Kerensky, an energetic leader and effective orator, became the cabinet's leading figure.

The Kerensky government was quickly attacked from left and right. The Bolsheviks criticized Kerensky at the first all-Russian Congress of Soviets in June but gained support from just over 100 of the 800 plus delegates. In July they attempted a coup in Petrograd. That was decisively defeated, and many of the coup leaders were arrested. Lenin fled to Finland. Meanwhile, cities were torn by strikes and demonstrations as the situation at the front grew more perilous. In the countryside, rioting peasants demanding land burned manor houses and murdered landlords.

Convinced that a strong military hand was what the nation needed, the army's commander in chief, General Lavr Kornilov, led an attack on Petrograd in September. Kerensky asked the soviets (and thus the Bolsheviks as well) to defend the government. Most of Kornilov's men had refused to follow his orders, and the threat passed quickly. But in the meantime Bolshevik leaders had been released from prison, and Bolshevist propaganda was gaining ground with simple slogans promising peace, land, and bread—issues at the heart of daily life and ones for which the provisional government had no clear solutions.

The Bolsheviks won control of the soviets in Moscow and Petrograd, electing Leon Trotsky chairman of the latter. Trotsky, who had worked with Lenin in exile, had until recently stood somewhat aloof from party conflicts. Now firmly in Lenin's camp, he proceeded to organize the armed forces in Petrograd. With the Social Revolutionaries supporting peasant expropriation of land, the provisional government was left politically alone in a city it could not control, trying to rule a nation in chaos and still at war.

The October Revolution   To the dismay of many in his party, Lenin, who had reentered Russia, boldly decided to seize power. When the second all-Russian Congress of Soviets met on November 7, he confronted it with a new government. Kerensky began countermeasures a few days before that date, but it was too late. On November 6, Red Guards (squads of armed workers), sailors, and soldiers captured the Winter Palace and strategic points throughout the city. A simultaneous movement in Moscow won control of the city in a week. Lenin announced to the Congress that the Bolsheviks held power and sent out a young officer to take command of the armies. At each stop along his route, the troops enthusiastically cheered his announcement of the Bolshevik coup. Their commanders could only acquiesce. Kerensky, who had escaped from the capital, tried to muster support, but the one group of Cossacks who moved on Petrograd was soundly defeated. The world's first communist government had taken office (see "Two Accounts of Revolution in Russia," p. 866).

"All power to the soviets!" had been one of the Bolsheviks' most effective slogans, and the Congress readily approved the one-party cabinet Lenin presented it. The rudiments of a new form of government emerged: The Congress of Soviets replaced parliament and elected a Central Executive committee to advise the Council of People's Commissars, or cabinet. From the very first, Bolshevik rule did not depend on any elected body. Elections for the promised constituent assembly, held at the end of November, would be the last open competition among parties for more than seventy years. The Bolsheviks won a quarter of the seats, other socialist parties more than 60 percent, conservatives and liberals the rest. As the assembly met on its second day, the military guards told it to adjourn.

Lenin provided a basis for such ruthlessness in his pamphlet "The State and Revolution," written in Finland in the summer of 1917. It used the Marxist conception that the state is the coercive organ of the ruling class to argue that, once the Bolsheviks held power, the proletariat would be that ruling class. The dictatorship of the proletariat, Lenin reasoned, was the only way to lead backward Russia through the transition to that higher historical stage that Marxists envisioned in which a state would no longer be necessary. The nationalization of land and factories would achieve socialism. Communism would follow once everyone learned to work for the good of society and once production met the needs of all. Until then, the single party, the "vanguard of the proletariat," would be model and guide.

Toward a Communist Society

Millions of workers, soldiers, and peasants had joined in pulling down the old system, and the Bolshevik leaders were determined to snatch their historical moment. The day after taking the Winter Palace, the new government decreed that land, livestock, and farm equipment belonged to the state but could be "temporarily" held by peasant committees, thereby legitimizing the rural revolution that was taking place anyway.

Initial Policies   No peasant was to work for hire, and committees of the poor would supervise the allocation of land and produce. Workers' committees would share in factory management, and everyone would be paid according to the work done (the state's new leaders assigned themselves laborers' salaries). All social titles and military ranks were abolished. "People's tribunals" and workers' militias replaced tsarist courts and police. Church and state were separated; the equality of the sexes was decreed and followed by regulations allowing divorce by mutual consent, measures that enhanced the reputation of Russian communism among progressives in Western Europe. Even the alphabet was reformed and the Gregorian calendar adopted.

In the next few months, railroads, banks, and shipping concerns were nationalized, foreign trade became a state monopoly, and Russia's debts were repudiated. The various nationalities of Russia were declared equal and granted the right of secession; Finland took advantage of that decree to separate from Russia in December 1917, while the Bolsheviks struggled to prevent the

TWO ACCOUNTS OF REVOLUTION IN RUSSIA

The culmination of the Russian Revolution came on November 7, 1917, when the Communists captured the Winter Palace, which was then the seat of the Kerensky government. Eyewitnesses saw the event very differently. The first account is by Pitirim Sorokin, a young member of the Social Revolutionary party, who would soon go into exile and have a distinguished career as a professor of sociology at Harvard. In his memoir, Leaves from a Russian Diary, *he recalled that day. The second description is from* Ten Days That Shook the World, *the famous book by John Reed, an American journalist who admired the Bolsheviks.*

"Lying ill all day on my bed, I listened to the steady booming of the cannon and the spatter of machine-guns and crack of rifles. Over the telephone I learned that the Bolsheviki had brought up from Kronstadt the warship *Aurora* and had opened fire on the Winter Palace, demanding the surrender of members of the Provisional Government, still barricaded there. At seven in the evening I went to the Municipal Duma. With many matters before us, the immediate horror that faced us was this situation at the Winter Palace. There was a regiment of women and the military cadets were bravely resisting an overwhelming force of Bolshevist troops, and over the telephone Minister Konovalov was appealing for aid. Poor women, poor lads, their situation was desperate, for we knew that the wild sailors, after taking the Palace, would probably tear them to pieces. What could we do? After breathless council it was decided that all of us, the Soviets, Municipalities, Committees of Socialist Parties, members of the Council of the Republic, should go in procession to the Winter Palace and do our utmost to rescue the Ministers, the women soldiers, and the cadets. Even as we prepared to go, over the telephone came the despairing shout: 'The gates of the Palace have been forced. The massacre has begun. . . . Hurry! The mob has reached the first floor. All is over. Goodbye. . . . They break in. They are. . . .' The last word . . . from the Winter Palace was a broken cry."

From Pitirim Alexandrovitch Sorokin, *Leaves from a Russian Diary*, exp. ed., 1920; Beacon Press, 1950.

"Carried along by the eager wave of men we were swept into the right-hand entrance, opening into a great bare vaulted room, the cellar of the east wing, from which issued a maze of corridors and staircases. A number of huge packing cases stood about, and upon these the Red Guards and soldiers fell furiously, battering them open with the butts of their rifles, and pulling out carpets, curtains, linen, porcelain plates, glassware. . . . One man went strutting around with a bronze clock perched on his shoulder; another found a plume of ostrich feathers, which he stuck in his hat. The looting was just beginning when somebody cried, 'Comrades! Don't touch anything! Don't take anything! This is the property of the People!' Immediately twenty voices were crying, 'Stop! Put everything back! Don't take anything! Property of the People!' Many hands dragged the spoilers down. Damask and tapestry were snatched from the arms of those who had them; two men took away the bronze clock. Roughly and hastily the things were crammed back in their cases, and self-appointed sentinels stood guard. It was all utterly spontaneous. Through corridors and up staircases the cry could be heard growing fainter and fainter in the distance, 'Revolutionary discipline! Property of the People'"

From John Reed, *Ten Days That Shook the World*, 1919.

Ukraine and the ethnic groups of the Baltic regions from following suit.

Revolutionary measures also made way for a reign of terror. A new secret police, the Cheka, differed from tsarist police in determination more than method. The citizens who sat on the new committees and tribunals often combined revolutionary enthusiasm with personal vengeance, and tens of thousands lost their property, their rights, and their lives for "mistaken" alliances, "false" ideas, or "suspect" gestures. Such practices, which helped the regime solidify support, also threatened to undermine the regular procedures of government.

Ending the War with Germany The most pressing issue was to find a way out of the war. In February 1918 a delegation headed by Trotsky, having failed to arrange terms of peace with Germany, proposed a policy of no peace, no war: Russia would just stop fighting. The following month, with the Germans just 100 miles from Petrograd, the Russians accepted the Treaty of Brest Litovsk. Russia surrendered more than 1 million square miles of territory to Germany, including a third of its arable land, a third of its factories, and three-quarters of its deposits of iron and coal. It granted the independence of Finland, Georgia, and the Ukraine; left to Germany the disposition of Russian Poland, Lithua-

CHRONOLOGY
The Conflicts That Resulted in Communist Victory

March 1917	February Revolution.
November 1917	October Revolution.
March 1918	Peace of Brest Litovsk.
1918–1920	Civil war.
1920–1921	War with Poland.
1921	Kronstadt mutiny.
1922	Japanese troops leave Russian territory.

nia, Latvia, and Estonia; and ceded parts of Transcaucasia to the Ottoman Empire. The Communists paid this high price for peace, confident that revolution in Germany would soon nullify the kaiser's gains.

The peace treaty, like the course of the revolution itself, exposed the discontent among non-Russian nationalities, and in July a new constitution tried to meet that problem by declaring Russia a federation—the Russian Soviet Federated Socialist Republic (R.S.F.S.R.). Great Russia, extending through Siberia, was the largest member. Ostensibly, political power rested with the local soviets, organized by occupation and elected by the votes of all men and women except for members of the clergy, former high officials, and those classified as bourgeois "nontoilers." These soviets elected delegates to the congress of soviets of their canton, the smallest administrative unit, and each of these congresses in turn sent delegates to a congress at the next administrative level. The system, which continued by steps up to the all-Russia Congress, allowed considerable control from the top. The constitution did not mention the Russian Communist party, as it was now named, although it was the real center of political authority. Its Central Committee elected the smaller **Politburo,** which shared ruling power with the governing Council of People's Commissars. Lenin was the dominant figure in both.

Civil War   The Bolsheviks were still surrounded by enemies. In March Allied troops in small numbers had landed in Murmansk, Archangel, and Vladivostok to prevent the supplies they had shipped to Russia from falling into German hands, but those detachments might also be used to support a change of regime (a move some Allied officials favored). At the same time, a number of tsarist generals, among them the army's

former commander-in-chief, Kornilov, were preparing to lead a small but excellent army of Cossacks against the Bolsheviks. It was the beginning of a civil war that would last for two terrible years.

While Trotsky undertook to organize the new regime's army, anti-Bolsheviks of every stripe, including the Social Revolutionaries, organized in hundreds of villages and towns. Across Russia, food riots, battles over land, skirmishes between workers and bourgeois, and ethnic hatred added to the violence. With the economy near collapse, the Bolsheviks adopted "War Communism," a program to extract from a country in chaos just enough men and supplies to fight a civil war through propaganda, requisitioning, police repression, and terror. With the firm leadership of Lenin, the military talent of Trotsky, and above all the mistakes of their enemies, they would eventually win.

By mid-1919 the major remaining threat came from armies under the command of former tsarist officers. One army pushed from the Urals toward Moscow but was stopped before it got there. Another took Kiev in August and reached within 300 miles of Moscow by October, while a third stood only 30 miles from Petrograd. These armies were weakened, however, by their conflicting ambitions; and they did little to win popular support. The areas under their control experienced a terror less efficient but at least as brutal as that conducted by the revolutionaries. With each defeat, more of the anticommunist soldiers melted away until hardly more than marauding bands were left. By the end of 1919, however, they were in general retreat. Their most important group withdrew to the Crimea early in 1920 and stubbornly fought on before finally heeding Allied advice and evacuating their remaining soldiers in November 1920.

The Last of the Fighting   The Communists had to fight against Poland as well. As provided by the Versailles treaty, an Allied commission had determined the Russo-Polish border, placing it along a line that assigned to Poland most areas in which Poles were a clear majority. Poland wanted more and insisted on its boundary of 1772, well to the east, citing cultural and historical arguments. Rejecting Russian offers of compromise, Poland sent an army into the Ukraine in March 1920. Within a month it took Kiev, but the Ukrainian nationalists who had fought the Russians were unwilling to fight for the Poles. In August the Red army, by now a relatively efficient military machine, launched an assault that soon threatened Warsaw. An effective Polish counterattack led in 1921 to a compromise settlement after all, one by which Poland gained considerable non-Polish territory in the Ukraine and in the adjacent region of White Russia. Once Russia's western border was settled, it was possible to agree on

Uncomfortable with the pomp of conventional armies, the Bolsheviks were nevertheless proud of the forces that had won the civil war. Here Trotsky reviews the Moscow Brigade of the Red Army.
Novosti/Sovfoto

a boundary with Turkey as well. It ignored local independence movements and assigned Armenia and Georgia to the Soviet federation, Kars and Ardahan to Turkey. Fighting continued in Asia until 1922, when Japan withdrew from eastern Siberia. By then, the Soviet Union was firmly in Communist hands.

Continuing Turmoil Under War Communism, regimentation and bloodshed were the means of survival, and by using them, the Communist party had become increasingly powerful; yet most of the countryside was still subject to the whims of local party officials and roving bands of armed men. Cities were partially empty, a million Russians had gone into exile, tens of millions more had died, manufacturing produced less in 1920 than in 1913, foreign trade had almost ceased, and poor harvests raised the specter of famine. Requisitions spurred resistance, and black markets flourished. Thus, the mutiny of sailors at the Kronstadt naval base in March 1921 was an ominous sign.[3] These sailors were the sort of men who had made the October Revo-

[3] Denounced as part of an international counterrevolutionary conspiracy, the members of the Kronstadt base who were captured after the mutiny was crushed were subject to executions and deportations, and for seventy years the event was cited in Soviet histories as an example of the kinds of forces arrayed against the revolution. In 1994 Boris Yeltsin announced the rehabilitation of these rebels, and the event was used as evidence that the brutality of Communist rule had begun with Lenin's ruthlessness.

lution possible; though their revolt was soon quelled and their demands for political liberty rejected, Lenin recognized the need for change.

The New Economic Policy Lenin announced the **New Economic Policy (NEP)**, a major turning point in the development of Communist Russia. To many, the NEP seemed a departure from Marxism, but Lenin saw Russia's problems as the result not of flaws in Marxist theory but of having stormed the "citadel of capitalism" too fast. Russia suffered from old habits hard to uproot and from a lack of the technical experts and managers that a modern economy required. With noteworthy pragmatism, Lenin proposed a moderate course that earlier the Bolsheviks would have opposed.

Under the NEP, peasants were no longer subject to requisitions but rather to a tax in kind. Businesses employing fewer than twenty workers could be run as private enterprises, and nationalized industries could be leased to foreigners as a way of training Russians in efficient methods. Fiscal reforms guaranteed a stable currency, helping Russia's external trade to emerge from the pattern of barter into which it had fallen. Recovery was slow. Millions died in the famine of 1920–1921 despite the extensive aid of the American Relief Administration, and not for another six years would production reach prewar levels.

Communist Rule Abandoning the hope of creating communism all at once, the NEP was nevertheless the reaffirmation of Communist determination. Every social institution was recruited to help create a stable new society. Cooperatives and trade unions, newspapers and public meetings taught efficiency and pride in class and nation, as did the school system, which was improved and extended. Its curriculum stressed official doctrines; workers' children were favored for admission to selective schools, and teachers were urged to abandon old-fashioned rote learning. Women were encouraged to work outside the home and were provided a whole series of programs aimed at their special needs as mothers. The problems of ruling over multiple nationalities had eased somewhat with the cession of so much territory in the Treaty of Brest Litovsk, and three-quarters of the remaining population could be called Russian. Officially non-Russian nationalities were given more recognition than ever before, as the Communist government reassembled much of the Russian Empire, and the Orthodox Church, while kept under tight supervision, was permitted to function.

In practice, the Communist party, which remained a restricted elite, was the most important instrument of rule. Organized in a hierarchy that paralleled the bureaucracy, it reached into every aspect of public life—factories, hundreds of new centers for adult education, and youth associations—propagandizing and encouraging, pressuring and explaining. In 1922 cultural activities were placed directly under the Ministry of Education, and the Western artistic movements recently welcomed were discouraged in favor of books and art that met the current definition of communist aesthetics: realistic in style, popular in appeal, and useful to the new order. Issues of practical policy were thrashed out within the government and the party, but to be on the losing side could be politically and sometimes personally fatal. Although the Communist government would never abandon the fear of foreign attack established during the civil war, it gave signs of seeking normal diplomatic relations; by 1924, the year of Lenin's death, every major power except the United States had recognized the new regime. An object of fear to liberals and conservatives, the new communist state became a source of inspiration and hope for the far left throughout the world.

Italian Fascism

Italy, too, experimented with a new form of government. Economically the least developed of the major Western powers, Italy and Russia had begun extensive industrialization at about the same time in the late nineteenth century, and there were many parallels between the two countries, despite Italy's more urban society, greater freedom, stronger constitutional tradition, and more responsive governments. With the end of the war, Italy was racked by inflation, unemployment, and talk of revolution. In many places peasants simply confiscated the land they had long been promised; when industrialists met a series of strikes with lockouts in 1920, workers answered by occupying factories, and many in the upper classes feared a communist revolution. Social conflicts that the state had largely ignored for twenty years now challenged the established system. The peace treaty, too, was disillusioning. Although granted considerable territory, Italy got less than expected, and its treatment by the other Allies was often humiliating. Disposition of the Dalmatian port of Fiume was still being argued in 1919 when a private expedition led by Gabriele d'Annunzio dramatically captured it for Italy. The nation's most famous living poet, d'Annunzio ruled Fiume for more than a year at the head of an "army" of the unemployed, whose nationalist frenzy and vulgar slogans were for many a welcome contrast to the wordy frustration of diplomacy. Eventually, the Italian government evicted him, but he had shown the effectiveness of direct action in a nationalist cause.

The Victory of Fascism   **Fascism** was born amid these crises. The term *fascio,* meaning "bundle," comes from an ancient Roman symbol of authority—a bundle of sticks, individually weak but strong in unity. Echoes of imperial Rome were part of the Fascist mystique. The movement centered around Benito Mussolini, whose polemical skills won him promotion to the editorship of the Socialist party newspaper until he was expelled in 1915 for favoring Italy's entry into the war. Mussolini, who established another paper, became one of Italy's noisiest nationalists, using the rhetoric of the left to denounce liberalism and parliamentary indecision and the slogans of nationalism to castigate Marxists. Fascism grew from this diverse heritage. Both a movement and a party, it employed propaganda, symbols, and activism in new ways, making party militants in their black shirts seem a civilian army.

At first the Fascists had little electoral success, but the changes in Italian politics offered them multiple opportunities. The elections of 1921 were the first in Italy with universal male suffrage, and two newer, well-organized mass parties overshadowed traditional leaders and groups. The Catholic Popular party demanded major reforms, but much of its real strength came from rural and conservative groups. The Socialists, for all their increased strength, were weakened by the split with their left wing, which formed a Communist party, inspired by the Bolsheviks' success in Russia.

The Fascists, who had won no seats in 1919, gained thirty-five in the new Chamber; and the aging Giolitti, who had been a dominating prime minister in the

Italian fascists frequently invoked the heritage of the Roman Empire as part of their intensely nationalist rhetoric. This photograph shows Mussolini commemorating the 2,698th anniversary of the city of Rome on April 21, 1936. How did this kind of public ritual help to consolidate fascist power? AP/Wide World Photos

prewar era, tried to patch together a personal coalition that included the Fascists in a "national bloc" of candidates. Giolitti thought the Fascists could thus be domesticated to parliamentary ways. Instead, they used the electoral campaign to demonstrate their style. Fascist squads in black shirts planted bombs, beat up opponents, and disrupted meetings, employing violence and intimidation while denouncing Marxists as a threat to order. And they benefited from the sympathy of many in the police and administration as well as the support of many property owners.

The Weakness of Opposition   When left-wing unions called a general strike in 1922, raising fears of revolution, Mussolini's Black Shirts grew more threatening and started taking over town councils by force. While politicians struggled to find a parliamentary majority, the Fascists staged a march on Rome in October. Motley squads of party militants moved on the capital in a grand gesture of revolt while Mussolini cautiously

waited in Milan. Belatedly, parliamentary leaders called for martial law, but King Victor Emmanuel III refused. Mussolini dashed to Rome, where the king invited him to form a cabinet; the largely symbolic revolt had been enough to capture power. Claiming the office both as a matter of perfect legality and by right of conquest, Mussolini at age thirty-nine became prime minister of a coalition government. In the elections of 1924, Fascists won a massive victory. Intimidation and fraud contributed to this success, but most Italians were willing to give the new party a chance.

It soon became clearer what a Fascist regime would mean. Giacomo Matteotti, a Socialist who bravely stood before the entire Chamber to enumerate Fascist crimes, was subsequently murdered in gangland style. As public condemnation mounted, Mussolini's government seemed about to topple, but the opponents of fascism were no more able to unite now than when they had been stronger. The Fascists gradually isolated first the Socialist and then the Popular party, which was weakened by the Vatican's distaste for its program of social reform. By 1925 all the opponents of fascism had been expelled from the legislature, and newspapers either printed what they were told or risked suppression. The Fascist period had begun.

To many in and out of Italy, it seemed merely that the nation at last had a strong, antisocialist leader. Some distinguished Italians were associated with the regime in various ways, men such as d'Annunzio, the sociologist Vilfredo Pareto, the composer Giacomo Puccini, the playwright Luigi Pirandello, and some of the avant-garde Futurist artists. Even moderates found it hard to believe that a party whose program contained so many contradictions—Fascists praised revolution and promised a strong state, defended property and called for social change, advocated order and used violence—could be dangerous for long.

Fascist Rule   Mussolini moved slowly to institutionalize his power. A series of special laws passed by 1926 declared the Duce (leader) of Fascism the head of state with the right to set the Chamber's agenda and to govern by decree. For twenty years, nearly all the laws of Italy would be issued in that way. Opposition parties were outlawed, scores of potential opponents arrested, and the civil service and judiciary purged of anyone thought too independent. Italy's newspapers were filled with pictures of Mussolini overawing visitors, captivating vast throngs, leaping hurdles on horseback, flying airplanes, harvesting grain. No story was too silly: The Duce recited the cantos of Dante from memory, he worked all night (the light in his office was carefully left on), he inspired philosophers and instructed economists, American razor blades were inadequate to the toughness of his beard, and his

These ten-year-old boys were not, official propaganda declared, just playing at being soldiers but were ready with half-size rifles and lunch kits to defend their country. Millions of Italian children were enrolled in five organizations: one for boys and girls 6 and 7 years old, two separate ones for boys and girls from the ages of 8 to 13, and two more for those from 14 to 17. For the four years after that, they could belong to the Young Fascists.
Bettmann/Corbis

speed in race cars frightened experts. Slogans such as "The Duce is always right" and "Believe, Obey, Fight" soon covered walls throughout Italy. The victory of an Italian athlete or the birth of a child to a prolific mother became an occasion for hailing the new order as Mussolini's propaganda pumped pride and confidence into a troubled nation.

Despite considerable skepticism, the good news and sense of energy were welcome. Mussolini's sensitivity to the masses brought to Italian government a popular touch that it had lacked. By 1931 when the government demanded that all professors sign a loyalty oath, only eleven refused. With most people frightened into silence and organized resistance shattered, the regime had little to fear from some secret Communist groups and an underground centered in France.

The authoritarian single party, completely subordinate to the Duce, reached into every city and town with its own militia, secret police, and tribunals. Recruited in its early years mainly from among the unemployed and alienated, the Fascist party soon won hundreds of thousands of new members eager for the advantages it offered, until by the 1930s the party decided to accept members more selectively in an effort to achieve internal discipline. There were associations for Fascist teachers, workers, and university students. In youth organizations for every age group over four years old, the next generation wore black shirts, marched, and recited official slogans. Citizens were to replace the handshake with the extended right arm of the Fascist salute,[4] and regulations established the Fascist names to give one's children and the form of address to use with one's friends.

Fascist doctrine, never wholly consistent, denounced the principles of the French Revolution and of majority rule but hailed "the people." The much-advertised principle of authority was reduced to simple obedience to the Duce. Authority itself was deemed purer when arbitrary. There was said to be a Fascist style in art and philosophy, sport and war. A candid irrationalism suspicious of intellectuals and traditional culture stressed the virtues of intuitive "thinking with the blood" and joy in war. As the antithesis of the decadent materialism of the democracies, Italy would influence the world and reclaim the heritage of imperial Rome (see "Fascist Doctrine," p. 872).

The Corporate State   The most discussed element of Fascism, the corporate state, was partly facade, partly an institutional expression of ideology. The intent was to organize each sector of production into a huge confederation, or corporation. Each corporation encompassed a syndicate of employers and one of workers, each headed by party members appointed by the government. Corporations were to establish industrywide policies and wage scales, and by 1926 the system was sufficiently in place to outlaw strikes, lockouts, and independent unions. In 1934 the number of corporations was set at twenty-two.[5] The Duce, as president

[4] The salute was a stylized form of the greeting used in ancient Rome and portrayed in the statue of Marcus Aurelius that since the Renaissance had stood on the Capitoline Hill in Rome, where Michelangelo designed a piazza to frame it. The salute quickly became an international symbol.

[5] A corporation covered an entire sphere of production, from raw materials to manufacture and distribution, and the corporations were divided into three groups: (1) grains, fruits and vegetables, wines, edible oils, beets and sugar, livestock, forestry and lumber, and textiles; (2) metals, chemicals, clothing, paper and printing, construction, utilities, mining, and glass and pottery; (3) insurance and banking, fine arts and liberal professions, sea and air transportation, land transportation, public entertainment, and public lodging.

FASCIST DOCTRINE

The most carefully constructed single statement of Fascist doctrine was the article "Fascism: Doctrine and Institutions," written in 1932 for the Enciclopedia Italiana, *one of the most impressive intellectual works accomplished under the Fascist regime. Although the article was officially listed as by Mussolini himself, most of it was written by Giovanni Gentile, a noted philosopher who was an early supporter of Fascism.*

"It [Fascism] is opposed to classical liberalism which arose as a reaction to absolutism and exhausted its historical function when the State became the expression of the conscience and will of the people. Liberalism denied the State in the name of the individual; Fascism reasserts the rights of the State as expressing the real essence of the individual. . . . The Fascist conception of the State is all-embracing; outside of it no human or spiritual values can exist, much less have value. Thus understood, Fascism is totalitarian, and the Fascist State—a synthesis and a unit inclusive of all values—interprets, develops, and potentiates the whole life of a people.

" . . . First of all, as regards the future development of mankind—and quite apart from present political considerations—Fascism does not, generally speaking, believe in the possibility or utility of perpetual peace. It therefore discards pacificism as a cloak for cowardly supine renunciation in contradistinction to self-sacrifice. War alone keys up all human energies to their maximum tension and sets the seal of nobility on those peoples who have the courage to face it. . . .

"Fascism denies the materialistic conception of happiness. . . . This means that Fascism denies the equation: well-being = happiness, which sees in men mere animals, content when they can feed and fatten, thus reducing them to a vegetative existence pure and simple.

"After socialism, Fascism trains its guns on the whole block of democratic ideologies, and rejects both their premises and their practical applications and implements. Fascism denies that numbers, as such, can be the determining factor in human society; it denies the right of numbers to govern by means of periodic consultations; it asserts the irremediable and fertile and beneficent inequality of men who cannot be leveled by any such mechanical and extrinsic device as universal suffrage.

" . . . The State, as conceived and realized by Fascism, is a spiritual and ethical entity for securing the political, juridical, and economic organization of the nation, an organization which in its origin and growth is a manifestation of the spirit. The State guarantees the internal and external safety of the country, but it also safeguards and transmits the spirit of the people, elaborated down the ages in its language, its customs, its faith. The State is not only the present, it is also the past and above all the future. Transcending the individual's brief spell of life, the State stands for the immanent conscience of the nation."

From S. William Halperin (ed.), *Mussolini and Italian Fascism,* Van Nostrand, 1964.

---

of each corporation, appointed its council of delegates, which then also sat in the National Council of Corporations. These institutions, which never attained real autonomy, were further undercut by the strength of established interests and by Mussolini's habit of legislating by decree. They were presented, however, as the Fascist alternative to liberal forms of representation, replacing conflict with coordination and eliminating class conflict.

Domestic Policies　Fascist economic policy sought *autarchy,* a self-sufficient national economy, and emphasized industrialization and technology. Initial distrust of big business soon lessened, but the government remained active in economic affairs and often favored nationalization. For reasons of prestige, the value of the lira was set to equal the French franc, which hurt Italian exports and required restrictions that led to a painful devaluation. In the interest of self-sufficiency, the government launched its famous battle of grain in 1926, which succeeded (with enormous hoopla) in doubling grain production at great cost in efficiency.

Output per capita declined in the Fascist era. Generally, the industrial giants in steel, automobiles, rubber, and chemicals found it easy to deal with (and often to manipulate) Fascist bureaucracy. At the same time, the Institute for Industrial Reconstruction (IRI) established in 1933 provided subsidies to weak industries and often ended up owning them, a significant extension of government ownership. By 1940 real wages were down in both industry and agriculture.

Efforts to keep peasants on the land and to increase the birthrate at most merely slowed the contrary

The techniques of modern art combined with evocations of ancient Rome in Fascist posters like this one for an exhibition in 1933 on the eleventh anniversary of the Fascist revolution.
Index s.a.s.

trends. But the regime did score some notable achievements, which it vigorously advertised. It suppressed the activities in Sicily of criminal groups called *mafia*, drained the malaria-infested marshes near Rome, built new railroads, and launched some superhighways. Enormous building projects contributed to employment. Workers benefited from the creation of centers with recreation halls, meeting rooms, and libraries in most towns and programs for vacations at seaside or mountain resorts. Family bonuses gave the poor an increased sense of security, and educational reforms put more people in school for longer periods.

The Lateran Agreements   Fascism's most publicized accomplishment was its accommodation with the Vatican. Although Mussolini and most of his early followers were thoroughly anticlerical, the Fascist government adopted many measures the Church would welcome,

putting crucifixes in classrooms and raising the budget for clerical salaries and church repairs. The Lateran treaties of 1929 ended sixty years of conflict between Italy and the Church. They recognized the tiny area of Vatican City as an independent state, and related agreements established religious teaching in public schools, guaranteed that marriage laws would conform to Catholic doctrine, promised to restrict Protestant activities, and determined the indemnity the Church should be paid for its losses during Italian unification. A dispute that had seared the consciences of millions of Italians was at last resolved.

Within the country, potential opponents of Fascism were baffled by Mussolini's apparent successes and, surrounded by propaganda, felt isolated and uncertain of what to believe. Indeed, most Italians probably shared some pride in their nation's heightened prestige. Outside Italy, important groups in all European and many South American nations sang the praises of Fascism's "bold experiment" that ended petty squabbling, ran the trains on time, kept order, and eliminated the threat of communism.

THE DISTINCTIVE CULTURE OF THE TWENTIETH CENTURY

The exciting intellectual and cultural movements of the 1920s built on those of the prewar period. Many of the works that marked new directions in science, philosophy, and the arts had appeared in the decades just before and after the turn of the century. These new trends, disquieting then, gained the momentum to become dominant in many fields after the war. Psychology, literature, and art explored the irrational and surreal. The sciences uncovered complexities in nature that made uncertainty a theoretical principle, and theories of society adopted a tough-minded "realism" that spoke of power and interest more than values. Norms of behavior that had been considered the essence of civilization just a generation earlier were now called into question.

Freudian Psychology

No one disturbed accepted views more deeply than Sigmund Freud, a Viennese physician whose clinical studies had taken him gradually from an interest in neurology to the study of psychiatry. Freud followed the method—close and detailed observation—of medical science, and his writings were as careful in their logic as in their literary elegance. Freud had done his most important work before 1914, and in many ways he was old-fashioned. For the most part, he accepted as socially necessary the norms of respectable behavior promulgated by the nineteenth-century middle class. He was deeply influenced by ideas of evolution, and his metaphors and assumptions betray the liberal economist's appreciation of self-discipline and calculated self-interest. His attention to the phenomenon of hysteria and his use of hypnosis built on the work of others to create a startling view of the human mind, which he insisted could be universally applied. His great impact, however, came in the twentieth century.

The Unconscious In treating neurotics, Freud found that they often experienced relief of their symptoms by recalling forgotten events under hypnosis. He concluded that the recollection itself was crucial, not for its accuracy, but as an expression of the psychic reality with which the patient had been unconsciously struggling. Within the unconscious, conflicting urges contended in what Freud labeled the *id*. Here universal basic desires (similar to instincts) seek satisfaction, and Freud found the most troublesome and psychologically significant desires to be sexual. The *ego* tries to channel and control these desires, directed to do so by the *superego*, which (rather like the conscience in more traditional conceptions) imposes a socially conditioned sense of what is acceptable behavior. Thus, mental life is marked by perpetual tension between the id and the superego.

This conflict, uncomfortably mediated by the ego, is unconscious, for one of the mind's responses is to repress from consciousness the id's desires. Most people remain unaware of their own deepest motivations. Repression, however, causes an enormous mental strain that often finds an outlet in neurotic behavior. As the patient comes to face and understand what is being repressed, neurosis is relieved.

Psychoanalysis From this conception of the human psyche, Freud developed an elaborate, subtle, and shocking theory that ascribed sexual lusts to every person at every age. The idea of infant sexuality was especially offensive to contemporaries, but so was the notion of the Oedipus or Electra complex, through which the boy's angry competition with his father (or the daughter's with her mother) could produce a child's unconscious guilt-ridden wish for the death of one parent in order to possess the other. Few in Freud's time could tolerate this ascription of base desires to decent people. Freudian theory proclaimed that such decent people were merely the most repressed. Similarly, religion provided satisfaction for infantile and obsessive needs. Even the greatest human achievements in art and science were the result of sublimation, by which Freud meant the diversion of the id's primitive demands to other, higher purposes.

Psychoanalysis, the name Freud gave his body of theory and his therapeutic technique, calls on the analyst not to pass judgments but rather to help the patient discover aspects of self that proper society held to be quite simply unmentionable. By implication, these ideas and therapeutic techniques called for a shift in aesthetic and intellectual standards. Freud considered whatever seemed real to the psyche to be important; dreams and slips of the tongue were serious expressions of psychic conflict. Hypnosis and free association (in which patients are encouraged to let their thoughts ramble) were valued as modes of expression in which hidden connections emerged without the intervention of narrative or logic. Freud pioneered new ways of comprehending life and literature on several levels at once and provided the model for doing so.

Wider Implications In the 1920s the broad implications of Freud's discoveries gained wider public recognition despite continued hostility. If repression leads to neuroses, one extrapolation went, then greater sexual freedom and, above all, greater candor will produce healthier people. This inference remains perhaps the most widespread popular notion drawn from Freudian teaching, though it was not a view he held. Related to this view is the belief that guilt is evil, a kind of Christian perversion of human nature. Freudian insights encouraged literary and personal introspection and supported the view that childhood is the most important phase of life. Although his theories stimulated new visions of a freer and happier life, Freud's dark conclusion was that "the price of progress in civilization is paid in forfeiting happiness." Civilization, then, is based on the repression of primitive and still very powerful drives, which may burst forth at any moment. Freud, who feared the explosion he foresaw, died in 1939, driven into exile by the anti-Semitism of the Nazis.

Freudians strove to maintain these doctrines whole as science and therapy, treating deviations as heresies; but there would be many deviations. The best known came from the Swiss psychologist Carl G. Jung, who soon broke from Freud and developed his theory of the collective unconscious, the common psychic inheritance of whole peoples, which they most commonly expressed in the symbols and rituals of religion. Jung's somewhat looser and more mystical perspectives have fascinated religious thinkers, attracted theorists of nation and race, and influenced philosophers and artists. More generally, the concepts and vocabulary of psychoanalysis penetrated much of Western culture, apparent in art and literature, journalism, and advertising.

The Humanities

Art and Literature   Some artists in the postwar period—the Surrealists, with their dreamlike canvases, are an example—applied Freudian ideas directly, and in his manifesto of Surrealism (1924), the writer André Breton proclaimed that art must liberate the subconscious. Quite independent of Freud, explorations of human irrationality fairly exploded in prose and poetry. The novels of Marcel Proust, Franz Kafka, and James Joyce most clearly mark the change in style and content.

Marcel Proust died in 1922, soon to be hailed as one of the great stylists of the French language. His long novel, *Remembrance of Things Past,* built an introverted and delicately detailed picture of upper-class Parisian life into a monumental and sensitive study of one man's quiet suffering, which became a model of interior monologue, of the novel in which the subject is not action seen from the outside but feelings observed from within.

Franz Kafka, who wrote in German though born in Prague, died in 1924, leaving instructions for his manuscripts to be burned. They were not, and they came to be accepted as quintessentially modern, with their realistic and reasonable descriptions of fantasies that convey the torture of anxiety. In *The Trial* the narrator tells of his arrest, conviction, and execution on charges he can never discover, an exploration of the psychology of guilt that foreshadows the totalitarian state.

James Joyce's international fame came with the publication of his novel *Ulysses* (1922), the presentation on a mythic scale of a single day in the life of a modest Dubliner, written in an exuberant, endlessly inventive game of words in which puns, cliché, parody, and poetry swirl in a dizzying stream of consciousness.

Virginia Woolf, who used related devices in her novels, was less widely read at the time, but her work would become very influential a generation later. A political activist and feminist who was prominent in England's intellectual circles, her book *A Room of One's Own* (1929) subtly explored the value of a female perspective and the ways in which women were discouraged from intellectual independence. Not all of the most important writers turned away from the objective tone and chronological clarity of traditional narrative. But even those who made use of more familiar techniques—like Thomas Mann in Germany, André Gide in France, and D. H. Lawrence in England—tended to explore topics and attitudes offensive to convention.

The Other Arts   In all the arts, shock became one of the points of creative expression. Dada, a movement that originated during World War I, put on displays, part theater and part art exhibition, of noisy nonsense and absurd juxtapositions that were intended to infuriate the Parisian bourgeoisie. Italian Futurists, poets and playwrights as well as artists, promised to build a new art for a technological age—"The world has been enriched by a new beauty: the beauty of speed"—and in their manifesto of 1909 had issued a call to "burn the libraries . . . demolish the venerated cities." The Fauves in France and the Expressionists in Germany and Scandinavia gloried in their reputation for wild and often brutal candor in the style and content of their paintings as well as in their conduct.

Works of art became more difficult to comprehend. Cubist and Expressionist painters, like composers using the twelve-tone scale and dissonance, deliberately eschewed the merely decorative or pleasant and seemed eager to incorporate violence and amorality. Even when more sober traditions prevailed—as in the carefully constructed, cerebral poetry of William Butler Yeats and of the younger Ezra Pound and T. S. Eliot— foreboding and obscurity intertwined. Today the richness and profundity of the greatest of these works are readily apparent. To contemporaries, however, they were more threatening than attractive, dangerously widening the chasm between "serious" art and the popular culture most intellectuals disdained.

Philosophy   The philosophical work most widely read in the 1920s was Oswald Spengler's *Decline of the West,* which had appeared in 1918. Spengler treated whole civilizations as biological organisms, each with a life cycle of its own, and presented his study of Western culture as an achievement of German philosophy. But his fame rested on the dire prediction of his title: World War I had begun the final act of Western civilization. José Ortega y Gasset's *The Revolt of the Masses,* published in 1930, was hardly more optimistic. The masses, he warned, were destined to use their rising power to destroy civilization's highest achievements. Scores of other writers joined in scorn for modern culture as vapid and directionless.

The most striking innovation in philosophy, however, came from another tradition entirely and was monumentally set forth in *Principia Mathematica* (1910) by Bertrand Russell and Alfred North Whitehead. It became the cornerstone of analytic philosophy, which holds that philosophers should concern themselves only with what is precise and empirically demonstrable. On the Continent a group known as the Vienna Circle developed a related system, logical positivism. The work of Ludwig Wittgenstein, especially his *Tractatus Logico-Philosophicus* (1921), influenced

Otto Dix
Grosstadt, **1927–1928**
Like many German Expressionists, Otto Dix challenged the public with a series of paintings that simultaneously lampooned and celebrated the decadence of life in Berlin in the Weimar era.
Kunstmuseum, Stuttgart, Germany. © 2005 Artists Rights Society (ARS), New York/Erich Lessing/Art Resource, NY

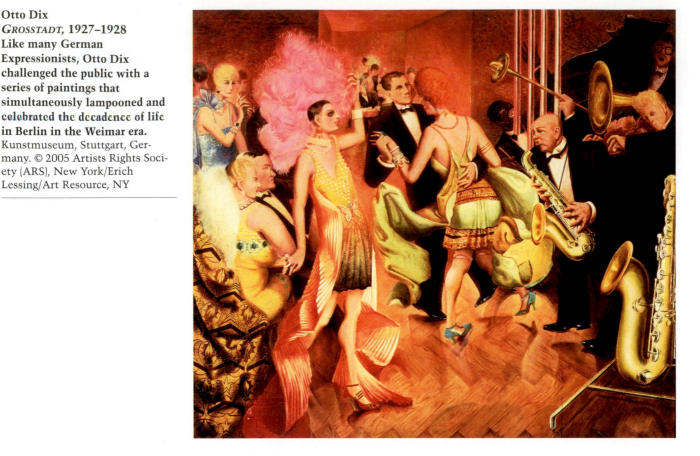

both schools of thought. According to Wittgenstein, the philosopher's task was to analyze every statement, stripping away those connotations and values, however appealing, that do not convey precise meaning.

The Sciences

Science had also moved beyond the layperson's comprehension since the late nineteenth century. Even when the achievements of science were apparent to everyone, they often rested on theoretical advances that overturned established certainties. And the fields in which scientists worked became ever more highly specialized.

The Nature of Matter   One line of scientific investigation stemmed from an experiment by two Americans, Albert A. Michelson and Edward W. Morley, in 1887. By demonstrating that the speed of light leaving earth was the same whether the light traveled in the direction of the earth's movement or against it, they challenged the established theory that the universe was filled with a motionless substance called "ether," which was thought necessary because waves could not function in empty space. The implications were fundamental, and exploring them led Albert Einstein to his

theory of **relativity,** which he set forth in two brief papers published in 1905 and 1915. They were of the highest philosophical as well as scientific interest: Space and time are not absolute, he said, but must be measured in relation to the observer and on the most fundamental levels are aspects of a single continuum.

As Einstein developed his theory of relativity, physicists were also achieving a new understanding of matter. Wilhelm Roentgen's discovery of x-rays in 1895 had given the first important insight into the world of subatomic particles. Within two years the English physicist J. J. Thomson showed the existence of the electron, the subatomic particle that carries a negative electrical charge. The atom was not the basic unit of matter. By the turn of the century, Pierre and Marie Curie, among others, had found radium and other materials to be radioactive; that is, they emitted both subatomic particles and a form of electromagnetic radiation. Soon, largely through the work of the English physicist Ernest Rutherford, radioactivity was identified with the breakdown of heavy and unstable atoms. These discoveries made it possible to link the structure of atoms with Dmitri Mendeleev's periodic table of elements. Elements with similar chemical properties were also similar in their atomic structures. A simpler and clear understanding of matter seemed in the offing.

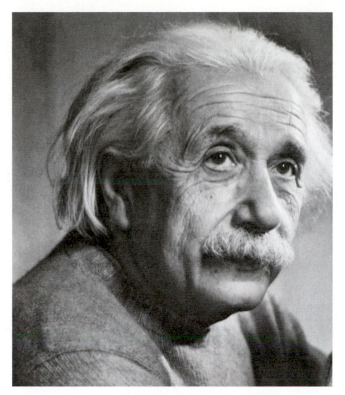

Einstein's face remains one of the best-known icons of the twentieth century, a symbol of humanity, universal genius, and Jewish exile.
Ottawa Karsh/Woodfin Camp & Associates

Quantum Physics But continuing research soon revealed phenomena that Newtonian physics could not explain. In 1902 the German physicist Max Planck challenged Newtonian assumptions by announcing that energy in the subatomic world was released or absorbed not in a continuous stream but in discrete, measurable, and apparently irreducible units, which Planck called quanta. Energy, in effect, possessed many of the properties of matter.

This finding implied that matter and energy might be interchangeable, and Einstein incorporated the insight into his theory of relativity in the famous equation $E = mc^2$. Energy (E) is equivalent to mass (m) times the square of the speed of light, a constant (c), which means that, at least in theory, small quantities of matter could be turned into enormous amounts of energy. In this respect Newtonian physics was wrong; matter could be transformed after all. In 1919 Rutherford produced changes in the structure of the nitrogen atom by bombarding it with subatomic particles, and other atomic changes were soon produced in the laboratory.

Uncertainty Principle By the mid-1920s, however, physicists had to face troubling anomalies. Planck's quantum theory, though verified in numerous experiments, considered particles to behave in probabilistic rather than absolutely regular patterns—a concept Einstein himself could never wholly accept. Furthermore, electromagnetic radiation, including visible light, seemed to behave like a flow of particles in some circumstances and in others as a wave—a regular disturbance of particles in which the particles themselves do not advance. Nor, the German physicist Werner Heisenberg argued, was it possible at the same time to determine a particle's position and its momentum, for at the subatomic level measurement interfered with the variables measured—a disturbing effect that Heisenberg appropriately named "the uncertainty principle." Conceptions of matter had been transformed in just a few years. Inside atoms there was mostly empty space and particles that did not behave with absolute regularity; and in both the subatomic world and the stellar universe, the position and purpose of the observer fundamentally affected what was observed.

The new theories proved powerful tools, but physicists who chose to philosophize about such matters now spoke in humbler and more tentative tones. Physics became one of the most prestigious, highly organized, and expensive of human activities, recognized rather than understood by the public through its applications: x-ray technology, the electron microscope, and eventually the controlled fission of atomic energy. Newtonian principles, physicists insisted, still obtained in most cases, as solid and predictable as ever. But there was a loss. The Western world had long looked to the sciences for confirmation of its philosophy and even its theology. In the twentieth century no popularizer would build a general outlook on society from the latest scientific discoveries as Voltaire had once done from the ideas of Newton.

The Biological and Social Sciences Although the new work in other fields of science was less revolutionary, it often had immediate impact. Knowledge of the mechanisms of heredity furthered scientific breeding of animals and the creation of plant hybrids that would greatly increase the productivity of agriculture. The isolation of viruses opened a new field of study, and the discovery of penicillin in 1928 by Englishmen Sir Alexander Fleming and Sir Howard Florey brought medicine a new armory of invaluable drugs.

The understanding of society was deeply affected by two giants of modern sociology, the Frenchman Émile Durkheim and the German Max Weber, whose work is central to modern social science. Durkheim's use of statistical tools and Weber's use of the "ideal type" to analyze how societies function remain influential, as does their concern with the customs and beliefs that hold society together. Both, for example, emphasized the importance of religion, although they were concerned not with its metaphysical truth but with its contribution to the development of the state and of capitalism. Both stressed the threat to society when group norms broke down, and both saw a danger of that breakdown in modern trends. Through this emphasis on the function of communal values rather than their validity and on the role of myth and ritual in all societies including our own, anthropology, sociology, and history have tended to share psychology's insistent relativism.

Public Culture

To the public at large, developments in science and the arts were associated with the prosperity and brash excitement of the twenties. Science meant the spread of automobiles, radios, and airplanes; new trends were known through colorful stylish advertising, risqué literature, and vibrant theater. The surprising crisp architecture and applied design of Walter Gropius' Bauhaus school in Germany, with its emphasis on relating form to function, began to win a following, and there was curiosity about the still more daring endeavors in France of Le Corbusier to envision a wholly modern city as a machine for living.

Cinema During the 1920s, motion pictures became more popular and more profitable than any form of entertainment had ever been. Germany, Britain, France, and Italy each built thousands of theaters, often on the most elegant streets of major cities. Many of these theaters gaudily combined the exoticism of a world's fair with reassuring luxury. Egyptian and Greek motifs, marble columns, fountains, and statues reinforced the fantasies on the screen.

People from every stratum of society attended the same films, and women often attended without male escorts. Influenced by the movies, middle-class and working-class families increasingly discussed the same topics and began to imagine different and better lives for themselves. Reviews and movie magazines helped to provide the publicity essential to success in a business that relied on stars and vast distribution networks. American companies did all this very effectively, filling screens around the world. The United States made the most films, followed by Japan and Germany.

The rapid transition to talking pictures between 1929 and 1930 underscored national differences, and every country had some ministry empowered to restrain the presentation on the screen of sex and violence. In 1919 an English Watch committee condemned a film of the Johnson-Jeffries fight, fearing it could "demoralize and brutalize the minds of young persons." Sunday showings were an issue for years. Pol-

Gaudy movie palaces like this Parisian theater, one of the first, became prominent monuments in every city, offering the masses an exotic luxury previously associated with the great opera houses.
Editions Tallandier

itics was present, too. Many countries restricted or banned German films in the 1920s; France, generally the most tolerant, in effect proscribed films made in the Soviet Union where, with Lenin's encouragement, the director Sergei Eisenstein brilliantly showed how well suited the medium was to depicting official views of the revolutionary power of the masses.

Consumerism While moralists worried about the cynicism of mass entertainment and the amoral excess of nightlife in cabarets and theaters, millions joined a kind of dizzying celebration. Middle-class families bought their first car; millions from every class, their first radio. Sophistication was a kind of shibboleth, used to justify lipstick, short skirts, alcohol, and one brash fad after another but also to underscore the cosmopolitanism that valued American jazz, openly learned from African art, and welcomed the new. For

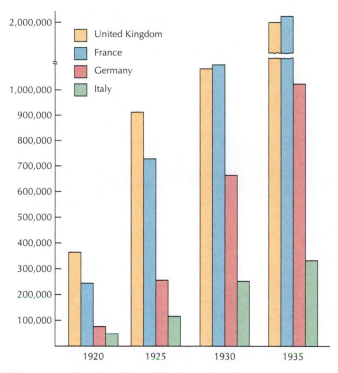

NUMBER OF MOTOR VEHICLES
The number of automobiles in a society reflects its general wealth, adaptation to a consumer economy, and changing patterns of communication. (Note that the United Kingdom, France, and Italy each had about 40 million people; Germany had 65 million.) This graph gives evidence of impressive prosperity and change; by 1935 France and the United Kingdom had one vehicle for every 20 people.

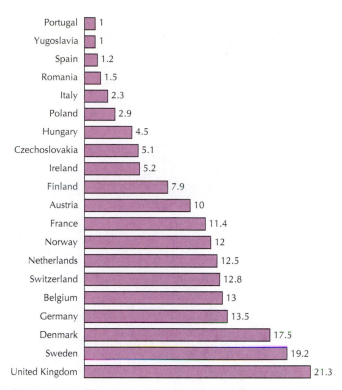

APPROXIMATE NUMBER OF RADIOS LICENSED FOR EVERY 100 PEOPLE IN 20 SELECTED COUNTRIES (1938)
Radio was an important new instrument of communication and propaganda. These statistics suggest that most families in the United Kingdom had a radio, that nearly everyone could sometimes listen to the radio in Finland and Austria, and that from Italy to Portugal millions of people heard the radio only on special occasions when speakers blared in public places.

perhaps the only time, Berlin rivaled Paris as a European artistic center, more famous as the home of acid satire in art and theater than for its thriving cultural institutions of a more traditional sort. Modernism turned its back on gentility.

THE GREAT DEPRESSION AND THE RETREAT FROM DEMOCRACY

Within less than a decade after the Paris Peace Conference, democracy was in retreat across Europe. By 1929 authoritarian regimes had violated or eliminated the liberal constitutions of Hungary, Spain, Albania, Portugal, Lithuania, Poland, and Yugoslavia as well as Italy. By 1936 political liberty had also been suppressed in Romania, Austria, Bulgaria, Estonia, Latvia, and Greece as well as Germany. Most of these countries were among the poorest in Europe, but their political difficulties illustrate the broader trend. Divided over issues of social reform, nationality, and religion—

differences amplified by new and angry socialist and peasant parties—they suffered increased disruption with each economic crisis and foreign threat.

Authoritarian Regimes

Authoritarian leaders often flirted with fascism on the Italian model, only to find it dangerously uncontrollable. They sought through decisiveness and force to achieve stability in societies riven by social conflict and where religious and ethnic loyalties could be readily fanned into anger and hatred by ambitious politicians.

The Monarchies of Central and Eastern Europe During the 1920s and 1930s, many Eastern European nations experimented with fascist policies and tactics. In Hungary, for example, a series of anti-Semitic governments, beginning with the regime of Admiral Miklos Horthy in 1920, discouraged democracy and introduced many fascist trappings. In Romania the government of King Carol

Police in Vienna prepare to confront socialists in 1927. The socialists were protesting the release of men believed to have murdered a socialist. In the ensuing riots, the palace of justice was burned and a hundred people were killed, part of the cycle of violence shaking the Austrian republic.
Bettmann/Corbis

II—an admirer of Mussolini—stripped most Jews of land and citizenship, tightened censorship, and imposed martial law. A 1934 coup by the military in Bulgaria abolished parliamentary government and free speech in that country. Similarly, in 1929 King Alexander I of Yugoslavia assumed dictatorial powers in an effort to tame the divisive forces of Serbian, Croatian, and Slovenian nationalism.

By the end of the 1930s, however, all of these countries had taken major steps to limit or suppress fascist activities. One reason for these policy shifts was opposition from France, on whose support these countries depended. In addition, the Eastern European authoritarian leaders found themselves threatened by both the ambitions of the fascists themselves and popular backlashes against fascism. Although these governments moved away from fascism, however, most of them remained authoritarian.

The Republics of Poland and Austria Events in Poland followed a somewhat different course. Like other European nations, Poland was wracked by internal conflicts: Catholics versus socialists, conservative landowners versus radical peasants. In 1926 Marshall Jozef Pilsudski assumed power in a military revolt. Once his followers attained a majority in parliament, Pilsudski resigned. However, men from the military continued to run the country.

In Austria the republic was undermined by the sharp division between a Catholic German countryside and a cosmopolitan imperial Vienna. The left-wing Social Democrats had little strength beyond Vienna. Meanwhile, the conservative Christian Socialists—whose nineteenth-century programs of welfare, nationalism, and anti-Semitism had influenced the young Hitler—moved steadily toward fascism. As violent clashes between the parties intensified, Chancellor Engelbert Dollfuss, a Christian Socialist, responded by suspending parliament, outlawing communists, and eventually banning all parties except his own Fatherland Front, a coalition of conservative groups. In 1934 he used military force to crush the Social Democrats. That same year, however, a group of Austrian Nazis assassinated Dollfuss, an act they hoped would lead to *Anschluss,* or union with Germany. Although the *Anschluss* did not take place until 1938, Austria's authoritarian government, having repressed the left, found if difficult to mobilize opposition to growing Nazi pressure.

International Fascism   Whether they won power or not, Europe's fascist movements had much in common. Generally influenced by Italian Fascism, they looked and sounded similar. They liked uniforms, starting with a shirt of one color. Cheap to buy and easy to adopt, it made a group of supporters (however few or poor) look like a movement, a historical force. They used paramilitary organization that promised decisive action to remake society through discipline and force. They created drama in the streets—noise, marches, colorful demonstrations, symbolic acts, and real violence—that undermined conventional standards of public behavior while advertising fascism as something new and powerful. They borrowed heavily from working-class movements and used all the devices of democratic politics, while seeming to stand outside the corrupting process of compromise and responsibility. Populist tactics were thus attached to the promise of order.

Fascists nostalgically evoked the enthusiastic patriotism of World War I to offer simple solutions to real problems. The disruption and inequity of capitalism, class conflict, a faltering economy, and aimless governments were the fault of enemies—liberal politicians, Marxist revolutionaries, Jews, and foreigners. Those enemies, although ridiculed and denounced in fascist propaganda, were credited with hidden powers that only the force of fascism could overcome. Fascism promised to create a united, orderly, prosperous community.

There was more to these movements than their simple myths, camaraderie, and sinister attraction to violence. Fascists addressed real fears. They spoke to a rural society that felt threatened by urbanization, to small-business people threatened by the competition of large corporations and to all business people threatened by workers' demands and government intervention, to a middle class threatened by socialism, to the privileged threatened by democracy, to the unemployed threatened by continuing economic depression, to the religious threatened by a secular society. Everywhere, they played on fear of a communist revolution.

The Appeal of Fascism   Fascists could do all this by borrowing freely from ideas current throughout Europe. They used socialist criticisms of liberalism and capitalism, conservative values of hierarchy and order, and intellectual denunciations of modern culture. They amplified a widespread contempt for parliamentary ineffectiveness, used doctrines of race made familiar by war and imperialism, and laid claim to the nationalism that every government liked to invoke. At the same time, as admirers of technology and organization, fascists promised to create more modern societies. And they laid claim to corporatism, which Mussolini's Italy advertised as the wave of the future.

Corporatist thought had a long and respectable history. Organizing society as well as parliament according to occupation promised to do away with the selfish competition of interests and parties characteristic of liberalism, to preserve social hierarchy, and to eliminate class conflict. The idea of so integrated a society gained attractiveness in the years of economic depression and prestige with Pope Pius XI's encyclical *Quadragesimo Anno* ("In the Fortieth Year") issued in 1931 on the fortieth anniversary of Leo XIII's *Rerum Novarum.* The new encyclical went further in rejecting the injustices of capitalism and the solutions of Marxism, and it called instead for harmony based on religion and cooperation through corporative organization. Many anxious people found in that papal pronouncement a sympathy for fascism that seemed to justify overlooking its deeply antireligious qualities.

The appeal of fascism was not limited to poor nations. Its ambiguities made it applicable everywhere. In Britain Sir Oswald Mosley, once considered a likely Labour prime minister, founded the British Union of Fascists. In Belgium fascism benefited from the antagonism between Catholics and anticlericals and between French-speaking Walloons and Dutch-speaking Flemings, who were increasingly sympathetic to fascism and to the Nazis. In the Netherlands a National Socialist movement rose to prominence in the 1930s, and there were a number of fascist and protofascist movements in France, including *Action Française,* which had become prominent in the furor of the Dreyfus case.

The Great Depression

Above all, fascist and Marxist movements benefited from a worldwide economic depression that undermined social and political stability and seemed to many the death knell of capitalism.

The Stock Market Crash On October 24, 1929, the price of stocks on the New York Exchange began to plummet. Suspecting that speculation had pushed stock prices too high, nervous investors sold their shares. Day after day tens of millions of dollars in paper assets disappeared. Such panics were not new, and they had spread from New York to Europe in the previous century. Now, however, the United States was the world's wealthiest nation and greatest creditor, and this panic settled into full-scale depression as banks failed, businesses cut back, consumption declined, factories closed, and unemployment rose. Its banks and exchanges shaken, the European economy suffered further from the decline in world trade and the withdrawal of American investments and loans. Financial panic hit Europe in May 1931 when Austria's largest bank nearly went under. The panic started a run on Austrian and German banks and then spread, as it had in the United States, to other sectors of the economy and to other nations.

The late 1920s had been years of boom in the United States and of general prosperity in much of Europe, but the Great Depression exposed deep-seated problems. Not all industries had recovered after the war. Coal and textile industries had long been sliding toward chronic depression. Former trade patterns had not revived, especially among the underdeveloped new countries of Eastern Europe, and economic difficulties were increased by Germany's inflation and Russia's withdrawal from commerce. Europe, which lost huge amounts of foreign investments during the war, had not regained its prewar percentage of world trade (about half), and American investments in Europe increased dramatically throughout the 1920s. Too much of the international economy rested on the unproductive passing of paper from the United States to Germany as loans, from Germany to the Allies as reparations, and from the Allies to the United States as payment of war debts; and the United States raised tariffs in 1922 and again in 1930 to levels that made it nearly impossible for Europeans to earn dollars by selling to Americans. Much of the prosperity of the 1920s rested on new processes and on new products, such as automobiles and synthetic fabrics, which proved vulnerable to the withdrawal of American investment and the decline in consumer confidence. The Great Depression underscored how uneven and artificial much of the preceding prosperity had been and showed that, for Europe, a decade had not been long enough to overcome the effects of World War I.

The Repercussions By 1932 the world's industrial production was two-thirds of what it had been in 1929. Unemployment climbed to more than 13 million in the United States, 6 million in Germany, and nearly 3 million in Great Britain. Among leading industrial nations, only France, with its balanced economy and lower fertility rate, escaped a crisis of unemployment. Since the war, and especially in democracies, governments were expected to provide solutions to economic problems. They looked first for international help. Because the reparations system had broken down amid the world economic crisis, European nations declared that they could no longer make debt payments to the United States. The United States refused to acknowledge the connection. Instead, President Hoover proposed that all intergovernment payments be suspended; his proposal, quickly accepted in 1932, was supposed to be temporary but in fact marked the end of both kinds of payments.

Other crises loomed. Austria's banking system had been saved from bankruptcy with British loans; but the deepening depression and other financial burdens forced Great Britain to abandon the gold standard, which meant it no longer guaranteed the value of the pound sterling. The important bloc of countries that traded in sterling followed suit. Tantamount to devaluation, these moves threatened chaos for international monetary exchanges and trade; and so the League of Nations sponsored a World Economic Conference that met in London in 1933. Begun with visions of high statesmanship, it ended in failure. When the United States also went off the gold standard, the structure of credit and exchange that had been one of the signal achievements of liberal finance fell apart. For a century, nations, like so many bankers, had supported international financial stability by honoring these rules of liberal economics, and that historic era had ended.[6]

National Responses In this crisis democracies responded first to domestic pressures. Austria and Germany sought a customs union, which was opposed by France and rejected by the World Court. Nearly everyone raised tariffs and import quotas, further reducing trade, while domestic programs protected political interests. Liberals were at a loss as to what else to do, and socialists were no better prepared to solve the problems of declining commerce, insufficient capital, and—most pressing of all—unemployment. Socialists could find some vindication in the evident weakness of capitalism, but their favorite nostrum, the nationalization of industry, was barely relevant. In practice, they adopted rather orthodox measures of budget reduction while supporting whatever palliatives for unemployment could be suggested, though the dole, the most common one, strained the budgets they wanted to balance.

---

[6] Karl Polanyi elaborated on the significance of abandoning the gold standard in a famous essay, *The Great Transformation: The Political and Economic Origins of Our Time.*

Most government policies, then, did little to help and may have made the situation worse; bankers and financiers, desperate to stem their losses, gave little attention to the international or social effects of their actions. And the millions of unemployed were more helpless still, standing in line for the dole, eating whatever they could get, taking any bits of work available. Growing communist parties let no one forget that while a whole international system had been collapsing, Soviet production advanced at a steady pace.

Gradually, economic conditions did improve; and by 1937 production in Germany, Britain, and Sweden was well above the 1929 level, though it remained below the 1929 level in the United States, Italy, Belgium, and France. Subsequent government intervention to shore up industries and provide employment did alleviate distress and improve morale. It also changed economic and political life and, at least in democracies, was often as socially divisive as the Depression itself. Democracies faced the dual threat of communism and fascism with a heavy burden of economic and social failure.

NAZI GERMANY AND THE USSR

In the 1930s Nazi Germany and the Soviet Union acquired unprecedented power over their own populations and used it in ways that changed the world. Understanding how these regimes evolved, their techniques of rule, and the policies they pursued remains a central challenge of twentieth-century history. Dictatorship has been recognized since ancient times as a specific political form. The most important dictatorships of this century, however, were different enough from previous examples to merit a separate term. They relied on a single political party, absolute devotion to a leader, domination of mass communications, direction of the economy, and the ruthless use of force—all in the name of an explicit, official ideology. The term **totalitarianism** refers to the combination of these characteristics and describes a system of rule more than specific policies, a system inclined to use oppression and terror to force citizens to participate in the regime's activities and belief system. In principle totalitarianism seeks to shape every aspect of life and to crush "enemies" identified by their race, occupation, region, or religion. Such a vision and the institutions that would attempt to carry it out did not develop all at once but evolved, primarily in Communist Russia, Fascist Italy, and Nazi Germany.

Useful as the concept of totalitarianism is, it has also come under heavy criticism for a number of reasons. In practice, none of the totalitarian regimes achieved total control. They often gave way before customs and institutions they could not afford to offend and negotiated with entrenched interests. Inefficiency and duplication were characteristic, even endemic, for these regimes were not monolithic. Officials and party members often bickered among themselves. No totalitarian ideology was entirely coherent or unanimously embraced, and there were important differences among totalitarian systems. The values promulgated and policies pursued in Soviet Russia were not at all the same as those of Nazi Germany. Italy's claim to be totalitarian was largely propaganda, and that is the point. *Totalitarianism* is a useful term not for describing how these regimes actually functioned but rather for describing the ambitions and techniques that made Europe's leading twentieth-century tyrannies a fundamentally new political form.

Hitler's Germany

The Nazi regime won power in a democracy with an advanced economy and a strong administrative tradition. It played upon selected elements of German history, from militarism and nationalism to the weakness of the Weimar Republic, and it took advantage of the social shocks Germany had recently suffered: defeat in war, failed revolutions, inflation, clashing ideologies, and a depression that brought the most extensive unemployment in Europe.

The Rise of Hitler   As a young man, Adolf Hitler was undistinguished, his ambition to be an artist thwarted when the Academy in Vienna rejected his application. Service in World War I had been a kind of salvation, providing comradeship and some accomplishment: He was promoted in the field. In Munich after the war, he found brief employment spying on the small German Worker's party, which the army considered dangerous. He also took to addressing political rallies in the beer halls, where he learned the potential of a movement that combined the personal loyalty of a paramilitary corps with mass appeal and where he molded the speaking style that would make him the most powerful figure in Germany.

His speeches combined crude accusations, a messianic tone, and simple themes repeated in a spiraling frenzy. Race and universal struggle were the core of his message. Germans were victims of vast conspiracies mounted by foreign powers, capitalists, Marxists, Freemasons, and (above all) Jews—the gutter anti-Semitism that Hitler had absorbed in Vienna. Jews were behind war profits, reparations, inflation, and depression; but Marxism was also Jewish, and communists were agents of the Jewish conspiracy. Internationalism and pacifism were Jewish ideas intended to destroy Germany as the bastion of Western civilization.

To Hitler, Western civilization was Aryan, an old term for the prehistoric peoples of Eurasia that he used to describe race. Germans and Nordic peoples were the purest Aryans, Jews their enemy. Life was a desperate struggle won by the ruthless, and Germany's destiny was victory over enemies who threatened the nation by means of the Versailles Treaty, economic disasters, communists, Jews, moral decay, and abstract art. All attacked the Germanic *Volk*, the German people whose primitive virtues must be welded into an irresistible force.

The Growth of the Nazi Party   Hitler named his party the National Socialist German Workers' party. *Nazi* was its acronym. The party was one of many such nationalist movements when in 1923 Hitler led them in the Munich *Putsch*, or rising. After it failed and Hitler was sent to prison, the book he wrote there, *Mein Kampf*, won little notice, for it was a turbulent, repetitious outpouring of his political views interlarded with demoniac statements about how human beings are manipulated by fear, big lies, and simplistic explanations. In prison and after his release in 1925, Hitler worked to reorganize and strengthen the party. To the SA, his street army of brown-shirted storm troopers, he added the SS, an elite corps in black uniforms who served as his bodyguards and special police.

Hitler's intensity and bad manners offended many, but others felt the fascination of a personality that radiated power. He soon gathered a group of absolutely loyal men: Hermann Göring, an air ace; Joseph Goebbels, journalist and party propagandist; and Heinrich Himmler. They worked ceaselessly to enlarge the party, orchestrate impressive rallies, and terrorize their opponents. The Nazis were gaining attention and support. In 1930 they became the second-largest party in the Reichstag, and the following year a group of Rhineland industrialists promised the Nazis financial support.

By the 1930s, the party was broadly based, and the issue of what social groups were first drawn to the Nazis has been the subject of historical controversy, because different interpretations of **Nazism** follow from the answer. Workers were probably the biggest single group of members, but most workers continued to favor socialists and communists. Disproportionately large numbers of Nazi supporters were small-business people and tradespeople, civil service employees, and (to a lesser extent) farmers—all groups fearful of losing income and status.

In the Depression, promises of recovery, higher agricultural prices, and more employment (tens of thousands found jobs in the SA and SS) had concrete appeal. Many people were drawn to the call to rebuild the army and to save society from socialism. In 1931 an array of right-wing nationalists joined the Nazis in a manifesto denouncing the "cultural Bolshevism" of the Weimar Republic and hinting that, once they seized power, the Nazis would protect only those who had joined them now. The Nazis spoke simultaneously like a government in office and like an underworld gang, and they demonstrated their seriousness by beating up Jews and socialists.

Collapse of the Weimar Republic   The Social Democrats led the government that faced the Great Depression and did the best they could with a shaky parliamentary majority and an uncooperative president. In 1930 the government resigned, to be replaced by the Center party and Heinrich Brüning, a cautious man with little popular appeal.

The elections of 1930 gave Nazis more than a hundred new seats, from which they contemptuously disrupted parliamentary proceedings. His confidence growing, Hitler became a candidate for president in 1932, when Hindenburg's term expired. Worried politicians persuaded the nearly senile field marshal to run for reelection. Ludicrously cast as the defender of the constitution, the eighty-four-year-old Hindenburg won handily, but Hitler got more than 13 million votes. When Brüning proposed a financial reform that included expropriation of some East Prussian estates, Hindenburg dismissed him and turned to Franz von Papen, a friend of important army officers and Junkers.

Hoping to create a right-wing coalition, von Papen lifted Brüning's ban on the SA and SS, named four barons and a count to his cabinet, and declared martial law in Prussia so he could unseat the socialist government there. The outcry led Hindenburg to call another election. This one resulted in a Nazi landslide. With 40 percent of the Reichstag's seats, the Nazis were by far its largest party. Hindenburg avoided naming Hitler chancellor by refusing to grant him the full decree powers he insisted on. The nation was sent to the polls again, and although the Nazis lost a little, they remained the largest party.

Hitler Takes Office   Hindenburg then named another chancellor, General Kurt von Schleicher, a conventional army officer. He made an easy target for the Communists, the disgruntled von Papen (who thought he saw his chance to regain power), and the Nazis. Von Papen, confident he could use Hitler but contain him, persuaded the men around Hindenburg to appoint Hitler the head of a coalition government. In fact Hitler was the only leader acceptable to the right who could also command a popular following. He took office in January 1933.

Hitler almost immediately called another election. Previous campaigns had been ugly, but this one was marked by systematic terror, especially in Prussia, where Hermann Göring was now minister-president and the police acted like electoral agents. The climax came with the burning of parliament, the Reichstag fire that the Nazis loudly blamed on the Communists. Hindenburg agreed to issue special laws—Ordinances for the Protection of the German State and Nation—that ended most civil liberties, including freedom of the press and assembly. The voters gave the Nazis 44 percent of the seats, enough, with the Nazis' nationalist allies, for a bare majority. Hitler pressed on. Communists were expelled from the Reichstag, conservatives wooed with calls to nationalism, and the Center party enticed with promises to respect the privileges of the Catholic Church. By March Hitler dared demand a special enabling act that gave him, as chancellor, the right to enact all laws and treaties independent of constitutional restraints for four years. Of the 566 deputies left in the Reichstag, only 94 Social Democrats (out of 121) voted no. Blandishment and terror had done their work, but the tragedy went deeper: German politics offered no clear alternative to Hitler.

Consolidating Nazi Rule   Hitler's regime moved quickly to destroy the potential for opposition. It established concentration camps, first on private estates and then in larger and more permanent institutions. The new order appeared to enjoy all but unanimous support. A campaign to boycott Jewish businesses was followed in April by laws eliminating most Jews from public service and limiting Jews to 1.5 percent and women to 10 percent of university enrollment. On May Day 1933, workers arrayed by occupation marched beside Nazi banners and slogans. By July all parties except the National Socialist had been outlawed, and soon all competing political organizations disappeared.

In the elections of November 1933, the Nazis won more than 90 percent of the vote. They restructured government, purged the civil service and judiciary, outlawed strikes, and clamped stricter controls on the press. In a few months Hitler had achieved fuller power than Mussolini had managed in years, and in the next few years Nazi policies on racial purity would be extended step by step throughout public life by ordinances, official policies, and police brutality.

Hitler's most serious potential rivals were within his own party, and his solution was barbarically simple.

Nazi party troops march out of the rally on Nuremberg Party Day, 1933, carrying victory banners proclaiming "Germany Awake."
AKG London

On a long weekend in June 1934, leaders of the Nazi left wing were shot or stabbed. Among hundreds of others, so were General von Schleicher and his wife, some Catholic leaders, some socialists, and some taken by mistake. Hitler admitted to seventy-four deaths; subsequent estimates raise the figure to as many as a thousand. The Night of the Long Knives proved that any horror was possible; and the purge, like the noisy accusations of homosexuality that accompanied it, established the tone of Germany's new order. When Hindenburg died in August, Germans voted overwhelmingly to unite presidency and chancellorship in the person of Adolf Hitler, who took the official title of *Führer* ("Leader").

Administrative and Economic Policies   The federal states lost their autonomy through a policy of *Gleichschaltung,* or coordination, and all government employees were made appointees of the Führer. New people's courts heard secret trials for treason, now very broadly defined, and rewritten statutes allowed prosecution for intent as well as for overt acts. Arrest and detention without charge or trial became a regular practice. At the same time, the Nazi party was restructured to parallel the state, with administrative *Gaue* ("regions") headed by a party *Gauleiter.* The party also had its own office of foreign affairs and its own secret police, the Gestapo, which infiltrated both the bureaucracy and the army.

Economic policies scored impressive successes. Unemployment dropped steadily thanks to great public works projects—government offices, highways, public housing, reclamation, and reforestation. Many of these projects used special labor battalions, in which one year's service was soon compulsory. Later the burgeoning armaments industry and growing armed forces eliminated the problem of joblessness entirely. By spending money when more traditional governments thought it essential to balance their budgets, the Nazis reduced unemployment more effectively than any other Western nation.

Paying the Cost   Such programs were expensive, and they were paid for in several ways. A currency scheme largely designed by Hjalmar Schacht, a brilliant economist, required that payments for foreign trade be made with special marks whose value changed according to the products and the nations involved. Goods that Germany bought were paid for in marks redeemable only through purchases in Germany. Tantamount to barter, this system increased Germany's self-sufficiency and its influence in countries that depended on German markets. Additional revenues came from property confiscated from Jews, high taxes, forced loans, and carefully staged campaigns urging patriotic Germans to contribute their personal jewelry to the state. Ultimately, costs would be covered by printing paper currency, with effects long hidden by a war economy and the exploitation of conquered lands. By 1945 the mark had fallen to about 1 percent of its 1933 value.

Labor policies met related goals. Strikes were outlawed and the mobility of workers regulated. The National Labor Front, which represented all workers and management, froze wages and directed personnel in the

The six-pointed star and the word *Jude* scrawled on this Berlin department store in 1938 were a warning to good Aryans not to shop there.
Bettmann/Corbis

interests of business and government. Industrialists were relieved of the uncertainties of the Weimar years.

Winning Approval   Meanwhile, the regime advertised the new benefits provided workers, including the summer camps and special cruises that were part of the Nazi program of Strength Through Joy. Nazi propaganda also reassured those ordinary people fearful of contemporary trends by denouncing modern art, the decadence of Berlin nightlife (and especially of homosexuality), and new roles for women. Special benefits to new families aided young couples in a depressed economy. Along with improved prenatal care and special honors for the most prolific mothers, such measures were part of the Nazi obsession with biology.

Initially, women were discouraged from working outside the home as a way to reduce unemployment among men, but the concern with women went far deeper. Wifely subordination was presented as a principle of social order and the foundation of the family. Women could not be lawyers or judges and could not constitute more than 10 percent of the learned professions. Social policies, schools, and clinics reinforced propaganda praising the role of Aryan women as breeders of a pure race. Severe penalties for performing abortions on healthy Aryans were accompanied by forced sterilization of the "unfit." Boys and girls were required to join the Hitler Youth.

The military had clear reasons for gratitude. Disregarding the disarmament clauses of the Treaty of Versailles (which Germany formally repudiated in 1935), Hitler pushed rearmament from the first. With the return of universal compulsory service in 1935 and the creation of an air force, Germany was soon spending several times as much on arms as Britain and France

combined. All military officers were required to take an oath of personal loyalty to Hitler. By 1938 Hitler had removed the minister of war, chief of staff, and more than a dozen generals, thereby consolidating his control over the military and the foreign service.

The Nazis and the Churches   The churches presented a different challenge. A concordat with the Vatican in 1933 gave the state some voice in the appointment of bishops while assuring the Church of its authority over Catholic orders and schools. Protestant denominations agreed to form a new body, the Evangelical Church, under a national bishop whom Hitler named; but when the bishop declared a need to "Aryanize" the church, dissidents formed the separate Confessional Church. The Minister for Church Affairs was authorized to confiscate ecclesiastical property, withhold funds, and have pastors arrested; but in practice the state kept religion in line more through the local harassment of individual clergy. Some priests and ministers cooperated with the regime—enthusiastically supporting war, race, and Reich. Most resisted at least the more outrageous demands made of them, and some individuals spoke out courageously. In 1937 Martin Niemoeller, the leader of the Confessional Church, was arrested for his opposition to Nazism; and Pope Pius XI condemned both the deification of the state and Nazi racial doctrine. In the following years some Catholic churches were burned, and members of religious orders were frequently tried on morals charges.

Anti-Semitism   Anti-Semitism was central to Nazi ideology and practice, and the Nuremberg laws of 1935 codified and extended previous regulations. Jews (anyone with one or more Jewish grandparents was consid-

GOEBBELS' POPULIST VIEW OF GERMAN CULTURE

As minister of propaganda in the German government, Joseph Goebbels was also president of the Reich Chamber of Culture, an organization divided into separate sections for the various arts and for film, radio, and the press. Artists had to belong in order to exhibit, perform, or be published. The speech quoted here was an address given by Goebbels to the annual Congress of the Chamber and of the Strength Through Joy organization held in Berlin in November 1937. Goebbels' efforts were at their peak, and he reported proudly on the campaign against decadent art (which included much of the modern art most admired today), on the abolition of art criticism, and on the new recreation homes for veterans and the elderly, saying, "Nothing similar has even been tried ever or anywhere else in the world."

"My Führer! Your excellencies!

"My racial comrades!

"Organization plays a decisive role in the lives of people. . . . For every organization must demand that its members surrender certain individual private rights for the benefit of a greater and more comprehensive law of life. . . .

"The purging of the cultural field has been accomplished with the least amount of legislation. The social estate of creative artists took this cleansing into its own hands. Nowhere did any serious obstructions emerge. Today we can assert with joy and satisfaction that the great development is once again set in motion. Everywhere people are painting, building, writing poetry, singing, and acting. The German artist has his feet on the ground. Art, taken out of its narrow and isolated circle, again stands in the midst of the people and from there exerts its strong influences on the whole nation.

". . . True culture is not bound up with wealth. On the contrary, wealth often makes one bored and decadent. It is frequently the cause of uncertainty in matters of the mind and of taste. Only in this way can we explain the terrible devastations of the degeneration of German art in the past. Had the representatives of decadence and decline turned their attention to the masses of the people, they would have come up against icy contempt and cold mockery. For the people have no fear of being scorned as out of step with the times and as reactionary by enraged Jewish literati. Only the wealthy classes have this fear. . . . These defects are familiar to us under the label 'snobbism.' The snob is an empty and hollow culture lackey. . . . He goes in black tie and tails to the theater in order to breathe the fragrance of poor people. He must see suffering, which he shudderingly and shiveringly enjoys. This is the final degeneration of the rabble-like amusement industry. . . . The Volk visits the theater, concerts, museums, and galleries for other reasons. It wants to see and enjoy the beautiful and the lofty. That which life so often and stubbornly withholds from the people . . . here ought to unfold before their eyes gleaming with astonishment. The people approach the illusions of art with a naïve and unbroken joyousness and imagine themselves to be in an enchanted world of the Ideal. . . . The people seek joy. They have a right to it.

". . . 'Hence bread and circuses!' croak the wiseacres. No: 'Strength Through Joy!' we reply to them.

"This is why we have thus named the movement for the organization of optimism. It has led all strata of the people by the million to the beauties of our country, to the treasures of our culture, our art, and our life. . . . The German artist of today feels himself freer and more untrammeled than ever before. With joy he serves the people and the state. . . . National Socialism has wholly won over German creative artists. They belong to us and we to them.

". . . In this hour, we all look reverently upon you, Führer, you who do not regard art as a ceremonial duty but as a sacred mission and a lofty task, the ultimate and mightiest documentation of human life."

From Salvator Attanasio et al. (trs.), "Speech of Goebbels," in George L. Mosse, *Nazi Culture: Intellectual, Cultural, and Social Life in the Third Reich*, Grosset & Dunlap, 1966.

ered a Jew) were declared to be mere subjects but no longer citizens. The Law for the Protection of German Blood and Honor prohibited marriage or sexual intercourse between Aryans and Jews, "Gypsies, negroes or their bastards." Subsequently, Jews were expelled from one activity after another, required to register with the state, and ordered to give their children identifiably Jewish names.

In 1938 the murder of a German diplomat by a young Jewish boy touched off a new round of terror. Many Jews were arrested, and the SS led an orgy of violence (named *Kristallnacht*, the "night of broken glass") in which Jews were beaten and murdered, their homes and businesses smashed, and synagogues burned. A fine of 1 billion marks was levied on the Jews of Germany, and they were barred from the theater and concerts, forbidden to buy jewelry, forced to sell their businesses or property, denied access to certain streets, and made to wear a yellow star. Worse would come.

For most Germans, life went on much as before but a little better, and there was a new excitement in the air. From the beginning, the Nazis' publicity had been flamboyant, their posters striking, and their rallies well staged; after the movement came to power, propaganda became a way of life. Torchlight parades, chorused shouts of *Sieg Heil!* ("Hail to victory!"), book burnings, the evocation of Norse gods, schoolyard calisthenics, the return to Gothic script—a thousand occasions offered Germans a feeling of participating, of being swept up and implicated in some great historical transformation. At the Reich Chamber of Culture, Joseph Goebbels saw to it that cinema, theater, literature, art, and music all promoted Nazism (see "Goebbels' Populist View of German Culture," p. 888). Things primitive and brutal were praised as Aryan; any who opposed or even doubted the Führer ceased to be German. For this new regime, warfare was its natural condition.

Stalin's Soviet Union

Communists held that dictatorship in the Soviet Union was incidental and supposedly temporary. The reality proved different. Communist rule became more systematically brutal and bloody after Lenin's death, but in the last decade historians have uncovered substantial evidence in newly opened Russian archives that Lenin had already laid the groundwork for such policies.

The Succession to Lenin   No one knew who Lenin's successors would be when he died in 1924 or even how the succession would be determined. For more than a year, Lenin had been ill and nearly incapacitated, but his prestige had precluded any public scramble for power, and many expected a more relaxed government by committee to follow. In a famous letter, Lenin had assessed two likely successors: Trotsky, whom he called overconfident but the best man in the Politburo, and Stalin, whom Lenin found "too rude" though an able organizer.

Over the next three years, Russia's leaders publicly debated complex issues of Communist theory and practical policy. Trotsky led those who clung to the traditional vision that revolution would spread across Europe, and he favored an uncompromisingly radical program at home and abroad. Stalin declared that the Soviet Revolution must survive alone, a "revolution in one country." No theoretician, and little informed about the world outside Russia, Stalin was not wholly at ease in these debates with more intellectual and experienced opponents. But they, in turn, underestimated his single-minded determination. When the Politburo formally adopted his position in December 1925, his victory rested on more than ideas.

The Rise of Stalin   As general secretary of the party's Central Committee, Stalin was the link between the Politburo and the party organization below it, and he could count on the loyalty of party officials, many of whom he had appointed. He played effectively on personal antagonisms and on resentment of Trotsky's tactless arrogance. When the Politburo elected three new members at that December meeting, all were Stalin's associates. He then effectively eliminated his opponents. When leading figures publicly sided with Trotsky, Stalin labeled the break in party solidarity a threat to communism. Trotsky and Grigori Zinoviev—the head of the Comintern, the organization of the Third International intended to lead communists around the world, whose prominence made him dangerous—were expelled from the Politburo in 1926 and from the party in 1927.

The left was broken, and the following year Zinoviev recanted his "mistake" in having supported Trotsky. Nikolai Bukharin, perhaps the party's subtlest theoretician and a leader of the right, recanted too. Trotsky, who refused to change his mind, was deported, continuing from abroad his criticism of Stalin's growing dictatorship. None of these veterans of the October Revolution had attempted to oust Stalin; even Trotsky, who built the Red Army, never tried to use it against him. Old Bolsheviks fervently accepted the need for party loyalty, and Stalin made sure that the open debates of those early years would not recur.

The First Five-Year Plan: Agriculture   In aims and enforcement, the First **Five-Year Plan** reflected some of the qualities that had brought Stalin to the top. It shamelessly incorporated ideas Stalin had denounced just months before, but it was thoroughly his in the bold assumption that Russia could be transformed into an industrial power by mobilizing every resource. By 1928, when the plan was launched, Russian production had regained prewar levels in most sectors. Lenin's New Economic Policy had depended heavily on private entrepreneurs in commerce and peasant owners in agriculture. The task now was to create a socialist economy, and the first step was to collectivize agriculture.

Using the improved techniques and the mechanization that peasants had on the whole resisted, Soviet agriculture could produce enough both to feed industrial workers and to export grain that in turn would pay for importing the machinery that industrialization required. The problem was that Russian peasants continued to withhold their goods from market when agricultural prices fell. Some 4 or 5 percent of them had the means to hire labor and lend money within their villages, which gave them a further hold over the local economy.

As famine threatened, the government mounted a sweeping campaign of propaganda and police action against these wealthier peasants, calling them *kulaks*—the old, pejorative term for grasping merchants and usurers. Their grain was seized (informers were given a quarter of any hoard uncovered), hundreds of thousands of people killed, and untold numbers deported to till the unbroken soil of Siberia. Peasants destroyed crops and animals rather than let the government have them.

The explosive antagonisms of rural society raged out of control, and Stalin had to intervene in 1930 to halt a virtual civil war. By then, more than half the peasants belonged to collective farms, but the strife had badly hurt production, which contributed to serious famine in 1932–1933. A kind of compromise followed. Even on collective farms peasants were permitted individual plots and privately owned tools. Larger machinery was concentrated at Machine Tractor Stations, which became the rural base for agricultural agents and party officials. By 1933 output was sufficiently reliable to permit the state to concentrate on the most massive and rapid industrialization in history.

The First Five-Year Plan: Industry According to the five-year forecast, industrial production was to double in less than five years, and in some critical areas, such as electrical power, it was to increase sixfold. More than 1,500 new factories were to be put into operation, including large automobile and tractor plants. Projects on a still grander scale included a Dnieper River power station and a great coal and iron complex in a whole new city, Magnitogorsk. These goals were met somewhat ahead of schedule, and there was only slight exaggeration in the government's proud claim to have made Russia an industrial nation almost overnight.

To pay for that achievement, indirect taxes were levied, wages allowed to increase only slightly, planned improvements postponed, peasants displaced, and peasant land collectivized. Food and most consumer items were rationed, with allotments varying according to one's contribution to the plan. Success required much more than money. Unskilled or poorly trained, laborers were unaccustomed to the pace now required: Turnover was high; output and quality, low. The state resorted to a continuous work week and moved special "shock brigades" of abler workers from plant to plant. Women and young people were urged into industrial jobs. "Socialist competition" pitted groups of workers and whole factories against each other for bonuses and prizes; piecework payment, once a hated symbol of capitalism, became increasingly common. Violators of shop rules were fined; malingering, pilfering, and sabotage (often loosely defined) became crimes against the state. "Corrective" labor camps, initially a mode of prison reform,

became another way to get more work done. Special courses within factories and enlarged technical schools trained new managers and engineers to replace the foreigners who were still essential to efficient industrial production.

In effect, an entire nation was mobilized, and the need for social discipline replaced an earlier emphasis on revolutionary enthusiasm. In schools, the formal examinations, homework, and academic degrees, recently abolished, began to return; classroom democracy gave way to greater authority for the teacher. The state stressed the importance of the family and praised the virtues of marriage, and the earlier emphasis on freedom for women gradually gave way to an emphasis on their contribution to Soviet productivity. Divorce was discouraged, and regulations on abortion, which had been legalized in 1920, became increasingly restrictive. Associations of writers, musicians, and artists worked on propaganda for the plan. Mass organizations of youth and workers met for indoctrination. Within the party, criticism or even skepticism was akin to treason. Hundreds of thousands of party members were expelled, and new recruits were carefully screened. "Overfulfillment" was triumphantly announced in 1932; the miracle of industrialization came with creation of a Russian totalitarianism.

Growth in the 1930s The Second (1933–1937) and Third (1938–1942) Five-Year Plans continued the push for industrialization at somewhat lower pressure. Consumer goods were more available, and rationing was eliminated by 1936. Standards of quality rose, and dramatic improvement in transportation, especially domestic aviation, made previously remote territories accessible. By 1939 Soviet Russia ranked third among the world's industrial producers behind only the United States and Germany, producing twenty-four times more electrical power and five times more coal and steel than in 1913. Literacy among people older than school age rose from below 50 percent in 1926 to more than 80 percent in 1939. As millions moved to cities, the number of higher schools, libraries, and hospitals doubled or tripled. In these years one-seventh of the population moved to the cities, making the country more urban than ever before. More than 90 percent of peasant households were on collective farms serviced by the Machine Tractor Stations.

Announcing that the stage of socialism had been reached, the Soviet Union adopted a new constitution in 1936. The changes it made were mainly formal. Direct voting by secret ballot replaced the cumbersome indirect elections for the Soviet of the Union. The other house, the Soviet of the Nationalities, represented the republics, which on paper had considerable autonomy. The two houses together elected the Coun-

Villagers watch with anticipation for the first light bulb in Bryansk Province to be switched on, an achievement of the First Five-Year Plan.
Novosti/Sovfoto

This Soviet poster of 1930 hails the International Day of Women Workers, part of the government's extended campaign to encourage women to work in factories.
Edimedia

cil of Ministers (the term *Commissars* thus passed away) as well as the Presidium, which legislated and whose chairman was head of state. The constitution recognized the Communist party as "the vanguard of the working people" and provided social and political guarantees that Communists hailed as the most democratic in the world. Ninety-six percent of the population voted in the next elections, 98 percent of them for the list the party presented.

Stalinism   A more confident government showed signs of relaxing its campaigns against potential enemies. Some political prisoners were amnestied in 1935, and a more controlled political police, the NKVD, replaced the sinister secret police. The campaign against religion abated. Opportunities for advancement in this expanding economy were great. White-collar classes got more respect, officers were restored to the army and navy, and supervisors were reinstalled in factories. Expression of opinion remained tightly controlled, however. Writers, Stalin commented ominously, were "engineers of human souls." Although harassed less than during the First Five-Year Plan, intellectuals had

long since learned the necessity of caution. The Russian Academy of Science, an important source of money and prestige, was never far from politics.

At the center of Soviet society stood Stalin, adulated as leader in every activity. Works of art were dedicated to him, factories named after him. His picture was everywhere. Patriotism overshadowed the socialist internationalism of an earlier generation, and Stalin was placed with Ivan the Terrible and Peter the Great as one of the molders of Russia. Although he held no official position other than party secretary, he demonstrated his awful power in the great purges of the late 1930s. Directed against engineers, Ukrainian separatists, former Mensheviks, and party members accused of being counterrevolutionaries, the purges were touched off by the assassination in 1934 of Sergei Kirov, a member of the Politburo who had been a close associate of Stalin's (in fact, Stalin himself was probably behind the assassination). Party and state mobilized to root out a great conspiracy. Zinoviev and members of the "left opposition" were twice tried for treason and were executed in 1937.

Other public trials followed: party leaders and army officers in 1937, members of the "right opposition," Nikolai Bukharin and other old Bolsheviks, in 1939. To the outside world, the indictments seemed vague and the evidence unconvincing. Yet the accused consistently confessed—the effect of torture perhaps, or the wish to protect their families, or maybe the final act of faith by men who were convinced of the inevitable course of history and believed that anyone resisting it was "objectively" a traitor. A reign of terror swept the country, feeding local vendettas until Stalin called a halt in 1939. The dead were countless; jails and labor camps were bursting with prisoners, perhaps 10 million. More than twice that many had gone into exile. Soviet totalitarianism had grown to be ominously like that of Germany and Italy, except for the values it professed.

THE DEMOCRACIES' WEAK RESPONSE

Confident Communist, Fascist, and Nazi regimes had moved dramatically to meet the challenge of the Depression and to forge social unity while tightening their hold on power. Europe's democracies responded more uncertainly, forever compromising and unable to disguise the social and ideological dissension that politics could not overcome.

Divisive Social Change

The Economy Economic recovery by the mid-1930s did not lessen these divisions, even though standards of living were rising again. Agriculture became more productive by becoming more mechanized and scientific, but those changes required increased capital (thus favoring larger holdings) and employed fewer laborers. Workers benefited from better transportation, mechanical refrigeration, cheaper clothes, and more leisure; but it took organized conflict for them to pry better wages from employers.

Many employees now enjoyed a shorter work week, but work itself was more subject to "American" efficiency on speeded-up assembly lines, forcing workers to repeat the same tasks at a pace set by factory managers (and known as Fordism, after the production methods of Henry Ford in Detroit). This form of production and the use of elaborate time and motion studies intended to reorganize work in ways that would further increase productivity (called Taylorism, after

studies by the American efficiency expert, Frederick W. Taylor) seemed to suggest that efficiency meant treating human beings like machines.

The middle classes recouped much that inflation and depression had undermined, but not their former confidence. While small businesses and craft industries remained insecure, larger corporations benefited first from the economic upturn and tended to form more powerful cartels, combining many firms within a single field so as to gain control of the entire production process from raw materials to marketing. And businesses large and small feared labor unions and socialist parties that were sounding increasingly militant.

Cultural Life Even cultural life lacked the healing qualities once expected of it. The scholars, scientists, and artists exiled from the new regimes in Russia, Italy, and Germany went to London, Paris, and especially the United States. They brought knowledge, methods, and artistic achievements that stimulated an explosion of creativity, and they brought their fears and disillusionment. Cultural movements seemed all the more foreign, politicized, and ideological. The new media did much to bridge the chasm between rural and urban life, but mass entertainment was not given to thoughtful discourse and moral uplift. The distinction between high and popular culture sharpened, and to many intellectuals culture itself was threatened as never before by the frothy commercialism of talking motion pictures and radio. Social scientists, poets, and novelists probed the theme of alienation, denounced faceless mass society, and engaged in radical politics.

In Paris, the Spanish painter Pablo Picasso became the dominant figure of twentieth-century art, restlessly experimenting with one new style after another. His most political work, *Guernica*, was a searing comment on war prepared for the Spanish pavilion at the Paris World's Fair of 1937 (see p. 893). Some artists defended the "experiments" of Hitler and Mussolini; far more joined Marxist groups, convinced that only socialism could create an acceptable society and preserve culture. The energy of the propaganda that advertised the transformation of Soviet society or the happy order, well-lit factories, and vacation resorts of Germany and Italy underscored the contrast between the ideologically coherent and purposeful societies of a single party and the aimless dislocation and dissension in the democracies.

The Argument for Liberty

Against the strident claims of radicals and fascists, four major groups of intellectuals—Marxists, Christian thinkers, liberals, and economists—expressed a revived commitment to freedom. The most prominent of these thinkers were the Marxists. The Russian Revolution

Pablo Picasso
Guernica, **1937**
Pablo Picasso used the still-new stylistic techniques he had mastered to protest the bombing of the Spanish town of Guernica by German planes in 1937. The huge, dark canvas, a political act in opposition to Franco and the Spanish Nationalists, foreshadowed modern warfare's brutal impact on civilian life. Kept in the United States for nearly fifty years, the painting can now be exhibited in a democratic Spain.
© 2005 The Estate of Pablo Picasso/Artists Rights Society (ARS), New York/Art Resource, NY

had enthralled millions of Europeans with visions of economic progress in a backward nation and of social equality and high culture in a mass society. This appeal grew as capitalist economies staggered, and it reached a peak with the promulgation of the Soviet constitution of 1936. At the same time, socialists and even communists insisted on the importance of justice, equality, and liberty, asserting that dictatorship in the Soviet Union was a special case.

Christians and Liberals

In Christian thought, traditional arguments against the idolatry of the state gained new meaning. The Protestant Karl Barth and the Catholic Jacques Maritain built on firm theological orthodoxy to stress the importance of individual freedom and social justice. Similar concerns emerged in the influential work of the Russian Orthodox Nikolai Berdyaev and the Jewish scholar Martin Buber.

From a more secular perspective, noted poets and novelists such as W. H. Auden, Thomas Mann, and André Malraux wrote powerfully in behalf of human dignity and social justice, warning of the dangers of power and the evils of war. Most vigorous in the politics and universities of Britain and France, liberals were also heard even in Fascist Italy. In his important *History of European Liberalism*, Guido de Ruggiero argued that liberal values, modified yet again, offered a practical path to stability and progress; and Benedetto Croce made liberty the central theme of his historical and philosophical writings.

Keynesian Economics

Economic theory also contributed to the argument for political freedom through the work of John Maynard Keynes, whose book *The General Theory of Employment, Interest, and Money* appeared in 1936. Keynes rejected classical views of economic man and the self-regulating economy. Few people, he argued, consistently act in their own financial interest, for no one is free of ideas, values, and tastes that shape actions. Nor do iron economic laws inexorably dictate a pattern of booms and busts. To Keynes, massive unemployment was not only intolerable but proof that capitalism must not be left to its own devices.

At the same time, he dismissed Marxism as outmoded. Instead, he offered a sophisticated theory that called on governments to smooth out the economic cycle. When the economy lagged, the government should lower interest rates to encourage production and should finance public works and social welfare to stimulate consumption. As the economy expanded, the opposite policies should check inflation and excessive speculation. Keynes advocated granting government a more active role while preserving free markets. In effect, he gave a theoretical foundation for practices already partially adopted under Swedish socialism, the French Popular Front (see later in this chapter), and the American New

Deal, President Franklin D. Roosevelt's program of social and economic reform inaugurated in 1933. An advocate of capitalism, Keynes defended it by denying that its social evils were inevitable; most capitalists denounced him as a socialist.

Few thinkers were neutral. With socialist anger, Auden, the British poet who chose to live in America, warned capitalists that "the game is up for you and for the others."[7] T. S. Eliot, the American poet who chose to live in Britain, proposed still tougher choices in a voice of Christian outrage: "The term 'democracy' . . . does not contain enough positive content to stand alone. . . . If you will not have God (and He is a jealous God) you should pay your respects to Hitler or Stalin."[8]

Domestic Politics

The Great Depression and rising international dangers undermined the traditional programs of democratic parties, left and right. Conservative parties pursued balanced budgets with results that embittered the unemployed. Liberals reluctantly accepted tariffs and subsidies that had few positive results. Socialists, weakened by competition from communists, antagonized workers by accepting weak welfare measures in the interest of better-balanced budgets. Issues of foreign policy had an even more paradoxical effect. Conservatives, historically supporters of military strength, were now inclined to downplay the dangers arising from Italy and Germany. Parties of the left, arguing that fascism must be resisted, tended to abandon their antimilitary rhetoric. As Finland and Czechoslovakia, whose economic growth and political freedom had made them models of the new postwar nations, felt the pressure from their stronger neighbors, the cause of democracy increasingly depended on Britain and France.

Cautious Compromise in Great Britain   Ramsay MacDonald became the British prime minister after a Labour victory in 1929. Following the advice of experts, he made drastic cuts in welfare and unemployment payments, measures that divided his own party. He then formed a national government with members from all three parties, in effect a conservative government in disguise, and was expelled from the Labour party amid bitter recriminations. His government adopted controls on foreign exchange and increased tariffs, policies that split the Liberals. When MacDonald resigned in 1935, tired and unloved, his coalition government had overseen a slow recovery of the British economy, redefined imperial relations, and initiated some cautious steps toward government planning. But it had done so by pursuing conservative policies, and it had devastated the proletarian movement to which MacDonald had devoted his life.

He was succeeded by Stanley Baldwin's Conservative government, his third time as prime minister. Baldwin campaigned as a strong supporter of the League of Nations, in which he actually had little interest; and, with a complacency that masked indecision, he steered clear of political extremes. The parliament elected with him, which would continue to sit through 1945 as the longest-lived in modern history, would later reveal a wealth of talent, testimony to the continued vitality of British political life.

In retrospect, even the crisis of 1936 could be seen as a comforting assertion of tradition. King Edward VIII, who had acceded to the throne, insisted on marrying an American divorcée. He was forced to abdicate, and the transition to George VI went smoothly, quelling talk of the end of the monarchy. At the time, however, British institutions appeared weak. As international affairs grew more ominous, Britain's uncertain foreign policy further undermined the capacity of continental states to resist the expansionist policies of Germany and Italy. Doubts about Britain's role increased in 1937 when Baldwin turned the prime ministership over to his earnest Chancellor of the Exchequer, Neville Chamberlain, who was convinced he could avoid the danger of war through caution and compromise.

Weak Government in France   France experienced the Depression later and less severely than other highly industrialized countries, but when the decline came, it lasted. The left won the legislative elections of 1932, as the economic slump began to be felt, but found it difficult to construct a reliable majority, for the Socialists refused to participate in bourgeois governments. The result was unstable governments committed to reducing expenditures and protecting established interests. Outside parliament, rightist factions, including the fascist Croix de Feu (Cross of Fire), grew increasingly noisy. On February 6, 1934, their uniformed militants led demonstrations against parliament that resulted in more bloodshed than Paris had seen since the Commune of 1871; many believe that the Third Republic nearly died that day. France seemed more bitterly divided than at any time since the Dreyfus affair at the turn of the century.

The exposure of a gigantic investment swindle perpetrated by one Serge Stavisky, who had important political connections, became the basis for a strident campaign against the republic by protofascist groups using the now familiar devices of uniforms, anti-

[7] W. H. Auden, "Consider This" and "In Our Time," in *A Little Treasury of Great Poetry*, Oscar Williams (ed.), New York: Charles Scribner's Sons, 1947, p. 689.

[8] T. S. Eliot, *The Idea of a Christian Society*, New York: Harcourt Brace, 1960.

Semitism, propaganda, and demonstrations. To meet the emergency, a former president of the republic, Gaston Doumergue, was recalled from retirement to take the premiership and empowered to govern by decree. The sober old man, supported by every party except the royalists and the Marxists, held office for nine calming months before giving way to a parliament that insisted on its prerogatives but little else.

The elections of 1936 brought a dramatic change. Moderate republicans, Socialists, and Communists formed an antifascist Popular Front (cooperation made possible by the decision of the Comintern directed from the Soviet Union to permit Communist alliances with other parties). Such rare solidarity brought the three parties a resounding victory and France its first Socialist premier, Léon Blum. He was a learned, humane intellectual and a Jew—attributes his enemies distrusted. Even as it took office, the new government faced a wave of strikes by workers determined to collect the fruits of their victory. They occupied factories, and many conservatives took that to be the revolution they dreaded. Eventually the strikes ended as the government pushed through legislation that provided for a general 12 percent increase in wages, two-week paid vacations, a forty-hour work week, and compulsory arbitration. Other reforms were soon added. Public works were launched, the Bank of France (long distrusted by the left) restructured, the arms industry nationalized, veterans given increased pensions, and small businesses offered subsidies. Each of these measures, like the devaluation of the franc, which in 1937 could no longer be avoided, frightened the business classes. New programs were hard to finance, and the economy proved more accessible to regulation than to stimulation. Blum's government—one of the Third Republic's most admired and most hated—had hardly begun the tax reforms its plans required when, after a year in office, it was defeated in the conservative senate. The Popular Front itself soon broke up. Subsequent governments were less daring amidst political feuds and public slander. Meanwhile, France's carefully constructed international position was collapsing.

The Failures of Diplomacy

The internationalism of the twenties had faded, and the sense of unreality in international affairs was underscored by the absence of the Soviet Union, which was effectively ostracized, and by the limited participation of the United States, which was absorbed in domestic affairs.

Italy and Germany Test Their Strength In October 1935 Italy invaded Ethiopia, seemingly an old-fashioned imperialistic venture preceded by carefully arranged understandings with Britain and France. But the racist propaganda and enthusiastic bombing of defenseless populations signaled something new. Europeans were shocked, and the League of Nations labeled Italy an aggressor and banned the sale to Italy of essential war materials. Most of Europe seemed united in this crucial test of the League's peacekeeping powers. Although the embargo angered Italy and caused some hardship, it did not stop the war, partly because the most important commodity of all, oil, was not included.

More important, some leaders in France and Britain considered Italy's friendship more important than the League, including the two foreign ministers: Pierre Laval, a slippery politician who had drifted steadily to the right, and Sir Samuel Hoare, an experienced conservative diplomat. Secretly, they arranged a settlement that would, in effect, give Italy most of Ethiopia. When the plan leaked to the press, public outrage forced both men to resign; but they had delayed efforts to add oil to the list of sanctions and undermined confidence in the two democracies. By May 1936, Ethiopia had capitulated, Italy could celebrate the lifting of the embargo, and all could see the ineffectiveness of the League of Nations.

Germany then began to exploit its opportunities. Everyone knew that Germany was rebuilding its fighting forces, and when German troops marched into the demilitarized Rhineland in 1936, there was no compelling international response. Italy this time did nothing. France, unwilling to act alone as it had in 1923, consulted the British, who urged acquiescence. The German troops were cheered by their countrymen in the Rhineland just as they had been the year before when France had turned over the Saar following a plebiscite overwhelmingly in favor of German rule. The fascist powers wanted radical changes in the international balance, and they had the initiative. Britain and France were internally divided, their leaders kept off balance by Germany's protests against the Versailles Treaty, by exuberant propaganda, and by shifting demands. Eastern European nations were torn between fear of the Soviet Union and fear of Germany.

The Spanish Civil War Civil war in Spain drove home the sense that all of Europe was divided between the fascist right and the Marxist left, destined for a life-and-death struggle. Spain had been a strife-torn nation since the end of World War I. In 1923 General Miguel Primo de Rivera assumed office as a de facto dictator and implemented a series of policies similar to the corporatist program of Mussolini. However, popular discontent, coupled with economic depression, forced Primo de Rivera into exile in 1930. In municipal elections held the following year, republicans and socialists triumphed, ushering in the second

Spanish republic. Meanwhile, political turmoil and violence continued as power shifted between leftist and conservative governments. The political climate became increasingly polarized, especially following the formation of the Falange—a movement modeled after Italian fascism—by José Antonio Primo de Rivera, the dictator's son. Finally, in July 1936, Spanish army officers stationed in Morocco rose up against the republic. The Spanish Civil War had begun.

General Francisco Franco soon emerged as their leader of the military revolt. The insurgent officers counted on support from Italy, Germany, and Portugal, where Antonio de Oliveira Salazar had already established his dominance over a single-party, corporative, conservative, and Catholic state. Little interested in doctrines or ideologies, Franco recognized the utility of a modern mass appeal and a disciplined movement. His supporters were called the Nationalists. Dominated by the army, they appealed to the monarchists and fascistic Falangists, to most of the clergy, and to all who favored desperate measures to escape from anarchy and communism. Italy and Germany quickly proffered their support and formed the Rome-Berlin Axis. Germany and Japan asserted their mutual sympathy and opposition to communism in the Anti-Comintern Pact. In addition to signing treaties, the fascist powers provided military support in the form of advisors, planes, tanks, and ammunition, as well as significant numbers of Italian troops. Mussolini welcomed the chance to enhance Italian prestige, and Hitler used the opportunity to test new German military technology. The Nationalist cause had become ideological and international.

The Spanish government's supporters included republicans, socialists, communists, anarchists, labor groups, and Catalan and Basque nationalists, a loose and badly split coalition. Known as the Loyalists, they saw themselves as the defenders of democracy against fascist aggression and of social justice against reaction; and they looked to the democracies for support. They received little except from the thousands of idealistic young men who went to Spain to fight as volunteers in national units like the Lincoln Brigade and the Garibaldi Brigade (which had its greatest moment when it defeated troops of the regular Italian army sent by Mussolini).

The Course of the Conflict　Among foreign nations, only the Soviet Union provided reliable, if limited, assistance to the Loyalists. Even this aid terminated in 1938, when Stalin decided to cut his losses. France, Britain, and the United States all adopted official policies of neutrality, even as aid to the Nationalists flowed in from Germany and Italy.

Foreign aid, trained troops, better military organization, and modern weapons made the victory of Franco's forces almost inevitable. They nearly won Madrid and the war itself in the summer of 1936, but the Loyalists held on and in a last-minute counterattack broke the Nationalists' assault. For more than two years, despite poor equipment and internal conflict, the republicans fought on, heartened by occasional victories. As the war progressed, the Loyalists became increasingly dependent on the Soviet Union for supplies, and that dependency plus the communists' organizational skills made them increasingly influential.

To the disgust of his Axis supporters, Franco conducted a war of attrition. Not until the spring of 1939, when Soviet supplies had ceased to come and Britain had signed special treaties of friendship with Italy, did the Spanish republic finally fall. Thousands of refugees wearily crossed into France while Franco filled Spain's capacious prisons with potential enemies, undid the republic's social measures, and restored the power of the Church over education. Franco then joined the Anti-Comintern Pact and took Spain out of the League of Nations. The civil war had taken more than a million Spanish lives, many at the hands of firing squads and mobs. The bombing of the town of Guernica by German aircraft in 1937 made people shudder before the vision of what war now meant for civilians, and the tales of atrocities on both sides fed the angry arguments between left and right throughout Europe and the United States. The one clear lesson was that the Western democracies, fearful and divided, had accepted defeat while the Axis acted.

Summary

For European societies the 1920s and 1930s were a period of innovation in cultural expression, social organization, and political mobilization. Where economic disaster, social failure, and political conflict were greatest, the response brought official ideologies, systematically enforced and apparently deeply believed. Using skillful mass propaganda disseminated on an unprecedented scale, governments found new ways to organize whole societies in the name of unanimity and efficiency, exercising powers rarely equaled even in wartime. That organization of society made the vague decencies of democracy with its social and ideological conflicts and the hypothetical opportunities of free markets seem limp in comparison. The anger, intolerance, and raw violence in European domestic life soon extended to international relations, creating a situation that clearly could not last. Optimists hoped that these crises might dissipate; pessimists could only wait for them to explode as states increased their military strength.

QUESTIONS FOR FURTHER THOUGHT

1. What are the significant similarities and differences between the revolutions in Russia and Italy, in the tactics that brought communists and fascists to power, and in the regimes they created?
2. On almost every front, cultural developments appeared to undermine established beliefs and values, but, looking back from today's perspective, is that a correct assessment?
3. Did the 1930s reveal inherent, and maybe universal, weaknesses in democracy and free markets or were those weaknesses the result of specific, and unusual, circumstances and the inadequacies of particular leaders?
4. Soviet Russia and Nazi Germany each set out to transform society and won fervent support at home and abroad. As models, each is now largely discredited, but are there aspects of their appeal and their policies that remain influential?

RECOMMENDED READING

Sources

*Adamthwaite, Anthony P. (ed.). *The Making of the Second World War.* 1979. A valuable collection of documents on the events and policies leading to war, with a useful introductory essay.

Ciano, Count Galiazzo. *Diary, 1937–1938.* 1952. *Diary, 1939–1943.* 1947. The diaries of Mussolini's son-in-law and, eventually, foreign minister are often self-serving, but they give a vivid picture of the intrigue and confusion at the center of the Fascist regime.

Engel, Barbara Alpern, and Anastasia Posadskaya-Vanderbeck (eds.). *A Revolution of Their Own: Voices of Soviet Women in Soviet History.* 1997. Interviews with eight women born before the Russian Revolution reveal the difficulties and gains experienced by women from different backgrounds under Russian communism.

Ortega y Gasset, José. *The Revolt of the Masses.* 1957. First published in 1932, this essay by one of Spain's leading philosophers and historians, an important work in its own right, is also a significant document of the disquiet that intellectual elites felt over the effects that increased specialization and mass society were having on the traditional culture of the West.

Reed, John. *Ten Days That Shook the World.* Available in many editions, this classic account of the Russian revolution was first published in 1922. John Reed went to Russia as a journalist and radical. His enthusiastic and perceptive report on the revolution captures both the excitement of the moment and the communist revolution's dramatic and international appeal.

Studies

Adamson, Walter. *Avant-Garde Florence: From Modernism to Fascism.* 1993. An insightful and provocative assessment of the links between prewar avant-garde literary movements and fascism.

*Allen, William S. *The Nazi Seizure of Power: The Experience of a Single German Town, 1930–1935.* 1965. A much-used microcosmic study.

*Arendt, Hannah. *The Origins of Totalitarianism.* 1958. This important study begins with a profoundly pessimistic application of hindsight to the imperialism and anti-Semitism of the late nineteenth century to make the case for Nazi totalitarianism as a phenomenon rooted in Western history.

*Bracher, Karl D. *The German Dictatorship.* Jean Steinberg (tr.). 1970. A major synthesis of work on the origins, structure, and impact of the Nazi movement.

*Bullock, Alan. *Hitler: A Study in Tyranny.* 1971. The best biography of Hitler and one that gives an effective picture of Nazi society.

Carr, Raymond. *The Civil War in Spain.* 1986. An unusually balanced study that puts the events of the war in the context of Spanish history and international relations.

Carsten, F. L. *The Rise of Fascism.* 1967. The careful synthesis of a distinguished scholar that looks at the varieties of fascist regimes.

Colton, Joel C. *Léon Blum: Humanist in Politics.* 1966. The biography of this appealing figure is particularly useful for the period of the Popular Front.

Fitzpatrick, Sheila. *The Russian Revolution, 1917–1932.* 1982. A valuable, fresh overview that emphasizes social conditions.

*Kershaw, Ian. *The Nazi Dictatorship: Problems and Perspectives of Interpretation.* 2000. A significant assessment that provides an excellent introduction to and interpretation of a vast literature.

*Kershaw, Ian, and Moshe Lewin (eds.). *Stalinism and Nazism: Dictatorships in Comparison.* 1997.

Kindleberger, Charles P. *The World in Depression, 1929–1939.* 1973. A study of the origins of the Depression and of responses to it in different countries.

*Kolb, Eberhard. *The Weimar Republic.* P. S. Falla (tr.). 1988. A comprehensive account of the difficulties and failures of Germany's experiment with democracy.

Koonz, Claudia. *Mothers in the Fatherland: Women, the Family, and Nazi Politics.* 1987. Shows the importance of gender policies to Nazi ideology and rule.

Lee, Stephen J. *The European Dictatorships: 1918–1945.* 1987. A comprehensive and systematic comparison of Communist Russia, Fascist Italy, and Nazi Germany.

Mack Smith, Denis. *Mussolini.* 1981. An informed, skeptical account by the leading English scholar of modern Italy.

*Nolte, Ernst. *Three Faces of Fascism.* Leila Vennewitz (tr.). 1965. A learned effort to place the intellectual history of fascism in France, Germany, and Italy in the mainstream of European thought.

Peukert, Detlev J. K. *Inside Nazi Germany: Conformity, Opposition, and Racism in Everyday Life.* 1987. Makes use of a great deal of recent research to explore the effects of Nazi tyranny on ordinary life and the difficulties of opposition to it.

*Pipes, Richard. *The Formation of the Soviet Union.* 1964. A clear, comprehensive, and very critical treatment of Soviet rule.

Tannenbaum, Edward R. *The Fascist Experience: Italian Society and Culture, 1922–1945.* 1972. A wide-ranging effort to recapture the meaning in practice of Fascist rule.

Thompson, John M. *Revolutionary Russia, 1917.* 1989. A good overview of what the revolution meant for ordinary life throughout the country.

*Ulam, Adam B. *Lenin and the Bolsheviks.* 1969. Combines the study of ideas and of policy to explain Lenin's triumph.

Weinberg, Gerhard L. *The Foreign Policy of Hitler's Germany.* 1970. A major study by a leading American diplomatic historian that helps explain Hitler's early successes.

*Available in paperback.

Leonard Henry Rosoman
A HOUSE COLLAPSING ON TWO FIREMEN, SHOE LANE LONDON EC4
This painting of a collapsing building captures the frightful devastation of aerial bombardment during World War II. The scene could have occurred in dozens of cities across Europe, such as Warsaw, Rotterdam, Liverpool, Hamburg, Dresden, or (in this case) London.
The Art Archive/Imperial War Museum

Chapter Twenty-Nine

THE NIGHTMARE: WORLD WAR II

THE YEARS OF AXIS VICTORY • THE GLOBAL WAR, 1942–1945
• BUILDING ON THE RUINS • EUROPEAN RECOVERY

World War II was the centerpiece of a long trial of European civilization. The outbreak of war followed a series of international crises, but in a larger sense it resulted from the kinds of governments brought to power by the social tensions of the era. For more than a decade a kind of ideological civil war undermined established institutions and exposed every weakness in the social fabric. New communist, fascist, and Nazi regimes carried those conflicts into international affairs, challenging the status quo and the democracies that defended it. The result was World War II, a war more total and more worldwide than its predecessor.

The war required massive organization, challenged national economies, and altered social relations. At first Germany gained everywhere, its preparations farther along, its tactics more ruthless. Slowly the Allies gained the upper hand, and the terrors of the battlefield were exceeded by the deliberate, systematic horrors of genocide, torture, and concentration camps. When peace finally came, Europe was a continent devastated, where millions had lost homes, family, health, and hope. It was a struggle just to make society function, and the achievement of stability and prosperity by the 1950s was a European miracle.

1935   1940   1945

Nuremberg trials of Nazi war criminals; fourth French Republic launched **1946** ●

Yalta Conference; Germany surrenders; socialist government elected in Britain; atomic bombing of Japan **1945** ●

Allied invasion of Normandy **1944** ●

Germans defeated at Stalingrad **1943** ●

Hitler invades USSR; Pearl Harbor **1941** ●

1947 —●
Berlin blockade; Marshall Plan; Indian independence

Fall of France **1940** ●

1939 ●
Hitler-Stalin Pact; outbreak of World War II

● **1938** Munich Agreement (height of appeasement)

THE YEARS OF AXIS VICTORY

The civil war in Spain had made the international situation frighteningly clear. Germany and Italy were allied, rearming, and aggressive. France and Britain, reluctantly rearming, still hoped to avoid war. The countries of Eastern Europe were effectively paralyzed, and the Soviet Union was an enigma, for no one knew whether it would eventually take sides or could fight effectively if it did. Once war began, German forces went from victory to victory.

The Path to War

For eighteen months Hitler orchestrated a series of escalating demands that culminated in the outbreak of World War II in September 1939.

The Anschluss   In February 1938, with the outcome of civil war in Spain still uncertain, Hitler began to pressure Austria. He summoned the Austrian chancellor, Kurt von Schuschnigg, to the Führer's secluded mountain retreat at Berchtesgaden and subjected him to a humiliating harangue. Schuschnigg promised to include Austrian Nazis in his cabinet. On returning home, he felt braver and decided to hold a plebiscite in the hope that public opinion would rally to save Austria's independence. Hitler, furious, massed the German army on the Austrian border, and Schuschnigg realized his position was hopeless. He had previously disbanded the Socialist party, the strongest opponent of union with Germany, and Italy warned that this time it would not oppose the German moves as it had a few years earlier. The friendless Austrian chancellor was replaced by a Nazi, who invited German troops to restore order. They did so on March 13, and Nazis indulged in the brutal public humiliation of Viennese Jews and in-

tellectuals. Within a month Austria's annexation to Germany was almost unanimously approved in a plebiscite run by the Nazis. The dream of union with Germany, *Anschluss,* had been fulfilled. Hitler's popularity at home rose still higher, and German influence spread more deeply into the Balkans. Britain and France merely protested.

Czechoslovakia   Two weeks after the Austrian plebiscite, Hitler demanded autonomy for the Sudetenland, an overwhelmingly German-speaking section of Czechoslovakia (see map 29.1). Once again, the claims that the Versailles settlement had been unfair and that Germans were being abused rallied support at home and weakened opposition abroad. Although this challenge to the Czech republic was far more daring— Czechoslovakia was a prosperous industrial state protected by a respectable army, well-fortified frontiers, and mutual-aid treaties with both France and Russia— the parallel with Austria was lost on no one. Supported by its allies, Czechoslovakia mobilized, and Hitler ordered the Sudeten Nazis to quiet down. But Czechoslovakia was vulnerable, and Hitler was adept at fanning ethnic resentments. The republic, dominated by the more prosperous Czech region, was barely able to maintain the loyalty of the Slovaks; a pro-Nazi party had won more votes than any other in the 1935 elections, and the great powers remained divided. Britain's prime minister, Neville Chamberlain, wanted to parlay directly with Germany, believing that no nonnegotiable British interest was at stake in the Sudetenland. Many in France and England, deeply alarmed at how close to war they were, doubted that fighting for Czechoslovakia's sovereignty over a German population was worth the risk. Throughout the summer, Sudeten Nazi leaders negotiated with the Czech state in an atmosphere heated by demonstrations there and in Germany.

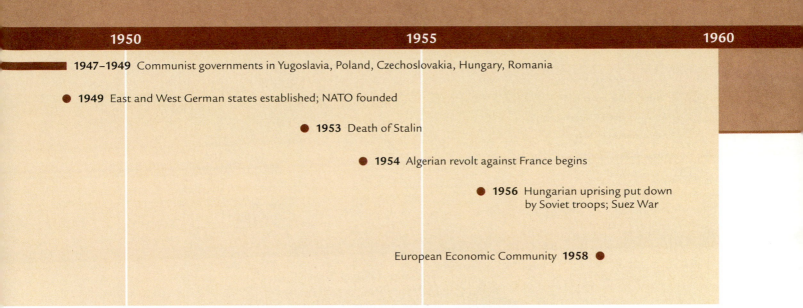

1950	1955	1960

1947–1949 Communist governments in Yugoslavia, Poland, Czechoslovakia, Hungary, Romania

● **1949** East and West German states established; NATO founded

● **1953** Death of Stalin

● **1954** Algerian revolt against France begins

● **1956** Hungarian uprising put down
by Soviet troops; Suez War

European Economic Community **1958** ●

Hitler and Mussolini on the way to the train station after the Munich conference. Count Galeazzo Ciano, the Italian foreign minister, is on Hitler's left; Hermann Göring is on Mussolini's right; General William Keitel, Rudolf Hess, and Heinrich Himmler are among those behind them.
Ullstein Bilderdienst

In August, Chamberlain, with French concurrence, sent his own emissary to mediate while German troops held maneuvers on the Czech border, and Hitler pointedly toured Germany's fortifications in the west. Hitler's speeches became more bellicose, and Chamberlain decided, once again with French support, to visit the Führer at Berchtesgaden. When they met on September 15, Hitler raised the stakes, demanding that Germany annex the Sudetenland. Britain and France advised Czechoslovakia to submit. Desperately, the Czechs sought some escape, but only the Soviet Union was ready to support Czech resistance. In a week Chamberlain flew back to Germany with the good news that Czechoslovakia had agreed to Hitler's terms, only to find them changed again: German troops must occupy the ceded territory immediately. The Czechs would have no time to move factories and military supplies or provide for citizens who wished to evacuate. A shocked Chamberlain said no, and for five days the world listened for war.

The Munich Agreement Then Mussolini persuaded Hitler to meet with the Duce and the prime ministers of Britain and France. They met on September 29, 1938, in Munich, where just fifteen years earlier Hitler had failed to capture the town hall. Now he dealt in terms of

903

MAP 29.1 EUROPE ON THE EVE OF WORLD WAR II
◆ For an online version, go to www.mhhe.com/chambers9 > chapter 29 > book maps

nations. During an afternoon and evening of discussions, Hitler was granted all he asked. Neither the Soviet Union nor Czechoslovakia was consulted. The next day Czechoslovakia submitted to Hitler's terms and accepted last-minute demands from Poland and Hungary for additional pieces of Czechoslovak territory that they had long coveted. At a single stroke, Czechoslovakia surrendered one-third of its population, its best military defenses, and much of its economic strength. Central Europe's strongest democracy was reduced to a German dependency, and a keystone of France's continental security was shattered. As the French prime minister's plane circled the Paris airport on his return from Munich, he watched the crowd below with dread. But it cheered him, and in Britain, Chamberlain became a hero. Peace, the newspapers trumpeted, had been preserved.

Poland and the Hitler-Stalin Pact German might, Hitler's speeches, virulent anti-Semitism, goose-stepping troops marching through central Europe, and news of what life was like in the newly annexed lands and in Germany itself—all gave Jews, ethnic groups the Nazis labeled inferior, peoples living along the German borders, and whole nations reason to be terrified. Early in 1939 German troops occupied Czechoslovakia and annexed the seaport of Memel from a frightened Lithuania. The pretext of absorbing only German peoples had now been abandoned.

Well-coordinated armored and mechanized infantry units spearheaded Germany's *blitzkrieg* (lightening war) against Poland.
AP/Wide World Photos

Chamberlain, believing that not even Nazis could want world war, was one of many in Europe who hoped concessions would appease Hitler; but most people in England and France had finally become resigned to the fact that Germany could only be stopped by force. Italy, inspired by Hitler's success, began a noisy campaign to get Nice and Corsica from France and in the summer of 1939 invaded and annexed Albania. The Rome-Berlin Axis was formally tightened into the "Pact of Steel," and Germany kept European chancelleries quaking with demands for nonaggression pacts. Late in August the leader of the Nazi party in German-speaking Danzig declared that his city, which the Versailles treaties had assigned to Poland, must be returned to the fatherland. The denunciations of the Versailles boundaries that poured from Germany, along with claims that Germans living within the Polish corridor were being persecuted, made it clear that Poland was next. As they had all summer, Britain and France renewed their pledges to protect Poland.

The summer's most important contest was for some alliance with the Soviet Union, and Hitler won that, too. Germany and the Soviet Union announced a nonaggression pact. The USSR had made overtures to Britain and France, suggesting that the territorial integrity of all the states between the Baltic and Black seas be guaranteed. The Western powers, reluctant to grant a communist nation such extensive influence, had responded weakly. Since 1935 the Soviet Union had advocated disarmament, supported the League of Nations, supplied Loyalist Spain, and offered support to Czechoslovakia, but Stalin feared that the democracies would welcome a war between Germany and the Soviet Union. In May 1939 he replaced his foreign minister, Maxim Litvinov, the eloquent spokesman for a pro-Western policy, with Vyacheslav Molotov, a tougher old ally. Hitler offered the Soviet Union a free hand in Finland, Estonia, Latvia, eastern Poland, and part of Romania should Germany seek any changes in its own eastern border. That became the basis for a nonaggression pact between the international sponsor of antifascist fronts and the creators of the Anti-Comintern Pact, a masterpiece of cynicism (and very old-fashioned diplomacy) that shocked a world still unaccustomed to totalitarian opportunism.

The last days of August resounded with formal warnings and clarifications from the major powers. On September 1, Germany invaded Poland. Britain and France mobilized, sent Germany an ultimatum, and declared war on September 3, 1939. One year after surrendering democratic Czechoslovakia, they would fight for authoritarian Poland.

The Last European War, 1939–1941

One argument for the policy of **appeasement** was that it had enabled Britain and France to buy time. They had been vigorously strengthening their armed forces, and the domestic consensus that war required was slowly taking shape. But much remained to be done; Germany had gained, too, in territory and power, and now there was no time left.

Blitzkrieg and Phony War   For two years the Axis scored one victory after another. Having carefully prepared the invasion, Germany attacked Poland with overwhelming force in September 1939, the first ***blitzkrieg,*** or "lightning war." Poland fell in less than a month, and Hitler suggested that the war could now end. Few were tempted by his hints of peace. Concerned to strengthen its frontiers against Germany, the Soviet Union attacked Finland in November and met such fierce resistance that the war lasted until the following spring. Having regained boundaries close to those of the last tsars, Russia could afford to wait. The Western powers had been waiting, too. Hitler refrained from attacking along the French border, and the Allied commanders resolved not to risk precious planes too soon or to repeat the pointless assaults of World War I. This was the period of the so-called phony war, during which arms production and mobilization speeded up, the world waited, and little happened. The strain was bad for morale.

With the Soviet Union standing aside from the conflict, French communists now said the war was a mistake; their party was suppressed. Paul Reynaud, energetic and determined, replaced Daladier as premier, and the Allies prepared to defend Norway, an obvious German target. But on April 9, 1940, Germany attacked Denmark, taking it in a day, and captured Norway's most important strategic points in short order, giving Germany bases for numerous assaults on British ships and cities. In Britain, Chamberlain resigned after a wide-ranging and often angry parliamentary debate, and Winston Churchill became prime minister of an all-party government on the day that the Germans attacked on the Western front. A Conservative who believed in empire and an opponent of appeasement, Churchill was a political maverick given his chance in the face of disaster. His decisiveness and eloquence made him one of England's greatest leaders.

The Fall of France   On May 10, and without warning, German troops flooded the Netherlands and Belgium. The Dutch, who had expected to escape this war as they had all others since the Napoleonic wars, surrendered in five days. The better-prepared and larger Belgian army held out for eighteen days. On May 14 a skillfully executed German offensive broke through the Ardennes forest, thought to be impervious to tanks, reached Sedan, and drove to the English Channel, trapping the Belgian and British forces fighting there along with much of the French army. The German air force, the Luftwaffe, controlled the skies, and the Allies' proudest achievement in the battle for France was the evacuation from the port town of Dunkirk of 340,000 troops pinned against the sea. They left for Britain in a motley flotilla of naval vessels, commercial ferries, and

French refugees with all the possessions they can carry clog the roads, expecting to be able to escape the German armies in 1940 as their parents had twenty-five years before.
Roger-Viollet/Getty Images

private sailboats, a symbol of heroism and inferior preparation.

The Allied defense of France was broken. German forces renewed the attack on June 5 and took Paris in a week. Anxious lest he miss the war entirely, Mussolini attacked France on June 10. France surrendered on June 16, 1940. The armistice was signed in the railway car used for Germany's surrender in 1918. More ironic still, the man who chose to sign for France was the World War I hero of Verdun, Marshal Henri Philippe Pétain.

Germany's Victory over France   Hitler seemed invincible and the blitzkrieg some terrible new Teutonic force, a totalitarian achievement other societies could not hope to equal. In fact, however, many of the tactical ideas on which it rested were first put forward by British and French experts, including a French officer, Charles de Gaulle. The blitzkrieg was the result not so much of new technology as new strategy. It combined air attacks with rapid movements of motorized columns to overcome the advantages that defensive positions had previously enjoyed. Tanks roared through and behind enemy lines, a maneuver requiring speed and precision that were alien to older theories. In the flat terrain of Poland, Germany's panzer tank divisions quickly encircled the enemy; in France, they often assaulted troops so far in the rear that they were not yet prepared for battle. The aim was less to capture ground than to break up communications. Then the Germans used air power to disorient and terrify the retreating army. The strafing of French roads clogged with civilian refugees and the bombing of Rotterdam had their place in the campaign to demoralize.

French strategy had relied too much on the defensive strength of the Maginot Line, a system of fortifications extending from the Belgian border to Switzerland, and on the assumption that Germany would respect the neutrality of Belgium and the Netherlands. The French had numerous tanks of their own but had been slow to deploy them; their air force was momentarily weakened because it was changing models. During the phony war, morale sagged with memories of the previous war and policy was undermined by politics rife with suspicion of the British, of the army, of the politicians, and of the left. Pétain, who believed France must now make its way in Hitler's Europe, blamed the Third Republic, and for a moment the nation turned to the octogenarian marshal with stunned unanimity.

He accepted terms of surrender that put three-fifths of the country under Nazi occupation and allowed 1.5 million French prisoners of war to be kept in Germany. The unoccupied southeastern part of France could have its own government, and that was established at Vichy. There, a reconvened parliament maneuvered by Pierre Laval named Pétain chief of state. The new regime, known as Vichy France, relied on a confused coalition of militant fascists and the traditional right and would never really be independent of Germany. After adopting bits of corporatism and some fascist trappings, it settled into a lethargy of its own, an often willing collaborator in Hitler's new order, ruling a truncated state as rife with intrigue, personal ambition, and shifting alliances as the Third Republic it so heartily denounced.

The Battle of Britain

Great Britain now stood alone. Unprepared for such enormous victories so soon, German officers planned their invasion of Britain while, beginning in June 1940, their bombers roared over England in sustained attacks that many believed would be enough to force surrender. Instead, in September the projected invasion was postponed, while the air attacks continued. The German navy had suffered enough damage in encounters with the British to favor caution, and by the next spring even the air raids were letting up.

Londoners sheltering in an underground subway station from the lethal destruction and sleep-destroying din of the German "Blitz" in 1940–1941.
© Corbis

The waves of German planes flying across the channel sustained losses far greater than those of Britain's Royal Air Force. British fighter planes, particularly the newer designs, proved at least the equal of the German; and they were aided by new techniques of antiaircraft defense, including radar, an English development that was the most critical addition to military technology in these years. At first the air raids concentrated on ports and shipping, then on airfields, and finally on cities, leaving great burning holes in London and completely destroying the industrial city of Coventry. But the diversity of targets dissipated the economic and military effects of the bombing, and the terror from the skies seemed to raise morale in a nation ever better organized and more fiercely determined to carry on. Merely to survive from June 1940 to June 1941 was a kind of victory in what Churchill memorably called Britain's "finest hour."

The Balkans

With all the Continent from Norway to Sicily and the Atlantic in their own hands or under friendly dictators in Spain and Portugal, the Axis powers looked eastward. In October 1940 Italian forces moved from Albania into Greece only to be pushed back, and Hitler had to bail out Mussolini by sending

The invading Germans laid siege to Moscow and Leningrad but finally met unyielding resistance. Soviet troops often engaged the enemy in ferocious close-quarter combat.
The Art Archive

in German troops and further squeezing the Balkan states, which were rapidly losing their independence. In June 1940 the Soviet Union, stretching the terms of its pact with Germany, took Bessarabia from Romania. Hungary and Bulgaria then took some of Romania for themselves, and Hitler announced that he would protect the rest of the country. In fact, all three Eastern European nations, already implicated in Hitler's mapmaking, were closely tied to Germany. It was no great step for them to join the Axis, welcome German troops in March 1941, and cooperate with Germany in invading Yugoslavia (which had hesitated too long over whether to join the Axis) and in attacking Greece, which had fought Mussolini too well.

The invasion was launched in April 1941 and swept through both countries within the month. Some Greek and British forces pulled back to Crete, only to be forced out almost immediately by German gliders and paratroops. The Allies retreated to Egypt, where British forces had held off an attack from Italy's neighboring colony of Libya. The Axis now threatened to dominate the Mediterranean, too.

The Invasion of the Soviet Union Having conquered so much, Hitler decided to complete his domination of the Continent. On June 22 German forces attacked the Soviet Union. The Soviets had long feared such a move, yet they appeared genuinely surprised, at least by the timing and the size of the German invasion. The assault, in three broad sectors, was the largest concentration of military power that had ever been assembled, and once more the blitzkrieg worked its magic. Germany's armored divisions ripped through Russian lines

and encircled astonishing numbers of troops. It looked to many observers as if the Soviet Union might collapse. Stalin, apparently in a state of shock, was silent for the first week after German forces invaded the Soviet Union. Finally, on July 3, 1941, he spoke by radio to the Soviet people. His address acknowledged initial defeats, invoked the example of Russian victories over invaders in the past, and emphasized that the Allies were fighting together against Nazi tyranny. But he also called in striking detail for ordinary citizens to continue the fight by destroying anything that might be helpful to the invaders (which became known as the "scorched earth" policy) and by constant sabotage.

German armies crossed the lands Russia had acquired since 1939, taking Riga and Smolensk in July, reaching the Dnieper in August, claiming Kiev and the whole Ukraine in September. Then the pace slowed, but while one German force lay siege to Leningrad in the north, a second hit Sevastopol in the south and moved into the Crimea. By December still another had penetrated to the suburbs of Moscow. There the German advance stopped temporarily, halted by an early and severe winter, by strained supply lines, and (at last) by sharp Russian counterattacks. The territory now held by Germany had accounted for nearly two-thirds of Russia's production of coal, iron, steel, and aluminum, as well as 40 percent of its grain and hogs.

As the war engulfed all of Europe,[1] German power at the end of 1941 was at its height, encompassing between 7 and 10 million soldiers, a superb air force, and a navy

---

[1]Only Sweden, Spain, Portugal, Switzerland, and Eire remained even technically neutral by grace of geography.

MAP 29.2 THE HEIGHT OF AXIS POWER, 1942
After the sweeping Axis conquests depicted in this map, the Battle of Britain (the struggle for supremacy in the air) thwarted Hitler's next invasion plan. But in actually turning the tide, how crucial do you suppose were the battles of El Alamein in North Africa and Stalingrad in Russia?
◆ For an online version, go to www.mhhe.com/chambers9 > chapter 29 > book maps

that included more than 150 submarines, which would sink nearly 400 Allied ships in the summer of 1942. Italy added sizable forces that were especially important in Africa. And yet Axis dominance was short-lived.

THE GLOBAL WAR, 1942–1945

From the 1930s on, the fascist powers had held the initiative in politics, international relations, and war. Germany's invasion of the Soviet Union extended the war across Europe and the Allied retreat carried it to North Africa. Japan's attack on the United States in 1941 continued the pattern of Axis surprises, but it also marked the beginning of a significant change. War in the Pacific made this a truly global war—involving Asia, the Middle East, and North Africa—and the addition of American power helped tip the balance toward the Allies, whose industrial capacity was far greater than their enemies'. Axis propaganda was losing effect in the face of the realities of German rule, which gave weight to Allied claims that they were fighting for civilization as Russia, the Americas, and the British Empire set out to reconquer Europe.

The Turn of the Tide

The United States Enters the War Despite its deep partisanship for France and Britain, the United States had remained technically at peace, even as the American government sold weapons to private firms for transfer to Great Britain and traded fifty old American destroyers for the lease of British bases in the western Atlantic. The United States, which Roosevelt called "the arsenal of democracy," also extended loans to Britain and then the Soviet Union. In August, Churchill and Roosevelt met at sea to draft the Atlantic Charter, which envisioned a world "after the destruction of the Nazi tyranny" that included collective security and self-determination for all nations, a world in which "all the men of all the lands may live out their lives in freedom from fear and want."

Ideological commitment, however, did not bring the United States into the war. Japan did that. Its attack on Manchuria in 1931 had been followed by a series of aggressive actions, from war with China starting in 1937 to the conquest of French Indochina in 1941. Tension between the United States and Japan increased with each new act of Japanese aggression, and America replied to the assault on Indochina with sanctions. Anticipating more, Japan gambled that the United States could be rendered nearly harmless in one blow, an attack on the American Pacific fleet at Pearl Harbor. The raid, on December 7, was devastating, and the United States declared it an act of war. All sides immediately recognized that the wars in Asia, Europe, and North Africa were one. Germany and Italy declared war on the United States three days later. Unless the Allies were driven from the seas, the industrial and military power of the United States might make a decisive difference in a war fought around the world.

Stalingrad Winter snows raised the specter of a continuing two-front war for Germany, which Hitler had sworn to avoid. For all its losses, Russia's Red Army was intact, and its scorched-earth policy in retreat left the German army little to live on. To secure its massive victories, Germany had to knock Russia out of the war. But the siege of Leningrad, the attacks on Moscow, and even a drive into southern Russia in the summer of 1942 that took Sevastopol (and desperately needed grain) did not accomplish that goal. The crucial battle of the Eastern front began around **Stalingrad** (now Volgograd) in August 1942. A breakthrough for the Germans at that strategic center would open the way to the oilfields of southern Russia.

By September the Germans had penetrated the city and fighting continued from building to building. The heroic defense gave Russia time to amass more troops than the Germans thought were available, and in the

CHRONOLOGY *Major Moments of World War II*	
March 1938	*Anschluss:* Germany annexes Austria.
September 1938	Munich Agreement, Germany takes Sudetenland.
August 1939	Hitler-Stalin Pact.
September 1939	Germany invades Poland; beginning of World War II.
April 1940	Germany invades Denmark, Norway.
May 1940	Germany invades Belgium, France, Netherlands.
June 1940	France surrenders.
October 1940	Italy invades Albania and Greece.
April 1941	Romania, Bulgaria, Hungary, and Germany invade Yugoslavia.
June 1941	Germany invades the USSR.
August 1941	Atlantic Charter.
December 1941	Japan attacks Pearl Harbor.
August 1942–February 1943	Battle of Stalingrad.
November 1942	Allies land in North Africa.
July 1943	Allies land in Sicily; Mussolini ousted.
November–December 1943	Teheran Conference.
June 1944	Allies land in Normandy.
February 1945	Yalta Conference.
May 1945	Germany surrenders.
July–August 1945	Potsdam Conference.
August 1945	U.S. drops atomic bombs and Japan surrenders.

meantime Germany's supplies dwindled. A Russian counterattack encircled the German army, which Hitler frantically ordered to stand its ground. When it finally surrendered, in February 1943, fewer than one-third of its 300,000 men were left. The giant Russian pincers had cost the Germans more than half a million casualties. Stalingrad was the turning point of the war on the Eastern front.

Strategic Bombing and the Invasion of North Africa
In the West, too, the Axis position was eroding. The

American servicemen survey the ruins on an airfield at Pearl Harbor; the United States had entered the war.
National Archives

losses that German submarines inflicted were less crippling after 1942, and Allied air supremacy extended to the Continent, where thousands of tons of explosives were dropped on Germany each month in 1942, a rate that would increase fivefold in 1943. The Americans bombed strategic targets during the day; the British preferred nighttime area bombing, with a city itself as the target. The inferno created by the firebombing of Hamburg in 1943 was a horror to be exceeded two years later in a yet more massive raid that leveled Dresden, a cultural center without important industry. Meanwhile, the Germans were unaware that the secret codes they believed unbreakable had been cracked in London as early as 1940, giving the Allies an advantage that would grow as the war progressed.[2]

[2]The code was cracked in a project named Ultra, using devices that foreshadowed the computer. The secret of Ultra was not revealed until long after the war, and historians are still assessing its impact. The information that the Allies gained through Ultra appears to have been especially important in the Battle of Britain, the protection of Atlantic shipping, later in the war in Egypt, and in the Normandy landing.

The Allies also regained control of the Mediterranean. Fighting had spread to Libya as soon as Italy entered the war, and battle lines then ebbed and flowed as each side balanced military needs elsewhere against the chance for victory in North Africa. In April 1941 Germany sent significant reinforcements, and General Erwin Rommel, the German "desert fox," began a drive toward the Egyptian border. In October 1942 his *Afrikakorps* reached El Alamein but was defeated there, allowing Britain's General Bernard Montgomery to launch a counteroffensive as British and American forces landed in Morocco and Algeria. That November invasion, the largest amphibious action yet attempted, and the campaign that followed was an important test of green American troops and of Allied coordination under an American commander, General Dwight D. Eisenhower. It succeeded. By May 1943, after heavy losses, the Axis powers had been pushed out of Africa.

Halting the Japanese Advance in the Pacific After costly stands at Bataan and Corregidor, the United States lost the Philippine Islands early in 1942. By March, the Japanese had conquered Malaya and the

Dutch East Indies (today's Indonesia), defeating the British and the Dutch in costly naval and land battles. The fall of Singapore, Britain's Pacific naval bastion, was a crippling blow. The rest of the war against Japan would be fought primarily by Australia and the United States. Stopping further Japanese expansion in the summer of 1942 was thus an important turning point. Although a naval engagement in the Coral Sea in May brought no clear-cut victory to either side, the United States was better able than Japan to replace its losses. A month later the Japanese suffered heavy losses of aircraft carriers at Midway in a naval battle they had sought.

In August American forces launched a relatively small invasion of their own in the Solomon Islands. Each side poured in reinforcements, and the fighting on Guadalcanal, which was especially bloody, continued for six months before the Japanese were defeated. The war was far from won, but these victories ended the threat that Japan might invade Australia or cut off supply lines from India to the Middle East. The Allies could feel comfortable with their agreement that the war in Europe should have priority—an acknowledgement of fear that the Soviet Union might not survive without massive help, of the importance of European industrial power, and of the bonds of Western culture.

Competing Political Systems

War on this scale required the coordination of entire economies and cooperation from every sector of society. After their slow start, Britain and the United States achieved that with impressive effect. The Soviet Union proved far stronger than expected, and Germany, the state that in theory was most devoted to militarism, managed in practice less well than its enemies.

The Allied Effort at Home   As bombs rained down on Britain, support for the war effort was nearly unanimous. Civilians accepted sacrifice and welcomed the end of unemployment. One-third of all males between 14 and 64 were in uniform, and unmarried women were mobilized. More women were employed in industry than ever before in both Britain and the United States. Labor unions signed a no-strike pledge, as they did in the United States. With tight rationing and government control of the economy, no society mobilized more thoroughly. Civilians accepted blackouts and suffered air raids and the temporary evacuation of 3.5 million women and children to the safer countryside. Even with that effort and that bravery, Britain increasingly depended on American aid. With its economic resources fully mobilized, the United States by the end of 1942 was producing more war matériel than all its enemies combined. Ships, planes, arms, and munitions from American factories and food from American farms flowed across the oceans to Britain and the Soviet Union.

Even before 1939 Stalin had adopted the policy of industrializing the more backward regions east of the Urals, a safe distance from Russia's western border, and in the months preceding Hitler's attack in 1941 hundreds of factories were moved there piece by piece. Despite its enormous losses of productive capacity, the Soviet Union was able throughout the war to produce most of the military supplies it needed. Central planning, rationing, military discipline, and the employment of women were not such a dramatic change in this communist regime, but the acceptance of rationing, the increased hours of labor, the destruction of homes, the death of loved ones, and the loss of men and territory required patriotism of a rather old-fashioned sort. Patriotism became the dominant theme of Soviet public life.

Nazi Rule   Until 1943 German civilians did not experience hardships comparable to the sacrifices of the Soviets or the lowered standard of living of the British. Nor was German output much greater than at the war's outset. The illusion, fed by military success and propaganda, that the war would soon be over encouraged interim measures. Competing elements of the Nazi party worked at cross purposes with each other and the government. Mutual distrust made it difficult for the Nazis to cooperate consistently with science and industry. Only when Albert Speer was given increased powers over the economy did coordination improve. In mid-July 1943 German production was twice what it had been in 1939, despite Allied bombing. A year later it was three times the prewar level.

Germany certainly benefited from its vast gains of territory rich in resources, industry, and personnel, but the system that took so naturally to ruthless conquest was less well adapted to ordinary life. The Nazis alienated those they conquered with their labor conscription, racial policies, and oppressive brutality. A high percentage of Ukrainians, for example, had welcomed liberation from Russian rule, but brief acquaintance with Nazi treatment of the "racially inferior" Slavs discouraged their cooperation. Nazi rule was most severe and most destructive in Eastern Europe and less harsh among the "Aryan" populations of the Nordic lands. But even in France food rations provided only about half the minimum that decent health requires. Germany's most crucial need was for workers, and slave labor was an answer in accord with Nazi racial theory. Eventually some 5 million Slavs were shipped like cattle to labor in Germany. By 1944 the 8 million foreign workers in Germany constituted one-fifth of the workforce.

The laborers' barracks at Buchenwald at the end of the war.
Bettmann/Corbis

Genocide   The hysteria of racial hatred got the better of rational planning. Brutalized and starving workers could hardly be efficient. Transporting and guarding slave laborers became an enormous, corrupting, and expensive enterprise. Many millions of people died in forced labor, perhaps 3 million Soviet prisoners of war were killed, and millions more Slavs in occupied territory starved to death. These deaths, evidence of massive brutality and consonant with Nazi ideas about inferior races, could be said to have had some connection with the exigencies of war, as could the German practice of killing large numbers of civilian hostages in occupied lands as a means of demoralizing resistance while reducing unworthy populations. Hounding Jews and Gypsies, cramming them into concentration camps, and killing them had less to do with the brutality of war (the massacre of prisoners taken on the Eastern front may have been a precedent) than with the implementation of Nazi racial theory. Throughout the fall of 1941 mobile SS squads executed Jews who had been rounded up on the Eastern front. Men and women, old and young were lined up, made to undress, and marched toward ditches to be shot by the SS (one squad reported having killed more than 200,000 people). The orders, equipment, and reports this slaughter required establish that many people had to have known about it.

The Holocaust   In January 1942, at a secret meeting of high officials held just outside Berlin, it was agreed that the systematic and efficient extermination of Jews should be made a general policy, "the **final solution** of the Jewish question" (see "A Gas Chamber," p. 914). By 1945, nearly 6 million Jews and as many other people (Poles, Gypsies, and Magyars especially) had died in concentration camps like Buchenwald and Dachau and the more recently constructed death camps like Auschwitz. Some of these camps were also supposed to be centers of production: A Krupp arms factory, an I. G. Farben chemical plant, and a coal mine were part of the Auschwitz

A GAS CHAMBER

At a meeting of high Nazi officials on January 20, 1942, Reinard Heydrich, Plenipotentiary for the Preparation of the Final Solution of the European Jewish Question, spoke proudly of the liquidation of the Jews already accomplished and of the concentration camps already established but called for a further step. "We have the means, the methods, the organization, experience, and people. And we have the will. This is a historic moment in the struggle against Jewry. The Führer has declared his determination . . . [and sees destruction of the Jews] as exterminating fatal bacteria to save the organism. . . . We will work effectively but silently." (Heydrich was later assassinated by the Czech resistance in Prague.) Nazi extermination camps indeed followed strikingly similar procedures, and the following description of the Birkenau camp is typical of hundreds of survivors' testimonies. It was written by a French doctor, André Lettich, who was a member of the "special commando" squad, whose job it was to empty the crematoria of corpses and make them ready for the next round.

"Until the end of January 1943, there were no crematoria in Birkenau. In the middle of a small birch forest, about two kilometres from the camp, was a peaceful looking house, where a Polish family had once lived before it had been either murdered or expelled. This cottage had been equipped as a gas chamber for a long time.

"More than five hundred metres further on were two barracks: the men stood on one side, the women on the other. They were addressed in a very polite and friendly way: 'You have been on a journey. You are dirty. You will take a bath. Get undressed quickly.' Towels and soap were handed out, and then suddenly the brutes woke up and showed their true faces: this horde of people, these men and women were driven outside with hard blows and forced both summer and winter to go the few hundred metres to the 'Shower Room'. Above the entry door was the word 'Shower'. One could even see shower heads on the ceiling which were cemented in but never had water flowing through them.

"These poor innocents were crammed together, pressed against each other. Then panic broke out, for at last they realised the fate in store for them. But blows with rifle butts and revolver shots soon restored order and finally they all entered the death chamber. The doors were shut and, ten minutes later, the temperature was high enough to facilitate the condensation of the hydrogen cyanide, for the condemned were gassed with hydrogen cyanide. This was the so-called 'Zyklon B', gravel pellets saturated with twenty per cent of hydrogen cyanide which was used by the German barbarians.

"Then, *SS Unterscharführer* Moll threw the gas in through a little vent. One could hear fearful screams, but a few moments later there was complete silence. Twenty to twenty-five minutes later, the doors and windows were opened to ventilate the rooms and the corpses were thrown at once into pits to be burnt. But, beforehand the dentists had searched every mouth to pull out the gold teeth. The women were also searched to see if they had not hidden jewelry in the intimate parts of their bodies, and their hair was cut off and methodically placed in sacks for industrial purposes."

From J. Noakes and G. Pridham (eds.), *Nazism, 1919–1945: A Documentary Reader*, Vol. 3: *Foreign Policy, War, and Racial Extermination*, University of Exeter Press.

complex. But the chief product of Auschwitz was corpses, at a rate that reached twelve thousand a day.

The extermination camps remain the ultimate nightmare of modern history. Beating and torturing prisoners of war was not new, though rarely so common as under the Nazis, but the industrial organization of death in Nazi camps raises terrifying questions about modern civilization. Hundreds of thousands of people were involved in operating those camps and in rounding up men, women, and children to be shipped to them. At first, the victims were primarily Slavs and Jews from the conquered lands of Eastern Europe; then Jews from Western Europe were hunted down and added to the flow. They came by trainload, huddled in boxcars, hungry, thirsty, frightened, and confused. Upon arrival at the camps, the weakest and least "use-

ful" (the ill, the elderly, children, and often women) were sent to showers that proved to be gas chambers. The others were given uniforms, often with patches that distinguished into neat categories the common criminals, political prisoners, homosexuals, communists, Jehovah's Witnesses, Slavs, and Jews, their identities transformed into serial numbers tattooed on their arms. Many were literally worked to death or were killed when they could work no longer. The prisoners themselves, reduced to blind survival, were caught up in this dehumanized world of beatings, limited rations, constant abuse, and contempt. Neither submission nor animal cunning guaranteed another day of life. Many inmates nevertheless managed haunting gestures of human feeling through a story told, a song sung, a bit of food shared.

German clerks and bureaucrats kept elaborate records of names, stolen possessions, and corpses, which were efficiently stripped of gold fillings and useful hair before being turned to ashes that could be used as fertilizer. Doctors invented new tortures under the guise of medical experiments to benefit the Aryan race. The sadistic pseudoscience of these doctors elaborated on the paranoid dream of purifying the Aryan race. Forced sterilization and euthanasia of the chronically ill, the physically handicapped, and the mentally retarded had been advocated and practiced by Nazis since they first came to power. In *Mein Kampf* Hitler had referred to Jews as a plague and like a bacillus weakening the Aryan race. Racial laws had extended that point to all aspects of social life, and brutal treatment helped to make prisoners seem inferior, even subhuman. Organized killing carried this denial of humanity one step further.

Yet even the SS guards—like the camp commandants, the people who arranged for trains, and the business people who bid for contracts to build gas ovens—employed euphemisms rather than acknowledge what was really happening. The residents of nearby towns rarely discussed what was carried in the trains rumbling by or asked about the odor that settled over the countryside from crematoria smokestacks. Nor did the Allies quite believe or choose to act on the stories that filtered out of Germany about atrocities on a scale too terrible to comprehend.

Resistance Movements   Millions of Europeans came to rely on the British Broadcasting Corporation for news and for encouragement in occupied lands, where every act of opposition—a speech not applauded, a whispered joke—took on symbolic significance. Gradually, against

HISTORICAL ISSUES: THE HISTORIANS' DEBATE ON GERMAN GENOCIDE

Over the past decade historians of Germany, particularly in Germany itself, have sustained a heated debate about the ways of understanding Nazi genocide. Among the issues in this debate, known as the Historikerstreit, are the role of racial theories, the example of the Soviet Union, and whether genocide had distinctly German roots. The citations here, from three well-known scholars, illustrate these positions.

HENRY FRIEDLANDER

"Historians investigating Nazi genocide have long debated who gave the order to commit mass murder, when it was issued, and how it was transmitted. Although the specific mechanism has been a matter of contention between rival groups of historians . . . , there now appears to be a general agreement that Hitler had a deciding voice, although no one has ever discovered, or is likely to discover, a smoking gun. Recently historians have focused on the specific dates when the idea to launch the physical annihilation of the European Jews was first advanced and when the decision to do so became irrevocable. . . . My own approach is somewhat different. I am not particularly interested in exact dates. Instead, I want to trace the sequential development of mass murder.

"I define Nazi genocide, what is now commonly called the Holocaust, as the mass murder of human beings because they belonged to a biologically defined group. Heredity determined the selection of victims. Although the regime persecuted and often killed men and women for their politics, nationality, religion, behavior, or activities, the Nazis applied a consistent and inclusive policy of extermination only against three groups of human beings: the handicapped, Jews, and Gypsies.

"The attack on these targeted groups drew on more than fifty years of political and scientific arguments hostile to the belief in the equality of man. Since the turn of the century, the German elite, that is the members of the educated professional classes, had increasingly accepted an ideology based on human inequality. Geneticists, anthropologists, and psychiatrists had advanced a theory of human heredity that had merged with the racist doctrine of *völkisch* nationalists to form a political ideology of a nation based on race. The Nazi movement both absorbed and advanced this ideology. After 1933 they created the political framework that made it possible to translate this ideology of inequality into a policy of exclusion, while the German bureaucratic, professional, and scientific elite provided the legitimacy the regime needed for the smooth implementation of this policy."

From Henry Friedlander, "Step by Step: The Expansion of Murder, 1939–1941," *German Studies Review* 17, October 1994.

ERNST NOLTE

"Auschwitz is not primarily a result of traditional anti-Semitism and was not, in its essential core, mere 'genocide'; rather, it was, above all, a reaction—born out of anxiety—to the annihilations which occurred during the Russian Revolution. This copy was far more irrational than the earlier original (because it was simply an absurd notion to imagine that 'the Jews' had ever wished to annihilate the German bourgeoisie or even the German people), and it is difficult to attribute to it even a perverted ethos. It was more horrifying than the original because it carried out the annihilation of human beings in a quasi-industrial manner. It was more repulsive than the original because it was based on mere suppositions, and was almost completely free of that mass hatred which, within the midst of horror, remains nonetheless an understandable—and thus, to a limited extent, reconciling—element. All this supports the notion of singularity, yet does not alter the fact that the so-called annihilation of the Jews during the Third Reich was a reaction or a distorted copy—and not a first act, not the original."

From Ernst Nolte, "Between Historical Myth and Revisionism," *Yad Vashem Studies* 19, 1988.

HANS-ULRICH WEHLER

"Nolte's thesis concerning the fatal consequences of the Bolsheviks' anxiety-producing class warfare is directed above all against a well-grounded interpretation: that Hitler and National Socialism were products of German and Austrian history. Only after factors rooted in that past have been assessed should the broader European context be considered. Nolte has sought to undermine this hard-won insight by displacing the 'primary historical guilt' onto Marx, the Russian Revolution, and the extermination policy of the Bolsheviks. I shall emphasize below the main points of the opposing view—a view that is better grounded empirically and more convincing in its interpretive approach than Nolte's theory:

"—Hitler and countless other National Socialists had internalized a fanatical anti-Marxism long before the First World War: that is, before the Russian Revolution, the civil war, and class warfare in the new Soviet Union could confirm and strengthen their hatred of the 'Reds.'

"—Social Darwinism in its vulgar (racist) form was one of the strongest forces driving the highly ideological 'worldview' of Hitler and many other Nazis well before 1917. Contemporary developments thereafter only served as confirmation to these confused minds.

continued

"—The poisonous morass of German and Austrian anti-Semitism was the source of the crazed ideas associated with the Nazi hatred of the Jews. The new racist, political anti-Semitism that flourished in the late 1870s quickly led to the explicit idea of extermination. For example, in its Hamburg resolutions of September 1899, the German Social Reform Party claimed publicly and without any embarrassment that 'in the course of the twentieth century, the Jewish question must be solved . . . once and for all by the complete separation and (if necessary for defensive purposes) the definitive extermination of the Jewish people.' What was new in the 1930s was 'only' that Hitler and his cohorts took this program literally—and brought with them the will to carry out the deed itself.

"—The Nazis effortlessly adopted the widespread, fully developed antidemocratic, antiliberal, and antiparliamentary political ideology that had already been fully developed by the German Right before 1917/18.

"—The Nazis were able to exploit the deeply corrosive anticapitalist resentments of the Protestant, provincial bourgeoisie and of peasant society. They were also able to counter the difficult conflicts of a modern class society with the hypertrophied idealization of an oft-evoked *Volksgemeinschaft* (national community).

"—National Socialism benefitted from long-term conditions in Germany: the antagonisms of Germany's social structure, an authoritarian mentality, the peculiarities of Prussian militarism, the Protestant subservience to the state, the national susceptibility to charismatic leaders, a particular kind of political philosophy, etc. Hitler's regime also profited from more recent conditions that stemmed from the experiences of the period 1914–33. Among these were 'the experience of war,' 'the nation in arms,' the 'total war' of 1916–18, the beginning of the defeat, the renunciation of all war aims, the stab-in-the-back myth, the 'disgraceful peace' at Versailles, the war reparations and postwar hyperinflation, and the destructive force of the Depression. These events belong to a long list of favorable factors with fatal consequences.

"Above all, the traditions and burdens of Germany's past influenced the course of National Socialism. Only after these have been identified should historians proceed to analyze the influence of the wider European and world-historical context."

From Hans-Ulrich Wehler, "Unburdening the German Past? A Preliminary Assessment," in Peter Baldwin (ed.), *Reworking the Past: Hitler, the Holocaust, and the Historians' Debate*, Beacon Press, 1990.

---

great odds, organized resistance movements formed. Some developed around neighborhood groups; many were connected to prewar political parties. Always composed of a small minority, these partisan movements achieved particular strength in Denmark and Norway, the Netherlands, France, and Yugoslavia. Many of them received material aid and guidance from governments-in-exile operating from London, the most notable being the Free French, headed by General de Gaulle.

Nazi reprisals for acts of resistance were meant to be horrible. When Czechs assassinated their new Nazi governor, Reinard Heydrich, in June 1942, the Germans retaliated by wiping out the village of Lidice, which they suspected of hiding the murderers: Every man was killed; every woman and child deported. On a single day in 1943, the Germans put 1,400 men to death in a Greek village. Hundreds of towns across occupied Europe have their memorials, a burned-out building or a ditch where clusters of civilians were massacred.

Yet the underground movements continued to grow, and their actions became a barometer of the course of the war. In France, partisan activities expanded from single exploits—smuggling Allied airmen out of the country, dynamiting a bridge, or attacking individual German officers—to large-scale intelligence and propaganda operations coordinated from London. Norway's resistance helped force the Germans to keep 300,000 troops there and away from more active fronts. In Yu-

goslavia, two groups of partisans maintained an active guerrilla war, although the British decision to support the group led by the communist Tito all but ensured his control of the country at the end of the war. After the Allied invasion of Italy, partisan groups there maintained an unnerving harassment of Fascist and Nazi forces. Even in Germany itself, some members of the army and the old aristocracy began to plot against Hitler. In July 1944 a group of conspirators planted a bomb under the table as the Führer conducted a conference with his staff. Hitler escaped serious injury, but the sense that he was doomed had spread to the heart of Germany.

These partisan movements were important for more than their immediate contribution to the war. The memory of their bravery partially eased the painful reality of defeat, and in countries like France, Italy, and Norway, where many had acquiesced in fascist regimes, the militant opposition of the resistance could be taken to express the real will of the people. In fact, many of the major political parties of the postwar era were formed in the resistance, and the ideas of democracy, freedom, and equality that circulated so passionately then would be repeated in constitutions and party platforms later. Most resistance fighters were young men, but many women, too, experienced the camaraderie of activism as secret couriers, provisioners, and occasionally group commanders. By joining in the resistance, women were being drawn into the rudimentary renewal of national political life.

Allied Strategy

By 1943 the Axis was on the defensive although it had the advantage of shorter, direct lines of supply. While Hitler continued to imagine that some daring thrust or miracle weapon would bring him victory, the Allies continued to disagree as to how they should attack Hitler's "fortress Europe."

A Second Front   The Soviet Union had repeatedly urged opening a **second front** on the Continent, and most of the American military command favored an immediate invasion. The British warned against the high cost of such an expedition, and, with Roosevelt's support, Churchill prevailed. The Allies invaded North Africa instead, ending the threat to Egypt. When that was not followed by landings on the Continent, the Soviets suspected that they and the Germans were being left to annihilate each other. The Americans continued to favor such an attack, but the British argued for tightening the blockade of Germany and for making more limited assaults in the Eastern Mediterranean and Southern Europe, on what Churchill called the "soft underbelly."

More than military strategy was at stake. The Allies had been less specific about their long-range goals than during World War I, and they were divided. Stalin looked forward to regaining the Polish territory lost in 1939 (Poland could be compensated with territory taken from a defeated Germany). The British recalled the earlier communist aim of revolution across the Continent (as well as imperial Russia's efforts before that to expand into Eastern Europe). The British hoped to place Anglo-American troops in such a way that, after the war, they could have a voice in the disposition of Eastern Europe. In London the exiled leaders of the Eastern European countries agitated for their own nationalist goals, alarmed by Stalin's references to the need for "friendly" governments along Russia's borders.

With such issues before them, Roosevelt and Churchill met at Casablanca in January 1943. There they decided (to the Soviets' disgust) to invade Sicily and agreed to demand the unconditional surrender of Italy, Germany, and Japan, an expression of moral outrage against fascism that was also meant to prevent the Soviet Union and the Western Allies from making any separate deals with the enemy. Welcomed by Allied public opinion at the time, the refusal to negotiate with the Axis was subsequently criticized for strengthening their desperate defense after defeat was inevitable.

The Invasion of Italy   In July a mammoth amphibious assault carried Anglo-American forces into Sicily. A victim of his own propaganda, Mussolini had consistently overestimated Italian strength. As the invaders advanced, the Fascist Grand Council in a secret session voted Mussolini out of office. The Duce was arrested, and Marshal Pietro Badoglio was named prime minister. A coalition of monarchists and moderate Fascists then sought an armistice. But Committees of National Liberation had sprung up throughout Italy; composed of anti-Fascists from liberals to communists, these Committees wanted nothing to do with Badoglio, a Fascist hero of the campaign in Ethiopia, or with the king, who had bowed to Mussolini for twenty years. Again the Allies were divided. Britain favored the monarchy and feared leftist influence in the Committees. The Americans leaned toward the Committees but agreed that representatives of the Soviet Union should be excluded from the Allied military government that would be installed in Italy.

In September Allied forces in Sicily invaded southern Italy, where they were well dug in by the end of the month. The German army, however, had snatched control of the rest of the peninsula. Although the Allies captured Naples in October, their campaign in Italy soon bogged down in difficult terrain and in the face of fierce German resistance. In a daring rescue, German paratroops snatched Mussolini from his mountaintop prison and took him to northern Italy, where he proclaimed a Fascist republic that was blatantly a German puppet. At the same time, Italy's anti-Fascist partisans were becoming increasingly effective. Italians, their country a battleground for foreign armies, were caught in civil war.

The Free French   Italy was not the first place in which the Allies indicated they might compromise with tainted regimes. At the moment of the North African invasion, Admiral Jean François Darlan, a former vice premier of Vichy France and commander of its armed forces, happened to be in Algiers. Eisenhower's staff quickly agreed to make him governor-general of French Africa provided his forces would not resist the Allied invasion. De Gaulle was outraged. He had claimed to represent a free France since his first call for continued resistance in 1940 when, from London, he organized French forces fighting with the Allies. His hauteur, his insistence on a voice in Allied policy, and his success in winning support in the French colonies had made his relations with Britain and the United States difficult at best. The assassination of Darlan in December 1942 eased the situation, and Germany's decision to occupy all of France in response to the Allied invasion of North Africa reduced de Gaulle's fears that the Allies might choose to deal with the Vichy regime. Monitoring events in Italy, the European governments-in-exile shared Stalin's concerns about the consistency and true aims of Allied policy.

Stalin, Roosevelt, and Churchill, meeting for the first time at Teheran, reached an understanding that laid the groundwork for Allied cooperation in pursuing the war.
Bettmann/Corbis

The Teheran Conference   Finally, at the end of November 1943, Roosevelt, Churchill, and Stalin met for the first time, at Teheran. The conversations were not easy. Previously, the British had mediated between the United States and the Soviet Union, but now the Americans took a middle position. The Allies reached a tentative understanding that the Soviet Union would accept a border with Poland similar to the one proposed in 1919, and they left open the question of what kind of government a liberated Poland might have. Their unity thus preserved by postponing the most difficult issues, the Allies could plan vigorous prosecution of the war. Stalin promised to declare war on Japan as soon as Germany surrendered, and Churchill's proposal for an invasion of the Dardanelles was rejected. The British and Americans agreed instead to land in France in the following year to open a true second front.

The Road to Victory

The Italian Front   The Allies progressed slowly in Italy, taking five months to fight their way past a costly new beachhead at Anzio. In December 1943, King Victor Emmanuel III announced that he would abdicate in favor of his son, and Badoglio gave way to a cabinet drawn from members of the Committees of National Liberation. Italy then officially joined the Allies. The Germans, however, held the advantage of entrenched positions on one mountain ridge after another. Northern Italy became another German-occupied country in which Jews were rounded up for death camps, and captured Italian soldiers were sent to slave labor in Ger-

many. The Allies slowly pushed northward, aided by partisan risings, while the main forces were held aside for the invasion of France. Only in May 1944 did Anglo-American armies finally seize the old Benedictine abbey of Monte Cassino, north of Naples, after a destructive bombardment. Rome, the first European capital to be liberated, was taken in June.

The Soviet Union   Soviet successes were more spectacular. In the spring of 1943 the Germans could still launch an offensive of their own, but it slowed within weeks. In July the Soviet army began a relentless advance that continued, with few setbacks, for almost two years. With armies now superior in numbers and matériel, Soviet forces reached the Dnieper and Kiev by November. In February 1944 they were at the Polish border. They retook the Crimea in the spring, Romania surrendered in August, and Finland and Bulgaria fell a few weeks later. Soviet power loomed over Eastern Europe.

The Western Front   For months Germany was subjected to constant pounding from the air, and the Germans knew an invasion across the English Channel was imminent. They believed it would come in the area around Calais, the shore closest to England, as a series of calculated feints seemed to indicate. Instead, on June 6, 1944, the Allies landed in Normandy. The largest amphibious landing in history, it put 150,000 men ashore within two days, supported by 5,000 ships and 1,500 tanks. In a complex series of landings, Eisenhower's Allied force poured onto the French beaches. Made

In February 1944 an American sergeant who spoke German, believing he faced six or seven Germans, called on them to surrender—fifty-six came forward.
Bettmann/Corbis

possible by overwhelming control of the air and helped by a poorly coordinated German defense, the landings nevertheless suffered heavy losses. Within a few months, more than a million men disembarked. In July they broke through the German defense and began a series of rapid drives through France. A second amphibious attack, in southern France in mid-August, led to swift advances inland that were greatly aided by well-organized French resistance groups. On August 24 the Parisian underground rose against the Germans, and French forces under Charles de Gaulle quickly entered the cheering city. Brussels fell a week later, and ten days after that, American troops crossed the German frontier.

Germany had launched its "miracle" weapon in June, the relatively ineffective V-1 pilotless plane, which was followed in September by the far more dangerous V-2 rocket. Had the Nazis recognized its potential earlier, the effects might have been devastating. The V-2 flew faster than the speed of sound and was almost impossible to intercept; but these rockets were

hard to aim, and too few and too late to be decisive. More threatening was a counterstroke through the Ardennes in December that rocked the Allied line back. The Battle of the Bulge, the last offensive the Germans would mount, cost about 70,000 men on each side before the Allies regained the initiative in January 1945.

The Yalta Conference   When Allied leaders held their last wartime meeting, at Yalta in February 1945, Russian troops occupied part of Czechoslovakia and stood on the German frontier of Poland. The decisions of the Big Three at Yalta, which were widely hailed at the time, later became the most controversial of World War II. The hurried meeting dealt with four broad issues, each a measure of the Allies' mutual distrust. They agreed to create a United Nations Organization. The Soviet Union asked for sixteen votes, one for each of its republics, to counterbalance the votes of the British Commonwealth and of Latin America, which the United States was expected to dominate. That request

General de Gaulle leading an informal victory parade down the Champs Elysées right after the liberation of Paris from the Nazis in August 1944. Towering over his compatriots from the resistance, the general was not hard to spot by the enthusiastic crowds.
AP/Wide World Photos

was reduced to three, and the Soviet Union got the veto it demanded but with some slight restrictions on its use. The USSR promised to declare war against Japan within ninety days of Germany's defeat in return for the territories Russia had surrendered to Japan in 1905 and for a sphere of influence in Manchuria.

A more contentious issue was the treatment of Germany. Each of the Big Three was assigned a zone of occupation, and Russia reluctantly agreed to the American and British plan to carve a zone for France from the areas under their control. Russia's demands for huge reparations and "labor services" were so troubling that specific terms had to be postponed. The form of Italy's government was in fact now largely set, as was de Gaulle's ascendance in an independent France. The main issue was Soviet dominance in Eastern Europe. The creation of new governments for the liberated nations, the most difficult issue of all, could not be postponed much longer, yet every proposal exposed fundamental differences between the Soviet Union and the Western powers.

In most of the countries they occupied, the Soviets were tolerating broad coalitions that included all the old antifascist parties, but they would not allow a role for the Western powers, even restricting Allied observers. When Churchill visited Moscow four months earlier, he had proposed a division of interests: The Soviet Union would have predominance in Romania and the largest influence in Bulgaria, Britain would have a free hand in Greece, and the two powers would recognize their equal interests in Yugoslavia and Hungary. Such crude understandings offered few guarantees, however, though Stalin remained silent when Britain intervened in the civil war raging in Greece in order to rout the leftists.

Stalin in turn exercised a free hand in Poland after the Polish underground arose against the Germans in August 1944. As Soviet troops approached Warsaw, the Russians simply halted their advance until the Germans had wiped out the resistance fighters, who were closely tied to the anticommunist Polish government in London. The Yalta Conference did not in fact adopt cynically drawn spheres of influence, but the conference's formulas, with their references to democratic governments and free elections, would in the end be interpreted by those who held the guns.

The Final Months   As the Allies pushed into Germany from all sides, it became clear that Berlin would be the final battleground. Fearing that Hitler planned a last desperate stand at his retreat at Berchtesgaden in the southern German mountains, Eisenhower halted the eastward advance of American and British armies at the Elbe River. The Russians took Berlin, where Hitler had ensured the maximum destruction by ordering a defense to the death. The Führer committed suicide on April 30, 1945, and his aides burned his body, which has never been found. Four days later a group of German officers signed the final unconditional surrender. The war in Europe was over.

World conflict would continue in Asia for four months more. It was expected to last much longer, even with the Russian help that had seemed so necessary when promised at Yalta. Despite massive bombing and repeated naval victories, Allied progress through the islands and jungles of the Pacific toward

MAP 29.3 THE ALLIED VICTORY IN WORLD WAR II
Armies of the Western allies converged with the forces of the Soviet Union at the Elbe River in Germany. How does this map help explain the postwar Soviet domination of Eastern Europe?

◆ For an online version, go to www.mhhe.com/chambers9 > chapter 29 > book maps

Japan had been laborious and bloody. Americans conquered Guam, landed in the Philippines, and took Iwo Jima but at great cost. The tactic of landing on some islands while skipping others, often leaving Japanese forces isolated and useless, created bases from which Allied planes threatened the Japanese fleet and the mainland itself. Eventual victory was no longer in doubt. During the three months following Germany's surrender, strategic bombing obliterated Japan's navy, industrial plants, and large parts of its cities. Firebombing killed nearly 200,000 people in Tokyo in just one week. But still the Japanese would not surrender, and estimates of Allied casualties from any invasion

of Japan's home islands reached into the hundreds of thousands.

On August 6 the new president of the United States, Harry Truman (Roosevelt had died in April), authorized the use of a new weapon that had been developed after years of secret research, the atomic bomb. In one blow, half of the city of Hiroshima disappeared from the face of the earth. A quarter of its 320,000 inhabitants were killed. On August 9 the Americans dropped an even more powerful atomic bomb on the city of Nagasaki. On August 8 the Soviet Union declared war on Japan; and on September 2, 1945, Japan surrendered unconditionally. The atomic bomb, an extraordinary achieve-

MAP 29.4 WORLD WAR II IN THE PACIFIC
As depicted in this map, what are the stories behind the incredible advance of Japanese power in the Pacific, its subsequent retreat under Allied pressure, and its eventual demise?

◆ For an online version, go to www.mhhe.com/chambers9 > chapter 29 > book maps

---

ment of science and technology made possible by great wealth and scores of European scientists driven to sanctuary in the United States, permitted a great democracy to end World War II by unleashing a new order of terror upon humanity. Later, many people would question the morality of using so terrible a weapon. Even in the jubilation of victory, leaders reordering a shattered world now knew that another war might bring the end of civilization.

BUILDING ON THE RUINS

For most Europeans the immediate postwar period brought little improvement in their living conditions, and for years individuals, institutions, and governments struggled with the effects of death, destruction, and the displacement of millions of people. Overcoming such fundamental problems on so vast a scale was the central

achievement of the next decade. Euphoria was brief even among the victors and the newly liberated, as people set about their daily tasks in an uncertain world of economic hardship, social dislocation, and political division. As European nations gained in political stability and economic strength, they remained distinctly subordinate to the United States and the Soviet Union in a world divided by the Cold War. And they had no choice but to give up their colonial empires.

Immediate Crises

The Devastation In contrast to World War I, a majority of the fatalities in World War II were civilian. About 4 million men died on battlefields; and for every soldier killed, two more were either wounded or taken captive. Civilian losses are harder to categorize, and often there was no one to do the counting. The Germans killed between 12 and 20 million people in occupied countries

Hiroshima, the victim of one of science's great achievements. The world had entered a new era of warfare, and for a generation the Japanese would suffer from the environmental destruction and the effects of radiation.
AP/Wide World Photos

and concentration camps. Across Europe millions more civilians died just for being where armies chose to bomb or shell or shoot. In all, the European casualties in World War II were five or six times greater than in World War I (only for Britain and France were they lower). The Soviet Union lost some 27 million people; Poland, about 6 million (including 3 million Jews); Germany, nearly 5 million. So the total European casualties of World War II—dead, wounded, or crippled by inhumane treatment—remain an estimate, a number hard to comprehend in its gruesome total or ghostly imprecision: some 45 to 55 million people.

Europe's industrial capability in 1945 was perhaps half what it had been in 1939, and only parts of such major cities as Frankfurt, Dresden, Brest, and Toulon were still standing. The Continent's most important ports, bridges, and rail lines had been all but destroyed. Agriculture was also hard hit. Large areas of farmland in France, Italy, and Germany could not be cultivated; the number of cattle in France had been reduced by half. In the winter of 1945–1946, starvation was a threat in many places, and in some, such as Vienna, thousands died of famine. Disease was an ever-present danger, too, although penicillin helped limit the epidemics that erupted. The rationing of food and clothes (and illegal black markets) continued in many countries into the 1950s, and Europeans looked to the United States and the Soviet Union for relief as Allied troops occupied the Continent.

Refugees   In addition to the millions without jobs or housing, there were more refugees in Europe than ever before in history. Some 8 million slave laborers

in the Third Reich and millions in concentration camps were put on trains headed back to where their homes had been. There were German prisoners of war and Allied prisoners in Germany. More than 7 million Soviet citizens in Germany, including defectors, had no place to go. Some 2 million Poles and Czechs returning from prison in the Soviet Union joined millions of Ukrainians and Poles who moved west to stay on the other side of the shifting border with the USSR. Romanians drove out Hungarians; Czechs expelled Hungarians and Germans. Millions of Germans whom the Nazis had transplanted to Poland in the interests of Germanization were forced to leave, and many of the 1.5 million Poles the Nazis had evicted wanted to go back home. The question of where national boundaries should be drawn, which had so troubled the peacemakers of Versailles, was settled now by first drawing the lines and then pushing inconvenient nationalities across them.

Most of the refugees who carried their few belongings along unfamiliar roads were civilians, perhaps 60 million in all, a majority of them women and children who had lost their homes and livelihood. Separated from kin and possessions, they struggled to survive in strange lands that were impoverished by war. We will never know how many died or were abused or robbed. Governments tried to make nice distinctions between the homeless (those in or near their own country) and displaced persons (who were mostly stateless—some 12 million were so registered in 1945), and they tried to separate criminals from others. Abandoned factories and warehouses, even former concentration camps, were used to house refugees, along with spe-

Citizens of Dresden, nearly a year after the war ended, making their way through the rubble from Allied saturation bombing.
Bettmann/Corbis

cially built crude barracks meant to be temporary. Bit by bit the fortunate were assigned a destination, but "unaccompanied children," the disabled, and the aged were harder to place.

The Terms of Peace: Potsdam No great peace conference took place after World War II. When the leaders of the Soviet Union, Great Britain, and the United States met at Potsdam for two weeks in July 1945, they hardly knew each other. President Harry Truman had been in office only three months following the death of Roosevelt, and in the midst of the meeting Clement Attlee replaced Churchill, who had been defeated in the British elections.

The Potsdam meeting outlined the future of Germany but left details for the future. The Allies readily agreed that all Nazi institutions must be abolished, German arms production prohibited, and German industry controlled. Democracy and free speech were to be re-stored. In the meantime Germany was divided into four zones of occupation, and so was Berlin, isolated in the Soviet zone. Germany's eastern border was moved westward to the Oder and Neisse rivers, enlarging Poland. During the next year, the foreign ministers of the four principal Allies (now including France) drafted treaties for the other defeated states, but their meetings soon became a forum for quarrels between the Soviets and the other three. Italy, Romania, Hungary, Bulgaria, and Finland each ceded minor territories to its neighbors. Austria, like Germany, remained divided into four occupied zones and without a formal treaty.

The Potsdam Conference had also laid down the terms for peace with Japan. The Soviet Union would get some territory, and the European nations would regain their Asian colonies. But the prime beneficiaries were China and, above all, the United States, whose troops already held most of the strategic islands in the Pacific and were to occupy Japan.

Göring, Hess, and von Ribbentrop (the first three on the left in the prison's dock) listen to the proceedings at the beginning of the Nuremberg trial for war crimes.
Bettmann/Corbis

War Crimes Trials   Within Europe, rooting out fascism was a major concern. In countries the Nazis had occupied, there were summary executions of collaborators and some public prosecutions, notably in France, where Pierre Laval and Marshal Pétain were tried. In Germany itself, however, the numbers involved made denazification difficult. Millions of forms were filled out and hundreds of trials held, but the drive against former Nazis soon waned. Determined to establish some lasting standard, the Allies created an international tribunal to try Hitler's closest associates for crimes against humanity. The trials, held in Nuremberg in 1945 and 1946, were also intended to inform the German people of the full horror of Nazi rule. The appalling revelations of those solemn hearings were followed by restrained judgments—only twelve of the twenty-two prime defendants were condemned to death, and three were acquitted.

International Agencies   The belief in international law that underlay the Nuremberg trials and the United

Nations Organization was tempered by a determination to learn from the past. This peace would not be punitive, and devastated nations, defeated enemies as well as those liberated from German rule, must be helped. Even before the UN had its charter, its first agency, the United Nations Relief and Rehabilitation Administration (UNRRA), was created, late in 1943. UNRRA played a major role in reconstructing postwar Europe, organizing relief of food and medical supplies, and coordinating international loans. To avoid the dangerous inflation that had followed World War I, a conference at Bretton Woods, New Hampshire, in 1944 created the International Monetary Fund and an International Bank for Reconstruction and Development (later the World Bank). Those institutions, with nearly $20 billion in assets, furthered reconstruction and capital investment by supporting stable currencies. They would become influential mechanisms for shaping the international capitalist economy.

But the main instrument of peace was to be the United Nations, and a few months after the Yalta meeting, fifty-one countries approved the United Nations Charter at a special conference held in San Francisco. The charter established a General Assembly of all members to determine policy, a decision-making Security Council of eleven nations to supervise "the maintenance of international peace," and various economic, social, and legal agencies. Permanent Security Council seats were reserved for the United States, the Soviet Union, China, Great Britain, and France, each with a right to veto any council action; the remaining six seats were filled by election from among the other member states. The fact that the United States and the Soviet Union belonged to the UN was a promising contrast to the League of Nations, but the conflict between them dominated international relations even within the UN, where the superpowers competed for the support of Asian, African, and Latin American nations.

Europe Divided

The conflict between communists and anticommunists divided Europe, domestically between the national parties of left and right, then more deeply between two sets of values and ideology, and ultimately between Eastern European nations dominated by the USSR and Western ones allied with the United States. With the fall of fascism, communists enjoyed the prestige of having played a central part in most resistance movements, and communist calls for social justice and greater democracy resonated with postwar idealism. Quickly, however, nearly every disagreement between communists and anticommunists became part of a larger power struggle.

Eastern Europe: New Communist Regimes   At war's end, Soviet troops occupied Eastern Europe from the Adriatic to the Baltic. The three formerly independent states of Estonia, Latvia, and Lithuania became Soviet republics, and Russia annexed territory from East Prussia, Poland, Hungary, and Romania. In the ostensibly autonomous nations of Eastern Europe, the Soviets discouraged independent revolutions like those that had followed World War I but skillfully used social issues and crude coercion to establish governments friendly to them. Communist parties had considerable support throughout the region, and the common pattern was to build on that base, excluding prominent anticommunists from the governing coalition, then using propaganda campaigns and sudden arrests to drive noncommunists from a share of power. The result was a series of single-party dictatorships on the Soviet model that consolidated their position through purge trials and use of the secret police (see "Churchill Sees an Iron Curtain," p. 928).

The USSR had an economic as well as a political purpose. Its production had sunk to less than two-thirds of prewar levels, and the new Five-Year Plan of 1946 openly depended on ransacking occupied areas, especially in the eastern zone of Germany. Early in 1946 the Russians forced a merger of East Germany's Social Democratic party with the smaller Communist party, and Soviet control was soon complete. After expropriating much of German industry and restricting trade with the West, the Russians gradually allowed increased industrial activity in the eastern zone and in 1949 gave it independent status as the German Democratic Republic. Germany had been divided in two.

Poland, where the communists were weakest, had been promised free elections, but repressive measures weakened the Peasant party in the elections of 1947. It was soon purged, and the largest party of Independent Socialists subordinated itself to the communist Workers' party. The government could then put a Russian in command of the army and attack the Catholic Church. The president and the foreign minister of Czechoslovakia, Eduard Beneš and Jan Masaryk, were the heirs of a notable democratic tradition. But the Communists were the largest party, and when in 1948 they threatened to take over the country, Beneš gave way and Masaryk died in a mysterious fall from a window. Hungary's coalition government, which had an anti-Communist majority, lost to the Communists in a dubious election in 1949. In each of these cases Britain and the United States protested, with little effect, and the new regimes established close links with the Soviet Union. By 1950 Romania, Albania, and Bulgaria were also solid members of the communist bloc.

Only Yugoslavia followed a different course. Marshal Tito easily won the 1945 national election, and communists dominated the government, but Tito resisted Soviet efforts to influence his foreign and domestic policies. After having joined the Cominform, which had replaced the Comintern and was similarly designed to coordinate international communist activity, Yugoslavia broke with its neighbors in 1948, using ties with the West to resist economic and political pressure from the East—an example to others of how small states could use the tense balance between the superpowers.

Western Europe: Postwar Politics   Although Spain and Portugal remained defiant dictatorships, the other countries of Western Europe returned to democratic political life and projects of social reform. The new constitutions of France and Italy spoke of the right to work, guaranteed social as well as civil rights, and at last gave women the vote. West Germany's federal structure and its two dominant parties, the Christian Democrats and the Social Democrats, recalled the

CHURCHILL SEES AN IRON CURTAIN

On March 5, 1946, Winston Churchill gave a speech at Westminster College in Fulton, Missouri, that immediately received worldwide attention. After years of official emphasis on the cooperation among the wartime Allies, its directness was shocking. In effect, it announced the Cold War.

"A shadow has fallen upon the scenes so lately lighted by the Allied victory. Nobody knows what Soviet Russia and its Communist international organization intends to do in the immediate future, or what are the limits, if any, to their expansive and proselytizing tendencies. I have a strong admiration and regard for the valiant Russian people and for my wartime comrade, Marshal Stalin. There is deep sympathy and goodwill in Britain—and I doubt not here also—towards the peoples of all the Russias and a resolve to persevere through many differences and rebuffs in establishing lasting friendships. We understand the Russian need to be secure on her western frontiers by the removal of all possibility of German aggression. We welcome Russia to her rightful place among the leading nations of the world. We welcome her flag upon the seas. Above all, we welcome constant, frequent and growing contacts between the Russian people and our own people on both sides of the Atlantic. It is my duty, however, for I am sure you would wish me to state the facts as I see them to you, to place before you certain facts about the present position in Europe.

"From Stettin in the Baltic to Trieste in the Adriatic, an iron curtain has descended across the Continent. Behind that line lie all the capitals of the ancient states of Central and Eastern Europe. Warsaw, Berlin, Prague, Vienna, Budapest, Belgrade, Bucharest and Sofia, all these famous cities and the populations around them lie in what I must call the Soviet sphere, and all are subject in one form or another, not only to Soviet influence but to a very high and, in many cases, increasing measure of control from Moscow.

". . . An attempt is being made by the Russians in Berlin to build up a quasi-Communist party in their zone of Occupied Germany by showing special favours to groups of left-wing German leaders. At the end of the fighting last June, the American and British Armies withdrew westwards, in accordance with an earlier agreement, to a depth at some points of one hundred and fifty miles upon a front of nearly four hundred miles, in order to allow our Russian allies to occupy this vast expanse of territory which the Western Democracies had conquered.

"If now the Soviet Government tries, by separate action, to build up a pro-Communist Germany in their areas, this will cause new serious difficulties in the British and American zones, and will give the defeated Germans the power of putting themselves up to auction between the Soviets and the Western Democracies. Whatever conclusions may be drawn from these facts—and facts they are—this is certainly not the Liberated Europe we fought to build up. Nor is it one which contains the essentials of permanent peace."

Reprinted in Brian MacArthur, *The Penguin Book of Twentieth-Century Speeches*, New York: Viking, 1992, and available in many other places.

pre-Nazi Weimar Republic. Everywhere social programs received much attention, but reconstruction took precedence over reform.

Ironically, at war's end Germany's industry was in better shape than that of any other continental nation, and the Allies soon relaxed restrictions on its economic activity. Early in 1949 they acknowledged the division of Germany and recognized the western sectors that Britain, France, and the United States had occupied as the Federal Republic of Germany. For the next fourteen years, Konrad Adenauer, the head of the Christian Democrats, served as chancellor. Mayor of Cologne from 1917 to 1933, he was seventy-three years old in 1949, a firm and conservative leader closely allied with the United States, who promoted an atmosphere of efficient calm.

Italy, too, became a republic when a majority of the electorate voted in 1946 to replace a monarchy tainted by Fascism. As the largest party, the Christian Democrats gave Alcide De Gasperi, prime minister from 1945 to 1953, a solid basis from which to govern. A wily politician, he successfully ostracized the Communists— the largest Communist party in the West—and took advantage of a split among Socialists to bring Italy into close alliance with the United States. Winning the crucial elections of 1948, with the help of heavy American pressure, he launched a program of moderate reform intended to lessen poverty in southern Italy and to stimulate industry in the north. Italian politics had returned to the unheroic tradition of parliamentary maneuver the Fascists had overturned.

France's Fourth Republic looked much like the Third. The new constitution kept the president subordinate to the legislature as in the past, and the domineering de Gaulle was soon pushed from office as provisional president. Although an effective program of

Family allowance payments for children of the working class began to arrive at local post offices in August 1946—a first installment on Britain's postwar "cradle to grave" welfare state.
Hulton Archive/Getty Images

massive reconstruction got quickly under way, the problems of unstable governments, labor agitation, and communist intransigence got more attention. The parliamentary maneuvers necessary to win thin and uncertain majorities soon fostered disillusionment with the Fourth Republic.

Without constitutional change, Britain's postwar politics brought dramatic innovation. Churchill, revered as a war leader, nonetheless lost the election of July 1945. With an enormous majority, the Labour party under Clement Attlee launched a massive program of **nationalization,** taking over the Bank of England and a wide range of major industries, including coal, transportation, electricity, and iron and steel. It also instituted extensive welfare programs and established public housing, national insurance, and free medical care for all. True to its principles, the Labour government also began Britain's withdrawal from the empire to which men like Churchill had been so attached.

The Cold War   A turning point came in 1947 when distrust between the Soviet Union and the United States hardened into a worldwide military, political, and ideological conflict quickly dubbed the Cold War. As Russia tightened its grip on Eastern Europe, the American president announced the Truman Doctrine, promising military and economic aid to nations in danger of communist takeover. His immediate concern was the civil war in Greece, where local communists were aided by neighboring Yugoslavia. The United States also sought bases in Turkey, for Britain could no longer sustain its power and influence in the Eastern

Mediterranean, and the United States replaced Britain as the leading anticommunist force there. American money and supplies poured into Greece, and this, combined with Yugoslavia's break with Russia, enabled the Greek government to crush the opposition by 1949. Turkey, slowly moving toward democracy, received similar assistance. Opposing communism and Soviet influence had become the focus of American policy.

A few months after the announcement of the Truman Doctrine, Secretary of State George Marshall unveiled a bold plan to stimulate European recovery and overcome the postwar economic crisis in which communism was likely to prosper. The United States would offer massive economic aid to all nations still recovering from the war. Remarkably, communist governments were eligible, too, but Russia forbade their participation and established its own Council of Mutual Economic Assistance (Comecon) instead. Even aid was a Cold War issue. In the West, communist parties opposed the Marshall Plan despite its obvious benefits, and the United States used its growing influence to see that communists were excluded from coalition governments in France and Italy. That happened in 1947, and West Germany banned the party itself in 1956. The two halves of Europe followed the lead of their powerful patrons.

Escalating Confrontation   Fearful of the growing German economy and of American support for anticommunist movements everywhere, the Soviet Union tightened its hold over the states of Eastern Europe. Suddenly, in June 1948, the Soviets closed off overland access to Berlin, which they saw as a dangerous outpost of Western power. War seemed imminent. The United States responded with an extraordinary airlift: For nearly a year, until the Soviets backed down, a steady stream of flights ferried in all of West Berlin's supplies.

When the Soviet Union tested its own atomic bomb in 1949, the United States announced that work had begun on the even more devastating hydrogen bomb. But the loss of a monopoly on atomic weapons made ground forces that did not depend on using them an essential deterrent to Soviet aggression. Consequently, in 1949 the **North Atlantic Treaty Organization (NATO)** was created to coordinate the military planning of the United States, Canada, and ten Western European nations,[3] which now received U.S. military aid. The Soviets replied with the **Warsaw Pact** of communist states in 1955.

[3] Great Britain, France, Belgium, the Netherlands, Luxemburg, Italy, Portugal, Denmark, Norway, and Iceland were the European members. Greece and Turkey would be added in 1952; West Germany, in 1955.

The world was as impressed as the children of Berlin by the airlift that carried supplies to the city and completed 277,264 flights in a year.
Fenno Jacobs/Black Star/StockPhoto

At first, the Cold War was primarily a conflict over Europe, waged as a competition for public opinion as well as international power. But with Eastern Europe isolated behind what Churchill called an "iron curtain" and communists excluded from political power in the West, the focus of the Cold War shifted. When the communist North Koreans invaded South Korea in 1950, the United States at once asked the United Nations to intervene, and the UN (with the USSR temporarily absent) called for an international army to stop the North Koreans. The Cold War was now worldwide, as it spread to colonial issues and conflicts in the Middle East and Asia (see "The Soviet Union Denounces the United States While Calling for Arms Reduction," p. 931).

Decolonization

Although many Allied leaders believed that with some concessions they could restore their empires, the contrary pressures proved too strong. During the war, Japan had taken the East Indies from the Dutch, Indochina from France, and Malaya from Britain. The Vichy government had lost touch with much of France's empire during the war, and both Stalin and President Roosevelt let de Gaulle know they did not favor France's return to Vietnam. Indeed, the United States was traditionally unsympathetic to European empires, and the Soviet Union not only denounced imperialism but frequently aided colonial uprisings.

The Opposition to Empire Nationalist movements opposed to colonial rule had been developing since before World War I, especially in Algeria, India, Indonesia, and Vietnam. These movements gained strength with their experience in combat during two world wars and with the wartime concessions won from their European rulers. European-educated statesmen and intellectuals—like Jawaharlal Nehru in India, Léopold Senghor in Senegal, Sékou Touré in Guinea, and Franz Fanon from the West Indies—built a powerful following at home and appealed to European intellectuals and reformers through writings that explored the profound destructiveness of imperialism. The language and tactics of these movements stressed liberty and self-determination while exposing injustice and selfish interests. Within the Netherlands, France, and Britain, the opponents of imperialism (primarily from parties on the left) grew stronger, their positions reinforced by the public's greater interest in having money spent on reconstruction at home.

For all that, withdrawal was piecemeal and often reluctant. Even in the Middle East, where during the war Britain and France had promised independence to Lebanon and Syria, the two imperial powers continued to jockey for position before withdrawing in 1946. Trans-Jordan became independent. Foreign troops left Iraq and Iran, and negotiations began for British forces to depart from Egypt and the Sudan. Great Britain also undertook to create separate Jewish and Arab states in

THE SOVIET UNION DENOUNCES THE UNITED STATES WHILE CALLING FOR ARMS REDUCTION

Andrei Vishinsky, the Russian delegate to the United Nations, spoke to the General Assembly on November 1, 1948, proposing steps toward arms reduction and control of atomic weapons. The address was testimony, however, to the global range of the Cold War. Most of it consisted of a lengthy denunciation of the policies of the United States, which was accused of undermining the United Nations; of intervening against democracy and peace in Korea, Greece, Indonesia, and Palestine; and of harming Europe's economy with the Marshall Plan while forming a military alliance with the nations of Western Europe aimed at the "freedom-loving" states of Eastern Europe.

"The policy of the USSR is a consistent and constant policy of expanding and strengthening international cooperation. This follows from the very nature of the Soviet State. A socialist State of workers and peasants deeply interested—a State, I repeat, which is deeply interested in the establishment of the most favorable conditions for peaceful creative work in the building of a socialist society. The foreign policy of the Soviet Union pursues the course of cooperation among all countries prepared for peaceful cooperation. The USSR consistently fights against any plan and measures and designs intended to create a gap, a cleavage, among peoples. It fights for the realization and implementation of democratic principles which were born out of the war.

"Such is not the case with the present foreign policy of the United States. After the termination of the recent war, the Government of the United States has changed its foreign policy: from a policy of fighting against aggressive forces, the United States has passed over to a policy of expansion. It is now attempting to realize plans for world domination. It is in open support in various countries of the most reactionary and monarchofascist regimes and groups and rendering to them systematic aid with money and armaments for the suppression of democratic national liberation movements in these countries; organization of military alliances or blocs, the construction of new military air and naval bases as well as the expansion and reconstruction in accordance with the newest military technical requirements of old bases established during the war with Germany, Japan, and Italy; furthermore, unchecked propaganda of a new war against the Soviet Union and the new democracies of Eastern Europe; a wild race of armaments; a true worship of the cult of the atomic bomb and allegedly a means of escape from all the dangers and misfortunes threatening the capitalistic world: these are the principal aspects, the characteristic features, of the foreign policy of the United States of America at present.

"Such a policy is inciting the psychosis of war, sowing restlessness and fear among the broad masses which strive for peace and peaceful creative labor. Such a policy has nothing in common whatsoever with a policy of peace.

"[A] . . . map by the ESSO Company of New York is of the same insolently arrogant and war-inciting nature. This map is published by the Standard Oil Company of New Jersey. It is called, quite provocatively, 'The Map of the Third World War.' That is what they are publishing in the United States—the Map of the Third World War! They are handing them out to motorists. This map, with provocatively militant appeals, carries the heading: 'Pacific Theatre of Military Operations.' The map is an example of the malicious war propaganda against the Soviet Union and the new democracies of East Europe.

". . . The reactionary circles of the United States and the United Kingdom as well as of countries such as France, Belgium, and others, do not confine themselves to slander and abuse alone. This campaign is now being headed not only by amateurs from the family of retired politicians, statesmen, Senators and Members of Parliament, but also by persons now holding high official posts in the Governments of the United States, the United Kingdom, France and some other countries.

". . . On the instructions of the Soviet Union Government the delegation of the USSR proposes to the General Assembly, for the purpose of strengthening the cause of peace and removing the menace of a new war which is being fomented by expansionists and other reactionary elements, the adoption of the following resolution:

". . . as the first step in the reduction of armaments and armed forces to reduce by one-third during one year all present land, naval, and air forces. . . .

". . . to prohibit atomic weapons as weapons intended for aims of aggression and not for those of defense;

". . . to establish within the framework of the Security Council an international control body for the purpose of the supervision and control of the implementation of . . . these measures. . . ."

Speech by Andrei Y. Vishinsky to the United Nations, November 1, 1948, from *Vital Speeches of the Day*, Vol. 15, No. 2, New York: City News Pub. Co., 1949.

Palestine, despite Arab hostility. They removed their troops in May 1948, amid mounting terror campaigns from both sides. Arab forces invaded the day the British left but were driven back. The United Nations, eager to provide Jews a refuge following Nazi persecution, endorsed the creation of an Israeli state, and UN

Lord Mountbatten, war hero and England's last Viceroy of India, speaks to India's Constituent Assembly on the day India became independent, August 18, 1947.
Hulton Archive/Getty Images

mediators were able to bring about a shaky truce that confirmed Israel's existence.

The Global Pattern   Where imperial rule was direct and of long standing, colonial officials offered concessions that somehow always came a little too late or led to demands for more. When they used force, opposition tended to increase, not only on the scene but around the world. News of effective resistance in one colony stimulated new protests and risings in others around the world. Efforts to censor the news and renewed campaigns against subversive agitators only increased their following and cost support of native local elites. Eventually it became clear that once fighting broke out, colonial rule was unlikely to survive, for the subject peoples were generally more determined and more willing to risk their lives than their former rulers.

But pulling out of empire was not easy. Mohandas K. Gandhi gained worldwide admiration for his credo of nonviolent resistance, which contributed greatly to the movement that forced Britain to grant independence to India in 1947. Neither Gandhi nor the British, however, could prevent the violent conflict between Hindus and Muslims that led to an independent Pakistan. Sri Lanka (Ceylon) and Burma gained their independence from Great Britain in the following year, but a major communist revolt broke out immediately afterward. Conflict in Malaya lasted from 1947 until complete British withdrawal in 1960, and Indonesia similarly won freedom from the Dutch in 1949 only after years of combat. Meanwhile, the French continued for a decade to fight for dominance over Indochina.

The campaign for independence became entangled with revolutionary movements and Cold War interests. India tried to steer a middle course, and Pakistan com-

mitted to the West, but in Vietnam the French-educated communist leader Ho Chi Minh organized a brilliant guerrilla campaign to unify the nation. The United States then encouraged France to defeat him, a costly war that ended only with the capture of a major French base at Dien Bien Phu in 1954 and French withdrawal from Vietnam. The Vietnamese communists got strong support from Russia and China. China was the most formidable of the newly communist states, where, after long civil conflict, the communists under Mao Zedong consolidated power in 1949. As a counterweight, the United States promoted the economic revival of a now democratic Japan and gave strong economic and military support to Taiwan (a large island off China still held by the Chinese nationalists). The Americans also promoted a Pacific equivalent to NATO in the Southeast Asia Treaty Organization (SEATO), in which Britain, Pakistan, Australia, New Zealand, and various Asian states joined with the United States in common defense. The Cold War, like **decolonization,** had a global reach.

In Africa, European officials, business people, and residents did what they could to prolong European rule with grants of autonomy and promises of aid, but they could only delay the inevitable. Britain acceded to Ghana's independence in 1957, but resistance and conflict were much greater where there were many residents of European descent. The fight over Algerian independence created a crisis in France (see below). Kenya won independence from Britain in 1963 only after years of brutal warfare and the systematic use of torture by the British to suppress the Mau Mau insurgency. Most African states had won formal independence by the 1960s, although Portugal held on to its colonies longer at the price of a decade of fighting. That ended only in 1974 when a military coup in Portugal forced it to abandon its empire. Its prize colony, Angola, was almost immediately caught up in a civil war in which the United States supported one side and the Soviet Union the other. Conflicts within the former colonies also tended to draw European states back into the political life of former colonies as local leaders appealed to old interests. Some African nations preferred to work with the European country from which they had gained independence rather than embrace the firm Cold War alignment that tended to come with American or Soviet aid.

Thus, Britain and France continued to influence affairs in their former colonies, especially in Africa, by taking advantage of diplomacy, economic interests, common languages, and similar educational, legal, and administrative institutions. Through the Commonwealth of Nations, Great Britain gathered its former colonies in an often influential international club, even if it could not always resolve conflicts between its own members. The *Union Française* even gave French-speaking former colonies a symbolic voice in France's domestic politics. Cold War competition, which increased the amount of economic and military aid available, also helped keep corrupt and dictatorial regimes in power by playing the superpowers against each other. Foreign intervention did not end with the passing of European empires.

EUROPEAN RECOVERY

By the early 1950s, European society had taken on a new look of health and stability. Amid a remarkable economic revival, political life settled into familiar national patterns. An easing of international tension made it possible to agree on a peace treaty for Austria and the withdrawal of occupation forces in 1955, and the USSR granted diplomatic recognition to West Germany despite its having joined NATO. This welcome recovery remained circumscribed, however, by postwar realities. Reinvigorated economies depended heavily on old industries, new state programs, and the policies of the two superpowers. Political stability remained vulnerable to sharp ideological divisions and crises of regime.

Economic Growth

Across Europe, extraordinary economic growth from 1947 to 1957 was connected to a distinctive European emphasis on the role of the state. National governments not only played a central economic role but developed social policies that set new standards for equity and well-being.

Postwar Gains   Despite the shortages of capital and supplies, the postwar situation provided some opportunities. European nations had access to a backlog of unexploited technology, including atomic power, the jet engine, television, antibiotics, and frozen foods. The very need to rebuild factories and transportation networks made it easier to adopt the most efficient methods and newest machinery. Similarly, the tragic displacement of millions of people increased the available skilled labor. Demographic developments also reflected Europe's remarkable resilience. A European "baby boom," though not so large as the simultaneous one in the United States, lasted until 1963, helping to replace some of the losses of war.

Stimulus from the Soviet Union and the United States
The recovery of Eastern Europe depended heavily on the Soviet Union. A strenuous effort enabled it to exceed prewar industrial output by 1953, and its leaders confidently predicted that the USSR would surpass the United States. As the economy expanded, however, the costs of administration increased disproportionately, and the inefficiencies of centralized management became more pronounced. Without a free market, planners had difficulty judging costs and performance. Agriculture was a major disappointment, and the grain harvest of 1953 was only slightly larger than in 1913.

The Soviet Union nevertheless provided an important market and economic stimulus for the countries of the Communist bloc, which organized their economies along the Russian model. All but Poland collectivized farmlands, and all instituted five-year plans to achieve rapid industrialization. In varying degrees, these governments adopted some elements of a mixed economic system—"goulash socialism,"as Hungary's compromise came to be called. The state retained ownership of most means of production, but managers operated within the structure of a largely free market and increased the production of consumer goods. Initially most successful in the already advanced economies of Czechoslovakia and East Germany, the model was generally adopted throughout Eastern Europe, which, although dramatically less prosperous than the West, experienced the highest economic growth rate in its history by the 1950s.

The Western European nations looked to the United States for help. In 1946 the United States extended $4.4 billion in long-term credit to Great Britain and, subsequently, $1.2 billion to France. A year later the United States acknowledged that Europe's economic problems existed on a scale that threatened to undermine recovery and announced the Marshall Plan. Over the next four years, more than $15 billion was channeled into Europe under the direction of the Organization for European Economic Cooperation (OEEC), which eighteen

Western states established for this purpose. That was followed by the European Payments Union, which regulated currency exchanges from 1950 to 1958. Europe's rapid recovery was made possible by this financial stability, by the planning the Marshall Plan required, and by the importation of goods from the United States the Plan provided for (which also benefited the American economy). In the three years from 1948 to 1950, the combined gross national product of the OEEC participants increased at an astonishing annual rate of 25 percent. By 1952 the gross product was approximately 50 percent higher than it had been in 1938, and per capita income was a third higher. Western Europe had never been wealthier.

The Economic Role of the State   The increased economic importance of the public sector resulted in part from the extension of wartime measures and from immediate social needs after the war, but it also reflected a changed attitude toward government's role. Britain and France nationalized utilities, transport, coal, and some of their heavy industry and their banking systems after the war, and in Italy the new state inherited from Fascism the ownership of huge conglomerates that directed hundreds of firms in some of the critical sections of industry. West Germany alone made no effort to expand the number of state-owned industries, but there, too, the government had an important role (as it had during the war) in coordinating economic growth. State ownership gave no assurance of efficient management, good labor relations, or a high return on capital, but it encouraged governments to develop economic policies to guide both public and private enterprises in the interests of overall growth.

With the Monnet Plan (1946–1950), France set the model of loose but effective economic direction from the state. Its advanced methods of national accounting and its highly trained corps of "technocrats" proved especially effective. Comparable plans were devised from Britain to Israel, especially in Scandinavian and Mediterranean countries. In West Germany the largest banks and a private trade association played a somewhat similar role through their close ties to government.

Nearly all European governments established programs to protect ordinary citizens and their families against sickness, impoverished old age, and unemployment. Great Britain provided the earliest and (Sweden excepted) probably the most complete example of what has come to be called the welfare state. Its cornerstone was the National Health Service, inaugurated in 1948, which assumed nearly the total cost of medical, dental, and hospital care for every citizen. Such programs were themselves an outcome of the war effort, which had lessened inequality in Britain (the diet of the very poor had actually improved). Continental governments also provided universal health care, family allowances with payments for minor children, housing programs, and a growing array of social services. By reducing insecurity, these measures also stimulated consumption. To meet their cost, states raised taxes and became more efficient in collecting them, in the process accumulating reserves that they used for investment according to their economic plans.

New Political Directions

Ironically, greater well-being tended to favor more conservative policies. Only in Scandinavia did socialists continue in office. In Britain the Conservatives regained power in 1951 and kept it for the next thirteen years, ending rationing and lowering taxes but not undoing most of Labour's social program. In 1953 the coronation of Queen Elizabeth II was celebrated as the symbol of a new era of prosperity. Italy's Christian Democrats turned more to the right while keeping Communists isolated, and West Germany under Adenauer became a model of stable prosperity. Political changes in France and the Soviet Union were more dramatic.

The Crisis of France's Fourth Republic   France's multiparty system tended not to produce strong governments; yet in many respects the Fourth Republic performed very well. In 1954 an able prime minister of the center-left, Pierre Mendès-France, announced a dynamic program of political reform and social modernization and at the same time set about extricating France from Indochina. To some on the right, that seemed dangerous weakness, and the reform measures further antagonized an angry movement of small shopkeepers and farmers—people bypassed by the benefits of modernization. The electorate shifted away from the center toward Charles de Gaulle, the very symbol of strength and order, and to the communist left.

Given these social strains, the colonial crisis in Algeria proved fatal. From 1954 to 1958 the Algerian problem brought down more French governments than any other issue, and the uprising against French rule was growing. A French colony since 1830, Algeria had a sizable French population that had lived there for generations, and their insistence that Algeria should remain French had a patriotic appeal to many people in France. The question of what to do added another bitter, ideological division. Supporters of French rule emphasized the loyalty of French settlers and the atrocities committed by Algerian nationalists. French army officers who had been fighting colonial uprisings in Africa and Asia since 1945 saw themselves, in the spirit of the Cold War, holding the line alone against worldwide communist plots. They denounced treacherous "politicians" ready to make concessions to Alger-

In January 1957 French paratroopers, searching for terrorists on the outskirts of Algiers, frisk a civilian in Arab clothing.
Bettmann/Corbis

ian nationalists. Leftists and intellectuals, however, were more outraged by the atrocities and torture committed by the French army and at a democracy that would wage war against Algerians seeking to govern themselves.

The Fifth Republic   When a group of French army officers seized political control in Algeria in 1958 and threatened to move against the French government, the National Assembly turned to de Gaulle as the man to unify the country and pacify the military insurgents. Saying he would once again serve the nation, he accepted extraordinary powers for six years (and led France for the next ten). De Gaulle then supported a new constitution, which was overwhelmingly approved by popular referendum in September 1958. It established the Fifth Republic as a presidential regime with a chief executive elected for a seven-year term. De Gaulle was chosen president two months later, and Gaullists became by far the largest party in parliament, where the Communists were reduced to a handful.

The president moved cautiously on the Algerian question, about which he had been shrewdly ambiguous. He quietly weakened and dispersed the leaders of the military revolt, only gradually revealing his willingness to accept Algerian self-determination, something three-quarters of the voters approved in a referendum held in January 1961. Infuriated, the most intransigent officers formed a secret army that for the next eighteen months employed terrorist tactics in both Algeria and France. Having arranged peace with the Algerian rebels, de Gaulle declared war on the army

rebels, and by the end of 1962, they had disbanded. Algeria was independent, and France enjoyed the stability its voters had wanted.

The Soviet Union   After thirty years of dictatorship, Joseph Stalin died of a stroke in 1953. The shock and sense of loss in the Soviet Union was compounded by the problem of succession, something its communist government had faced only once before. It went surprisingly smoothly, and a form of collective leadership emerged. Only in 1956–1957 did it become clear that Nikita Khrushchev was the dominant figure. The competition for leadership involved two principal issues. Stalin's last years had brought heavy repression (with terror), ugly anti-Semitism, and a party line enforced on everything from socialist realism in the arts to the fallacious genetic theories of Trofim Lysenko. Many Russians wanted an end to such policies. The second issue was the standard of living, which had been sacrificed to the demanding goals of the latest five-year plan. Even Stalin had hinted that it might be time to increase consumption as well as build industry. Khrushchev had seemed conservative on the need for change, and his triumph showed again that control of the Communist party remained the key to power. Still, the infighting that brought him to the top, which included sudden dismissals and even executions, was followed not by purges but by the reassignment of his opponents to less prominent positions.

With a speech to the Twentieth Party Congress in 1956, Khrushchev established his surprising new direction. He attacked the "cult of personality" under Stalin, naming many of Stalin's excesses, his paranoid distrust, his interference in the conduct of war, and his responsibility for the purge trials of the 1930s. Nothing like it had occurred before. Myths that for a generation had been central to the nation's enormous sacrifices were suddenly unmasked. Khrushchev's charges circulated widely in secret and then more openly, with unsettling effects in the Soviet Union, Eastern Europe, and communist movements everywhere. Streets and squares were renamed; statues and pictures disappeared. With the thaw following Stalin's death, a freer and more open society appeared in prospect. Although Khrushchev quickly clamped down on criticism amid rising complaints about domestic problems and rumblings from within the Soviet bloc, restraints were never again so rigid or arbitrary as they had been under Stalin. When the Soviet Union celebrated the fortieth anniversary of the Russian Revolution in 1957 by launching the world's first space satellite, *Sputnik*, the USSR's status as a state both powerful and stable seemed dramatically confirmed.

The International Context

Although Britain and France were on the Security Council and Scandinavians served as the UN's general secretaries until 1961, the United Nations reflected a redistribution of international power in which Europe no longer dominated. Economic strength made Western European nations prominent in such international economic organizations as the International Monetary Fund and in arms sales but did not lessen their subordination to the superpowers. Often restive individual nations sought to follow distinctive paths.

The Suez Crisis　Great Britain asserted its independence during a crisis in relations with Egypt, once a part of their empire. Gamal Abdel Nasser's government was distrusted in the West for its nationalism, its radical domestic program, and its willingness to accept aid from nations in the Communist bloc. When the Western powers, following the United States, refused aid for the construction of a high dam across the Nile at Aswan, Nasser nationalized the Suez Canal, still owned by a British-controlled company. Britain responded strongly and, after efforts at compromise broke down, conspired with Israel and France to take military action. Israel attacked Egypt in October 1956 and occupied the banks of the canal, aided by an Anglo-French bombardment. Because both the Soviet Union and the United States opposed the entire venture, the United Nations was able to force a ceasefire within a week and the withdrawal of foreign troops shortly afterward. This return to old imperialist tactics merely demonstrated that such tactics no longer worked and

that British and French action required American acquiescence. That remained true even though Britain soon became the third nation to possess a hydrogen bomb and France would later be the fourth.

The Soviet Bloc　The Communist governments of Eastern Europe had closely mimicked Soviet rule in the ruthless use of secret police and internment camps, in the idolization of Stalin, and in general policy. But resentment of the USSR's exploitation became more public after Stalin's death. Within three months, the workers of East Berlin took to the streets in a general strike, protesting the increased production quotas they blamed on the Soviet Union. Russian tanks rushed in to put down the revolt, but it had long-lasting effects. Walter Ulbricht became the new leader of East Germany and offered a program of higher wages and better living conditions even while strengthening the dictatorship. Although still tightly tied to the Soviet Union, East Germany expanded its trade with West Germany and developed a voice of its own in the councils of communist countries.

A workers' protest in Poland in 1956 even won support from nationalists within the Communist party. Once again Soviet forces intervened, this time to public jeers. The Polish Communist party then elected its secretary, Wladyslaw Gomulka, in preference to the pro-Russian candidate. Gomulka retained power until 1970 by convincing the Soviets of his loyalty while arguing that socialist states needed to follow distinctive national paths. Poland demanded and got a share of the war reparations that Germany paid, negotiated economic aid from the United States, and mitigated its repression of the Catholic Church and of Polish intellectuals.

Risings in Hungary ended more tragically. Riots in October 1956 were fiercely anti-Russian, and the Soviet troops at first withdrew from Budapest, seemingly disposed to accept Hungary's increased autonomy. Then Imre Nagy, who had been arrested the year before for "right-wing deviationism," became premier. Bowing to popular pressure, he agreed to replace the alliance with Russia with a policy of neutrality. The Soviet leaders pressured, threatened, and finally sent their army to crush the revolution. It did so in ten days of bitter fighting while rebel radio stations pleaded for the Western aid that many Hungarians expected. None came. Hungary suffered a heavy-handed, repressive Soviet occupation, and a new wave of refugees left the country. Nagy himself was eventually executed, yet his successor, Janos Kadar, slowly led the country on a more national course.

Washington denounced Russian imperialism but remained preoccupied with the crisis over the Suez Canal within its own alliance, in effect acknowledging a So-

Soviet tanks occupy the streets of Budapest; the uprising of October 1956 had been crushed.
Bettmann/Corbis

viet sphere of influence. The USSR would not allow satellite regimes to defy Soviet policy. Yugoslavia remained the great exception, and improved relations with Khrushchev did not affect Yugoslavia's trade with the West nor its experiments at decentralization. Albania, isolated from the Soviet sphere by geography, and the most backward country on the Continent, formed closer ties to communist China as a kind of challenge to the USSR. Romania, like Bulgaria among the most Stalinist of the satellite regimes, distanced itself slightly by seeking better relations with the West. Little more was possible.

Bipolar Stability   The Warsaw Pact and the NATO alliance institutionalized the armed confrontation between the superpowers in Europe. For some thirty years their competition shaped international relations, at times becoming a rigid opposition and at others allowing some flexibility. In 1961 East-West tension was literally cast in stone when East Germany built a long gray wall across the center of Berlin, eventually extending it along East Germany's entire western border. As a symbol and as a device to keep East Germans from leaving, the wall fostered international distrust. There was a still more ominous crisis in 1961, when the United States sponsored an invasion of Cuba aimed at the overthrow of Fidel Castro. It failed, and in the following year the Russians began to base missiles in Cuba. War seemed imminent until, as the Americans massed their fleet, the Soviets withdrew their missiles. There was, after all, a mutual interest in not disturbing the balance of power, and the Soviet Union was facing a growing rift

with China that made diplomatic exchanges with the United States more attractive.

Literally in the middle, European governments used their influence to favor East-West negotiations at summit conferences and on specific issues. They promoted agreements on space exploration in 1967, the beginning of the Strategic Arms Limitation Talks in 1969, and on the principles of human rights at the Helsinki Conference in 1975. Through trade, loans, and technical agreements, the governments of Western Europe encouraged those of Eastern Europe toward whatever autonomy from the Soviet Union they were willing to attempt.

National Interests   Individual states continued to probe ways to serve their interests. West Germany gradually asserted some of the political weight that its wealth implied. Less committed to the Cold War than Adenauer had been, Willy Brandt skillfully negotiated a new opening to the East. The resulting treaty between West Germany and the Soviet Union, signed in 1970, was a milestone that earned Brandt the Nobel Peace Prize. While allowing for a peaceful reunification of Germany as a possibility, it accepted West Germany's eastern boundary, pointed to a normalization of the status of Berlin (still divided between Soviet and Western occupation), and paved the way for extensive relations between West Germany and the governments of Eastern Europe.

Great Britain emphasized its close ties to the United States rather than to Europe, and the Scandinavian countries tended to position themselves as friends of nonaligned countries and mediators between the superpowers. The most flamboyant search for an independent policy was de Gaulle's. Resentful of American policy toward France, he set upon a course that by 1966 led to the withdrawal of French forces from NATO command (and of NATO forces from French soil), although France remained a member of the alliance. France also strengthened its relations with Eastern Europe and increased its aid to developing nations. Greater independence from American policy appealed to many others in the West, especially on the left, and in 1981 nearly half a million young people in Bonn and perhaps another million in other capitals marched to demand that Europe be freed of the nuclear weapons of either side.

Summary

Europe's war, like its ideological divisions, had spread around the world, and it had taken a worldwide mobilization to defeat the Axis. The exhausting victory over Fascism, Nazism, and Japanese militarism took an immense toll in lives and resources. Yet European nations rebounded with remarkable speed after 1945, and the dominant states on the whole adjusted realistically to the loss of their empires and of their former international preeminence. The Cold War's ideological and geographical division of Europe became a basic fact of life. But disillusionment could be found on both sides of the divide. The new welfare states of the democracies scarcely solved all their problems, and in the Communist block, one-party dictatorship and repression continued long after Stalin's demise. Europe had recovered from the nightmare of World War II, but its economic, social, and cultural place in the modern world remained unclear.

QUESTIONS FOR FURTHER THOUGHT

1. Initially, new technologies and tactics made a crucial difference in the course of the war, but was the later course of the war reminiscent of, even a continuation of, World War I?
2. How would you compare the problems of reconstruction after World War II and the responses to them to the period of reconstruction after World War I? What was learned from that recent history?
3. To what extent were American and Western European policies partly responsible for the Cold War? To what extent did the actions of the Soviet Union precipitate the Cold War?

RECOMMENDED READING

Sources

*Churchill, Sir Winston S. *The Second World War.* 6 vols. 1948–1954. Each volume of Churchill's detailed account can be read singly. His masterly prose recaptures the drama and meaning of the century's greatest war.

*Frank, Anne. *Diary of a Young Girl.* 1947. The unvarnished thoughts of a doomed Jewish girl hiding in Amsterdam during the Nazi occupation.

*Hitler's *Table-Talk.* Hugh Trevor-Roper (ed.). 1988. Recorded by his aides, Hitler's opinionated ramblings and reminiscences have a chilling fascination.

Monnet, Jean. *Memoires.* 1978. The chief architect of the European Community here reveals the roots of his vision and the personal style that made him so effective.

Studies

*Aron, Raymond. *The Imperial Republic: The United States and the World, 1945–1973.* 1974. A leading French thinker of the time analyzes the period of American dominance.

Brown, Colin, and Peter J. Mooney. *Cold War to Détente, 1945–1980.* 1981. A largely narrative account of relations between the superpowers.

Calder, Angus. *The People's War: Britain 1939–1945.* 1969. A spirited account of the British home front.

Chambers, John Whiteclay II, and David Culbert (eds.). *World War II, Film and History,* 1996. A study of the formation of popular images.

*Clendinnen, Inga. *Reading the Holocaust.* 1999. A discussion of what the Holocaust meant to perpetrators and victims, as reflected in memoirs and fiction.

*Crossman, Richard H. (ed.). *The God That Failed.* 1950. The moving testimony of former Marxists about their lost faith during the era of Stalin.

*Crouzet, Maurice. *The European Renaissance since 1945.* 1971. An optimistic essay on postwar Europe and the growth of the European Community.

Dawidowicz, Lucy S. *The War against the Jews, 1933–1945.* 1976. An extensive consideration of the twentieth century's greatest horror.

*DePorte, A. W. *Europe between the Superpowers.* 1979. An assessment of Europe's place in the postwar bipolar system.

Elkins, Caroline. *Imperial Reckoning. The Untold Story of Britain's Gulag in Kenya.* 2004. Documents the brutal British campaign of torture and forced removal against the independence revolt in Kenya in the 1950s.

Fejto, François. *A History of the People's Democracies: Eastern Europe since Stalin.* 1971. The conflicts and variety among Eastern European states under Soviet dominance.

Gross, Jan. *Neighbors: The Destruction of the Jewish Community in Jedwabne, Poland.* 2001. A case study of murderous anti-Semitism and its appalling results.

Grosser, Alfred. *The Western Alliance: European-American Relations since 1945.* 1983. A clear-headed account of how international relations have worked in practice.

Hennessy, Peter. *Never Again: Britain, 1945–1951.* 1993. A balanced narrative of the triumphs and failures of Britain's postwar socialist government.

Jackson, Julian. *France: The Dark Years, 1940–1944.* 2001. A comprehensive and balanced account of collaboration and resistance.

La Feber, Walter. *America, Russia, and the Cold War.* 1967. Argues for the responsibility of the United States in creating the Cold War.

Lagrou, Pieter. *The Legacy of Nazi Occupation: Patriotic Memory and National Recovery in Western Europe, 1945–1965.* 1999. A comparative study of how France, Belgium, and the Netherlands dealt with the impact of Nazi occupation as they undertook postwar reconstruction.

*Laqueur, Walter. *Europe since Hitler.* 1982. One of the ablest surveys of the foundations of contemporary Europe that sees Europe as a whole.

*Liddell-Hart, Basil H. *History of the Second World War.* 1980. The crowning work of this renowned strategist and military historian.

*Maier, Charles S. (ed.). *The Origins of the Cold War and Contemporary Europe.* 1978. Essays seeking not so much to lay blame for the Cold War but to study its connection to domestic societies.

*Mason, Tim, and Jane Caplan (eds.). *Nazism, Fascism, and the Working Class.* 1995. Ten essays engage leading historical interpretations on fascism and social class.

*Mazower, Mark. *Dark Continent: Europe's Twentieth Century.* 1999. An original and critical interpretation.

Milward, Alan S. *The Reconstruction of Western Europe, 1945–1951.* 1984. Concludes that the economic boom of the 1950s and 1960s began as early as 1945, when government policy established international economic interdependence.

*Neff, Donal. *Warriors at Suez.* 1981. This dramatic account by a journalist focuses on the political leaders of the nations involved in the crisis of 1956.

Rioux, Jean-Pierre. *The Fourth Republic, 1945–1958.* 1987. A close look at and a critical assessment of the period before de Gaulle's reemergence.

Sherwin, M. J. A. *A World Destroyed: The Atomic Bomb and the Grand Alliance.* 1975. A scholarly and balanced account of this controversial subject.

*Ulam, Adam B. *Expansion and Coexistence: The History of Soviet Foreign Policy, 1917–1973.* 1974. An expert appraisal of the consistent patterns and political pressures underlying Soviet policy.

Weinberg, Gerhard. *A World at Arms: A Global History of World War II.* 1994. Remarkably balanced synthesis, attentive to political and economic as well as military aspects of the war.

Wilkinson, James D. *The Intellectual Resistance in Europe.* 1981. A wide-ranging assessment of the content and legacy of the antifascist resistance and its place in contemporary thought.

*Winter, Jay, and Emmanuel Sivan. *War and Remembrance in the Twentieth Century.* 2000. Essays on the cultural and psychological impact of war as a major element of modern history.

*Available in paperback.

In November 1989 the East German government suddenly granted free access to West Berlin; the spontaneous celebrations that followed became the symbol of one of history's great turning points.

Chapter Thirty

THE NEW EUROPE

THE NEW INSTITUTIONS • POSTINDUSTRIAL SOCIETY • THE POLITICS OF PROSPERITY
• THE END OF AN ERA • CONTEMPORARY CULTURE

In the last third of the twentieth century, Europe entered on a new course, and 1957 marked a quiet turning point. The Soviet Union's achievement in launching *Sputnik* confirmed the equilibrium between the two superpowers and allowed renewed emphasis on raising the standard of living in the USSR and the Eastern European nations firmly in the Soviet orbit. In Western Europe the struggles over Algeria and Egypt were the last flurry of old imperial dreams and brought a new constitution in France and new policies and leaders in Britain. In retrospect, however, the event of 1957 with the greatest importance for the future was a treaty signed by six nations meeting in Rome. That agreement would grow into the European Union (EU), which has steadily expanded in authority and membership. To some of its members, the EU remains merely a set of international agreements. To others the new institutions constitute a fundamental change in the body politic.

Despite the economic "miracles" of the 1950s, there was good reason to wonder whether European economies could match the economic transformation occurring in North America or meet the demands of

global capitalism. That Western Europe was able to do that requires explanation. At the same time, the social changes accompanying this transformation created new strains and highlighted issues of the environment, immigration, and persistent unemployment. Political systems had to deal with these challenges amidst increasing demands for greater democracy and social justice. The nations of Western Europe weathered the domestic crises of the 1960s and 1970s with new policies and awkward compromises. Communist governments responded first with repression; then in the 1980s they, too, tried desperate compromise. Its outcome was their sudden collapse—a sweeping and unexpected transformation that affected all of Europe and much of the world.

This new Europe of open markets, international institutions, and easy movement across boundaries fosters a lively, self-aware culture. Affected by increased leisure, the growth in higher education, and the spread of mass media, it critically addresses new questions about the role of women, the meaning of identity, and the nature of culture itself.

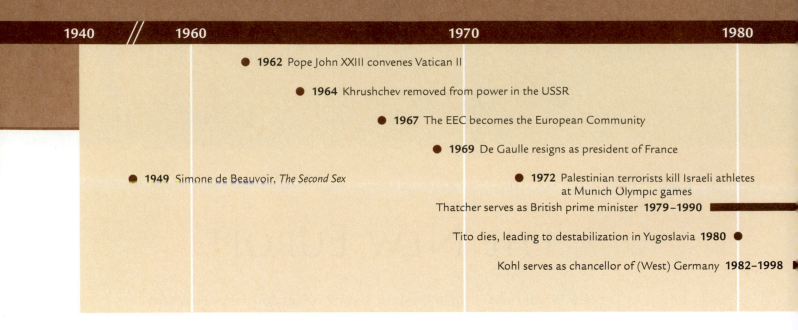

1962 Pope John XXIII convenes Vatican II

1964 Khrushchev removed from power in the USSR

1967 The EEC becomes the European Community

1969 De Gaulle resigns as president of France

1949 Simone de Beauvoir, *The Second Sex*

1972 Palestinian terrorists kill Israeli athletes at Munich Olympic games

Thatcher serves as British prime minister **1979–1990**

Tito dies, leading to destabilization in Yugoslavia **1980**

Kohl serves as chancellor of (West) Germany **1982–1998**

THE NEW INSTITUTIONS

Paradoxically, the bloodshed of World War II made it easier to see Western Europe as a cultural unit.[1] The Allies had talked a lot about the shared values of Western civilization. Postwar recovery in Western Europe featured transnational programs like the Marshall Plan, and the Cold War engendered further measures of cooperation, as in NATO. Thus, economic and military needs, cultural change, and an older idealism came together in the creation of new European institutions. Some doubt the durability of these new ventures; some see them as beginning a historic transformation, a new body politic. All agree that today, at least, they are a central fact of European life.

Cautious Beginnings

The Council of Europe Movements calling for some kind of European integration sprang up in many parts of Europe in the postwar period, and in 1948 a conference met in The Hague to consider the possibilities. A thousand delegates from twenty countries gathered for the meeting, which was chaired by Winston Churchill, who had spoken a few years earlier about the need for a United States of Europe. Division that continues to this day appeared from the first. Some countries (initially led by France and Belgium) wanted to create a European body with real political power, while others (primarily Great Britain and the Scandinavian countries) favored a kind of continuing conference.

The Council of Europe founded in the following year was a compromise. The foreign ministers of the member states, meeting in private, would constitute the Council. There would also be a merely consultative assembly, whose delegates eventually came to be selected by their national parliaments. Headquarters were established in Strasbourg; ten nations joined.[2] The new organization had no binding powers over its members; yet it did come to exercise some influence. A declaration of human rights, drawn up in 1950, went into effect in 1953 to safeguard "the ideals and principles of . . . [the members'] common heritage," and a European Court of Human Rights held its first hearing in 1960. Maintaining individual freedom and the rule of law was a requirement that excluded all the nations of Eastern Europe as well as Spain, Portugal, and Greece while they were ruled by dictators.

Remarkably, the decisions of the Council and its Court of Justice have been obeyed by member states. By 1970 eight more nations had joined. The Council has gained authority over the years, playing an active part in aiding the nations of Eastern Europe before and after the breakup of communist regimes there. Today, some forty-one nations, from Russia to the Atlantic, including all the smallest ones, belong to the Council. Its assembly meets regularly in Strasbourg to establish general policies, where complaints against any member state are adjudicated.

[1] Geographers list nineteen nations as belonging to Western Europe: Austria, Belgium, Denmark, Finland, France, Greece, Iceland, Ireland, Italy, Lichtenstein, Luxemburg, the Netherlands, Norway, Portugal, Spain, Sweden, Switzerland, the United Kingdom, and Germany. All of these countries save Finland now belong to the Council of Europe, which also includes Cyprus, Malta, and Turkey.

Belgium, Denmark, Iceland, Germany, Italy, Luxemburg, the Netherlands, Norway, Portugal, Turkey, the United Kingdom, Canada, and the United States belong to NATO. France and Greece are also NATO members, although their armed forces no longer are under NATO command.

[2] Belgium, France, the Netherlands, Luxemburg, the United Kingdom, Ireland, Italy, Denmark, Norway, and Sweden.

- **1985** Gorbachev becomes leader of the Soviet Union
- **1986** Single Europe Act begins to integrate Europe into a single market
- **1987** Soviet troops begin to withdraw from Afghanistan
- **1989** Havel elected president of Czechoslovakia
- **1990** East and West Germany reunited
- **1991** USSR officially dissolves
- **1992** Maastricht Treaty converts the EC to the European Union (EU)
- **1993** Czechoslovakia divides into the Czech Republic and Slovakia

- **1999** Euro is introduced as a common currency
- **2000** Milosovic removed from power in Yugoslavia; Putin elected president of Russia
- **2001** September 11 terrorist attacks in the United States
- **2003** Invasion of Iraq divides the United States from many European allies
- **2004** Terrorist bombing in Madrid kills almost 200 people
- **2005** Pope John Paul II dies; Benedict XVI selected; France and the Netherlands reject the European constitution

The Coal and Steel Community Stronger transnational institutions proved hard to establish, however, and so two leaders who envisioned a more integrated Europe decided to begin with small steps. Jean Monnet, a leading French economist, and Robert Schuman, France's foreign minister, proposed creating the French-German Coal and Steel Authority, which was established in 1950. A year later, propelled by the euphoria of recovery, Italy and the three Benelux countries (Belgium, Luxemburg, and the Netherlands) joined to establish the European Coal and Steel Community (ECSC), which was given the power to coordinate the production and distribution of the coal and steel critical to industrial growth. That became the kernel of a common market.

As the ECSC demonstrated its economic value and as its authority increased, further steps became possible, just as Monnet and Schuman had hoped. In the Treaty of Rome, signed in 1957, the six members of the ECSC created a new agency to coordinate the development of atomic energy (EURATOM) and agreed in gradual steps to eliminate tariffs between each other and to establish a common tariff toward goods from other nations. This was the European Economic Community (EEC), also known as the Common Market. Its prospects were anything but certain. Britain refused to take part, and de Gaulle was less internationalist than his predecessors. Nevertheless, six nations that had often been at war now declared that they were "determined to lay the foundations of ever-closer union among the peoples of Europe . . . and to ensure economic and social progress by common action."

EEC vs. EFTA A dramatic rivalry followed. Reluctant to accept permanent political ties to the Continent or to loosen its Commonwealth connections, Great Britain fostered the creation of the European Free Trade Association (EFTA). This looser association, which set more limited goals (free trade among its members, for example, but not a common tariff) and had very limited powers of enforcement, was joined by Sweden, Norway, Denmark, Austria, Switzerland, and Portugal.

In the ensuing years the states of the EEC enjoyed the highest increases in per capita productivity, more than 4 percent a year. By 1968 all tariffs among the member states had been abolished. Continued economic growth among its members made the organization ever more attractive. In 1967 the EEC's three organizations—the EEC, the ECSC, and EURATOM—were folded into a single entity, the European Community (EC). Its name, like its goals, now explicitly reached beyond the merely economic.

The European Community After extended negotiations, Great Britain, Ireland, and Denmark joined the EC in 1973. Together, the nine members of the European Community surpassed the United States in the production of automobiles and steel, and by 1979 in total gross national product (GNP) as well. Fuller integration among the nine member-states came slowly, however.

Once again, the momentum for growth came more from evolving practices than dramatic decisions. The EC's executive is the Commission, to which each member nation appoints at least one member and the larger countries more. Members of the Commission are independent of any national government. The programs adopted by the Commission often set new precedents and have led to a large bureaucracy at its headquarters in Brussels. The heads of government of the EC countries began in 1972 to hold meetings several times a year as the European Council, in itself an important step toward more coordinated policies. Every six months the head of a different government serves as president, and a tendency developed for presidents of the European Council to seek some new accomplishment to mark their term, another stimulus to expanded activity. New legislation proposed by the Commission must be approved by a Council of Ministers, specialists in the relevant fields, such as agriculture or finance, appointed by and responsible to the member governments. Clearly intended as a check on the EC's autonomy, the Council of Ministers was nevertheless empowered in the 1980s to set some policies by majority vote rather than unanimity.

At the same time the European Parliament has gradually become more assertive. Despite its very limited powers, the creation of an elected parliament was hailed as "the birth of the European citizen." In 1979 the citizens of each member nation began voting directly for delegates to the Community's parliament, where the representatives sit according to political party rather than nationality. Over the years the European Parliament has begun to assert itself and to supervise the Commission more closely. The process of integration continued, with creation of a mechanism for regulating exchange rates and through the rulings of the EC's court. Thus, uniform regulations have spread to many fields (on standards of product quality, insurance, and environmental issues, for instance) and common legal rights (in the case, for example, of migrant workers).

Agricultural policy was especially controversial. The EC's subsidies, which had strong domestic support from farmers, resulted in costly stockpiles of unsold produce. Because Britain imports most of its food and has a smaller farm population, it contributed far more toward these costs than the EC spent in Britain. Its vigorous protests forced adjustments and then some reform of agricultural policies in 1981; but the issue was complicated by the further enlargement of the Community to include Greece in 1981 and Spain and Portugal in 1986, all countries with competing agricultural interests. Special grants to poorer regions—including the northwestern part of the British Isles, southern Italy, and the poorer members generally (Ireland, Portugal, Spain, and Greece)—have helped to bring those regions closer to the EC's general level of prosperity. As the Community gained a voice in matters traditionally considered the exclusive concern of national governments, especially social issues, domestic opposition to the EC tended to become more vocal.

Toward European Union

The Single Europe Act In 1986 Jacques Delors, the president of the Commission, succeeded in winning support for the Single European Act, an agreement to create a single market. The act declared that by the end of 1992 there would no longer be any restrictions within the Community on the movement of goods, services, workers, or capital. These terms were met, with minor exceptions, and they brought striking changes in the lives of ordinary people. Most of the border checkpoints between member states on the continent have disappeared. All citizens of the member states carry a community passport, crossing national boundaries without restriction. Any of them can open a bank account, take out a mortgage, receive medical care, or practice a profession anywhere in the EC, for, in principle at least, the licenses and university degrees of one country are recognized in all the others.

The Single European Act required that vast arrays of national regulations be made uniform. Social practice, however, was as important as any new directives. Anticipating European integration, businesses, government agencies, and schools set about on their own to bring their practices in line with those of the EC, forming ties with colleagues in other countries. Organizations and individuals began to think and operate in terms of the Community as a whole; and sensing this momentum, the leaders of the EC pressed for more.

The European Union The **Maastricht Treaty** of 1992 changed the name of the EC to the European Union (EU) to indicate its greater integration. The treaty also enlarged the powers of its parliament and called for a coordinated foreign policy and the adoption of a common European currency by 1999. The public found all these changes and requirements a little overwhelming. Attitudes toward the EU tended to turn more negative wherever domestic economies faltered, and public opinion on the complex Maastricht Treaty was so evenly divided in most countries that many questioned support for the EU itself. Within member states, opposition to the EU was joined by those opposed to any surrender of national sovereignty, by opponents of the EU's bureaucratic regulations, by those fearful of foreign immigrants, and by a variety of special interests. Advocates of the EU, on the other hand, have tended to include the most prominent political leaders, economic interests, and intellectuals.

In 1995 Austria, Finland, and Sweden joined the EU, and, remarkably, all of the fifteen member states except Greece met the Maastricht Treaty's stringent requirements. That willingness to raise taxes and cut budgets is testimony to widespread faith in the future of the EU. Great Britain, Denmark, and Sweden opted, however, not to join the common currency on the first wave. In the rest of the EU, banks, businesses, and governments began in 1999 to keep accounts in Euros, and in 2002 the traditional coins and bills emblazoned with national symbols gave way to currency in Euros (only the coins have national emblems, on one side).

MAP 30.1 GROWTH OF THE EUROPEAN UNION TO 2005
Established in 1967 as the European Economic Community (or Common Market), the European Union originally comprised six nations and by 2004 had grown to twenty-five. In what year did these nations adopt one common currency? What other nations do you suppose may join?
◆ For an online version, go to www.mhhe.com/chambers9 > chapter 30 > book maps

CHRONOLOGY
The Making of the European Union

1950 Germany and France form the Coal and Steel Authority.

1951 Italy and the Benelux nations join.

1957 The Treaty of Rome creates the European Economic Community of six nations.

1965 The EEC becomes the European Community.

1973 Great Britain, Ireland, and Denmark join the EC.

1979 Citizens elect the EC parliament.

1981 Greece joins the EC.

1986 Spain and Portugal join the EC.

1987 The Single Europe Act.

1992 Maastricht Treaty calls for European Union, common currency.

1995 Austria, Finland, and Sweden join the EU.

1999 Common currency, central bank take effect.

2004 The EU adds ten new members, primarily from Eastern Europe.

2005 Voters in France and the Netherlands reject the European constitution.

By the end of the century, thirteen additional nations were in line to join the EU, leading to further prolonged negotiations as each state struggled to meet the EU's requirements for limited national debt, low inflation, political freedoms, and accommodation to hundreds of complex regulations. Decision making remained cumbersome, however, and reform difficult. Nevertheless, the EU's authority continued to grow. Its idealism is represented in EU policies requiring that all members protect freedom of speech and movement and have a system of equal justice (with no death penalty) and in its many pronouncements on such matters as human rights, opposition to racism, protection of children, and "the full participation of women in civic, political, social, and economic life."

In 2004 the EU significantly expanded its size and domain by incorporating ten new states: Poland, the Czech Republic, Slovakia, Slovenia, Hungary, Estonia, Latvia, Lithuania, Cyprus, and Malta. Most of these countries either were located in Eastern Europe or were former Soviet republics. Generally speaking, they were smaller and poorer than the original member states. With the addition of these new countries, the EU expanded its boundaries far to the east. It also became a massive organization. Its twenty-five member states had a total population of 450 million and an aggregate economy that was roughly equal to the United States.

To help manage the organization's expanded size and promote greater unity, European leaders initiated

Flags of the member states fly outside the Brussels headquarters of the European Union.
Steve Vidler/eStock Photo

a convention in 2002 under former French President Valery Giscard d'Estaing to draft a European constitution. After two years of deliberation, the convention finalized the document. The constitution was designed to streamline the decision-making process while encouraging members to adopt common policies regarding defense, immigration, and foreign affairs. Among its provisions were a longer term for its president, a written bill of rights, and new laws to deal with terrorism. On October 29, 2004, representatives of the member states signed the constitution.

To become law, however, the constitution had to be ratified by all twenty-five countries within two years. On May 29 and June 1, 2005, voters in France and the Netherlands, respectively, rejected the constitution by large margins. Voters argued that the new system would lead to a loss of national sovereignty and increased immigration. In addition, left-wing opponents feared that the constitution would jeopardize the **social welfare** state and diminish workers' rights. Some observers also interpreted the vote as a protest against continued high unemployment and weak job growth in many European nations, including France. The rejection of the constitution generated uncertainty regarding the future of European integration.

POSTINDUSTRIAL SOCIETY

The European Union's importance in Europe today rests on a half-century of economic growth and on the political and social changes that accompanied it. Standards of living rose, despite important setbacks, and every nation grew richer than it had ever been before. But the ways of creating wealth changed and so did lifestyles. Industrial production no longer dominated the economy, for the service sector employed more and more people in office work, sales, and personal services. Societies so structured have come to be called, a little misleadingly, *postindustrial*, to indicate the importance of these changes with their emphasis on new technologies. Exuberantly embraced in North America and by the elites of Western Europe, the transformation was slower and encountered greater difficulty in Eastern Europe. Everywhere, it brought painful dislocations, unemployment, and greater inequality as well as greater wealth.

Europe's Advantage

The coal fields of Britain, West Germany, and Eastern Europe and the iron ore fields of France and Sweden were once critical to industrialization, and they have been supplemented by other sources of energy such as natural gas and oilfields in the North Sea. Except for the Soviet Union, however, much of Europe has historically been disadvantaged by its limited natural resources. That is now less crucial. Economies today create wealth primarily through efficient production and services; and Europe, like the United States, excels in the factors that matter most: great amounts of capital and institutions to facilitate its rapid movement, advanced technology, experienced managers, skilled and willing workers, efficient marketing, rapid communication, high levels of education, adaptable societies, and high consumption.

Infrastructure During the 1960s every European nation launched new road-building projects, and by 1980 the most important of them had been completed. Superhighways now run from Stockholm to south of Valencia and from Naples to Hamburg. Railroads, valued

High-speed electric trains poised for their dash from Paris to Lyons.
Liaison International/Getty Images

for passenger travel as well as for transport (and usually considered a service to be provided by the state) have been extensively modernized. In 1981 French trains, which hold world speed records, began to carry passengers from Paris to Lyons at 165 miles per hour. A tunnel under the English Channel, a project considered for centuries, opened in 1994 to provide direct automobile and rail links between Britain and the Continent. Water transport along Europe's coasts, rivers, and canals is relatively inexpensive, and air travel, dense throughout the Continent, is especially important across the expanses of Russia.

In the face of American and Japanese competition, Western European nations remain among the technological leaders in electronic communication, especially wireless telephones and satellite communication. On average, one-third of EU households are connected to the Internet. Europe's banks and stock markets, important sources of stability, began in the 1980s to become more flexible and in the 1990s to join international and global mergers. In 2000 the Frankfurt and London stock markets joined forces. Until the 1980s, in much of Western Europe as well as the communist nations outside the USSR, economic growth rested on mixed economies, with an important role for state planning in the West and some room for private enterprise in Eastern Europe. Since then, a strong trend toward privatization has brought more rapid growth and painful social adjustments that include cost cutting, rising unemployment, and international competition. The emphasis on productive efficiency, new products, marketing, and personal consumption that once seemed characteristically American now dominates most of Europe.

In the West agricultural productivity has increased as well, while the number of people who work on the land has continued to decline (in Ireland, until very recently one of the West's least developed nations, 60 percent of the workforce were employed in agriculture in 1960 and fewer than 8 percent are today). Modern farming, too, requires new investment and mechanization. With only about 3 percent of the world's farmland, Western Europe produces nearly one-third of the world's dairy products and 15 percent of the world's eggs, potatoes, and wheat (of which France is one of the world's largest producers).

Education   Modern societies require citizens to be more highly educated than ever before. That has led to extensive and controversial reforms that in the late 1960s and early 1970s often led to angry demonstrations and even riots. Traditionally in Europe, secondary education has been the great mark of social difference. A small fraction of students went to secondary schools noted for their demanding and usually classical curriculums. These schools were the gateway to a univer-

The skyscrapers of Frankfurt, one of Europe's greatest commercial centers, loom over the statue of Schiller, Germany's great eighteenth-century playwright.
Liaison International/Getty Images

sity. A larger proportion of students went to vocational secondary schools, and half or more of the youths beyond the ages of twelve and fourteen went directly to work. Despite efforts to make this segregation an effect of academic performance, in practice social class made a critical difference.

Educational reforms intended to make the system more democratic were offensive to defenders of the older curriculum, while not going far enough to satisfy student radicals, but they instituted important changes. In the West enrollments in the more prestigious forms of secondary education doubled and trebled, and a trend toward "comprehensive" schools more like the American high school allowed many of the graduates of those schools to go on to higher education. The number of university students has increased enormously, and more women than men now receive postsecondary education in most developed countries. In communist societies the children of workers and party members had priority for admission to such schools, but total enrollments increased more slowly than in the West before 1989. This expansion in the years of schooling and access to it requires increased state expenditure and families able to support children for a longer period before they begin to work. It helps to make social mobility become a more universal goal and makes education the subject of intense debate about fairness, culture, and employment.

Educational systems have tended to become more similar across Western Europe, although important differences in national traditions remain. Despite the creation of hundreds of new institutions of higher education, often with American-style campuses, enrollments in many countries swelled beyond capacity. Among European nations, the Scandinavian countries, France, Italy, Belgium, and the Netherlands have the highest proportion of young adults in some form of postsecondary education, with the proportion somewhat lower in Great Britain and Germany.

The Changing Roles of Women As women's lives changed even more than men's, European institutions have gradually adapted. Women have become more prominent in all the professions and in politics. Most European women over the age of fifteen engage in economic activity (the proportion ranges from about half in Italy, Spain, and Ireland to more than 80 percent of them in the Czech Republic, Poland, and the Scandinavian countries). Women make up from one-fifth to half of all managers in most countries, especially in smaller enterprises and rarely in top positions. Labor unions thus pay more attention to their needs: in Italy, for example, pressing employers to grant released time with pay to take special courses. Women constitute from one-half to nearly two-thirds of professional and technical workers. European governments and employers have made child care available to most women, in effect, encouraging mothers to have careers. On the average, however, women workers continue to earn less than men (between two-thirds as much in Britain and four-fifths as much in France).

Young women expect to have a freedom of movement that their mothers did not as they train, travel, work, and socialize outside their families. The availability of contraception and, by the 1970s, abortion (changes more accepted in Europe than in the United States) has added to this sense that women have the right to plan their life course. Gender discrimination nevertheless remains a serious problem and source of tension. The EU and many governments have adopted strong statements for equality and against sexual harassment, but their effect is limited, making the difference between ideal and reality all the more apparent as women wrestle with the pressure of multiple responsibilities.

Urban Planning Postindustrial society is heavily urban, and Europe has long experience in making its well-organized cities function well. The threat was clear: As urban agglomerations expanded across the surrounding suburbs, the inner core of older cities tended to lose population as people with greater wealth and leisure sought more space and privacy. The new highways, extended subways, and bus lines that push the cities outward rarely keep pace with the congestion of traffic at their heart. As similar-looking skyscrapers rise in the city centers and in new business centers around what had been the periphery, similar residential districts sprawl across the outskirts. One-fifth of the population of France lives within an hour's drive of Paris, and nearly that proportion of Britain's population is similarly close to London. Volgograd stretches for forty-five miles along the river after which it was named, and some fourteen cities of the former Soviet Union have a population of more than a million.

European states were accustomed to spending money to maintain city services, but governments were unsure how best to build. In the 1950s new housing in both the East and West tended to look like dreary concrete barracks and often provided few of the services necessary to create a sense of community. In nearly every country, whole new cities, often bleak and artificial, surround the metropolis: Five towns of 24,000 people each were placed around Paris; twenty-four such towns surround Moscow. Since the 1970s the trend has shifted to new urban hubs on a smaller scale, carefully planned to have shopping, recreational, and cultural centers of their own as well as some light industry so that much of the working population need not commute. Many of these ventures—those in Scandinavia were among the first—have proved to be attractive models, widely imitated, mixing large and small modern buildings, pleasant streets, and restful green spaces. War damage forced German governments into expensive projects of urban renewal, and from the 1960s on governments across much of Western Europe have invested in refurbishing urban centers and creating some of the world's most interesting experiments in urban planning, often with stunning effects.

Cities like Rome and Vienna found that banning traffic from the narrow, medieval streets of their old centers made them more attractive (and expensive) for shops and housing. Loud laments were heard at the

The glass structures that replaced Paris' central market evoke the iron and glass pavilions built a century earlier but now contain shops, museums, and a media center. New apartment buildings stand in the background. Leveling the crowded old mercantile buildings surrounding the market also provided a view of the Gothic church of St. Eustache that had not been seen for centuries.
Charles Graham/eStock Photo

razing of Les Halles in Paris, handsome wrought iron sheds built in the Second Empire to provision the capital with food, but the gains in efficiency and improved traffic were undeniable. The exciting new cultural center built in the 1970s as part of the area's renewal has become the most visited site in Paris. In London, the produce sellers of Covent Garden also had to give way to a cultural center, and Billingsgate, the fishmarket that gave the language a word for verbal abuse, closed in 1981. Everywhere, new projects are under way in the expectation that, like the stunning Guggenheim museum in Bilbao or bridge in Lisbon, they will keep Europe's great cities among the most livable and attractive in the world.

Social Welfare Although the gap between the wealthiest and poorest segments of society is less in Europe than in the United States, large pockets of unemployment and poverty remain. In communist Europe professional people and officials lived at a much higher standard and with far greater freedom of choice than workers or peasants, an important element in the unpopularity and ultimate downfall of those governments. The full impact of these inequalities is softened throughout

Europe by complex provisions for social security, minimal fees for education, universal medical care, many provisions for the elderly, and a wide variety of family benefits and services. Not surprisingly, rates of infant mortality have declined and longevity rates have improved in Western Europe to be among the most favorable in the world. Because birthrates in Europe are now generally the lowest in the world and the elderly are an ever-increasing proportion of the population as people live longer, social expenditures necessarily increase.

In the 1970s unemployment had begun to rise, depressing regions dependent on declining industries as well as those that had never enjoyed industrial prosperity. By the 1990s, endemic unemployment had become one of Europe's most pressing social problems, generally averaging more than 10 percent and hitting young people and immigrants the hardest. On the whole, programs of special subsidies and tax incentives have had disappointing results. With taxation already relatively high, governments have had little new to offer, while demands for lower taxes became a mainstay of the political center and right. Subsidized housing had mixed results. Although relatively cheap in communist Europe, good housing remained scarce, leading to long waiting lists for cramped apartments. In the West, where much new housing was subsidized by governments (in the 1980s about one-third of new housing in Germany, one-half in Great Britain, two-thirds in Sweden and France), the result was segregation in isolated and dismal surroundings.

New Issues

Foreign Workers   A massive movement of people began to alter European society in the 1960s. With jobs available in the industrial zones, many men and somewhat fewer women moved from the less developed to the more prosperous regions. At first, it seemed a continuation of older patterns, but immigrants now crossed national boundaries more freely than in the past. Southern Italians went to northern Italy but also to Switzerland and Germany; Spaniards, Portuguese, and North Africans to France; Yugoslavs and Turks to Germany; African and Caribbean blacks, Indians, and Pakistanis to England. These people, too, contributed to Europe's economic miracle although they were most often employed as domestic servants, street sweepers, and the least skilled industrial workers. By the 1970s foreign immigrants made up 17 percent of the workforce in Switzerland, some 8 percent in Germany, and only slightly less than that in France.

Often different in physical appearance, language, and culture from the majority of those around them, immigrants were drawn together and forced by poverty to live in slums that quickly became ghetto subcultures resistant to and misunderstood by the larger society. Lacking the full protection of citizenship, resented by native workers competing for jobs and higher pay,

despised as sources of crime and heavy welfare costs, these migrants re-created some of the gravest social problems of the early nineteenth century, now exacerbated by prejudices of race and color. Many gradually came to see themselves as permanent residents, and many acquired citizenship, as their children automatically did (except in Germany). This second generation went to local schools and for the most part adopted local ways, yet these families often remained partially dependent on government programs and were the first to feel the effects of any economic downturn. Their plight and the prejudice against them were problems for which most European societies were ill prepared (see "A Turkish Girl Arrives in Germany," p. 952).

The Environment   Economic growth also brought pollution that contaminated the air, waterways, and countryside as it poured from factories and automobiles and littered the landscape. Monuments and scenic places revered for centuries came to be seriously threatened. Western Europe was slow to respond, and in Eastern Europe the problem was ruthlessly ignored. The Rhine became one of the most polluted international waterways, and high concentrations of mercury were recorded in Geneva's Lac Leman. Escaped industrial gases caused illness and death in the outskirts of Milan, and the magnificent palaces of Venice were discovered to be slowly sinking, apparently because the earth beneath their pilings gives way as underground water is pumped up on the mainland for industrial use. Acid rain is destroying Germany's Black Forest, and it is now dangerous to bathe in or eat fish from much of the Baltic and Mediterranean seas. The remaining monuments of ancient Greece and Rome and the ornate facades of

Many German cities have districts, like this one in Cologne, that look almost as if they were in Turkey.
Regis Bossu/Corbis Sygma

A Turkish Girl Arrives in Germany

Aynur, a young Turkish girl, published in a Turkish newspaper a very personal and frank account of her life in Germany. She had gone to Germany with her mother to live with her father, who had worked there several years. Leaving her village elementary school behind, she went to a Turkish school in Germany and lived there into her teens. As she adopted new ways, she became alienated from her family, found German friends only among groups of homosexuals and drug addicts, and eventually made several visits to Turkey in search of old ties to her extended family and native culture. She ends her account with the comment, "On my birth certificate it is written that I am a 'Turk.' But in the full sense, more correctly, with my thinking, I am not completely a Turk. I do not want to be a German either." In the passage quoted here, she describes her first days in Germany.

"A bustle of activity commenced as soon as the plane landed in Berlin. Everyone wanted to disembark. I looked for the sun as soon as we went out, but it wasn't to be seen. I thought I was before a gray wall. The weather was cloudy and rainy. Later on I started looking for blond people. I always thought that all Germans were blond.

"We took a taxi. I was watching out of the window. I was trying to see the white houses which I had dreamed about. All around were large brick buildings. There were no people in sight on the wide boulevards. I was constantly asking my father, 'Which one looks like our house?'

"Finally we got out of the taxi. I was looking around to find the house that they lived in. My father, pointing to a somewhat larger door, said, 'You enter here.' An old door, all the edges of which were broken, and a somewhat large building from which the plaster was falling. After we entered through the large door and went through the small concrete courtyard, we started climbing the stairs. The holding-on places were broken.

"Suddenly all of my illusions were shattered. Pessimism and dejection overcame me. We climbed until the fourth floor. My father opened the door. A small hallway, a living room, and a kitchen. That was all there was to the home. The toilet was outside, they said.

"I asked myself, 'Is this our house?' I withdrew to a corner and started to investigate the living room. In the middle a faded rug was laid. Around it stood a few old armchairs. The only new thing was a fairly large television that stood in the corner. Forgetting everything, we started playing with the television. At each press of a button, a different film appeared.

"Six of us started to live together in the one-room house. This situation did not strike me as odd. In our village, too, we used to live all together. Since I had not had any different living experience, this did not seem unusual.

"My older sister and I did not get out of the room for a period of three months. We were afraid, and moreover, our father was not giving us permission. Our only tie to the outside was a window facing the courtyard. Children were playing in the courtyard. My only wish was to play with them. From time to time I was able to talk through the kitchen window with our neighbor's daughter, who was a year older than I. I was impatiently waiting for her return from school. My first friend in Germany was this girl.

"Her hair was cut very short. She looked like a very modern girl. We went down together to the courtyard entrance to play. I gained a little courage. After that I started going to their home.

"We used to wear skirts over pajamas in our village. My father had bought slacks for us in Istanbul. From then on we wore slacks under our skirts instead of pajamas. Slowly I began to imitate my friend. When no one was at home, I would take off my skirt and walk around in my slacks. At other times, I would take off my slacks and walk around in just my skirt. My older sister was not able to dare to do this. She would sit at the window as my look-out.

"For a long time when we went outside, we wore slacks under our skirts."

From Akural Aynur (tr.), in Ilhan Basgöz and Norman Furniss (eds.), *Turkish Workers in Europe*, Turkish Studies Publications, 1985. Reprinted by permission.

Gothic churches in city after city crumble and crack from the vibrations and fumes of modern traffic.

Governments intent upon stimulating growth were reluctant to impose the restrictions and to undertake the expense that protecting the environment required until strong ecology movements in Germany, Britain, the Low Countries, and France forced their hand. Political parties, known everywhere as the Greens, focused on these environmental issues, and several international agencies now enforce European standards against pollution. Although much more remains to be done, the gains have been impressive. Stern regulations eliminated the smog that had plagued London since the sixteenth century, killing thousands of people as recently as 1952. The Thames has become a clean river for the first time in centuries. In the 1960s and 1970s, nearly every building in Paris was stripped of the somber, dark patina of soot accumulated through 150 years of industrialization (to begin darkening anew from automotive exhaust). By the 1980s, citizens' movements, well-organized programs for recycling, and strict regulations were changing the landscape across Europe, and European states had become leaders in international measures to protect the environment. Green parties have remained small, even in Germany, where the movement is strongest, but the larger parties have adopted much of the Green's program.

THE POLITICS OF PROSPERITY

In retrospect, the basis for Europe's greater integration and economic transformation was established by 1957, but that prospect was often called into question between then and 1989. At the time, the tensions of the Cold War in a divided continent and domestic social and political conflicts were more obvious. Two periods of crisis stand out, one culminating in 1968 and the other beginning in 1973; both challenged established economic and political systems.

Waves of Protest

Greater well-being seemed to strengthen moral outrage. Many Western Europeans were appalled by the rising commercialism and inequality that accompanied prosperity. Many Eastern Europeans were determined to win some of the advantages that their Western neighbors enjoyed. A number of otherwise very different movements sought alternatives.

The Revolutions of 1968   For a few weeks in May 1968 the students of Paris seemed to recapture the rev-olutionary spirit of 1848, with their barricades of paving stones and trees, imaginative posters, and mocking slogans. In Germany, Italy, Great Britain, and the United States as well, students briefly acted as an independent political force in 1968 and 1969. Inspired by the movements of national liberation in Africa and Asia and outraged by the war in Vietnam, they denounced imperialism as a product of capitalist societies that used consumer goods to mask inequality and injustice.

More specifically, they excoriated the rigidities and inadequacies of the educational system to which they were subject. Their elders noted with surprise that these angry protesters were in fact the beneficiaries of expanded educational opportunities and increased prosperity. As revolutions, these movements failed. Labor unions and the traditional left were suspicious of privileged college students; liberals and conservatives were offended by rudeness and violence. In elections following these upheavals, the majority of voters turned to parties that emphasized order. These protest movements nevertheless stimulated important reforms, especially of education; and their style of protest, their challenges to middle-class values, and their questioning of authority have remained important elements in public discourse and in a distinctive youth culture. Ever since, movements of social criticism have used the organizing skills and tactics of satire and street theater that worked so well in 1968 to win the attention of a complacent society. The Greens are very much the heirs of those student activists.

In Czechoslovakia the optimism of 1968, when Alexander Dubček came to power, was short-lived. As

University of Paris students riot in the streets May 14, 1968, to protest police brutality. Within days, the unrest spread throughout France, sparking off strikes and riots among students and dissatisfied workers.
Hulton Archive/Getty Images

Communist party secretary, he was able to adopt a program of liberalization including greater autonomy for Slovakia and freedom of speech, assembly, and religion. Students were noisily enthusiastic for this "communism with a human face," but Moscow saw it as an intolerable danger. In the largest military operation in Europe since World War II, troops from the Soviet Union, East Germany, Hungary, and Poland invaded Czechoslovakia in August. Dubček was soon ousted; of his springtime program, only Slovakian autonomy was allowed to stand.

The Women's Movement   Women were prominent in the student demonstrations across Europe and the United States, but many discovered that male radicals, despite their rhetoric of equality in matters of race and class, tended to allocate subordinate roles to women. Simone de Beauvoir's *The Second Sex* and Betty Friedan's *The Feminine Mystique* helped women identify the problem.

When her book first appeared in 1949, Beauvoir was well established in French intellectual circles but best known as the intimate friend of Jean-Paul Sartre, the most admired intellectual of the day. *The Second Sex*, a memoir of her own experiences, made her famous. The book gained power in the context of the 1960s, for it reflected on the ways in which society tends to make women ancillary to others (institutions, families, husbands). Beauvoir wondered whether equality for women, even if possible, would be enough to overcome this subordination to other interests or whether women did not need to establish their own distinctive voice. Her questions and her candor pushed the women's movement in new directions.

The Feminine Mystique appeared in 1963. Betty Friedan, an experienced American journalist and mother of three, wrote about what she saw as the split between the idealized vision of the perfect homemaker and the reality of women's lives. In the years after World War II, women were expected to find personal fulfillment as wives and mothers. Instead, Friedan identified women as suffering from "the problem that has no name" and a profound crisis in identity. Along with *The Second Sex*, *The Feminine Mystique* became a handbook of the women's movement in the 1960s and 1970s. The new politics centering on women's needs and women's rights became one of the important developments of the latter half of the twentieth century.

Terrorism   Rather than abandon fading hope for revolution, some radical groups turned to terrorism. The skills and equipment necessary for a terrorist campaign were not hard to come by in the semisecret world of international crime, espionage, and arms deals that flourished during the Cold War. Although terrorists were few in number, modern urban society is vulnerable to their anonymity and surprise tactics. These small groups did not aim to capture power but rather to provoke the authorities into repressive acts that would alienate the public. German terrorists shot at business leaders as well as politicians until caught by severely efficient police. Basque terrorists shook several Spanish governments with their bombs and murders but accomplished little more.

In Italy, Marxist and neo-Fascist underground bands competed in kidnappings and bombings accompanied by revolutionary proclamations. In 1978 the best-known of the radical groups, the Red Brigades, climaxed a series of attention-getting exploits by kidnapping Aldo Moro, a prominent politician. Police searched for him in vain as the nation held its breath until his bullet-riddled body was found in an abandoned car. Across the political spectrum, the public responded with outrage against terrorism rather than anger at the state. Although the Red Brigades remained active, they were on the wane by the time their leaders were arrested a few years later. Such incidents, like the shooting of Pope John Paul II by a Turkish terrorist in 1981, provoked outcries about the alienation and violence of modern society but did little to change it.

Terrorism was more effective where local hatreds gave it a popular base. Irish Protestants, determined to maintain British rule in Northern Ireland, had long clashed with their Catholic neighbors who wanted Northern Ireland to be part of the Irish Republic. Neither side had much faith in the British government's proposed compromises permitting local rule, proposals never tested because terrorism reached the level of continuous war. Underground organizations on each side killed hundreds of innocent people. Although a majority of people said they favored some workable solution, loyalty to neighbors, nationalism, and recollections of past injustice, discrimination, and repression permitted violence to prevent a resolution. Even by the end of the century, the truce established in the 1990s remained uncertain.

More distant religious strife brought terrorists to the Continent, too. Supporters of the Palestine Liberation Organization, seeking a Palestinian state, killed Israeli athletes at the Munich Olympic Games in 1972, and in the 1970s Muslim terrorists placed bombs in Paris stores. Terrorists gained little for their various causes, but heightened urban fear made tough security measures and heavily armed police a prominent part of European city life.

Eurocommunism   By the 1980s, communist parties in Western Europe realized that they had to broaden their appeal. Throughout Western Europe years of electoral and union activity had led communist parties to form coalitions and take positions on scores of practical issues. Arguing for social justice and political freedom invited commitment to pluralism and democracy. The French and Italian parties had objected to the Soviet invasion of Czechoslovakia in 1968, and the Italian party even accepted NATO. Criticizing Soviet policies in Eastern Europe opened prospects for an alternative program.

That alternative came to be known as **Eurocommunism,** and Italy's Communist party was its model and major proponent.[3] It proclaimed its commitment to civil rights, multiple parties, and free elections; and its increased electoral successes stimulated a trend toward Eurocommunism on the left. The French Communist party, traditionally among Europe's most rigid, and a newly revived Spanish Communist party adopted Eurocommunist positions despite pressure from the Soviet Union to preserve the unity of communism and remain loyal to Soviet leadership. By the sixtieth anniversary of the Russian Revolution in 1977, Eurocommunism represented a schism within the communist movement. But suspicion of communist parties ran deep, and even limited electoral success stimulated opposition on the right.

The End of Dictatorship in Greece, Portugal, and Spain While the Western European Left was moderating its goals, opposition to anti-Communist dictatorships grew stronger. In Greece army officers had overthrown the unstable parliamentary system and eventually the monarchy itself in 1967, but in 1973, civilian leaders were able to force the restoration of democracy. To strengthen a fragile but modernizing economy, Greece's repressive military rulers had needed to draw closer to Western Europe, where they found little inclination to deal with dictators. That Greece was clearly on a course leading toward democracy and economic growth was confirmed by its acceptance as a member of the European Community in 1981.

In Portugal the Salazar regime, which had paralleled Franco's long period of rule in Spain, continued in milder form even after Salazar became incapacitated in 1968. While opposition remained stymied at home, it grew stronger in Portuguese Guinea, Angola, and Mozambique, where Portugal relied on brute force to hold on to its empire. Condemned in the United Nations, by African states, and by most European nations, the overtaxed government was suddenly seized in April

1974 by a group of army officers promising full freedom and civil rights for Portugal and self-determination for the colonies. The response was overwhelming. Crowds danced in the streets and cheered smiling soldiers whose rifles were decorated with flowers.

The euphoria could not last. A poor and backward country, Portugal faced raging inflation and declining production. While peasants claimed the land they had long coveted, socialist and communist unions competed for support among the workers, business groups struggled to defend their interests, and many prominent businesspersons left the country. For two years new cabinets fell after a few months in the face of revolts from left and right. Nevertheless, the nationalization of banks and industry was followed by free elections in 1975 and 1976 and relatively moderate socialist governments that brought Portugal closer to other countries in Western Europe. With elections that gave Portugal its first democratically elected civilian president in sixty years, Portugal was able to join the European Community in 1986.

In contrast, the political transformation in Spain was more gradual. Franco retired in 1973 but skillfully kept his influence until his death two years later. In 1969 he had called on Juan Carlos, the grandson of Spain's last king, to take the empty throne, in effect as Franco's heir. Juan Carlos showed himself more committed to democracy and more adept than expected. In 1978 Spanish voters approved a new constitution. An attempted military coup failed, and greater regional autonomy reduced agitation from separatists.

Suddenly, a society long dormant came alive. A stagnant economy caught fire in the 1970s and 1980s under the premiership of the extremely popular socialist Felipe Gonzales. Although his decision to join NATO was not popular, his success in joining the European Community in 1986 and ending Spain's fifty years of relative isolation was widely cheered. The prosperous democracies of Western Europe, capitalist but committed to programs of social welfare, were the models other Europeans wanted to follow.

Capitalist Countries: The Challenge of Recession

When economic growth slowed, political conflict sharpened. Traditional political programs lost relevance, and weakened governments struggled with problems deeply embedded in their social and economic systems. Nearly everywhere the crisis brought a change of government as opposition parties gained power.

The Energy Crisis European economies were instantly vulnerable when in October 1973 the oil-exporting nations (mainly in the Middle East) banded

---

[3] Communist parties had traditionally attracted nearly one-third of the electorate in Italy, one-fifth in France and Finland, one-eighth in Spain, and much less elsewhere: about 5 percent in Sweden, 4 percent in Denmark, 3 percent in Belgium, 2 percent in Greece and the Netherlands, and less than 1 percent in West Germany and Great Britain. The parties in Portugal, briefly powerful after the revolution there, and in Finland were the two least inclined to Eurocommunism.

France invested more heavily in nuclear energy than did any other country. Well run and efficient, the French plants provoked little public opposition, but not even a mural of a child at the beach could make the giant stacks seem to belong in their bucolic surroundings.
Liaison International/Getty Images

together in a cartel to raise international prices. Europe imported nearly two-thirds of its energy in the form of petroleum, and only the Soviet Union could meet its own energy needs through domestic production. In response to higher prices, Western nations redoubled efforts to develop domestic sources of energy. Over the next decade the exploitation of North Sea oilfields made Norway self-sufficient and Britain nearly so, and the Netherlands developed Europe's largest fields of natural gas. But Europe's energy consumption continued to rise, and greater self-sufficiency depended heavily on nuclear energy. By 1976 more than half the world's nuclear power plants operating or under construction were in Europe, where France became the world leader. These measures and the collapse of oil prices in 1986 eased the immediate economic crisis, but its effects remained.

Opposition to reliance on nuclear power, long led by the Greens, increased after the meltdown of a nuclear reactor at Chernobyl in the Soviet Union in 1986. Radioactive clouds swept over much of Central Europe, creating concern for safety that increased in the following years as the full extent of the casualties within the Soviet Union came to be known.

Stagflation The high cost of energy added to inflationary pressures. Among major capitalist nations, only West Germany consistently managed to hold the rate of inflation below 5 percent a year. It rose to more than 20 percent in Britain and Italy in 1975–1976 (30 percent in Portugal) and undermined planning, savings, and trade, while squeezing salaried employees and many workers. This widespread inflation called into question

practices on which prosperity had seemed to rest: deficit financing by governments, increased imports, and business reliance on raising prices to maintain profits. Efforts to change these policies initiated conflicts and class conflicts over social programs, especially in Britain and Italy. Economists identified a new condition, *stagflation*, the paradoxical combination of economic stagnation and rising prices, and worried about a more familiar one, recession.

Where strong anti-inflationary measures were imposed, as in Britain, unemployment rose, and in Europe generally became higher in the 1980s than at any time since World War II (although it would rise higher still a decade later). Europe was undergoing a major and painful economic transition. Its now-aging industries faced increased competition from the Japanese and from new plants in other parts of the world, and the state's capacity to respond was limited. The public supported social programs but opposed still higher taxes, leaving little room for maneuver, and an unexpected rise in regionalism brought new accusations that central governments disadvantaged local interests. Thus, long-accepted national policies were called into question amid new divisions. Although each country evolved its own response, the central issues were similar.

Opening to the Left: France The student revolt in May 1968 shook de Gaulle's government. It weathered the storm through firmness and promises of reform because student radicals had frightened French voters, but the Fifth Republic was never the same. The government passed education reforms, broadened social programs, and made the civil service more responsive; but when a referendum on de Gaulle's vague but far-reaching plans for decentralizing the state was defeated in 1969, he resigned. The next two presidents from the center-right differed from him more in style than policy, winning close elections with promises of stability and moderation, while the opposition criticized the political system as isolated from public opinion in its reliance on highly trained experts, however brilliant. Although most French voters were centrist, the division between a more or less Marxist left and a technocratic right dominated politics.

In 1981 the socialist leader of that opposition, François Mitterrand, won the presidential election by attempting to bridge that divide. He promised a new emphasis on issues of culture, leisure, and urban life but maintained his alliance with the Communists and supported the traditional demands of the left for the nationalization of many industries and for a more equitable distribution of income. On election night there was dancing in the streets and optimistic talk of a post-Gaullist era. The new government began with dramatic measures, nationalizing many heavy industries and most banks, raising wages and benefits, and increasing social expenditures. The daring gamble failed to stimulate an economy hurt by business distrust, the fall of the franc, and an unfavorable international economy. Within a few years, separated from the Communists, Mitterrand adopted policies of austerity, deflation, and investment in high technology that were more like those of his predecessors than his own platform. As the right gained in elections, France found a socialist president leading a government of the center that was concerned with economic modernization, military strength, and support of the European Community. As to the new social problems—large pockets of endemic unemployment, drug addiction, and racial conflict—politicians had few solutions.

Opening to the Left: Italy

In 1983 Bettino Craxi became Italy's first Socialist prime minister. A wily politician who had rebuilt the Socialist party, his arrival in power was the culmination of two long-term political trends. The Christian Democrats had dominated Italian politics since the founding of the republic in 1946, relying on a system of semisecret negotiations and labyrinthine deals. The Communists continued to be excluded from these coalitions, as were the Socialists until 1963. While the economy boomed—Italy had enjoyed the longest period of economic growth of any European nation—this domination was acceptable. As restiveness increased, so did restiveness with this closed and often corrupt system. Meanwhile, the growing respectability of the Communist party helped it win local offices in much of the north, especially in the newly established regional administrations and in most

The bicentennial of the French Revolution, which had once divided all of Europe, was the occasion in 1989 for celebrations of patriotism and the importance of human rights.
D. Aubert/Corbis Sygma

of Italy's largest cities. Having gained a reputation for probity and efficiency, they argued for a "historic compromise," in which Communists and Christian Democrats would govern together in the interests of stability and reform.

Some such compromise seemed all but inevitable until Craxi set the Socialists on the opposite course and made his party indispensable to a governing coalition. He became prime minister and brought a new decisiveness to government, but the hoped-for reforms gave way to more immediate economic issues. His government brought stability, an impressive achievement in a tension-filled nation undergoing rapid social change, but one that fell far short of the significant changes promised.

A Shift to the Right: West Germany

In West Germany political issues tended to be overshadowed by the satisfying fact of prosperity as the Federal Republic surpassed the United States in world trade. Even the significant shift in 1969 to a government led by the Social Democrats did not lessen the commitment to encouraging investment, expanding trade, and preventing inflation. Often surprisingly conservative in their economic policies, the Social Democrats pursued democratization in other ways, carrying through educational reforms, expanding social services, and requiring large firms to have elected labor representatives on a central board of directors. Then in 1982 an unfavorable economic climate helped the Christian Democrats to regain office under Helmut Kohl, who would remain prime minister for longer than anyone since Bismarck. Kohl's government was more closely tied to the United States and friendlier to business but almost as eager as its predecessors to maintain good relations with the East. Like France and Italy, Germany looked more and more to the European Community to provide a program for the future and to shape its international role.

A Shift to the Right: Great Britain

Continuity had characterized British policy for thirty years until Margaret Thatcher became prime minister in 1979. When the Conservatives were in power, they favored the private sector but largely accepted the extensive welfare programs and mixed economy they inherited. Constrained by the plight of the British economy, Labour governments in their turn reduced public expenditures and pressured trade unions to accept wage limits, while improving transport and expanding higher education.

Britain's overwhelming problem was the economy, and neither North Sea oil nor membership in the European Community solved it. Businesses failed to modernize plants or raise productivity at the pace of other industrial nations. Inflation depressed the rate of investment. Analysts found it easier to lay the blame—on the enormous cost to Britain of World War II, unimaginative and weak business managers, an inadequate educational system, the selfish conservatism of labor unions, and the high costs of welfare and defense—than to prescribe remedies. In office as the recession got worse, the Labour party lost the 1979 election.

Margaret Thatcher

A doctrinaire advocate of free enterprise, Thatcher reversed the course of British domestic policy, and the two major parties became more ideological. Out of power, Labour was dominated by its left wing, a fact that divided opposition, helping the Conservatives to stay in office. The results of Thatcher's decisive policies were impressive. The British economy restructured, and productivity rose in the late 1980s, increasing prosperity and reducing still-high unemployment. That restructuring, combined with reductions in social services, including education, also increased social inequality.

Even her opponents—and she was widely disliked—grudgingly admired Thatcher's outspokenness and fearless consistency, and there was no arguing with economic growth. She strengthened her position by appealing to nationalist fervor in 1983 when Argentina suddenly attacked the Falkland Islands (which Britain had held and Argentina had claimed for more than a century), and she took much of the credit for Britain's victory. In 1990 she won her third consecutive election, something no prime minister had done for 160 years. But her unbending defense of unrestrained capitalism and her view of Britain's national interest made for abrasive relations with many leaders at home and with the European Community. A revolt in her own party forced her to resign soon after her last electoral victory. Her less divisive successor kept his party in power until Labour's overwhelming victory in the elections of 1997, but the Thatcher years remain a turning point in modern British history.

Communist Rule: The Problem of Rigidity

Khrushchev's Effort

The Soviet Union's most impressive achievement, admired throughout the world, had been its industrial growth. By the 1960s its economy was second in overall production and wealth only to that of the United States. It sent the first person into orbit around the earth in 1961; and as the world's largest producer of steel, iron, and, more recently, oil, the USSR was apparently gaining in the economic competition with the West. Brashly confident, Khrushchev, who declared that the Soviet Union "would bury" the United States, promised that his government was now able to give more attention to consumer products and adequate housing. Like his campaign of de-Stalinization, such policies opened the possibility of a new evolution in Soviet rule, but that proved difficult.

Khrushchev's plans to increase agricultural production failed, and the issue of whether to invest in consumer goods or heavy industry reopened long-standing conflicts within the highest circles. Many Kremlin leaders worried as well about the growing restiveness in Eastern Europe and the rift with China, which since 1956 had consistently denounced the Soviet Union's international policies as a betrayal of communism. When, in the process of solidifying his authority, Khrushchev antagonized the military, they and his opponents in the Politburo and the Central Committee felt strong enough to speak against him. In 1964 they voted him out of office and sent him into quiet retirement.

Signs of Failure

The orderly transition was promising in itself, but Khrushchev's successors, led by Leonid

Brezhnev, were tough party technicians who held a firm grip on power and offered no fresh solutions. The cold-blooded invasion of Czechoslovakia, the continuing agricultural crisis (which required the purchase of American grain in 1972 and 1975), and the need to import industrial technology, particularly from Italy and France, were all signs of a system failing to adapt to change.

Evidence of arbitrary repression continued to tarnish the country's international image. Throughout the West the press revealed the plight of Soviet Jews, subject to discrimination and attack and intermittently permitted to emigrate. When Boris Pasternak's novel *Doctor Zhivago* exposed the seamy aspects of Soviet life and earned him the Nobel Prize for Literature in 1958, Pasternak was not permitted to go to Stockholm to receive it. Significantly, the case of Alexander Solzhenitsyn in 1970 caused still greater international furor. He, too, was prevented from receiving the Nobel Prize he won that year for his story of the *Gulag Archipelago*, a haunting account of the terrors of Soviet concentration camps. Four years later he was arrested and deported, joining a chorus of Russian writers and scientists whose criticisms were widely published outside the USSR and increasingly well known at home.

Gorbachev's Gamble   When Brezhnev died in 1982, he was succeeded by elderly and ailing party figures who exemplified the bureaucratic grayness of Soviet rule. Thus, the appointment in 1985 of Mikhail Gorbachev to be general secretary of the Communist party marked a new era. At fifty-four, the youngest man to lead the Soviet Union since Stalin, Gorbachev gradually revealed a personality and daring that led him in startling new directions. He spoke openly about problems of inefficiency and alienation (absenteeism and alcoholism among the workforce reached alarming levels), and he recognized the importance of radical reform in order to meet the growing demand for consumer goods and to sustain the arms race with the United States. The cost, and risk, of that competition went up as the president of the United States, Ronald Reagan, poured more money into new weapons. Meanwhile, the contrast between East and West in both agricultural and industrial production had grown more striking, and the USSR's earlier achievements in heavy industry now counted for less economically than the newer technologies and services in which it lagged.

Gorbachev confronted these problems on three fronts. He set about to restructure Soviet society by decentralizing decision making, which required more open communication, greater authority for local managers, and a reduction in the role of the Communist party. Gorbachev had to overcome entrenched resistance at all levels, but his efforts made ***perestroika*** (political and economic restructuring) and ***glasnost*** (greater openness) international words and won him admirers around the world.

Internationally, his foreign policy made him the most popular figure in Soviet history. He campaigned against the threat of nuclear war; and at a summit meeting with Reagan in 1986, Gorbachev suddenly proposed breathtaking reductions in nuclear arms that nearly won Reagan's acquiescence before aides hurriedly dissuaded him. Gorbachev also knew that he must end the war in Afghanistan. Soviet troops had gone there in 1979 to support a Communist government entangled in a bloody guerrilla war against rebels heavily supported by the United States. The war was a dangerous drain on Soviet lives, wealth, and morale, and in 1987 Gorbachev began a staged withdrawal.

Remarkably, he also extended glasnost to Eastern Europe. Gorbachev realized that those governments, too, needed to restructure; and he was glad to end costly barter arrangements with the Comecon nations, which permitted them to buy Soviet oil at prices below the world market in exchange for Eastern European products that the Soviet Union did not want. But once launched, glasnost was hard to contain. When some of the East European nations began to request that Soviet troops leave their territory and to replace their Communist regimes, Gorbachev accepted those changes, too. However necessary, such concessions troubled hostile hard-liners at home, and each step toward reform revealed the need for more and the resistance from officials.

Ethnic Conflict in the USSR   A still greater danger to Soviet stability arose from the explosion of nationalist unrest in 1988. Demonstrations and violent clashes occurred around the perimeter: on the Eastern frontier (in Georgia, Moldavia, and the Ukraine), among the Baltic republics (Latvia, Lithuania, and Estonia), and in the southern republics. The Baltic states created at the end of World War I had lost their independence in World War II, becoming part of the Soviet Union by war's end. Demonstrations there now revived passionate memories of independence, and formerly rubber-stamp representative bodies began to act like parliaments. While they wrote new laws and constitutions, Gorbachev offered general promises, argued for the benefits of membership in the USSR, restrained his own army, and delayed any final stand on their status.

In the southern republics, Azerbaijanis and Armenians engaged in open war, inflamed by conflicts that were ethnic (Azeri and Armenians had fought for centuries), religious (Shia Muslims and Armenian Orthodox Christians), social (the Armenians had generally been wealthier and better educated), political (involving territorial claims and relations with Moscow), and

For years Gorbachev was mobbed by enthusiastic well-wishers whenever he visited Western Europe and the United States; his trip to West Germany in 1990, where he was accompanied by Chancellor Kohl, was one of his last triumphal tours.
R. Bossu/Corbis Sygma

economic (Azerbaijan's oil industry, its principal source of wealth, was declining). Eventually, Soviet troops attempted to separate the combatants but did not try to exercise sovereign authority over them.

Russians constituted the largest ethnic group in the multinational USSR, and theirs was the largest republic. They had long enjoyed privileged status throughout the federation. Now, Russian nationalists fanned the fears of losing that status with a campaign in the name of culture (with appeals to the Orthodox Church), order (attractive to the military and some party members), and race (including virulent anti-Semitism). Nationalism was as grave a challenge to Gorbachev as bloated bureaucracy and stores with empty shelves. The bonds of ideology, institutions, and custom that had held a great state together were beginning to look weak.

Pressure for Change in Eastern Europe   In 1968 the "Brezhnev doctrine" had declared that a "threat to socialism" in one country was a threat to all. He had followed the invasion of Czechoslovakia with efforts to strengthen the economic ties binding the Comecon countries, but the nations of Eastern Europe were looking westward for increased trade and badly needed loans. Romania, not content with its allotted role as a Soviet granary, had launched its own course of industrialization and an independent foreign policy that made its brutal dictator, Nicolae Ceausescu, welcome in the West. East Germany, the second industrial power among communist states (and the seventh in Europe), oscillated between friendly overtures toward and suspicious rejection of West Germany much as it alternated between concessions and repression at home, where there were riots against the government in the early 1970s.

The pressures for change were stronger still in Czechoslovakia, Hungary, and Poland, where cultural ties to Western Europe remained strong and the Catholic Church became an outlet for growing restiveness. Riots against the police took place in Hungary, which had one of the strongest and most consumer-oriented economies of Eastern Europe. Riots in Poland in 1976 forced postponement of a projected rise in food prices, and four years later strikes led to the recognition of Solidarity, an organization of independent trade unions, whose leader, Lech Walesa, became a national hero. With support from the Catholic Church, the Solidarity movement grew strong enough to prompt a change of government. In a world in which public protest was dangerous and rare, events in Poland gained significance. But there was no telling where they would lead. The new head of the Polish Communist party, General Wojciech Jaruzelski, resorted to martial law and clamped down on Solidarity. East European governments continued to rely on force in the face of rising public resentment.

Yugoslavia was the maverick among communist states. Its limited market economy and its independence from the Soviet Union had once suggested another kind of communism. Weakened by Tito's death in 1980 and by contention among its member republics, Yugoslavia could not manage the reforms necessary to shake its economy out of a prolonged economic downturn. There was, in fact, no model of how to make desired changes and preserve communist rule. Soviet presence remained the central fact of life in Eastern Europe.

THE END OF AN ERA

International relations, domestic politics, culture, and trade had all been shaped by forty years of Cold War. In one of history's sudden great turns, communist governments fell across Europe, bringing new regimes in the East and easing domestic divisions in the West by undermining ideologies of left and right. Market economies and mass, parliamentary democracies were the order of the day.

The Miracles of 1989

Although the contradictions had become obvious, no one expected communist rule to collapse completely. Eastern Europe governments had for years eased up on controls and repression when greater efficiency or popular anger seemed to require it. When, however, those steps exposed institutional blockage and threatening dissent, communist governments had moved to stifle reform and silence opposition. In 1989 they did not, and one by one communist regimes were swept away.

Poland   In Poland, despite martial law, Solidarity continued its underground propaganda with wit and daring. It turned the visit of the pope, who was Polish, into the occasion for more demonstrations. Placards and pamphlets, rumors and clandestine radio broadcasts nourished rising agitation. And the government did not call out the army. Gorbachev had told the United Nations in 1988 that the Soviet Union would allow its allies to go their own way. Now that policy was tested. Sensing Walesa's popularity and the power of Solidar-

ity, Jaruzelski relaxed martial law and released some political prisoners. But public anger and frustration increased, and the economy worsened. In February 1989 the government, in a major concession, acknowledged Solidarity's legitimacy, but Solidarity demanded free elections. The government hesitated, and Gorbachev signaled that Poland was on its own. In April, when elections took place, Solidarity won almost all the seats in the parliament. Stunned and frightened, Communist party members did not know what to do. After various formulas for compromise failed, Solidarity took over the cabinet in August, the first noncommunist government in the Soviet bloc.

Hungary   Hungarians were well aware of events in Poland, for the irrepressible flow of information was an important factor in the events of 1989. Political discussion, like economic activity, was already freer in Hungary than other Eastern European countries, and by April even some party officials joined in public discussions of the need for free speech, civil rights, and the protection of private property. At the annual May Day celebrations, international communism's grandest occasion, opponents dwarfed the official celebration, and a huge demonstration in June dared to honor the uprising of 1956. Even some members of the government chose to attend. In October the Hungarian Communist party flexibly changed its name to the Socialist party and promised free elections for the following year. The power of people aroused seemed irresistible.

East Germany   Many old-line Communist leaders remained convinced that a good show of force would

MAP 30.2 EUROPE SINCE WORLD WAR II

This map shows the dramatic border changes and the emergence of new countries in Europe since World War II. Can you name a few of the newest countries in Europe? What were some of the events that led to their independence?

◆ For an online version, go to www.mhhe.com/chambers9 > chapter 30 > book maps

restore order and keep the party in power. In October Erich Honecker, the head of East Germany's Communist party and its prime minister, took that tack. His soldiers beat and arrested demonstrators in East Berlin. A week later, however, he resigned, for Gorbachev announced that he disapproved such use of force; worse, the East German republic was walking away. Every day hundreds of people, especially the young and those with marketable skills, abandoned their country. Most went to Hungary, where they mobbed the West German embassy, seeking visas. Embarrassed Hungarian and West German governments arranged for special trains to carry them west, and more people came, pushing and shouting and climbing over embassy walls.

On November 9, 1989, Honecker's successor announced that East Germany's border with West Berlin would be opened that very day. The guards could not believe their orders. Then late that night they shrugged and stepped aside as hoards of people pushed through the gates of the Berlin Wall. Hundreds, then thousands, cheered and waved from atop that symbol of oppression before strolling past the well-stocked shops of West Berlin. The celebrations continued in front of the television cameras for days, even after work crews began dismantling the wall. Thousands continued to come each day, some just testing what it felt like to be that free and looking in store windows, others seeking a different life in West Germany. Throughout East Germany, meetings that would have been illegal a few weeks earlier took place in churches and public squares as the police watched and then withdrew. The government's promises for reform and official pleas for order were drowned in revelations of past corruption and talk of uniting the two Germanies.

The Final Round in Eastern Europe   For a while the harsher East European governments—in Czechoslovakia, Bulgaria, and Romania—remained unscathed by the changes around them, but that isolation did not last. Crowds of protesters were filling Wenceslas Square in Prague, 40,000 people in October, then 200,000 after a riot in which police beat up demonstrating students. A few days later 300,000 came to shout, sing, and jingle keys as a good-humored suggestion that it was time for the Communists to leave. In now familiar rites, slogans were scrawled everywhere, posters covered the walls, and new political groups formed. By December 1989 the best organized of these, Civic Forum, had won power and elected as president of Czechoslovakia its leader, Vaclav Havel, the popular playwright whose works had long been banned (see "Havel's Inaugural Address," p. 964).

Even Bulgaria and Romania, with less-developed economies and weaker traditions of political participation, could not escape the historic pressure. They met

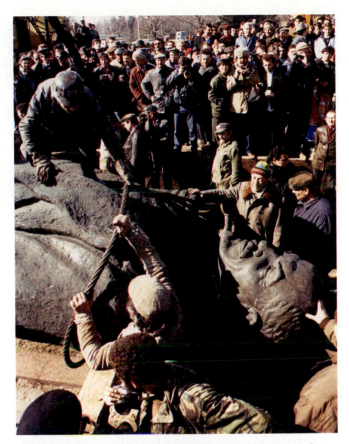

May 1990: Having pulled a statue of Lenin to the ground, Romanian workers remove the cable from his neck.
Bettmann/Corbis

it very differently. Bulgaria's Communist party took its cues from the Soviet Union and in November forced from office Todor Zhivkov, party secretary for thirty-five years and head of state for twenty-seven. He was jailed and plans for free elections announced. Romania, in contrast, suffered weeks of bloodshed. When in December crowds gathered in Bucharest, the government gave the order to shoot. Still the crowds formed and violence increased. Romania's dictator, Ceausescu, tried to make his escape but was caught and executed by firing squad on Christmas Day. Fighting continued for a week between the army and special police loyal to Ceausescu. Everywhere Romanians waved flags with a conspicuous hole in the center where the Communist hammer and sickle had been.

Rarely has there been so sudden a political collapse and on such a scale. Economic failure and resentment of Soviet dominance explain a good deal. Workers and Catholics in Poland, party members and entrepreneurs in Hungary, students and intellectuals in Czechoslovakia mobilized their fellow citizens with surprising speed and skill. For years radio and television had conveyed the knowledge that life was better in the West,

HAVEL'S INAUGURAL ADDRESS

Vaclav Havel was perhaps the most widely admired of the new leaders of Eastern Europe, and his literary skill and philosophic bent made him a particularly effective spokesperson. In his inaugural address on January 1, 1990, as president of the Czech Republic, he commented on the historical meaning of the dramatic changes that brought him to office.

"My dear fellow citizens, for forty years you heard from my predecessors on this day different variations of the same theme: how our country flourished, how many million tons of steel we produced, how happy we all were, how we trusted our government, and what bright perspectives were unfolding in front of us.

"I assume you did not propose me for this office so that I, too, would lie to you.

"Our country is not flourishing. The enormous creative and spiritual potential of our nation is not being used sensibly. Entire branches of industry are producing goods which are of no interest to anyone, while we are lacking the things we need. A state which calls itself a workers' state humiliates and exploits workers. Our obsolete economy is wasting the little energy we have available. A country that once could be proud of the educational level of its citizens spends so little on education that it ranks today as seventy-second in the world. We have polluted our soil, our rivers and forests, bequeathed to us by our ancestors, and we have today the most contaminated environment in Europe. Adult people in our country die earlier than in most other European countries. . . .

"But all this is still not the main problem. The worst thing is that we live in a contaminated moral environment. We fell morally ill because we became used to saying something different from what we thought. We learned not to believe in anything, to ignore each other, to care only about ourselves. Concepts such as love, friendship, compassion, humility, or forgiveness lost their depth and dimensions, and for many of us they represented only psychological peculiarities, or they resembled gone-astray greetings from ancient times, a little ridiculous in the era of computers and spaceships. Only a few of us were able to cry out loud that the powers that be should not be all-powerful, and that special farms, which produce ecologically pure and top-quality food just for them, should send their produce to schools, children's homes, and hospitals if our agriculture was unable to offer them to all. The previous regime—armed with its arrogant and intolerant ideology—reduced man to a force of production and nature to a tool of production. In this it attacked both their very substance and their mutual relationship. It reduced gifted and autonomous people, skillfully working in their own country, to nuts and bolts of some monstrously huge, noisy, and stinking machine, whose real meaning is not clear to anyone. It cannot do more than slowly but inexorably wear down itself and all its nuts and bolts."

From Brian MacArthur (ed.), *The Penguin Book of Twentieth-Century Speeches*, New York: Viking, 1992.

despite all the efforts at censorship; and in the fall of 1989 images of cheering or rioting crowds spread the contagion of revolt. In the face of such diffuse anger, officials remarkably ready to quit and citizens determined to push revealed shockingly widespread cynicism about these regimes. The frequent comparisons to the revolutions across Europe in 1848 made sense. Young men and women, especially students, echoed the events of 1968 and revealed the impact of an international youth culture in their clothes and music, their sense of theater and use of mockery, and their slogans. As crowds lost their fear, a massive contempt and a universal hunger for freedom washed away the pomp of officialdom, the claims of party ideology, and the power of the police.

Freedom illumined not only the appalling failures and corruption of the fallen regimes but also the problems still to be faced. Within months, unaccustomed freedoms resurrected old divisions—ethnic, social, and ideological. All at once, the Eastern Europe of 1990 looked much like that of the 1920s. Moderate conservatives gained the lead among Hungary's multiple parties and expressed nationalist resentment at the treatment Romania accorded Hungarians living in its territory. Czechoslovakia was soon debating yet again the relations of Czechs and Slovaks. As Poland risked the drastic medicine of sudden conversion to a market economy, rifts appeared within Solidarity. In Bulgaria, Communist party members won most of the seats in free elections, and in Romania leaders who claimed no longer to be Communists showed little willingness to allow real democracy. East Germans voted for those who promised the most rapid assimilation into the German Federal Republic.

The Disintegration of the USSR

A hero in Western Europe and the United States, Gorbachev was never so popular at home. Efforts to create more of a market economy threatened jobs. Attempts to make one sector more efficient were stymied by re-

A Lithuanian crowd holds up a banner that says "Ivan Go Home" and cheers as a Soviet soldier is burned in effigy. This demonstration in April 1990 followed two years of similar agitation.
Bettmann/Corbis

lated sectors that operated in the old ways. The new price structure increased inflation, uncertainty, and hoarding. Many party members and the army resented the erosion of their own authority and the weakening of the Soviet Union's international position.

The Opposition to Gorbachev   Seeking a strong political base, Gorbachev called for a huge Congress of People's Deputies as a step toward greater democracy. It met in 1989 and elected Gorbachev president of the Soviet Union. It also rejected the constitution's assertion that the Communist party must be preeminent (like all Soviet leaders since Stalin, Gorbachev's power had previously come from his position as party secretary). Discussions were more open than ever before. Deputies attacked old abuses, denounced the KGB, and gave vent to a rising chorus of competing ethnic demands. Solzhenitsyn warned against allowing Western decadence to infiltrate Russian society. Caught in the middle, Gorbachev clamped down on the media and allowed the army to threaten that it might restore order in the Baltic republics.

Among the opponents of this authoritarian turn, Boris Yeltsin, the head of the Communist party in Moscow, stood out. An outspoken populist, he reached ordinary people as Gorbachev never had, and in 1991 he was elected by popular vote president of the Russian republic, the largest in the Soviet Union. Other ene-

mies of Gorbachev were active, too. When Gorbachev took his August vacation in the Crimea, hard-liners in his own government, in the military, and in the KGB staged a coup. Tanks filled the streets, and the coup leaders announced that Gorbachev had been replaced. Beyond that, they seemed to have no plan. Yeltsin held firm against the coup with remarkable support from public opinion. Crowds pleaded with the soldiers not to act, miners in Siberia went on a strike, demonstrators marched in city after city, and some army officers declared their support of Yeltsin.

Within two days, the leaders of the coup were in prison and Gorbachev was back in Moscow, but he was now overshadowed by Yeltsin. He had no party, for across the nation, people pulled down the symbols of communism, closed and sometimes looted Communist party offices. Only eight of the fifteen Soviet republics responded to his call for a meeting. In October 1991 Russia, Ukraine, Belarus, and Kazakhstan declared that the Soviet Union had ceased to exist. No significant group fought to save it, and it was replaced by the looser Confederation of Independent States. Gorbachev resigned, a victim of the revolution he had unleashed.

Europe without Cold War

The fall of communism and the collapse of the Soviet Union meant the end of the Cold War. The policies of

BOUNDARY CHANGES SINCE 1989

— Former boundary of Soviet Union

Former area of Soviet Union

— Former boundary of Czechoslovakia

— Former boundary of Yugoslavia

----- Former boundary between
East & West Germany

All other boundaries as of 1998

SIGNIFICANT NATIONALIST MOVEMENTS

France (Brittany)

France (Corsica)

Great Britain (Scotland)

Great Britain (Wales)

Italy (Sardinia)

Italy (Tyrol)

Spain (Basque Region)

Spain (Catalonia)

AREAS OF VIOLENT CONFLICT OR OPEN WAR

Armenia-Azerbaijan

Georgia-Abkhazia

Moldova

Bosnia-Herzegovina, former Yugoslavia

Northern Ireland

Persian Gulf War

Israeli-Palestinian conflict

Kurdish-Turkish-Iraqi conflict

Chechnya

ETHNIC-BASED DISPUTES

Hungarian populations in Slovakia

Hungarian poulations in Romania

Russian populations in Crimea (Ukraine)

Russian populations in Georgia

Russian populations in Azerbaijan

Russian populations in Baltic States

Map 30.3 Ethnic and Territorial Conflict in Europe and the Middle East
Examine the movements, conflicts, and disputes illustrated on this map within the context of political developments, changing borders, and ongoing strife. Have any of these conflicts been resolved or do they continue still?

◆ For an online version, go to www.mhhe.com/chambers9 > chapter 30 > book maps

fifty years had to be rethought, as did the hard-headed assumptions on which they had rested. No one could know the implications of such fundamental changes, but it was clear that domestic politics, economic policies, and international relations would all now be different.

German Unification   The fall of communism affected Germany right away. Chancellor Kohl pushed for the immediate unification of East and West Germany, moving faster than many Germans thought wise, outmaneuvering the opposition parties, and capturing popular enthusiasm. By the end of 1989, he had gained the support of the United States and then of France, in effect, forcing a reluctant Britain to join in negotiations aimed at winning Soviet acceptance of German unification. Many were frightened at the prospect, but Kohl reassured the West with the promise that an enlarged Germany would be fully integrated into the European Community. The Soviet Union feared the increase in NATO's strength, but such concerns were rooted in an era quickly passing. In August 1990 the victors of World War II—the Soviet Union, the United States, Britain, and France—signed a treaty with the two Germanies. In return for the promise to respect its boundary with Poland and to limit the size of its combined army, Germany could unify and remain in NATO as Europe's richest and most powerful state.

For Germans, however, the benefits were not immediate. The East German economy, which had been the most productive in Eastern Europe, revealed enormous weakness. Its outmoded and inefficient industry could not compete in the dynamic economy of the West, and unemployment rose. East Germans, suffering high unemployment, resented what felt like subordinate status, and West Germans struggled with the unexpectedly high cost of unification as well as a flood of German immigrants. Confidently, parliament voted to make Berlin once again the capital of a united Germany, launching a building boom there that has made it one of Europe's most exciting and dynamic cities. Nevertheless, by 1998 German unemployment hit a postwar high at 12.6 percent, and in the election of that year the Christian Democrats lost to the Social Democrats. Shortly after that Helmut Kohl, the hero of unification, was disgraced by revelations of corrupt practices in party finance, and the Christian Democrats chose Angela Merkel to lead them in opposition. She was the first woman to lead a major German party.

New Political Alignments and Immigration   The collapse of communist regimes had important repercussions elsewhere, too. Italian politics since World War II had been shaped by the presence of a powerful Communist party that was excluded from power. Increas-

ingly moderate, it responded to the events of 1989 by making a final break with old-line communism and changing its name. The Christian Democrats, however, lost their principal reason for being, which had been to keep the Communists out of power. When charges of corruption uncovered a vast network of graft, the Christian Democratic party and their Socialist allies both simply disintegrated. In the next parliament, two-thirds of the deputies had never held any elective office and most belonged to new parties with new leaders. Public contempt for the old political class and a new electoral system (reducing the effects of proportional representation) opened the way for a restructuring of the political system.

Throughout Europe, politics was affected by the enfeeblement of the Marxist left, by the weakening of the anticommunist right, and by resentment of foreigners. The result was a shift toward the political center during the 1990s and early 2000s. For example, in France, Jacques Chirac, the head of a conservative coalition, defeated the Socialist Lionel Jospin in 1995 to become president. In Italy, media mogul Silvio Berlusconi defeated Romano Prodi of the center-left "Olive Tree Coalition" to become prime minister in 2001. In Great Britain, Tony Blair was elected to three consecutive terms as prime minister as the leader of the "New Labour" Party. Under Blair's leadership the party moved toward the center and embraced the basic principles of free enterprise.

Perhaps the dominant political development during these years was a widespread movement to cut back the large-scale social welfare states that had evolved over the course of the twentieth century. One major impetus for this policy was the Maastricht Treaty, which required all EU members to agree to restrictions on inflation rates, budget deficits, and public debt. Significantly, governments undertook these efforts regardless of which party was in power. For example, in France, the conservative Chirac government reduced taxes and sought to privatize the state pension system. At the same time, in Germany, the Social Democratic government of Gerhard Schröder attempted to reduce spending by cutting unemployment benefits and government pensions. Similarly, while serving as prime minister of Italy during the 1990s, Prodi introduced an austerity budget and trimmed social welfare spending. In some cases these policies generated opposition from labor unions and other groups. The role of the government in promoting social welfare loomed as a major issue in the opening years of the twenty-first century.

On the right, noisy new groups, often with neofascist tendencies, played on the fear of foreigners, gaining attention and many votes from Russia through the West. Heightened by unemployment and by the increased number of immigrants from Eastern Europe,

Turkey, the Middle East, and Africa, antiforeign feeling fed on the competition for space and ill-paying jobs. In Italy a new party, the Northern League, gained ground in the prosperous north by combining in one program opposition to immigration and denunciation of the central government's corruption and high taxes. In France unemployed industrial workers who had voted communist in the past were often sympathetic to the xenophobic but influential campaigns of the National Front. Aimed especially at Muslims, whose population in Europe was approaching 15 million, these campaigns made immigration a national issue that influenced governmental policies. And in Germany, where hundreds of thousands of people made their way from the faltering economies of Eastern Europe, incidents in which gangs of skinheads and neo-Nazis burned immigrant housing were an ominous reminder of Germany's past.

These movements were denounced by the left and by most figures of authority. Nevertheless, they did achieve some electoral success in certain countries. For example, in 2000, an Austrian party led by Joerg Haider, who had expressed admiration for Hitler, gained a share in the ruling coalition. The other EU nations responded by refusing formal cooperation with the Austrian government. Although that effort had limited effect, it raised new concern that the EU might infringe on national sovereignty, especially in smaller nations.

In other countries, anti-immigrant movements and parties attracted new followers following the September 11, 2001, terrorist attacks against the United States by Islamic militants. For example, in Denmark, a country with a historical reputation for tolerance, an anti-immigrant party known as the Danish People's Party won 12 percent of the vote in the parliamentary elections of November 2001. The following year, a prominent Dutch political figure named Pim Fortuyn, who had denounced Islam as a "backward culture" and campaigned for immigration restrictions in the Netherlands, ran for prime minister. He was assassinated shortly before the election, but his party captured the second-highest total of seats in the Dutch parliament.

The most dramatic and widely publicized illustration of the growing prominence of the far right occurred during the French presidential election of 2002. In the first round of elections, Jean-Marie Le Pen, the leader of the National Front, finished second to President Chirac in a field of sixteen candidates that included the Socialist Prime Minister Lionel Jospin. Capitalizing on voters' fears concerning unemployment, rising crime rates, and the presence of a "foreign" population within their country, Le Pen identified immigration as the cause of all of these problems. His proposed solutions included terminating legal immigration and expelling all illegal immigrants, constructing more prisons, reinstating the death penalty, and extending preference to native-born French citizens in such areas as employment, benefits, and housing. He also argued that France should reconsider its relationship with the European Union. Significantly, Le Pen received his greatest support in regions that had both substantial minority populations—particularly Arab—and high crime rates. Le Pen's electoral success shocked many observers and galvanized French voters, many of whom took to the streets in protest. On May Day, almost 1.5 million people throughout France demonstrated against the National Front. Determined to prevent Le Pen from achieving a respectable showing in the election, the French left joined with the moderate right to support Chirac. As a result, Chirac won the election with an overwhelming 82 percent of the vote.

Overall, the far-right, anti-immigrant parties achieved only limited success, and some experts claimed that their threat to European politics was exaggerated. Nevertheless, in a few countries such as Denmark and the Netherlands, they did achieve representation in the national legislature. More important, however, their growing popularity—Le Pen won more than 5 million votes in the election—pressured the mainstream parties to respond to widespread concerns regarding immigration, crime, and terrorism. As a result, many European governments began to propose restrictions on immigration and reductions in benefits for their immigrant populations.

The Transition from Communism The governments of Eastern Europe turned out to have heavier debts and more outmoded industries than even the critics of communism had suspected, and industrial pollution on an enormous, sometimes life-threatening, scale was a difficult problem for new governments in strapped economies. Unsure of the loyalty or competence of their own administrations, they attempted painful reforms while subject to unfamiliar public criticism. The capitalism suddenly unleashed was often socially disruptive, and the search for a new sense of community encouraged appeals to ethnic identity.

Poland undertook the most radical shift to a market economy, and economic indicators showed dramatic improvement. Ordinary citizens often suffered, however, and former Communists gained in the elections of 1993 by promising to slow the transition. Russia, Hungary, Poland, and the Czech Republic pleaded for more foreign aid and foreign investment. The relentless drive to capitalism in prosperous Czech regions and the cynical ambitions of Slovak politicians had forced the breakup of Czechoslovakia, creating the Czech Republic and Slovakia, although opinion polls indicated a majority in each country would have preferred to stay together. Elsewhere, too, economic strains reinforced ethnic and religious conflict, something nationalist parties were quick to use, especially in Romania.

The Breakup of Yugoslavia   Former Communists, in fact, proved particularly adept at stirring ethnic resentments, especially in the former Soviet Union and, most tragically of all, in Yugoslavia. Ethnic differences had not prevented Yugoslavia's six republics from effectively functioning together even after the death of Tito. By the 1980s Croatia and Slovenia, economically the most developed Yugoslav republics, openly attacked the economic and political policies of the Serbian-dominated government of Yugoslavia. As demands for reform grew stronger with the fall of communism elsewhere, Serbian communists resisted by raising support at home through appeals to Serbian nationalism. In 1990–1991 Slovenia and Macedonia joined Croatia and Bosnia-Herzegovina in declaring their independence. But large numbers of Serbs lived in sections of the latter two lands. Efforts to expel them and their own armed resistance, supported by the Yugoslav government under Slobodan Milošević, created civil war. Regional, economic, and ideological differences transmuted into ethnic hatred as each side, recalling past injustices, committed new atrocities. Truces were signed and broken. Uncontrolled local units could count on support no matter what horrors they committed. Slaughter and rape destroyed whole villages. By 1993 Serb forces had recaptured about one-third of Croatia and nearly two-thirds of Bosnia-Herzegovina, a republic in which Serbs, Croatians, and Muslims had once been proud of living peacefully together.

Despite these horrors and the risk that war could spread, NATO and the EU responded weakly, denouncing ethnic violence but not wanting to be drawn into a Balkan war. Slowly, the United States assumed a cautious leadership, pressuring the contending parties to accept a truce signed in 1995 in Dayton, Ohio. American and even some Russian troops then joined European and UN forces as peacekeepers with limited roles. Although Milošević faced opposition at home, militant nationalism and alert police squelched voices of moderation. Meanwhile, ethnic Albanians grew increasingly restive in Kosovo, a Yugoslav province historically tied to Serb identity. Milošević followed a familiar pattern, tightening control, using nationalist rhetoric, and in 1998 launching an assault to drive the Albanians out. It was called **ethnic cleansing,** and it pushed more than 600,000 refugees out of the country. NATO forces, led by the United States, responded in March 1999 with an air assault that lasted three months before the Serbs withdrew. Yugoslavia, its infrastructure badly damaged, was reduced to Serbia and a discontented Montenegro. The uneasy peace in the Balkans depended on the presence of foreign troops keeping ethnic groups

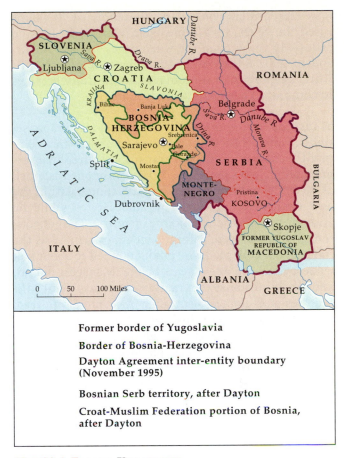

MAP 30.4 FORMER YUGOSLAVIA
In 1990 and 1991, Slovenia, Croatia, Bosnia-Herzegovina, and Macedonia declared their independence from Slobodan Milošević's Yugoslavian government, sparking a brutal civil war. The country of Yugoslavia was created in 1919 as a result of World War I peace treaties. How do you suppose this history contributed to the bloody Serbian policy of ethnic cleansing?
◆ For an online version, go to www.mhhe.com/chambers9 > chapter 30 > book maps

apart, while most of those accused of war crimes remained out of reach.

Hope for a more principled outcome revived in the fall of 2000, however, when Milošević was forced from power. His efforts to manipulate elections had brought the opposition parties, students, and farmers together in demonstrations reminiscent of Warsaw and Prague a decade earlier. Police and propaganda lost effectiveness, and Europe's last communist government fell. Its shaky replacement looked to the EU for economic and political support. Yugoslavia had to deal with a devastated economy and do so—like much of Eastern Europe—with ramshackle institutions, administrators and police from the previous regime, and a populace in poverty, harboring tragic memories and bitter resentments only partially repressed. Tensions eased, however, in a more open regime. It allowed Milošević to be tried for war crimes in The Hague, and in 2002 Serbia and Montenegro agreed to split while keeping their diplomatic and military services in common. Yugoslavia was no more.

Transition in Russia   Only Yugoslavia faced more serious ethnic conflicts than Russia, and no former communist country found the transition to free markets more difficult. As president, Yeltsin postponed as much as he could and tried to moderate disputes within the new Confederation of Independent States while he pushed for drastic economic reform. The effects, though limited, were painful. Unemployment rose, the ruble all but collapsed, and production fell to about half what it had been a few years before. Managers did not know how to adjust to a market economy; many officials resisted change altogether. As repression eased, corruption spread, criminal gangs flourished, and ugly groups of nationalists grew louder.

Free elections in 1991 produced a Congress of People's Deputies in which Yeltsin's opponents—communists, nationalists, members of the military, and representatives of regional movements—outnumbered his supporters. Yeltsin compromised when possible and ignored the Congress when he could. As parliamentary resistance stiffened and his own popularity declined, Yeltsin risked a national presidential election in the spring of 1993 and won. A few months later Yeltsin declared the parliament dissolved. Several hundred delegates refused to obey. Holed up in their offices, they collected arms and called on the people and the army for support. The army remained silent, but the delegates were heartened when groups of Yeltsin's opponents gathered outside the parliament building. Amid calls to bring the government down, shots were fired from within. Finally, the army bombarded and then stormed the building. A hundred or more people died, more bloodshed than Moscow had seen since 1917.

Reliance on the military, like Yeltsin's measures against parliament and his indifference to the rulings of the supreme court, was troubling proof that Russia had not achieved a constitutional system or the rule of law. Although seemingly rather indifferent, the public supported Yeltsin when forced to choose, and he surprised pollsters by winning reelection in 1996. By then the economy was improving slightly, and Russia could take its place in meetings of the nations with the largest economies. Ill and exhausted, Yeltsin named Vladimir Putin his successor and stepped down on December 31, 1999. Putin, a former KGB officer who had entered politics in 1990, won the presidential election in March 2000. Combining insistence on order, cryptic statements in favor of democracy, shrewd deals at

Members of the cabinet and presidential staff applaud as Prime Minister Vladimir Putin, front left, shakes hands with President Boris Yeltsin in Moscow's Kremlin on Friday December 31, 1999. In a television speech that stunned Russia, Yeltsin announced he was stepping down six months before his term was supposed to finish.
AP/Wide World Photos

home, and assertion of Russia's importance abroad, he brought an air of firmness to a still unstable polity.

International Implications   The end of the Cold War affected international affairs around the world. The United Nations, no longer hobbled by a Security Council in which the United States and Russia nearly always disagreed, began to function more in the way envisioned at its founding, pacifying local conflicts and providing humanitarian aid. When Iraq invaded Kuwait in 1991, Russia supported the American-led attack on Iraq. Unable to play on superpower competition, all sides in the Middle East had to reassess their positions. Without Soviet support, the Muslim states could only lose by diplomatic intransigence, and once Israel was no longer a Cold War bastion, it could be less certain of unending American aid. After decades of stalemate, Palestinians and Israelis agreed in 1993 to negotiate on limited autonomy for Palestine. Just as some resolution seemed imminent in 2000, however, fear and violence flared again, threatening to undo the peace process.

Ironically, the diplomatic implications of the Cold War's end were less clear in Europe, where that confrontation had begun. The future of NATO was a major issue, and its failure to act in Yugoslavia increased public doubts about its continued usefulness. The United States, with British support, insisted it was still needed; Germany and France appeared tempted by the idea of a more autonomous European force. Reacting to its initially feeble response to the Balkan crisis, the EU

The wreckage of the World Trade Center in New York City. Searing images of airplanes slamming into the twin towers and of the resulting destruction burned into the American consciousness.
Sipa Press

agreed in 2000 to create its own rapid-response force to serve as peacekeepers in just such situations. NATO also decided to expand, including nations once in the Soviet bloc (Hungary, Poland, and the Czech Republic were to be the first to join and others indicated a wish to do so). That would ensure American involvement on the Continent and protect East European nations from Russia. It might also prevent those nations from fighting each other over boundaries that had changed many times in the recent past and often been a cause of war. There were risks, however, in isolating Russia, selecting certain states to become NATO members, and requiring them to invest in the modern arms NATO membership required. Meanwhile, the slowly moving negotiations to dismantle nuclear warheads in the three former Soviet republics that harbored them remained an encouraging sign of the changes brought by the end of the Cold War. So did Russia's agreement to take part in NATO deliberations.

A New War on Terrorism   The overarching international reality was that the United States had become the world's only superpower. While maintaining close relations with the United States, members of the Euro-pean Union sought collectively and individually to establish some independence in world affairs. Greater tensions arose in areas beyond Europe. In Asia, Latin America, and the Middle East, issues were often defined as reactions to U.S. policy, even though that policy was not always consistent or clear. Efforts to unseat or at least discipline the Iraqi regime had limited effect, were often distrusted in Europe, and fed rising resentment in the Muslim world. America's hesitant interventions to end civil war and foster democracy in Africa, the Caribbean, and the Balkans had mixed results and garnered more criticism than support at home. But if the "Vietnam syndrome" made the United States cautious about military intervention, America's economic power and pervasive mass culture were felt everywhere.

On taking office in January 2001, the administration of George W. Bush appeared to be setting a new course. With little consultation of other nations, the United States declared its determination to stand alone in rejecting international agreements, those on the environment and nuclear arms, among many others. It also broke from previous administrations by announcing that it would not undertake "nation building" in unstable societies and would no longer serve as the active intermediary in the Israeli-Palestinian conflict. These and similar measures brought denunciations from Russia and cries of protest from Europe against American "unilateralism."

Then on September 11, 2001, nineteen men highjacked four domestic flights. One plane crashed, one flew into the Pentagon, and the other two deliberately smashed into the twin towers of the World Trade Center in New York City. The effects were catastrophic. The planes, loaded with fuel for transcontinental flights, were incendiary bombs, setting fires that blasted people out of the buildings and melted steel girders, causing the towers to crumble in a fountain of debris. Some three thousand people died from these assaults on symbols of American economic and military strength. Almost from the beginning, television carried images around the world of the largely futile rescue efforts in an inferno of flames and smoke that lasted for days. Expressions of sympathy and outrage poured in from nearly every nation, and the public learned that this devastating act of terrorism had apparently been the work of a network of Muslim extremists known as al Qaeda. Their headquarters were in Afghanistan, where they were led by Osama bin Laden, a wealthy Saudi opposed to the Saudi Arabian government, which he denounced as a repressive agent of the American infidel. In Afghanistan he cooperated with the fanatically intolerant Taliban regime that gained control of most of the country in the aftermath of the Afghan war against the Soviet Union.

Religion, geopolitics, a global economy, and global communications came together in the training camps Osama bin Laden maintained. His group was responsible for at least three major attacks on American forces and embassies in the Middle East and Africa starting in 1993. While he escaped American efforts to hunt him down, he gained sympathy in the Muslim world by fanning resentment of American policy in the Middle East, especially its support for Israel, and by denouncing America's "immoral" culture and selfish economic power. With a network of agents and funds scattered across Europe and into Asia, he had accomplished the first important attack on American soil since the War of 1812.

Americans responded with patriotic fervor, and President Bush declared the focus of his administration to be the war against terrorism around the world. NATO, for the first time in its history, invoked a treaty clause that considered an attack on one member as an attack on all. Britain and France offered their armed forces as did other members of NATO. Russia announced its willingness to join (recalling that it considered the Chechnyan rebels to be terrorists, too). The United Nations unanimously supported the United States (which had recently agreed to pay most of its back dues), while

Muslim nations and leaders cautiously distanced themselves from the Afghan government and the terrorists it harbored. As the United States assembled its military force, governments everywhere began to freeze bank accounts the terrorists might use and to round up Middle Easterners suspected of ties to terrorists. Amid remarkable international cooperation and many hopeful signs, people everywhere wondered what else they had to fear. No one knew quite how this new kind of war would be fought, how extensive it might become, or how long it would last.

Under U.S. leadership, the response to terrorism quickly assumed the form of conventional warfare. Shortly after 9/11, the U.S. government demanded that the Taliban turn over bin Laden and shut down all al Qaeda operations in Afghanistan. When the government refused, the United States and Great Britain began a massive and sustained bombing attack that supported a ground offensive by anti-Taliban forces. By the end of the year the Taliban had been overthrown, a new and more moderate government had been established in Kabul, and the UN had authorized a multination peacekeeping force for the country. A presidential election finally was held in October 2004, with Hamid Karzai winning an overwhelming victory.

The next target of the U.S. offensive was Iraq. The United States had accused the brutal dictatorial regime of Saddam Hussein of stockpiling weapons of mass destruction (WMDs) and cooperating with al Qaeda and other terrorist groups. Under pressure from the United States and Great Britain, the UN Security Council unanimously passed Resolution 1441 in November 2002. This resolution declared Iraq to be in violation of numerous UN rulings, and it demanded that the Iraqi government permit UN inspectors to search the country for WMDs. In March 2003, the United States and Britain declared Saddam Hussein to be in violation of the resolution. Coalition forces from these and other countries invaded Iraq and, within a short time, removed Saddam Hussein's regime from power. In June 2004 the coalition helped to create an interim government. The following January, Iraq held national elections. Due to disputes among rival factions, however, the new government was not sworn in until May. Meanwhile, violent resistance to both the occupation forces and the new government—much of it directed against civilians—remained widespread.

The aggressive policies of the United States created a fissure between that country and most of its traditional European allies. This tension was evident as early as November 2001, when German Chancellor Schröder narrowly survived a vote of no confidence as a result of his decision to send peacekeeping troops into Afghanistan. The truly divisive event, however, was the decision to invade Iraq. Many European countries, par-

Red Cross helpers lift a body bag containing the victim of a bomb blast from a train about one kilometer outside the main train station in Madrid, March 11, 2004. Ten simultaneous explosions killed 182 people on packed Madrid commuter trains in Europe's bloodiest attack in more than 15 years.
© Kali Pfaffenbach/Reuters/Corbis

ticularly France, Germany, and Russia, felt strongly that the UN weapons inspectors under Hans Blix should have been given more time to complete their mission. Although Britain had drafted a new resolution that explicitly authorized the use of force against Saddam Hussein, it never submitted the draft to the Security Council for a vote. As a result, the invasion proceeded despite the opposition of many Council members.

The Iraq War thus generated negative feelings on both sides. To many European nations, the decision to invade reflected a growing unilateralism and militarism on the part of the Bush administration. These sentiments were reinforced by the ongoing violence in Iraq, the inability of the coalition forces to locate any major stockpiles of WMDs, and the continued failure to apprehend Osama bin Laden. At the same time, many Americans interpreted European opposition to its policies as evidence of Europe's unwillingness to use military force against dangerous enemies.

The consequences of this dispute permeated European politics throughout this period. For example, in 2002, Schröder was reelected despite the poor performance of the German economy due in large part to his opposition to U.S. plans for a possible invasion. In Spain, a terrorist bombing in Madrid three days before the 2004 election killed nearly 200 civilians. The government of Prime Minister Jose Maria Aznar Lopez initially blamed the incident on the Basque separatist group ETA but then conceded that the attack was the work of Islamic extremists. Anger over this misinformation, combined with widespread opposition to Aznar's decision to support the invasion of Iraq, led to a victory by the Social-

ist Workers Party. Newly elected Prime Minister Luis Rodriguez Zapatero then withdrew all Spanish troops from Iraq. In 2005 Tony Blair—Bush's closest European ally—became the first member of the Labour Party ever to be elected to a third term. However, polls indicated that Blair won despite his support for the war. (The polls also suggested that Iraq figured far less prominently in the British elections than in the 2004 U.S. elections, in which Bush was victorious.) In addition, the Labour Party's share of the popular vote declined, as did its majority in Parliament. The divisions between Europe and the United States brought about by the Iraq War posed a major challenge to both sides in the opening years of the twenty-first century.

CONTEMPORARY CULTURE

The burst of artistic creativity that followed World War II embraced new trends and styles in all the arts. At the same time, the global expansion of a dynamic popular culture is one of the hallmarks of the second half of the twentieth century. Gradually interwoven into modern social thought, these developments have contributed to new ideas about culture that have spread through the humanities and social sciences and influenced modern social movements.

Postwar Creativity

With the end of the war, European artists could reflect more freely on the searing experiences of repression and bloodshed that had darkened the previous decade. They could take part in artistic movements that had been banned under fascist governments, and they could catch up on the new ideas and styles coming from America, where the many European artists and intellectuals who fled the continent had helped to make New York the cultural capital of the Western world. Figures already famous in the 1930s, like the painter Pablo Picasso and the poet T. S. Eliot, could now be simultaneously honored as founders of modern art and savored with a freshness usually reserved for the newly discovered. The works most admired in the 1950s and 1960s showed considerable continuity with the avant-garde works of the prewar period.

Authors wanting to show how ordinary people had experienced dictatorship, war, and postwar dislocation favored a style noted for its directness and telling detail. Called neorealism, this style flourished especially in Italy, where the novels of Ignazio Silone and Alberto Moravia gave incisive, often bitter, yet affectionate accounts of the daily struggles of people buffeted by movements and events beyond their control, and where the films of Roberto Rossellini and Vittorio de Sica combined the harsh eye of the candid camera with sympathy for the minor characters who are society's victims and its strength.

These forms gradually gave way to ones that built on more radical prewar art and presented several points of view simultaneously, challenging any assumption of a single reality. In Germany the plays of Bertolt Brecht used such devices for a firm Marxist purpose (in 1949 Brecht left the West to live in East Berlin), and the savagely satirical novels of Heinrich Böll extended the once-shocking surrealism of Franz Kafka to convey Central Europe's experience of the twentieth century. Stimulus from outside Europe was also important. The most admired sculptor, the English artist Henry Moore, was directly influenced by African art in designing huge reclining figures that combined clean lines, solid masses, and provocative empty spaces.

Adapting Traditional Values The arguments for human decency needed restatement following the horrors of genocide, totalitarianism, and war. **Existentialism,** one of the most influential movements of the postwar period, offered a radical solution to the problem of ethics. Life may be absurd and meaningless, the French philosopher Jean-Paul Sartre reasoned, but to take any action is to make a decision, and doing so is to make a personal moral choice. Building on the prewar work of Karl Jaspers and Martin Heidegger in Germany, Sartre constructed a radical individualism that centered on moral responsibility. Even in the worst of circumstances, the sum of the choices made give each life its moral mean-

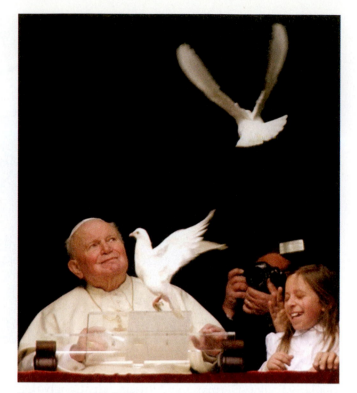

Pope John Paul II looks on as two white doves are freed at the end of the Angelus prayer in St. Peter's square, at the Vatican, January 30, 2005.
AP/Wide World Photos

ing. The soldier could refuse to torture; the civilian could choose to resist custom or authority. Underneath its relentless pessimism, Sartre's existentialism—set forth in essays, dramas, and criticism—held out the possibility of moral heroism.

Christian voices shared in the postwar anguish over values. Leading theologians—also mainly men of an older generation, like Jaspers, Karl Barth, and Jacques Maritain—were studied with renewed interest. The Protestant Paul Tillich and the Catholic Pierre Teilhard de Chardin achieved a large following with their systematic claims for Christianity's relevance to modern life. This confidence, reflected in the postwar vigor of Christian political parties, illuminated the papacy (1958–1963) of Pope John XXIII. He was extraordinarily popular, admired by Protestants as well as Catholics and by peasants and workers as well as intellectuals. Determined to recast the Church's position in the modern world, he called the Vatican Council known as **Vatican II,** which opened in 1962. Devoted to *aggiornamento,* the Council sought to bring the Catholic Church up to date not just organizationally but in social policy as well. It made the leadership of the Church far more international, directed attention to the concerns of developing nations, made respect for Jews a formal policy, and expressed belief in religious liberty. Putting more emphasis on individual understanding than institutional uniformity, it ordered that Masses be conducted in the vernacular instead of Latin. These changes encountered resistance, and with Pope John's death before the Council was completed, the Church turned to more cautious consolidation of doctrine and structure.

After Pope John XXIII died on June 3, 1963, the Council continued to meet under his successor, Paul VI, until 1965. Although many Catholics embraced the changes encouraged by the Council, others became concerned that the Church had deviated too far from its traditional teachings. In 1978 Karol Wojtyla of Poland became Pope John Paul II. John Paul became a strong critic of Western materialism and a proponent of social justice. He openly identified with the Solidarity movement in his native country, and he made numerous trips to Africa and Asia. At the same time, he staunchly defended Catholic orthodoxy and papal authority. He alienated many liberal Catholics with his continued opposition to homosexuality, abortion and birth control, and the ordination of female priests.

After John Paul II died on April 2, 2005, Benedict XVI was quickly chosen as his successor. Formerly the Cardinal Joseph Ratzinger, he had been appointed prefect of the Congregation for the Doctrine of the Faith in 1981. In this position Ratzinger moved to enforce orthodoxy within the Church while denouncing the "dictatorship of relativism." Many people interpreted his elevation to the papacy as a sign that the Church would continue to move in a more traditional direction.

These developments within the Catholic Church coincided with a global movement toward religious fundamentalism. In the United States, the growing numbers of evangelical Protestants emerged as a major political force. George Bush's reelection in 2004 was due in part to his ability to appeal to both Protestant fundamentalists and conservative Catholics. At the same time, Islamic fundamentalism played a vital role in shaping political and social life in the Middle East. The effects of this movement were also felt in European countries such as France and Germany that contained significant Muslim minority populations.

The Explosion of Popular Culture

American Influence   A very large part of the commercial entertainment that Europeans watch and listen to comes from the United States. American dominance in the motion picture industry, apparent in the 1930s, has grown since World War II. Although European governments have tried a variety of measures to reduce the proportion of American productions in their movie theaters and on television, they have failed. In the 1950s over half of the movies that Europeans attended were from the United States, and by the 1990s the figure was more than 80 percent. American films had some commercial advantages. They could be offered cheaply because the large American market had already covered most of their production costs. American movie companies were masters at distribution, and the American government was willing to pressure other countries to provide access to American films. American productions have had similar success on European television, as privately owned television networks compete with government-run networks by filling a majority of their airtime with inexpensive American reruns.

In fact, American television productions have demonstrated remarkably wide appeal. The television series *Dallas* was as popular and well known in Europe as in the United States, and Italian judges have found themselves explaining to defendants more familiar with *Perry Mason* than with their own justice system that "your honor" is not a term used in Italian courts. By the 1990s, soap operas from Brazil (especially popular in Portugal and Spain) and Australia (especially popular in Great Britain) were added to American shows as regular fare on European television networks owned by Italian, French, and German media tycoons. Theme parks, too, have spread from the United States to Europe. Denmark has its Legoland; and *Parc Asterix*, based on a series of French comic books, is located on the outskirts of Paris, not far from the European Disneyland.

An International Youth Culture   Much criticized on both sides of the Atlantic, such commercial entertainment had been especially troubling to many European intellectuals who feared that their societies would follow the American example. Conservatives worried that American-style democracy undermined the values that supported high culture; Marxists believed that ruthless capitalism made culture a commodity, mass produced, cheap, and aimed at the lowest taste. The signs that something more was at stake—the creation of an international youth culture—became clearer in the 1950s with the international appeal of rock and roll and the fashions that went with it.

American jazz had been popular in Europe since the 1920s, especially in France, and after the war, the presence of American troops and the programs of Armed Forces Radio did much to disseminate American popular music. The new musical culture did not come exclusively from the United States, however. The Beatles, who combined American influences with those of the British music hall, were by far the most influential popular music group of the 1960s and, along with the Rolling Stones, helped to create a transatlantic style that was at home on the Continent and in Latin America as well as in Britain and the United States. By the 1980s an international tour was a normal part of star status in pop music. In each country, performances were usually preceded by local groups, adding to the sense of a single culture with national variants. When in 1997 the Irish band U2 performed in Rome and Sarajevo, or when Bob Dylan and gospel singers appeared with the pope at a eucharistic congress, national origin hardly seemed to matter.

Globalization   These trends were part of a larger pattern known as globalization, in which communications, cultural exchanges, and economic activity increasingly take place on a worldwide scale. The last decades of the twentieth century witnessed a global revolution in communications and information technology. New inventions such as desktop and laptop computers, the In-

Inspired by American musicians such as Chuck Berry, Little Richard, and Elvis Presely, the Beatles took the United States by storm in the 1960s.
© Hulton-Deutsch Collection/Corbis

Once the imperial palace to Ming and Qing Dynasty emperors, the Forbidden City now hosts a Starbucks coffee shop.
© Macduff Everton/Corbis

ternet, cellular telephones, personal digital assistants (PDAs), CD and DVD players, digital photography, and satellite-based systems dramatically enhanced the flow of ideas, making information available instantaneously across the globe. One consequence of the communications revolution was that Western culture, whether based in the United States or in Europe, became accessible to people on every continent.

Global economic activity became more tightly integrated as well. Jobs, goods and services, and capital increasingly flowed over and beyond national borders. One key element in economic globalization was the emergence of large-scale enterprises that are based in one country but have operations in many countries. Known as multinational corporations (MNCs) or transnational corporations (TNCs), these firms increasingly dominated many sectors of the global economy. Significantly, more than 90 percent of the largest TNCs were based in either Western Europe, the United States, or Japan. Among the most prominent European-based TNCs were BP (Great Britain), Nestlé (Switzerland), Siemens (Germany), and Nokia (Finland). Of course, the globalization of economic activity encouraged greater cultural and ideological exchanges between Western and non-Western peoples.

New Directions   The arts had never been more international than after World War II, and they were necessarily affected by the energy of new forms of popular culture. One response was to turn away from the fast-paced plots of American cinema in favor of a more reflective mood. The novels of Alain Robbe-Grillet and the films of Jean François Truffaut and Ingmar Bergman were contemplative personal essays, held together by the sensitivity and imagination of a single creator and by images simultaneously surreal and real. Identified in France as the *nouvelle vague* of the 1960s, this style had its counterpart in all the arts.

Postmodernism   The change of attitude as the arts tended to become less austere and less concerned with the formal principles that academies taught and critics favored was dramatically obvious in architecture. Modern architecture, influenced by the Bauhaus school, had developed an international style that favored the pure and simple, geometric forms and unadorned walls of glass. By the 1970s, however, newer styles rejected that aesthetic and instead deliberately featured unexpected shapes, pitched roofs with gables, echoes of many older styles, and whimsical ornamentation. Because the element that this eclectic architecture most obviously shared was its rejection of modernism, it came to be called *postmodern*, a term soon applied to many other fields as well.

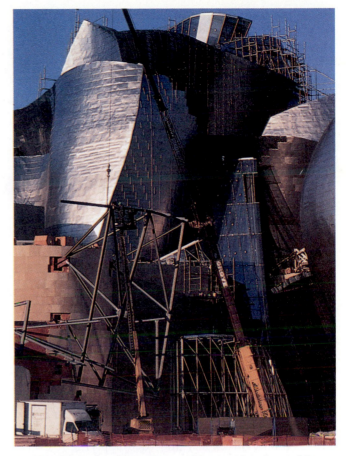

A monument of a postmodern and international age, this Guggenheim museum was designed by the American architect Frank Gehry and opened in 1997 in Bilbao, Spain, a city once known primarily as a grim industrial town.
J. Pavlovsky/Corbis Sygma

A preference for playful attitudes and individualistic innovation more than a formal school of thought, **postmodernism** reflected important cultural tendencies. Labeling regularity, rigid logic, and the control of nature or human beings as modern made postmodernism a convenient way to describe a new direction in the arts and social sciences.

Social Thought

Following World War II, the major schools of social thought had generally assumed that rational analysis could explain social behavior with a certain objectivity that would lead to beneficial policies. From the 1970s on, however, students of society have been increasingly inclined to show instead how programs for social improvement, how claims to objective knowledge, and how the promotion of high culture may actually be exercises that preserve the dominance of elites.

Modernization and Marxism Social and political thought in the 1950s used historical and social analysis to prescribe solutions for current problems. Theories of modernization traced a line of development from the era of absolute monarchy to a modern age of liberal democracy, and in doing so sought to explain what went wrong in nations like Germany, Italy, and Spain that had not sustained democracy. The answers to these historical questions were then offered as a guide for developing nations around the world as the means to democratic stability.

Writings on modernization, especially pervasive in the United States, influenced the social sciences throughout the West. They demonstrated the connection between political freedom and economic growth and showed that these developments in turn were intricately related to social changes, such as literacy and urbanization. Discussions of modernization tended to advocate for all societies the values, legal systems, and social practices identified as characteristic of Western Europe and the United States. Studies of modernization fostered greater attention to the non-Western world and favored interdisciplinary research that used sophisticated social scientific theories and methods (including quantitative analysis and opinion surveys). By the 1970s, however, these theories had come under heavy attack for creating an idealized description of Western (often American) society and then applying it everywhere, for stressing consensus and compromise while largely ignoring social conflicts and injustice, and for serving as a Cold War ideology in competition with Soviet Marxism.

Marxist thought, which also incorporated ideas of progress, provided the principal alternative to theories of modernization. Varieties of Marxism less rigid than Soviet communism were influential throughout European intellectual life, especially in England and Italy in the late 1960s and 1970s. In their flexibility and subtle insights, these neo-Marxist analyses made lasting contributions to the understanding of society and culture, especially through ideas associated with the so-called Frankfurt school and with Antonio Gramsci. A group of innovative and Marxian social scientists and philosophers had flourished in Frankfurt under Germany's Weimar republic until Hitler forced its leaders into exile. Although their writings were rigorous and difficult, they gained a wide readership in the postwar period. And their analyses, whether of the arts or social structure, interlaced modern sociology and psychology (especially Freudian ideas) with a profound distaste for mass culture and contemporary society. One of their members, Herbert Marcuse, became a hero to leaders of the student revolts of 1968 because of his powerful criticism of the commercialism and illusory freedom of modern society.

The pervasiveness of Marxist thinking also owed a great deal to the work of Antonio Gramsci. Like the more doctrinaire Hungarian Georg Lukács, Gramsci was a communist intellectual who took culture seriously, not simply as a reflection of society's material structure but as the collection of values that held it together. One of Italy's leading communist activists, Gramsci was imprisoned by the Fascist authorities; most of his writing consists of notebooks and letters written in prison during the 1920s and 1930s and published after the war. Gramsci, while recognizing the importance of religion and the arts, sought to explain why peasants and workers accept inequality. He developed the concept of cultural hegemony, exploring how the values and styles invented and promulgated by elites come to be shared across social classes and thus shape the thought and action of entire societies. Radicals, Gramsci argued, must provide an alternative culture that matches the qualities of the culture they wish to overturn.

Cultural Studies English, French, German, and American scholars applied these ideas to their own histories and to current political debates, exposing a bias toward the status quo in liberal ideology and elitism in much current scholarship. The field of cultural studies has evolved from this line of attack on dominant ideologies while distancing itself from Marxism and gaining momentum from worldwide changes in politics as well as culture. Decolonization invited a new look at how imperialism functions and provoked renewed interest in how non-Western societies wrestle with Western cultural and economic domination. The self-serving assumptions built into European assessments of non-European cultures (a topic that dominates anthropology today) had become easier to identify. Movements in behalf of ethnic minorities—African Americans in the United States and other ethnic groups in the United States and Europe—undermined claims that society's established institutions and authorities were neutral. Cultural studies has also made popular culture the object of serious study, especially in Britain, welcoming its irreverence and finding within it a yearning for freedom and the creative expression of marginalized people alienated from consumer society.

Michel Foucault The methods, insights, and vocabulary of cultural studies owe a great deal to the work of the Frenchman Michel Foucault, perhaps the most influential thinker of the 1980s, particularly in the United States and England. Foucault was trained as a philosopher, and his work achieved international resonance much as Sartre's had done a generation earlier. Foucault consistently acknowledged his debt to Nietzsche and was clearly influenced by Marx, the new social history,[4] and the work of the French anthropologist Claude Lévi-Strauss. Lévi-Strauss believed that every aspect of a supposedly primitive society—its kinship systems, customs, rituals, and myths—can be understood as the extension of unstated, complex, and integrated structures of thought. These hidden structures, he declared, reflect the nature of the human mind, a view that led him to an admiration of premodern societies comparable to that felt by many modern artists.

All these currents were present in Foucault's thought, but most of all he built on the rising science of semiotics, the study of the signs by which human beings communicate. In Foucault's hands, semiotics provided the means for reinterpreting modern history and civilization. His periodization was conventional: Modernity emerged in the late eighteenth century and was heralded by the French Revolution. But he upended the conventional interpretations of what modernity meant. Medicine, psychology, and prison reform were not simply the progressive results of increased knowledge but instruments of a new social discipline. The scientific observation of other people, however neutral or objective it claims to be, is a means of controlling behavior through shared *discourse*—a crucial Foucauldian term. By *discourse* Foucault means a framework of understanding used consciously and unconsciously that automatically excludes some possibilities and urges others. To talk about certain behavior as an illness, for example, is a form of power, and power is one of Foucault's central concerns. Discourse functions within society to make power diffuse and pervasive, independent of public intent. Foucault's ideas (like his witty, perceptive, and involuted style) provided a new and effective way to challenge not just the acknowledged evils of modern society but the laws, institutions, practices, and conception of knowledge on which society rests. Without proffering solutions, Foucault's works offer an arsenal of weapons with which to unmask intellectual claims to authority or objectivity.

Poststructuralism A further powerful attack on the apparent neutrality of scientific categories and logical reason is heavily indebted to French intellectual Jacques Derrida. Like Foucault, Derrida uses the tools of semiotics and philosophy and has more followers in the United States than in Europe. The two have been called the philosophers of 1968 because of their ties to the student movement of those years. Derrida studies

literature by concentrating on the text and subjecting it to a technique he named *deconstruction*. For deconstructionists, texts contain linguistic signs that are not straightforward—not *transparent*, to use their term—but instead carry multiple associations with individual words, with style and syntax, and with all the literary, cultural, social, and personal contexts from which a given text has emerged. Necessarily, the signs on the page must be (mis)translated in the mind of the reader. Thus, no text has one stable meaning but communicates differently to different people and on many levels at once. Deconstruction, the exploration of multiple and hidden signification, directly denies the existence of absolutes and any pretense to objectivity.

These currents of contemporary thought, obviously related to postmodernism, are often referred to as *poststructuralism* because they have moved beyond logical structures, scientific models, and fixed categories. Under the influence of poststructuralism, the techniques of literary analysis have become important to contemporary writings about society. Social custom, forms of courtesy and dress, organizations and law, education and religion can all be studied like a text for the multiple messages they convey.

Gender Studies In no field has the large body of poststructuralist theory had greater impact than in gender studies, which looks beyond biological or sexual differences to the social construction of different roles for men and women, differences fabricated from custom, from views about the nature of women and men, and above all, from seemingly neutral dichotomies such as strength/weakness, rationality/irrationality, and public/private, which when associated with male/female become constraints on the roles thought proper for women. Such studies have made it necessary to rethink and rewrite a great deal of history, anthropology, and sociology. If the theoretical base has been heavily European, its application has been more extensive in the United States, where the structure of universities, the rapid opening of careers to women, and public preoccupation with oppressed groups have fostered the development of gender studies. In Europe, too, however, similar reinterpretations of society and culture have given new strength to feminist movements and to campaigns in behalf of groups previously marginalized (see "A Reflection on Contemporary Feminism," pp. 980).

Europe's admired, established culture and the institutions that sustain it have come under attack from many quarters, and those attacks have made their own contributions to culture. That established culture, which remains at the core of education, religion, and much of public life, meanwhile draws millions of people each year to museums and concert halls.

---

[4] French historians centered around the journal *Annales* began before World War II to develop approaches to social history that influenced historical study around the world in the 1960s and 1970s and continue to make important contributions to the social sciences and humanities. Foucault himself was close to, although not part of, the *Annales* group.

A Reflection on Contemporary Feminism

Julia Kristeva arrived in Paris in 1966 as a twenty-six-year-old Bulgarian scholar trained in linguistics. She quickly became an important contributor to the semiotics movement in France. In addition to widely acclaimed scholarly works, essays, and novels, she writes frequently on women's issues. Provocative and controversial, her studies are nevertheless representative of European feminist writings in several respects: their engagement with European philosophy from Plato through Hegel and Nietzsche; their sophisticated use of psychoanalysis and literary criticism, including deconstruction; their analysis of the contemporary historical context; and their search for a new feminism through close attention to immediate, practical, and personal issues. Following are excerpts from "Women's Time," an essay first published in French in 1979.

"When the women's movement began as the struggle of suffragists and existential feminists, it sought to stake out its place in the linear time of planning and history. As a result, although the movement was universalist from the start, it was deeply rooted in the sociopolitical life of nations. The political demands of women, their struggles for equal pay for equal work and for the right to the same opportunities as men have, as well as the rejection of feminine or maternal traits considered incompatible with participation in such a history, all stem from the *logic of identification* with values that are not ideological (such values have been rightly criticized as too reactionary) but logical and ontological with regard to the dominant rationality of the nation and the state.

"It is unnecessary to enumerate all the benefits that this logic of identification and spirited protest have offered and still offer to women (abortion rights, contraception, equal pay, professional recognition, and others). These benefits have had or will soon prove to have even more significant effects than those of the Industrial Revolution. This current of feminism, which is universalist in scope, *globalizes* the problems of women of various social categories, ages, civilizations, or simply psychic structures under the banner of Universal Woman. In this world, a reflection about generations of women could only be conceived of as a succession, a progression that sought to implement the program set out by its founding members.

"A second phase is associated with women who have come to feminism since May 1968 and who have brought their aesthetic or psychoanalytic experiences with them. This phase is characterized by a quasi-universal rejection of linear temporality and by a highly pronounced mistrust of political life. Although it is true that this current of feminism still has an allegiance to its founding members and still focuses (by necessity) on the struggle for the sociocultural recognition of women, in a *qualitative* sense, it sees itself in a different light than did the prior generation of feminists.

"The 'second phase' women, who are primarily interested in the specificity of feminine psychology and its symbolic manifestations, seek a language for their corporeal and intersubjective experiences, which have been silenced by the cultures of the past. As artists or writers, they have undertaken a veritable exploration of the *dynamics of signs*. At least on the level of its intentions, their exploration is comparable to the most ambitious projects for religious and artistic upheaval. . . . For more than a century, anthropologists and sociologists have attracted our attention to the society-sacrifice that works behind 'savage thought,' wars, dream discourse, or great writers. . . . Today's women have proclaimed that this sacrificial contract imposes itself against their will, which has compelled them to attempt a revolt that they perceive to be a resurrection. Society as a whole, however, considers this revolt to be a refusal and it can result in violence between the sexes (a murderous hatred, the break-up of the couple and the family) or in cultural innovation. In fact, it probably leads to them both. In any event, that is where the stakes are, and they are of enormous consequence. By fighting against evil, we reproduce it, this time at the core of the social bond—the bond between men and women."

From Julia Kristeva, *New Maladies of the Soul.* Copyright © 1995 by Columbia University Press. Reprinted with permission of the publisher.

Summary

Without the harsh simplicity of bipolar conflict, European affairs looked more complex after the collapse of the Soviet Union and the end of the Cold War, but that complexity also reflected the astounding gains of fifty years of peace. The promise of well-being was never more universal or real. To be sure, capitalism brought dangerous dislocation across the Continent, and freedom allowed ethnic conflict. But political and ideological differences were now less important and the distinction between Eastern and Western Europe less relevant. Intellectual creativity has generated excitement but no clear consensus; questions of values remain painfully unresolved. Whereas social equality has yet to be achieved, increased wealth has been accompanied by the signs of alienation revealed in drug abuse and xenophobia. There are troubling indications every day of the anger, frustration, and disillusionment many people feel. Nevertheless, Eastern Europe is freer than ever before in its history and Western Europe more united than it has ever been. A half-century ago few people expected that by the end of the twentieth century, in an increasingly global society, Europe would remain a favored continent, enviable in its wealth, liberty, and culture.

QUESTIONS FOR FURTHER THOUGHT

1. How do you explain the growth of the European Union despite hesitant beginnings, frequent disagreements, and continual setbacks that all along the way have led most commentators to predict its failure?
2. Are postindustrial society and the new economy really so different from the past?

3. Why have European dictatorships fallen?
4. What do you see as the strengths and weaknesses of contemporary culture? Is it likely to produce a backlash comparable to that of the 1930s?

RECOMMENDED READING

Sources

Ash, Timothy Garton. *The Magic Lantern: The Revolution of '89 Witnessed in Warsaw, Budapest, Berlin, and Prague.* 1990. An eyewitness account by a particularly keen and informed observer.

de Beauvoir, Simone. *Memoirs of a Dutiful Daughter.* James Kickup (tr.). 1959. *All Said and Done.* Patrick O'Brian (tr.). 1974. Important to the history of contemporary feminism, Beauvoir's memoirs also give a sense of the intellectual life of the times.

Gorbachev, Mikhail. *Perestroika: New Thinking for Our Country and the World.* 1989. This presentation of Gorbachev's vision of the future is as revealing for the issues it does not address as for its specific recommendations.

Studies

*Albertini, Rudolf von. *Decolonization: The Administration and Future of the Colonies, 1919–1960.* Francisca Garvie (tr.). 1982. A solid account that focuses on Britain and France and is especially valuable for its historical depth.

*Ash, Timothy Garton. *The Polish Revolution: Solidarity.* 1984. Rich in insights into the social roots, techniques, ideas, and effectiveness of a moment that captured worldwide attention.

*Burgess, Michael. *Federalism and the European Union.* 2000. Reviews the history of the European Union to make the case for the continuing importance of the national states within it.

*Caplan, Richard, and John Feffer. *Europe's New Nationalism: States and Minorities in Conflict.* 1996. Essays on regions from Scotland to Eastern Europe that discuss the important historical issues raised by some of the less-familiar outbursts of nationalism since the end of the Cold War.

*Fink, Carole, Philipp Gassert, and Detlef Junker (eds.). *1968: The World Transformed.* 1998. Essays on the worldwide phenomenon of the protest movements from China and the United States to Eastern Europe, attentive not only to global influences and their use of common themes but to the variety of specific issues, including race, women, and consumerism.

Hennessy, Peter, and Anthony Seldons. *Ruling Performance: British Governments from Attlee to Thatcher.* 1987. Contrasting perspectives on British politics in radically different governments.

Hoffman, Stanley, et al. *In Search of France.* 1965. A group of scholars attempt to define the unique patterns of French political and social life.

Hoffmann, Stanley, and Paschalis Kitromilides. *Culture and Society in Contemporary Europe.* 1981. An anthology of essays by leading intellectuals attempting to evaluate the interplay of tradition and modernity in Europe.

Hoskins, Geoffrey. *The Awakening of the Soviet Union.* 1990. An excellent overview of how change came to a society that had resisted it for so long.

*Hughes, H. Stuart. *Sophisticated Rebels.* 1990. An intellectual historian considers the nature of dissent in the West as well as in Eastern Europe during the critical years of 1988 and 1989.

*Hulsberg, Werner. *The German Greens: A Social and Political Profile.* 1988. A systematic treatment of the strongest of the European environmental movements.

*Jarausch, Konrad H. *The Rush to German Unity.* 1994. Uses recently opened archives to provide a historian's assessment of the complicated events that united the two Germanies.

Katzenstein, Mary F., and Carol M. Mueller (eds.). *The Women's Movements of the United States and Western Europe.* 1987. These collected essays make for a book with wide coverage that underscores some striking national differences.

*Kavanagh, Dennis, and Anthony Seldon (eds.). *The Thatcher Effect.* 1989. A variety of critical appraisals of Thatcher's policies.

Kennedy, Paul. *Preparing for the Twenty-First Century.* 1993. A historian's skeptical look at power relations in the near future.

Lewin, Moshe. *The Gorbachev Phenomenon.* 1988. A brilliant analysis written as the phenomenon was unfolding that relates current events to the developments in Soviet society over the previous fifty years.

*Maier, Charles S. *Dissolution: The Crisis of Communism and the End of East Germany.* 1997. Connects domestic and international politics to ideology and social conditions to explain the collapse of communism and the German unification.

*Modood, Tariq, and Pnina Werbner. *The Politics of Multiculturalism in the New Europe: Racism, Identity, and Community.* 1997. Essays present multiculturalism as the result of the change in domestic politics.

*Panayi, Panikos. *An Ethnic History of Europe since 1945.* 2000. Compares the experience of ethnic minorities across Europe.

*Parker, Geoffrey. *The Logic of Unity.* 1975. Usefully analyzes the forces for European unity from a geographer's perspective.

Silber, Laura, and Allan Little. *The Death of Yugoslavia.* 1995. A moving, penetrating, and unusually balanced account.

*Available in paperback.

Glossary

absolutism Political doctrine that the monarch is the source of all authority and government in a kingdom.

Academy Quarter of Athens in which Plato established a school.

Aeneid Epic poem by Roman poet Virgil about the founding of Rome.

agora Central market of a polis.

Allah Islamic term for God that derives from the Arabic word *al ilah*, meaning "The God."

Amon-Re "Hidden"; an unseen, universal god of Egypt.

Anabaptists Individuals who, pointing out that the Bible nowhere mentions infant baptism, argued that the sacrament was effective only if the believer understood what was happening and that therefore adults ought to be rebaptized. Opponents argued that infant baptism was necessary so that a baby would not be denied salvation if it died young.

anarchists Radical activists who called for the abolition of the state, sometimes by violent means.

anti-Semitism Anti-Jewish sentiment used to reinforce conservative, antiliberal and nationalist politics.

appeasement The policy by antiwar governments in Britain and France to placate Nazi Germany. Culminated in the Munich conference giving Germany control of Czechoslovakia in 1938; encouraged further German aggression.

apprenticeship Method by which young candidates, or apprentices, studied a particular trade under a master of that skill before admittance into the guild.

Areopagus Rock in central Athens that gave its name to a powerful governing council.

Arianism Heresy based on the teaching of Arius, an Alexandrian priest, which denied that Jesus was coequal with God the Father.

assignats Paper money issued by the French revolutionary governments, whose value was backed by nationalized church lands.

aton Disk of the sun, worshiped by Akhnaton, an Egyptian pharaoh.

Augustus "Most honored"; name conferred on the first emperor of Rome.

balance of power The belief that no one state should be permitted a dominant role in international affairs, and that alliances among their neighbors ought to restrain ambitious rulers.

Baroque Ornate style of art, music, literature, and architecture that emerged in the seventeenth century, characterized by an emphasis on grandeur, power, drama, and rich color.

Bastille A fortress prison seized on July 14, 1789, by Parisians looking for munitions to repulse the royal army; the event symbolized the Revolution's popular support.

Beguines Pious laywomen who lived in communities outside of convents.

Beowulf Anglo-Saxon epic that illustrates the weakness of tribal kingship.

Bill of Rights Document (usually only in a constitutional system) listing the protections from government oppression enjoyed by individual citizens.

billeting Providing board and lodging for troops by making ordinary citizens house and feed soldiers in their homes.

biometry The application of statistical methods to the analysis of biology and medicine.

Bismarck, Otto von The chief minister of Prussia's king, he masterminded the unification of Germany through military aggression and nationalist appeals.

Black Death Great plague of the fourteenth century that spread throughout Europe and resulted in huge loss of human life.

blitzkrieg "Lightning war"; German military tactic in which enemies were overrun with lightning speed using tanks and air power; led to the quick defeat of Poland in 1939 and France in 1940.

Bolsheviks "Majority faction"; the Leninist wing of the Russian Marxist party; after 1917, the Communist party.

broadsides Brief pamphlets or leaflets, often satiric, making sharp comments about a major issue of the day.

Brumaire The coup d'état in 1799 that overthrew the Directory and led to the dictatorship of Napoleon Bonaparte.

cahiers Grievance petitions written by local electoral assemblies, to be presented to the king by the deputies attending the Estates General in France.

Caliph In the Middle Ages, he was the religious and civil ruler of the Muslim empires, as in the Abbasid Caliphate.

Carolingian minuscule New form of formal, literary writing that used capital letters for the beginning of sentences and lowercase letters for the text.

cartel An informal association of manufacturers or suppliers who maintain prices at a high level and set production limits to control market demand.

Central Powers Name given to the coalition including Germany, Austria-Hungary, Turkey (the Ottoman Empire), and Bulgaria in World War I.

Chartism A mass working-class movement in Britain between 1837 and 1848 that derived its name from the People's Charter, a document calling for universal male suffrage, frequent elections by secret ballot, and other democratic reforms.

chivalry A new code of behavior that refined the manners of knights and nobles and adapted them to life in a noble household.

Cistercians Monastic order founded in 1098; they emphasized the emotional devotion to Christ's and Mary's humility.

Civil Code (Napoleonic Code) A grand codification of French law under Napoleon, which preserved certain gains of the Revolution such as legal equality and the abolition of seigneurial property, while clarifying contract and family law.

Civil Constitution of the Clergy The French Revolution's 1790 reform of the Catholic Church under which priests and bishops were elected by the laity, and parishes and dioceses were redrawn; created opposition to the Revolution and a schism within French Catholicism.

Classicism A movement in the arts that seeks to recapture the style and the subjects associated with ancient Greece and Rome.

Colonial Mandate Designation for the former colonial possessions of Germany and the Ottoman Empire, which the League of Nations placed under the control of the various Allied nations after World War I.

colonus In the Roman Empire, a free man who was settled as a worker on the land of another.

comitatus A Germanic warrior band organized under the leadership of an established chief.

Committee of Public Safety A committee of deputies to the National Convention that set political and military strategy and formed the hub of the revolutionary dictatorship of 1793–1794.

common law Laws that applied to the entire kingdom and were thus distinct from local customs, especially associated with England.

commune In medieval and Renaissance Europe, a self-governing association created by townsmen and headed by elected officials.

Concert of Europe A loose agreement by the major European powers to act together to maintain the conservative order in Europe and repress liberal and nationalistic uprisings after 1815.

Conciliar Movement Advocates of the authority of General Councils, rather than the papacy, in the Roman Church, especially active in the 1400s.

Concordat (of 1801) The religious settlement with Pope Pius VII that made Catholicism the "preferred" religion in France but protected religious freedom for non-Catholics.

confraternity A voluntary association of people; in earlier times, usually associations of laymen who wanted to intensify their religious piety.

Congress of Vienna An international congress that met from 1814 to 1815 to set peace terms for continental Europe after the Napoleonic Wars; notable for its creation of a European balance of power and the restoration of old dynasties.

conquistador A Spanish minor nobleman who led his country's expeditions of conquest into Central and South America in the sixteenth century.

conscription Policy of requiring all males of a certain age to sign up for a nation's army.

Constitutionalism The political doctrine that authority in a state depends on consent by the governed, or at least by the leaders of the society.

consuls Supreme magistrates in the Roman Republic, always holding office in pairs.

Continental System Economic sanctions established by Napoleon under which all ships carrying British goods or trading with Britain, even those from neutral countries, were banned from European ports and subject to seizure.

Corn Laws British grain tariffs seen as benefiting the landed gentry at the expense of higher bread prices for urban consumers; an opposition movement by middle-class reformers led to the repeal of nearly all duties in 1846.

Cortes The legislatures of the Spanish kingdoms—Aragon, Castile, and Navarre—which were made up of representatives of the Church, the aristocracy, and towns.

Counter-Reformation Refers to those who see the Catholic revival of the sixteenth century as a response to the Reformation. Those who consider it a natural development within the Church refer to the revival as the Catholic Reformation.

courtly love The polite relations between men and women.

crusades In the eleventh through thirteenth centuries, a series of armed expeditions of Christians to the East to overturn Islamic rule of the Holy Land.

Cubism Art form pioneered by Pablo Picasso and Georges Braque in the early twentieth century that rejected the artistic conventions of three-dimensional perspective and naturalistic representation for a flat, two-dimensional perspective and an abstract style.

Cuneiform System of writing by pressing wedge (Lat. *cuneus*) into clay.

curia regis An assembly of men who advised the king and acted as his principal court.

curiales Councilors in the Roman Empire.

curia Town council in the Roman Empire; later means royal court and central directing body of the Roman Catholic Church.

Cyrillic alphabet Developed by Cyril, a Slavonic script based on Greek letters.

danse macabre "Dance of death"; popular artist motif that depicted people from all different walks of life dancing with a skeleton as a foretaste of their deaths.

decolonization The gradual postwar withdrawal of European nations from colonial empires and the rise of national self-determination in former colonies; initiated a new era of global politics that intersected with the Cold War.

deism Belief in the existence of a supreme being but arising from reason rather than revelation.

Delian League Alliance of Greek states headed by Athens; became the Athenian Empire.

demesne land Land, worked by serfs, that the lord held for his own crops and profit.

demographic transition A pattern of declining birth rate accompanied by a more rapidly falling mortality rate that is characteristic of modern societies.

dialectic The art of analyzing logical relationships among propositions in a dialogue or discourse. Later, a philosophical term for Hegel, who applies the term simultaneously to both world history and ideas. It describes the development from one stage of consciousness to a superior one through a dynamic process of the fusion of contradictions into a higher truth.

dictator In the Roman Republic, a supreme officer whose term was limited to six months; this limit was broken by Sulla and Julius Caesar.

Diet The legislature of the Holy Roman Empire and many German states, bringing together representatives of princes, cities, and the Church.

Directory The centrist republican regime in France between 1795 and 1799; characterized by a weak executive, political polarization, and instability.

Divine Comedy Written by Dante, a medieval poem of personal spiritual exploration.

divine right of kings The belief that a monarch's powers derived directly from God, and thus that treason was a kind of blasphemy.

Doctrine of Petrine Succession The traditional Catholic (and medieval) view that Jesus himself endowed the apostle Peter with supreme responsibility for his church.

doctrine of survivals A term first employed by the anthropologist Edward Tyler (1832–1917) to refer to vertigial cultural phenomena from the past that continue to survive even though they have lost their utility.

Dorian Greeks Last wave of Greeks to immigrate, speaking the Doric dialect.

dynasty A family, usually of rulers, that maintains its authority from generation to generation.

East India Co. (British) A corporation that initially traded with native groups in India but eventually exercised an oppressive colonial dominance over Indian affairs.

enclosure The act of consolidating and fencing in land used in open-field agriculture or village common land.

Entente Powers Name of the members of the Triple Entente of 1907—Britain, France, and Russia—which expanded during World War I to include Belgium, Serbia, Greece, Italy, Romania, the Soviet Union, and the United States.

entrepreneur A person who organizes and assumes risk in a business venture in hopes of making a profit.

Epicureans Followers of the philosopher Epicurus who taught that everything is made of atoms (*a-toma* in Greek) and recommended a quiet life free of powerful emotional attachments.

epicycles In traditional astronomy, small circular orbits, revolving around the main circular orbit, that planets follow as they move through the sky.

epistemology Theory of how one obtains and verifies knowledge or truth.

equestrians Originally the Roman cavalry; became the business class of Rome.

Estates In a number of countries in Europe, representative assemblies that were composed of three houses of representatives: the clergy, the nobility, and townsmen.

Estates General An assembly convened by Louis XVI in 1789 that represented the clergy, the nobility, and the Third Estate; once used to win support for royal policy, it had not met since 1614.

ethnic cleansing A coordinated assault to drive members of a specific ethnicity out of a particular region.

Eucharist Also known as communion; Christian sacrament offered during a religious service in which consecrated bread and wine are consumed in celebration of the Lord's Last Supper.

eugenics The study of the improvement of the human race through selective breeding to eradicate less desirable traits in society. An extrapolation from the work of Charles Darwin, it was popularized by his cousin Francis Galton (1821–1911), in the nineteenth century.

Eurocommunism An alternative program for Western Europeans who disagreed with Soviet policies (particularly the invasion of Czechoslovakia) in Eastern Europe.

evolution The process by which species develop through the natural selection of traits best adapted to the environment.

existentialism A twentieth-century philosophy asserting that individuals are responsible for their own values and meanings in an indifferent universe.

famine Period of severe food scarcity due to too much or too little rainfall.

fascism A philosophy or system of government that advocates a dictatorship of the extreme right together with an ideology of belligerent nationalism.

fealty An oath, often accompanying the oath of homage, in which the vassal swears to uphold his homage.

feudalism An economic, political, and social organization of medieval Europe. Land was held by vassals from more powerful overlords in exchange for military and other services.

fief Land given to a vassal from his lord in exchange for specified terms of service; sometimes called benefice.

"Final Solution" Based on Nazi theories of racial inferiority, the systematic extermination of Jews in German-occupied Europe in massacres and death camps like Auschwitz from 1941 to 1945. Also known as the Holocaust or the Shoah.

Five-Year Plans Plans for the rapid, massive industrialization of the nation under the direction of the state initiated by the Soviet Union in the late 1920s.

forms In the thought of Plato, perfect models of all things; any object we see in life is only an imperfect imitation of the object's form (in Greek, *idea*, meaning something that can be seen).

Franco-Prussian War The conflict from 1870 to 1871 that led to the unification of Germany and (indirectly) to the creation of the French Third Republic; signaled the rise of Germany as a military power.

Frankfurt Parliament The assembly elected in 1848 to unify the various states of Germany under a new liberal constitution and a single monarch; it was dissolved in 1849 when Prussia spurned its projects.

Freikorps German postwar paramilitary groups, consisting mainly of war veterans, employed by both the new republican government and especially by far-right political movements such as the Nazis; literally "volunteer troops."

"general will" Rousseau's idealized concept of popular consensus, under which individual interests are subordinated to the public good.

gentry Owners of significant country estates in England, forming a distinct social group immediately below the nobility.

glasnost A Soviet policy under Mikhail Gorbachev permitting a more open discussion of political and social issues and freer dissemination of news and information.

Golden Horde The capital of a division of the Mongol Empire at Sarai, on the lower Volga River.

Gothic Style of Western European architecture and art that developed in the twelfth century; the style is characterized by vaulting and pointed arches.

Great Schism Major split of the Church in the period of 1378–1417, in which two, and later three, popes fought over the rule of the Church.

Greek Orthodox Church Modern term for the Eastern Orthodox Church, whose main departure from Catholicism is their belief that, in the Holy Trinity, the Holy Spirit proceeds only from the father.

guerillas In Spain during the Napoleonic occupation, groups of irregular fighters who harassed French troops, restricted access to supplies, and punished collaborators; a pioneering model for modern guerrilla warfare.

guilds Associations formed by merchants and master artisans to defend and promote their interests and to regulate the quality of the goods they produced and sold.

Hanseatic League Association of northern European trading cities that by the fourteenth century had imposed a monopoly over cities trading in the Baltic and North Seas.

heavy-wheeled plow A heavy, powerful plow that cut more deeply into the ground, forming furrows that drained excess water. It permitted cultivation of heavier river valley soils.

Hellenistic Age In Greek history, the period 323–330 B.C.

helots Publicly owned slaves in Sparta.

heresy Any belief contrary to church dogma; from Greek *hairesis*, "choice."

hieroglyphs "Sacred carvings"; Egyptian style of writing using pictures.

hijra Muhammad's migration from Mecca to Medina in 622; it marks the beginning of the Islamic calendar.

homage An oath of allegiance sworn by a vassal to his lord.

home front In the new time of total war during World War I, civilians—mostly women and men ineligible for military duty—remaining at home assumed a primary role in the national economy; their continued efforts were held up as indispensable to the war being fought on the military front.

Homo erectus   "Erect human being"; predecessor of the modern human species *Homo sapiens.*

Humanism   An intellectual movement of the Renaissance that emphasized the importance of having the ability to read, understand, and appreciate the writings of the ancient world.

Hundred Years' War   War between France and England fought in the fourteenth and fifteenth centuries. Allegedly sparked by a dispute over French royal succession.

Hussites   Followers of Hus, the Bohemian priest whose practices attempted to reduce the distinction between priest and worshippers.

iconoclasm   In the Byzantine Empire, a rejection of religious icons or pictures of Jesus, Mary, and the saints that led to the destruction of a number of these religious images.

imperium   Power of command held by Roman officers.

Impressionists   A group of artists who conveyed subjective experiences by capturing the effects of light and color on canvas.

induction   Starting with observation, the logical process by which one moves to general principles.

indulgences   Grants to sinners by the Roman Catholic Church that reduce time for their souls in purgatory before they can ascend to heaven.

Inquisition   A special papal court instituted by Pope Gregory IX for the purpose of rooting out heresy.

intendants   French officials who ruled the country's provinces as direct representatives of the king.

Investiture Controversy   Conflict between the German emperor and the pope over who had the authority to appoint bishops and "invest" them with their spiritual symbols of office, the ring and the staff.

Islam   Strong monotheistic religion founded by Muhammad.

itinerant justices   English justices who traveled and heard both criminal and civil pleas. In both cases, they relied on the testimony of a jury.

iurisprudentes or **iurisconsulti**   Jurists or advisers in the Roman legal system whose opinions shaped laws.

ius civile   "Civil law," or law relating to Roman citizens.

ius gentium   "Law of the nations"; Roman law as applied to noncitizens or to all cultures.

Jacobin Club   An influential political club whose leaders propelled the French Revolution toward a democratic republic and supported the use of severe repression against the Revolution's enemies.

Jacquerie   French peasant revolt in 1358.

jingoism   Attitude of extreme and belligerent patriotism often used to gain popular support for war and other political causes.

Julio-Claudians   Dynasty of related rulers from 27 B.C. to A.D. 68 in Rome.

July Monarchy   The liberal constitutional monarchy established in France from 1830 to 1848, in which the House of Orléans replaced the Bourbons; its modest reforms benefited most the wealthy middle class.

June Days   An uprising in Paris in 1848 by radicals and workers that was brutally suppressed by government forces of France's new republic; the event symbolized the conflict between liberal democracy and working-class militancy.

Junkers   Prussian aristocrats whose large estates and tradition of military and bureaucratic service ensured their dominance within the Prussian state.

justification by faith   A central tenet of Luther's theology: belief that one is saved through the grace of God rather than good deeds.

Justinian's Code   Known as the *Corpus Iuris Civilis*, this was the codification of Roman law undertaken by the Byzantine Emperor Justinian in 528.

Keynesian economics   Economic theories and programs ascribed to John M. Keynes and his followers. Keynes argued against a totally laissez-faire economy, urging governments to minimize the effects of boom-and-bust economic cycles by manipulating interest rates and employment (through public works projects).

Koran   The Muslim holy book that contains the prophecies Allah revealed to Muhammad; it was written between 651 and 652.

kyrios   Greek, roughly "master"—for example, head of a family; used for Christian God.

laissez-faire   The theory in which individual self-interest and free markets, rather than state regulation or guild protection, stimulate economic progress.

"last decree"   *Senatus consultum ultimum*, "final resolution of the Senate"; an instruction to a consul to "see that the state suffers no harm"; a declaration of martial law, first used in 121 B.C. in Rome.

latifundia   Large plantations in the Roman world, worked mainly by slaves.

League of Nations   International organization created in the wake of the end of World War I and located in Geneva; the forerunner to the modern-day United Nations.

legion   Main unit of the Roman army, in principle 6,000 men.

levée en masse A military draft by the French National Convention in August 1793 of unmarried men between the ages of eighteen and twenty-five that recruited about 300,000 new soldiers.

Linear B Script used on Crete, as well as in Greece, to write the early form of Greek.

Lollards Followers of Wycliffe, a vocal dissenter of the church's leadership. This group became an underground rural movement.

Lyceum School established by Aristotle, meeting in and taking its name from a grove in Athens.

Maastricht Treaty Changed the name of the European Community (EC) to the European Union (EU) in 1992. It also enlarged the powers of its parliament and called for a coordinated foreign policy and a common European currency by 1999.

maat Egyptian concept of right order.

Magna Carta "The Great Charter"; English royal charter of liberties granted by King John in 1215. Intended to settle disputes over the rights and privileges of England's nobility.

Magyars The Hungarian-speaking population of the Hapsburg Empire who began to push for Hungary's independence in the 1840s.

Mannerism Art style that emerged in the sixteenth century in response to the serenity and idealization of the High Renaissance. Mannerism is characterized by distorted, esoteric imagery and a sense of artificiality.

manor An estate held by the lord that included land, the people on the land, and a village, usually with a mill. A fief might contain a number of manors or sometimes just part of one.

manorialism An agricultural, legal, and social organization of land, including a nucleated village, large fields for agriculture, and serfs to work the land.

Marxism The political philosophy of Karl Marx, based on the premise that economic conditions determine the nature of society. Marxists advocate the overthrow of capitalism, which they believe will lead to the establishment of a classless society.

memsahib A term of respect used by Indians to address female social superiors. Used in the nineteenth century to refer to British women in colonial India, the term came to connote the blatant ethnocentrism and spoiled behavior associated with these women.

mendicant Orders of religious men, followers of Sts. Dominic and Francis of Assisi, who preached among the poor townsmen and lived a life of begging.

mercantilism The belief that the amount of wealth in the world was fixed, and that a nation should try to gain as much as it could at the expense of other nations, either by accumulating more gold or, in a more sophisticated version, by improving its balance of trade— that is, by exporting more than it imported. This doctrine led to some governmental regulation of commerce in a number of countries in the seventeenth and eighteenth centuries.

Mesopotamia "Land between the [Tigris and Euphrates] rivers," home of early civilizations.

Messiah In Hebrew, *mashiah:* one anointed by God to rule; title given by Christians to Jesus.

metropole Term used to describe European countries in the context of the dominant economic and cultural relationships they had with their colonies.

Middle Passage The harsh voyage of slaving ships from Africa to the Americas during which an average of 10 percent of the slaves perished.

Minoan Name for civilization on Crete, derived from legendary King Minos.

monasticism Practice of withdrawing from daily life to devote oneself to prayer in isolated communities.

Muslims Those who submit to the will of Allah. In Western Europe, often referred to as Saracens.

nationalism A social and political outlook insisting that the state should embody a national community united by some or all of the following: history, ethnicity, religion, common culture, and language.

nationalization State takeover of privately owned businesses; used in fascist Italy and the Soviet Union, but also in postwar Britain and France, to promote greater economic efficiency and social justice.

natural history The science of the earth's development accomplished through the study of geology, zoology, and botany.

natural rights Liberties that should be common to all people by virtue of their nature as human beings; one basis for the French Declaration of the Rights of Man and Citizen of 1789.

natural selection A central feature of Charles Darwin's (1809–1882) theory of evolution that suggests that only organisms best adapted to their environment survive and transmit their genes to succeeding generations, whereas those less adapted are eliminated.

Nazism The body of political and economic doctrines put into effect by the National Socialist German Workers' party in the Third German Reich. A fascist form of government based on state control of all industry, predominance of groups assumed to be racially superior, and supremacy of the Führer.

Neoclassicism A style of art and poetry inspired by themes from antiquity and its conceptions of form and beauty.

Neolithic Age New Stone Age; date of beginning of agriculture, about 11,000 B.C.

Neoplatonism Influential school of thought during the Renaissance, based on Plato's belief that truth lay in essential but hidden forms.

Neostoicism A sixteenth- and seventeenth-century school of philosophy dedicated to the revival of moral values, such as calmness, self-discipline, and steadfastness, first advanced by the Stoics in ancient Greece and Rome.

New Economic Policy (NEP) Lenin's compromise on economic and social policy for the USSR during the 1920s.

New World Name given to the Americas by sixteenth-century explorers and settlers.

Nicene Creed Declaration made at Nicaea in 325 that Jesus was coeternal with God.

Nominalists Indviduals who subscribed to a school of thought in medieval Europe that rejected abstractions as the subject matter of philosophy and focused instead on one's experience of individual, distinct beings and objects.

North Atlantic Treaty Organization (NATO) Created in 1949 to coordinate military forces from the United States, Canada, and ten Western European nations in response to perceived Soviet threats in Europe.

notables Locally prominent and wealthy individuals whose support for Napoleon and subsequent French governments was encouraged by state recognition and honors.

novus homo A "new man"; in Roman politics, a man elected consul with no ancestor who had held this office.

October Manifesto Declaration by the tsar of Russia in 1905 that provided Russia with a written constitution and guaranteed freedom of speech and assembly.

oligarchy The rule of a state by a small number, often the Wealthy citizens.

open-field system The division of agricultural land on a manor into three large fields. The lord held land for his direct profit in these, and his serfs also had strips of land in all three fields. The land farmed by each individual was therefore mixed in with, and open to, neighboring plots. The medieval system lasted long after serfdom ended in England and France.

oral tradition Tales, songs, and adages passed on orally that were the core of traditional popular culture.

Osiris Egyptian god of fertility.

ostracism Procedure in ancient Athens by which men could be banished from the city; voting was done by scratching names on *ostraka* (potsherds).

Ottoman Empire Powerful and much feared empire of the Ottoman Turks, whose holdings stretched across the Middle East and Europe; began as a small state in the fourteenth century but soon took over Asia Minor and surrounded Byzantine territory, resulting in the fall of Constantinople in 1453.

Paleolithic Age Old Stone Age; age of stone tools, ending about 11,000 B.C.

papal bulls Papal letters, closed with a lead seal, or *bulla*.

papal *curia* The central bureaucracy of the pope; it served as the central financial and judicial administration and selected the new pope.

parlements The chief law courts in the regions of France; the members, who owned their offices, claimed the right to approve royal legislation for their regions, and sometimes clashed with the king.

Parliament English legislature, consisting of a House of Lords whose members were nobles and bishops, and a House of Commons whose members were elected gentry and townsmen.

patricians Upper class, a small minority, in Rome; the status was heredity.

perestroika A policy of economic and governmental reform instituted by Mikhail Gorbachev in the Soviet Union during the mid-1980s.

pharaoh Title of Egyptian kings from the New Kingdom onward.

Pharisees Jewish sect that believed in resurrection and accepted non-Jewish converts.

Philippics Orations by the Athenian politician, Demosthenes, attacking King Philip II of Macedonia; used also to refer to speeches of Cicero against Mark Antony.

philosophes A group of French intellectuals who used rational inquiry to advocate intellectual and religious freedom and a variety of practical reforms.

plebeians The great mass of Roman citizens; they were not blocked from holding office.

polis Especially in classical Greece, a city that was also an independent state, not sharing citizenship with any other state.

Politburo The principal policy-making and executive committee of the Russian Communist party.

postmodernism A later twentieth-century approach to the arts stressing relativism and multiple interpretations.

predestination The belief that God has preordained whether a person will be saved or damned, and nothing can be done to reverse this fate.

prefect The chief administrator in each French department appointed by the central government; a hallmark of centralization established by Napoleon but lasting into the twentieth century.

Principate The Roman Empire from Augustus down to Diocletian, so named from the republican term *princeps*, roughly "first citizen."

protoindustrialization Heavy concentrations of pre-factory manufacturing, in which urban merchants employed rural households to produce goods, especially textiles.

psychoanalysis A method of analyzing psychic phenomena and treating emotional disorders that involves treatment sessions during which the patient is encouraged to talk freely about personal experiences and especially about early childhood and dreams.

public sphere Forums outside the royal court, such as newspapers, salons, and academies, in which the educated public could participate in debate on the issues of the day.

Puritans Devout Protestants who believed in a stern moral code and rejected all hints of Catholic ritual or organization.

raj British rule in India, which had spread through most of the subcontinent by the mid-nineteenth century.

realism The depiction of ordinary, everyday subjects in art and literature as part of a broader social commentary; a reaction against the themes and styles typical of Romanticism or of academic painting.

reasons of state Often known by its French name, *raison d'état,* the doctrine that, especially in foreign affairs, a state is bound by no restraint when pursuing its interests.

Reformation The period of major change and variance in the fundamental beliefs of Christianity. The demands of the faithful varied and intensified throughout Western Europe, making it difficult for the Roman Catholic Church alone to accommodate all of them.

relativity Einstein's theory that all aspects of the physical universe must be defined in relative terms.

Renaissance Rebirth of classical culture that occurred in Italy after 1350.

Restorations Attempts by the powers in Europe to restore the dynasties and monarchical institutions (including the Bourbons in France) disrupted by the revolutionary and Napoleonic upheavals.

risorgimento A term meaning "resurgence," used to describe the liberal nationalist movement that led to the unification of Italy by 1870.

Roman Catholic "Universal" church; Christian church headed by a pope.

Romanesque Style of Western European architecture and art developed after 1000; the style is characterized by rounded arches, massive walls, and relatively simple ornamentation.

Romanticism An artistic movement that rejected classical aesthetic forms and norms, and which emphasized personal experience, emotion, or spirituality.

sacrament Means by which God distributes grace. Luther retained only baptism and the Eucharist.

Sadducees Conservative Jewish sect that did not believe in angels or resurrection because such teachings were not found in the five books of the Old Testament, known as the Pentateuch.

sagas Adventure stories told in prose that cover the Viking period to about 1000, when Iceland converted to Christianity.

Saint-Simonians A nineteenth-century movement that called for the reorganization of society by scientists and industrialists to achieve planned progress and prosperity.

salons Social gatherings, usually organized by elite women, that sought to promote discussion of Enlightenment ideas.

sans-culottes Parisian militants, mainly artisans and shopkeepers, who called for repression of counter-revolutionaries, price controls, and direct democracy; helped bring the Jacobins to power in 1793.

satyr play Comic, often vulgar, play performed after an ancient Greek tragedy.

Schlieffen Plan In World War I, the German military plan specifying how the army would fight a two-front war: Germany would invade Belgium and the Netherlands on its way to France, score a quick defeat in the west, and then concentrate its forces against Russia in the east.

Scholasticism A form of argument, or dialectic, developed in the Middle Ages, particularly with Abelard and Thomas Aquinas.

Scientific Revolution The succession of discoveries and the transformation of the investigation of nature that was brought about in the fields of astronomy, physics, and anatomy during the sixteenth and seventeenth centuries.

Second Empire The reign of Napoleon III in France from 1852 to 1870; while authoritarian in nature, the regime fostered popular support through social programs and nationalist sentiment.

second front In World War II, the establishment of an Allied front in Western Europe to match the Russians battling the Nazis in the East; after several delays, the Allies launched the second front with the Normandy invasion in June 1944.

seigneurialism A system prevalent in Western Europe by which peasants owed various fees and dues to the local lord even if the peasants owned their land.

serf or villein Peasant who was personally free, but bound to the lord of a manor and worked the land on the manor.

serfdom A feudal system of agricultural exploitation in which peasants were bound to their lord's estate and owed him forced labor.

sexagesimal System of mathematics based on the number 60.

sexual selection The theory that the traits that increase an organism's (typically male's) success in mating and transmitting its genes are selected and perpetuated. Differs from natural selection, which focuses only on traits that influence survival.

shell shock New psychological diagnosis applied to those soldiers exhibiting signs of psychic distress during the First World War, thought to be caused by the near-constant shelling experienced in the trenches.

sister republics States and territories that fell under French control during the Directory and were reconstituted as republics in collaboration with native revolutionaries.

Skepticism Philosophy that questions whether human beings can ever achieve certain knowledge.

Slavophiles Russian intellectuals who opposed Westernization and saw Russia's unique institutions and culture as superior; some supported autocracy but also favored emancipation of the serfs.

social Darwinism The application of Darwin's scientific theory of evolution to society, often in the service of reactionary and even racist ideas.

social welfare State-run programs for social security, education, medical care, and family benefits.

Sophists Teachers of rhetoric in classical Greece, especially in Athens.

Stalingrad The place where Russians fought ferociously, street by street, to halt the German advance in 1942; marked the turning point of the war on the Eastern front.

state of nature Description in political theory of the condition of humanity before the creation of governments.

steam engine A machine patented in 1782 that converted steam into mechanical energy; provided a cheap and flexible source of power critical for early industrialization.

Stoics Followers, in Greece and Rome, of thought of Zeno, who taught that the wise man leads a life of moderation, unmoved by joy or grief, and stands by his duty according to natural law.

strategic bombing A military doctrine of aerial bombardment of populated and industrial areas; intended to destroy morale and the industrial capacity to fight. Initiated by the Germans on Britain, but most fully used by the British and U.S. air forces.

Sturm und Drang A literary and artistic movement in Germany that emphasized strong artistic emotion; a precursor of the Romantic movement.

subinfeudation The grant of a fief by a vassal to a subordinate who becomes his vassal.

Sunni-Shiite schism Division within the Islamic religion over who should rule after Mohammad's death.

syndicalism A movement in which worker's organizations attempted to destroy bourgeois capitalism and gain control of industry by general strikes.

Talmud General body of Jewish tradition.

tariff A duty or custom fee imposed on imports, often to protect local agriculture or industry from competition.

Tetrarchy Rule of four co-emperors of Rome under Diocletian.

Thermidorian reaction The period between the fall of Robespierre and the establishment of the Directory during which the Convention dismantled the Terror and attacked egalitarian politics.

thermodynamics The study of the relationships between heat and other forms of energy; becomes one of the bases of nineteenth-century physics.

three-field system Agricultural system in which two-thirds of the land was cultivated on a rotating basis; it replaced the two-field system and resulted in increased productivity.

Tory English political party committed to a strong monarch and a strong Anglican Church.

total war Unprecedented type of warfare in which all segments of society, civilians and soldiers, men and women, were mobilized in the hope of ensuring victory.

totalitarianism A twentieth-century form of authoritarian government using force, technology, and bureaucracy to effect rule by a single party and controlling most aspects of the lives of the population.

tragedy The supreme dramatic form in ancient Greece, usually treating a mythological theme and leading to catastrophe for some of the characters.

transubstantiation Belief that bread and wine are transformed into the body and blood of Christ during the Eucharist.

Treaty of Paris (1763) Peace treaty ending the British and French war for empire in which France surrendered Canada to the British and lost its foothold in India.

Treaty of Tordesillas Signed in 1494, the treaty confirmed the pope's division of the world between the Portuguese and Spanish for exploration and conquest. Under its terms, a line was drawn some 1,200 miles west of the Cape Verde Islands, with Portugal granted all lands to the west and Spain granted all lands to the east.

trench warfare Static, defensive type of combat seen mostly on the Western front of World War I, where a war of attrition was fought in a complex system of underground trenches and supply lines.

triangular trade A complex pattern of colonial commerce between the home country (Britain or France) and its colonies in which refined or manufactured goods were exchanged for raw materials or slaves from West Africa.

tribunes Ten Roman plebeians, elected to protect the common people; some of them became powerful political activists.

triremes Greek warship, powered by three banks of oars.

triumvirate "Body of three men," a term applied to two such cabals in the Roman Republic.

trivium and quadrivium School curriculum that became the standard program of study in universities. The trivium comprised the verbal arts (grammar, rhetoric, and logic), while the quadrivium comprised the mathematical arts (arithmetic, astronomy, geometry, and music).

troubadour A writer of vernacular romantic lyrics or tales who enjoyed the patronage of nobles around Europe in the twelfth through fifteenth centuries.

tsar Title adopted by the Russian king; the term was the Slavic equivalent of the Latin term *caesar*.

tyrant In ancient Greek states, a powerful man who ruled in a polis without legal sanction, not necessarily a cruel despot.

ultraroyalists French reactionaries who not only supported divine-right monarchy but called for the return of lands taken from the émigrés during the Revolution.

usury Interest of profit on a loan; it was prohibited by the Church.

Utilitarianism British reform movement that believed that society should be based on "the greatest happiness for the greatest number," and that sound governments could make such calculations.

utopian Having to do with an ideal society, as presented in Sir Thomas More's book *Utopia*, which means "nowhere" in Greek.

vassal A free warrior who places himself under a lord, accepting the terms of loyal service, fighting in times of war, and counseling in times of peace.

Vatican II Vatican council called by Pope John XXIII in 1962. Vatican II made the leadership of the Church more international, directed attention to the concerns of developing nations, and ordered that Masses be conducted in the vernacular instead of Latin.

Vulgate The Latin translation of the Bible in the fourth century, identified with St. Jerome, which became the medieval Church's standard text and was deemed holy in the sixteenth century.

war guilt clause Article 231 of the Treaty of Versailles, specifying that Germany alone was responsible for causing the First World War.

Warsaw Pact The Russian response to NATO; an international military organization established in 1955 that included the Soviet Union and Eastern European communist states.

Weimar Republic Left-liberal German government established after the war, named for the city where German politicians formed the republic; instituted universal suffrage, and wrote a new democratic constitution.

Wergeld Literally, "man-payment"; in Germanic tribes, as a means to prevent feuds, payments given in compensation for crimes committed; the amount of compensation depended on the social rank of the individual.

Whig English political party committed to a strong Parliament and religious toleration.

Yalta Conference In February 1945, the meeting between Roosevelt, Churchill, and Stalin to set the postwar order in Europe. The conference agreed on the creation of the United Nations but was unable to counter future Soviet dominance in Eastern Europe.

Zeus Sky god; the chief god in Greek myth.

ziggurat Terraced tower built of baked brick in Mesopotamia.

Zollverein A customs union established by Prussia among most states in the German Confederation that allowed for free movement of goods; promoted the economic unification of Germany.

Text Credits

Chapter 19

Page 559 From C. A. Macartney (ed.), *The Habsburg and Hohenzollern Dynasties in the 17th and 18th Centuries*, pp. 151 and 155–157. Copyright © 1970 by C. A. Macartney. Reprinted by permission of HarperCollins Publishers. **Page 565** From Sandra M. Gilbert and Susan Gubar (eds.), *The Norton Anthology of Literature by Women: The Tradition in English*, W. W. Norton Co., 1985. Reprinted by permission. **Page 566** From Jean-Jacques Rousseau, *The Social Contract*, Book 1, David Campbell Publishers. Reprinted by permission.

Chapter 20

Page 588 Georges Lefebvre, *The Coming of the French Revolution.* © 1947 Princeton University Press, 1975 renewed PUP. Reprinted by permission of Princeton University Press. **Page 588** From William Doyle, *Origins of the French Revolution*, 1988. Reprinted by permission of Oxford University Press. **Page 594** R. R. Palmer, *The Age of Democratic Revolution.* © 1959 Princeton University Press, 1987 renewed PUP. Reprinted by permission of Princeton University Press. **Page 594** From R.R. Palmer (trans.), *The Age of Democratic Revolution*, Princeton University Press, 1959, pp. 510–511.

Chapter 21

Page 633 From *Political Constitution of the Spanish Monarchy*, proclaimed in Cadiz, March 19, 1812, (trans. James B. Tueller). **Page 638** From B. Las Cases (ed.), *Mémorial de Sainte-Hélène.*

Chapter 22

Page 650 From Louis L. Snyder (ed.), *Documents of German History*, Rutgers University Press, 1958, pp. 158–159. **Page 655** From B. R. Mitchel, *European Historical Statistics, 1750–1970*, 1975, Columbia University Press. Reproduced with permission of Palgrave Macmillan. **Page 663** From Sidney Pollard and Colin Holmes (eds.), *Documents of European Economic History, Vol. 1*, St. Martin's Press. Reprinted by permission of Palgrave Macmillan. **Page 665** From Thomas S. Ashton, "The Standard of Life of the Workers in England, 1790–1830," *Journal of Economic History*, Vol. 9, 1949. Reprinted by permission. **Page 665** From Eric J. Hobsbawm, "The British Standard of Living, 1790–1850," *Economic History Review*, 1957. Reprinted by permission. **Page 666** From Ronald M. Hartwell, "The Rising Standard of Living in England, 1800–1850," *Economic History Review*, 1961. Reprinted by permission. **Page 666** From Theodore S. Hamerow, *The Birth of a New Europe, State and Society in the Nineteenth Century*, University of North Carolina Press, 1983, pp. 140–141. Reprinted by permission.

Chapter 24

Page 713 From Louis L. Snyder (ed.), *The Documents of German History*, New Brunswick: Rutgers University Press, 1958. **Page 720** From Giuseppe Massini, *On the Duties of Man*, Greenwood Publishing Group. **Page 728** From Louis L. Snyder (ed.), *The Documents of German History*, New Brunswick: Rutgers University Press, 1958.

Chapter 25

Page 740 From Karl Wittgensteing, "Kartelle in Österreich," in Gustav Schmoller (ed.), *Über wirtschaftliche Kartelle in Deutschland und im Auslande* (Leipzig, 1894); as quoted in Carroll and Embree, *Readings in European History since 1814* (1930). **Page 742** From P. Bairoch et al., *The Working Population and Its Structure*, Gordon V. Breach, 1968, p. 119. Reprinted by permission. **Page 748** From Thomas H. Huxley, *Evolution and Ethics and Other Essays*, New York: D. Appleton and Company, 1916. **Page 757** From Richard Levy, *Antisemitism in the Modern World.* Copyright © 1991 by D.C. Heath and Company. Used with permission of Houghton Mifflin Company.

Chapter 27

Page 824 Reprinted with the permission of Scribner, an imprint of Simon & Schuster Adult Publishing Group from *Origins of the World War, Volume II, Revised Edition* by Sidney B. Fay. Copyright © 1930 by The Macmillan Company; copyright renewed © 1958 by Sidney Bradshaw Fay. **Page 840** From Harold Owen and John Bell (eds.), *Wilfred Owen: The Collected Letters*, Oxford University Press, 1967. Reprinted by permission. **Page 853** From Sidney Pollard and Colin Holmes (eds.), *Documents of European Economic History, Vol. 3: The End of Old Europe, 1914–1939* (St. Martin's Press, 1972). Reprinted by permission of Palgrave Macmillan.

Chapter 28

Page 872 From S. William Halperin (ed.), *Mussolini and Italian Fascism* (Van Nostrand, 1964). **Page 889** From Salvator Attanasio et al. (trs.), Speech of Goebbels, in George L. Mosse, *Nazi Culture: Intellectual, Cultural, and Social Life in the Third Reich*, University of Wisconsin Press, 1966. Reprinted by permission.

Chapter 29

Page 914 From J. Noakes and G. Pridham (eds.), *Nazism 1919–1945 Volume Two, State Economy and Society 1933–1939: A Documentary Reader.* ISBN: 0 85989 599 8 Reprinted by permission of the University of Exeter Press. **Page 916** From

Volume C Index